★ABOUT THIS BOOK

This year's principal font is Georgia, the first seriffed typeface to be used as body copy in *Guinness World Records* for over 15 years. (Serifs are the small slabs or hooks at the ends of the letters; historically, type designers believed that they increased the readability of text.) Matthew Carter of Microsoft created Georgia in order that a seriffed font could be read more easily on a computer screen, where certain fonts were considered more difficult to read.

The overwhelming body of evidence – researched since the 1930s – reveals, however, that serifs do nothing to improve readability. This year's font choice, then, is purely an aesthetic one.

The display font is **BLACKSTOCK**, created by Aerotype of Glendale, California, USA. Reproduced "warts and all" from a source dating to the 1820s, this distressed face is reminiscent of old letterpressed or screen-printed circus and "wanted" posters. This chunky and bold feel is extended into the design of the pages, and lends the book a fun, nostalgic, vaudeville vibe.

The cover uses a laser-cut holographic flame effect – designed in the UK and rendered in metallic foil in California, USA – with a photographic fire printed on top. Incorporated into the foil is a holographic lens with the new-look spherical Guinness World Records text block.

INTRODUCTION
FIRE!

HIT!
THE RECORD FOR THE MOST FLAMING TORCHES JUGGLED AT THE SAME TIME IS HELD BY ANTHONY GATTO (USA), WHO JUGGLED SEVEN TORCHES IN 1989.

MISS!
DELIBERATELY STARTED FOREST FIRES MADE 1997 THE WORST YEAR IN RECORDED HISTORY FOR THE DESTRUCTION OF THE ENVIRONMENT BY FIRE.

FARTHEST DISTANCE FIREWALKING

Trever McGhee (Canada) walked 181.9 m (597 ft) over embers with temperatures in excess of 657.67°C (1,215.80°F) at Symons Valley Rodeo Grounds in Calgary, Alberta, Canada, on 9 November 2007.

★LONGEST RUN DURING A FULL-BODY BURN

The greatest distance run while performing a full-body burn is 78.9 m (259 ft) and was achieved by professional stunt performer Keith Malcolm (UK) of The Stannage International Stunt Team at the Alton Show in Hampshire, UK, on 5 July 2009.

LONGEST-BURNING FIRE

A burning coal seam lying beneath Mount Wingen in New South Wales, Australia, is thought to have started around 5,000 years ago when lightning struck the coal seam at the point where it reached the Earth's surface. The fire is still burning, around 30 m (100 ft) underground, as it has slowly eaten away at the seam.

LARGEST FIREWORKS DISPLAY

A fireworks display featuring 66,326 fireworks was achieved by Macedo's Pirotecnia, Lda. in Funchal, Madeira, Portugal, on 31 December 2006. The display, which was part of the New Year celebrations on the island of Madeira, was launched from 40 different sites and was over in just eight minutes.

WORST FIREWORKS DISASTER

An estimated 800 people died as a result of an accident during a fireworks display staged beside the river Seine in Paris, France, on 16 May 1770 to mark the marriage of the future Louis XIV.

MOST PEOPLE BURNED AT THE STAKE

The burning of "witches" at the stake reached its greatest intensity in Germany in the 16th and 17th centuries. At Quedlinburg, near Leipzig, 133 witches were burned in one day in 1589. Elsewhere, in the towns of Wurzburg and Bamberg, at least 1,500 witches were burned in less than a decade during the mid-17th century.

★LARGEST BURNING MAN FESTIVAL

The annual Burning Man festival staged in the Black Rock Desert in Nevada, USA, attracted a record 49,599 visitors to the 2008 event. The week-long festival is named after the giant wooden effigy that is burned during the Saturday of Labor Day weekend. The event dates back to 1986.

★LONGEST FULL-BODY BURN (NO OXYGEN)

On 25 February 2010, stuntman Ted A Batchelor (USA) endured a full-body burn without oxygen for 2 min 57 sec on the set of *Lo Show dei Record* in Rome, Italy. Previously, on 19 September 2009, Ted had led a group of 17 in the **largest simultaneous body burn**, when members of his team and the "Ohio Burns Unit" (USA) set themselves alight for 43 seconds in South Russell, Ohio, USA.

DID YOU KNOW?

THE LONGEST MOTORCYCLE RIDE THROUGH A TUNNEL OF FIRE WAS BY CLINT EWING (USA) AND MEASURED 60.9 M (200 FT) LONG ON 27 JANUARY 2008.

TRIVIA

The earliest use of fire by humans has been traced back approximately 1.5 million years to locations in East Africa.

HIGHEST FLAME BLOWN BY A FIRE BREATHER

Tim Black (Australia) blew a 7.2-m-high (23-ft 7-in) flame for *Zheng Da Zong Yi – Guinness World Records Special* in Beijing, China, on 15 September 2007.

NEW RECORD ★ UPDATED RECORD

★MOST PEOPLE SPINNING FIRE

On 15 August 2009, in an event organized by The Arts Factory Lodge in New South Wales, Australia, 102 participants span fire brands for a total of six-and-a-half minutes. The high-temperature twirling was accompanied by a group of drummers, who kept track of time by beating on their instruments. A crowd of more than 300 people cheered on the fire spinners.

★TALLEST VOLCANIC FIRE FOUNTAIN

When the Izu-Oshima volcano, Japan, erupted in November 1986, it launched a fountain of fire into the air that was recorded as reaching 1,600 m (5,250 ft) in height. A volcanic fire fountain is characterized by a violent, geyser-like eruption of incandescent lava, rather than an ash column.

★LARGEST GATHERING OF FIRE BREATHERS

On 15 October 2008, 269 people got hot under the collar together in Eindhoven, the Netherlands, when they set the record for the largest gathering of fire breathers. The event was coordinated by the Dutch student association Intermate.

★LARGEST FLAMING IMAGE USING CANDLES

On 10 December 2009, 118 employees of the Sandoz (Pakistan) company created a flaming image with 35,478 candles at the Hotel Serena in Faisalabad, Pakistan. The image depicted the Sandoz logo and motto and had an area of 910.45 m² (9,800 ft²).

WORST TUNNEL FIRE

On 12 November 2000, 155 skiers died in a tunnel fire on the Kaprun railway, which took passengers up the Kitzsteinhorn Glacier in the Austrian Alps. The fire occurred when a blocked heating ventilator caused leaking hydraulic oil to ignite.

★LONGEST WALL OF FIRE

A wall of fire measuring 3,102.3 m (10,178 ft 3 in) long was created by the Marine Corps Community Services (USA) during the 2009 MCAS Yuma Air Show in Yuma, Arizona, USA, on 14 March 2009.

FASTEST JET-POWERED FIRE TRUCK

The jet-powered *Hawaiian Eagle*, owned by Shannen Seydel of Navarre, Florida, USA, attained a speed of 655 km/h (407 mph) in Ontario, Canada, on 11 July 1998. The truck is a red 1940 Ford, powered by two Rolls-Royce Bristol Viper engines boasting 4,470 kW (6,000 hp) per engine and generating 5,443 kg (12,000 lb) of thrust.

LARGEST BONFIRE

A bonfire with a volume of 1,715.7 m³ (60,589 ft³) was built by ŠKD Mladi Boštanj and lit on 30 April 2007 in Boštanj, Slovenia, to celebrate Labour Day. Its 43.44-m (142-ft 6.2-in) height also qualifies the conflagration as the **tallest bonfire**.

INSTANT EXPERT

✪ FIRE RESULTS FROM A CHEMICAL REACTION BETWEEN OXYGEN AND A SOURCE OF FUEL THAT HAS BEEN HEATED TO ITS IGNITION TEMPERATURE.

✪ THE HOTTEST FLAME CREATED IN A LABORATORY IS PRODUCED BY CARBON SUBNITRIDE (C_4N_2). AT 1 ATMOSPHERE PRESSURE, IT BURNS WITH A FLAME CALCULATED TO REACH 4,988°C (9,010°F).

✪ "GREEK FIRE" WAS CREATED IN THE 7TH CENTURY AD. PROJECTED AS BURNING LIQUID JETS, IT COULD BURN ON, OR EVEN UNDER, WATER. THE FORMULA FOR ITS CREATION HAS BEEN LOST FOR CENTURIES.

British Library Cataloguing-in-Publication Data:
A catalogue record for this book is available from the British Library

ISBN: 978-1-904994-57-2

For a complete list of credits and acknowledgements, turn to p.278.

If you wish to make a record claim, find out how on p.18. Always contact us before making a record attempt.

Check the official website **www.guinnessworldrecords.com** regularly for record-breaking news, plus video footage of record attempts. You can also join and interact with the GWR online community.

Sustainability
The trees that are harvested to print *Guinness World Records* are carefully selected from managed forests to avoid the devastation of the landscape. For every tree harvested, at least one other is planted.

The paper contained within this edition is manufactured by UPM Kymi, Finland. The production site has been awarded the EU Flower Licence, is Chain-of-Custody certified, and operates environmental systems certified to both ISO 14001 and EMAS in order to ensure sustainable production.

The European Eco-label distinguishes products that meet high standards of both performance and environmental quality. Every product awarded the European Eco-label must pass rigorous environmental fitness trials, with results verified by an independent body.

Made of paper awarded the European Union Eco-label
reg.nr FI/11/1

Pictured opposite is Francisco Domingo Joaquim – aka Mr Bongo – of Angola. He rose to fame in the past few years thanks to his appearance on YouTube demonstrating his record for the **widest mouth**. Find out just how far apart he can stretch his lips on pp.74–75.

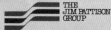

THE JIM PATTISON GROUP

EDITOR-IN-CHIEF
Craig Glenday

MANAGING EDITORS
Matt Boulton, Ben Way

EDITORIAL TEAM
Chris Bernstein (index), Rob Cave, Rob Dimery, Carla Masson, Joel Meadows, Matthew White

DESIGN
Keren Turner and Lisa Garner at Itonic Design Ltd, Brighton, UK

COVER PRODUCTION
API; Simon Thompson

COVER DESIGN
Simon Jones

DIRECTOR OF PUBLISHING
Mina Patria

PRODUCTION MANAGER
Jane Boatfield

PRODUCTION ASSISTANT
Erica Holmes-Attivor

PRODUCTION CONSULTANTS
Patricia Magill, Roger Hawkins, Esteve Font Canadell, Salvador Pujol, Julian Townsend

PRINTING & BINDING
Printer Industria Gráfica, Barcelona, Spain

ORIGINAL COMIC ART
Jimmy Rumble

PICTURE EDITOR
Michael Whitty

DEPUTY PICTURE EDITOR
Laura Jackson

PICTURE RESEARCHER
Fran Morales

ORIGINAL PHOTOGRAPHY
Tim Anderson, Richard Bradbury, Jacob Chinn, Maria Elisa Duque, Paul Michael Hughes, Jonathan Lewis, Ranald Mackechnie, John Wright

COLOUR ORIGINATION
Resmiye Kahraman at FMG, London, UK

EDITORIAL CONSULTANTS
Earth, Science & Technology: David Hawksett
Life on Earth: Dr Karl Shuker
Human Body: Dr Eleanor Clarke; Robert Young (gerontology)
Adventure/Exploration: Ocean Rowing Society; World Speed Sailing Records Council
Weapons & Warfare: Stephen Wrigley
Arts & Entertainment: Dick Fiddy (TV); Thomasina Gibson
Society: Mike Flynn
Music: Dave McAleer
Sports & Games: Christian Marais; David Fischer (US sports)

GUINNESS WORLD RECORDS
Managing Director: Alistair Richards

SVP Finance: Alison Ozanne
Finance Managers:
UK: Neelish Dawett
USA: Jason Curran
Accounts Payable Manager: Kimberley Dennis/Laura Hetherington
Accounts Receivable Manager/Contracts Administrator: Lisa Gibbs
Legal and Business Affairs: Raymond Marshall
Global Director of HR: Kelly Garrett

RECORDS MANAGEMENT
VP OF RECORDS
Marco Frigatti (Italy)
HEAD OF ADJUDICATIONS
Andrea Bánfi (Hungary)
ADJUDICATIONS TEAM
Jack Brockbank (UK)
Danny Girton, Jr (USA)
Amanda Mochan (USA)
Talal Omar (Yemen)
Tarika Vara (UK)
Lucia Sinigagliesi (Italy)
HEAD OF RECORDS MANAGEMENT
UK: Mariamarta Ruano-Graham (Guatemala)
USA: Carlos Martínez (Spain)
RECORDS MANAGEMENT
Gareth Deaves (UK)
Ralph Hannah (UK)
Louise Ireland (Wales)
Kaoru Ishikawa (Japan)
Mike Janela (USA)
Olaf Kuchenbecker (Germany)
Kimberly Partrick (USA)
Chris Sheedy (Australia)
Kristian Teufel (Germany)
Louise Toms (UK)
Aleksandr Vipirailenko (Lithuania)
Wu Xiaohong (China)

Director of IT: Katie Forde
Web Developer: Daniel Sharkey
IT Analyst: Paul Bentley
Developer: Imran Javed
System Analyst: Jawad Ahmed Butt
Director of Television: Rob Molloy
Digital Content Manager: Denise Anlander
Television Assistant: Jimmy Rumble
Director of GWR LIVE!: Paul O'Neill

SALES AND MARKETING
Senior VP Sales & Marketing: Samantha Fay
US Marketing Director: Laura Plunkett
US PR Executive: Jamie Panas
US PR & Marketing Assistant: Sara Wilcox
English Language Sales & Marketing Director: Nadine Causey

Licensing Director: Frank Chambers
Senior National Accounts Manager: John Pilley
National Accounts Executive: Lisa Gills
English Language Marketing Executive: Tom Harris

PR Manager: Amarilis Espinoza
International Licensing Manager: Beatriz Fernandez
US Licensing Manager: Jennifer Gilmour
Business Development Managers:
USA: Stuart Claxton
Japan: Erika Ogawa
International Marketing Manager: Justine Bourdariat
PR Manager: Karolina Davison
PR Executive: Damian Field

Office Administrators/Reception:
Jennifer Robson (UK)
Morgan Wilber (US)

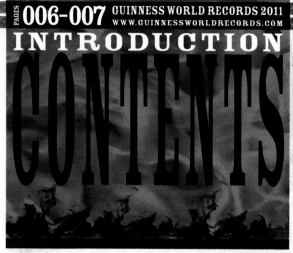

INTRODUCTION
CONTENTS

TRIVIA SCATTERED THROUGHOUT THE BOOK ARE THESE FUN, FACT-FILLED NUGGETS OF RECORD-RELATED TRIVIA.

RECORDS BY CITY

At the foot of every page, you'll find records associated with different cities. Starting in the UK, from London's Greenwich meridian at 0°00'E, these cities are arranged in order of their longitude (distance from the meridian), so as you read the book, you can read your way around the world, eastwards, city by city.

QUIZ!
WHAT ARE THESE? THEY'RE SIMPLE QUIZ QUESTIONS TO TEST YOUR FAMILY AND FRIENDS.
SEE P.278 FOR ALL THE ANSWERS.

INTRODUCTION
EDITOR'S LETTER

★ ★ ★ ★ ★ ★ ★ ★ ★ ★ ★ ★ ★ ★

WELCOME TO THE EXPLOSIVE NEW EDITION OF THE WORLD'S BIGGEST-SELLING COPYRIGHT BOOK. WHAT A YEAR IT'S BEEN - WE'VE LITERALLY GONE FROM ONE EXTREME TO ANOTHER TO BRING YOU MORE PICTURES, MORE RECORDS AND MORE INCREDIBLE ACHIEVEMENTS THAN EVER...

It's been a roller coaster of a year here at Guinness World Records (for actual **roller coaster** records, see p.196). We've witnessed some fantastic highs and experienced some poignant lows, but we've survived the ride for another year and the result is *Guinness World Records 2011*, the first edition of the new decade.

As ever, the **biggest-selling copyright book** is crammed with record-breaking facts and feats from up and down the country and from all around the world.

THE SUN

Thanks again to *The Sun*, the UK's biggest-selling daily paper, for their on-going commitment to record-breaking. Look out for *The Sun Bus* for your chance to get involved and maybe get your name in *the* record book!

The UK is a major player in the league table of record claimants and record holders, with 464 successful attempts ratified out of 7,111 claims, so we've tried to include as many of these records as possible. Well done to everyone who was selected – and commiserations to those who weren't lucky enough to make the grade.

If you didn't make it into the book, perhaps you featured on one of our TV shows? Guinness World Records has rarely been off our screens, adjudicating records on programmes such as *Blue Peter*, *The Paul O'Grady Show*, *The Gadget Show* and *The Alan Titchmarsh Show*. So, a massive thank you goes out

THE SIMPSONS: A highlight of the year was meeting *The Simpsons* creators Al Jean (left) and Matt Groening at the San Diego Comic Con 2009. See more on p.174.

PADDLE POWER

Hats off to *Blue Peter*'s Helen Skelton (UK), who made the ★**longest journey by canoe** this year! Her solo effort – to raise funds for Sport Relief – saw her cover 3,234.79 km (2,010 miles), or 60 miles a day for six weeks, travelling from Peru and arriving in St John in the Amazon Delta, Brazil, on 28 February 2010.

ANNE-MARIE

Blue Peter

HELE

★ NEW RECORD
★ UPDATED RECORD

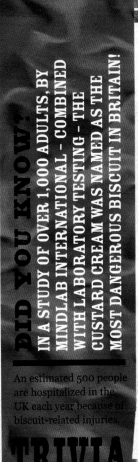
An estimated 500 people are hospitalized in the UK each year because of biscuit-related injuries.

TRIVIA

to all the hosts, producers, directors, assistants and, of course, claimants, who made these records happen.

Thanks also to the two major teams that source the records. Our worldwide adjudicators and consultants have been busier than ever dealing with claims from every country – and made my job as Editor-in-Chief ever more difficult by unearthing ever more fascinating records. Find out more in our special feature on p.12– *Adjudicators & Consultants*.

Did you know that there's a new way to get *your* name into the records books – it's called *GWR Live!* and

GADGET SHOW: It's one of our fave TV shows, so it's been a privilege to take part in *The Gadget Show* (Five). Congrats to Jason, Suzi and the gang for all their success!

PAUL O'GRADY: A big thank you again to Paul and his production team for attempting, setting and breaking so many records on his award-winning TV show!

AROUND THE WORLD WITH THE TALL MAN

Sultan Kösen (Turkey), the world's **tallest living human being**, stopped off in London on the first leg of his 2010 round-the-world tour. The jolly giant's been everywhere, from New York and Madrid to Reykjavik and Vienna. Here he is having the sun kept off his back during a photoshoot outside the GWR offices. Such a superstar! Turn to pp.72–73 to find out more about his trip.

GADGETS GALORE
OVER THE YEARS *THE GADGET SHOW* HAS SET FOUR GUINNESS WORLD RECORDS, INCLUDING ONE FOR THE ★FASTEST SLOT CAR (1,583.4 SCALE KM/H; 983.88 SCALE MPH).

ON THE UP
IT APPEARS THAT SULTAN IS STARTING TO STRAIGHTEN UP – THANKS TO A MEDICAL SUPPLIER WHO PROVIDED HIM WITH OUT-SIZED CRUTCHES, ALLOWING HIM TO STAND UPRIGHT FOR THE FIRST TIME IN YEARS.

SOLE MAN
SULTAN WOULD LIKE TO SAY HOW INDEBTED HE IS TO SHOEMAKER GEORGE WESSELS (GERMANY) FOR SUPPLYING HIM WITH MADE-TO-MEASURE SHOES. "IT MAKES SUCH A BIG DIFFERENCE TO HAVE SHOES THAT FIT!" SAYS SULTAN.

LE MANS, FRANCE
The **fastest lap in the Le Mans 24-hour race** is 3 min 21.27 sec (average speed 242.093 km/h; 150.429 mph) by Alain Ferté (France) in a Jaguar XJR-9LM on 10 June 1989.

48°00'N
0°11'E

INTRODUCTION
EDITOR'S LETTER

★ ★ ★ ★ ★ ★ ★ ★ ★ ★ ★ ★ ★ ★ ★

> *"I've always wanted to achieve great things, and for the first time in my entire career I feel I've accomplished something now that my name is in* The Guinness Book of World Records.*"*
>
> **Michael Jackson, at a GWR party held in his honour in 1984**

PETER CROUCH: England's famed robotic dancer led a group of 429 players from the Danone Nations Cup in the ★largest robot dance on 17 May 2010.

DISNEY: How better to mark the London premiere of Robert Zemeckis' A Christmas Carol movie than by organizing the ★largest group of carol singers? Leading the 14,100-strong choir was tenor Andrea Bocelli.

you can learn more about this travelling, hands-on record-breaking roadshow on pp.16–17. And never mind *other* people's TV shows – another way to get your name listed here is by setting or breaking a record on one of our *own* global TV progammes. For a summary of *GWR TV* filmed this year, see p.14.

With all these exciting ways to source Guinness World Records, it's been a task and a half trying to squeeze them all in. Still, it's helped me to create some exciting new sections for this year's book:
• Did you miss the very first spread on *Fire!*? If so, check back to pp.2–3 now for an explosive start to *2011*.

• We bid a fond farewell to the *Space Shuttle* programme on pp.28–29 as NASA confirms the end of an era for its iconic reusable space craft.
• Sultan update! Learn the latest about the **tallest living man**'s world tour on p.72 (and check out the latest on the **shortest living mobile man** on p.76).

• Animal fans: check out the *two* chapters on pets and wildlife: *Living Planet* (pp.46–69) and *Animal Magic* (pp.148–157).
• Armchair detectives who can't get enough *Cop & crime shows* should turn to p.168; if true crime is more your thing, check out pp.130–131.
• Thanks to James Cameron's *Avatar* (the **most successful movie of all time***; see p.158), the world's gone mad for *3D cinema*, so don't miss our special feature on pp.180–181.

• I spent a fascinating week at the San Diego Comic Con researching lots of new material on *Sci-fi & fantasy TV* (pp.170–171) and *Comics & graphic novels* (pp.164–165) as well as seizing the opportunity to meet the legendary Matt Groening (*see Toons & animation*, pp.174–175).
• Along the bottom of every page you'll find our *Records GPS* feature: go on a city-by-city world tour, starting in the "home of time" itself – Greenwich in London, at 0° on the map – and travel east around the world to various cities in order of longitude.
• And, as usual, you'll find every major sporting record listed in our *Sports Reference* section, starting on p.268.

VIRGIN LONDON MARATHON

Sherlock Holmes beat Wally and Zorro? Fred Flintstone beat Woody and Buzz Lightyear? It can mean only one thing: the Virgin London Marathon! On 25 April 2010, GWR once again lent its support to this fantastic fund-raising race, ratifying 19 new records – a record in itself! Find out more on pp.246–247.

'APPY TALK
GWR HAS GONE APP MAD, CREATING UNIQUE DIGITAL CONTENT FOR THE IPAD AND IPHONE PLATFORMS – CHECK US OUT ON APPLE'S APP STORE.

HE PINGPING

He might have been small in stature, but He Pingping (right) had the personality of a giant. The news of his passing made headlines around the world; the iconic Pingping was adored by millions of people, many of whom wrote to us to express their sadness.

Many of you also asked who would fill Pingping's small shoes as the new **shortest living mobile man**. The answer is Edward Niño Hernandez (left) of Colombia – you'll find his record on p.77.

WITNESS
EDWARD NIÑO HERNANDEZ (COLOMBIA) WAS MEASURED IN APRIL 2010 BY DOCTORS IN BOGOTÁ. PRESENT WAS GWR JUDGE CARLOS MARTINEZ (ON THE LEFT IN THE PICTURE ABOVE).

DANCER
EDWARD LISTS AMONG HIS HOBBIES DANCING TO REGGAETON IN CLUBS, KEEPING FIT, DRESSING UP AND IMPERSONATING MICHAEL JACKSON, AND (NO PUN INTENDED) THE TV SHOW *SMALLVILLE!*

COMICS LEGEND
TURN TO P.164 FOR ALL THE BEST COMICS & GRAPHIC NOVELS RECORDS. CHECK OUT THE SPECIAL HEADER CREATED FOR US BY LETTERING GURU TODD KLEIN. THANKS TODD!

> *"There are few jobs in which you end the day teaching the world's smallest man how to play the drums!"*
>
> Craig Glenday,
> GWR Editor-in-Chief

IN MEMORIA

This year's edition is a particularly poignant one for us at GWR as it serves as our tribute to two very important record holders who died this year: Michael Jackson (p.187) and He Pingping (p.77).

Michael Jackson was a big fan of the book, and he was always willing to give up his time for us, whether it was to open a new GWR Museum or just to pop into the office to say hello. I was honoured to be considered Michael's friend, and I'll always cherish the memories of his visit to the London office in 2006, and presenting him with his award for *Thriller* at that year's World Music Awards.

A more recent addition to the GWR family was He Pingping, the world's **shortest living mobile man**. The cheeky, impish Pingping first lit up our lives in 2009 when he made the pages of our book, before going on to become an international superstar. I was lucky enough to visit Inner Mongolia to measure the little man for the first time, and I knew from the moment I set eyes on him that he was going to be... well, a big hit!

As we travelled together to introduce him to his new global fans, it was clear that his short stature was always going to have health implications. Yet, he never let his size get in the way of having a good time, and he refused to be treated as an invalid. He wrung all he could out of the precious time he had, inspiring those with troubles of their own.

So, what better message to take into the new decade than this: life is there to be lived! Enjoy every frightening bank and turn of that roller coaster, and feel the thrill of the unknown highs and lows ahead of you. And if you break some records along the way, so much the better! Have a fantastic 2011...

Craig Glenday
Editor-in-Chief.

Follow me at twitter.com/ craigglenday

LOOSE WOMEN: The TV ladies who lunch couldn't wait to witness the most stripper trousers ripped off in one minute. Host Coleen Nolan (above) was speechless!

HEART FM: Commiserations to DJ Jamie Theakston at Heart FM for his gallant effort at popping the most balloons in a minute. His failure only goes to show how difficult it can be to become a record holder!

DUBLIN'S 98: Siobhan O'Connor, co-host of the Morning Crew radio show, at last joined her fellow presenters as a record holder this year after hugging a record 5,000 people in 24 hours!

IPSWICH, UK

The most "hop the fence" yo-yo tricks in one minute is 144, set by Arron Sparks (UK) during an event in Ipswich, Suffolk, UK, on 27 July 2008.

52°03'N
1°09'E

INTRODUCTION
ADJUDICATORS & CONSULTANTS

★ ★ ★ ★ ★ ★ ★ ★ ★ ★ ★ ★ ★

MEET THE TWO TEAMS THAT CAN TURN YOUR DREAMS INTO REALITY... THE RECORDS ADJUDICATORS WITH THE POWER TO SAY "YES" OR "NO" TO YOUR CLAIM, AND THE CONSULTANTS, WHO USE THEIR SPECIALIST KNOWLEDGE TO FIND WORLD RECORD FACTS AND SUPERLATIVES ALL YEAR ROUND.

Information flows into the *Guinness World Records* office in one of two main ways. The first is via our **Adjudicators**, who manage the 65,000 claims we receive each year.

This multilingual team divides itself between the GWR offices and visiting record attempts all around the world. As each record application comes in, it is assigned to one of the team, who will work on approving or rejecting the claim. These are the guys who also write the official rules – often in conjunction with a relevant governing body or acknowledged expert or consultant *(see next page)*.

Pictured here are some of the team. You might recognize one or two of the adjudicators – they are often the judges you see on GWR TV shows!

ADJUDICATOR ON SITE
Here's GWR Adjudicator Carlos Martínez (Spain) assessing a record claim for the **highest gas pipeline** on location in Peru. To find out how you can apply to have a judge on site, visit **www.guinnessworldrecords.com**.

The Adjudicators
1. Louise Toms (UK)
2. Lucia Sinigagliesi (Italy)
3. Ralph Hannah (UK)
4. Louise Ireland (UK)
5. Aleksandr Vypirailenko (Ukraine)
6. Andrea Bánfi (Hungary)
7. Talal Omar (Yemen)
8. Marco Frigatti (Italy)
9. Jack Brockbank (UK)
10. Mariamarta Ruano-Graham (Guatemala)
11. Kristian Teufel (Germany)
12. Gareth Deaves (UK)
13. Amanda Mochan (USA)
14. Tarika Vara (UK)

WE SEEK
GWR FOUNDING EDITOR NORRIS McWHIRTER ONCE DESCRIBED HIS JOB AS "FINDING THE -ESTS FROM THE -ISTS" – THAT IS, FINDING SUPERLATIVES FROM THE EXPERTS.

WE SPEAK
ENGLISH, SPANISH, JAPANESE, GERMAN, DUTCH, PORTUGUESE, FRENCH, RUSSIAN, UKRAINIAN, HUNGARIAN, ROMANIAN, ITALIAN, KOREAN, ARABIC, CHINESE AND WELSH.

THE ADJUDICATORS

TOULOUSE, FRANCE
The **highest-capacity jet airliner** is the double-deck Airbus 380, which first flew in Toulouse, France, on 27 April 2005. While it has a nominal seating capacity of 555, it has a potential maximum seating capacity of 853 depending on the interior fuselage fit.

YOUNG AND OLD

Among those missing from the group photo below are gerontologist Robert Young (left), pictured here with last year's **oldest woman** Gertrude Baines (USA, 1894–2009) in Los Angeles, California, USA, and our TV historian Dick Fiddy (inset) of the British Film Institute.

Without all of these people – and feedback from you, the public – we wouldn't be able to produce such a compelling and diverse snapshot of our record-breaking year. So thanks to everyone who contributes to making the book – it's because of *you* that it continues to be the planet's **biggest-selling copyright book**!

Supporting the Adjudications team – and also playing a crucial role helping the editorial team research new records – are the **Consultants**. This is the international panel of experts who use their specialist knowledge to proactively research records on behalf of Guinness World Records.

The spectrum of topics covered by the Consultants is what gives Guinness World Records its unique appeal – from the latest scientific breakthroughs, via all the most important sporting achievements, to the very latest gossip and showbiz news from the entertainment industry. In between, we have medical expertise from a range of specialists (including a gerontologist who researches old age and longevity, a trichologist – that's a "hair" doctor! – and an endocrinologist who advises us on giants and dwarves), as well as engineers, mountain climbers, retired Air Force officers, sailors, musicians, a couple of very on-the-ball sports experts – one of whom specializes in US sports – and a TV historian from the British Film Institute.

Rounding off the list of experts are the countless (and often uncredited) academics, scientists, researchers and inventors who help us ratify records across our wide range of topics.

The Consultants
1. Kenneth (and Tatiana, not in shot) Crutchlow: Ocean Rowing Society
2. Thomasina Gibson: showbiz, movies, entertainments
3. Christian Marais: world sports, gambling, games
4. Craig Glenday: Editor-in-Chief, Guinness World Records
5. David Hawksett: planets, science, technology, engineering
6. Stephen Wrigley: aircraft, military, crime, judiciary, society
7. Dr Eleanor Clarke: anatomy, medicine, human body
8. Dave McAleer: music
9. Mike Flynn: journeys, adventuring.

SHUKER
MISSING FROM THE GROUP SHOT IS OUR ZOOLOGY CONSULTANT (AND CRYPTOZOOLOGIST) DR KARL SHUKER, WHO WAS ON A FIELD TRIP TO JAPAN AT THE TIME.

THE CONSULTANTS

SHOOT
ALAS, THE WEEK IN WHICH WE PLANNED TO PHOTOGRAPH ALL OUR ADJUDICATORS AND CONSULTANTS WAS THE WEEK IN WHICH THE ICELANDIC VOLCANO EYJAFJALLAJÖKULL ERUPTED – SO SOME OF THEM COULDN'T MAKE IT.

VERSAILLES, FRANCE

The **largest garden** is that created by André Le Nôtre (France) at Versailles, France, in the late 17th century for King Louis XIV. It covers over 6,070 ha (15,000 acres), of which the famous formal garden covers 100 ha (247 acres).

48°48'N
2°08'E

INTRODUCTION

GWR TV

★ ★ ★ ★ ★ ★ ★ ★ ★ ★ ★ ★ ☆

THE LAST 12 MONTHS HAVE SEEN US FILMING BREATH-TAKING FEATS IN 17 COUNTRIES, PUTTING TOGETHER 120 HOURS OF DYNAMIC, PRIMETIME ENTERTAINMENT FOR SHOWS SEEN IN 85 COUNTRIES AND FEATURING OVER 250 RECORD ATTEMPTS.

★ NEW RECORD
☆ UPDATED RECORD

"Travelling to different shows around the world I get to meet truly talented people that inspire me and make my job fun!"

GWR's Marco Frigatti

★OLDEST BODYBUILDER

On *Lo Show dei Record* in Italy on 18 March 2010, Ernestine Shepherd (USA, b. 16 June 1936) set a record for the **oldest competitive female bodybuilder**. She was 73 years 9 months and 2 days old at that time, and still competes in international bodybuilding competitions.

JAPAN

In Japan we have a series called *Guinness World Records Special* featuring talented individuals such as competitive eater extraordinaire Takeru Kobayashi (Japan, right), who munched six hot dogs in 3 minutes in Kashiwanohakoen Stadium just outside Tokyo on 25 August 2009 (see p.138 for other food feats carried out against the clock).

GREECE

The second series of *Guinness World Records* in Greece saw an audience share of over 25% of the country's viewing public! The show, broadcast by MEGA, the country's largest broadcaster, stars Kostas Fragolias, Lorentzo Cariere and Giorgos Lianos, pictured here celebrating with new record holder Daniele Seccarecci (Italy), the **heaviest competitive bodybuilder (male)** at 135 kg (297 lb 9.9 oz).

AUSTRALIA

Produced by Eyeworks and airing on the Seven Network, Australia's *Guinness World Records* takes record-breaking to the masses, with locations shoots where attempts are performed live before an astounded public. Studio feats included Mon Tanner's record for **fire eating – most torches extinguished in one minute**, with 88. But like so many before him he lost his record just a few months later...

CHINA

This was our fifth year working with CCTV, China's state broadcaster, and record breaking has never been so popular: *Zheng Da Zong Yi – Guinness World Records Special* has a regular audience of over 50 million! The show mixes highly competitive record-breaking spectaculars with popular acts and demonstrations of skill, such as an exhilarating performance by the Shaolin warrior monks, pictured centre.

ZOO
THE LATEST ITALIAN SERIES WAS VERY "ANIMAL-FRIENDLY" – IT FEATURED GIANT CENTIPEDES, TARANTULAS, KING COBRAS, RATTLE SNAKES, DOGS AND A WHITE OX!

WHO
GWR COMMISSION PHOTOGRAPHERS TO ATTEND FILMING AT OUR TV SHOWS TO ENSURE WE HAVE THE BEST AND MOST UP-TO-DATE PICTURES OF OUR RECORD HOLDERS.

POLAND

Broadcast by Polsat, Poland's second biggest television channel, *Guinness World Records* is a localized Polish edition of our popular Italian *Lo Show dei Record* show featuring many of the same record-breaking guests as the Italian programme. Now in its second series, our Polish show is presented by the former TV sports news presenter Maciej Dowbor. He is pictured here, in a return to his sporting roots, talking to Federica Pellegrini (Italy), women's 200 m freestyle (long course and short course) and 400 m (long course) freestyle world record holder.

NEW ZEALAND

Hosted by Marc Ellis, former All Black player and a Guinness World Record holder, TV2's *NZ Smashes Guinness World Records* saw a slight twist to our format – Eyeworks, the production company behind the show, handpicked record attempts that had featured in other TV shows, and lined up ambitious Kiwis to try to claim the record as their own! The success of this format in New Zealand – it frequently got an audience twice as large as that of *The Simpsons* (see p.175) when shown in NZ – led to a similar production in Australia, whereby these famously competitive nations could go head-to-head to see who could break the most Guinness World Records. The picture to the left shows 121 New Zealanders attempting the record for the **largest human mattress dominoes**.

ITALY

Euro Produzione, our long-standing production partners in Europe, hit gold with *Lo Show dei Record* in Italy, with 143 fresh record attempts and a new hostess in the shapely form of former model Paola Perego. Paola's personal touch was key to getting all the people who are "unici almondo" (unique in the world) to reveal the stories behind their attempts and achievements. Among the many successful record breakers were White Rope Skippers (all UK, pictured left) setting the record for the **most consecutive Double Dutch style skips by a team**, with 362.

FRANCE

Le Monde des Records is now in its 11th year in France and is as popular as ever. We broadcast more programmes by volume in this country than any other territory, and have also featured on more TV channels here than anywhere else. Pictured is Bruno Wattier's attempt at the **most stripper trousers worn and removed in one minute**. He set this record with five on 29 September 2009, but lost it on 18 March 2010 when it was beaten on the set of *Lo Show dei Record* in Rome, Italy!

★HEAVIEST SHOES WALKED IN

Physical fitness fan Zhang Zhenghui (China) appeared on the set of *Lo Show dei Record* in Rome, Italy, on 18 March 2010, where he managed to walk 10 m (32 ft 9 in) while wearing cast-iron shoes weighing a hefty 122.8 kg (270 lb 11.6 oz).

INTERVIEW MEET MR MOLLOY...

Rob Molloy (pictured right with champion gurner Tommy Mattinson) is Director of Television at Guinness World Records He took time out from his busy schedule to tell us what it's like on the set of a Guinness World Records show...
Well, each show is different. Many of them reflect the cultures of the country they are based in, and that's always interesting to see. Sometimes filming can be stressful, but it's always entertaining.

What are your favourite records that have featured on GWR TV programmes?
My personal favourite is the man who ran through 15 sheets of tempered glass on our New Zealand show. Or the record for the longest duration for three contortionists in a box – that was pretty crazy, they were filmed in countries all over Europe doing that!

What exciting new projects can we expect in the next year?
As well as our studio-based shows we are planning on taking audiences behind the scenes and on the road with our adjudicators, allowing them to see world records as they happen!

BEHIND THE SCENES AT GWR TV

There were 11 cameras on set at all times during the making of *Lo Show dei Record* in Rome, Italy, which began filming on 25 February and wrapped on 29 April 2010. It had a production team of 118 behind it (they ate 150 kg, or 330 lb 9.6 oz, of food between them while working), and it took 40 days to construct the set, which measured 40 x 40 m (131 ft 2 in x 131 ft 2 in).

EXTRA! FOR MORE RECORD-BREAKING TV, TURN TO PP.166-167.

Isabelle Dinoire (France) underwent the **first partial face transplant** at Amiens University Hospital, Amiens, France, on 27 November 2005. Ms Dinoire was left with severe facial disfigurement after her pet dog ripped off her nose, lips and chin trying to wake her after she accidentally overdosed on pills in May 2005.

INTRODUCTION

GUINNESS WORLD RECORDS LIVE!

GUINNESS WORLD RECORDS LIVE! IS ALL ABOUT TAKING RECORD BREAKING ON THE ROAD. WE'VE INVITED PEOPLE FROM ALL AROUND THE GLOBE TO COME TO OUR CHALLENGE FAIRS - THE ONLY PLACES IN THE WORLD WHERE YOU CAN WALK IN A HUMBLE MORTAL, AND WALK OUT A GENUINE GUINNESS WORLD RECORDS RECORD HOLDER!

★ **NEW RECORD**
☆ **UPDATED RECORD**

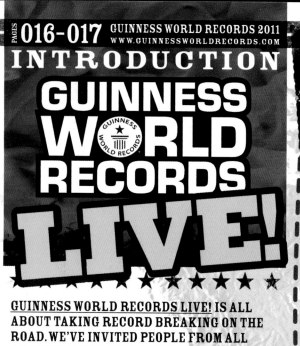
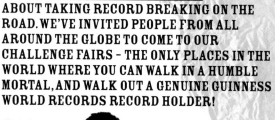

DALLAS, USA

★**MOST POINTS SCORED AS KOBE BRYANT PLAYING 2K SPORTS NBA 2K10 VIDEO GAME**
Chico Kora (USA, above) scored 29 points playing as Kobe Bryant on *NBA 2K10* at the NBA Jam in Dallas, Texas, USA, on 13 February 2010.

X GAMES
LA, CALIFORNIA & ASPEN, COLORADO, USA
GWR Live! got involved once again in the Summer and Winter X Games. Various BMX records were attempted (above and below), and Phil Smage (USA, below right) set the record for the **highest ollie on a snowskate**, at 72.4 cm (28.5 in).

CROWD PLEASERS
REDCOATS MICHEALA LORMIER AND DAVE CLARK HOSTED THE GUINNESS WORLD RECORD LIVE! AT BUTLINS RESORT IN BOGNOR REGIS, UK.

TRIVIA
DID YOU KNOW?
GWR LIVE! HAS WITNESSED OVER 250 RECORDS BEING BROKEN IN EIGHT COUNTRIES. THE MOST CULTURALLY DIVERSE CHALLENGE FAIR WAS AT GLOBAL VILLAGE IN DUBAI, UAE, WHICH WAS ATTENDED BY 34 DIFFERENT NATIONALITIES.

BED HEADS
A TEAM OF SIX (ALL UK) MADE UP A BUNK BED IN 1 MIN 11 SEC AT A GWR LIVE! EVENT AT BUTLINS, MINEHEAD, UK, ON 7 MARCH 2010.

BOGNOR REGIS, UK
★FASTEST TIME TO DRESS A BARBIE DOLL

This challenge proved endlessly fascinating for younger guests (above) at Butlins. The record to dress a Barbie in three items of clothing, shoes and an accessory is jointly held by Andrea Benjamin (UK) and Debbie Watson (UK), with a time of 36.99 sec on 15 April 2010.

OSAKA, JAPAN
★MOST BALLS CAUGHT, NO HANDS

The Guinness World Records Live! Challenge in the Park in Tokyo Midtown saw massive crowds trying their hand at rolling, spinning, throwing, sorting, folding, recycling and leap-frogging as they attempted to win a place in history. Pictured is 61-year-old Tsuyoshi Kitazawa from Akasaka, Tokyo, who set the record for the ★**most tennis balls caught with no hands in one minute**, with 15.

TURKEY
CAN STACKING

The GWR Live! Challenge Fair for Multi Corporation in Turkey started at Europe's largest shopping mall, the Forum Istanbul, and then toured Forum malls in cities across Turkey. Pictured is Deniz Özeskici (Turkey), who built a 20-can pyramid in just 6.49 sec on 4 April 2010.

BIG IN JAPAN
THE GWR LIVE! PARK CHALLENGE LAUNCHED IN TOKYO MIDTOWN, AKASAKA, TOKYO, ON 29 APRIL 2010. ON THE VERY FIRST DAY, EIGHT NEW GUINNESS WORLD RECORDS WERE SET.

SCREAM

DUBAI
LOUDEST SHOUT...

At Global Village in Dubai, UAE, members of the public broke 61 records over 110 days throughout early 2010. One of the most popular challenges was the **loudest shout** (pictured left), but no one was able to equal Annalisa Wray (UK), who achieved a shout of 121.7 dBA way back on 16 April 1994. It's still the record to beat...

DUNKIRK, FRANCE

The **greatest evacuation in military history** was carried out by 1,200 Allied naval and civil craft from Dunkerque (Dunkirk), France, between 26 May and 4 June 1940. A total of 338,226 British and French troops were rescued.

51°02′N 2°22′E

INTRODUCTION
HOW TO BE A
RECORD
BREAKER

★ ★ ★ ★ ★ ★ ★ ★ ★ ★ ★

SO, YOU FANCY YOURSELF AS
A RECORD BREAKER? WANT
TO GET YOUR NAME IN PRINT?
HERE'S OUR IDIOT'S GUIDE TO
TURNING YOUR IDEAS INTO
ACTION. APPLYING IS FREE
AND EASY, SO YOU'VE GOT
NO EXCUSES...

EXTRA!
IF ANIMATION GETS
YOU ANIMATED, TAKE
A TRIP TO TOON WORLD
ON P.174.

NEW CATEGORY: This is what we
call a record claim that we've never seen before (as opposed
to an "existing category"). But you have to convince us that
your idea is a good one before we open a new category!

STEP 1
Think of a record! Or better,
flick through a copy of the
GWR book and find a record
you think you can break.
Looking through the book
will also give you an idea of
the kinds of records we like.

STEP 2
Visit **www.guinnessworld
records.com** and click on
"APPLY NOW" – then tell us
about your record
idea. Give us as
much notice as
you can (about
three months
is ideal!).

STEP 6
Now you practise, practise,
practise. This is Luke, by
the way, and he wants to try
the **longest time juggling
three objects blindfolded**.

STEP 7
When you're ready, attempt
your record as per the
guidelines. Be sure to have
at least two independent
witnesses, and film the entire
event. Invite the press, too!

STEP 8
Next, mail us your evidence,
your video footage, your
signed witness statements
and whatever else we've
requested in the guidelines.
Then there's more
waiting to do...

SNAP!
IF YOU REALLY WANT
TO SEE YOUR RECORD
IN THE BOOK, BE SURE
TO SUBMIT THE BEST
POSSIBLE PHOTOS – WE
LOVE RECORDS WITH
EXCITING, DYNAMIC
PHOTOGRAPHY!

36°42'N
3°13'E
ALGIERS, ALGERIA
The world's **largest bowl of couscous** weighed 6.04 tonnes (13,315 lb) and was made by Semoulerie
Industrielle de la Mitidja and displayed at the International Fair of Algiers, Algeria, on 3 June 2004.

STEP 3

The next bit's easy – you just have to wait while our Records Management Team (RMT) plough through their (enormous) inbox and get to your claim. This is why we need the time – also, we might need expert help assessing your idea.

FAST TRACK
IF YOU'RE IN A RUSH, WHY NOT TRY OUR THREE-DAY FAST TRACK SERVICE? YOU PAY A FEE FOR A DEDICATED RECORDS MANAGER TO PROCESS YOUR CLAIM ASAP.

STEP 4

If your record category already exists, we'll email you the guidelines that the last claimant followed. If it's a new category – and we like it – we'll create new guidelines and email them to you asap.

STEP 5

Congratulations, we like your idea and you've got the guidelines. Read and follow them carefully – if you ignore them, you're unlikely to succeed.

If you get a "no" from Marco's Records Management Team, don't despair – rethink your idea and then re-apply. We reject about 85% of claims because they're too dangerous or too stupid... or just not impressive enough!

STEP 9

Back at GWR Towers, we'll watch your video, assess your witness statements and consult with any necessary governing body or expert. Have you followed the guidelines? Have you beaten the record?

STEP 10

Congratulations – if you're a record breaker, we'll send you your official GWR certificate. You're now a member of an elite group, a special family of high achievers, a crack squad of record holders!

STEP 11

There's one last stage: if you're *really* lucky, your record will be selected for the annual GWR book. Not every record makes it – only the best of the best! Good luck, everyone!

GHENT, BELGIUM
Jos de Troyer (Belgium) created the **largest hanging basket** measuring 10.5 m (34 ft 5 in) in diameter and weighing 45 tonnes (99,208 lb) in Ghent, Belgium. It went on display in April 2000 above the Emile Braunplein Square.

51°03'N
3°44'E

INTRODUCTION

GWR DAY

★ **NEW RECORD**
★ **UPDATED RECORD**

★ ★ ★ ★ ★ ★ ★ ★ ★ ★ ★ ★ ★

GUINNESS WORLD RECORDS DAY IS OUR ANNUAL, GLOBAL CELEBRATION OF RECORD BREAKING, WHEN HUNDREDS OF THOUSANDS OF PEOPLE AROUND THE WORLD GET TOGETHER TO SET OR BREAK RECORDS. HERE IS JUST A SMALL SELECTION OF FEATS ATTEMPTED ON AND AROUND GWR DAY 2009!

GWR DAY 2009

RECORD	NAME	COUNTRY OF ORIGIN
Most push ups with claps (73)	Stephen Buttler	UK
Tallest matchstick model (6.53 m; 6 million matches)	Toufic Daher	Lebanon
Largest sports lesson (884)	multiple	Ireland
Fastest hot water bottle burst (18.81 seconds)	Shaun Jones	UK
Fastest time to peel and eat three lemons (28.5 seconds)	Jim Lyngvild	Denmark
Largest cup of hot chocolate (4.5 litres; 4 gallons)	Serendipity 3	USA
Largest paintbrush mosaic (10 x 2.6 m; 32 ft 9 in x 8 ft 6 in)	Saimir Strati	Albania
Highest wall climb on darts (5 m; 16 ft 4 in)	Maiko Kiesewetter	Germany

UK

★ FARTHEST DISTANCE TO PULL A BUS WITH THE HAIR

Manjit Singh (UK), the "Iron Man of Leicester", pulled an 8-tonne (8.8-ton) double-decker bus 21.2 m (69 ft 6 in) using just his hair as part of the GWR celebrations in London. He tried the same stunt in 2007 using his ears but failed to move the bus the required distance.

NORTHERN IRELAND

★ STORYBOOK CHARACTERS

The largest gathering of people dressed as storybook characters is 300, achieved by Carr's Glen Primary School in Belfast, Northern Ireland, UK.

ITALY

★ FASTEST TIME TO EAT PASTA

Ernesto Cesario (Italy) ate his way into the record books on GWR Day 2009 by eating a 150-g (5.2-oz) bowl of pasta in 1 min 30 sec in Milan.

USA

★ LARGEST CHEERLEADING DANCE

GWR Day is now so popular in America, it takes up the entire week! One of our favourite events from last year involved 297 participants from the University Cheerleaders Association (USA) performing the largest cheerleading dance at the University of Memphis in Tennessee. Each participant danced for a muscle-pounding 5 min 43 sec!

GERMANY

★ FARTHEST JOURNEY BY WATERSLIDE

To commemorate GWR Day in Germany, a team of 10 (all Germany) broke the 24-hour water-slide distance record, covering a fantastic 1,357.22 km (843.33 miles) at the Galaxy Erding indoor waterpark, the largest of its kind in Europe.

52°04'N 4°18'E

THE HAGUE, THE NETHERLANDS

The **largest clog dance** involved 475 participants at an event organized by Introdans Education and Dance and Child International at the Spuiplein in the Hague, the Netherlands, on 8 July 2006.

FINLAND
★ FASTEST 40 M BY HUMAN WHEELBARROW

The truly international team of Adrian Rodriguez (Mexico, standing) and Sergiy Vetrogonov (Ukraine) achieved the fastest 40 m (131 ft) by a human wheelbarrow, taking just 17 seconds in Helsinki, Finland. The dynamic duo averaged a speed of 0.29 m/s (0.951 ft/s).

NETHERLANDS
★ MOST BASKETBALL BOUNCES (1 MIN)

Congratulations to Kiran Harpal (Netherlands) who broke the one-minute basketball-bounce record at the Hiernasst Youth Center in Wijchen with 384 consecutive bounces in the allotted time!

TURKEY
★ MOST CONCRETE BLOCKS BROKEN (30 SEC)

Martial arts expert Ali Bahçetepe (Turkey) broke 655 blocks using just his hands in 30 seconds in Datça Cumhuriyet Meydani, Turkey, on 11 November 2009.

UK
★ MOST PEOPLE HUGGING (1 MIN)

To kick off GWR Day in the UK, a total of 112 morning commuters hugged one another at St Pancras station in London for one minute.

FREE HUGS

ORGANIC WORLD

EXTRA!
FOR MORE SHOWS OF STRENGTH, FLEX YOUR MUSCLES AND TURN TO PP.90-91.

NORWAY
★ LARGEST GINGERBREAD MAN

Getting in on the action was IKEA Furuset in Oslo, Norway, where this ginormous gingerbread man weighing 651 kg (1,435 lb 3 oz) was baked and decorated.

ITALY
★ LONGEST PLATFORM-TO-PLATFORM BICYCLE JUMP

Bicycle daredevil Vittorio Brumotti (Italy) successfully cleared a jump of 4.02 m (13 ft 2 in) between the top of two trucks in Fiera Milano, Milan, Italy.

NEW ZEALAND
FARTHEST MALTESER BLOW

Over in NZ, we could rely on multiple record holder Alistair Galpin to lead the charge. First off was the **farthest distance to blow a Malteser** (a chocolate covered honeycomb malt ball) **using a straw** – 11.29 m (37 ft).
- Later the same day, Alistair achieved the ★**farthest distance to spit a champagne cork** at 5 m (16 ft 3 in).
- He then rounded the day off with the ★**farthest distance to blow a coin** – an epic 37.6 cm (14 ft 4 in).

TN

BRUSSELS, BELGIUM
The **largest deliberately buried hoard of coins** ever found was the so-called Brussels hoard of 1908, comprising approximately 150,000 coins.

50°50N 4°21E

SPACE

CONTENTS

LARGEST SPACE TELESCOPE

NASA's Hubble Space Telescope (HST, inset), named after the eminent American astronomer Edwin P Hubble, celebrated its 20th anniversary in April 2010. The telescope, which weighs 11 tonnes (24,250 lb) and is 13.1 m (43 ft) in overall length, with a 240-cm (94.8-in) reflector, was launched into space by the US space shuttle *Discovery* on 24 April 1990. It has been serviced five times while in orbit and is currently due to remain in use until at least 2014. During its operational lifespan, the HST has captured spectacular images of many deep-space objects, such as this image of R136, a young stellar grouping in the 30 Doradus Nebula.

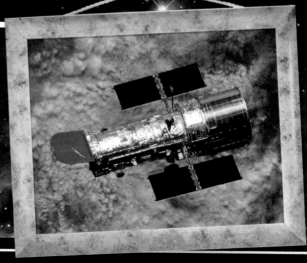

NÎMES, FRANCE

48°50'N 4°21'E

The **largest surviving ancient Roman aqueduct** is the Pont du Gard near Nîmes in southern France, which stands 47 m (155 ft) tall and is 275 m (902 ft) long at its highest level. It was built in the late 1st century BC or the early 1st century AD and carried water across the river Gard.

52°01'N
4°22'E

DELFT, THE NETHERLANDS

The **largest flying paper aircraft**, with a wing-span of 13.97 m (45 ft 10 in),
was constructed by a team of students from the Faculty of Aerospace Engineering at
Delft University of Technology, the Netherlands, and flown on 16 May 1995.

SPACE
A SENSE OF SCALE

TRIVIA

DID YOU KNOW?
THE EARTH HAS A DIAMETER OF 12,756 KM (7926 MILES) AND A MASS OF 5,974,000,000,000,000,000,000,000 KG. IT'S 149 MILLION KM (92.9 MILLION MILES) FROM THE SUN, BUT HOW DOES IT COMPARE WITH OTHER BODIES IN THE UNIVERSE?

★ NEW RECORD
★ UPDATED RECORD

LARGEST SPIRAL GALAXY

Discovered in 1986, from photographs taken by the Anglo-Australian astronomer David Malin, and later named after him, Malin 1 is a spiral galaxy some 1.1 billion light-years away. In terms of its diameter, it is the largest known spiral galaxy in the Universe, measuring around 650,000 light-years across – several times the size of our Milky Way, which has a diameter of around 100,000 light-years. Malin 1 contains some 50 billion suns'-worth of free-floating hydrogen.

LARGEST GLOBULAR CLUSTER

Omega Centauri, in the southern constellation of Centaurus, is the most massive of the roughly 140 globular clusters surrounding our galaxy. Consisting of several million stars with a combined mass equivalent to 5 million Suns, it is visible to the naked eye as a hazy star. However big this might seem, though, it would still take around 100,000 Omega Centauris to equal just one spiral galaxy such as the galaxy in which we live, the Milky Way.

LARGEST STAR

Due to the physical difficulties in directly measuring the size of a distant star, not all astronomers agree on the identity of the largest star, but the most likely candidate is VY Canis Majoris, a red supergiant some 5,000 light-years away. Estimates of its size give it a diameter of between 2.5 and 3 billion km (1.55–1.86 billion miles) or 1,800–2,100 times the size of the Sun. If placed at the centre of the Solar System, its outer surface would reach beyond the orbit of Jupiter.

LARGEST GALAXY

The central galaxy of the Abell 2029 galaxy cluster, located 1,070 million light-years away from the Earth in the constellation of Virgo has a major diameter of 5,600,000 light-years – 80 times the diameter of our own Milky Way galaxy – and a light output equivalent to 2,000,000,000,000 (two trillion) Suns. Scientists suspect Abell 2029 attained its massive size by pulling in nearby galaxies.

LARGEST STRUCTURE IN THE UNIVERSE

A team of astronomers led by Richard Gott III and Mario Juric (both USA) of Princeton University, Princeton, New Jersey, USA, have discovered a huge wall of galaxies some 1.37 billion light-years long. They used data from the Sloan Digital Sky Survey, which is mapping the locations of one million galaxies in the universe. Their discovery was announced in October 2003.

= 16,000 LIGHT-

= 560,000 LIGHT-YEARS

= 100 MILLION LIGHT-YEARS

LARGEST STAR WITH A PLANET

In January 2003, astronomers announced their discovery of a planet orbiting the orange giant star HD 47536. This star is expanding at the end of its life and now measures around 33 million km (20.5 million miles, or 23 times the size of the Sun) across. The planet is some 300 million km (186 million miles) from its star but will be consumed in

ANTWERP, BELGIUM
51°13'N 4°24'E
The **largest ever gem theft** occurred at the Antwerp Diamond Centre, Belgium, when 123 of the 160 vaults were emptied in a weekend raid between 15–16 February 2003, resulting in an estimated loss of $100 million (£62 million).

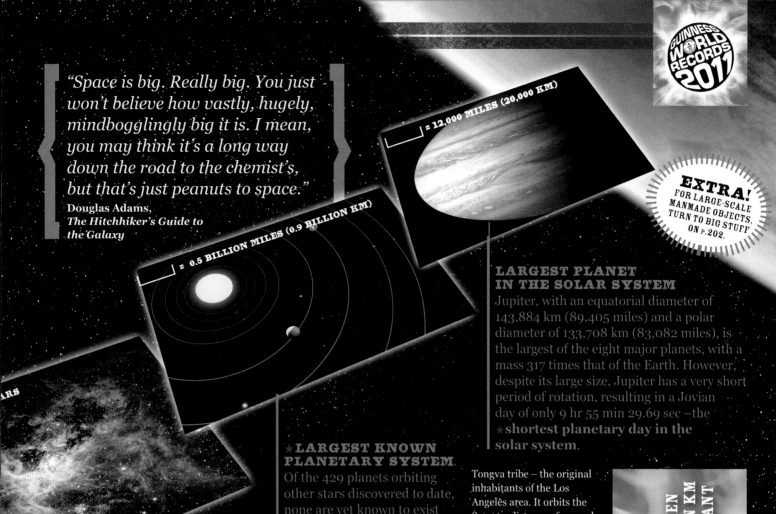

> "Space is big. Really big. You just won't believe how vastly, hugely, mindbogglingly big it is. I mean, you may think it's a long way down the road to the chemist's, but that's just peanuts to space."

Douglas Adams,
The Hitchhiker's Guide to the Galaxy

= 12,000 MILES (20,000 KM)

= 0.5 BILLION MILES (0.9 BILLION KM)

EXTRA!
FOR LARGE-SCALE MANMADE OBJECTS, TURN TO BIG STUFF ON P.202.

LARGEST PLANET IN THE SOLAR SYSTEM

Jupiter, with an equatorial diameter of 143,884 km (89,405 miles) and a polar diameter of 133,708 km (83,082 miles), is the largest of the eight major planets, with a mass 317 times that of the Earth. However, despite its large size, Jupiter has a very short period of rotation, resulting in a Jovian day of only 9 hr 55 min 29.69 sec –the ★ **shortest planetary day in the solar system**.

★ LARGEST KNOWN PLANETARY SYSTEM

Of the 429 planets orbiting other stars discovered to date, none are yet known to exist within a planetary system as large as our own Solar System, which is thought to be 100,000 AU (15 billion km; 9.3 billion miles) across.

LARGEST NEBULA VISIBLE TO THE NAKED EYE

The Tarantula Nebula in the constellation of Doradus, in the southern sky, is large and bright enough to be visible to the naked eye, despite being at a distance of 170,000 light-years (10.7 billion AU). The huge cloud of glowing gas and dust has a diameter of around 1,000 light-years (63 million AU) and is the only nebula outside our galaxy visible to the naked eye.

Tongva tribe – the original inhabitants of the Los Angeles area. It orbits the Sun at a distance of around 6 billion km (4 billion miles) and has an orbital period of 288 years.

LARGEST ASTEROID IN THE ASTEROID BELT

Among all the objects in the asteroid belt between Mars and Jupiter, Ceres is the largest, with an average diameter of 941 km (584.7 miles). Discovered by Giuseppe Piazzi at Palermo, Sicily, on 1 January 1801, Ceres is large enough to have an almost spherical shape: It is classified as the **smallest dwarf planet** and is due to be visited by NASA's *Dawn* probe in 2015.

and a diameter of around 2,400 km (1,490 miles). Before the reclassification of Pluto as a dwarf planet, Eris was regarded by many as the tenth planet of the Solar System. Eris has a small moon, Dysnomia, around 350 km (217 miles) across.

LARGEST KUIPER BELT OBJECT

The Kuiper belt is the cloud of frozen gases and debris at the edges of our solar system around 55 AU (8.1 billion km; 5 billion miles) from the Sun. The Kuiper Belt object 50000 Quaoar measures around 1,300 km (800 miles) across and was discovered by Chad Trujillo and Mike Brown (both USA) at Caltech, Pasadena, California, USA, on 4 June 2002. The object, originally dubbed 2002 LM60, is named after a creation god of the

★ LARGEST ASTEROID VISITED BY SPACECRAFT

First discovered in 1885, 253 Mathilde, like Ceres, is found in the Asteroid Belt. The asteroid measures 66 x 48 x 46 km (41 x 29 x 28 miles) and became the third and largest asteroid to be encountered by a spacecraft in June 1997, when it was passed by NASA's *NEAR Shoemaker* spacecraft.

a few tens of millions of years as the star continues to expand into a red giant.

★ LARGEST EXTRASOLAR PLANET

Discovered in 2006, TrES-4 is an extrasolar planet some 1,400 light-years away, orbiting its parent star GSC 02620-006648 once every 3.5 days. It was discovered using the transit method, where the planet eclipses its star during its

short orbit as seen from Earth. With a diameter of around 240,000 km (150,00 miles), it is some 1.7 times the size of Jupiter.

LARGEST DWARF PLANET

The icy world Eris was discovered in January 2005. It has a highly elliptical orbit, with its distance from the Sun ranging from between 5.6 and 14.6 billion km (3.4–9.07 billion miles),

DID YOU KNOW?

AN ASTRONOMICAL UNIT (AU) IS A UNIT OF MEASUREMENT EQUAL TO THE DISTANCE BETWEEN THE EARTH AND THE SUN. ONE AU IS 149 MILLION KM (92 MILLION MILES) – NEPTUNE, THE MOST DISTANT PLANET TO EARTH, IS 30 AU AWAY.

TRIVIA

A light-year – the distance light travels in a year – is equivalent to 9.4 trillion km (5.8 trillion miles).

SPACE
SATURN

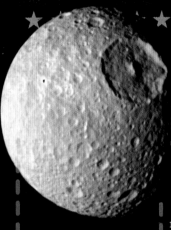

★ ★ ★ ★ ★ ★ ★

LEAST ROUND PLANET

A combination of its low density (less than water) and rapid rotation (10.6 hours) gives Saturn the most oblate shape among the planets. Its equatorial diameter is 120,536 km (74,897.5 miles) while its polar diameter is just 108,728 km (67,560 miles).

★ SMALLEST ROUND WORLD

Mimas, the 20th largest moon in the Solar System, is just 396.6 km (246.4 miles) across. It is the smallest known body in the Solar System whose shape has been rounded due to its own gravity. The largest crater on Mimas is Herschel, which is 130 km (80 miles) across. It has 5-km-high (3-mile) walls, and a 6-km-high (4-mile) high central peak.

★ LONGEST-LASTING LIGHTNING STORM

A lightning storm in Saturn's upper atmosphere raged for more than eight months in 2009. Monitored by the *Cassini* spacecraft, the storm, with a diameter of a few thousand kilometres, caused lightning flashes in Saturn's atmosphere around 10,000 times the intensity of their terrestrial counterparts.

★ LARGEST ERUPTIVE ICE PLUMES

Active cryovolcanism on Enceladus, Saturn's sixth-largest moon, had been predicted by scientists ever since the encounters by the two *Voyager* spacecraft in the early 1980s had revealed the geologically young surface of this icy moon. In 2005, observations from the *Cassini* spacecraft showed immense plumes of water ice above the moon's south pole. They are formed by the eruption of pressurized water reservoirs beneath the ice, forced to the surface by volcanic activity. They are at least as tall as the moon's 505-km (313-mile) diameter.

★ CLOSEST MOON TO SATURN

Discovered in July 2009 using observations from the *Cassini* spacecraft, S/2009 S 1 is a tiny moon just 300 m (985 ft) across that orbits Saturn at a distance of just 56,732 km (35,251 miles), less than the radius of the planet. It orbits within the outer B Ring and was discovered using the shadow it cast across the rings themselves.

★ OUTERMOST DISCRETE RING

The most outwardly discrete ring, as opposed to a diffuse dust disc, is the contorted F Ring, with an orbital radius of 141,000 km (87,600 miles). It lies some 4,000 km (2,500 miles) beyond the edge of the main ring system and is probably the most dynamically active ring in the Solar System. Just a few hundred kilometres wide, the F Ring is held in place by two shepherd moons, Pandora and Prometheus, whose gravitational interactions with the ring particles produce twisted knots within the ring that can change appearance over just a few hours.

★ LARGEST PLANETARY RING

The Phoebe ring, discovered by NASA's Spitzer Infrared Telescope and announced on 6 October 2009, is a sparse disc of dust that extends to the orbit of the moon Phoebe, some 12,955,759 km (8,050,335 miles) from Saturn itself. It is believed to be formed by dust kicked off the surface of Phoebe by micrometeorite impacts.

GREATEST RING SYSTEM

The intricate system of rings around Saturn have a combined mass of around 4×10^{19} kg (9×10^{19} lb) – equivalent to the mass of an icy moon around 400 km (250 miles) across, or 1,800 times less massive than our Moon. Gaps in the ring (such as the Colombo Gap) are caused by the gravitational influence of Saturn's moons. Rings G and E are more distant and not shown below.

Colombo Gap

Maxwell Gap

EXTRA!
TURN THE PAGE FOR EVERYTHING YOU NEED TO KNOW ABOUT THE SPACE SHUTTLE.

D RING

C RING

LEAST DENSE PLANET

Saturn is composed mostly of hydrogen and helium, the two lightest elements in the universe. It has an average density of only 0.71 times that of water. As Saturn is actually less dense than water, it would float – if there were an area of water in the Solar System large enough to accommodate it!

HOT! THE PASTEL AND YELLOW HUES ON THE PLANET REVEAL MANY CONTRASTING BRIGHT AND DARKER BANDS IN BOTH HEMISPHERES OF SATURN'S WEATHER SYSTEM.

SHOT! THIS TRUE COLOUR PHOTOGRAPH WAS ASSEMBLED FROM *VOYAGER 2* SATURN IMAGES OBTAINED ON 4 AUGUST 1998 FROM A DISTANCE OF 21 MILLION KM (13 MILLION MILES).

DID YOU KNOW?

THE BOTTOM RIGHT IMAGE SHOWS A FLASH OF SUNLIGHT REFLECTED OFF A METHANE LAKE ON SATURN'S MOON TITAN. THIS TYPE OF GLINT IS KNOWN AS A SPECULAR REFLECTION.

Cassini took the image of Kraken Mare on 8 July 2009 from 200,000 km (120,000 miles).

TRIVIA

TALLEST RIDGE IN THE SOLAR SYSTEM

Observations of Saturn's moon Iapetus by the NASA/ESA spacecraft *Cassini-Huygens* on 31 December 2004 revealed a ridge at least 1,300 km (800 miles) long, reaching an altitude of around 20 km (12 miles) above the surface. Iapetus is just 1,400 km (890 miles) across.

LARGEST CHAOTICALLY ROTATING OBJECT

Saturn's moon Hyperion measures 410 x 260 x 220 km (254 x 161 x 136 miles) and is the largest highly irregularly shaped body in the Solar System. It is one of only two bodies in the Solar System discovered to have completely chaotic rotation, tumbling in its orbit around Saturn. The other is asteroid 4179 Toutatis, measuring 4.5 x 2.4 x 1.9 km (2.7 x 1.5 x 1.1 miles).

CLOSEST MOONS TO EACH OTHER

Janus and Epimetheus share the same average orbit some 91,000 km (56,500 miles) above Saturn. As their orbital paths are only 50 km (31 miles) apart, one of the moons is always catching the other up. Every four years they come within 10,000 km (6,200 miles) of each other and swap orbits, before drifting apart again.

SATELLITE WITH THE THICKEST ATMOSPHERE

Saturn's large moon Titan has the thickest atmosphere of any moon in the Solar System, exerting a surface pressure of 1.44 bar. It consists mainly of nitrogen gas and is the most similar atmosphere to our own in the Solar System.

★ **NEW RECORD**
★ **UPDATED RECORD**

★LARGEST METHANE SEA

Kraken Mare, on Titan, is a body of liquid methane 1,170 km (727 miles) across and with an area similar to that of the Caspian Sea on Earth (3,626,000 km²; 1,400,000 miles²). In July 2009, *Cassini* imaged the glint of reflected sunlight off Kraken Mare.

Huygens Gap

Encke Gap

Keeler Gap

B RING

A RING

F RING

LYON, FRANCE

An international team of eight surgeons carried out the **earliest hand transplant operation** when they stitched the hand of a dead man to the wrist of 48-year-old Clint Hallam (New Zealand) in 1998, after he had suffered a chainsaw accident nine years previously.

FEATURE
SPACE SHUTTLES

★ ★ ★ ★ ★ ★ ★ ★ ★ ★ ★ ★

THE SPACE SHUTTLE – or, more accurately, the Shuttle Transportation System (STS) – made its first test flights in 1981, and orbital missions began the following year. It is the world's first – and to date only – spacecraft to make multiple orbital flights and landings.

Now, nearly 30 years later, NASA has announced the retirement of the space shuttle programme. With its end in sight, we take a look at the shuttle's record-breaking history and its major achievements.

★ MOST REUSED SPACECRAFT

NASA's space shuttle *Discovery* was last launched on 5 April 2010, beginning its 38th space flight, STS-131. *Discovery*, the third orbiter in the shuttle fleet, first flew in August 1984.

★ FIRST SPACECRAFT WITH A GLASS COCKPIT

Glass cockpits are characterized by electronic instrument displays, replacing older consoles that relied on mechanical gauges to display flight information. All three of NASA's operational shuttles have glass cockpits, the first to receive one being *Atlantis*, which flew with the new interface in 2000 during STS-101.

LARGEST SOLID ROCKET BOOSTER

The two boosters that assist the launch of the US space shuttle use solid rather than liquid fuel. They are the largest solid rocket boosters (SRBs) ever flown. Each booster is 45.4 m (149 ft) long and 3.6 m (12 ft) wide. Each contains more than 450,000 kg (1,000,000 lb) of propellant and provides a thrust of 1.49 million kg (3.3 million lb), or around 83% of lift-off power. Unlike the shuttle's external fuel tank, the SRBs are reusable.

LONGEST SHUTTLE FLIGHT

The lengthiest shuttle flight was by *Columbia* and its crew of five astronauts during the STS-80 mission. Launched on 19 November 1996, it had 17 days 15 hr 53 min 26 sec of mission elapsed time.

LARGEST SHUTTLE CREW

The shuttle mission with the largest crew to date was STS-61-A, which launched on 30 October 1985, carrying eight astronauts on board *Challenger*. This flight carried the West German Spacelab D-1 laboratory. The flight lasted 7 days 44 min 51 sec.

★ NEW RECORD
★ UPDATED RECORD

FIRST! SPACE SHUTTLE *COLUMBIA* WAS THE FIRST SPACECRAFT TO LAND ON WHEELS. BEFORE THIS, SPACECRAFT USED PARACHUTES TO REACH EARTH.

LAST! AT THE TIME OF GOING TO PRESS, THE LAST SHUTTLE MISSION PLANNED BY NASA, *DISCOVERY* STS-133, IS PLANNED FOR 16 SEPTEMBER 2010.

QUIZ!
WHAT WAS THE NAME GIVEN TO NASA'S FIRST SPACE SHUTTLE?
SEE p.278 FOR THE ANSWER.

LARGEST OBJECTS TRANSPORTED BY AIR

Although not the heaviest, the largest single objects to be transported by air are the 37.23-m (122-ft 2-in) space shuttles, which are "piggy-backed" on top of modified Boeing 747 jets from alternative landing strips back to Cape Canaveral in Florida, USA. *Discovery*, *Atlantis* and *Endeavour* each weigh around 100 tonnes (110 tons) when transported.

SPACE TOILET:

The toilet on the space shuttle uses foot straps and thigh bars to hold the user in place. Solids are stored on board until landing and waste liquids are vented into space.

LARGEST DOOR

Each of the four doors in the NASA Vehicle Assembly Building near Cape Canaveral, Florida, USA, is 140 m (460 ft) high, as tall as a 35-storey building. Their massive size was originally to allow fully assembled Saturn V rockets to pass through them.

★MOST PEOPLE ON A SPACEWALK

The first flight of *Endeavour* on 7 May 1992 was to repair the failing *Intelsat VI* satellite. Retrieving the satellite proved problematic until Pierre Thuot, Richard Hieb and Thomas Akers (all USA) performed a spacewalk and were able to capture *Intelsat VI* by hand. In the meantime, mission commander Daniel Brandenstein (USA) manoeuvred *Endeavour* to within a few feet of the stricken satellite. This is the only occasion in history that three people have walked in space at the same time.

★FIRST MANNED MAIDEN SPACE FLIGHT

The first ever shuttle launch was a test flight by astronauts John Young and Robert Crippen (both USA) on 12 April 1981. This was the first time a new spacecraft system had ever flown in space without a prior unmanned space flight.

★HEAVIEST GLIDER

The heaviest shuttle landing was *Columbia* during the STS-83 mission, which touched down on 8 April 1997 with a mass of 96,642 kg (213,060 lb). To return to Earth, the shuttle fires its orbital manoeuvring engines to slow down and decrease its altitude, and uses friction to reduce speed in the upper atmosphere. From then on the landing sequence is unpowered, with the shuttle acting as a glider, performing a series of high-altitude turns to dissipate speed, and eventually approaching the runway and touching down with the rear wheels first.

★HEAVIEST COMPONENT

At lift-off, the space shuttle consists of the orbiter itself, the external fuel tank that feeds its main engines and two solid rocket boosters attached to the tank that provide additional thrust. The heaviest component at lift-off is the tank, weighing 760,000 kg (1,680,000 lb).

HEAVIEST PAYLOAD LAUNCHED

The *Chandra X-ray Observatory* was launched by *Columbia* on 23 July 1999. With a mass of 22,753 kg (50,161 lb), this was the heaviest satellite that has ever been launched by the space shuttle.

★FIRST SHUTTLE DOCKING

On 29 June 1995, *Atlantis* docked with the Russian *Mir* space station, beginning the Shuttle-*Mir* Programme. This was the 100th space flight by the USA. *Atlantis* brought cosmonauts Anatoly Solovyev and Nikolai Budarin to *Mir*, and returned Vladimir Dezhurov, Gennady Strekalov (both Russia) and Norm Thagard (USA) to Earth. This was the first time a shuttle crew had changed in orbit.

★FIRST INFLIGHT REPAIR

On 26 July 2005, the shuttle *Discovery* launched on the STS-114 mission. During a spacewalk, Stephen Robinson (USA) was able to manually pull out two protruding "gap fillers" between the thermal tiles on *Discovery*'s underbelly. This photograph was taken by Robinson using a digital camera. It shows the thermal tiles on the underside of the shuttle, reflected in the visor of his helmet.

DID YOU KNOW? THE FIRST ORBITAL SPACE SHUTTLE MISSION – STS-1 – WAS THE 54.5-HOUR MAIDEN FLIGHT OF *COLUMBIA*, COMMANDED BY NASA ASTRONAUT JOHN YOUNG.

SPACE
THE SUN

EXTRA!
TAKE A TRIP TO SATURN BY TURNING BACK TO PP.26-27.

★ ★ ★ ★ ★ ★ ★ ★ ★ ★ ★ ★

★ FIRST FLY-BY OF THE SUN'S POLES

The joint NASA/ESA *Ulysses* spacecraft was launched from the space shuttle *Discovery* in 1990. It headed out to Jupiter, where it used a gravitational slingshot to send it into a polar orbit around the Sun, from where it has directly observed both solar poles. The spacecraft ceased operations on 30 June 2009.

★ LARGEST SUNSPOT GROUP

On 8 April 1947, the largest sunspot group ever identified was found in the Sun's southern hemisphere. At its greatest length, it measured 300,000 km (187,000 miles), with a maximum width of 145,000 km (90,000 miles). It was roughly 36 times greater than the surface area of the Earth and was even visible to the naked eye, close to sunset.

LARGEST SOLAR FLARE

On 4 November 2003, a solar flare – seen at the lower right-hand side of this photograph – erupted from the surface of the Sun. It was rated as an X28 event by the Space Environment Center of the National Oceanic and Atmospheric Administration (NOAA), in Boulder, Colorado, USA.

★ LONGEST LASTING SUNSPOT GROUP

Between June and December 1943, a group of sunspots was observed to last for 200 days. The smallest sunspots, known as pores, and less than 2,500 km (1,553 miles) across, can last less than one hour.

★ LONGEST AND SHORTEST SOLAR CYCLES

The solar cycle is a periodic change in the number of sunspots on the surface of the Sun and relates directly to solar magnetic activity. It was first discovered in 1843 and, by examining older observations of sunspots, astronomers now have data on sunspot activity going back to the early 17th century. The cycle lasts an average of 11 years, with the longest so far ending in 1798 having lasted 13.7 years, and the shortest ending in 1775, having lasted just nine years.

★ BIGGEST OBJECT IN THE SOLAR SYSTEM

The Sun has a mass 332,900 times greater than that of Earth, and a diameter of 1,392,000 km (865,000 miles). It accounts for 99.86% of the mass of the whole Solar System.

★ CLOSEST APPROACH TO THE SUN BY A SPACECRAFT

The unmanned spacecraft *Helios 2* approached within 43.5 million km (27 million miles) of the Sun, carrying both US and West German instrumentation, on 16 April 1976.

Due for launch in 2015, NASA's *Solar Probe+* will attempt to study the Sun from as close as 6.2 million km (3.9 million miles), from within the Sun's outer atmosphere or corona. Travelling at a speed of 200 km/sec (125 miles/sec), the spacecraft will have to survive temperatures of up to 1,420°C (2,600°F).

SOL: The scientific term for the Sun. It is found in Latin, among other languages, as is the word for the Moon: "Luna".

★ HIGHEST-RESOLUTION SOLAR TELESCOPE

The Swedish 1-m (3-ft 2-in) Solar Telescope on La Palma in the Canary Islands uses a mirror in the path of the sunlight that minutely changes shape a thousand times per second to counter the effects of atmospheric turbulence. It can see details on the surface of the Sun (inset) as small as 70 km (43 miles) across.

MARSEILLE, FRANCE

48°18'N 5°22'E

The **last use of the guillotine** was on 10 September 1977 at Baumettes Prison, Marseille, France, for the torturer and murderer Hamida Djandoubi, who was aged 28 at the time.

CONVECTIVE ZONE
Energy from the core moves through this zone by convection, similar to the turbulent movement in boiling water.

HOTTEST PLACE IN THE SOLAR SYSTEM
The very centre of the Sun is the hottest place in the Solar System. The latest estimates of the temperature put it at 15,600,000°C (28,080,000°F). The pressure in the core is also immense, around 250 billion times the pressure at sea level on Earth. These conditions allow nuclear fusion to take place, which is what makes the Sun shine.

RADIATIVE ZONE
Radiation produced in the core can "bounce around" among the matter in the radiative zone for millions of years.

★ NEW RECORD
★ UPDATED RECORD

GALACTIC
THE SUN ORBITS THE CENTRE OF OUR MILKY WAY GALAXY AT AROUND 220 KM/SEC (136 MILES/SEC). IT TAKES 225–250 MILLION YEARS TO COMPLETE ONE ORBIT.

CORE
The Sun's core is approximately 15,600,000°C (28,080,000°F). Around 600 million tonnes of hydrogen are fused into around 596 million tonnes of helium every second by nuclear fusion.

★ NEAREST STAR
The pioneering work of Father Angelo Secchi (Italy, 1818–78) in spectroscopy led to his classification scheme for stars, and to his conclusion that our own Sun was a star and not a phenomenon unique to the Solar System. At just 149,000,000 km (93,000,000 miles) from Earth, the Sun is astronomically close. The next nearest star, Proxima Centauri, is 4.2 light years away, or 40,000,000,000,000 km (24,000,000,000,000 miles),

★ LARGEST TORNADOES IN THE SOLAR SYSTEM
In April 1998, scientists announced the discovery of rotating tornado-like storms in the atmosphere of the Sun, using observations made by the *SOHO* satellite. Occurring mainly near to the poles of the Sun, these phenomena are around the size of Earth and the ionized gas within them moves at around 500,000 km/h (300,000 mph).

PROMINENCE
Vast eruptions of plasma from the photosphere can extend into space for hundreds of thousands of kilometres.

PHOTOSPHERE
The visible surface of the Sun is where we see phenomena such as sunspots. Its average temperature is around 5,500°C (9,932°F). Sunspots are cooler, at around 3,000°C (5,432°F).

★ STRONGEST GEOMAGNETIC STORM
At 11:18 a.m. on 1 September 1859, British astronomer Richard Carrington observed two blinding explosions occurring on the surface of the Sun. The following dawn, all over the world the skies were ablaze with aurorae caused by the charged particles from the eruptions interacting with Earth's magnetosphere, having taken just 18 hours to cross the space between the Sun and the Earth (the journey normally takes three or four days).

The study of ice cores suggest that events of this magnitude occur roughly every 500 years. The magnetic disruptions caused by the "Carrington Event" affected telegraph systems all over Europe and North America.

MOST DESTRUCTIVE GEOMAGNETIC STORM
The "Great Geomagnetic Storm" of 13 March 1989 was the most destructive geomagnetic storm ever recorded. The record-breaking event was classified G5 (the most severe rating) on the space weather scale. The result of an abnormally strong solar wind, it caused large-scale disruption to the power grid in Canada and the USA, and even changed the orbit of a satellite. The power outages – caused by failures at the Hydro-Québec systems in Canada – saw 6 million people losing electricity for nine hours.

DID YOU KNOW?
THE MEAN DISTANCE BETWEEN THE SUN AND THE EARTH IS AROUND 149 MILLION KM (93 MILLION MILES). AT THIS DISTANCE, IT TAKES LIGHT 8 MIN 19 SEC TO REACH THE EARTH.

The sun formed 4.57 billion years ago. In another 5 billion years it will start to run out of fuel and swell into a red giant.

TRIVIA

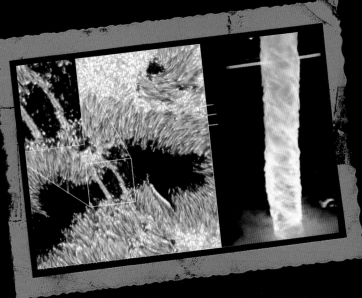

EARTH

★ ★ ★ ★ ★ ★ ★ ★ ★ ★ ★ ★ ★ ★ ✩

CONTENTS

43°22'N
5°27'E

AIX-EN-PROVENCE, FRANCE

The **largest known dinosaur eggs** are those of *Hypselosaurus priscus* ("high ridge lizard"), a 12-m-long
(40-ft) titanosaurid that lived about 80 million years ago. Examples found in the Durance valley near
Aix-en-Provence, France, in October 1961 would have had, uncrushed, a length of 30 cm (12 in).

LIGHT
PICTURED (AND INSET) IS ANTELOPE CANYON, NEAR PAGE IN ARIZONA, USA - THE MOST VISITED SLOT CANYON IN THE SOUTH-WEST OF AMERICA.

DARK
THE MAIN PICTURE SHOWS A VIEW FROM THE BOTTOM OF THE UPPER ANTELOPE CANYON LOOKING UP THROUGH A CHANNEL TO THE OUTSIDE WORLD.

★LARGEST CONCENTRATION OF SLOT CANYONS

Slot canyons are deep, narrow, winding passages that have been carved into sedimentary rock by millions of years of erosion from sandstorms, rain and fast-flowing waters. They are characterized by narrow openings and deep sides, often with cavernous interiors and beautifully coloured striations.

According to SummitPost, the climbing and outdoor activity group, the Colorado Plateau in south-western North America has a greater number of slots than anywhere on Earth, perhaps as many as 10,000.

GRENOBLE, FRANCE

45°12'N
5°42'E

The late Michel Lotito (France) of Grenoble, France, known as Monsieur Mangetout, ate metal and glass from the age of nine – without doubt the **strangest diet** on record. Gastroenterologists who had X-rayed his stomach described his ability to consume 900 g (2 lb) of metal per day as unique.

EARTH
PEAKS & TROUGHS

★ ★ ★ ★ ★ ★ ★ ★ ★ ★ ★ ★ ★

HIGHS

TALLEST MOUNTAIN

Mauna Kea on the island of Hawaii, USA, is the world's tallest mountain. Measured from its submarine base in the Hawaiian Trough to its peak, it has a height of 10,205 m (33,480 ft), of which 4,205 m (13,796 ft) is above sea level.

TALLEST UNCLIMBED MOUNTAIN

At 7,570 m (24,835 ft), Gangkar Punsum in Bhutan is ranked as the world's 40th highest peak, and the highest mountain yet to be climbed. Unsuccessful attempts were made to summit the peak in the 1980s, then in 1994, a partial ban of mountaineering in the country was declared. Since 2003, all climbing in Bhutan has been outlawed – for religious reasons – so it could remain unclimbed for many years to come.

TALLEST MOUNTAIN FACE

The Rupal face of Nanga Parbat, in the western Himalayas, Pakistan, is a single rise of some 4,600 m (15,000 ft) from the valley floor to the summit. The mountain itself, with a summit of 8,125 m (26,656 ft), is the world's ninth highest mountain.

★HIGHEST POLAR ICE CAP

Dome Argus is a vast ice plateau near the centre of East Antarctica. Its highest point is some 4,093 m (13,428 ft) above sea level. It is the highest ice feature on Antarctica and it overlies the 1,200-km-long (745-mile) Gamburtsev Mountain Range.

★HIGHEST HISTORICALLY ACTIVE VOLCANO

Llullaillaco, on the Argentina–Chile border, is a stratovolcano on a plateau within the Atacama Desert. At 6,739 m (22,109 ft) high, it is the highest recorded active volcano; its last eruption was in 1877.

LONGEST UNDERWATER CAVE SYSTEM

Sistema Ox Bel Ha (meaning "Three Paths of Water" in the Mayan language), in the state of Quintana Roo, Mexico, is a complex series of underwater passages accessible by exposed lakes called cenotes. As of May 2009, some 180.038 km (111.870 miles) of underwater passages had been explored and mapped by cave divers.

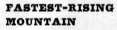

FASTEST-RISING MOUNTAIN

Nanga Parbat in Pakistan is growing taller at a rate of 7 mm (0.27 in) per year. Part of the Himalayan Plateau, it formed when India began colliding with the Eurasian continental plate between 30 and 50 million years ago.

LARGEST SUBGLACIAL MOUNTAIN RANGE

The Gamburtsev Mountains in eastern Antarctica extend for approximately 1,200 km (745 miles) across the continent. They reach up to 2,700 m (8,850 ft) high and are permanently buried under more than 600 m (1,968 ft) of ice. Discovered by a Soviet team in 1958, the mountains are believed to be around 500 million years old.

LONGEST SUBMARINE MOUNTAIN RANGE

The Mid-Ocean Ridge extends some 65,000 km (40,000 miles) from the Arctic Ocean to the Atlantic Ocean, around Africa, Asia and Australia, and under the Pacific Ocean to the west coast of North America. It has a maximum height of 4,200 m (13,800 ft) above the base ocean depth.

EXTRA! EXPLORE FASCINATING FISH & SEA LIFE BY TURNING TO pp.58–59.

★DEEPEST MINE

TauTona, which means "great lion" in the Setswana language, is a gold mine situated near Carletonville, South Africa, owned by AngloGold Ashanti. Originally built by the Anglo American Corporation, the 2-km (1.24-mile) original main shaft was sunk in 1957. The mine began operation in 1962 and, by 2008, had reached a depth of 3.9 km (2.4 miles). At this depth, the temperature of the rock faces can reach 60°C (140°F). The mine now has around 800 km (497 miles) of tunnels and employs 5,600 miners.

★HIGHEST ACTIVE CARBONATITE VOLCANO

Oldoinyo Llengai, Tanzania, is a rare type of volcano that erupts natrocarbonatite lava. At 2,962 m (9,718 ft) high, it is the only active volcano of this type on Earth. It erupts a bizarre runny lava that appears like molten chocolate at 500–600°C (930–1,110°F) and turns white upon cooling.

INSTANT EXPERT

✪ THE TIBETAN PLATEAU IS THE LARGEST AND HIGHEST ON EARTH, WITH AN AREA OF 1,850,000 KM² (715,000 MILES²) AND AN AVERAGE ALTITUDE OF 4,900 M (16,000 FT).

✪ IT CONTAINS THE HIMALAYA MOUNTAIN RANGE ON ITS SOUTHERN EDGE, WHICH CONTAINS EVEREST, THE WORLD'S <u>HIGHEST MOUNTAIN</u>, AT 8,848 M (29,029 FT).

✪ THE GREATER HIMALAYA CONTAINS 100 MOUNTAINS TALLER THAN 7,200 M (23,622 FT).

✪ THE EARTH'S CRUST IS THE THICKEST IN THE WORLD AT THE HIMALAYAS, WITH A THICKNESS OF AROUND 75 KM (46 MILES).

LOWS

DEEPEST CAVE

In September 2007, cavers from the Ukrainian Speleological Association reached a record depth of 2,191 m (7,188 ft 3 in) in the Krubera Cave (also known as the Voronya Cave) in the Arabika Massif, Georgia. Over 2.5 km (8,202 ft) of new cave passages were explored during this 29-day underground expedition.

DEEPEST PENETRATION INTO THE EARTH'S CRUST

A geological exploratory borehole near Zapolyarny on the Kola peninsula of Arctic Russia, which began on 24 May 1970, had reached a depth of 12,261 m (40,236 ft) by 1983, when funding stopped. The temperature of the rocks at the bottom of the hole is about 210°C (410°F).

LARGEST SEA CAVE

The Sea Lion Caves, close to Florence on the coast of Oregon, USA, have a chamber 95 m (310 ft) long, 50 m (165 ft) wide and around 15 m (50 ft) high in a wave-cut passage measuring 400 m (1,315 ft) long.

DEEPEST VALLEY

The Yarlung Zangbo valley in Tibet has an average depth of 5,000 m (16,400 ft), but in 1994 explorers discovered that its deepest point was 5,382 m (17,657 ft). This is more than three times deeper than the Grand Canyon, which is the **largest land gorge** with a depth of 1.6 km (1 mile) and a width ranging from 0.5 km to 29 km (0.25–8 miles).

The peaks on either side of the Yarlung Zangbo valley are Namche Barwa (7,753 m; 25,436 ft) and Jala Peri (7,282 m; 23,891 ft). They are just 21 km (13 miles) apart, with the Yarlung Zangbo River flowing between them at an elevation of 2,440 m (8,000 ft).

LARGEST CAVE OPENING

The entrance to Cathedral Caverns in Grant, Alabama, USA, is the world's largest cave opening. At 38.4 m (126 ft) wide and 7.6 m (25 ft) high, Cathedral Caverns was originally known as the Bat Cave until it was developed into a tourist attraction in 1955.

DEEPEST LAVA CAVE

Kazumura Cave in Hawaii, USA, is both the deepest and also the longest lava cave – an open tube down the inside of a lava flow. It is 59.3 km (36.9 miles) long and descends 1,099 m (3,605 ft) down the eastern flank of Kilauea volcano.

★GREATEST VERTICAL DROP

Mount Thor on Baffin Island, Nunavut, Canada, is a granite peak whose west face consists of a vertical drop of 1,250 m (4,101 ft). It is technically an overhang, with the average angle of repose of the cliff being at 105° – 15° beyond the vertical. The mountain was first climbed in 1953 by a team from the Arctic Institute of North America (AINA).

Over fifty Andes peaks exceed 6,000 m (20,000 ft) – 18.5 times higher than France's Eiffel Tower.

TRIVIA

UP! MOUNT THOR HAS AN AVERAGE ANGLE OF 105°, WHICH MAKES IT VERY POPULAR WITH CLIMBERS. IT WAS FIRST SCALED IN 1953.

DOWN! MOUNT THOR IS MADE OF GRANITE AND IS PART OF THE BAFFIN MOUNTAINS. THESE, IN TURN, FORM PART OF THE ARCTIC CORDILLERA MOUNTAIN RANGE.

★ NEW RECORD
UPDATED RECORD

GENEVA, SWITZERLAND
The **most expensive mobile phone** was designed by GoldVish of Geneva, Switzerland, and was sold for €1,000,000 ($1,287,200; £675,123) at the Millionaire Fair in Cannes, France, on 2 September 2006.

46°12'N
6°09'E

EARTH
RIVERS & LAKES

★ ★ ★ ★ ★ ★ ★ ☆ ★ ★ ★ ☆

HIGHEST LEVEL OF ALKALINITY IN A LAKE SYSTEM

The Magadi–Natron basin in the Great Rift Valley of Kenya–Tanzania contains saline (salt) bodies of water with temperatures as high as 50°C (120°F) and alkalinity that reaches levels as high as pH 10-12 – strong enough to burn the skin. The corrosiveness of these lakes – notably Natron, Magadi and Nakuru – is caused by high concentrations of minerals from hot springs, along with a high evaporation rate. Lake Natron's characteristic deep-red colour is the result of pigments produced by algae that live in the hypersaline environment.

★ LARGEST RAPIDS BY FLOW RATE

Inga Falls, on the Congo River in the Democratic Republic of Congo, drops in height by 96 m (315 ft) over a length of around 15 km (9 miles). The average flow rate has been measured at around 42,400 m³/sec (1,500,000 ft³/sec), enough to fill London's Albert Hall in around two seconds. Inga Falls has a maximum flow rate of around 70,800 m³/sec (2,500,000 ft³/sec).

★ LARGEST INLAND DELTA

The Okavango Delta in Botswana is formed by the Okavango river as it enters an endorheic basin in the Kalahari Desert. (The term "endorheic" means it has no outlets other than evaporation for its water.) Millions of years ago it emptied into an inland sea until tectonic activity interrupted the river and formed the delta. The size of the delta varies seasonally from around 16,000 km² (6,100 miles²) to around 9,000 km² (3,400 miles²).

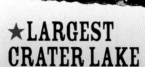

★ LARGEST CRATER LAKE

Lake Toba, on the Indonesian island of Sumatra, is the site of a supervolcanic eruption around 75,000 years ago that was probably the largest anywhere on Earth during the last 25 million years. The crater formed by the eruption is now filled with water that makes Lake Toba, which is around 100 km (60 miles) by 30 km (18 miles) in extent, and 505 m (1,656 ft) deep at its deepest point.

★ LARGEST TIDAL BORE

Tidal bores are formed when the front of the incoming tide forms a wave or series of waves that travels up a river against its direction of flow. This phenomenon occurs in several dozen locations around the world, but by far the largest and most spectacular happens in the Qiantang river, China, where it can form a massive wave of water up to 9 m (30 ft) high and travelling upstream at up to 40 km/h (25 mph). The bore is so dangerous that it is thought only a handful of people have been able to surf it.

★ LARGEST DESERT LAKE

Lake Turkana in the Great Rift Valley, Kenya, has a surface area of 6,405 km² (2,472 miles²) and an average depth of 30.2 m (99 ft). It is the fourth largest salt lake in the world and is fed by the Omo, Turkwel and Kerio rivers. There is no outflow from Lake Turkana and the only method of water loss is by evaporation.

LARGEST TROPICAL LAKE

With a surface area of around 68,800 km² (26,563 miles²), Lake Victoria is the biggest lake in the world that lies within the tropics. Containing some 2,750 km³ (659 miles³) of water, it is ranked as the seventh largest freshwater lake in the world. It is the main source of the Nile, the **longest river**.

The deepest point on the bed of the Dead Sea is located 800 m (2,624 ft) below sea level.

TRIVIA

★ DEEPEST HYPERSALINE LAKE

The Dead Sea on the Israel–Jordan border is the deepest hypersaline (very salty) lake in the world, with a maximum depth of 378 m (1,240 ft). The Dead Sea has an average salinity of more than 8.5 times that of sea water. Dead Sea mud is believed by many people to have healing properties when rubbed on to the skin (right).

SALTIEST LAKE

Don Juan Pond in Wright Valley, Antarctica, has such a high salt content that it remains a liquid even at temperatures as low as -53°C (-63.4°F). At its saltiest, the lake's percentage of salt by weight is 40.2%, compared to 23.1% in the Dead Sea and a 3.38% average in the world's oceans as a whole.

GREATEST RIVER FLOW

The Amazon river in South America has the greatest flow of any river, discharging an amazing average of 200,000 m³/sec (7,100,000 ft³/sec) into the Atlantic Ocean, which increases to more than 340,000 m³/sec (12,000,000 ft³/sec) in full flood. The lower 1,450 km (900 miles) averages 17 m (55 ft) in depth, but the river has a maximum depth of 124 m (407 ft).

The Amazon is fed by over 1,000 tributaries and its flow is 60 times greater than that of the Nile. The Amazon accounts for about 20% of all the fresh water that drains into the world's oceans.

★LARGEST WATERFALL (VERTICAL AREA)

Victoria Falls, on the Zambezi river between Zimbabwe and Zambia, is neither the tallest nor widest in the world, but it is the largest by vertical area. Being 1,708 m (5,604 ft) wide and 108 m (354 ft) high, it creates a sheet of falling water with an area of around 184,400 m² (1,984,000 ft²).

FAST!
VICTORIA FALLS IS ALSO KNOWN AS MOSI-OA-TUNYA – "THE MIST THAT THUNDERS". IT HAS AN AVERAGE ANNUAL FLOW RATE OF 1,088 M³/SEC (38,422 FT³/SEC).

FLUSH!
THE INCREDIBLE VOLUME OF WATER GOING OVER THE FALLS EACH SECOND IS ENOUGH TO FLUSH 83,692 TOILETS, OR 7,230,988,800 TOILETS EVERY DAY!

★LARGEST EPHEMERAL LAKE

Like Lake Turkana (see p.36), Lake Eyre – which is located in the lowest point in Australia – is an example of an endorheic system. It usually contains little or no water but occasionally floods due to heavy monsoon rains. In 1974, the greatest flooding of this salt flat basin created a temporary inland sea with an area of around 9,500 km² (3,600 miles²).

The **longest journey by car using alternative fuel** is 38,137 km (23,697 miles), by a team of four (all Germany) in a Volkswagen Caddy EcoFuel using natural gas. The journey started in Cologne, Germany, on 15 October 2006 and finished in Leipzig, Germany, on 12 April 2007.

EARTH
OCEANS & SEAS

★ NEW RECORD ★ UPDATED RECORD

SMALLEST COASTLINES

	STATE/NATION	DISTANCE (METRIC)	DISTANCE (IMPERIAL)
1	Monaco (below left)	5.6 km	3.5 miles
2	Nauru (below right)	19 km	12 miles
3	Bosnia	20 km	13 miles
4	Jordan	25 km	16 miles
5	Slovenia	30 km	19 miles

★ OLDEST SEAWATER

The seawater at the bottom of the 3,800-m-deep (12,400-ft) Canada Basin has remained unstirred for several thousand years. The Basin, which is north of Canada and Alaska, USA, is connected to the Pacific Ocean only by the 70-m-deep (230-ft) Bering Strait and is protected from the power of the Atlantic Ocean by tall submarine ridges.

★ FIRST PROVEN ROGUE WAVE

Rogue waves are waves with abnormal height compared to others, and were long believed to be legendary. On 1 January 1995, the first confirmed measurement of this phenomenon occurred as a wave with a height of 25.6 m (84 ft) struck the Draupner platform in the North Sea.

★ LARGEST DEAD ZONE

Regions of coastal waters where seawater is depleted of oxygen are called "dead zones". More than 400 have been mapped around the world, but the Baltic Sea, with an area of around 377,000 km^2 (145,000 miles^2), is the largest. The bottom of the Baltic lacks oxygen year-round.

WIDEST CONTINENTAL SHELF

The Siberian continental shelf extends 1,210 km (750 miles) off the coast of Siberia, Russia, into the Arctic Ocean. Huge concentrations of methane exist beneath this shelf. In 2008, scientists found evidence that global warming is starting to allow this trapped methane to enter the atmosphere.

★ YOUNGEST OCEAN

Of the major oceans of the world, the Southern Ocean (also known as the Antarctic Ocean and the South Polar Ocean) is the youngest. It formed when Antarctica split away from Australia and South America around 30 million years ago, also forming the Drake Passage in the process.

★ LARGEST VOLCANIC ZONE

The Pacific Ring of Fire is a huge horseshoe-shaped arc of concentrated earthquake and volcanic activity around 40,000 km (24,800 miles) long, located in the Pacific Ocean. It contains some 452 volcanoes and more than 75% of the world's active and dormant volcanoes.

At 10,911 m (35,797 ft), the Marianas Trench in the Pacific is the **deepest point in any ocean**.

TRIVIA

★LARGEST AREA OF GLOWING SEA

In 1995, scientists at the US Naval Research Laboratory discovered an area of luminous sea in the Indian Ocean off the coast of Somalia using satellite images. The patch of water (pictured) measured over 250 km (155 miles) long, with an area of around 14,000 km² (5,400 miles²). Bioluminescent bacteria are thought to have been responsible for the water's appearance.

★WARMEST OCEAN

The Indian Ocean has the warmest surface temperature of all the world's oceans, as most of it is found in the tropics. Its minimum surface temperature is around 22°C (72°F), but can be as high as 28°C (82°F) towards the east; temperatures in the south can be considerably lower. At 73,556,000 km² (28,400,000 miles²) the Indian Ocean is the third largest of the Earth's oceanic divisions, covering approximately 20% of the Earth's surface.

★DEEPEST OBSERVED VOLCANIC ERUPTION

On 18 December 2009, US scientists announced the discovery of a volcanic eruption around 1,200 m (3,900 ft) deep in the Pacific Ocean. The footage, captured in May 2009 by a robotic submersible, shows molten lava erupting from the West Mata volcano, which is 200 km (125 miles) south-west of the Samoas and is one of the most active submarine volcanoes in the world.

★NEWEST FORMING OCEAN

In 2005, a rift some 56 km (35 miles) long opened up in the Afar Depression (also known as the Danakil Depression, the lowest point in Africa) in Ethiopia. In November 2009, scientists announced that results of their analysis showed that this rift is the beginning of the formation of a new ocean. The tectonic processes occurring under Afar are the same as those on the ocean floor at the ridges where new crust is formed and existing crust is pushed apart.

It is expected that, around a million years from now, seawater from the Red Sea will pour into the Afar Depression as it stretches and thins, and the resulting body of sea will gradually grow, possibly to become as large as the Atlantic or Pacific Oceans.

LARGEST SUBMARINE TAR FLOW

In 2003, a team of scientists led by Texas A&M University, USA, discovered the world's first asphalt-erupting volcano 3,000 m (9,842 ft) deep on the sea-floor of the Gulf of Mexico. Using a remotely operated camera, the team found tar flows from the volcano, named Chapopote, covering at least 1 km² (0.4 miles²). Their results were published in the journal *Science* in May 2004.

★SHALLOWEST OCEAN

The Arctic Ocean is the shallowest (and smallest) of the five main oceans. At 14,056,000 km² (5,426,000 miles²) it is roughly the size of Russia and covers 2.8% of the Earth's surface, but has an average depth of 1,050 m (3,450 ft).

★HIGHEST OCEAN TEMPERATURE

In August 2008, an international team of scientists announced they had recorded water at a temperature of 464°C (867°F) spewing from a hydrothermal vent on the ocean floor, 3,000 m (9,842 ft) deep at the Mid-Atlantic Ridge. Above 407°C (764°F) at this depth, water becomes "supercritical" and lighter than normal water. The water at the "black smoker" was measured using sensors on a remote-controlled robot.

★FASTEST SEA-FLOOR SPREADING CENTRE

The East Pacific Rise is a tectonic plate boundary that runs from Antarctica to the west coast of the USA. At this boundary a new crust is being created and the continental plates are moving apart. A portion of the East Pacific Rise – the Pacific-Nazca boundary – is pushing continental plates apart at a rate of around 150 km/million years (93 miles/million years).

KRAKA- PICTURED IS ISLAND-VOLCANO KRAKATOA ERUPTING IN MAY 2009. AN ERUPTION ON 27 AUGUST 1883 WAS THE LOUDEST NOISE EVER RECORDED...

-TOA! ...THE EXPLOSION WAS HEARD FROM MORE THAN 5,000 KM (3,100 MILES) AWAY. THAT'S 8% OF THE EARTH'S SURFACE!

EARTH
ISLANDS & REEFS

★ ★ ★ ★ ★ ★ ★ ★ ★ ★ ★ ★ ★ ★ ★

LARGEST ISLAND

Greenland, the largest island, is about 2,175,600 km² (840,000 miles²) in size – just over three times larger than the US state of Texas.

At around 103,000 km² (39,768 miles²), the **largest volcanic island** is Iceland, formed from eruptions from the Mid-Atlantic Ridge, on which it sits. Iceland is essentially sea-floor exposed above the ocean.

★LARGEST RIVER ISLAND

Majuli, in the Brahmaputra River in north-east India, covers around 880 km² (340 miles²) – twice the size of Barbados. Many years ago, the island was a long, thin strip of land called Majoli ("land between two parallel rivers") until earthquakes and floods in the 17th and 18th centuries changed the rivers' flow.

★LONGEST BARRIER ISLAND

Barrier islands are narrow, run parallel to mainland coasts and are formed by the action of waves and currents.

★LARGEST ISLAND IN A LAKE ON AN ISLAND IN A LAKE ON AN ISLAND

The island of Luzon in the Philippines is home to Lake Taal, and within the lake lies the Taal volcano; the central volcanic crater of Taal is now a lake, called Crater Lake, and Vulcan Point is an island, approximately 40 m (130 ft) across, situated within Crater Lake.

LONGEST REEF

The Great Barrier Reef off Queensland, north-eastern Australia, is 2,027 km (1,260 miles) in length. This mammoth feature is not actually a single structure, but consists of thousands of separate reefs.

The reef is the **largest marine structure built by living creatures**, as it consists of countless billions of dead and living stony corals (order Madreporaria and Scleractinia).

Padre Island in the Gulf of Mexico, off the Texas coast, formed just a few thousand years ago and is around 210 km (130 miles) long.

★ARCHIPELAGO WITH THE MOST ISLANDS

The Archipelago Sea lies within Finnish waters in the Baltic Sea and contains around 40,000 islands. The whole archipelago – or chain or group of islands – is slowly rising as the land is still "rebounding" since the weight of ice from the last Ice Age was removed.

★LARGEST ATOLL

An atoll is a marine structure that comprises

a body of water (lagoon) enclosed by a ring (or partial ring) of coral. The Great Chagos Bank in the Indian Ocean is an atoll covering 12,642 km² (4,881 miles²) – yet the seven named islands that form its rim have an area of just 4.5 km² (1.7 miles²).

★MOST ISLANDS WITHIN AN ATOLL

Huvadhu Atoll in the Indian Ocean contains around 255 islands and covers an area of 2,900 km² (1,120 miles²).

LIFE
THE CROWN-OF-THORNS STARFISH FEEDS ON THE CORAL POLYPS THAT MAKE UP THE GREAT BARRIER REEF. IN 2000, AN OUTBREAK KILLED 66% OF LIVE CORAL COVER.

SUPPORT
THE GREAT BARRIER REEF SUPPORTS AN EXTRAORDINARY DIVERSITY OF LIFE, INCLUDING 1,500 SPECIES OF FISH AND MORE THAN 125 SPECIES OF SHARKS.

REEFS:

USS Oriskany, the largest artificial reef, is affectionately known as the "Great Carrier Reef". Why? See below...

★YOUNGEST ISLAND

The island of Surtsey, off the south coast of Iceland, formed on 14 November 1963 when the new land being created by an undersea volcano finally breached the surface of the ocean. The volcanic activity, which had begun 130 m (426 ft) below the surface, lasted until 5 June 1967. By this time, Surtsey had grown to around 2.7 km² (1 mile²). Since then, the island has been gradually shrinking because of erosion.

★LARGEST SUBMERGED BANK

The reef Saya de Malha Bank in the Indian Ocean covers 40,808 km² (15,756 miles²). It rises to within 7 m (22 ft) of the surface and would be the world's largest atoll – three times the size of the Great Chagos Bank – if it were above sea level.

★OLDEST CORAL REEF

The Chazy Reef Formation is a fossilized coral reef that extends from the US state of Tennessee to Newfoundland in Canada. Its most significant outcrop occurs at Isle La Motte in Vermont, USA. It originally formed c. 450 million years ago in what was then the Iapetus Ocean. It is the oldest known example of structures built by coral.

★LARGEST FRINGING REEF

Fringing reefs occur right off the shoreline of a landmass – unlike a barrier reef, which occurs farther out into the ocean and often forms a lagoon. Ningaloo Reef, on the shore of Western Australia, extends for around 300 km (180 miles) in length and is just 100 m (330 ft) from the shore at its closest point.

LARGEST ARTIFICIAL REEF

The US Navy's attack aircraft carrier USS *Oriskany* (aka the "Mighty O", laid 1944) was decommissioned in 1976 after a long service, and was scheduled for scrapping until the decision was made to sink it as an artificial reef in the Gulf of Mexico, 38 km (24 miles) off Pensacola, Florida, USA. It was sunk on 17 May 2006, using 226 kg (500 lb) of C4 explosives, and took 37 minutes to reach the sea bed.

It is around 45 m (150 ft) tall and 270 m (888 ft) long and attracts an abundance of marine life rarely seen in the northern Gulf of Mexico.

In 2009, Surtsey got a webcam. For info, footage and some amazing photos, go to www.surtsey.is

TRIVIA

★ **NEW RECORD**
★ **UPDATED RECORD**

★OLDEST ISLAND

Madagascar, in the Indian Ocean off the south-eastern coast of Africa, became an island around 80–100 million years ago, when it split off from the Indian subcontinent. With an area of 587,041 km² (226,657 miles²), it ranks as the fourth largest island in the world and is home to 5% of the world's plant and animal species.

EXTRA! FOR A REVIEW OF THE WORLD'S WORST NATURAL DISASTERS, GO TO PP.44-45.

ALESSANDRIA, ITALY
The **largest chocolate bar** weighed 3,580 kg (7,892 lb 8 oz) and was made by Elah Dufour-Novi in Alessandria, Piemonte, Italy, on 11 October 2007.

44°55'N
8°37'E

EARTH
WEATHER & CLIMATE

★HIGHEST STORM PHENOMENA

Elves are ethereal reddish phenomena that occur above thunderstorms. They were discovered in 1992 using a low-level camera on board the space shuttle. Lasting less than a millisecond, they appear as disc-shaped luminous regions up to 480 km (300 miles) across and occur at altitudes of around 97 km (60 miles).

GREATEST SNOWFALL (DEPTH)

The deepest snowfall recorded to date measured 11.46 m (37 ft 7 in) at Tamarac, California, USA, in March 1911. The **greatest snowfall in 12 months** fell between 1971 and 1972, when a total of 31,102 mm (1,224 in) was recorded at Paradise, Mount Rainier, Washington, USA.

MOST TREES DESTROYED BY STORMS

A record 270 million trees were felled or split by storms that hit France on 26–27 December 1999.

FASTEST WIND SPEED

On 10 April 1996, a wind speed of 408 km/h (253 mph) was recorded at Barrow Island, Australia, during Tropical Cyclone Olivia. This is the fastest wind speed ever recorded on Earth not associated with a tornado.

HOTTEST PLACE ON EARTH

For a fraction of a second, the air around a lightning strike is heated to around 30,000°C (54,000°F), or roughly five times hotter than the visible surface of the Sun.

EXTRA! WHAT HAPPENS WHEN THE NATURAL WORLD TURNS VIOLENT? TO FIND OUT, TURN THE PAGE…

MOST VIOLENT PLACE IN A TROPICAL CYCLONE

Just beyond the calm eye of a hurricane or typhoon is the eye wall. This is a complete circle of storm clouds, often in a towering vertical structure, whirling around the eye. It is here that the highest winds and strongest rainfall occur. In cyclones with very high wind speeds of above 177 km/h (110 mph), a second eye wall will often form around the first.

WORST DAMAGE TOLL FROM AN ICE STORM

The most damaging ice storm on record occurred in the first week of January 1998 in eastern Canada and adjoining parts of the USA. The storm, which began on 6 January, shut down airports and trains, blocked highways and cut off power to 3 million people – almost 40% of the population of Québec. Over five days, freezing rain coated power lines with 10 cm (4 in) of ice, more weight than they could carry, and tens of thousands of poles were toppled. The bill was estimated at a massive CAN$1 billion ($650 million; £406 million).

★FIRST CLOUD SEEDING EXPERIMENT ON A TROPICAL CYCLONE

On 13 October 1947, the US military dumped 36 kg (80 lb) of dry ice into an Atlantic hurricane. "Pronounced modification of the cloud deck seeded" was recorded by the crew before the hurricane changed direction and hit the coast of Georgia. The damage caused by the cyclone was blamed on the experiment and the programme, Project Cirrus, was cancelled.

★MOST RECENTLY CLASSIFIED CLOUD FORMATION

The last cloud type to be recognized as distinct was cirrus intortus in 1951. In 2009, a new type, undulatus asperatus, was proposed by experts as a new type of cloud formation. Its characteristic appearance (pictured) resembles ocean waves, although it is rare. Undulatus asperatus clouds tend to dissipate without forming storms.

MAINZ, GERMANY
50°01'N 8°14'E

It is widely accepted that the **oldest mechanically printed book** was the Gutenberg Bible, printed in Mainz, Germany, c. 1455, by Johann Henne zum Gensfleisch zur Laden (c. 1398–1468), who was known as zu Gutenberg.

DID YOU KNOW?

LIGHTNING IS A DISCHARGE OF ELECTRICAL CURRENT IN THE ATMOSPHERE. ALTHOUGH SEVERAL THEORIES EXIST, SCIENTISTS ARE NOT SURE OF ITS PRECISE CAUSE.

Up to 16 million lightning storms occur each year. Some lightning forks may be 8 km (5 miles) long.

TRIVIA

POW!
POSITIVE LIGHTNING STRIKES ARE KNOWN AS "BOLTS FROM THE BLUE", AS THEY OFTEN BREAK FORTH OUT OF CLEAR OR ONLY SLIGHTLY CLOUDY SKIES.

ZAP!
AS WELL AS THUNDER STORMS, LIGHTNING CAN BE CAUSED BY VOLCANO ERUPTIONS AND FOREST FIRES, WHICH CAN CREATE ENOUGH DUST IN THE ATMOSPHERE TO GENERATE A STATIC CHARGE.

★ MOST POWERFUL LIGHTNING

No one knows exactly how lightning is created, but ice in clouds may be a factor, perhaps helping to divide electrical current into positive and negative charges. Less than 5% of all lightning strikes involve positive lightning – in which the net transfer of charge from the cloud to the ground is positive. Positive lightning outlasts normal (negative) lightning strikes and causes a stronger electrical field, giving rise to strikes of up to a billion volts and an electrical current that may reach 300,000 amperes.

★ GREATEST CLOUD COVER DUE TO HUMAN ACTIVITY

Contrails are condensation trails in the atmosphere left by aircraft. Depending upon local atmospheric conditions, they can last between seconds and hours. In the busiest air corridors, the combined effect of aircraft contrails can increase the cloud cover by up to 20%.

★ NEW RECORD
★ UPDATED RECORD

★ STRONGEST HURRICANE

The category-5 Hurricane Wilma, which occurred during October 2005 and caused damage to the Yucatán Peninsula, Mexico, was the strongest hurricane since records began in 1851. A hurricane hunter plane measured a barometric pressure in the eye of just 882 millibars – the lowest ever recorded for a hurricane. Wind speeds in Wilma's eye wall reached 270 km/h (165 mph).

★ LARGEST BLUE JET

Blue jets are electrical phenomena that project upwards in a cone from the tops of cumulonimbus clouds during thunderstorms. They were discovered in 1989. On 14 September 2001, scientists in Puerto Rico recorded a blue jet that reached around 80 km (49 miles) above a storm, and lasted less than a second.

★ FIRST IDENTICAL SNOW CRYSTALS

One often heard statement about snow is that no two snowflakes are ever alike. However, in 1988, Nancy Knight (USA), a scientist at the National Center for Atmosphere Research in Boulder, Colorado, USA, found two identical examples while using a microscope to study snow crystals from a storm in Wisconsin, USA.

CLOUDS WITH THE GREATEST VERTICAL RANGE

Cumulonimbus clouds have been observed to reach a vertical height of almost 20,000 m (65,600 ft – or nearly three times the height of Mount Everest) in the tropics.

MOST COWS KILLED BY LIGHTNING

A single bolt of lightning killed 68 Jersey cows that were sheltering under a tree at Warwick Marks' farm near Dorrigo, NSW, Australia, on 31 October 2005. So, don't shelter under trees in a storm!

EARTH
NATURAL DISASTERS

★FASTEST VOLCANIC HAZARD

Pyroclastic flows are the most dangerous of volcanic hazards. They are a mixture of gas and rock that travel down and away from a volcano at temperatures of up to 1,000°C (1,830°F) and speeds of up to 720 km/h (450 mph). In 1902, a pyroclastic flow at Mount Pelee on Martinique overwhelmed the city of Saint-Pierre, killing 30,000 people.

★HIGHEST DEATH TOLL FROM A BLIZZARD

A week-long blizzard from 3 to 9 February 1972 dumped more than 3 m (10 ft) of snow across parts of rural Iran, ending a four-year drought. Approximately 4,000 people are estimated to have died as a result of the blizzard.

★HIGHEST DEATH TOLL FROM A WILDFIRE

On 8 October 1871, forest fires burned through north-east Wisconsin and upper Michigan, USA, killing an estimated 1,200 to 2,500 people. More than 3,800 km² (1,500 miles²) of forest and farmland was destroyed. The event is known as the "Peshtigo tragedy", after a village that lost half its population in the fire.

MOST DAMAGE CAUSED BY A CYCLONE

Hurricane Katrina, which devastated the coast of Louisiana, USA, and surrounding states on 29 August 2005, caused damage estimated to be as high as $156 billion (£90 billion). At least 1,836 people lost their lives in the hurricane and subsequent floods. Katrina was the first category-5 hurricane of the 2005 season, the sixth strongest Atlantic hurricane ever recorded and represents the **costliest natural disaster**.

★CLOSEST POINT TO HUMAN EXTINCTION

The eruption of the Toba supervolcano around 75,000 years ago threw some 800 km³ (191 miles³) of ash into the atmosphere, creating Earth's largest volcanic crater. The resulting tsunamis and volcanic winter are thought to have reduced the human population to 10,000.

COSTLIEST YEAR FOR NATURAL DISASTERS

According to reinsurers Swiss Re, the Asian tsunami, an unusually active hurricane season and disasters such as floods pushed the total economic loss for 2005 to $225 billion (£128 billion).

DID YOU KNOW?

A PYROCLASTIC FLOW IS LIKE A FAST-MOVING LIQUID, WITH ROCKS AND DEBRIS SUSPENDED IN IT BY HOT, EXPANDING GASES AND ITS FORWARD MOMENTUM. IT FLOWS LIKE A SNOW AVALANCHE.

More people have been killed by pyroclastic flow than any other type of volcanic hazard.

TRIVIA

HIGHEST DEATH TOLL FROM A TSUNAMI

On 26 December 2004, an earthquake with a magnitude of 9 occurred under the Indian Ocean, off the coast of Indonesia. The resulting tsunami wave inundated the coastlines of nine different countries around the Indian Ocean. The total death toll will never be known but, as of 20 January 2005, at least 226,000 people are known to have perished.

EXTRA! TURN BACK TO PP.30-31 TO READ ABOUT THE AWESOME POWER OF THE SUN.

★HIGHEST DEATH TOLL FROM A HEAT WAVE

The hottest August on record for the northern hemisphere was in 2003. At least 35,000 fatalities are thought to have resulted from the extreme heat, with some estimates as high as 52,000. France suffered worst, with 14,802 deaths, mainly among the elderly; the temperature reached 40°C (104°F) on seven consecutive days there.

★HIGHEST DEATH TOLL FROM A FIRE WHIRL

Under the right circumstances, tornado-like phenomena can occur within fires. The deadliest example on record happened as a result of the Great Kanto Earthquake of 1 September 1923, which devastated the Kanto region of Honshu, Japan. Around 38,000 people were incinerated by a fire whirl while packed into the Former Army Clothing Depot in Tokyo.

WORST AVALANCHE DISASTER – MOST PEOPLE TRAPPED

At least 265 people died and over 45,000 were trapped on 20 January 1951 during the "Winter of Terror", when a series of 649 reported avalanches, caused by a combination of hurricane-force winds and wet snow overlaying powder snow, thundered through the Swiss, Austrian and Italian Alps.

MOST EXTENSIVE FLOOD DAMAGE

Flooding from the Hwai and Yangtze rivers in China in August 1950 destroyed 890,000 homes and left 490 people dead and 10 million homeless. Around 2 million ha (5 million acres) of land was left under water, rendering 1.4 million ha (3.5 million acres) unfit for the planting season.

MOST POWERFUL EARTHQUAKE

The Valdivia earthquake or Great Chilean Earthquake of 22 May 1960 had a magnitude of 9.5 on the moment magnitude scale. (Like the Richter scale, this records the amount of energy released in an earthquake.) It is estimated to have killed between 2,231 and 5,700 people and left 2 million homeless.

★HIGHEST MUDSLIDE DEATH TOLL

In December 1999, a torrential storm dumped 911 mm (35 in) of rain on Vargas state, Venezuela, in just a few days. The resulting mudslides from the mountainous areas close to the coast caused massive loss of life and infrastructure damage. Estimates of the death toll range from 10,000 to as high as 30,000, though — as with all natural disasters — exact figures are practically impossible to determine.

BRICKS TOWNS THAT WERE COMPLETELY DESTROYED BY THE MUDSLIDE WERE NOT REBUILT. INSTEAD, THEY WERE TURNED INTO PARKS AND COMMUNITY FACILITIES.

MORTAR THE MUDSLIDE DAMAGED AROUND 60% OF THE REGION'S INFRASTRUCTURE – ROADS, BRIDGES AND UTILITY SERVICES, ETC – AT AN ESTIMATED COST OF $3.2 BILLION (£1.9 BILLION).

★ **NEW RECORD**
UPDATED RECORD

HEIDELBERG, GERMANY

The **largest wooden wine cask** is the Heidelberg Tun, which lies in the cellar of the Friedrichsbau in Heidelberg Castle, Heidelberg, Germany. Installed in 1751, it is 7 m (23 ft) tall and 8.5 m (28 ft) across, with a capacity of 221,726 litres (48,773 gallons)

49°24'N 8°42'E

LIVING PLANET

★ ★ ★ ★ ★ ★ ★ ★ ★ ★ ★ ★ ★ ★ ★

LARGEST NOCTURNAL PRIMATE

The aye-aye (*Daubentonia madagascariensis*) of Madagascar has a body length of 40 cm (16 in), a tail length of 50.5 cm (20 in) and weighs approximately 2.76 kg (6 lb). These solitary animals spend up to 80% of the night foraging for food in the tree canopies and most of the daytime sleeping in tree nests.

Aye-ayes are also known for their skeletal, dexterous middle finger, which is used to tap tree bark to listen for evidence of edible insect larvae inside. They then make a hole in the tree trunk and use the middle finger to hook out the larvae – the primate equivalent of the woodpecker!

AYE! AYE-AYES ARE THOUGHT TO USE ECHOLOCATION TO SEEK OUT PREY – LIKE BATS. THEY ARE THE ONLY PRIMATES TO DO SO.

AYE! THESE NOCTURNAL LEMURS HAVE SQUIRREL-LIKE FRONT INCISOR TEETH THAT CONTINUE TO GROW AND NEVER WEAR DOWN.

BREMEN, GERMANY

53°04'N 8°47'E

Visible to the eye, *Thiomargarita namibiensis* is the **largest bacterium**. Heide Schulz, from Bremen's Max Planck Institute for Marine Microbiology found samples up to 0.029 in (0.75 mm) wide off the Namibian coast.

QUIZ!
NO TALL TALES –
HOW LONG IS THE
AYE AYE'S TAIL?
SEE P.278 FOR THE ANSWER.

CONTENTS

★ **NEW RECORD**
★ **UPDATED RECORD**

STUTTGART, GERMANY

The **most tap dancers in a single routine** was 6,951, who gathered at the City Square,
Stuttgart, Germany, on 24 May 1998. The routine, choreographed by Ray Lynch (USA), lasted
2 min 15 sec and was performed to the tune "Klicke-di-Klack", which Ray had composed.

48°48'N
9°10'E

LIVING PLANET
EARLY LIFE

★★★★★★★★★★★★★★

★ LARGEST LAND ARTHROPOD

Known from fossils discovered in North America and Europe, *Arthropleura* was a large arthropod that resembled a giant centipede and lived between 340 and 280 million years ago. Scientists estimate that the creature, whose body was made up of around 30 plates, each with its own pair of legs, could grow to between 0.3 m and 2.6 m (1 ft–8 ft 6 in) long.

LARGEST TRILOBITE

Announced on 9 October 2000, a 445-million-year-old trilobite more than 70 cm (27.5 in) long was discovered in northern Manitoba, Canada, by a group of Canadian scientists led by Dr Graham Young.

★ FIRST LIFE ON EARTH

The earliest life for which there is strong evidence are the microfossils of reef-building cyanobacteria found in the Apex Chert, Western Australia, and estimated to be 3.465 billion years old.

LONGEST FOSSIL RECORD

Stromatolites have the longest fossil record of any form of life on Earth. These cauliflower-shaped, rock-like structures are formed by the activity of cyanobacteria and are thought to have appeared on Earth some 3.5 billion years ago.

In 1954, a colony of living stromatolites was found in Shark Bay, Australia.

ROCK
BEDROCK FROM THE NUVVUAGITTUQ GREENSTONE BELT ON THE EASTERN SHORE OF HUDSON BAY, CANADA, DATES BACK SOME 4.28 BILLION YEARS. IT IS THE OLDEST SURVIVING ROCK.

★ FIRST ANIMAL TRAILS

On 3 February 2010, scientists announced a series of 70 newly discovered fossil trails visible on rocks from Newfoundland, Canada, dating back 565 million years. Scientists have speculated that the trails might have been made by a relative of modern sea anemones.

OLDEST CHORDATE

Pikaia gracilens is the oldest known chordate (a member of the animal group to which humans and all vertebrates belong). It lived during the mid-Cambrian, more than 500 million years ago. The first *P. gracilens* specimen was found in the Burgess Shale fossil site, British Columbia, Canada. *P. gracilens* resembled a contemporary jawless marine invertebrate called the lancet (*Dicrocoelium dendriticum*).

DID YOU KNOW?

THE OLDEST FOSSILIZED PENIS DATES BACK AROUND 100 MILLION YEARS. IT BELONGS TO A TYPE OF CRUSTACEAN CALLED AN OSTRACOD, AND MEASURES JUST 1 MM ACROSS.

The primitive squid-like animal *Cameroceras* was the largest creature in the ocean up until around 438 million years ago.

TRIVIA

PRECAMBRIAN (4,600–543 MILLION YEARS AGO [MYA]) *geological time before life; accounts for 87% of all geological time*

HADEAN* (4,600–4,000 MYA)   ARCHAEAN (4,000–2,500 MYA)   PROTEROZOIC (2,500–542 MYA)

PERIOD ERA EON				

4,600 MYA
Formation of the Earth and Moon, probably through accretion (the gathering of rock and gas), though there are theories that the Moon was formed as a result of an object hitting the Earth

4,000 MYA
Earth is wracked by volcanic activity; geological time begins as the ★first rocks form. The beginning of the Archaean is estimated rather than known, because of insufficient evidence: few rocks from this period remain

2,500 MYA
Early life confined to the seas, as very little oxygen is available on land

3,500 MYA
Stromatolites have the ★oldest fossil record of any life on Earth

CAMBRIAN (542–488 MYA)

530 MYA
Hard-shelled life (e.g. trilobites) emerges; the ★oldest known vertebrate, *Haikouichthys*, is also our ★oldest known ancestor

*Source: International Commission on Stratigraphy; *informal, not ratified by the ICS; colours defined by the Commission for the Geological Map of the World*

BREGENZ, AUSTRIA
47°30'N 9°45'E

The **longest table football marathon** lasted 51 hr 52 min and was set by Alexander Gruber, Roman Schelling, Enrico Lechtaler and Christian Nägele (all Austria) in Bregenz, Austria, between 27 and 29 June 2008.

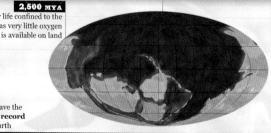

LARGEST PLACODERM

Placoderms constitute a class of prehistoric armoured fish known today only from fossils, and lived from the mid-/late-Silurian Period to the close of the Devonian Period (430–360 million years ago). They were characterized by the thick articulated plates of armour that covered their head and body. The largest species, often looked upon as the world's first vertebrate super-predator, was *Dunkleosteus telleri*, which was 8–11 m (26 ft 2 in–36 ft) long and had a near-worldwide distribution.

★ NEW RECORD
☆ UPDATED RECORD

★FIRST TRUE INSECT

Rhyniognatha hirsti lived in what is now Aberdeen, Scotland, UK, approximately 410 million years ago. The specimen was first described in 1926 by entomologist Robin John Tillyard (Australia), who regarded it as unremarkable and left it to London's Natural History Museum, UK. Entomologists David Grimaldi and Michael Engel (both USA) re-studied the fossil 80 years later using modern microscopes and spotted the creature's classic insect features. They published their research in *Nature* on 12 February 2004.

★FIRST LAND ANIMAL

The fossil of a 1-cm-long (0.25-in) centipede found near Stonehaven, Scotland, UK, by bus driver and amateur palaeontologist Mike Newman (UK) is thought to be 428 million years old and the earliest evidence of a creature living on land. Formally named *Pneumodesmus newmani* in 2004, the arthropod had spiracles – primitive air-breathing structures – on the outside of its body.

★LARGEST ARTHROPOD

The largest arthropod (jointed, limbed invertebrate) currently known is *Jaekelopterus rhenaniae*, a huge species of eurypterid, or sea scorpion, formally described in November 2007. Based upon the finding of a 46-cm-long (1-ft 6-in) fossilized chelicera, a claw-like mouthpart, the whole animal is thought to have measured up to 2.6 m (8 ft 6 in) in length.

FIRST WILDFIRE

The earliest wildfire smouldered approximately 419 million years ago during the Silurian period, when oxygen levels may have been higher than today's. A team of scientists from Cardiff University's School of Earth, Ocean and Planetary Science (UK) found evidence of a low-intensity burn, probably started by lightning, while studying three-dimensional charred fossils of small plants found in rocks near Ludlow, in the Welsh borderland, UK, in April 2004.

★FIRST AQUATIC REPTILE

Mesosaurus, which lived in South African and South American fresh water some 320–280 million years ago, is believed to be the first aquatic reptile. Less than 2 m (6 ft 6 in) long at most, *Mesosaurus* possessed a pair of slender jaws brimming with needle-like teeth, a long tail that was possibly finned and webbed feet.

★FIRST LAND PLANT

The earliest vascular land plant (one with a circulatory system) is *Cooksonia*, which appeared approximately 425 million years ago during the mid-Silurian Period. The plants had a branching stalk terminating in several spore-bearing structures called sporangiums.

V. 27439

PHANEROZOIC (543–0 MYA) *from the Greek for "make life appear"; our current eon, defined by abundant animal life*

PALAEOZOIC (542–251 MYA) *from the Greek for "early life"*

ORDOVICIAN (488–443 MYA)	SILURIAN (443–416 MYA)	DEVONIAN (416–359 MYA)	CARBONIFEROUS (359–290 MYA)	PERMIAN (290–251 MYA)

480 MYA Land still barren except for lichen and slime mould; first signs of arthropods making tentative steps on land

435 MYA Arthropods still dominant life-form

440 MYA Complex coral reefs form at tropical regions

400 MYA Enormous jawed fish dominate the seas

410 MYA Life begins major shift to colonize land; first plants and fungi grow by streams and rivers

370 MYA Forests emerge on land; land animals dominated by millipedes and early spiders; fish move from the sea to produce air-breathing, four-legged amphibians

320 MYA Sharks and bony fish dominate the seas

330 MYA Arthropods reach giant proportions but amphibians dominate land; first reptiles appear

290 MYA Global ice age; dry-adapted reptiles dominate

248 MYA Extreme climate change results in **largest mass extinction**; 95% of all life dies

---

HAMBURG, GERMANY
The **largest fashion catalogue** had 212 pages and measured 1.2 m x 1.5 m (3 ft 11 in x 4 ft 11 in) when unveiled in Hamburg, Germany, on 30 August 2003. It was a replica of the Bon Prix S2 catalogue *Voila!*.

53°35'N 9°59'E

LIVING PLANET
DINOSAURS

BIG
ANOTHER TITANOSAURID, *ANTARCTOSAURUS GIGANTEUS* (GIANT ANTARCTIC LIZARD), FOUND IN ARGENTINA AND INDIA, IS ESTIMATED TO HAVE WEIGHED BETWEEN 40 AND 80 TONNES (44 AND 88 TONS).

SMALL
THE ★SMALLEST SPECIES OF DINOSAUR IS THE FEATHERED MICRORAPTOR *ZHAOIANUS*. IT HAS A TOTAL LENGTH OF 39 CM (15.3 IN), OF WHICH 24 CM (9.4 IN) IS ACCOUNTED FOR BY ITS TAIL.

★ **NEW RECORD**
★ **UPDATED RECORD**

LONG
THE ★LONGEST DINOSAUR TAIL WAS THAT OF THE NORTH AMERICAN SAUROPOD *DIPLODOCUS*. IT MEASURED UP TO 13 M (42 FT 7 IN) IN LENGTH.

HEAVIEST DINOSAUR

In 1994, dinosaur researcher Gregory Paul used the fossil remains of a titanosaurid from Argentina called *Argentinosaurus* (above) to calculate that it had originally weighed up to 100 tonnes (110 tons), making it the heaviest dinosaur to have walked the Earth. Paul based his calculations on the creature's vertebrae.

★ **LARGEST AMMONITE**
An incomplete fossil shell of the ammonite *Parapuzosia*

seppenradensis discovered in Germany in 1895 measured 1.95 m (6 ft 3 in) across, but the complete shell is thought to have been around 2.55 m (8 ft 4 in). Ammonites were related to squids and octopuses but lived inside coiled shells, and this particular species was alive during the late Cretaceous Period (99.6 million to 65.5 million years ago).

LARGEST DINOSAUR FOOTPRINT
In 1932, the gigantic footprints of a large bipedal hadrosaurid ("duckbill") measuring 136 cm (53.5 in) in length and 81 cm (32 in) wide were discovered in Salt Lake City, Utah, USA.

LARGEST LAND-BASED CARNIVORES

The therapods (beast-footed) are the group of dinosaurs that many scientists believe evolved into birds. They included the fearsome *Tyrannosaurus rex*, *Allosaurus* and the even bigger *Giganotosaurus* (left), which lived 93–89 million years ago and could grow to an estimated 13 m (43 ft) long with a weight of 6 tonnes (13,230 lb).

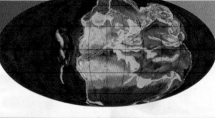

PERIOD	ERA	EON			
				PHANEROZOIC (543–0 MILLION YEARS AGO [MYA])	
				MESOZOIC (251–65 MYA)	
			TRIASSIC (251–206 MYA)		**JURASSIC** (206–144 MYA)

245 MYA Globe is dominated by the "supercontinent" Pangea, the **largest ever continent**

230 MYA First dinosaurs – in the form of small, bipedal predators – emerge

225 MYA The shrew-like *Adelobasileus cromptoni* is the **first known mammal**

225 MYA Pterosaurs take to the skies; giant reptiles such as the ichthyosaur *Cymbospondylus* dominate seas

200 MYA Extinction event, but dinosaurs flourish and dominate life

210 MYA **Longest dinosaur**, *Amphicoelias*, estimated at around 60 m (197 ft)

180 MYA Archosaurs (dinosaurs, pterosaurs, crocodilians) dominant on land; marine reptiles continue to rule the waves

*Source: International Commission on Stratigraphy; *informal, not ratified by the ICS; colours defined by the Commission for the Geological Map of the World*

59°57'N 10°45'E

OSLO, NORWAY
The **largest band** ever assembled was one of 20,100 bandsmen from Norges Musikkorps Forbund bands, who came together at the Ullevaal Stadium, Oslo, Norway, on 28 June 1964.

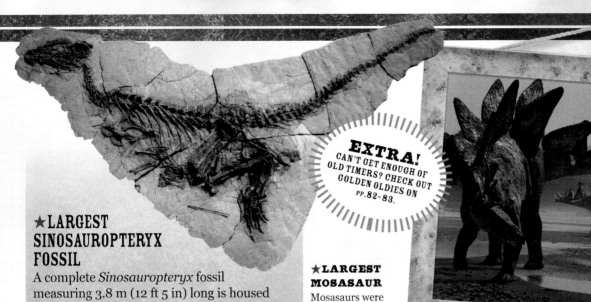

EXTRA!
CAN'T GET ENOUGH OF OLD TIMERS? CHECK OUT GOLDEN OLDIES ON PP. 82–83.

★ LARGEST SINOSAUROPTERYX FOSSIL

A complete *Sinosauropteryx* fossil measuring 3.8 m (12 ft 5 in) long is housed at the Shandong Tianyu Natural History Museum in Shandong province, China. The *Sinosauropteryx* is the first dinosaur found that displayed evidence of having had feathers.

LARGEST AND MOST COMPLETE TYRANNOSAURUS REX SKELETON

The largest, most complete and best-preserved *Tyrannosaurus rex* skeleton ever found is "Sue", measuring 4 m (13 ft) tall and 12.5 m (41 ft) long and approximately 90% complete. It was found in South Dakota, USA, on 12 August 1990 by explorer Sue Hendrickson (USA), after whom the skeleton has been named.

LONGEST DINOSAUR GENUS NAME

Micropachycephalosaurus, meaning "small thick-headed lizard", is the longest generic name for a dinosaur, with an impressive 23 letters and nine syllables. Named in 1978 by Chinese palaeontologists, this very small dinosaur, only 50–100 cm (6–12 in) long, is a thick-skulled plant-eater that lived in China around 83–73 million years ago, in the Cretaceous Period.

★ LARGEST PREHISTORIC CARNIVOROUS BIRD

Brontornis burmeisteri, which lived in Patagonia, South America, during the Miocene Epoch, is recognized as the largest carnivorous bird ever. Standing approximately 2.8 m tall (9 ft 3 in), this huge flightless bird weighed 350–400 kg (770–880 lb), more than twice the weight of today's largest bird, the ostrich (*Struthio camelus*).

★ LARGEST MOSASAUR

Mosasaurs were prehistoric sea lizards, related to modern-day varanids or monitor lizards. The largest mosasaur known to science is *Hainosaurus*, which had a total length of up to 15 m (49 ft 2.5 in).

★ LONGEST DINOSAUR HORNS

The longest horns of any dinosaur were the paired horns borne above the eyes by the North American ceratopsian dinosaur *Triceratops*. Each horn measured up to 1 m (39 in) long, and may have been used in courtship jousting bouts.

LARGEST CROCODILE EVER

Sarcosuchus imperator was a prehistoric species of crocodile that lived approximately 110 million years ago. Recent fossilized remains found in the Sahara Desert, Africa, suggest that this creature took 50–60 years to grow to its full length of around 11–12 m (37–40 ft) and its maximum weight of approximately 8 tonnes (17,636 lb).

★ SMALLEST-BRAINED DINOSAUR

The *Stegosaurus* ("plated lizard") – which, about 150 million years ago, roamed the lands that comprise the present-day US states of Colorado, Oklahoma, Utah and Wyoming – measured up to 9 m (30 ft) in length but had a walnut-sized brain weighing only 70 g (2.5 oz). This represented 0.002% of its computed body weight of 3.3 tonnes (7,275 lb) – compared to 0.06% for an elephant, or 1.88% for a human.

from the Greek for "make life appear"; our current eon, defined by abundant animal life

from the Greek for "middle life"

CRETACEOUS (144–65 MYA)

160 MYA Global warming leads to humid climates and lush jungles; large trees (conifers) and cycads common

155 MYA *Allosaurus* among the largest land predators of the Jurassic Period

150 MYA Emergence of *Archaeopteryx* marks the start of the evolution of the **first birds** from therapod dinosaurs

130 MYA Earth is now the land of the giants, with the appearance of *Giganotosaurus* and *Argentinosaurus*, the **largest-ever land animals**

115 MYA Mammals remain small in size but increasingly large in number; their size, shape and diversity is restricted by the dominance of the dinosaurs

100 MYA Dinosaurs, the most dominant land vertebrates since the Jurassic Period, are at their most diverse

90 MYA Flowering plants diversify thanks to the emergence of pollinating insects

65 MYA Mass extinction event at the end of the Cretaceous Period removes 40% of animal families, including dinosaurs; the Age of the Reptile is over

LIVING PLANET
BEASTS

★★★★★★★★★★★★★★

★ LARGEST BEAR

The giant short-faced bear (*Arctodus simus*) was the largest bear of all time. This prehistoric species, also known as the bulldog bear, had an estimated weight of 600–800 kg (1,322–1,763 lb). Males were bigger than females, and when on all fours would have stood around 1.6 m (5 ft 3 in) at the shoulder.

SMALLEST HOMINID

Discovered by Indonesian and Australian scientists in a cave on the island of Flores, Indonesia, in 2003, *Homo floresiensis* stood just 1 m (3 ft 3 in) tall. A species of great ape, *Homo floresiensis* lived on Flores as recently as 13,000 years ago.

★ LONGEST MASTODON TUSK

A mastodon tusk measuring 5.02 m (16 ft 6 in) was excavated between 17 and 28 July 2007 at a dig in Milia, Grevena, Greece, supervised by Evangelia Tsoukala, Dick Mol and a palaeontological team from the Aristotle University of Thessaloniki and the School of Geology.

★ **NEW RECORD**
★ **UPDATED RECORD**

★ MOST COMPLETE FOSSIL PRIMATE

On 19 May 2009, an international team of scientists unveiled the fossilized remains of a primate dating back 47 million years – the most complete fossil of an early primate found to date. The 1-m-long (3-ft) female specimen, closely resembling a modern-day lemur and named *Darwinius masillae*, had been found in Germany in 1993. The lengthy delay between discovery and announcement was the consequence of many years spent authenticating and preparing the specimen for sale. Time will tell how significant this fossil find proves to be.

FOSSIL
THE JARKOV MAMMOTH – NAMED AFTER GUENADI JARKOV, THE NINE-YEAR-OLD REINDEER HERDER WHO FOUND IT – IS THE OLDEST INTACT MAMMOTH. IT IS AN ESTIMATED 23,000 YEARS OLD.

FAMILY
ELEPHANTS AND MAMMOTHS ARE CLASSIFIED AS PART OF THE FAMILY ELEPHANTIDAE. THE ASIAN ELEPHANT IS A CLOSER RELATIVE TO THE MAMMOTH THAN THE AFRICAN ELEPHANT.

LARGEST ELEPHANT EVER

The Steppe mammoth *Mamuthus trogontherii* roamed over what is now central Europe a million years ago. A fragmentary skeleton of this species found in Mosbach, Germany, indicates a shoulder height of 4.5 m (14 ft 9 in) – this compares to the largest African elephant recorded, which had a shoulder height of 3.6 m (12 ft) and weighed over 8.1 tonnes (9 tons).

PERIOD ERA EON

PHANEROZOIC (543–0 MILLION YEARS AGO [MYA])

CENOZOIC (65–0 MYA)

PALEOGENE (65–23 MYA)

64 MYA
Continents continue to drift towards their present position; supercontinent Laurasia not yet divided

60 MYA
Following mass extinction, only animals smaller than a crocodile remain alive; birds are the largest creatures and biggest predators

55 MYA
Explosion in (often giant) mammalian life as environment niches filled; elephants, rodents, primates and whales appear

36 MYA
Antarctica begins to freeze over, cooling the oceans' climate; 25% of life on Earth perishes

30 MYA
New mammal species (ancestors of modern horses, pigs and camels) emerge, many dinosaur-sized, such as the **largest-ever land mammal**, *Indricotherium*

23 MYA
First true carnivores appear; grassland becomes a dominant part of the landscape, covering one-fifth of the planet

*Source: International Commission on Stratigraphy; *informal, not ratified by the ICS; colours defined by the Commission for the Geological Map of the World*

46°04'N 11°08'E

TRENTO, ITALY

The ★ **longest-running international speed skating competition** is the Alberto Nicolodi Trophy, organized by Sportivi Ghiaccio Trento, Trento, Italy, which started in 1961 and had its 49th anniversary event on 20–21 February 2010.

EXTRA!
ALL THESE BEASTS ARE LONG EXTINCT. FOR MUCH MORE ON MODERN MAMMALS LOOK LIVELY AND TURN TO PP. 66-67.

★LARGEST SLOTH

Megatherium, a giant ground sloth, lived in what is now South America during the Pliocene and Pleistocene epochs for around 5.3 million years. It stood 5.1 m (16 ft 8 in) high on its hind legs, and had an estimated average weight of 4.5 tonnes (4.9 tons).

LARGEST PREHISTORIC MAMMAL

Indricotherium, of the family Hyrachyidae, was a long-necked, hornless rhinocerotid that lived in western Asia and Europe about 35 million years ago. It measured 5.41 m (17 ft 9 in) to the top of the shoulder hump and was 11.27 m (37 ft) long.

★LARGEST SABRE-TOOTHED CAT

Smilodon populator lived in what is now South America from around 1 million years ago to around 10,000 years ago and stood 1.56 m (5 ft 5 in) at the shoulder. Each of its two serrated sabre-like canine teeth were up to 30 cm (12 in) long.

★LARGEST THUNDER BEAST

Also known as *brontotheres* or *titanotheres*, thunder beasts were huge prehistoric odd-toed ungulates (mammals that, like horses, walk on their toenails) that resembled rhinoceroses. The largest thunder beast was *Brontotherium*, which lived in North America around 55.8–33.9 million years ago. Characterized by a very large Y-shaped, horn-like structure of bone on its nose, this mighty herbivorous mammal stood around 2.5 m (8 ft 2 in) high at the shoulder, and may have weighed up to 1,000 kg (2,200 lb). When native American Indians first found the huge fossilized bones of this mammal, they mistook them for those of a legendary beast called the thunder horse that jumped down from the sky to Earth and made loud noises during thunderstorms. Based on this folklore, scientists named the animal *Brontotherium* ("thunder beast").

★LARGEST EGG-LAYING MAMMAL

Hackett's long-beaked echidna (*Zaglossus hacketti*), known from fossil remains in Western Australia, weighed up to 100 kg (220 lb) and was the size of a sheep. A massive relative of modern echidna, or spiny anteaters, it lived around 2.6 million to 12,000 years ago.

DID YOU KNOW?
KNOWN AS THE WEST RUNTON ELEPHANT, THE LARGEST COMPLETE MAMMOTH SKELETON WAS DISCOVERED IN CROMER, NORFOLK, UK, IN 1990. IT STANDS 4 M (13 FT) AT THE SHOULDER.

The giant deer *Megaloceros giganteus* had 4.3-m (14-ft) antlers – similar in size to the length of an adult American alligator.

TRIVIA

from the Greek for "make life appear"; our current eon, defined by abundant animal life

from the Greek for "new life"

NEOGENE (23–5 MYA)				QUARTERNARY (5–0 MYA)		

20 MYA
Herbivores evolve new teeth and digestive systems to deal with the abundance of grass; they also herd and migrate with the seasons

15 MYA
Golden era for *Deinotherium* – the second largest land mammal ever – a proboscidian related to the modern-day elephant

10 MYA
The ★largest ever predatory shark is *Carcharodon megalodon*, around 16 m (53 ft) long, with a mouth perhaps 2 m (6 ft) wide

4 MYA
Our ancestors are prey to the sabre-toothed *Dinofelis*, a successful carnivore mammal of the felid (cat) family

2.5 MYA
The tool-using *Homo habilis*, the ★first recognizable human, evolves from a hominid such as *Australopithecus afarensis*

2 MYA
The elephantine woolly mammoth *Mammuthus* appears; its shaggy coat and thick skin is perfect for surviving harsh winters during the last Ice Age

190,000 YA
Homo sapiens – yes, that's us – evolves in eastern Africa; within 40,000 years, we have spread across Asia, Europe and the Far East

PADUA, ITALY
The world's **oldest botanical garden** that remains on its original site is the Orto Botanico in Padua, Italy, which was created in 1545. The original design of a circular central plot (symbolizing the world) surrounded by a ring of water remains intact to this day.

45°25'N
11°52'E

LIVING PLANET
INSECTS & ARACHNIDS

BEETLE: Beware - beetles can bite! Their name comes from the German for "little biter".

STRANGEST DEFENCE MECHANISM

The bombardier beetle (genus *Brachinus*) stores two harmless chemicals in a special chamber in its abdomen. When it feels threatened, the liquids are released into a second chamber and mix with an enzyme, resulting in a violent chemical reaction and the release of considerable heat (up to 100°C, or 212°F) from the anus.

★HARDIEST BEETLE

The world's most indestructible beetle is a small species known as *Niptus hololeucus*. Researcher Malcolm Burr revealed that 1,547 specimens were discovered alive and thriving inside a bottle of casein (a chemical present in milk) that had been stoppered for 12 years. Burr also discovered another collection found living for 15 years inside a tin of leaves from the powerful poison plant *Datura stramontium*.

★LONGEST ANT MEMORY

Worker ants of two different species – *Formica selysi* and *Manica rubida* – that had been reared together for three months and then separated could still recognize one another after 18 months – the most tenacious ant memory demonstrated.

DEADLIEST ANT

The bulldog ant (*Myrmecia pyriformis*), found in coastal regions of Australia, uses its sting and jaws simultaneously. It has caused at least three human fatalities since 1936.

LARGEST BEETLE

The largest beetle in terms of weight, and indeed the **heaviest insect**, is Africa's goliath beetle (*Goliathus goliathus*), which can obtain larval weights (that is, its weight during its juvenile stage) up to 100 g (3.5 oz).

★LARGEST CRANE-FLY

The world's largest species of crane-fly or daddy long-legs is *Holorusia brobdignagius*, which can grow up to 23 cm (9 in) long, but is exceedingly slender and fragile.

★LONGEST SNOUT ON A BEETLE

South Africa's long-snouted cycad weevil (*Antliarhinus zamiae*) has the longest snout of any beetle. The 2-cm-long (0.79-in) snout is used for drilling holes in cycad seeds, inside which the 3-cm-long (1.18-in) weevil can then lay its eggs.

★LONGEST ANIMAL NAME

The longest scientific binomial (two-part) name given to any animal is *Parastratiosphecomyia stratiosphecomyioides* (containing 42 letters), aka the soldier fly, which is a species of stratiomyid fly with a metallic green thorax and abdomen.

★LARGEST ANIMAL FAMILY

The largest taxonomic family of animals is the weevil or snout beetle family, Curculionidae, which contains over 60,000 species currently known to science.

LARGEST MILLIPEDE

A fully grown African giant black millipede (*Archispirostreptus gigas*) owned by Jim Klinger of Coppell, Texas, USA, measures 38.7 cm (15.2 in) in length, 6.7 cm (2.6 in) in circumference, and has 256 legs.

100s
DESPITE THEIR NAMES, CENTIPEDES (MEANING "100 FEET") DON'T HAVE 100 LEGS, AND MILLIPEDES ("1,000 FEET") DON'T HAVE 1,000 LEGS!

1,000s
THE RECORD FOR THE ANIMAL WITH MOST LEGS GOES TO A SPECIMEN OF *ILLACME PLENIPES* - A MILLIPEDE FROM CALIFORNIA, USA, WHICH HAD 750 LEGS.

ACTUAL SIZE

"Pedipalps" (pincers) are used to catch prey and dig burrows, as well as playing a role in mating and defence.

LARGEST SCORPION

A specimen of *Heterometrus swannerdami* found during World War II in Krishnarajapuram, India, measured 29.2 cm (11.5 in) in overall length, from its stinger to its "pincer".

★ LARGEST ORB-WEB SPIDER

In 2000, an enormous female specimen of orb-web spider was discovered by Slovenian biologist Dr Matjaz Kuntner in a collection of specimens owned by the Plant Protection Institute in Pretoria, South Africa. Not only did it prove to belong to a hitherto unknown species – which Dr Kuntner later formally described, naming it *Nephila komaci* – but it was also found to constitute the world's largest orb-web spider species.

Further specimens have since been obtained, some from the island of Madagascar, revealing that females have a leg-span of up to 12 cm (4.7 in), and can spin webs up to 1 m (3 ft 3.3 in) wide. Males are about a quarter of the size of females.

LARGEST SPIDER

A male goliath bird-eating spider (*Theraphosa blondi*) collected at Rio Cavro, Venezuela, in April 1965 had a record leg-span of 28 cm (11 in) – long enough to cover a dinner plate.

STRONGEST SPIDER WEBS

The extremely tough webs spun by spiders of the genus *Nephila* can catch small birds and frogs (pictured), and are even capable of slowing down the passage of mammals up to the size of humans.

Spiders of the tropical African species *N. senegalensis* have a special garbage line in their web, in which the sucked-out remains of small birds have been found.

EXTRA! CHECK OUT SOME CREEPY CRUSTACEANS ON PP. 56-57 AND AMAZING MAMMALS ON PP. 66-67.

★ NEW RECORD
UPDATED RECORD

"Dear GWR, my giant millipede is 15¼ inches - is this a world record?"
Jim Klinger, Jungle Jim's Bugs of the World. Erm, yes!

LIVING PLANET
CRUSTACEANS & MOLLUSCS

QUIZ!
TO WHICH GROUP DO THE FOLLOWING CREATURES BELONG, MOLLUSC OR CRUSTACEAN?
A. CRAB B. OCTOPUS C. SLUG
SEE P. 278 FOR THE ANSWER.

★SHARPEST NIGHT VISION

Gigantocypris is a marine crustacean (pictured) that lives at depths of more than 1,000 m (3,300 ft), where there is virtually no sunlight. Luckily, this genus of ostracod has the best night vision of any animal, boasting eyes with an f-number (a measure of light sensitivity) of 0.25 (humans measure around f-2.55). Each eye possesses a pair of high-powered parabolic reflectors that direct the very dim available light on to the retina at their centre.

ACTUAL SIZE

★LARGEST COPEPOD

Copepods are small marine crustaceans, typically 1–2 mm (0.04–0.07 in) in length, that constitute the biggest biomass in the oceans. The largest species of copepod is *Pennella balaeonpterae*, which lives exclusively as a parasite upon the backs of fin whales (*Balaenoptera physalus*). It can attain a maximum length of 32 cm (12.5 in).

LARGEST LAND CRUSTACEAN

The robber or coconut crab (*Birgus latro*), which lives on tropical islands and atolls in the Indo-Pacific, is the largest land-living crustacean. Weights of up to 4.1 kg (9 lb) and leg-spans of up to 1 m (39 in) have been recorded. The **largest crustacean** is the giant spider crab (*Macrocheira kaempferi*), with a claw-span of up to 3.7 m (12 ft 1.6 in).

★MOST RECENTLY DESCRIBED CLASS OF CRUSTACEANS

In 1979, while diving in Lucayan Cavern beneath the island of Grand Bahama, biologist Dr Jill Yager (USA) encountered tiny worm-like crustaceans that proved to be a new species, dubbed *Speleonectes lucayensis*. So different was *S. lucayensis* from all crustaceans that, in 1981, an entirely new taxonomic class -- Remipedia -- was created in order to accommodate it. Several additional, related species have since been discovered, all of which are blind and characterized by their oar-like limbs, hence these crustaceans are termed remipedes ("oar-footed").

★MOST MATERNAL CRAB

The Jamaican bromeliad crab (*Metopaulius depressus*), which actually lives on land in mountainous forests, is the world's most maternal crab. The female lays her eggs in puddles of rainwater that collect in the large leaves of bromeliad plants, and three months after the eggs hatch she feeds her offspring with small insects and also chases away would-be predators such as lizards and large spiders.

BOOT!
THE GIANT CHITON IS ALSO KNOWN AS THE GUMBOOT CHITON, AS IT RESEMBLES EITHER THE SOLE OF A RUBBER BOOT, OR THE BOOT ITSELF!

FOOT!
LIKE A SLUG, THE CHITON IS EFFECTIVELY JUST ONE BIG FOOT. A NOCTURNAL CREATURE, IT CLINGS TO ROCKS AND EATS ALGAE AND KELP.

★LARGEST CHITON

Chitons (from the Greek for "tunic") are primitive marine molluscs. The largest is the gumshoe or giant Pacific chiton (*Cryptochiton stelleri*), found off the Pacific coasts of North America and Japan, which grows up to 33 cm (1 ft) long and 13 cm (0.43 in) wide. Its red, leathery mantle (or "girdle") wraps around its body (like a tunic, hence its name), covering a series of armoured plates that run down the chiton's back.

LARGEST CLAM

The largest of all existing bivalve shells is that of the marine giant clam (*Tridacna gigas*), found on the Indo-Pacific coral reefs. One specimen measuring 1.15 m (3 ft 9.25 in) in length and weighing 333 kg (734 lb) was collected off Ishigaki Island, Okinawa, Japan, in 1956; it probably weighed just over 340 kg (750 lb) when it was alive.

Slugs like beer! Research at Colorado University in the USA in 1987 identified Kingsbury Malt Beverage to be the slug's top tipple.

TRIVIA

CHOMP! SOME SLUGS POSSESS TENS OF THOUSANDS OF TINY, RAZOR-SHARP TEETH THAT ARE CONTINUALLY BEING REPLACED.

★LARGEST BARNACLE

Barnacles are marine crustaceans that "encrust" themselves to surfaces. The largest is the giant acorn barnacle, *Balanus nubilis*, standing up to 12.7 cm (5 in) high.

★LARGEST MOLLUSC

An adult male colossal squid (*Mesonychoteuthis hamiltoni*) weighing around 450 kg (990 lb) and measuring 10 m (33 ft) long was caught by fishermen in the Ross Sea of Antarctica. It was taken to New Zealand for research, and the catch was announced on 22 February 2007. Colossal squid are usually shorter than giant squid, but much heavier.

MOST VENOMOUS MOLLUSC

The two closely related species of blue-ringed octopus, *Hapalochlaena maculosa* and *H. lunulata,* are found around the coasts of Australia and parts of south-east Asia. They carry a neurotoxic venom so potent that their relatively painless bite can kill in a matter of minutes. It has been estimated that each individual carries sufficient venom to cause the paralysis or death of 10 adult people. Fortunately, blue-ringed octopuses are not considered aggressive and normally bite only when they are taken out of the water and provoked. These molluscs have a radial spread of just 100–200 mm (4–8 in).

LARGEST EYE-TO-BODY RATIO

The vampire squid (*Vampyroteuthis infernalis*) has the largest eye-to-body ratio of any animal. Its body can reach a length of 28 cm (11 in), while its eyes may have a diameter of 2.5 cm (0.9 in).

OLDEST MOLLUSC

In 2006, a quahog clam (*Arctica islandica*) that had been living on the seabed off the north coast of Iceland was dredged by a team from Bangor University's School of Ocean Sciences, Wales, UK. On 28 October 2007, researchers revealed that it was between 405 and 410 years old. The clam was nicknamed "Ming", after the Chinese dynasty in power when it was born!

GASTROPOD: From the Greek for "stomach foot", on the misunderstanding that slugs glide around on their bellies.

ACTUAL SIZE

★LARGEST SLUG

The world's largest species of terrestrial slug is the ash-black slug, *Limax cinereoniger*. Found in ancient woodlands throughout all but the most northerly regions of Europe, this gastropod mollusc can grow to a length of up to 30 cm (12 in), and eats fungi.

VATICAN CITY

41°54'N 12°27'E

The **oldest army** is the Pontifical Swiss Guard in the Vatican City, which comprises 80 to 90 individuals. The unit's foundation dates back to 21 January 1506; its earliest origins, however, predate 1400.

LIVING PLANET
FISH & SEALIFE

★ HOTTEST FISH EYES

Swordfish (*Xiphias gladius*) have special organs that heat up their eyes to as much as 28°C (82°F), improving their efficiency in cold water and enabling them to spot prey swiftly.

QUIZ!
OF ALL THE FISH IN THE SEA, WHICH IS THE LARGEST?
SEE P.278 FOR THE ANSWER.

★ SMALLEST SEA URCHIN

The *Echinocyamus scaber* species of sea urchin, which is native to the seas off New South Wales, Australia, has a test (shell) diameter of just 5.5 mm (0.22 in).

★ LARGEST FAMILY OF FISH

Family Cyprinidae, the carp family of freshwater fish, contains over 2,400 species, housed in approximately 220 genera. Among its most familiar members are the carps (including goldfish), tench, barbs, minnows and barbels.

LONGEST FISH FIN

All three species of thresher shark (family Alopiidae) have huge scythe-shaped caudal (tail) fins that are roughly as long as their entire bodies. The largest of the three species is the common thresher shark (*Alopias vulpinus*), which is found worldwide in temperate and tropical seas. Common threshers may grow to a length of 6 m (19 ft 8 in), of which almost 3 m (9 ft 10 in) consists of its greatly elongated upper tail fin; the fish's body itself is sleek and slender.

FASTEST FISH

In short-distance speed trials carried out at the Long Key Fishing Camp, Florida, USA, a cosmopolitan sailfish (*Istiophorus platypterus*) took out 91 m (300 ft) of line in 3 seconds, equivalent to a velocity of 109 km/h (68 mph). By comparison, cheetahs run at 100 km/h (62 mph). Sailfish achieve their incredible bursts of speed thanks to their highly oxygenated red muscles.

MOST VENOMOUS JELLYFISH

The box jellyfish (*Chironex fleckeri*), aka Flecker's sea wasp, found off the north coast of Australia, typically contains enough venom to kill 60 humans and is responsible for one death per year, on average.

★ LARGEST FAMILY OF MARINE FISH

Family Gobiidae, the goby family, contains over 2,000 species (including the whip coral goby *Bryaninops yongei*, below). Gobies range in length from less than 1 cm to 30 cm (0.2–12 in), their most distinctive feature being their disc-shaped sucker derived from their fused pelvic fins.

★ LARGEST SEA LILY

Despite their flower-like appearance, sea lilies are animals, not plants. The largest species (genus *Metacrinus*) inhabit the Pacific Ocean. They have a maximum stalk height of 61 cm (2 ft), with a 15.2-cm (5.98-in) arm length.

★ LARGEST BARRACUDA

A barracuda specimen weighing 38.6 kg (85 lb 1 oz) was caught on 11 April 2002 off Christmas Island, Kiribati, in the Pacific Ocean.

LARGEST FISH EGG

The crew of a shrimp trawler in the Gulf of Mexico found a whale shark egg (*Rhincodon typus*) measuring 30.5 x 14 x 8.9 cm (12 x 5.5 x 3.5 in) on 29 June 1953.

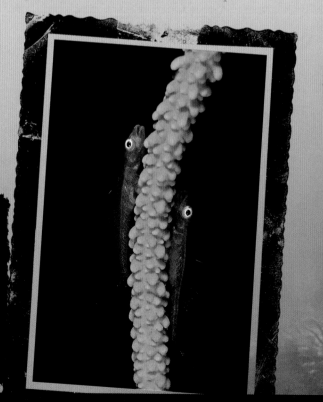

★ LONGEST PREGNANCY

The common frilled shark (*Chlamydoselachus anguineus*), a primitive species native to all oceans, has a longer gestation period (pregnancy) than any other animal: an average of 3.5 years.

★ **NEW RECORD**
★ **UPDATED RECORD**

URCHIN:
An old-fashioned word for the spiny hedgehogs that sea urchins resemble!

★ HEAVIEST STARFISH

On 14 September 1969, a specimen of *Thromidia catalai*, a hefty five-armed species of starfish native to the western Pacific, was caught off Ilot Amédée, New Caledonia. The starfish, which weighed an estimated 6 kg (13 lb 3 oz), was later deposited at New Caledonia's Nouméa Aquarium.

★ LARGEST BRAIN CORAL COLONY

As large as a truck, a brain coral approximately 3 m (9 ft 10 in) high and 5 m (16 ft 4 in) across can be found on a dive site called Kelleston Drain, south of the island of Little Tobago, Trinidad and Tobago. Like all colonial corals, brain corals are not a single organism but composed of millions of individual coral polyps living together.

★ HEAVIEST FISH

A scientifically recorded specimen of whale shark (*Rhincodon typus*) captured off Baba Island, near Karachi, Pakistan, on 11 November 1949 measured 12.65 m (41 ft 6 in) long, making it the **largest fish**, but it also weighed an estimated 15–21 tonnes (33,000–46,200 lb), giving it the record for heaviest fish too. Sharks and rays are cartilaginous fish – their skeletons are composed of cartilage instead of the hard bone of many other fish species. The **heaviest bony fish** is the ocean sunfish (*Mola mola*), which has been recorded as weighing 2 tonnes (4,400 lb) and measuring 3 m (10 ft) from fin tip to fin tip.

LONGEST FISH MIGRATION

A bluefin tuna (*Thunnus thynnus*) was tagged off Baja California, Mexico, in 1958 and was caught again 483 km (300 miles) south of Tokyo, Japan, in April 1963, by which time it had travelled a straight-line distance of at least 9,335 km (5,800 miles). Its weight also increased from 16 kg (35 lb) to 121 kg (267 lb) between catches.

LONGEST SURVIVAL OUT OF WATER FOR A FISH

Six species of lungfish live in freshwater swamps that dry out for months or even years at a time. Two of the four species found in Africa (*Protopterus annectens*, *P. aethiopicus*, *P. dolloi* and *P. amphibius*) are considered to be real survival experts. As their swamp water recedes, they burrow deep into the ground and secrete mucus to form a moisture-saving cocoon around their bodies. They then build a porous mud plug at the entrance of the burrow – and wait. Abandoning gill breathing in favour of their air-breathing lungs, they can live for up to four years in this dormant position.

LARGEST JELLYFISH

Most jellyfish have a body diameter, or bell, ranging from 2 cm to 40 cm (0.8–15.8 in), but some species grow considerably larger. The largest recorded specimen was an Arctic giant jellyfish (*Cyanea capillata arctica*) that washed up in Massachusetts Bay, USA, in 1870; it had a bell diameter of 2.28 m (7 ft 6 in) and tentacles stretching 36.5 m (120 ft).

DID YOU KNOW?

SIPHONOPHORES RESEMBLE TRUE JELLYFISH, ALTHOUGH THE TWO ARE ONLY DISTANTLY RELATED. ONE SIPHONOPHORE SPECIES, *PRAYA DUBIA*, IS THE WORLD'S LONGEST ANIMAL, AT 30–50 M (100–160 FT).

TRIVIA

By way of comparison to *Praya dubai*, the blue whale, the world's **largest animal**, is 25–27 m (82–88 ft 6 in) long.

UP
THE HIGHEST-LIVING FISH IS THE TIBETAN LOACH (FAMILY COBITIDAE), FOUND AT AN ALTITUDE OF 5,200 M (17,060 FT) IN THE HIMALAYAS!

DOWN
THE DEEPEST-LIVING FISH IS THE *ABYSSOBROTULA GALATHEAE* SPECIES OF CUSK EEL, WHICH LIVES AT A DEPTH OF 8,370 M (27,460 FT).

COPENHAGEN, DENMARK
Bakken, located in Klampenborg, north of Copenhagen in Denmark, opened in 1583 and is the **oldest operating amusement park** in the world. The park claims to have over 150 attractions, including a wooden roller coaster built in 1932.

55°40'N 12°34'E

LIVING PLANET
AMPHI-BIANS

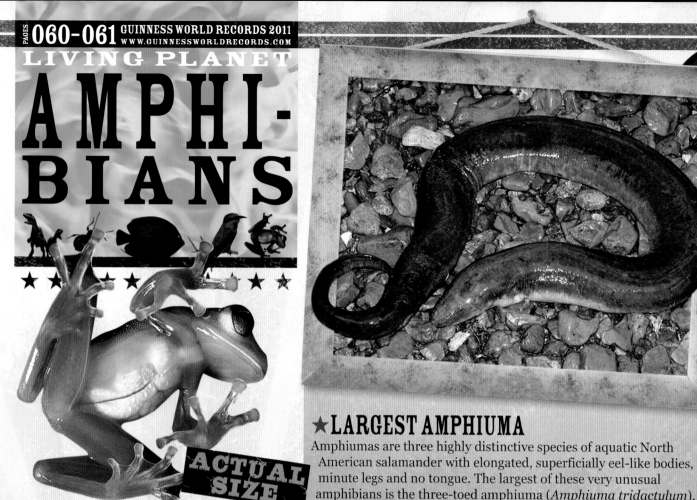

ACTUAL SIZE

★LARGEST AMPHIUMA

Amphiumas are three highly distinctive species of aquatic North American salamander with elongated, superficially eel-like bodies, minute legs and no tongue. The largest of these very unusual amphibians is the three-toed amphiuma (*Amphiuma tridactylum*), pictured. It can grow to 1 m (3 ft 3 in) long, possesses gill slits but lacks eyelids, and lives in marshes and lakes within the south-eastern USA.

★MOST TRANSPARENT AMPHIBIAN

Some so-called glass frogs (of the family Centrolenidae), native to the rainforests of Central and South America, have partially transparent abdominal skin that resembles frosted glass. Their heart, liver and gut can be readily seen through it when viewed from underneath. The remainder of their skin is usually lime green.

LARGEST FROG

A specimen of the African goliath frog (*Conraua goliath*), captured in April 1899 on the Sanaga River, Cameroon, had a snout-to-vent length of 36.83 cm (14.5 in) and an overall length of 87.63 cm (34.5 in) with its legs extended, about the size of a house rabbit.

The world's **smallest frog**, and the **smallest known amphibian**, is *Eleutherodactylus limbatus* of Cuba, which is 8.5–12 mm (0.33–0.47 in) long from snout to vent.

★RAREST AMPHIBIANS

The Red List of Threatened Species lists two toads as "Extinct in the Wild":
• The Wyoming toad (*Bufo baxteri*) exists only within the Mortenson Lake National Wildlife Refuge in Wyoming, USA; believed extinct in 1980, it was rediscovered in 1987 but no known mating in the wild has occurred since 1991.
• The hundreds of remaining Kihansi spray toads (*Nectophrynoides asperginis*), a dwarf toad native to Tanzania, live at the Bronx Zoo, New York City, USA.

★LEAST FECUND AMPHIBIAN

Fecundity is the capacity for producing offspring. The world's least fecund frog is the Cuban frog (*Sminthillus limbatus*), a tiny species of poison-dart frog whose female lays only a single egg.

In stark contrast, a single female of the world's **most fecund amphibian**, the cane toad (*Bufo marinus*), will lay as many as 30,000–35,000 eggs per spawning.

MOST POISONOUS...

Frog: The golden poison-dart frog (*Phyllobates terribilis*) of South and Central America may measure only 4–5 cm (1.6–2 in) long, but it secretes enough toxin to provide a lethal dose to 10 adult humans or 20,000 lab mice.

QUIZ!
WHICH CLASSIC ARCADE VIDEOGAME FEATURES AN AMPHIBIAN ATTEMPTING TO CROSS A BUSY ROAD AND A FAST-FLOWING RIVER?
SEE P.278 FOR THE ANSWER.

★LARGEST GENUS OF FROG

The *Pristimantis* genus of frog contains more than 400 species, with new ones being discovered each year. These small frogs are native to southern Central and northern South America, and are notable for laying their eggs on land. These hatch directly as froglets, thus bypassing the tadpole stage.

UDINE, ITALY
46°03'N 13°14'E
The **most participants in a cycling event** is 48,615 for the 29.3-km-long (18.2-mile) Udine Pedala 2000, organized by Rolo Banca 1473, at Udine, Italy, on 11 June 2000.

★ **NEW RECORD**
★ **UPDATED RECORD**

LAND
THE WORD AMPHIBIAN COMES FROM THE GREEK *AMPHI-*, MEANING "BOTH KINDS", AND *BIOS*, MEANING "LIFE" – BOTH KINDS OF LIFE...

WATER
..."BOTH KINDS OF LIFE" REFERS TO THE AMPHIBIANS' ABILITY TO EXIST ON LAND AND IN THE WATER – A CLASS BETWEEN FISH AND REPTILES.

★LARGEST CAECILIAN

Extant (living) amphibians can be divided into Anura (frogs and toads), Caudata (newts and salamanders) and Gymnophiona (caecilians). This last order are limbless tropical amphibians that generally resemble earthworms, and have eyes hidden beneath a layer of skin. The world's largest is Thompson's caecilian (*Caecilia thompsoni*), a Colombian species that can attain a length of 1.51 m (4 ft 11 in). It is native to moist tropical and subtropical lowland forests as well as plantations and even rural gardens.

LARGEST AMPHIBIAN

The giant salamanders (family Cryptobranchidae) are the greatest of the amphibians. The record-holder is the Chinese giant salamander (*Andrias davidianus*, pictured), which lives in mountain streams in north-eastern, central and southern China. One record-breaking specimen collected in Hunan Province measured 1.8 m (5 ft 11 in) in length and weighed 65 kg (143 lb).

DID YOU KNOW? THROUGHOUT JUNE 2009, CITIZENS OF ISHIKAWA PREFECTURE IN JAPAN REPORTED NUMEROUS EXAMPLES OF FROGS AND TADPOLES RAINING OUT OF THE SKY!

Frogs feature prominently in the classic 1980s videogame *Frogger*, in which players guide frogs to safety.

TRIVIA

Newt: One drop of blood from the California newt (*Taricha torosa*), which contains the toxic and powerful nerve poison tetrodotoxin, could kill several thousand mice.

LARGEST NEWT

The Spanish ribbed newt (*Pleurodeles waltl*), found in central and southern Iberia and Morocco, is 15–30 cm (6–12 in) long.

The world's **smallest newt** or **salamander** is the Mexican lungless salamander (*Bolitoglossa mexicana*), which attains a maximum length of approximately 2.54 cm (1 in).

★HIGHEST FROG CROAK

The concave-eared torrent frog (*Odorrana tormota*) of eastern China emits a croak of 128 kHz – well beyond the range of human hearing, which cannot detect sound frequencies above 20 kHz.

ACTUAL SIZE

EXTRA! DISCOVER MORE ABOUT HUMANITY'S RELATIONSHIP WITH ANIMALS IN OUR ANIMAL MAGIC CHAPTER, FROM P.148.

LIVING PLANET
REPTILES

ACTUAL SIZE

★ SMALLEST CHELONIAN

Of all the chelonians – turtles, tortoises and terrapins – the smallest is the speckled cape tortoise or speckled padloper (*Homopus signatus*). It has a shell length of 6–9.6 cm (2.3–3.7 in) – so small that the tortoise can hide in tiny gaps between rocks.

★ FASTEST CROCODILE ON LAND

The freshwater crocodile (*Crocodylus johnstoni*) can attain speeds reaching 17 km/h (10.56 mph) when in full gallop – a mode of terrestrial locomotion that only a few species of crocodile can accomplish. Native to Australia, this crocodile rarely grows larger than 2.5–3 m (8–10 ft).

★ LARGEST GECKO

Delcourt's giant gecko (*Hoplodactylus delcourti*) is known from only a single mounted and stuffed specimen measuring 61 cm (2 ft) long. It had been on display at the Marseille Natural History Museum in France for more than a century before, in 1979, it was recognized by curator Alain Delcourt as representing a species unknown to science. The gecko was formally named and described in 1986.

FASTEST LIZARD

In a series of experiments conducted by Professor Raymond Huey from the University of Washington, USA, and colleagues at the University of California at Berkeley, USA, the highest burst speed recorded for any reptile on land was 34.9 km/h (21.7 mph), achieved by *Ctenosaura*, a spiny-tailed iguana from Central America.

★ LONGEST REPTILIAN INCUBATION PERIOD

Of all the egg-laying reptiles the tuataras (see *Instant Expert*, p.63) have to keep their eggs warm the longest before they are ready to hatch. Scientists have recorded tuataras incubating eggs for as long as 13 to 15 months before their offspring emerge from their shells.

★ LARGEST CROCODILE EGGS

The false gharial (*Tomiostoma schlegelii*), a crocodilian with long, narrow jaws and a slender snout native to south-east Asia, lays eggs that typically measure 10 x 7 cm (3.94 x 2.76 in). Despite its name, recent studies have shown that the false gharial is more closely related to other gharials than crocodiles and alligators.

★ LARGEST VENOMOUS LIZARD

Measuring up to 3.13 m (10 ft 3 in) and weighing around 70 kg (154 lb 5 oz), the Komodo dragon (*Varanus komodoensis*) is the **largest lizard**. In 2009, researchers at Melbourne University, Australia, discovered that the reptile also possesses a pair of venom glands in its lower jaw that secretes a venom containing several different toxic proteins.

HORNS
HORNED LIZARDS OF THE GENUS *PHRYNOSOMA* CAN SQUIRT BLOOD OUT OF THEIR EYES TO FRIGHTEN POTENTIAL PREDATORS.

THORNS
AS ITS NAME MIGHT SUGGEST, THE THORNY DEVIL (*MOLOCH HORRIDUS*) IS COVERED IN SHARP SPINES THAT MAKE IT HARD FOR PREDATORS TO SWALLOW.

BERLIN, GERMANY

The **largest single rock concert**, in terms of participants and organization, was Roger Waters's production of Pink Floyd's *The Wall*, staged on 21 July 1990 in Potsdamer Platz, straddling East and West Berlin, Germany, when 600 people performed on stage.

DID YOU KNOW?

LIKE THE KOMODO DRAGON, THE GILA MONSTER (*HELODERMA SUSPECTUM*) AND THE MEXICAN BEADED LIZARD (*HELODERMA HORRIDUM*) ARE ALSO VENOMOUS.

Of all the reptile groups, the crocodilians – crocodiles, alligators and gharials – are the closest living relatives to birds.

TRIVIA

LARGEST TORTOISE

The giant tortoises (*Chelonoidis nigra*) of the Galápagos Islands are the largest tortoise species. A specimen named Goliath, who resided at the Life Fellowship Bird Sanctuary in Seffner, Florida, USA, from 1960 until his death in November 2002, was 1.35 m (4 ft 5.5 in) long, 1.02 m (3 ft 3.6 in) wide, 68.5 cm (2 ft 3 in) tall and weighed 417 kg (920 lb).

EXTRA!
FOR MORE COLD-BLOODED CREATURES, PLOD ALONG TO PP.50-51 TO EXPLORE THE LAND OF THE DINOSAURS.

★ MOST ACUTE NOCTURNAL COLOUR VISION

Unlike most other animals with nocturnal vision, the helmeted gecko (*Tarentola chazaliae*) can perceive colours at night. This is thought to be due to the higher density of colour-sensitive large cone cells in the lizard's retinas.

★ COUNTRY WITH MOST VENOMOUS SNAKE SPECIES

Australia not only contains more species of venomous snake than any other country on Earth, but also includes among those snakes no less than nine of the world's top 10 most venomous snake species. These include such (in)famous serpents as the inland taipan (*Oxyuranus microlepidotus*) – perhaps the world's most venomous snake – the eastern brown snake (*Pseudonaja textilis*) at the number two spot, the coastal taipan (*Oxyuranus scutellatus*) third and the tiger snake (*Notechis scutatus*) fourth.

OLDEST SNAKE

The greatest reliable age recorded for a snake in captivity is 40 years 3 months 14 days for a male common boa (*Boa constrictor*) named Popeye, who died at Philadelphia Zoo, Pennsylvania, USA, on 15 April 1977.

LARGEST CROCODILIAN

The estuarine, or saltwater, crocodile (*Crocodylus porosus*) is found throughout the tropical regions of Asia and the Pacific. The Bhitarkanika Wildlife Sanctuary in Orissa State, India, houses four measuring more than 6 m (19 ft 8 in) in length, the largest being over 7 m (23 ft) long. There are several unauthenticated reports of specimens up to 10 m (33 ft) in length. Adult males average 4.2–4.8 m (14–16 ft) in length and weigh about 408–520 kg (900–1,150 lb).

SMALLEST CROCODILIAN

The dwarf caiman (*Paleosuchus palpebrosus*) of northern South America is the smallest crocodilian in the world today. Females rarely exceed a length of 1.2 m (4 ft) and males rarely grow to more than 1.5 m (4 ft 11 in).

★ **NEW RECORD**
UPDATED RECORD

RAREST LIZARD

Until it was rediscovered in 1990, the Jamaican iguana (*Cyclura collei*) was thought to be extinct. With no more than 100 adult specimens located since 1990, the species is considered critically endangered and it is clinging to survival in southern Jamaica's remote Hellshire Hills -- the only sizeable area of dry forest remaining on the island.

LONGEST VENOMOUS SNAKE

The venom of a single bite from the king cobra (*Ophiophagus hannah*), found in south-east Asia and India, is enough to kill an elephant, or 20 people. What's more, it can grow to 3.65–4.5 m (12–15 ft) in length and can stand tall enough to look an adult human in the eye.

RAREST CROCODILIAN

There were fewer than 200 Chinese alligators (*Alligator sinensis*) living in the wild in 2002. Found in the lower parts of the Yangtze River in wetlands, the species can grow to 2 m (6 ft 6 in) and weigh 40 kg (88 lb). Their numbers have dwindled over time due to habitat destruction and killing by local farmers.

INSTANT EXPERT

✪ TUATARAS MIGHT LOOK LIKE LIZARDS, BUT THEY ARE ACTUALLY THE ONLY LIVING REPRESENTATIVES OF AN OTHERWISE EXTINCT GROUP OF REPTILES CALLED THE SPHENODONTIDS, A GROUP THAT THRIVED AT THE TIME OF THE DINOSAURS.

✪ NOT ALL REPTILES LIVE ON DRY LAND. THE MARINE IGUANA (*AMBLYRHYNCHUS CRISTATUS*) AND VARIOUS SPECIES OF SEA SNAKE LIVE IN SALT WATER.

✪ THE COMMON BASILISK (*BASILISCUS BASILISCUS*) IS KNOWN AS THE "JESUS LIZARD" FOR ITS ABILITY TO RUN ON WATER!

★ LARGEST TUATARA

There are only two species of tuatara, both of which are found exclusively in the islands off the main coast of New Zealand. Of the two, the greatly endangered Brothers Island tuatara (*Sphenodon guntheri*) is the largest. It can grow up to 76 cm (2 ft 6 in) long and have a maximum weight of 1.4 kg (3 lb 1 oz).

LIVING PLANET
BIRDS

EXTRA!
SEE HOW WELL WE HUMANS DO WHEN WE TAKE TO THE SKIES BY VISITING PP.116-117.

DID YOU KNOW?

NORTH AMERICAN PASSENGER PIGEONS ONCE FLOCKED IN THEIR TENS OF MILLIONS – BUT IN LESS THAN 100 YEARS, THEY WERE HUNTED BY MAN TO EXTINCTION.

There is a bird known as the vampire finch (*Geospiza difficilis septentrionalis*) – and yes, its favourite food is blood!

TRIVIA

KEENEST SMELL FOR A BIRD

Few birds have a developed sense of smell, but the black-footed albatross (*Diomedea nigripes*) can smell bacon fat poured into the ocean from at least 30 km (18 miles) away.

★HUNGRIEST BIRDS

The world's hungriest birds are the hummingbirds (family Trochilidae), which have such high metabolic rates that they need to consume at least half of their total body weight in food every day in order to survive. Their food consists mostly of tiny insects and nectar.

FASTEST BIRDS

• **In level flight**: The mean estimated speed recorded for a satellite-tagged grey-headed albatross (*Thalassarche chrysostoma*) is 127 km/h (78.9 mph) sustained for more than eight hours.

• **In a dive**: A peregrine falcon (*Falco peregrinus*) was recorded at a velocity of 270 km/h (168 mph) at a 30° angle of stoop, rising to a maximum of 350 km/h (217 mph) at 45°.

• **On land**: The **fastest (flightless) bird on land** is the ostrich (*Struthio camelus*), which can reach 72 km/h (45 mph) when running.

• **In water**: The fastest bird swimmer is the gentoo penguin (*Pygoscelis papua*), which has a burst of speed of about 27 km/h (17 mph).

STRONGEST BIRD OF PREY

The female harpy eagle (*Harpia harpyja*) regularly kills and carries away animals equal or superior to its 9 kg (20 lb) weight.

SMALLEST BIRDS

Male bee hummingbirds (*Mellisuga helenae*) of Cuba and the Isle of Youth measure 57 mm (2.24 in) in total length, half of which is taken up by the bill and tail, and weigh just 1.6 g (0.056 oz). Females are slightly larger.

Hummingbirds also have the **fastest wing-beat**. The ruby-throated hummingbird (*Archilochus colubris*) can produce a wing-beat rate of 200 beats per second (bps).

HEAVIEST BIRDS

The **heaviest bird of prey** is the Andean condor (*Vultur gryphus*, pictured), males of which average 9–12 kg (20–27 lb) and have a wing-span of 3 m (10 ft). The **heaviest flying bird** is the kori bustard (*Ardeotis kori*) of south and east Africa; males can reach 18.2 kg (40 lb). The **heaviest (and largest) of all birds** is the ratite male ostrich (*Struthio camelus camelus*). It can grow 2.75 m (9 ft) tall and may weigh 156.5 kg (345 lb).

★ **NEW RECORD**
■ **UPDATED RECORD**

LAZY!
KORI BUSTARDS – THE HEAVIEST FLYING BIRDS – ARE RARELY SEEN IN THE AIR: THEY ARE SO HEAVY, THEY PREFER TO WALK EVERYWHERE!

BONES!
ANDEAN NATIVES COLLECT THE BONES OF THE ANDEAN CONDOR – THE HEAVIEST BIRD OF PREY – BELIEVING THAT THEY HAVE HEALING POWERS.

RATITE: "Flightless". The name is from the Latin for "raft": just as a raft has no keel, these birds have no keel (length-wise ridge) in their breast bone.

★HIGHEST YOLK CONTENT

The bird eggs with the highest yolk content to egg volume are those of New Zealand's kiwis (order Apterygiformes). Some 60% of a kiwi egg's volume is taken up by yolk (compared with 31% of a hen's egg), and contains so much nutrient that the kiwi chick does not have to eat for several days after hatching.

SMALLEST NEST

The nest of the vervain hummingbird (*Mellisuga minima*) is about half the size of a walnut shell, while the deeper but narrower one of the bee hummingbird (*M. helenae*) is thimble sized.

LARGEST COMMUNAL NEST

The sociable weaver (*Philetairus socius*) of south-western Africa builds a nest that can be up to 8 m (26 ft) long and 2 m (6 ft 6 in) high. Resembling a giant haystack that hangs from a tree or telegraph pole, it contains up to 300 individual nests. Not surprisingly, these enormous communal nests can get so heavy that the tree on which they are built sometimes collapses under the weight!

★HIGHEST NESTS

The highest tree nest constructed by any bird is that of the marbled murrelet (*Brachyramphus marmoratus*), a small North Pacific member of the auk family of seabirds. Its nests have been discovered as high as 45 m (147 ft), usually on moss-covered branches of old conifer trees.

This may explain why the first formally identified nest from this species was not recorded by science until as recently as 1961, in Asia; the first North American example was not found until 1974.

★MOST BIRD SONGS RECORDED

The red-eyed vireo (*Vireo olivaceus*), a small New World species of songbird, has been recorded singing 22,197 songs in a 10-hour period, an average of over 2,000 songs per hour!

★LOWEST NESTING ALTITUDE

The little green bee-eater (*Merops orientalis*) nests at 400 m (1,312 ft) below sea level in the Dead Sea area of the Middle East. This is the lowest nesting altitude recorded for any species of bird.

★SMALLEST EGGS

Surprisingly, bearing in mind that it lays the **largest eggs** of any bird, the bird that lays the smallest eggs relative to body weight is the ostrich (*Struthio camelus*). This is because the egg's weight is only 1.4–1.5% of the ostrich's total weight. A comparable percentage has also been recorded for the emperor penguin (*Aptenodytes forsteri*).

★SHORTEST MIGRATION

In stark contrast to the thousands of kilometres flown by certain migrating birds, North America's blue grouse (*Dendragapus obscurus*) descends a mere 300 m (984 ft) from its winter home in the mountainous pine forests to deciduous woodlands in order to feed upon the early crop of seeds and fresh leaves.

JINX!

BECAUSE A WRYNECK CAN TWIST ITS HEAD AND NECK THROUGH NEARLY 180°, SOME PEOPLE BELIEVED THAT WITCHES USED THE BIRD TO MAKE CURSES. THE WORD "JINX" DERIVES FROM THEIR LATIN GENUS NAME: *JYNX!*

★LONGEST BIRD TONGUE

Relative to body size, the longest tongue of any bird is that of the wryneck (*Jynx torquilla*), a European relative of woodpeckers. Its tongue is two-thirds of its 16.5-cm (6.4-in) body length. On a human scale, this would mean you could lick your knees without bending over!

VIENNA, AUSTRIA

The **longest human beatbox marathon** is 24 hours and was achieved by Michael Krappel (Austria) during the event Vienna Recordia, in Vienna, Austria, on 30 September 2007.

48°12'N
16°22'E

LIVING PLANET
MAMMALS

★STRONGEST MAMMAL BITE

In tests, the Tasmanian devil (*Sarcophilus harrisii*) produced a bite force quotient (the scientific measure of the power of an animal's bite relative to its size) of 181. By comparison, the tiger's bite force quotient is 127 and the lion's a mere 112.

★LARGEST MAMMAL FAMILY

Family Muridae, a group containing many rodents, is the largest of all mammal families. The group contains more than 600 species, including the true mice and rats, as well as the gerbils and jirds. Rodents were already widely distributed globally, but have since been introduced by man to many islands that were previously rodent-free.

EXTRA!
FOR MORE ON MAMMALS, DON'T FORGET TO CHECK OUT LIFE DOWN ON THE FARM ON PP. 156-157.

TALLEST MAMMAL

Native to the dry savannah and open woodland areas of sub-Saharan Africa, a typical adult male giraffe (*Giraffa camelopardalis*) measures between 4.6 m and 5.5 m (15–18 ft) tall. The tallest recorded giraffe was a 5.8-m (19-ft) Masai bull (*G. c. tippelskirchi*) named George, received by Chester Zoo, UK, on 8 January 1959.

SLOWEST MAMMAL

Despite its undeserved reputation, the three-toed sloth (*Bradypus tridactylus*) of tropical South America is not really a lazy creature – it is just very slow. On the ground its average speed is 1.8–2.4 m (6–8 ft) per minute (0.1–0.16 km/h; 0.07–0.1 mph), but in the trees it can accelerate to 4.6 m (15 ft) per minute (0.27 km/h; 0.17 mph)!

★SMALLEST HYRAX

Africa's hyraces are small mammals that superficially resemble rodents but are most closely related to the African elephant (*Loxodonta africana*) – the **largest land mammal** at 4–7 tonnes (8,800–15,400 lb). Despite links to the biggest of land beasts, the yellow-spotted rock hyrax (*Heterohyrax brucei*), is no bigger than 47 cm (18.5 in) in total length – adult specimens can be as short as 32.5 cm (12.7 in) – and weighs a mere 2.4 kg (5.29 lb), at most.

By comparison, the **smallest land-dwelling mammal** is Savi's pygmy shrew (*Suncus etruscus*), a tiny insect-eating mammal that inhabits the Mediterranean and southern Asia regions. The shrew is about the size of a human thumb, with an average body length of 36–53 mm (1.4–2 in), tail length of 24–29 mm (0.9–1 in) and weighs just 1.5–2.6 g (0.05–0.09 oz).

★LIGHTEST EGG-LAYING MAMMAL

Of the five species of monotreme (see *Did You Know?*), the platypus (*Ornithorhynchus anatinus*) of mainland Australia and Tasmania is the lightest. Male platypuses typically weigh 1.0–2.4 kg (2.2–5.2 lb) while females weigh just 0.7–1.6 kg (1.5–3.5 lb).

★FASTEST-PANTING WILD DOG

The big-eared fennec fox (*Fennecus zerda*) has a novel way of cooling down in its Saharan home. When the temperature reaches 38°C (100°F), it loses heat by panting at a rapid rate of 690 breaths per minute!

★HUNGRIEST BEAR

The giant panda (*Ailuropoda melanoleuca*) can only digest around 21% of all the bamboo that it consumes. Consequently, it must eat up to 38% of its own weight in bamboo shoots each day.

★ NEW RECORD
★ UPDATED RECORD

DID YOU KNOW?

MOST MAMMALS GIVE BIRTH TO LIVE YOUNG – EXCEPT FOR THE EGG-LAYING MONOTREMES: THE DUCK-BILLED PLATYPUS AND THE LONG- AND SHORT-NOSED ECHIDNAS.

Giant pandas do not hibernate and have to eat all year round because of their inefficient diet.

TRIVIA

★ LARGEST MAMMAL GENOME

An animal's genome is the map of all of its genetic information and is found in the nucleus of every cell in its body. The red vizcacha rat (*Tympanoctomys barrerae*) has a genome containing 16.8 picograms (1 picogram = 1 trillionth of a gram) of DNA. Most other mammals have a genome containing only 6–8 picograms. The red vizcacha also has the ★ **most chromosomes of any mammal** with a total of 102 chromosomes, split into 51 pairs. By comparison, humans have only 46 chromosomes, divided into 23 pairs.

★ LONGEST-LIVED RODENT

The naked mole rat (*Heterocephalus glaber*) is a bizarre-looking mammal that spends its life in underground burrow systems beneath East Africa's drier tropical grasslands. An extremely social creature, mole rats reside in colonies and can live for up to 28 years.

FASTEST

When measured over a short distance, the cheetah (*Acinonyx jubatus*) can maintain a steady maximum speed of approximately 100 km/h (62 mph) on level ground, making it the **fastest land mammal over short distances**.

A prime example of a speedy cheetah is Sarah, an eight-year-old that ran 100 m (328 ft) in 6.13 seconds at Cincinnati Zoo, Ohio, USA, on 10 September 2009, giving her the record for the ★ **fastest 100 m by a land mammal**, trouncing Usain Bolt's (Jamaica) 100 m time of 9.59 seconds (see p.268).

However, Sarah's speed has no staying power compared with that of a pronghorn (*Antilocapra americana*). Native to western North America, pronghorns have been recorded travelling continuously at 56 km/h (35 mph) for as far as 6 km (4 miles), giving them the title of the **fastest land mammal over long distances**.

Finally, the **fastest marine mammal** is the bull killer whale (*Orcinus orca*). On 12 October 1958, one specimen was recorded travelling at 55.5 km/h (34.5 mph) in the north-eastern Pacific.

★ BONIEST MAMMAL TAIL

The long-tailed pangolin (*Manis tetradactylus*) has up to 47 vertebrae in its tail – more than any other mammal. All eight species of pangolin, or scaly anteater, have impressive spines and claws that are composed of keratin, the same substance as human fingernails.

★ LONGEST WHALE TOOTH

The ivory tusk of the male narwhal (*Monodon monoceros*) grows to an average length of roughly 2 m (6 ft 6 in) but can exceed 3 m (9 ft 10 in) and weigh up to 10 kg (22 lb). In past centuries, the single (or, very rarely, paired) spiralled tusks were sometimes thought to be unicorn horns when found washed up on the beach.

BIG! THE LARGEST MAMMAL IS THE BLUE WHALE (*BALAENOPTERA MUSCULUS*), WITH AN AVERAGE LENGTH OF 24 M (80 FT)!

SMALL! THE SMALLEST MAMMAL IS THE BUMBLEBEE BAT (*CRASEONYCTERIS THONGLONGYAI*), WITH A HEAD-BODY LENGTH OF ONLY 29–33 MM (1.14–1.29 IN).

LIVING PLANET
PLANT LIFE

EXTRA! FOR THE FASTEST TIME TO EAT VARIOUS FRUIT, VEGETABLES AND OTHER FOODSTUFFS, CHECK OUT THE CHOMP-IONS ON P.140.

> "[The corpse flower] smells like a dead person... I happen to be a nurse and that is exactly what it smells like."
>
> **A visitor to Huntington Botanical Gardens, San Marino, California, USA, tells it like it is**

★ RAREST FLAX PLANT

Flax is a fibrous plant that has long been used to make fabric. The rarest species of flax plant is the Floreana flax (*Linum cratericola*), native to the Galápagos Islands. Only discovered by science in the 1960s, then feared extinct from 1981 until rediscovered in 1997, this small subshrub is presently limited to three small groups on Floreana Island. Here it is threatened with extinction by feral goats, invasive plants and periods of dry weather.

SMALLEST PLANT KINGDOM

Of the six biogeographical plant zones – Boreal, Neotropical, Paleotropical, South African, Australian and Antarctic – the South African is the smallest.

★ MOST CHROMOSOMES IN A PLANT

All living organisms contain chromosomes – the part of a cell that contains all the genetic information that determines what characteristics the organism will possess. While humans have 46 chromosomes in 23 pairs, many other organisms have far more. The adder's tongue fern (*Ophioglossum reticulatum*) is reported to have 1,440 chromosomes arranged into 720 pairs, making it the record holder for both the greatest number of chromosomes in a plant and the ★ **most chromosomes in an organism**.

MOST SELECTIVE CARNIVOROUS PLANT

Nepenthes albomarginata is a carnivorous plant that grows in Malaysia and Indonesia and feeds only on *Hospitalitermes bicolor* termites. The termites are attracted to edible hairs, called trichomes, on the plant, but sometimes slip down the plant's "throat" and are digested by liquids at the bottom of the flower.

HIGHEST CONCENTRATION OF ENDANGERED PLANT SPECIES

South Africa's Cape Flats hosts 15 species per square kilometre that are threatened by extinction.

★ RAREST WILLOW

Deciduous willows are a common tree throughout the northern hemisphere. However, one species, the Tarragonès willow (*Salix tarraconensis*), is considered critically endangered and is known only from a few dispersed populations of 10 to 40 specimens located between Castellón and Tarragona in Spain.

★ OLDEST YEW

The world's oldest yew tree is a specimen of common yew (*Taxus baccata*) that grows in the churchyard of St Digain's parish church in Llangernyw, North Wales, UK. It is estimated to be 4,000 years old.

HIGHEST CONCENTRATION OF HEATHERS

The fynbos (Afrikaans for "fine bush") plant ecosystem, exclusive to South Africa's Cape floristic region, contains more than 600 species of heather (genus *Erica*). Only 26 species of heather occur in the rest of the world.

★ RAREST ONION

The rarest member of the onion genus *Allium* is *Allium rouyi*, a Spanish species with fewer than 300 known specimens fragmented among five subpopulations confined within a very small area of Bética province in Andalusia, Spain.

MOST TOXIC PLANT

Based on the amount it takes to kill a human, the most toxic common plant in the world is the castor bean (*Ricinus communis*). The toxin – ricin – causes the clumping and breakdown of red blood cells and internal bleeding. It is 6,000 times more toxic than cyanide and 12,000 times more toxic than rattlesnake venom.

SMELLIEST PLANT

Native to the Sumatran rainforests, the "corpse flower", or titan arum, *Amorphophallus titanum*, is believed to be the smelliest plant on Earth. When it blooms, it releases a foul odour similar to that of rotting flesh to attract flies to aid in its pollination. The stench can be smelled up to half a mile (0.8 km) away.

ONION: Comes from the Latin *unionem*, which literally means "unity", and describes the many layers of an onion's skin.

★RAREST CLUB MOSS

Club mosses are a primitive form of plant endemic to wet forests and cliffside shrublands. The wawae'iole (*Huperzia nutans*) is the rarest variety and only grows on Koolau Mountain on Oahu in Hawaii, USA.

★OLDEST CYPRESS

A cypress tree (*Cupressus sempervirens*) known as Sarv-e-Abarkooh, or Zoroastrian Sarv, is a tourist attraction in Abarkooh, Yazd, Iran. It is estimated to be over 4,000 years old and has been declared a national monument.

FASTEST ENTRAPMENT BY A PLANT

Carnivorous plants trap their prey in movements considered to be among the fastest in the entire plant kingdom. On land, the clamshell-like leaves of the Venus flytrap (*Dionaea muscipula*) shut in one-tenth of a second (100 milliseconds) from the moment they are stimulated. Underwater, the hinged trapdoor of the bladderwort (*Utricularia vulgaris*) captures its victim in 1/15,000th of a second.

LARGEST SEED COLLECTION

The Millennium Seed Bank Project, housed at the Wellcome Trust Millennium Building, Wakehurst Place, West Sussex, UK, had 24,200 species collected as of 20 March 2010.

SMALLEST ORCHID

The platystele (*Platystele jungermannioides*) found in the lower cloud forest of Mexico, Guatemala, Costa Rica and Panama at an elevation of 200–1,000 m (656–3,280 ft) grows around 6.3 mm (0.25 in) high and 20 mm (0.78 in) wide. This smallest of orchid species blooms in the spring with just two or three tiny flowers that are a mere 2.5 mm (0.09 in) wide. With roughly 25,000 species, the orchid family is also the second largest flowering plant family behind the Compositae family of daisies, the ★**largest family of flowering plants**, with more than 26,000 species.

MOST VISITED GARDEN (PAYING VISITORS)

The Royal Botanic Gardens, Kew, Surrey, UK, has an average of 1 million paying visitors per year. The 132-ha (326-acre) site has 40 historically important buildings and collections of over 40,000 species of plants. Kew Gardens became a United Nations World Heritage site on 3 July 2003.

★TALLEST HARDWOOD TREE

A specimen of Australian swamp gum tree (*Eucalyptus regnans*) known as "Centurion" stands 101 m (331.36 ft) tall and has a diameter of 4 m (13.12 ft). It is located just 80 km (49 miles) from Tasmania's capital, Hobart.

★ NEW RECORD
★ UPDATED RECORD

FAST! SOME SPECIES OF BAMBOO GROW AT A RATE OF UP TO 91 CM (35 IN) PER DAY, OR 0.00003 KM/H (0.00002 MPH). THIS MAKES THEM THE FASTEST-GROWING PLANTS.

SLOW! THE SLOWEST-GROWING TREE IS THE WHITE CEDAR (*THUJA OCCIDENTALIS*). IT TOOK 155 YEARS FOR ONE TREE TO REACH A HEIGHT OF JUST 10.2 CM (4 IN).

TARANTO, ITALY
The **largest focaccia bread** weighed 2,800 kg (6,172 lb) and was made by Catucci Pietro and Latte Antonio (both Italy) in the Piazza Mercato, Mottola, Taranto, Italy, on 6 August 2005.

40°28'N 17°14'E

HUMAN BEINGS

★ ★ ★ ★ ★ ★ ★ ★ ★ ★ ★ ★ ☆

LABRET: A piercing or adornment of the lip, and in particular the lower lip. Ornaments range from simple studs to enormous clay plates.

HOOK!
BEFORE BECOMING THE MOST PIERCED MAN, JOHN LYNCH WAS A BANK MANAGER. AFTER QUITTING HIS JOB, HE BECAME HOOKED ON PIERCINGS AND TATTOOS.

COOK!
ELAINE DAVIDSON RAN A BRAZIL-THEMED CAFE/RESTAURANT IN EDINBURGH, SCOTLAND, UK, BEFORE BECOMING A FULL-TIME HUMAN PINBOARD!

{ *"People often just want to look at me or touch me. Some even want to kiss me."* }
**Elaine Davidson,
most pierced woman**

STOCKHOLM, SWEDEN
The world's **first banknotes** (or *banco-sedlar*) were issued in Stockholm, Sweden, in July 1661 by the Bank of Palmstruch. The oldest surviving note is one of five dalers dated 6 December 1662.

MOST PIERCED PEOPLE

Since having her first piercing in January 1997, Elaine Davidson (UK) has had 4,225 pieces of metal attached to, and inside, her body. Elaine is the world's most pierced person. Her male equivalent is John Lynch (UK, aka Prince Albert), who had, at the last count, 241 piercings, including 151 in his head and neck.

CONTENTS

CAPE TOWN, SOUTH AFRICA

The **first heart transplant operation** was performed on Louis Washkansky (South Africa) at the Groote Schuur Hospital, Cape Town, South Africa, on 3 December 1967, by a team of 30 headed by Prof. Christiaan Neethling Barnard (South Africa).

33°55'S 18°25'E

FEATURE
TALLEST MAN

SULTAN IN LONDON

The first stop on Sultan's whirlwind worldwide tour was London (right) and the Guinness World Records HQ. It was in London, at the iconic Tower Bridge, that Sultan was introduced to a frenzied world media. Luckily, he had a few days to get his breath back before heading to New York, USA.

TALL TOUR 2009

Sultan once lived a quiet life on a farm in the Mardin region of Turkey. Now, he's an international jet-setter! Here he is making a big impression in London, UK (above left), Madrid, Spain (above) and Milan, Italy (above right). He also travelled to Reykjavik, Iceland, where he enjoyed a spa bath, and Vienna, Austria, where he became a media star!

MILAN

MADRID

LONDON

EXTRA!
FOR MORE TALL TALES AND SHORT STORIES, TURN TO P.76.

DID YOU KNOW?

SULTAN HAS GROWN SO TALL BECAUSE OF A TUMOUR ON HIS PITUITARY GLAND. THE TUMOUR HAS NOW BEEN REMOVED, AND HE HAS FINALLY STOPPED GROWING.

TRIVIA

The pituitary gland controls the release of growth hormone: too much and you're a giant; too little, you're a dwarf.

HIGH HOPES

So what are the newly famous gentle giant's dreams for the future? "I want what everyone else wants," says Sultan. "A wife, a family, a nice home. I'd also like the chance to find some decent clothes that fit! I've already had a suit made for me, and at least one dream has come true: I now own a pair of jeans made specially for me!"

TALL
SULTAN IS PICTURED HERE MEETING 2-YEAR-OLD MATILDA NIEBERG DURING HIS VISIT TO THE UK. AT 66 CM (2 FT 2 IN) TALL, SHE IS 3.5 TIMES SMALLER THAN SULTAN.

TALES
SULTAN DIDN'T START HIS INCREDIBLE GROWTH SPURT UNTIL HE WAS 10 YEARS OLD. HE ONLY STOPPED GROWING IN 2007, AGED 24!

TALLEST LIVING MAN

At 246.5 cm (8 ft 1 in), Sultan is the world's **tallest living man** and **tallest living human being**. Indeed, he is the tallest person to exceed 8 ft (243.8 cm) in 20 years, and only the 11th person in history to be officially ratified as over 8 ft by Guinness World Records.

Sultan was first measured by GWR's Editor-in-Chief, Craig Glenday, in Ankara, Turkey, on 11 February 2009. "To avoid any controversy, I had to measure him myself," said Craig. "It's the only way to be totally sure of a claimant's height. There is too much at stake to leave it to anyone other than a GWR representative."

One of the most difficult aspects of being so tall, says Sultan, is finding clothes and shoes to fit. His 36.5-cm-long (1-ft 2-in) feet – the **largest feet on a living person** – require extra-large shoes (inset, compared with a UK size-9 trainer), which are expensive to make.

Sultan also holds the record for the ★ **largest hands on a living person**, measuring 27.5 cm (10.83 in) from the wrist to the tip of the middle finger.

HUMAN BEINGS
BODY PARTS

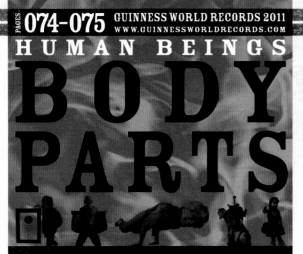

★ WIDEST TONGUE

Here's a record that will take some lickin'! The tongue of Jay Sloot (Australia) was measured to be 7.9 cm (3.1 in) at its widest point on the set of *Lo Show dei Record* in Rome, Italy, on 18 March 2010.

ACTUAL SIZE

LONGEST TONGUE

Jay might have the edge in width, but when it comes to length, Stephen Taylor (UK) is the tongue champ. Stephen's tongue was 9.8 cm (3.86 in) from its tip to the middle of his closed top lip when it was measured at the Westwood Medical Centre, Coventry, UK, on 11 February 2009.

★ LONGEST TOOTH REMOVED

Loo Hui Jing (Singapore) had a tooth measuring 3.2 cm (1.26 in) extracted by Dr Ng Lay Choo at the Eli Dental Surgery in Singapore on 6 April 2009.

ACTUAL SIZE

★ MOST TEETH IN THE MOUTH

The record for the most teeth in the mouth belongs to Kanchan Rajawat (India) and Luca Meriano (Italy), both of whom had 35 adult teeth as of 17 October 2008.

★ SMALLEST TOOTH EXTRACTED

A primary tooth extracted from Colton Laub (USA) on 30 October 2002 by Dr Scott Harden at Fountain View Family Dentistry, Acworth, Georgia, USA, measured 3 mm (0.1 in).

LONGEST MILK TOOTH

Ahmed Afrah Ismail (Maldives) had a milk tooth measuring 2.3 cm (0.9 in). The tooth was measured in Male, Republic of Maldives, on 28 December 2000.

LONGEST TOENAILS

Since 1982, Louise Hollis (USA) has been growing her toenails to exceedingly great lengths. When measured at their longest in 1991, the combined length of all 10 toenails came to 220.98 cm (87 in).

AHH! LOUISE WAS INSPIRED TO GROW HER TOENAILS IN 1982, AFTER SEEING A TV PROGRAMME FEATURING THE LONGEST FINGERNAILS.

★ MOST ELASTIC MOUTH

The lips (oral labia) and cheeks (buccal cavity) of Francisco Domingo Joaquim "Chiquinho" (Angola), were measured, at full stretch, to be 17 cm (6.69 in) wide on 18 March 2010. Incredibly, he does not have the widest gape (see p.75). Chiquinho suffers from a connective tissues disorder.

AHH! CHIQUINHO'S MALLEABLE MOUTH IS SO BIG THAT IT CAN COMFORTABLY ACCOMMODATE A WHOLE 330 ML DRINKS CAN!

"I'd seen a video of him on the internet, but nothing compares to the experience of measuring him in real life."
Vice President of Records Marco Frigatti on meeting Chiquinho

BELGRADE, SERBIA

Chess masters Goran Arsovic and Ivan Nikolic (both Yugoslavia, now Serbia) played a game with 269 moves on 17 February 1989 – the **most moves in a chess game**. The drawn game was played in Belgrade, Yugoslavia (now Serbia), and took 20 hr 15 min.

LONGEST FINGERNAILS EVER (MALE)

We were saddened in December 2009 to learn of the passing of Melvin Boothe (USA). Melvin first contacted us about his fantastic fingernails in 2006, and when last measured on 30 May 2009 at his home in Troy, Michigan, USA, they had a combined length of 9.85 m (32 ft 3.8 in).

EXTRA! FOR MORE MEDICAL RECORDS, GO TO PP.84-85.

★ **NEW RECORD**
★ **UPDATED RECORD**

LONGEST LEGS (FEMALE)

Svetlana Pankratova's (Russia) legs measured 132 cm (51.9 in) long in Torremolinos, Spain, on 8 July 2003. Her unique gift presents certain challenges – she has to have some clothes specially made, she ducks through doorways, and needs lots of legroom when travelling in cars and planes.

NARROWEST WAIST

Cathie Jung (USA) is 1.73 m (5 ft 8 in) tall but her waist is much smaller than you might expect – just 53.34 cm (21 in). And that figure narrows to just 38.1 cm (15 in) when she is wearing a corset, which pulls in the lower ribs. Cathie developed her tiny waist as part of her enthusiasm for Victorian clothing. Look at pictures of ladies in the Victorian era, when corsets were normal attire, and see how narrow their waists were!

LARGEST FEET EVER

Robert Wadlow (USA) wore US size 37 AA shoes (UK 36; approx. European 75), equivalent to 47 cm (18.5 in) long. To say thanks to the International Shoe Company (USA), who provided his $100 shoes (equivalent today of £1,120) for free, Wadlow visited an estimated 800 US cities on a goodwill promotional tour.

LARGEST HANDS

Robert Wadlow (USA, 1918–40), the **tallest man ever** (see pp.76–77 to discover the heights he reached) had hands that measured 32.3 cm (12.75 in) from the wrist to the tip of his middle finger. He wore a size 25 ring.

LONGEST FINGERNAILS ON A SINGLE HAND

The aggregate measurement of the five nails on the left hand of Shridhar Chillal (India, b. 18 August 1937) was 705 cm (23 ft 1.5 in) on 4 February 2004. His thumb measured 158 cm (62.2 in), his index finger 131 cm (51.5 in), his middle finger 138 cm (54.3 in), his ring finger 140 cm (55.1 in) and his little finger 138 cm (54.3 in). Chillal last cut his fingernails in 1952.

LONGEST FINGERNAILS EVER (FEMALE)

Lee Redmond (USA) started to seriously grow her fingernails in 1979 and, over the years, she carefully manicured them to reach a total length of 8.65 m (28 ft 4.5 in), as measured on the set of *Lo Show dei Record* in Madrid, Spain, on 23 February 2008. Sadly, Lee lost her nails in a car accident in early 2009, but since that time no one has beaten her all-time record.

FEWEST TOES

The two-toed ("ostrich-foot") syndrome exhibited by some members of the Wadomo tribe of the Zambezi Valley in Zimbabwe, and the Kalanga tribe of the eastern Kalahari Desert in Botswana, is hereditary via a single mutated gene.

LARGEST GAPE

J J Bittner (USA) is able to open his jaw to a gap of 8.4 cm (3.4 in). His gape was measured from the incisal edge of his maxillary central incisors to the incisal edge of his mandibular central incisors -- that is, between the tips of the front teeth in his upper and lower jaws.

DID YOU KNOW?
THE ADULT LIVER CAN WEIGH BETWEEN 1.2 AND 1.5 KG (2.64 AND 3.3 LB) – ABOUT ONE THIRTY-SIXTH OF THE AVERAGE TOTAL BODY WEIGHT.

The liver is the **largest gland**, and the **largest solid organ**, in the body.

TRIVIA

LONGEST NOSE ON A LIVING PERSON

The nose of Mehmet Ozyurek (Turkey) was measured at 8.8 cm (3.46 in) long from bridge to tip on the set of *Lo Show dei Record* in Rome, Italy, on 18 March 2010.

CHOO! IT IS CLAIMED THAT THOMAS WEDDERS, WHO LIVED IN ENGLAND DURING THE 1770s, HAD A NOSE MEASURING 19 CM (7.5 IN) LONG.

HUMAN BEINGS
SIZE

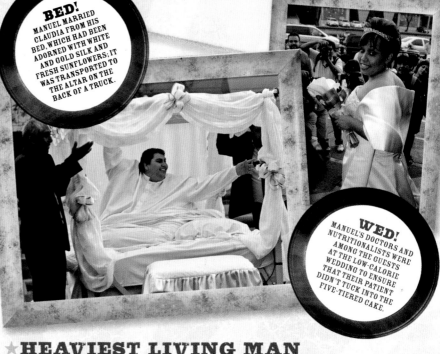

BED! MANUEL MARRIED CLAUDIA FROM HIS BED, WHICH HAD BEEN ADORNED WITH WHITE AND GOLD SILK AND FRESH SUNFLOWERS; IT WAS TRANSPORTED TO THE ALTAR ON THE BACK OF A TRUCK.

WED! MANUEL'S DOCTORS AND NUTRITIONALISTS WERE AMONG THE GUESTS AT THE LOW-CALORIE WEDDING TO ENSURE THAT THEIR PATIENT DIDN'T TUCK INTO THE FIVE-TIERED CAKE.

★ SHORTEST TEENAGE GIRL

The shortest known female teenager is Jyoti Amge (India, b. 16 December 1993), who was measured on 6 September 2009 in Tokyo, Japan, for *Bikkuri Chojin 100 Special #2* (Fuji TV) and found to be 61.95 cm (2 ft). Born in Nagpur, India, Jyoti's ambition is to become an actress.

SHORTEST MAN

Ever: The shortest mature human of whom there is independent evidence was Gul Mohammed (India, 1957–97). On 19 July 1990, he was examined at Ram Manohar Hospital, New Delhi, India, and found to measure a height of 57 cm (22.5 in).

Living: Lin Yih-Chih (Taiwan), who is wheelchair-bound owing to osteogenesis imperfecta, measures 67.5 cm (27 in).

Living (mobile): *See p.77.*

SHORTEST WOMAN

Ever: Pauline Musters (Netherlands, 1876–95) measured 30 cm (12 in) at birth; when she died of pneumonia with meningitis at the age of 19, she had reached a height of just 61 cm (2 ft).

★ HEAVIEST LIVING MAN

At his last weigh-in (December 2009), Mexico's Manuel Uribe registered 416.5 kg (918 lb; 65.5 st) – a reversal of fortune for the dieting 43-year-old, who had been experiencing regular weight loss since peaking at 560 kg (1,235 lb; 88 st) in 2006. Despite being bed-bound, Uribe married his second wife Claudia Solis (above right) in 2008.

Living: Madge Bester (South Africa) measures 65 cm (2 ft 1.5 in) tall. A sufferer of the skeletal disorder type III osteogenesis imperfecta, she has extremely brittle bones and is confined to a wheelchair in a home in Bloemfontein, South Africa. Her mother Winnie (d. 2001), also a sufferer, measured 70 cm (2 ft 3.5 in).

Living (mobile): This category remains unfilled as of 1 April 2010.

LIGHTEST PERSON

Lucia Xarate (Mexico, 1863–89) of San Carlos, Mexico, an emaciated ateleiotic dwarf of 67 cm (26.8 in), weighed 1.1 kg (2.8 lb) at birth and only 2.13 kg (4 lb 11 oz) at the age of 17. She fattened up to 5.9 kg (13 lb) by her 20th birthday.

CERTIFICATE

A Guinness World Record was achieved on the set of *Lo Show Dei Record* in Rome, Italy in 2010

GUINNESS WORLD RECORDS LTD

★ SHORTEST TEENAGE BOY

The shortest known male teenager is Khagendra Thapa Magar (Nepal, b. 14 October 1992), who, on 25 February 2010, was measured by a team of doctors in Rome, Italy, for *Lo show dei record* and found to be 65.58 cm (2 ft 1.8 in). In October 2010, he is due to turn 18, at which point he will be considered by Guinness World Records to be the **shortest living (mobile) man**.

KOSICE, SLOVAKIA
48°42'N 21°15'E

The **largest litter of brown bears** (*Ursus arctos*) born in captivity is five. Miso, Tapik, Dazzle, Bubu and Cindy (three males, two females) were born on 6 January 2002 in Zoo Kosice, Kosice-Kavecany, Slovakia.

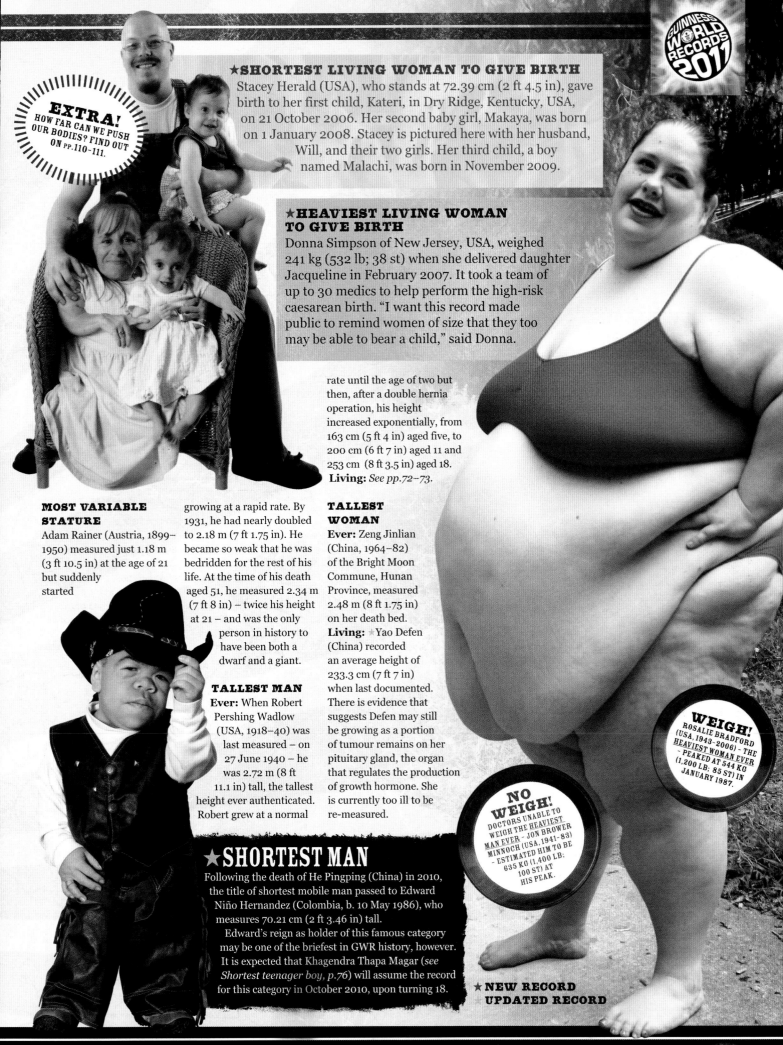

EXTRA!
HOW FAR CAN WE PUSH OUR BODIES? FIND OUT ON PP.110–111.

★SHORTEST LIVING WOMAN TO GIVE BIRTH

Stacey Herald (USA), who stands at 72.39 cm (2 ft 4.5 in), gave birth to her first child, Kateri, in Dry Ridge, Kentucky, USA, on 21 October 2006. Her second baby girl, Makaya, was born on 1 January 2008. Stacey is pictured here with her husband, Will, and their two girls. Her third child, a boy named Malachi, was born in November 2009.

★HEAVIEST LIVING WOMAN TO GIVE BIRTH

Donna Simpson of New Jersey, USA, weighed 241 kg (532 lb; 38 st) when she delivered daughter Jacqueline in February 2007. It took a team of up to 30 medics to help perform the high-risk caesarean birth. "I want this record made public to remind women of size that they too may be able to bear a child," said Donna.

MOST VARIABLE STATURE

Adam Rainer (Austria, 1899–1950) measured just 1.18 m (3 ft 10.5 in) at the age of 21 but suddenly started growing at a rapid rate. By 1931, he had nearly doubled to 2.18 m (7 ft 1.75 in). He became so weak that he was bedridden for the rest of his life. At the time of his death aged 51, he measured 2.34 m (7 ft 8 in) – twice his height at 21 – and was the only person in history to have been both a dwarf and a giant.

TALLEST MAN

Ever: When Robert Pershing Wadlow (USA, 1918–40) was last measured – on 27 June 1940 – he was 2.72 m (8 ft 11.1 in) tall, the tallest height ever authenticated. Robert grew at a normal rate until the age of two but then, after a double hernia operation, his height increased exponentially, from 163 cm (5 ft 4 in) aged five, to 200 cm (6 ft 7 in) aged 11 and 253 cm (8 ft 3.5 in) aged 18. **Living:** *See pp.72–73.*

TALLEST WOMAN

Ever: Zeng Jinlian (China, 1964–82) of the Bright Moon Commune, Hunan Province, measured 2.48 m (8 ft 1.75 in) on her death bed. **Living:** ★Yao Defen (China) recorded an average height of 233.3 cm (7 ft 7 in) when last documented. There is evidence that suggests Defen may still be growing as a portion of tumour remains on her pituitary gland, the organ that regulates the production of growth hormone. She is currently too ill to be re-measured.

★SHORTEST MAN

Following the death of He Pingping (China) in 2010, the title of shortest mobile man passed to Edward Niño Hernandez (Colombia, b. 10 May 1986), who measures 70.21 cm (2 ft 3.46 in) tall.

Edward's reign as holder of this famous category may be one of the briefest in GWR history, however. It is expected that Khagendra Thapa Magar (*see Shortest teenager boy, p.76*) will assume the record for this category in October 2010, upon turning 18.

NO WEIGH! DOCTORS UNABLE TO WEIGH THE HEAVIEST MAN EVER – JON BROWER MINNOCH (USA, 1941–83) – ESTIMATED HIM TO BE 635 KG (1,400 LB; 100 ST) AT HIS PEAK.

WEIGH! ROSALIE BRADFORD (USA, 1943–2006) – THE HEAVIEST WOMAN EVER – PEAKED AT 544 KG (1,200 LB; 85 ST) IN JANUARY 1987.

★ **NEW RECORD**
  UPDATED RECORD

HUMAN BEINGS
SKIN DEEP

EXTRA!
IF YOU'RE A SUCKER FOR SIDESHOW ARTS, DON'T HANG AROUND – TURN TO P.96.

★ MOST NEEDLES IN THE HEAD

Wei Shengchu (China) had 2,009 needles inserted into his head on the set of *Lo Show dei Record* in Milan, Italy, on 11 April 2009.

EARLIEST PLASTIC SURGERY

Walter Yeo (UK) was the first person in the world to have plastic surgery. In 1917, skin grafts were transferred from his shoulder to his face in order to replace his upper and lower eyelids. He had lost them while manning the guns aboard HMS *Warspite* in 1916, in the Battle of Jutland, during World War I.

★ FARTHEST DISTANCE TO PULL A VEHICLE USING MEAT HOOKS

Hannibal Helmurto (Germany) pulled a 4-tonne (8,818-lb) van a total of 107 m (360 ft) using two meat hooks inserted through the skin in the small of his back in Edinburgh, UK, on 13 August 2007.

MOST BODY PIERCINGS IN ONE SESSION

Josh Brown and Yuri Dubon (both USA) carried out 1,200 piercings in one session lasting 2 hr 53 min at the Sign of the Times, Norco, California, USA, on 16 August 2009.

MOST TATTOOED SENIOR CITIZENS

The **most tattooed female senior citizen** is 73-year-old grandmother Isobel Varley (UK). Isobel had her first tattoo – a small bird on her right shoulderblade – on 14 August 1986 after a visit to a tattoo convention in Hammersmith, London, UK. As of April 2010, she had a 93% body coverage.

The ★**most tattooed male senior citizen** is Tom Leppard (UK) – see opposite.

★ MOST PEOPLE TATTOOED SIMULTANEOUSLY

A total of 178 people were tattooed at the same time at the 5th annual London Tattoo Convention 2009, held at the Tobacco Dock in London, UK, on 24 September 2009.

★ MOST TATTOOED WOMAN

Julia Gnuse (USA, below) has had approximately 95% of her body decorated with tattoos; her first tattoo was in 1991. She shares her ink-redible record with Krystyne Kolorful (Canada), who has taken 10 years to achieve 95% coverage.

The skin (the **largest organ**) protects us against infection, and helps us to retain moisture and regulate body temperature.

TRIVIA

★ LONGEST TATTOO SESSION

Andy Kynes (UK) underwent a gruelling 48-hr 11-min tattoo session under the needle of Lady Kaz Wilson (UK) at the Diamond Tattoo Studio in Wigan, Lancashire, UK, on 18–21 November 2009. The event was organized to raise money for UK charity Children in Need.

METAL TEETH

Gone are Lucky's original teeth and in their place are silver fangs.

WHITE INK

Lucky has started inking white tattoos on top of the black.

OUCH!
LUCKY IS TATTOOED ON THE EYELIDS, THE DELICATE SKIN BETWEEN THE TOES, AND DOWN INTO THE EARS. HE EVEN HAS HIS GUMS TATTOOED!

★ MOST TATTOOED SENIOR CITIZEN

Former **most tattooed man** Tom Leppard (aka Tom Woodbridge, UK), has 99.9% of his body covered in a saffron-yellow and black leopard-print tattoo. The 73-year-old ex-soldier lived for 20 years in the wilds of the island of Skye in the Scottish Hebrides before finally changing his spots and moving into a sheltered housing scheme in the Skye village of Broadford in 2008.

★ MOST TATTOOS BY A SINGLE ARTIST (24 HOURS)

Hollis Cantrell (USA) created 801 tattoos in 24 hours at Artistic Tattoo in Phoenix, Arizona, USA, on 16 November 2008.

STRETCHIEST SKIN

Garry Turner (UK) is able to stretch the skin of his stomach to a length of 15.8 cm (6.25 in) thanks to a rare medical condition called Ehlers-Danlos Syndrome, a disorder of the connective tissues affecting the skin, ligaments and internal organs. With this condition, the collagen that strengthens the skin and determines its elasticity becomes defective, resulting in, among other things, a loosening of the skin, and "hypermobility" of the joints. In more serious cases, it can cause the rupturing of blood vessels.

CICATRIX: A healed scar, hence the term "cicatrization" – the deliberate cutting of the skin to create decorative scar tissue.

COLOURED INK

Inked in red across his face and scalp is the Tibetan mantra "Om Mani Padme Hum", usually translated as "Praise to the Jewel in the Lotus".

SCALP

Lucky has gouged out three strips of skin from his scalp, revealing the skull beneath!

STRETCHED EARLOBES

Lucky's ears are not just pierced, they're stretched and fitted with a spacer or "flesh tunnel".

BLACK INK

An all-over "body suit" of black ink.

CHEST IMPLANTS

Through his pectoral muscles, Lucky has placed two titanium rods; these will eventually be removed, creating a hollow through which he can attach weights and hooks.

★ MOST EXTENSIVE SCARIFICATION

Women of both the Tiv and Nuba peoples of Nigeria, in West Africa, endure extreme scarification rituals as part of a rite of passage (as in the case of the Nuba) or to accentuate their beauty. The scars are made using a knife, or, more traditionally, stones, shards of glass or coconut shell. The deep wounds that result are rubbed with toxic plant juices to create swollen welts, or "keloids".

Scarification – or "cicatrization" – of the torso begins in young Nuba females when their breasts first develop. Further scarring of the entire torso coincides with the onset of menses. Finally, the back, arms, legs and neck are decoratively scarred once the woman weans her first child.

For the Tiv, scars are closely associated with sexuality. The more scars a woman bears, the more sexually demanding she is perceived to be. Within Tiv culture, this carries implications about her desire to reproduce.

MOST TATTOOED PERSON

Lucky Diamond Rich (Australia, b. NZ) has spent over 1,000 hours having an entire "body-suit" of tattoos (plus a layer of solid black) applied – coverage in excess of 200%.

RIGA, LATVIA
The **most Mentos and soda fountains** created in the same place is 1,911 and was achieved by the people of Latvia and students of TURIBA in Riga, Latvia, on 19 June 2008.

56°56'N 24°06'E

HUMAN BEINGS
HAIR

★ ★ ★ ★ ★ ★ ★ ★ ★ ★ ★ ★

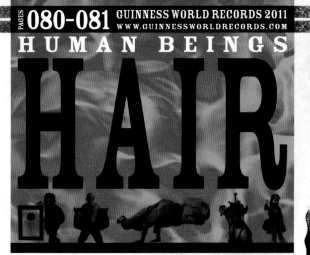

TRIM
CHUY – PRONOUNCED "CHEWIE" – IS SHOWN HERE RECEIVING A TRIM AT THE I GRI.SIANI HAIR SALON IN ROME BEFORE HIS FIRST APPEARANCE ON ITALIAN TV.

★LARGEST BALL OF HUMAN HAIR

Over the past 50 years, Henry Coffer (USA) has been collecting human hair and amassing a giant hairball that, as of 8 December 2008, weighs 75.7 kg (167 lb) and measures 4.26 m (14 ft) in circumference. Coffer, a 77-year-old barber from Charleston, Missouri, began saving hair at the request of a customer. Over the years he has been collecting, he has found many uses for his hair clippings, including patching potholes, gardening and fertilizing soil.

LARGEST HUMAN HAIRBALL

"Trichobezoar" is the medical name for a hairball, which occurs as a result of Rapunzel Syndrome or "trichophagia" – the eating of one's own hair (from the Greek for "hair eating"). The largest trichobezoar surgically removed from a human was a hairball weighing 4.5 kg (10 lb) found in the stomach of an unnamed 18-year-old woman treated at Rush University Medical Center in Chicago, Illinois, USA, in November 2007.

HAIRIEST FAMILY

Pictured is "Chuy" Jesus Fajardo Aceves, one of a family of 19 – covering five generations – from Mexico that suffers from hypertrichosis, aka "werewolf syndrome". The women are covered with a light to medium coat of hair, while the men of the family have thick hair on every inch of their body, apart from their hands and feet.

★MOST HAIRSTYLES APPLIED (8 HOURS)

Rachel Brown (USA) of Salon Mimosa in Lake Park, Florida, USA, styled the hair of 32 customers in eight hours on 16 February 2009. Each client had to have his/her hair washed and rinsed, and then cut, completely dried and styled before Rachel moved on to the next client.

★MOST HAIRCUTS BY A TEAM (24 HOURS)

Ten hairdressers from Supercuts in Houston, Texas, USA, cut 349 heads of hair on 10 October 2009.

★LONGEST BEARD

On 4 March 2010, Sarwan Singh's (Canada) beard was measured at 2.37 m (7 ft 9 in) on the set of *Lo Show dei Record* in Rome, Italy, the longest beard on a living person. The iconic Sikh – head Giani (priest) at Guru Nanak Sikh Temple in Surrey, Canada – said, "It's not a talent, like playing music... It's a gift from God."

DID YOU KNOW?
THE SIKH FAITH OPPOSES THE CUTTING OF FACIAL HAIR, SO SARWAN SINGH HAS NEVER SHAVED IN HIS LIFE. "MY BEARD IS MY FAVOURITE BODY PART."

In 2001, Ismael Rivas Falcon (Spain) pulled a train weighing 2,753.1 kg (6,069 lb) with his beard.

TRIVIA

QUIZ!
WHICH OF THESE MEASURES THE MOST: THE LONGEST BEARD, LONGEST MOUSTACHE OR HIGHEST HAIRSTYLE?
SEE p.278 FOR THE ANSWER.

EXTRA!
THE HUMAN BODY IS MORE AMAZING THAN YOU CAN IMAGINE. FIND OUT MORE ON PP.74–75.

59°26'N 24°44'E
TALLINN, ESTONIA
Intan Pragi (Estonia) spun a roulette wheel more than 1,650 times over 48 hours during the **longest croupier marathon** at the Olympic Casino in Tallinn, Estonia, on 18–20 February 2005.

★HAIRIEST TEENAGE GIRL

The most hirsute female teen – according to the Ferriman-Gallwey method – is Supatra "Nat" Sasuphan (Thailand). She was assessed on the set of *Lo Show dei Record* in Rome, Italy, on 4 March 2010. The Ferriman-Gallwey score is a method of quantifying hirsutism (hairiness) in women.

★TALLEST MOHICAN
The tallest mohawk measures 80 cm (31.5 in) and belongs to Stefan Srocka (Germany). The length was verified at Hairgallery Daniela Schorn in Marktrodach, Germany, on 2 June 2009.

★LONGEST MOUSTACHE
Ram Singh Chauhan (India) has a moustache that measured 4.29 m (14 ft) on the set of *Lo Show dei Record* in Rome, Italy, on 4 March 2010.

HAIR
WITH THE FERRIMAN-GALLWEY METHOD, FEMALE HAIR GROWTH IS RATED FROM 0 (NO GROWTH) TO 4 (HEAVY COVERAGE) IN NINE LOCATIONS.

WHERE
THE NINE LOCATIONS ARE THE UPPER LIP, CHIN, CHEST, UPPER BACK, LOWER BACK, UPPER ABDOMEN, LOWER ABDOMEN, UPPER ARMS AND THIGHS.

★LONGEST FEMALE DREAD-LOCKS
The dreadlocks of Asha Mandela (USA) reached a record 5.96 m (19 ft 6.5 in) when professionally unknotted and measured on CBS's *The Early Show* in New York City, USA, on 11 November 2009 for GWR Day.

★HIGHEST HAIRSTYLE
A hair-do measuring 2.66 m (8 ft 8 in) high was created by several hairdressers in an event organized by KLIPP unser Frisör in Wels, Austria, on 21 June 2009.

★TALLEST WIG
An enormous wig of human hair was made by Emilio Minnicelli (Italy) and modelled in the main square of the Bologna Piazza Maggiore in Italy on 15 May 2004. It measured 14.3 m (46 ft 11 in) tall and weighed 26 kg (57 lb).

LONGEST EXTENSIONS
A hair extension piece of 16.25 m (53 ft 10 in) in length was applied by Kay Meinecke (Germany) to the hair of a model at a shopping centre in Hamburg, Germany, on 10 November 2007.

MOST EXPENSIVE HAIRCUT
An Italian customer of the Stuart Phillips Salon in Covent Garden, London, UK, paid £8,000 ($16,420) on 29 October 2007 for a luxury haircut.

★MOST HAIR DYED (24 HOURS)
Ten hairdressers and their assistants from Schwarzkopf & Sergio & Margarida Hair Salon in Lisbon, Portugal, dyed 380 heads of hair in 24 hours on 21 October 2009.

LONGEST HAIRS

Arm: 14.61 cm (5.75 in), Justin Shaw (USA), 7 October 2009.
Chest: 22.8 cm (9 in), Richard Condo (USA), 29 April 2007.
Ear: 18.1 cm (7.12 in), Anthony Victor (India), 17 September 2007.
Eyebrow: 17.8 cm (7.01 in), Toshie Kawakami (Japan), 22 July 2008.
Eyelash: 6.99 cm (2.75 in), Stuart Muller (USA), 7 December 2007.
Leg: 16.51 cm (6.5 in), Wesley Pemberton (USA), 9 February 2008.
Nipple: 12.9 cm (5.07 in), Douglas Williams (USA), 26 May 2007.

LONGEST HAIR
The world's longest documented hair belongs to Xie Qiuping (China), at 5.627 m (18 ft 5.54 in) when measured on 8 May 2004. She has been growing her hair since 1973, from the age of 13. "It's no trouble at all. I'm used to it," she said. "But you need patience and you need to hold yourself straight when you have hair like this."

LONGEST BEARD (FEMALE)

Melinda Maxie – the stage name of Vivian Elaine Wheeler (USA) – has a beard that, when last measured in 2000, had a maximum length of 27.9 cm (11 in). "A sideshow wouldn't be a sideshow without the bearded lady," said Melinda, who has been in and out of circuses since the age of 8 years old.

★ NEW RECORD
★ UPDATED RECORD

HELSINKI, FINLAND
As of 19 June 2008, Seppo Mäkinen (Finland) had amassed 30,105 different badges from more than 50 countries, the **largest collection of badges**. He began his record-breaking collection in 1994.

60°10'N 24°56'E

HUMAN BEINGS
GOLDEN OLDIES

★ ★ ★ ★ ★ ★ ★ ★ ★ ★ ★ ★ ★

OLDEST LIVING

	NAME	AGE	DATE OF BIRTH
1	Eugénie Blanchard (St Barts/France)	114	16 Feb 1896
2	Eunice Sanborn (USA)	113	20 Jul 1896
3	Besse Cooper (USA)	113	26 Aug 1896
4	Walter Breuning (USA) **m**	113	21 Sep 1896
5	Chiyono Hasegawa (Japan)	113	20 Nov 1896
6	Venere Pizzinato-Papo (Italy)	113	23 Nov 1896
7	Shige Hirooka (Japan)	113	16 Jan 1897
8	Mississippi Winn (USA)	113	31 Mar 1897
9	Dina Manfredini (USA)	113	4 Apr 1897
10	Mineno Yamamoto (Japan)	113	8 Apr 1897

Source: Gerontology Research Group, extracted 11 May 2010   **m** = male

OLDEST LIVING...
★**Person** (and ★**woman**): Eugénie Blanchard, who lives on the French-owned island of St Barthélemy in the Caribbean, was born on 16 February 1896 and became the world's oldest human at the age of 114 years old 75 days; *see table left for the top 10 oldest living people as of 11 May 2010.*
★**Man:** Walter Breuning (USA). *See opposite page.*
★**Twin:** The oldest living single twin is 110-year-old

★OLDEST SIBLINGS
With a combined age of 325 years 289 days, the Thornton sisters of Shreveport, Louisiana, USA, are the oldest ever siblings. All three passed away within a few weeks of each other: Rosie Thornton Warren (left) on 18 December 2009; Carrie Thornton Miller (right) on 5 January 2010; and Maggie Lee Thornton Renfro (pictured middle) on 22 January 2010.

Ruth Peter Anderson (USA, b. 24 July 1899). Her fraternal twin Abel died in 1900 at the age of one year. *To our knowledge, no pair of twins has ever reached supercentenarian status (over 110).*
Twins: As we go to press, Guinness World Records is attempting to identify the holders of the record for the **oldest identical twins.** Widespread media coverage has been devoted to the

claim of Cao Daqiao and Cao Xiaoqiao (China, b. 3 October 1905), said to be 104 years old, though GWR is still to secure documentary evidence confirming this age. The twins live in Weifang in east China's Shandong province.

★LONGEST WORKING ICE-CREAM SELLER
Charlie D'Angelo (b. 26 September 1919) of Clifton, New Jersey, USA, has been working as an ice-cream man non-stop for 30 years, delivering confections from his Iggy's Igloo ice-cream truck since 1979. He has worked in the ice-cream trade intermittently since the age of 12!

EXTRA! NOT OLD ENOUGH FOR YOU? SHUFFLE ON OVER TO DINOSAURS ON PP. 50-51.

CAUTION: CHILDREN

DID YOU KNOW?
ON 20 FEBRUARY 2010, THERE WERE 76 PEOPLE CONFIRMED AND AUTHENTICATED AS BEING OVER THE AGE OF 110. OF THESE, ONLY THREE WERE MEN!

The chance of you living to 128 years old is about 1 in 2,560,000,000,000 (that's 1 in 2.56 trillion)!

TRIVIA

DAME THE OLDEST PERSON – AND OLDEST WOMAN – WHOSE AGE HAS BEEN AUTHENTICATED WAS JEANNE CALMENT (FRANCE), WHO DIED AGED 122 YEARS.

The title of oldest man ever, then, passes to Thomas Peter Thorvald Kristian Ferdinand "Christian" Mortensen (Denmark/USA, 16 August 1882–25 April 1998), who died aged 115 years 252 days – the only Nordic person to live beyond the age of 113.

★OLDEST MICHELIN THREE-STAR CHEF

Jiro Ono (Japan, b. 27 October 1925), owner of the Sukiyabashi Jiro sushi restaurant in Tokyo, Japan, was first acknowledged as a three-star chef in the *Michelin Guide Tokyo 2008* when he was 82.

★OLDEST SALSA DANCER

In December 2009, salsa dancer Sarah Paddy Jones (UK, born 1 July 1935) and her partner, Nicko, took first prize on the Spanish TV talent show *Tu Si Que Vales*.

OLDEST LIVING MAN

On the death of Henry Allingham (UK, 1896–2009), the title of oldest living man passed to 113-year-old Walter Breuning (b. 21 September 1896, above) of Great Falls, Montana, USA. At his last birthday, he became only the 12th man in history verified to reach 113 or older.

Conjoined twins: Ronnie and Donnie Galyon (USA, b. 25 October 1951) are the oldest living conjoined twins. For 36 years, they travelled in circuses, but retired in 1991. They share a passport but can cast two votes.

Married couple (aggregate age): Karl Dølven (Norway, b. 31 August 1897) married Gudrun Haug (Norway, b. 14 October 1900) on 4 June 1927. They were married until Gudrun's death on 24 April 2004, when she was 103 years 193 days and

Karl was 106 years 237 days – an aggregate age of 210 years 65 days.

The ★**longest current marriage** is that of Herbert and Zelmyra Fisher (both USA). For details of their remarkable feat, turn to p.122.

★OLDEST MAN EVER

New evidence has come to light that casts doubt on the long-standing longevity record held by Shigechiyo Izumi (Japan). The birth certificate submitted as evidence might actually belong to his older brother, who died at a young age; if the family used Izumi as a "necronym" – that is, gave him his dead brother's name, as the new research suggests – this means his final age was 105 years old, not 120.

★OLDEST FEMALE ATHLETICS RECORD HOLDER

On 11 October 2009, 100-year-old Ruth Frith (Australia) threw a record 4.07-m (13-ft 4-in) shot put in the over-100s category at the World Masters Games in Sydney, Australia. The Games are open to athletes of all abilities.

GAMES THE WORLD MASTERS GAMES ARE THE ★LARGEST PARTICIPATORY MULTI-SPORT EVENT ON THE PLANET. THE 2002 GAMES ATTRACTED A RECORD 24,886 ATHLETES.

★OLDEST FEMALE YOGA TEACHER

At 83 years old, Australia's Bette Calman is the oldest woman to teach the Indian mental and physical discipline of yoga.

YOGA GRANDMOTHER BETTE HAS TAUGHT YOGA FOR 40 YEARS. HERE SHE IS PICTURED IN THE (DEMANDING) PEACOCK POSITION!

★ **NEW RECORD**
UPDATED RECORD

EDIRNE, TURKEY
The world's **oldest continuously sanctioned sporting competition** is the Kırkpınar Oil Wrestling Festival, which has been held since 1460. The event is currently staged on the Sarayiçi Peninsula near Edirne, Turkey.

41°40'N 26°34'E

HUMAN BEINGS

MEDICAL RECORDS

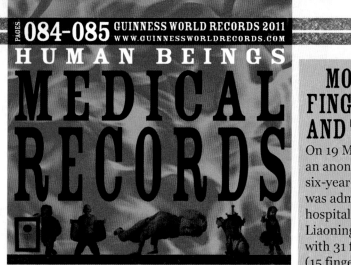

★ ★ ★ ★ ★ ★ ★ ★ ★ ★ ★ ★ ★ ★ ★

> "We chose him because he is tenacious, motivated and persistent."
>
> **Arm transplant surgeon Dr Jean-Michel Dubernard on his patient, Denis Chatelier (see below)**

★FIRST DOUBLE ARM TRANSPLANT

In January 2000, an international team of 18 surgeons and 32 support staff led by Professor Jean-Michel Dubernard (France) made history by performing the first double arm transplant. The recipient – Denis Chatelier, a 33-year-old French explosives worker (pictured) who had lost his arms in an accident four years previously – received the forearms of an 18-year-old cadaveric donor.

The procedure took 17 hours to complete and was performed at the Edouard-Herriot Hospital in Lyon, France. Dubernard had previously performed the **first arm transplant** back in 1998.

ARGH!
STUNT RIDER EVEL KNIEVEL (USA) HAD ENDURED 433 BONE FRACTURES BY THE END OF 1975. HIS LAST YEAR OF MAJOR STUNTS – THE **MOST BROKEN BONES IN A LIFETIME**.

AHH!
BALAMURALI AMBATI (USA, B. 29 JULY 1977) BECAME THE WORLD'S **YOUNGEST DOCTOR** ON 19 MAY 1995 AT THE AGE OF 17 YEARS 294 DAYS.

EXTRA!
FOR THE LOWDOWN ON SOME BIZARRELY BIG BODY PARTS, GO TO P.74!

MOST FINGERS AND TOES

On 19 March 2010, an anonymous six-year-old boy was admitted to a hospital in Shenyang, Liaoning province, China, with 31 fingers and toes (15 fingers and 16 toes). Three fingers on each hand are fused; however, x-rays show each finger had full skeletal development.

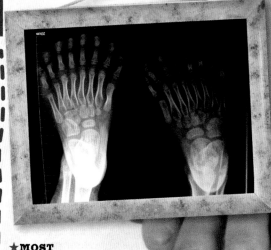

★MOST EYE TESTS CARRIED OUT IN AN HOUR

Volunteers from Specsavers International BV conducted a total of 648 eye tests in 92 locations throughout the Netherlands on 15 May 2009.

LARGEST TUMMY TUCK OPERATION PERFORMED ON A WOMAN

Plastic surgeons at the Hospital de Cruces in Barakaldo, Spain, removed an "apron" of fat weighing 60 kg (132 lb) from a morbidly obese woman in March 2006. During the nine-hour operation, surgeons needed small cranes to help support the fat and skin removed from her stomach. The weight removed is similar to that of an average 17-year-old girl, and had an energy content of 462,000 calories.

HIGHEST PERCENTAGE OF BURNS TO THE BODY

• Tony Yarijanian (USA, right) underwent 25 surgical procedures after suffering burns to 90% of his body in an explosion at his wife's beauty spa on 15 February 2004.
• David Chapman (UK) also survived 90% burns after an accident with a petrol canister on 2 July 1996.

38°25'N 27°08'E **IZMIR, TURKEY**

The world's **oldest datable bridge** still in use is the slab-stone single-arch bridge over the river Meles in Izmir (formerly Smyrna), Turkey, which dates from c. 850 BC. Remnants of Mycenaean bridges dated c. 1600 BC exist in the neighbourhood of Mycenae, Greece, over the River Havos.

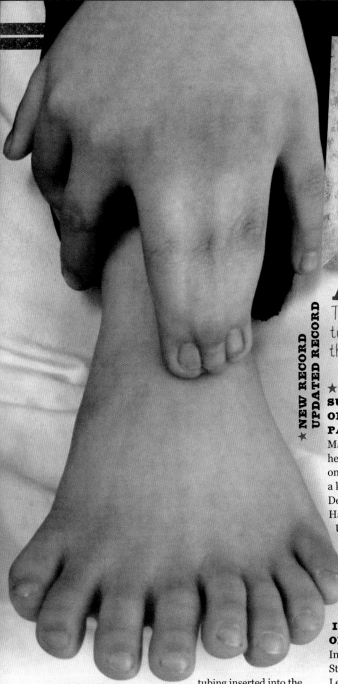

ABDOMINOPLASTY:

The medical term for a tummy tuck. A small tummy tuck is called an apronectomy, after the "apron" of skin and fat removed.

★LONGEST SURVIVING MULTI-ORGAN TRANSPLANT PATIENT

Mark Dolby (UK) received a heart-lung-liver transplant on 21 August 1987 and a kidney transplant in December 2005, all at Harefield Hospital, London, UK. As of 22 April 2009, he had survived 21 years 244 days as a multi-organ transplantee.

LEAST BLOOD TRANSFUSED IN A TRANSPLANT OPERATION

In June 1996, a team from St James University Hospital, Leeds, UK, performed a liver transplant on 47-year-old housewife Linda Pearson (USA) without any blood being transfused. Such an operation usually requires 2.3–3.4 litres (4–6 pints) of blood, but as a Jehovah's Witness Mrs Pearson chose to refuse the transfusion on religious grounds.

MOST HAND AMPUTATIONS ON THE SAME ARM

Clint Hallam (New Zealand) has had his right hand amputated a total of three times. He first lost his hand in 1984 after an accident with a circular saw. Surgeons managed to reattach the severed limb but an infection developed and it was removed in 1988. In September 1998, doctors gave him a hand transplant but Clint later requested that it be amputated.

YOUNGEST MULTI-ORGAN TRANSPLANT PATIENT

Sarah Marshall (Canada, b. 14 February 1997) became the youngest patient to receive a multi-organ transplant when, on 7 August 1997, she was given a liver, a bowel, a stomach and a pancreas at the Children's Hospital in London, Western Ontario, Canada.

★LARGEST TUMMY TUCK

According to Russian news website www.life.ru, in early 2010 a 49-year-old man known only as Petr F (pictured above, before and after) underwent a three-hour operation to remove 120 kg (264 lb) of fat and skin in Voronezh, Russia. Prior to the operation, Petr weighed 240 kg (529 lb), but his inability to walk for prolonged periods drove him to seek medical help.

★LONGEST-LIVING HYDROCEPHALIC

The medical condition hydrocephalus is marked by excess cerebrospinal fluid in the skull, which puts pressure on the brain, often harming it. The most common treatment is a "shunt", a technique developed in 1952 that uses tubing inserted into the skull to carry the excess fluid safely to another part of the body. In 1985, the death rate for sufferers was 52%, making the case of Theresa Alvina Schaan (Canada, b. 17 March 1941) all the more striking. As of 7 August 2009, she's been living with the condition for 68 years 143 days.

JAN 2004

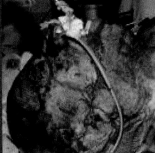

FEB 2004

AUG 2004

JAN 2007

OCT 2007

VARNA, BULGARIA

43°13'N
27°55'E

The **largest legal document** is an insurance policy measuring 9 x 6 m (29 ft 4 in x 19 ft 8 in), issued by ING Asigurari de Viata (Romania) and signed in Varna, Bulgaria, on 15 March 2008.

SUPER STUNTS

(SOME OF) ASHRITA'S ACHIEVEMENTS

1. Fastest 100-m egg-and-spoon race (19.90 seconds)
2. Fastest mile balancing a baseball bat on the finger (7 min 5 sec)
3. Fastest 1-mile sack race (16 min 41 sec)
4. Longest balance board duration (1 hr 49 min 5 sec)
5. Longest duration on a Swiss ball (3 hr 38 min 30 sec)
6. Fastest 1-mile fireman's carry (15 min 11.87 sec)
7. Fastest 10-km hula hooping (1 hr 25 min 9 sec)
8. Fastest mile on a pogo stick while juggling balls (23 min 28 sec)
9. Fastest 1-mile piggyback race (13 min 1 sec)
10. Longest table-tennis-bat-and-ball duration (3 hr 7 sec)
11. Fastest mile on spring-loaded stilts (7 min 13 sec)
12. Fastest mile on a space hopper (15 min 3 sec)
13. Greatest distance travelled with a pool cue balanced on the chin (1,668 m; 5,472 ft)
14. Most starjumps in 1 minute (61)

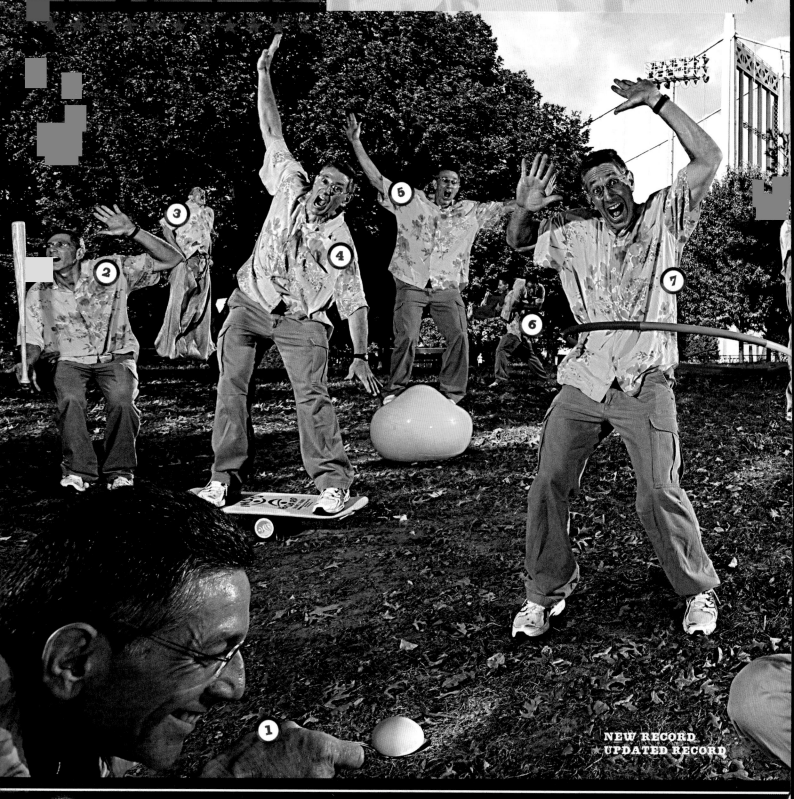

NEW RECORD
UPDATED RECORD

JOHANNESBURG, SOUTH AFRICA

26°12'S
28°02'E

Vic Toweel (South Africa) knocked down Danny O'Sullivan (UK) 14 times in 10 rounds in their world bantamweight fight at Johannesburg, South Africa, on 2 December 1950, before the latter retired. You can hardly blame O'Sullivan for retiring –he'd just suffered the **most knockdowns in a boxing match**.

FUNAMBULIST:

Another name for "tightrope walker". It comes from the Latin "funambulus", meaning "rope walker".

HEAVIEST ELEPHANT LIFTED

In 1975 while performing with Gerry Cottle's Circus (UK), Khalil Oghaby (Iran) lifted an elephant off the ground using a harness and platform above the animal. At 2 tonnes (4,400 lb), this is the heaviest elephant ever lifted by a human.

LONGEST-RUNNING CIRCUS

Ringling Bros. and Barnum & Bailey Circus (USA) is the world's longest running, with Barnum Bailey's "Greatest Show on Earth", established in 1870 and later merging with the Ringling Brothers in 1919. At its height, the circus had around 1,200 employees and travelled across the USA by railroad in 100 double-length carriages.

LARGEST CIRCUS AUDIENCE

A crowd of 52,385 people gathered to see the Ringling Bros. and Barnum & Bailey Circus, at the Superdome, New Orleans, Louisiana, USA, on 14 September 1975.

HIGHEST SHALLOW DIVE

On 9 October 2009, Darren Taylor (USA) performed a shallow dive from a height of 10.9 m (35 ft 9 in) at the Gwinnett Arena, Atlanta, Georgia, USA. In doing so, he broke his own record by 2.5 cm (1 in).

★MOST 360° SPINS ON A TIGHTROPE (TWO MINUTES)

On 20 September 2007, Maimaitiaili Abula (China) performed 41 full-circle spins on a tightrope on the set of *Zheng Da Zong Yi – Guinness World Records Special* in Beijing, China.

★MOST ROTATIONS HUNG FROM THE NECK OF ANOTHER PERSON (30 SECONDS)

Liu Xiaogao and Liu Jiangshan (both China), from the Shenyang Jinying Youth Acrobatic Troupe, performed 82 rotations suspended from each other's neck by a belt in 30 seconds on the set of *Zheng Da Zong Yi – Guinness World Records Special* in Beijing, China, on 21 November 2009.

★MOST BULLWHIP CRACKS (ONE MINUTE)

Adam Winrich (USA) carried out 257 bullwhip cracks in a minute at The Stone's Throw Bar in Eau Claire, Wisconsin, USA, on 20 June 2009.

MOST CONSECUTIVE SOMERSAULTS HORSEBACK RIDING

In 1856, James Robinson (USA) performed 23 consecutive somersaults on horseback at Spalding Rogers Circus, Pittsburgh, Pennsylvania, USA.

FARTHEST JUMP RIDING A LION

Edgard and Askold Zapashny (both Russia), of the Russian State Circus Company, performed a 2.3-m (7-ft 6-in) jump astride a lion named Michael on 28 July 2006.

HUMAN BILLED AS "ALAR", THE FIRST HUMAN ARROW WAS TONY ZEDORAS (USA), AT THE BARNUM & BAILEY CIRCUS IN THE USA IN 1896.

ARROW VESTA GUESCHKOVA (BULGARIA) WAS FIRED 22.9 M (75 FT) ON 27 DECEMBER 1995, THE FARTHEST A HUMAN ARROW HAS BEEN FIRED.

> *"Pain lasts for a minute. The glory lasts for a lifetime."*
> **Shallow-dive supremo Darren Taylor, aka Professor Splash**

★LONGEST DISTANCE BY A HORSE ON HIND LEGS

The greatest distance covered by a horse walking on only two legs is 30 m (95 ft 5 in) and was achieved by a horse named Doc, ridden by Gregory Ancelotti (Italy), on the set of *Lo Show dei Record*, in Milan, Italy, on 25 April 2009.

KUWAIT CITY, KUWAIT

The **largest kite flown** had a lifting area of 950 m² (10,225.7 ft²). Laid flat, it had a total area of 1,019 m² (10,968.4 ft²) and was 25.475 m (83 ft 7 in) long and 40 m (131 ft 3 in) wide. The kite was made by Abdulrahman Al Farsi and Faris Al Farsi (both Kuwait) and flown at the Kuwait Hala Festival in Flag Square, Kuwait City, Kuwait, on 15 February 2005.

29°22'N 47°58'E

SUPER STUNTS
MASS PARTICIPATION

★★★★★★★★★★★★

LARGEST "THRILLER" DANCE

The largest Michael Jackson "Thriller" dance was performed by 13,597 participants at an event organized by the Instituto de la Juventud del Gobierno del Distrito Federal at the Monumento a la Revolución, Mexico City, Mexico, on 29 August 2009.

★ LARGEST BACKWARDS RACE

The record for the largest backwards race was achieved by 539 people at an event organized by Mater Salvatoris Institute in Kapellen, Belgium, on 13 March 2009.

★ LARGEST BIKINI PARADE

A bikini parade involving 287 women set a world record at an event held by Kellogg's Special K in Johannesburg, South Africa, on 7 November 2009.

★ MOST PEOPLE CRAMMED INTO A SMART CAR

A total of 16 members of the Candy Lane Dancers troupe (all New Zealand) squeezed into a standard Smart Car at the Sylvia Park shopping mall in Auckland, New Zealand, on 23 August 2009.

★ LARGEST FAMILY REUNION

The largest family reunion is 2,585 and was achieved by the Lilly family at Flat Top, West Virginia, USA, on 9 August 2009.

★ LARGEST HUMAN BEATBOX ENSEMBLE

Michael Krappel (Austria) assembled a beatbox ensemble with 327 participants in Vienna, Austria, on 27 September 2009.

★ MOST PEOPLE GOLD PANNING

The greatest number of people gold panning at the same time was 100, at an event organized by Primaria Rosia Montana in Rosia Montana, Romania, on 30 August 2009.

★ MOST PEOPLE CHANTING

At an event held in Gärdet Park, Stockholm, Sweden, 2,558 people chanted together on 15 August 2009.

★ LARGEST BOLLYWOOD DANCE

A Bollywood dance featuring 1,082 students and teachers of the Anglo Chinese School was performed in Singapore on 29 April 2009.

★ MOST PEOPLE DRESSED AS BEES

A total of 1,901 participants dressed up as bees on 15 July 2009 in Staffordshire, UK.

★ MOST PEOPLE HOLDING THEIR BREATH UNDERWATER

On 11 October 2009, a total of 280 people held their breath underwater in Torri del Benaco, Verona, Italy. The record was achieved by "La Scuola del Mare 2" (Italy).

★ LARGEST CHRISTMAS-CRACKER PULLING

A group of 1,478 people engaged in a mass Christmas-cracker pull in Tochigi, Japan, on 18 October 2009.

★ LARGEST CHARITY WALK

A charity walk by 1,903 people took place at an event in Rathcoole Park, Rathcoole, County Dublin, Ireland, on 5 September 2009.

★ LARGEST GROUP HUG

A group of 9,758 people combined to encircle the citadel of Alba Iulia in Transylvania, Romania, in a communal hug on 29 May 2009.

★ LARGEST DANCE CLASS

The biggest dance class was achieved by an unprecedented 7,770 participants at an event organized by DanceSport Team Cebu International Inc. at the Cebu City Sports Center in Cebu City, the Philippines, on 27 June 2009. The participants were trained more than three weeks prior to the event to ensure the success of the attempt.

MINI
A GROUP OF 21 MALAYSIAN STUDENTS FITTED INTO AN OLD-STYLE MINI COOPER ON 17 JUNE 2006. THE MOST PEOPLE CRAMMED INTO A MINI COOPER.

MAXI
THE MOST PEOPLE CRAMMED INTO A NEW-MODEL MINI IS 24, AT AN EVENT SET UP BY GRUPO LOGAX, S.A. DE C.V. IN MEXICO CITY, MEXICO, ON 19 AUGUST 2009.

TEHRAN, IRAN
Official Iranian estimates gave the size of the crowds lining the 32-km (20-mile) route to Tehran's Behesht-e Zahra cemetery on 11 June 1989, for the funeral of Ayatollah Ruhollah Khomeini, as 10,200,000 people. That figure represented one-sixth of Iran's population, the **largest percentage of a population to attend a funeral**.

MOST KITES FLOWN SIMULTANEOUSLY

For an initiative organized by United Nations Relief and Works Agency (UNRWA), children at Al-Waha beach, Gaza Strip, on 30 July 2009, flew 3,710 kites, the greatest number in the air together at one time.

★ LARGEST COFFEE PARTY (SINGLE VENUE)

A coffee party comprising an incredible 8,162 participants was held by Krüger GmbH & Co. KG (Germany) at the Jugendpark in Cologne, Germany, on 30 August 2009.

★ MOST PEOPLE EXERCISING TO A VIDEOGAME

On 22 May 2009, 605 people performed an exercise routine to a videogame at the Electronic Arts Burnaby Campus Sports Field in Burnaby, British Columbia, Canada.

LARGEST MARTIAL ARTS DISPLAY

A martial arts display featuring 33,996 participants practicing tai chi took place at an event organized by Beijing Municipal Bureau of Sports in Beijing, China, on 8 August 2009.

★ MOST PEOPLE KNITTING

On 7 August 2009, at the "Sock Summit" in Portland, Oregon, USA, 937 people took part in a mass knitting event.

★ LARGEST ANNUAL GATHERING OF WOMEN

Attukal Pongala in Kerala, India, is a celebration of womenhood in which offerings (*pongala*) are made to Attukal Amma, the mother goddess. The 2010 event attracted more than three million women.

★ LARGEST PICNIC (MULTIPLE VENUE)

A total of 12,934 picnickers assembled across 79 venues in a record attempt organized in the UK for National Family Week on 25 May 2009.

★ MOST PEOPLE IN A MULTI-LEGGED RACE

The greatest number of participants in a multi-legged race was achieved by 261 people at an event held by Nogata North Elementary School in Nogata, Japan, on 21 November 2008.

★ MOST PEOPLE DRESSED AS STAR TREK CHARACTERS

On 14 February 2010, 99 people dressed as characters from *Star Trek* assembled at the Millennium Bridge, London, UK. The event was staged by Namco Bandai Partners in association with Atari to help celebrate the arrival of new MMORPG *Star Trek Online*.

LARGEST GATHERING OF SMURFS

The most people dressed as Smurfs was 2,510 and was achieved by Jokers' Masquerade with the help of Swansea University at Swansea Oceana in Swansea, UK, on 8 June 2009. Everyone's faces, arms and legs had to be painted blue to qualify.

DID YOU KNOW?

TAI CHI CHUAN, TO GIVE IT ITS FULL NAME, IS A CHINESE MARTIAL ART. THE NAME MEANS "SUPREME ULTIMATE FIST", AND IT DATES BACK TO AROUND 1580.

Ken Dickenson and Kevin Bartolo performed a tai chi marathon for a record 25 hr 5 min in Australia on 17–18 March 2006.

TRIVIA

The **most expensive car number plate** -- made up of the single digit "1" – was sold to Saeed Abdul Ghaffar Khouri (UAE) for Dh52.2 million ($14.2 million; £7.2 million) at a special number-plate auction organized by Emirates Auction Company, and held at Emirates Palace, Abu Dhabi, UAE, on 16 February 2008.

SUPER STUNTS
MASS PARTICIPATION

★MOST PARTICIPANTS IN A BADMINTON RALLY

A total of 96 participants played in a badminton rally on 23 May 2009. The record was set by Aviva (Singapore), in Raffles City Mall, Singapore.

★LARGEST SCUBA DIVING LESSON

A "class" of 2,465 people took part in a scuba lesson in the water of Malalayang beach in Manado, Indonesia, on 16 August 2009.

MOST...

★MODELS IN A FASHION SHOW

The Muaa Summer 2010 show in Buenos Aires, Argentina, saw 260 models take to the catwalk on 8 October 2009.

★BACKING DANCERS TO A SINGER

A total of 251 members of an audience were trained to perform a choreographed routine for singer Alesha Dixon (UK) in London, UK, on 2 April 2009.

★CARS WASHED IN EIGHT HOURS (MULTIPLE VENUES)

During the Soaps It Up! National Car Wash Fundraiser event coordinated by Victory Management Group (USA) on 20 June 2009, 4,105 people gathered in multiple venues across the USA to wash cars and raise money for cystic fibrosis research.

★GOLF BALLS HIT SIMULTANEOUSLY

A record 1,873 balls were hit simultaneously at the Real Federacion Español de Golf course in Madrid, Spain, on 27 September 2009.

★CHAMPAGNE BOTTLES SABRED SIMULTANEOUSLY

At an event organized by International Sabrageurs Anonymous in Portarlington, Co. Laois, Ireland, on 18 July 2009, 152 participants simultaneously sabred bottles of champagne.

★SKY LANTERNS FLOWN SIMULTANEOUSLY

An amazing 10,318 sky lanterns were launched at an event organized by Freedom Faithnet Global (Indonesia) in Ancol Carnaval Beach, Jakarta, Indonesia, on 5 December 2009.

★KARAOKE PARTICIPANTS

The largest karaoke session took place at Bristol Motor Speedway in Bristol, Tennessee, USA, on 22 August 2009, when 160,000 people sang "Friends in Low Places", by Garth Brooks (USA), before the start of the NASCAR Sharpie 500 race.

★LARGEST PARADE OF MINIS

The London & Surrey Mini Owners Club organized a parade of Mini cars consisting of 1,450 vehicles, as part of the London to Brighton Mini Run, in Crystal Palace, London, UK, on 17 May 2009.

MINIS: Made by British Motor Corporation (BMC), these old-style Minis were in production between 1959 and 2000.

ICON THE MINI WAS VOTED THE SECOND MOST INFLUENTIAL CAR OF THE 20TH CENTURY IN 1999. THE FORD MODEL T CLAIMED FIRST PLACE.

MI 5YCO

GUINNESS WORLD RECORDS 2011

★ LARGEST GATHERING OF SUPERHEROES

A record 1,091 people gathered at Twickenham Stadium, London, UK, while dressed as superheroes at an event organized by the Rugby Football Union and facilitated by event360 at the Emirates Airline London Sevens on 23 May 2010. Various hulks, bananamen and ninja turtles attended, but Elvis and Santas were disqualified!

EXTRA! FOR MORE ECCENTRIC BEHAVIOUR, TURN TO PP.142-143 FOR SOME RECORD-BREAKING COLLECTORS!

LARGEST...

★ HALLOWEEN GATHERING

A group of 508 people in scary costumes assembled in Bloomington, Indiana, USA, on Halloween 2009.

On 24 September 2009, the ★largest gathering of skeletons featured 197 people, in London, UK.

★ GATHERING OF PEOPLE DRESSED AS STORYBOOK CHARACTERS

On 12 November 2009, a group of 300 people dressed up as storybook characters in celebration of Guinness World Records Day. The record was set by Carr's Glen Primary School in Belfast, Northern Ireland, UK.

★ SPORTS LESSON

A record 882 students at Ballyclare High School in Northern Ireland took part in a sports lesson on 12 November 2009. Also top of the class were 5,401 participants who enjoyed the ★largest physics lesson in Denver, Colorado, USA, on 7 May 2009.

LONGEST CONGA ON ICE

An impressive 252 participants performed a conga on ice at the Alexandra Palace Ice Rink in London, UK, to celebrate Guinness World Records Day on 11 November 2009.

★ LARGEST FOOTBALL TOURNAMENT

Copa Telmex 2009 was contested by 187,765 players, in 11,280 teams, and held in Mexico between 1 May and 29 November 2009. It was staged with the aim of providing a brighter future for Mexican youth.

ON ICE THE LARGEST ICE SKATING PINWHEEL WAS SET BY 70 PARTICIPANTS IN EINDHOVEN, THE NETHERLANDS, ON 14 MARCH 2010.

MUSCAT, OMAN

Made from Swarovski crystal, the world's **largest chandelier** hangs in the Sultan Qaboos Grand Mosque in Muscat, Oman. It is 14.1 m (46 ft) tall and 8 m (26 ft) in diameter, with 1,114 bulbs.

23°37'N 58°35'E

HUMAN ENDEAVOURS

★ ★ ★ ★ ★ ★ ★ ★ ★ ★ ★ ★

★ YOUNGEST FEMALE TO ROW THE INDIAN OCEAN

Sarah Outen (UK, b. 26 May 1985) single-handedly crossed the Indian Ocean, east to west, between 1 April and 3 August 2009 in her boat *Serendipity* (which she affectionately termed *Dippers*). At the start of her trip, Sarah was aged 23 years 310 days. Her journey began in Australia and ended 4,180 nautical miles (7,740 km; 4,810 miles) later in Mauritius. During the epic trip, she lost 20 kg (44 lb) in weight – despite scoffing a stomach-bulging 500 chocolate bars – and also broke two oars.

EXTRA!
IF YOU LOVE RECORD-BREAKING TALES OF THE HIGH SEAS, TURN TO P.118.

SSR 136912

SARAH OUTEN
SOLO ACROSS THE INDIAN - 2009
www.sarahouten.co.uk

★ **NEW RECORD**
★ **UPDATED RECORD**

CONTENTS

"If you're strong up-top and have prepared well, then you have the best chance – stubborn and strong, and with a bit of luck, you'll weather the worst of the storms. It's all about attitude, endurance and keeping happy."
Sarah Outen, ocean rower

24°51'N 67°00'E

KARACHI, PAKISTAN

Nargis Bhimji of Karachi, Pakistan, celebrated her birthday for 35 hr 25 min by crossing time zones, flying from Karachi to Singapore and then to San Francisco, USA, on 27 June 1998 – thereby giving her the record for the **longest birthday**.

MEN
THE INDIAN OCEAN HAS ONLY BEEN CONQUERED TWICE BY SOLO MALE ROWERS – MORE MEN HAVE CLIMBED EVEREST THAN HAVE TRIED TO ROW THIS FEARSOME SEA.

WOMEN
ONLY 10 WOMEN HAVE SUCCESSFULLY ROWED ACROSS AN OCEAN SOLO; OF THESE, ONLY TWO HAVE CHOSEN TO ROW A SECOND OCEAN. NONE CHOSE THE INDIAN!

INDIAN OCEAN

The Indian Ocean is the third largest ocean, representing 20% of Earth's surface water. It is also the second deepest ocean, after the Pacific, with an average depth of 3,736 m (12,260 ft).

The direct route from Australia to Mauritius is 3,100 nautical miles (5,740 km; 3,560 miles) – see green line (right). Sarah clocked up 4,180 nautical miles, though (see red line), thanks to "feisty currents, teasing winds and general unpredictable weather".

MUMBAI, INDIA

The **longest dosa** (rice flour pancake) measured 9.14 m (30 ft) and was prepared by chefs at the Sankalp Restaurant in Andheri, Mumbai, India, on 12 February 2006.

18°57'N
72°49'E

HUMAN ENDEAVOURS
GRAND TOURS

★GREATEST DISTANCE ON A HAND-CRANKED CYCLE IN 24 HOURS

Thomas Lange (Germany) covered 649.85 km (403.80 miles) on a hand-cranked cycle in 24 hours during the Bike Sebring 12/24 Hours, in Sebring, Florida, USA, from 14 to 15 February 2009.

(4,975.93 miles) by powered paraglider flying west to east across Canada from Tofino (British Columbia) to Bay St Lawrence (Nova Scotia) from 15 May 2009 to 24 August 2009. He landed and took off from Canadian schools along the way, where he gave presentations to the children to encourage them to challenge their fears and realize their own dreams.

PUNT

Aided by four other crew members John Pearse (UK) travelled by punt from Oxford, UK, to Leeds, UK, and back to Oxford from 19 June to 10 August 1965, a total of 1,160 km (721 miles).

WHEELCHAIR

Rick Hansen (Canada) wheeled his wheelchair 40,075 km (24,901 miles) through four continents and 34 countries, starting from Vancouver, BC, Canada, on 21 March 1985 and returning there on 22 May 1987.

FASTEST...

PARIS-LONDON JOURNEY

David Boyce of Stewart Wrightson (Aviation) Ltd travelled the 344 km (214 miles) from central Paris, France, to central London, UK (BBC TV Centre), in 38 min 58 sec on 24 September 1983. He travelled by motorcycle and helicopter to Le Bourget, France; then via jet (piloted by the late Michael Carlton) to Biggin Hill, UK; and lastly by helicopter to the TV Centre car park.

EXTRA!
MORE OF A HOMEBODY THAN A GLOBE-TROTTING GRAND TOURIST? THEN SWITCH TO P.166 TO FIND OUT WHAT'S ON TV.

★LONGEST JOURNEY SWIMMING

Martin Strel (Slovenia) covered a distance of 5,268 km (3,273.38 miles) when he swam the entire length of the Amazon River, in Peru and Brazil, from 1 February to 8 April 2007.

LONGEST JOURNEY BY...

carrying a 3.7-m-tall (12-ft) wooden cross and preaching from the Bible throughout.

★MOTORIZED BICYCLE

Eddie Sedgemore (UK) cycled 3,077 km (1,912.1 miles) on a motorized bicycle in 28 days from 9 May to 5 June 2009.

★A PILGRIM

The greatest distance claimed for a "round the world" pilgrimage is 61,319 km (38,102 miles) by Arthur Blessitt (USA) since 25 December 1969. He has crossed 315 "nations, island groups and territories"

★POWERED PARAGLIDER

Benjamin Jordan (Canada) travelled 8,008 km

WALKING BACKWARDS

Aged 36, Plennie L Wingo (USA) completed a 12,875-km (8,000-mile) backwards walk from Santa Monica, California, USA, to Istanbul, Turkey, in 517 days between 15 April 1931 and 24 October 1932. Wingo averaged 24.89 km (15.47 miles) each day of his trip.

FASTEST TIME TO CYCLE THE LENGTH OF THE PAN-AMERICAN HIGHWAY

Scott Napier (UK) cycled the Pan-American highway from Prudhoe Bay, Alaska, USA, to Ushuaia, Argentina, in 125 days from 22 June to 25 October 2009. Napier cycled a total of 22,690.36 km (14,099.11 miles) on his trip.

DID YOU KNOW?

GIAMPIETRO MARION (ITALY) CYCLED THE SOUTH AMERICAN PORTION OF THE PAN-AMERICAN HIGHWAY, FROM CHIGORODO, COLOMBIA, TO USHUAIA, ARGENTINA, IN 59 DAYS IN 2000.

The Pan-American highway is broken by a small impassable section called the Darién Gap.

TRIVIA

CLASSIC JOURNEYS

On every continent there is a classic journey to be found; it may be from one extreme point to another, or it may be between two points that have an historical or even romantic association. Whatever the journey may be, you can be sure that someone is going to attempt to complete that journey using either an outlandish mode of transport, or in the quickest time possible, and more often than not both! These are a few of our favourite fastest journeys.

JOURNEY	FROM	TO	DISTANCE	HOW	WHO	TIME	WHEN
Cairo to Cape	Cairo, Egypt	Cape Town, South Africa	approximately 11,000 km (6,835 miles)	Bicycle	Chris Evans, David Genders, Michael Kennedy (all UK), Paul Reynaert (Belgium), Jeremy Wex, Steve Topham, Scotty Robinson, Andrew Griffin (all Canada) and Sascha Hartl (Austria)	119 days 1 hr 32 min	18 January to 17 May 2003
John O'Groats to Land's End	John O'Groats, Scotland, UK	Land's End, England, UK	1,407 km (874 miles)	Foot	Andrew Rivett (UK)	9 days 2 hr 26 min	4 to 13 May 2002
Land's End to John O'Groats	Land's End, England, UK	John O'Groats, Scotland, UK	1,407 km (874 miles)	Unicycle	Robert Ambrose (UK)	12 days 1 hr 59 min	13 to 25 August 2000
Pan-American Highway	Ushuaia, Argentina	Prudhoe Bay, Alaska	30,431 km (19,019 miles)	Foot	George Meegan (UK)	2,426 days	26 January 1977 to 18 September 2009
Trans-Australia	Perth, Western Australia	Sydney, New South Wales	approximately 4,000 km (2,485 miles)	Bicycle	Richard Vollebregt (Australia)	8 days 10 hr 57 min	13 to 21 October 2006
Trans-USA	Jacksonville, Florida	San Diego, California	4,175 km (2,595 miles)	Inline skates	Russell "Rusty" Moncrief (USA)	69 days 8 hr 45 min	5 January to 15 March 2002
Trans-USA	Newport, Oregon	Washington, DC	5,248 km (3,261 miles)	Unicycle	Akira Matsushima (Japan)	43 days	10 July to 22 August 1992
Trans-USA	San Francisco, California	New York City	4,989 km (3,100 miles)	Foot	Frank Giannino, Jr (USA)	46 days 8 hr 36 min	1 September to 17 October 1980

UNPOWERED CROSSING OF THE BERING STRAIT

The fastest crossing of the Bering Strait – the sea channel that separates Asia from North America -- on foot and skis was completed by Dmitry Shparo and his son Matvey (both Russia), achieved when they reached Chariot, Alaska, USA, on 20 March 1998.

They had begun their journey in Mys Dezhneva, East Cape, Russia, on 1 March and travelled a total distance of approximately 290 km (180 miles).

★ TIME TO VISIT ALL SOVEREIGN COUNTRIES

Kashi Samaddar (India) visited all 194 United Nations member countries in 6 years, 10 months and 7 days, between 18 July 2002 and 24 May 2009.

RELAY CYCLE AROUND AUSTRALIA

Starting and finishing in Brisbane, Queensland, a team of eight cyclists took 18 days 8 hr 39 min to cycle 14,314 km (8,894 miles) around Australia between 22 October and 9 November 2001, taking in 19 coastal cities along the way.

LONGEST JOURNEY BY SKATEBOARD

Starting in Leysin, Switzerland, on 24 June 2007 and finishing in Shanghai, China, on 28 September 2008, Rob Thomson (New Zealand) travelled a staggering 12,159 km (7,555 miles) on his skateboard in 463 days.

★ LONGEST JOURNEY ON A POCKETBIKE (MINIMOTO)

Ryan Galbraith and Chris Stinson (both USA) travelled a record 716.58 km (445.26 miles) on pocketbikes (minimotos) from 5 to 8 August 2009. Galbraith and Stinson began their journey in Colorado, USA, and ended in South Dakota, USA.

★ NEW RECORD
UPDATED RECORD

PUSH! IN 2001, 30 SOUTH AFRICAN SCHOOL PUPILS PUSHED AN UNPOWERED SOAPBOX CART 2,061 KM (1,280 MILES) BETWEEN KOMATIPOORT AND CAPE TOWN, SOUTH AFRICA, IN 19 DAYS.

CRAWL! ARULANANTHAM SURESH JOACHIM (CANADA) CRAWLED FOR A RECORD 56.62 KM (35.18 MILES) AROUND A CIRCUIT IN SYDNEY, NEW SOUTH WALES, AUSTRALIA, ON 18-19 MAY 2001.

NEW DELHI, INDIA

The **highest road** in the world is in Khardungla pass at an altitude of 5,682 m (18,640 ft). It is one of the three passes of the Leh–Manali road in Kashmir, completed in 1976 by the Border Roads Organization, New Delhi, India. Motor vehicles have been able to use it since 1988.

28°37'N 77°12'E

HUMAN ENDEAVOURS
AROUND THE WORLD

> "There is no way they would send me off without me being fully prepared."
>
> **Michael Perham, on his parents' support for his record-breaking feat**

★ YOUNGEST PERSON TO SAIL AROUND THE WORLD SOLO AND UNSUPPORTED

Michael Perham (UK, b. 16 March 1992) sailed non-stop around the world in *TotallyMoney.com*, starting and finishing at the Ushant/Lizard line, in 284 days from 15 November 2008 to 27 August 2009, arriving aged 16 years 7 months 30 days. It is a record that is unlikely to be beaten as GWR no longer accepts claims for this category by anyone under 16 years of age.

FIRST...

CIRCUMNAVIGATION BY AIRCRAFT WITHOUT REFUELLING

Richard G "Dick" Rutan and Jeana Yeager (both USA) travelled the globe westward from Edwards Air Force Base, California, USA, in nine days from 14 to 23 December 1986 without refuelling. The key to their success was their aircraft *Voyager* – created by Dick's brother Burt, the man behind *SpaceShipOne*, the vehicle used in the **first privately funded manned spaceflight**.

CIRCUMNAVIGATION BY BALLOON SOLO

Steve Fossett (USA) circled the globe in *Bud Light Spirit of Freedom*, a 42.6-m-tall (140-ft) mixed-gas balloon, from 19 June to 2 July 2002. He took off from Northam, Western Australia, and landed at Eromanga, Queensland, Australia, after covering 33,195 km (20,627 miles) over 14 days 19 hr 50 min – the **longest duration flown by a balloon solo**.

PERSON TO SAIL AROUND THE WORLD (SOLO AND NON-STOP)

Robin Knox-Johnston (UK) set sail from Falmouth, Cornwall, UK, in his yacht *Suhaili* on 14 June 1968 as one of nine participants in the *Sunday Times* Golden Globe Race. By the time he returned to Falmouth on 22 April 1969, he was the only remaining competitor and claimed both the record and the £5,000 ($8,070) prize money.

WOMAN TO SAIL NON-STOP AROUND THE WORLD IN BOTH DIRECTIONS

On 16 February 2009, former PE teacher Dee Caffari (UK) finished the Vendée Globe round-the-world yacht race in sixth place. This achievement means that Dee is the first woman to sail both ways around the world, alone and unaided.

FIRST UNPOWERED EQUATORIAL CIRCUMNAVIGATION

Mike Horn (South Africa) circumnavigated the globe along the Equator by bicycle, dugout canoe, sailing trimaran and on foot in 513 days between 2 June 1999 and 27 October 2000. His journey started and finished near Libreville in the west African state of Gabon, and proceeded in six legs that included crossing the Amazon and central Africa.

FIRST CIRCUMNAVIGATION BY AIRCRAFT

Two US Army Douglas DWC seaplanes, the *Chicago*, piloted by Lt Lowell H Smith (right), and the *New Orleans*, flown by Leslie P Arnold, flew around the world in 57 "hops" between 6 April and 28 September 1924, beginning and ending at Seattle, Washington, USA.

EXTRA!
ALL THESE RECORD HOLDERS HAVE SKIPPED OVER OCEANS - MAKE SURE YOU DON'T BY SETTING SAIL FOR PP.38-39.

VOCALINK

FIRST CIRCUMNAVIGATION BY AMPHIBIOUS CAR

Ben Carlin (Australia) and his American wife Elinore left Montreal, Canada, in *Half-Safe*, a modified amphibious jeep, on 24 July 1950 intent on going around the world. It was an eventful trip – Elinore left her husband in India and filed for divorce – but eventually Ben arrived back in Montreal on 8 May 1958, after travelling 62,765 km (39,000 miles) over land and 15,450 km (9,600 miles) by water.

What's more, she is only the fourth person ever to do so.

This remarkable feat is now added to her previous achievement of becoming the **first woman to circumnavigate westwards solo and non-stop** in May 2006.

FASTEST...

CIRCUMNAVIGATION BY PASSENGER AIRCRAFT

The fastest flight under the Fédération Aéronautique Internationale (FAI)

FASTEST TIME AROUND THE WORLD BY A SAILING CREW

Bruno Peyron (France) captained a crew of 14 around the world in 50 days 16 hr 20 min 4 sec aboard the maxi catamaran *Orange II* from 24 January to 16 March 2005. The journey started and finished in Ushant, France.

rules, which permit flights that exceed the length of the Tropic of Cancer or Capricorn (36,787.6 km; 22,858.8 miles), was one of 31 hr 27 min 49 sec, set by an Air France Concorde, flight AF1995 (Capts Michel Dupont and Claude Hetru, both France). The Concorde flew from JFK airport in New York, USA, eastbound via Toulouse, Dubai, Bangkok, Guam, Honolulu and Acapulco on 15 and 16 August 1995 with a crew of 18 plus an additional 80 passengers.

Also according to the FAI rules, the **fastest time to fly around the world on scheduled flights** is 44 hr 6 min by David J Springbett (UK). His route took him over a course of 37,124 km (23,068 miles) from Los Angeles, California, USA, eastbound via London, Bahrain, Singapore, Bangkok, Manila, Tokyo and Honolulu from 8 to 10 January 1980.

FIRST CIRCUMNAVIGATION

While Ferdinand Magellan is often credited with the first round-the-world voyage, he died on the way and never completed the journey. He led a fleet of five ships that left Spain on 20 September 1519. Of these, only the *Vittoria* returned, on 8 September 1522, under the command of navigator Juan Sebastian de Elcano and with just 17 of the original crew.

CIRCUMNAVIGATION BY HELICOPTER

John Williams and Ron Bower (both USA) flew west around the world (against the prevailing winds) in a Bell 430 helicopter in 17 days 6 hr 14 min 25 sec from 17 August to 3 September 1996, starting and finishing in Fair Oaks, London, UK.

CIRCUMNAVIGATION BY CAR

The record for the first and fastest man and woman to have circumnavigated the Earth by car covering six continents under the rules applicable in 1989 and 1991 embracing more than an equator's length of driving (40,075 km; 24,901 road miles), is held by Saloo Choudhury and his wife Neena Choudhury (both India). The journey took 69 days 19 hours 5 minutes from 9 September to 17 November 1989. The couple drove a 1989 Hindustan "Contessa Classic" starting and finishing in Delhi, India.

ON YER BIKE! PHILIP WHITE (UK) WENT AROUND THE WORLD ON A BICYCLE BETWEEN 19 JUNE 2004 AND 24 APRIL 2005, AT A RECORD-BREAKING AGE OF 24 YEARS & 125 DAYS.

Orange

★ **NEW RECORD**
★ **UPDATED RECORD**

ENDURANCE

★ MOST CONSECUTIVE POGO-STICK JUMPS (MALE)

The greatest number of consecutive jumps achieved on a pogo stick is 186,152, by James Roumeliotis (USA) in Massachusetts, USA, on 22–23 September 2007.

TREADMILL RUNS

The ★**farthest distance run on a treadmill in 48 hours (team)** is 868.64 km (539.86 miles), by the 12-strong Porsche Human Performance (UK) team at the Festival of Speed, Goodwood, UK, on 3–5 July 2009.

Lee Chamberlain (UK) travelled 753.24 km (468.04 miles) on a treadmill at the Camberley Shopping Centre, Surrey, UK, from 18 to 25 July 2009, the ★**farthest distance run on a treadmill in a week.**

FARTHEST...

★ DISTANCE TO SURF ON A RIVER BORE

On 8 June 2009, Sergio Laus (Brazil) surfed the Pororoca bore on the Araguari River, Amapa, Brazil, for 36 minutes, covering 11.8 km (7.33 miles).

★ LONGEST TIME TO HOLD THE BREATH VOLUNTARILY (FEMALE)

Karoline Mariechen Meyer (Brazil) held her breath underwater for an astonishing 18 min 32.59 sec at the Racer Academy swimming pool, Florianopolis, Brazil, on 10 July 2009. A professional freediver, Karoline trained for four months to try to break the record. Prior to the attempt, she inhaled oxygen for 24 minutes.

★ PADDLEBOARD JOURNEY (TEAM)

Stephanie Geyer-Barneix, Alexandra Lux and Flora Manciet (all France) completed a paddleboard journey extending 4,830 km (3,2001 miles; 2,607 nautical miles), from the island of Cap Breton (Canada) to Capbreton (France) on 28 August 2009. The journey took 54 days to complete and the three women paddled from a kneeling or lying position using only their hands to propel them through the water.

★ DISTANCE BY MOTORCYCLE IN 24 HOURS

Omar Hilal Al-Mamari (Oman) rode 2,127 km (1,321.65 miles) on a motorcycle on a road between Marmool and Thamrait in Oman, on 18–19 August 2009.

★ DISTANCE RUN IN ONE HOUR (FEMALE)

Dire Tune (Ethiopia) ran 18,517 m (60,751 ft) in one hour at the IAAF World Athletics Grand Prix meeting in Ostrava, Czech Republic, on 12 June 2008.

★ OPEN-WATER SWIM RELAY

A team of 200 participants swam a total of 684.75 km (425.48 miles) in an open-water relay at Lake Camlough, Camlough, Northern Ireland, UK, held between 9 and 19 September 2009.

DISTANCE WALKED OVER HOT PLATES

Rolf Iven (Germany) walked 22.90 m (75 ft 1 in) over hot plates on the set of *Lo Show dei Record*, in Milan, Italy, on 18 April 2009.

★ FASTEST MILE IN A BOMB DISPOSAL SUIT

Lt Jonathan Kehoe (USA) ran a mile wearing a bomb disposal suit in a time of 10 min 16 sec at Camp ECHO in Diwaniyah provence, Iraq, on 2 February 2009. Jonathan is a lieutenant in the US Navy Explosive Ordnance Disposal (USN EOD). He wore a 34-kg (75-lb) EOD 9 bomb suit.

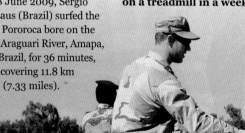

EXTRA! FOR AERIAL DAREDEVILRY, TAKE OFF FOR P.116. AND FOR TALES OF BRAVERY AND ENDURANCE ON THE WORLD'S OCEANS, WAVE HELLO TO P.118.

MEDAN, NORTH SUMATRA, INDONESIA

A young pointer puppy named Judy was captured by the Japanese in 1942 and interned at a makeshift POW camp at Medan, Indonesia, along with the captured crew of HMS *Grasshopper*, of which she was the mascot. The upside of this is that she achieved a Guinness World Record — as history's **only ever POW**

The ★**first modern triathlon** (a swim, cycle and run) was held in San Diego, USA, in 1974.

TRIVIA

★GREATEST DISTANCE RUN BY A RELAY TEAM

The longest distance run by a relay team is 3,096 km (1,923 miles) and was achieved by the Gillette Phenomenal Tour over 14 days, from 21 September 2009 to 5 October 2009.

LONGEST STATIC CYCLING MARATHON

Switzerland's Mehrzad Shirvani rode a static cycle for a record eight days (192 hours) at the Kortrijk Xpo, Kortrijk, Belgium, from 17 to 25 January 2009. Shirvani beat the previous record by more than six hours.

IRON
IF CONVENTIONAL TRIATHLONS AREN'T TESTING ENOUGH, TRY AN IRONMAN: A 3.86-KM (2.4-MILE) SWIM AND A 180.25-KM (112-MILE) CYCLE, FOLLOWED BY A MARATHON!

LONGEST...

★READING-ALOUD MARATHON (TEAM)

Elizabeth Sánchez Vegas, Ana María Leonardi, María Cristina Alarcón, Lilly Blanco, Devorah Sasha and Isabel Viera, from International Solidarity for Human Rights, read the Universal Declaration of Human Rights aloud at the InterAmerican Campus of the Miami Dade College in Miami, Florida, USA, for 240 hr 15 min 27 sec from 3 to 13 November 2009.

★DANCE MARATHON (INDIVIDUAL)

Dr Vattikotta Yadagiriacharya (India) danced for 108 hours continuously at the Ravindra Bharathi Auditorium, Hyderabad, India, from 25 to 29 November 2008.

TENNIS MARATHONS

The ★**longest doubles tennis match** lasted 50 hr 00 min 8 sec and was played between Vince Johnson, Bill Geideman, Brad Ansley and Allen Finley (all USA) at the YMCA of Catawba Valley, Hickory, North Carolina, USA, from 7 to 9 November 2008.

The ★**longest singles tennis match** lasted 36 hours and was achieved by Dennis Schrader and Bart Hendriks (both Netherlands), in Zandvoort, the Netherlands, on 10–11 September 2009.

★STAND-UP COMEDY SHOW (INDIVIDUAL)

Comedian Tommy Tiernan (Ireland) performed a stand-up set lasting 36 hr 15 min at Nuns Island Theatre, Galway, Ireland. The event began at 3 p.m. on Friday, 10 April 2009, and ended two days later, at 3:15 a.m.

★TIME TO HOLD A LIVE SCORPION IN THE MOUTH

Kanchana Ketkaew (Thailand) held a living scorpion in her mouth for 2 min 23 sec on the set of *Lo Show dei Record* in Milan, Italy, on 11 April 2009. Her husband placed the scorpion in her mouth.

★FULL-BODY ICE CONTACT

Chen Kecai (China) spent 1 hr 48 min 21 sec in direct contact with ice in the frozen Jingbo Lake, Mudanjiang City, China, on 14 March 2010.

★HANDSHAKE

• On 21 September 2009, Jack Tsonis and Lindsay Morrison (Australia) shook hands for 12 hr 34 min 56 sec in Sydney, Australia.
• George Posner and John-Clark Levin (both USA) then shook for 15 hours in California, USA, on 4 October 2009.
• And on 21 November 2009, Matthew Rosen and Joe Ackerman (both UK) shook for 15 hr 30 min 45 sec in London, UK.

MAN
THE FASTEST TIME TO COMPLETE AN IRONMAN RACE IS 7 HR 50 MIN 27 SEC, BY LUC VAN LIERDE (BELGIUM) AT ROTH, GERMANY, ON 13 JULY 1997.

velofollies

★ **NEW RECORD**
★ **UPDATED RECORD**

BANGKOK, THAILAND

13°45'N 100°29'E

In its most scholarly transliteration, Krungthep Mahanakhon, the official name for Bangkok, the capital of Thailand, has 168 letters and is the **longest place name**. The official short version (without capital letters, which are not used in Thai) is: krungthephphramahanakhon bowonratanakosin mahintharayuthaya mahadilokphiphobnovpharad radchataniburirom udomsantisug *(111 letters)*.

FEATURE
LAND SPEED RECORD

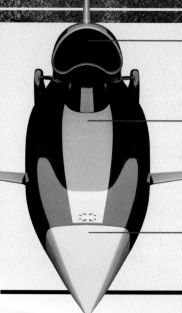

INTAKE DUCT

A single, central intake duct delivers airflow to the engine. The procedure is: 1. air enters; 2. air is compressed and pressurized; 3. fuel is added, then ignited; 4. expanded air is forced through the turbines; 5. gases are expelled through a nozzle out of the back of the engine.

COCKPIT

The driver is secured in a rigid carbon-fibre safety cell based on the design of a fighter plane cockpit. Its designer Andy Green, who will drive the *Bloodhound*, calls it the "world's fastest office"!

WINGLETS

Dynamic (computer-controlled) winglets above the wheels help to maintain a constant wheel load – i.e., they keep the car on the ground!

BODYWORK

The carbon-fibre and aluminium shell can withstand an air pressure of more than 12 tons/m² (2,457 lb/ft²). Changes to the bodywork are constantly fed to the onboard computer.

★ ★ ★ ★ ★ ★ ★ ★ ★ ★ ★ ★ ☆

IN LATE 2011 (OR EARLY 2012), A NEW ATTEMPT WILL BE MADE AT THE LAND SPEED RECORD. THE TEAM BEHIND THE ATTEMPT IS LED BY THE UK'S RICHARD NOBLE (BELOW RIGHT) AND ANDY GREEN (BELOW LEFT), WHO SET THE CURRENT RECORD OF NEARLY 1,228 KM/H (763 MPH) IN 1997. THIS TIME, THE AIM IS TO BREAK THE 1,000 MPH (1,609 KM/H) BARRIER...

LAND SPEED RECORD

The official land speed record (measured over one mile) is 1,227.985 km/h (763.035 mph; Mach 1.020), set by Andy Green (UK) on 15 October 1997 in the Black Rock Desert, Nevada, USA, in *Thrust SSC* (SuperSonic Car).

Thrust SSC was the brainchild of former land speed record-holder Richard Noble (UK).

★ FIRST CAR TO BREAK THE SOUND BARRIER

When Andy Green set the land speed record in 1997 in the Black Rock Desert, it was the first time that anyone on land had gone faster than the speed of sound – usually around 1,236 km/h (768 mph) in dry air at 20°C (68°F). The resultant sonic boom shook a school and caused sprinkler covers to fall off in the nearby town of Gerlach.

Pilot Green achieved the record 50 years and a day after the sound barrier was broken in the air by pilot Chuck Yeager (USA).

FASTEST SPEED ON A CONVENTIONAL MOTORCYCLE

John Noonan (USA) reached a speed of 406.62 km/h (252.662 mph) on a modified 1,350 cc Suzuki Hayabusa at Bonneville Salt Flats, Utah, USA, on 7 September 2005.

FASTEST ROCKET CAR

The highest speed ever attained in a rocket-powered car is 1,016.086 km/h (631.367 mph) over the first measured kilometre by *The Blue Flame*, on the Bonneville Salt Flats, Utah, USA, driven by Gary Gabelich (USA) on 23 October 1970. Momentarily, Gabelich exceeded 1,046 km/h (650 mph). The car was powered by a liquid natural gas/hydrogen peroxide rocket engine.

QUIZ!
WHAT WAS THE NAME OF THE VEHICLE THAT BROKE THE SPEED OF SOUND ON LAND AND WHO WAS ITS PILOT?
SEE P.278 FOR THE ANSWER.

WHIZZ!
AS HE SLOWS DOWN, ANDY WILL FEEL A FORCE OF 3 ɢ IN THE OPPOSITE DIRECTION, DRAINING THE BLOOD FROM HIS HEAD TO HIS FEET. HOPEFULLY, HE WON'T LOSE CONSCIOUSNESS!

GEE!
AS HE ACCELERATES, DRIVER ANDY GREEN WILL EXPERIENCE A G-FORCE OF 2.5 ɢ, WHICH WILL PUSH HIM BACK INTO HIS SEAT AND FORCE THE BLOOD INTO HIS HEAD.

NEW RECORD
★ UPDATED RECORD

KUALA LUMPUR, MALAYSIA
3°08'N 101°41'E
The 130-m-tall (425-ft) tower at Kuala Lumpur International Airport (KLIA) in Malaysia is the **tallest air traffic control tower** in the world. The design, by a local architect, is shaped like a giant Olympic torch.

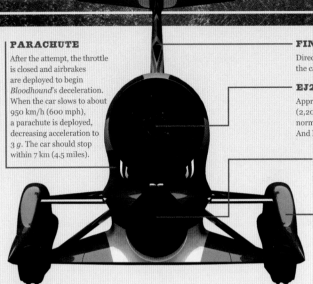

PARACHUTE

After the attempt, the throttle is closed and airbrakes are deployed to begin *Bloodhound*'s deceleration. When the car slows to about 950 km/h (600 mph), a parachute is deployed, decreasing acceleration to 3 *g*. The car should stop within 7 km (4.5 miles).

FIN

Directional stability is provided by a relatively small fin – too big and the car can be affected by crosswinds; too small and it will be unstable.

EJ200 ENGINE

Approximately half of the thrust is provided by a 1,000-kg (2,204-lb) Rolls-Royce EJ200 engine – a military turbofan normally found in the engine bay of a Eurofighter Typhoon. And located beneath the engine is the...

HYBRID SOLID-FUEL ROCKET

At 563 km/h (350 mph), the 400-kg (882-lb) hybrid solid-fuel rocket kicks in; together, the jet and rocket has a power of 212 kN (47,500 lb) – equivalent to 180 Formula One cars.

REAR WHEELS

The 90-cm (35.8-in) solid-aluminium wheels turn 12,000 times a minute. They are protected by front- and rear-pointing covers that not only reduce drag but also protect the wheels from debris.

SUPER-SONIC CAR

Shown here is a CGI of the 6,422-kg (14,148-lb), 12.8-m-long (50-ft) *Bloodhound*, the SuperSonic Car (SSC) that Richard Noble hopes will jet driver Andy Green to more than 1,609 km/h (1,000 mph) – faster than the current low-altitude air speed record. The target set for *Bloodhound* is a 31% improvement on the team's previous record-breaking *Thrust SSC* time!

FASTEST WHEEL-DRIVEN CAR

The fastest speed reached by a vehicle powered through its wheels – i.e., where the power of the engine is directed to the car's wheels, as opposed to jet power, which provides the thrust – is 737.794 km/h (458.444 mph) by the turbine-powered *Vesco Turbinator*, driven by Don Vesco (USA) at Bonneville Salt Flats, Utah, USA, on 18 October 2001.

FASTEST CAR CRASH SURVIVED

In September 1960, during trials to set a new land speed record at Bonneville, multiple world-record-holder Donald Campbell (UK) crashed his car *Bluebird* while travelling at a speed of 579 km/h (360 mph). The vehicle rolled over and Campbell fractured his skull; against all the odds, the daredevil driver survived.

LONGEST SKIDMARK

The skidmark made by the jet-powered *Spirit of America*, driven by Norman Craig Breedlove (USA), after the car went out of control at Bonneville in Utah, USA, on 15 October 1964, was nearly 10 km (6 miles) long.

TRACK! THE *BLOODHOUND* TEAM HAVE CHOSEN TO ATTEMPT THE RECORD ON A DRIED-UP LAKE BED KNOWN AS THE HAKSKEEN PAN IN THE NORTHERN CAPE OF SOUTH AFRICA.

MACH NUMBER:

The speed of an object in relation to (i.e., divided by) the speed of sound – so a car at Mach 1 is travelling at the speed of sound. *Bloodhound* is designed to reach Mach 1.4.

LAND SPEED MILESTONES

MPH	KM/H	YEAR	CAR	DRIVER	LOCATION
39.24	63.15	1898	*Jeantaud*	Gaston de Chasseloup-Laubat (France)	Achères, France
103.56	166.66	1904	*Gobron Brillié*	Louis Rigolly (France)	Ostend, Belgium
203.7	327.82	1927	*Sunbeam*	Henry Segrave (USA)	Daytona, Florida, USA
301.12	484.60	1935	*Bluebird*	Donald Campbell (UK)	Bonneville, Utah, USA
407.45	655.72	1963	*Spirit of America*	Craig Breedlove (USA)	Bonneville
526.28	846.96	1964	*Spirit of America*	Craig Breedlove (USA)	Bonneville
600.60	966.57	1965	*Spirit of America*	Craig Breedlove (USA)	Bonneville
763.03	1,227.98	1997	*Thrust SSC*	Andy Green (UK)	Black Rock Desert, USA
1,000+	1,609+	2011?	Bloodhound *SSC*	Andy Green (UK)	Hakskeen, SA

The selected entries show the progression of the land speed record as each 100-mph milestone is reached.

HUMAN ENDEAVOURS
HIGH ACHIEVERS

"It will be a case of mind over matter. We want to show people that if we can do it anyone can."

Amputee John Sandford Hart (UK), preparing to climb Kilimanjaro on crutches

FEMALE
TAMAE WATANABE (JAPAN) REACHED THE SUMMIT OF MOUNT EVEREST AT THE AGE OF 63 YEARS 177 DAYS ON 16 MAY 2002, BECOMING THE OLDEST WOMAN EVER TO DO SO.

★ MOST CONQUESTS OF MOUNT EVEREST

Apa Sherpa (Nepal) reached the summit of Mount Everest, on the Nepal–Tibet border, for the 19th time on 21 May 2009, the most times anyone has ever successfully climbed the world's highest mountain.

Apa began climbing in the late 1980s because he, like many other Sherpa people, found that being a guide was a good way to make money to support a family.

★ OLDEST MAN TO CLIMB MOUNT KILIMANJARO

Reginald W Alexander (UK, b. 1 October 1930) reached the summit of Mount Kilimanjaro, Tanzania, on 3 August 2009, aged 78 years 306 days.

★ NEW RECORD
★ UPDATED RECORD

DID YOU KNOW?

EIGHT RAF FIREFIGHTERS CLIMBED THE HEIGHT OF EVEREST (8,848 M; 29,028 FT) ON A "VERSACLIMBER" MACHINE IN A RECORD 1 HR 56 MIN 8 SEC AT MOUNT PLEASANT AIRFIELD, FALKLAND ISLANDS, ON 27 APRIL 2004.

The first published height of Everest, then known as Peak XV, was 8,840 m (29,002 ft) in 1856.

TRIVIA

★ HIGHEST ALTITUDE SCUBA DIVING

Scuba dives have been made on several occasions at an altitude of 5,900 m (19,357 ft), in a lagoon in the crater of Licancabur, a volcano on the border between Chile and Bolivia. One diver to investigate the lagoon was Henri Garcia of the Chilean Expedición America team; he spent 1 hr 8 min at depths of 5–7 m (16–23 ft) on 16 January 1995.

HIGHEST ALTITUDE REACHED BY MOTORCYCLE

A team of six from the North Calcutta Disha Motorcycle Club (all India) rode their Hero Honda motorcycles to an altitude of 6,245 m (20,488 ft) on the Changchemno Range near Marsemikla, India, on 29 August 2008.

HIGHEST MARATHON

The Everest Marathon, first run on 27 November 1987, begins at Gorak Shep, (5,212 m; 17,100 ft) and ends at Namche Bazar, (3,444 m; 11,300 ft). The fastest time for a man to complete this race is 3 hr 50 min 23 sec by Hari Roka (Nepal) in 2000, and the fastest time for a woman is 4 hr 35 min 4 sec by Anna Frost (New Zealand) in 2009.

FIRST WOMAN TO CLIMB MOUNT EVEREST

Junko Tabei (Japan) reached the summit of Mount Everest on 16 May 1975.

MALE
ACCORDING TO THE SENIOR CITIZEN MOUNT EVEREST EXPEDITION, MIN BAHADUR SHERCHAN (NEPAL) REACHED THE TOP OF EVEREST ON 25 MAY 2008 AT THE RECORD AGE OF 76 YEARS 340 DAYS.

★ FIRST MARRIED COUPLE TO REACH THE SUMMIT OF MOUNT EVEREST

Phil and Susan Ershler (USA) were the first married couple to successfully climb Mount Everest, reaching the summit on Thursday 16 May 2002 – the same day that a record 54 people reached the top.

21°05'N
105°55'E
CHENGDU, CHINA

The **largest panda cub born in captivity** weighed 218 g (7.6 oz) when he was born at the Wolong Giant Panda Research Centre, Chengdu, Sichuan province, China, on 7 August 2006. The cub is the first offspring of Zhang Ka, who was in labour for 34 hours, itself the **longest recorded labour for captive pandas**.

FIRST PEOPLE TO CLIMB EACH OF THE 8,000ERS

The 8,000ers are the 14 mountains on Earth that rise to more than 8,000 m (26,247 ft) above sea level. They are all located in the Himalayan and Karakoram mountain ranges in Asia. Reinhold Messner (Italy) became the **first person to climb all of the 8,000ers** when he summited Lhotse on the Nepal/Tibet border on 16 October 1986, having begun his quest in June 1970 – a total of 16 years 3 months 19 days. By the end of 2009, only 18 people had completed the feat. The ★**fastest person to climb all 8,000ers** is Jerzy Kukuczka (Poland), who took 7 years 11 months 14 days to complete the feat, between 4 October 1979 and 18 September 1987.

(source for table: www.8000ers.com)

MOUNTAIN	HEIGHT	DATE	EXPEDITION NATIONALITY	FIRST TO CLIMB (nationality as Expedition unless stated)
Everest	8,848 m (29,028 ft)	29 May 1953	British	Edmund Hillary (New Zealand), Tenzing Norgay (India/Sherpa)
K2	8,611 m (28,251 ft)	31 July 1954	Italian	Achille Compagnoni, Lino Lacedelli
Kangchenjunga	8,586 m (28,169 ft)	25 May 1955	British	George Band, Joe Brown
Lhotse	8,516 m (27,939 ft)	18 May 1956	Swiss	Fritz Luchsinger, Ernst Reiss
Makalu	8,485 m (27,837 ft)	15 May 1955	French	Jean Couzy, Lionel Terray
Cho Oyu	8,188 m (26,863 ft)	19 May 1954	Austrian	Josef Jöchler, Herbert Tichy, Pasang Dawa Lama (India/Sherpa)
Dhaulagiri I	8,167 m (26,794 ft)	13 May 1960	Swiss	Kurt Diemberger (Austria), Peter Diener (Germany), Ernst Forrer, Albin Schelbert, Nawang Dorje (Nepal/Sherpa), Dorji (Nepal/Sherpa)
Manaslu	8,163 m (26,781 ft)	9 May 1956	Japanese	Toshio Imanishi, Gyalzen Norbu (India/Sherpa)
Nanga Parbat	8,125 m (26,656 ft)	3 July 1953	Austro-German	Hermann Buhl (Austria)
Annapurna I	8,091 m (26,545 ft)	3 June 1950	French	Maurice Herzog, Louis Lachenal
Gasherbrum I	8,080 m (26,509 ft)	5 July 1958	American	Andrew Kauffman, Peter Schoening
Broad Peak	8,051 m (26,414 ft)	9 June 1957	Austrian	Hermann Buhl, Kurt Diemberger, Marcus Schmuck, Fritz Wintersteller
Gasherbrum II	8,035 m (26,362 ft)	7 July 1956	Austrian	Josef Larch, Fritz Moravec, Johann Willenpart
Shisha Pangma	8,027 m (26,335 ft)	2 May 1964	Chinese	Hsu Ching, Chang Chun-yen, Wang Fu-zhou, Chen Sam, Cheng Tien-liang, Wu Tsung-yue, Sodnam Doji, Migmar, Trashi, Doji, Yonten

★FASTEST ASCENT OF MOUNT KILIMANJARO ON CRUTCHES

John Sandford Hart (UK, below centre) completed an ascent of Mount Kilimanjaro on crutches in 4 days 20 hr 30 min. Sandford Hart, who had his right leg amputated as the result of a boating accident, completed the challenge from 24 to 29 October 2009.

★HIGHEST ALTITUDE CYCLING

Gil Bretschneider and Peer Schepanski (both Germany) rode their mountain bikes at an altitude of 7,211 m (23,658 ft) on the slopes of the Muztagata peak in Xinjiang province, China, on 10 July 2009.

The challenge started on 23 June 2009, when the pair were at an altitude of 5,350 m (17,552 ft), and it took them 17 days to reach their goal.

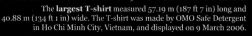

HO CHI MINH CITY, VIETNAM

10°46'N 106°41'E

The **largest T-shirt** measured 57.19 m (187 ft 7 in) long and 40.88 m (134 ft 1 in) wide. The T-shirt was made by OMO Safe Detergent in Ho Chi Minh City, Vietnam, and displayed on 9 March 2006.

HUMAN ENDEAVOURS
REACH FOR THE SKIES

⭐ ⭐ ⭐ ⭐ ⭐ ⭐ ⭐ ⭐ ⭐ ⭐ ⭐ ⭐

★ MOST TANDEM JUMPS BY ONE INSTRUCTOR IN 24 HOURS

Harold "Chip" Bowlin, with his passenger Kristine Gould (both USA), achieved 103 tandem parachute jumps in 24 hours, the record for a single instructor. The attempt was undertaken in Zephyrhills Skydive City, Florida, USA, between 14 and 15 April 2009.

FIRST AIRCRAFT FLIGHT OVER THE NORTH POLE

Roald Amundsen (Norway) made the first verified flight over the North Pole on 12 May 1926 in the airship *Norge*. Amundsen was accompanied on the flight from Spitzbergen, Norway, to Alaska, USA, by 15 crew members, including Umberto Nobile (Italy), the airship's designer and pilot, American explorer Lincoln Ellsworth and Oscar Wisting (Norway), a polar explorer who was also the helmsman.

★ FIRST LANDING ON AN AIRCRAFT CARRIER

Flying a Sea Vampire of the Royal Navy registration LZ551/G, Eric "Winkle" Brown (UK) became the first person to land and take off in a jet aircraft from an aircraft carrier (HMS *Ocean*) on 3 December 1945.

★ FIRST CORPS OF MILITARY BALLOONISTS

The French Army established a corps of balloonists – known as The Aérostiers – on 2 April 1794. The corps was a reconnaissance unit that used its elevated position to plot the location of the enemy on the battlefield.

★ FARTHEST FLIGHT BY A PARAGLIDER (FEMALE)

Kamira Pereira (Brazil) flew her paraglider 324.5 km (201.63 miles) in a straight line west from Quixada, Brazil, on 14 November 2009. In doing so, she beat her own record of 323 km (200.7 miles), which she had set just six days earlier.

★ OLDEST SOLO PILOT HELICOPTER FLIGHT

Peter Chantler (UK) completed a solo helicopter flight over Rosebank Farm in Tarporley, UK, on 8 April 2009 at the age of 83 years 2 months and 11 days.

EXTRA! WANT TO LOOK EVEN FARTHER AFIELD? CHECK OUT THE SPACE CHAPTER, FROM P.22.

★ GREATEST VERTICAL DISTANCE FREEFALLING IN 24 HOURS

The greatest accumulated vertical distance covered while freefalling in 24 hours is 102 km (63.38 miles) and was achieved by the Nagual Freefly Team – Daniele Fraternali, Cristian Giorgi and Alessandro Mitrugno (all Italy) – in Fano, Italy, on 28 June 2009.

DID YOU KNOW?

CAPTAIN ELGEN M LONG (USA) ACHIEVED THE FIRST CIRCUM-POLAR FLIGHT IN A PIPER PA-31 NAVAJO FROM 5 NOVEMBER TO 3 DECEMBER 1971. HE COVERED 62,597 KM (38,896 MILES) IN 215 FLYING HOURS.

TRIVIA

Mark Malkoff (USA) completed a record 135 scheduled flight journeys in 30 days from 1 to 30 June 2009.

"Once you've learned the skills, your muscles remember."

Peter Chantler (right)

HEAVIEST ITEM AIRLIFTED

A power plant generator weighing 187.6 tonnes (206.7 tons) was airlifted by an Antonov Airlines 225 "Mriya" aircraft at Frankfurt Hahn Airport, in Frankfurt, Germany, on 11 August 2009.

★LARGEST CIVILIAN FORMATION FLIGHT

A record 37 Van's RV Aircraft led by Stu McCurdy (USA) flew in different close formations during the AirVenture09 Airshow in Oshkosh, Wisconsin, USA, on 28–29 July 2009.

FIRST FLIGHT OVER EVEREST

On 3 April 1933, two aircraft, a Houston-Westland and a Westland-Wallace – both open cockpit biplanes fitted with Bristol Pegasus SIII engines – made the first manned flights over Mount Everest (8,848 m; 29,029 ft), the **highest mountain** in the world. The aircraft took off from Lalbalu aerodrome, near Purnea, India, crewed by Colonel L V S Blacker and Squadron Leader the Lord Clydesdale in one and Flight Lieutenant D F MacIntyre and S R Bonnet (all UK) in the other.

The flight cleared the mountain by a reported 30.48 m (100 ft). Close-range photographs of Everest proved the achievement.

★ **NEW RECORD**
UPDATED RECORD

★FASTEST HANG-GLIDER

Dustin Martin (USA) completed a circuit of a 100-km (62.14-mile) triangular course in a hang-glider at an average speed of 49 km/h (30.45 mph). A US national hang-gliding team member, Martin completed his flight over Zapata, Texas, USA, on 26 July 2009 in his Wills Wing T2C 144.

QUIZ!
IN 1911, NORWAY'S ROALD AMUNDSEN BECAME THE FIRST MAN TO REACH THE SOUTH POLE. WHAT OTHER POLAR RECORD DID HE ACHIEVE 15 YEARS LATER?
SEE P.278 FOR THE ANSWER.

★FIRST PUBLIC DEMONSTRATION OF A STEERABLE LIGHTER-THAN-AIR CRAFT

On 24 September 1852, engineer Henri Giffard (France) travelled 27 km (16.7 miles), from Paris to Trappes (both France), in his hydrogen-filled dirigible. He controlled the aircraft using a tiny steam engine, and maintained a speed of just 5 km/h (3 mph).

★LONGEST HOT-AIR BALLOON FLIGHT BY A FEMALE TEAM

On 8 September 2009, Dr Ann Webb and Dr Janet Folkes (both UK) set a new world record for the longest balloon flight by an all-female team, breaking the previous record of 60 hr 12 min by just over nine hours. They set the record during the annual Coupe Aéronautique Gordon Bennett.

FASTEST TIME TO FLY A HELICOPTER AROUND THE WORLD (EASTBOUND)

Simon Oliphant-Hope (UK) flew around the world in a time of 17 days 14 hr 2 min 27 sec, at an average speed of 88.9 km/h (55.2 mph), in a MD Hughes HU/50 - MD500E single-engined helicopter from 3 to 21 June 2004. His start and finishing point was Shoreham, West Sussex, UK.

HIGHEST FLIGHT BY AN AIRSHIP

David Hempleman-Adams (UK) flew a Boland Rover A-2 airship over Rosedale, Alberta, Canada, reaching an altitude ratified by the Fédération Aéronautique Internationale (FAI) at 6,614 m (21,699 ft) on 13 December 2004.

LONGEST TIME FLYING AN AIRSHIP

In November 1928, Hugo Eckener (Germany) flew the Graf Zeppelin for 71 hours, covering a total of 6,384.5 km (3,967 miles), between Lakehurst, New Jersey, USA, and Friedrichshafen, Germany. This is the longest non-stop flight by an airship, both in distance and duration.

★FASTEST ELECTRIC AIRCRAFT

On 12 June 2009, Maurizio Cheli (Italy) piloted the electrically powered SkySpark light aircraft at the World Air Games 2009 in Turin, Italy. During the eight-minute flight, Cheli achieved a record-breaking maximum speed of 250 km/h (155 mph).

NORTH!
IVAN ANDRÉ TRIFONOV (AUSTRIA) FLEW A ONE-MAN THUNDER AND COLT CLOUDHOPPER BALLOON OVER THE GEOGRAPHIC NORTH POLE ON 20 APRIL 1996...

SOUTH!
...ON 8 JANUARY 2000, TRIFONOV BALLOONED OVER THE GEOGRAPHIC SOUTH POLE, ANTARTICA. HE IS THE FIRST MAN TO ACHIEVE BOTH FEATS.

HUMAN ENDEAVOURS

ALL AT SEA

ATLANTIC OCEAN

The **first person to row any ocean solo** is John Fairfax (UK), who rowed the Atlantic east to west in *Britannia* from 20 January to 19 July 1969. He and Sylvia Cook (UK) were also the **first team to row the Pacific Ocean**, in *Britannia II*, between 26 April 1971 and 22 April 1972.

John Fairfax also holds the record for the **first person to row two oceans**.

The **youngest person to sail the Atlantic Ocean solo** is David Sandeman (UK), who sailed between Jersey, UK, and Newport, Rhode Island, USA, aged 17 years 176 days in 1976.

★FIRST TANDEM ROW ACROSS THE INDIAN OCEAN

Guy Watts and Andrew Delaney (both UK) rowed across the Indian Ocean aboard their boat *Flying Ferkins* in 102 days 13 hr 40 min between 19 April and 30 July 2009. Guy and Andrew's incredible achievement secured the pair Guinness World Records recognition for the **first** and the **★fastest tandem row across the Indian Ocean**.

David's boat was the 10.67-m-long (35-ft) *Sea Raider* and his voyage lasted 43 days. *Guinness World Records does not endorse or sanction any attempts under the age of 16 for this category.*

INDIAN OCEAN

The **★first row across the Indian Ocean by a four-man-strong team** was completed by team Row 4 Charity – Phil McCorry, Matt Hellier, Ian Allen and Nick McCorry (all UK) – who completed the journey aboard the *Bexhill Trust Challenger* between 19 April and 26 June 2009.

The **★first row across the Indian Ocean by a female team of four** was by the Ocean Angels – Sarah Duff, Fiona Waller, Elin Haf Davis and Joanna Jackson (all UK) – who

made the crossing from 19 April to 6 July 2009 in the *Pura Vida*.

The Ocean Angels quartet completed their trip in 78 days – making it the **★fastest row across the Indian Ocean by a team of four (female)**.

The **★fastest row across the Indian Ocean** took 58 days 15 hr 8 min, between 28 April and 25 June 2009. The feat was accomplished by team Pirate Row – Angela Madsen, Doug Tumminello, Brian Flick (all USA), Helen Taylor, Paul Cannon, Ian Couch, Simon Chalk (all UK) and Bernard Fissett (Belgium) – in their boat *Aud Eamus*. The trip also gave them another record – see p.119!

PACIFIC OCEAN

Mick Dawson and Chris Martin (UK) were the **★first team to row the Pacific Ocean (west to east)**. They made the journey from Choshi, Japan, to the Golden Gate Bridge, San Francisco, California, USA, aboard their craft *Bojangles* in 189 days 10 hr 39 min, from 8 May 2009 to 13 November 2009.

WORLD
APPROXIMATELY 70% OF THE EARTH'S SURFACE IS COVERED BY WATER – AROUND 360,000,000 KM² (138,000,000 MILES²).

WATER
AT 166,241,000 KM² (64,186,000 MILES²), THE PACIFIC OCEAN IS ABOUT TWICE THE SIZE OF THE ATLANTIC (86,557,000 KM²; 33,420,000 MILES²).

FASTEST ATLANTIC CROSSING WALK ON WATER

Rémy Bricka (France) "walked" across the Atlantic Ocean between Tenerife, Canary Islands, and Trinidad on 4.2-m-long (13-ft 9-in) skis in 59 days from 2 April to 31 May 1988. He covered 5,636 km (3,502 miles), towing a platform housing supplies and essentials such as a water still. Rémy is also a seasoned musician, and has produced a string of albums and singles since the 1970s.

The Pacific Ocean is the **oldest ocean**. The rocks at the bottom are around 200 million years old.

TRIVIA

Born on 19 February 1947, Peter Bird (UK) was the ★**youngest person to row solo (east to west) across the Pacific Ocean** in his boat, *Hele-on-Britannia*. He left San Francisco, USA, on 23 August 1982 and arrived at the Great Barrier Reef, Australia, on 14 June 1983 at the age of 36 years 114 days. In doing so, he also became the **first person to row the Pacific Ocean solo**.

The **fastest solo row (west to east) across the Pacific Ocean** is 134 days 12 hr 15 min, by Gerard d'Aboville (France). He departed from Choshi, Japan, on 11 July 1991 and arrived in Ilwaco, Washington, USA,

on 21 November 1991, after covering 6,200 nautical miles (11,482 km; 7,134 miles).

The raft *Nord*, captained by Andrew Urbanczyk (USA), sailed from Half Moon Bay, California, USA, to the Pacific island of Guam, a straight-line distance of 5,110 nautical miles (9,463 km; 5,880 miles), in 136 days from 26 August 2002 to 28 January 2003. This represents the **longest non-stop journey by raft**.

ENGLISH CHANNEL

The **fastest swim of the English Channel**, and the **fastest swim of the England–France route**, is 6 hr 57 min 50 sec and was achieved by Petar Stoychev (Bulgaria), who crossed from Shakespeare Beach, Dover, UK, to Cap Gris Nez, France, on 24 August 2007.

On 24 May 2007, Micha Robyn (Belgium) achieved the

★**fastest crossing of the English Channel by waterski**, in 29 min 26 sec.

The **oldest person to swim the English Channel** was George Brunstad (USA, b. 25 August 1934), who was aged 70 years 4 days when he completed the crossing, in a time of 15 hr 59 min, on 29 August 2004.

Simon Paterson (UK) travelled underwater from France to England with an air hose attached to a pilot boat in 14 hr 50 min

on 28 July 1962, the **fastest time to swim the English Channel underwater**.

The ★**fastest crossing of the English Channel by a single canoe/kayak** is 2 hr 59 min, by Ian Wynne (UK), between Shakespeare Beach, Dover, UK, and Cap Gris Nez, France, on 5 October 2007.

★FASTEST NORTH SEA CROSSING BY A DOUBLE SEA KAYAK (CANOEING)

On 4 July 2009, Ian Castro and Simon Worsley (both UK) crossed the North Sea in a double kayak in 17 hr 53 min. They began in Southwold, UK, and ended in Zeebrugge, Belgium. The pair also achieved the **fastest North Sea crossing in single sea kayaks**: 24 hr 20 min, ending on 28 August 1999.

★FIRST CROSSING OF THE INDIAN OCEAN (TEAM)

The eight-strong team Pirate Row — comprising one Belgian, four Brits and three Americans – rowed across the Indian Ocean between 28 April and 25 June 2009 in their craft the *Aud Eamus*.

KAYAK: From the Inuit "qayak", describing a wooden canoe covered in sealskin and propelled with a paddle.

EXTRA!
IF WE'VE WHETTED YOUR APPETITE FOR ADVENTURE, TURN TO P.110 FOR MORE AMAZING FEATS OF ENDURANCE.

BEIJING, CHINA
The Imperial Palace in the centre of Beijing, China, covers a rectangle measuring 960 x 750 m (3,150 x 2,460 ft) over an area of 72 ha (178 acres). It is the **largest palace** on Earth. The outline survives from the construction of the third Ming emperor, Yongle (1403–24).

39°54'N 116°24'E

HUMAN SOCIETY

EXTRA!
TURN TO PP.126-127
FOR MORE ON
NATIONS &
POLITICS.

★ **NEW RECORD**
★ **UPDATED RECORD**

UNICEF: After World War II, children in Europe were at great risk of famine and disease, so the United Nations Children's Fund (UNICEF) was created in December 1946 to provide them with food, clothing and health care. Today, the organization provides humanitarian aid to children in developing countries world wide.

WHO?
IN JULY 2009, THE POPULATION OF AFGHANISTAN WAS ESTIMATED AT 28,395,716, OF WHOM 43.6% ARE AGED BETWEEN 0 AND 14 YEARS. (MALE, 6,343,611; FEMALE, 6,036,673.)

WHERE?
AFGHANISTAN IS SITUATED IN SOUTHERN ASIA, NORTH AND WEST OF PAKISTAN AND EAST OF IRAN. IT HAS AN AREA OF 652,230 KM² 251,827 MILES²), WHICH IS SLIGHTLY SMALLER THAN TEXAS, USA.

★MOST DANGEROUS COUNTRY IN WHICH TO BE BORN

According to the UNICEF Annual Report *The State of the World's Children*, Afghanistan is the worst country in which a child can be born. The infant mortality rate in the country is 157 deaths for every 1,000 live births. Apart from the danger posed by military operations against Taliban insurgents, the lack of access to clean water and growing insecurity in the country often make it impossible to carry out vital life-saving vaccination programmes against diseases such as poliomyelitis and measles. Afghanistan also has the world's
★**lowest adult life expectancy**: 43.8 years.

**22°59'N
120°11'E**

TAINAN, TAIWAN
The **largest display of lanterns** in a single venue numbered 47,759, at an event organized by Tainan County Government at Solar City in the "Prayer for Peace" area of Tainan Science Park in Tainan, Taiwan, on 24 February 2008.

CONTENTS

MANILA, THE PHILIPPINES

On 22 May 1998, the Central Bank of Manila, in the Philippines, issued a special commemorative 100,000-peso legal-tender banknote, measuring 22 x 33 cm (8 ½ x 11 in), printed by Giesecke Devrient of Munich, Germany. It is the **largest legal banknote**, in terms of size.

14°35'N
120°58'E

HUMAN SOCIETY
THAT'S LIFE

EXTRA! FOR MORE BIZARRE BODY RECORDS, VISIT "SKIN DEEP" ON PP.78-79.

★ **NEW RECORD**
☆ **UPDATED RECORD**

★ LONGEST MARRIAGE

Herbert Fisher (USA, b. 10 June 1905) and Zelmyra Fisher (USA, b. 10 December 1907) were married on 13 May 1924 in North Carolina, USA. They had been married for 85 years, 10 months and 8 days as of 21 March 2010.

MOST PROLIFIC MOTHER

The greatest recorded number of children born to one mother is 69, to the first wife of Feodor Vassilyev (Russia). In 27 pregnancies between 1725 and 1765, she gave birth to 16 pairs of twins, seven sets of triplets and four sets of quadruplets. Only two of the children failed to survive their infancy.

The mother also holds the records for giving birth to the most sets of twins and the most sets of quadruplets.

MOST SETS OF TRIPLETS

Maddalena Granata (Italy, 1839–1886) gave birth to 15 sets of triplets during her lifetime.

MOST ALBINO SIBLINGS

All four children of Canada's Mario and Angie Gaulin – Sarah (b. 1981), Christopher (b. 1983), Joshua (b. 1987) and Brendan (b. 1989) – were born with the rare genetic condition oculocutaneous albinism. Their father also has the condition and their mother carries the gene. Pictured above are the family's three brothers.

MOST GENERATIONS BORN ON THE SAME DAY

Five families hold the record for having four generations born on the same day: Ralph Betram Williams (USA, b. 4 July 1982), Veera Tuulia Tuijantyär Kivistö (Finland, b. 21 March 1997), Maureen Werner (USA, b. 13 October 1998), Jacob Camren Hildebrandt (USA, b. 23 August 2001) and Mion Masuda (Japan, b. 26 March 2005) all share their birthday with a parent, grandparent and great-grandparent.

MOST TWINS BORN ON THE SAME DAY

There are only two verified examples of a mother producing two sets of twins with coincident birthdays. The first is that of Laura Shelley (USA), who gave birth to Melissa Nicole and Mark Fredrick Julian, Jr on 25 March 1990 and Kayla May and Jonathan Price Moore on the same date in 2003.

The second is that of Caroline Cargado (USA), who gave birth to Keilani Marie and Kahleah Mae on 30 May 1996 and Mikayla Anee and Malia Abigail on the same date in 2003.

SILVER SURFERS FOR TIPS ON A LONG, HEALTHY MARRIAGE, FOLLOW HERBERT AND ZELMYRA'S TWITTER FEED AT HTTP://TWITTER.COM/LONGESTMARRIED

DID YOU KNOW?

THE MEDIAN AGE ON EARTH IS 28.2 YEARS OLD – HALF OF THE PLANET IS YOUNGER THAN THIS AGE, AND HALF IS OLDER. WHICH HALF ARE YOU IN?

There are, on average, 6,200 weddings every day in the USA; one-third have been married before.

TRIVIA

★ MOST "MULTIPLES" IN ONE CLASS

The 2009–10 tenth-grade class (above) at J J Pearce High School in Richardson, Texas, USA, boasts 10 sets of twins and one set of triplets. Having 10 sets of twins in one academic year is also a record, shared with the 7th grade of the 2006–07 year at Raymond J Grey Jr High School in Acton, Massachusetts, USA. At the Louis Marshall School in Brooklyn, New York City, USA, there were 29 sets of twins for the 1999–2000 school year (the **most twins in one school**).

★ MOST COUPLES MARRIED IN 24 HR

A total of 163 couples were married, one after the other, at the Singapore Botanic Gardens in Singapore on 20 September 2009.

★ LARGEST VOW RENEWAL CEREMONY

On 20 June 2009, 1,087 married couples amassed at Miami University in Oxford, Ohio, USA, for the "Miami Merger Moment", a wedding-vow-renewal event that formed part of the university's Alumni Weekend.

★ LONGEST BRIDAL VEIL

A wedding veil measuring 3,358 m (11,017 ft) long was worn by Sandra Mechleb at her wedding to Chady Abi Younis (both Lebanon) in Arnaoon, Lebanon, on 18 October 2009. The veil was longer than 140 tennis courts laid end to end.

★ SMALLEST AGE DIFFERENTIAL IN A MARRIED COUPLE

The married couple with the smallest known age difference is Allan Ramirez (b. 19 December 1980, 12:14 p.m.) and Elizabeth Ramirez (b. 19 December 1980, 12:16 p.m.) of Texas, USA, who were born just two minutes apart. They wed on 4 November 2000 in Plantersville, Texas, USA.

★ MOST EXPENSIVE DIVORCE

When media mogul Rupert Murdoch and his wife Anna (both Australia) divorced in 1999 – after 32 years of marriage – he agreed to let his ex-wife have $1.7 billion (£1.09 billion) worth of his assets as well as $110 million (£71 million) in cash. He remarried soon after.

★ FIRST ZERO-GRAVITY WEDDING

On 23 June 2009, Erin Finnegan and Noah Fulmor (both USA) wed in zero-gravity in a modified Boeing 727-200. Weightlessness was achieved by flying the plane in repeated dives from 10,970 m (36,000 ft) to 7,315 m (24,000 ft).

★ MOST SETS OF MIXED TWINS

Lightning struck twice for mixed-race parents Dean Durrant (UK, of West Indian descent) and Alison Spooner (UK) when, in March 2009, Alison delivered her second set of mixed twins: Leah and Miya. In 2001, she gave birth to mixed twins – the dark-skinned Hayleigh and fair-skinned Layren.

ODDS
A MIXED-RACE COUPLE HAS A 1-IN-500,000 CHANCE OF HAVING A SET OF MIXED TWINS, BUT NO STATISTICS EXIST FOR LEAH AND MIYA - TWO SETS IS SUCH A RARE OCCURRENCE!

TAIPEI, TAIWAN

The **largest gathering of twins** took place in Taiwan on 12 November 1999, when 3,961 pairs converged on the square of Taipei City Hall. The twins came from as far away as the UK, Germany, India and the USA, and ranged in age from one month to 88 years.

25°02'N
121°38'E

DEATH

QUIZ!
ON AVERAGE, HOW MANY GRAVES DID JOHANN HEINRICH KARL THIME DIG A YEAR IN HIS 50-YEAR CAREER?

SEE P.278 FOR THE ANSWER.

★ MOST EXPENSIVE GHOSTS

Two vials supposedly containing the exorcized spirits of an old man and a young girl were sold at an online auction in March 2010 for NZ$2,830 ($1,990; £1,300). New Zealander Avie Woodbury claimed to have enlisted the help of an exorcist and a ouija board to contact and trap the spirits in July 2009.

★ OLDEST KNOWN CATACOMBS

The first burial chambers to be referred to directly as catacombs were those beneath San Sebastiano ad Catacumbas (aka Sebastiano fuori le mura) in Rome, Italy, which was built in the early 4th century. There are many such tombs along the Via Appia (Appian Way) – the ancient road that leads from Rome to Brindisi – as burials were considered Christian and outlawed within the walls of Rome.

★ LARGEST AUTOMATED TOMB FACILITY

The six-storey Kouanji Buddhist Temple in Tokyo, Japan, is an automated tomb facility that, as of 1 January 2010, houses 6,850 human remains. Square marble boxes – which can contain the cremated remains ("cremains") of up to nine relatives – are accessed by visitors using a swipe card that identifies the location of the remains and delivers them via a conveyor-belt system. Each burial costs around Y800,000 (£5,370; $8,800).

★ LARGEST GATHERING OF ZOMBIES

The Big Chill music festival in Ledbury, Herefordshire, UK, was swamped by 4,026 zombies on 6 August 2009. The living dead were taking part in filming for the forthcoming Film4/Warp Films production *I Spit on Your Rave*. Set nine years in the future, the movie stars comedian Noel Fielding (UK) as a zombie king in a Britain wiped out by a virus.

CATACOMB: Underground tomb or burial chamber, suspected to derive from the Latin *cata tumbas* – "among the tombs".

LARGEST COMMUNAL TOMB

A communal tomb housing 180,000 World War II dead on Okinawa, Japan, was enlarged in 1985 to accommodate another 9,000 bodies thought to be buried on the island.

FARTHEST RESTING PLACE

On 31 July 1999, America's *Lunar Prospector* spacecraft crashed into the Moon after 18 months of successful mission operations. Incorporated into this orbiter was a small (3.8-cm; 1.5-in) polycarbonate container holding 28.3 g (1 oz) of the remains of the pioneering planetary scientist Dr Eugene Shoemaker (USA). Wrapped around the container was a piece of foil inscribed with some of Shoemaker's work.

LARGEST MASS CREMATION

In December 1997, at a temple in Smut Scom, Thailand, tonnes of bones (including 21,347 skulls) were cremated to mark the end of urban burials in Bangkok, the overcrowded Thai capital. The bones represented unclaimed remains from a Chinese cemetery in Bangkok.

GENEROUS SPIRITS
PROCEEDS FROM THE SALE OF THE EXPENSIVE SPIRITS – TRAPPED IN BOTTLES WITH HOLY WATER – WILL GO TO AN ANIMAL CHARITY... ONCE THE EXORCIST'S FEE HAS BEEN PAID!

41°47′N 123°27′E

SHENYANG, CHINA
A brush measuring 5.6 m (18 ft 4 in) long and 2.06 m (6 ft 9 in) wide – the **largest calligraphy brush** – was used by calligrapher Zhang Kesi (China) to paint the Chinese character for "long" (which means "dragon") at the China International Horticultural Exposition on 6 May 2006.

★LARGEST OSSUARY

The skeletal remains of 6 million people lie, neatly arranged, in subterranean catacombs – aka ossuaries or charnel houses – beneath the streets of Paris, France. The city is riddled with an estimated 300 km (186 miles) of tunnels and pathways, of which 11,000 m^2 (nearly 3 acres) are packed tightly with the bones of those re-interred from the city's overflowing cemeteries in the late 1700s.

LARGEST LIVE TV AUDIENCE

The worldwide TV audience for the funeral of Diana, Princess of Wales (UK, 1961–97) on 6 September 1997 at Westminster Abbey, London, UK, was watched by an estimated global audience of 2.5 billion.

LARGEST VIRTUAL FUNERAL

In October 2005, an avid computer gamer known only as Snowly (China) indulged in a three-day non-stop marathon of the Massively Multiplayer Online Role-Playing Game *World of Warcraft* (Blizzard, USA). While attempting a particularly challenging task in the game, Snowly died of fatigue in the real world. Over 100 gamers visited a virtual cathedral inside the game, where a service was held in her memory.

FASTEST HEARSE

Joe Gosschalk (Australia) covered a quarter mile in his 1979 Ford LTD P6 hearse in 13.7 seconds at 158 km/h (98 mph) at Willowbank Raceway in Queensland, Australia, on 10 June 2005. The hearse has a 5.7-litre (351-cu-in) engine with nitrous oxide boost. Its licence plates read "Undead".

LONGEST CAREER AS A GRAVE DIGGER

It is recorded that Johann Heinrich Karl Thieme, sexton of Aldenburg, Germany, dug 23,311 graves during a 50-year career. After his death in 1826, his understudy dug *his* grave!

LARGEST FUNERALS

The funeral of India's charismatic C N Annadurai (above, d. 3 Feb 1969), a Chennai Chief Minister, was attended by 15 million people, according to police sources.

• The queue at the grave of the popular Russian singer Vladimir Visotsky (d. 28 Jul 1980) stretched for 10 km (6 miles).

★ NEW RECORD ★ UPDATED RECORD

★LONGEST-RUNNING FESTIVAL OF THE DEAD

In one form or another, Día de los Muertos (Day of the Dead) in Mexico has been celebrated in this part of the world for over 3,500 years. To honour their dead, and the goddess Mictecacihuatl (the "Lady of the Dead"), the Aztecs and other Meso-Americans would perform rites and rituals, often involving skulls. Today, the tradition continues on 1 and 2 November each year, with the emphasis on partying and celebrating with the family, often in flamboyant costumes and masks.

DEATH
IN THE 16TH CENTURY, THE SPANISH CONQUISTADORS, UNABLE TO STOP THE "PAGAN" CEREMONY, MOVED DAY OF THE DEAD TO COINCIDE WITH HALLOWEEN, BUT THE TWO ARE NOT REALLY CONNECTED.

MASK
REVELLERS WISHING TO COMMEMORATE DECEASED RELATIVES AND FRIENDS DON WOODEN SKULL MASKS OR CALACAS AND TAKE PART IN FEASTING AND DANCING.

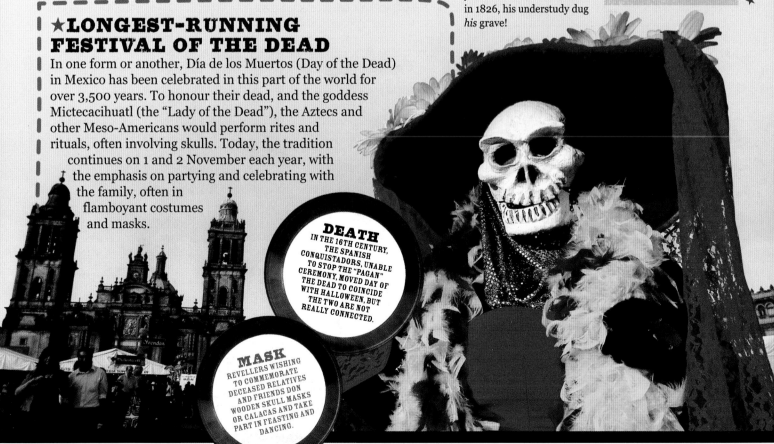

PYONGYANG, NORTH KOREA

The world's **longest train journey without changing trains** is one of 10,214 km (6,346 miles) from Moscow, Russia, to Pyongyang in North Korea. One train a week makes the journey by this route, which includes sections of the famous Trans-Siberian line. It is scheduled to take 7 days 20 hr 25 min.

39°00'N
125°30'E

HUMAN SOCIETY
NATIONS & POLITICS

★LONGEST-SERVING DEMOCRATIC HEAD

Lee Kuan Yew was Prime Minister of Singapore from 1959 to 1990 – a total of 31 consecutive years. Despite leaving power, Kuan Yew remains an important political figure in Singapore and is "Minister Mentor" to the current Prime Minister, his son Lee Hsien Loong.

★HIGHEST DEATH RATE FROM AIDS (COUNTRY)

In 2007, incidence of AIDS-related deaths in Zimbabwe reached a shocking 1,060 people per 100,000 population. An estimated 15.3% of Zimbabwe's population is living with AIDS but drought, famine and a poor economy have all made matters worse.

★LARGEST COUNTRY WITHOUT AN AIRPORT

With an area of 468 km² (180 m²) and a population of 71,822, Andorra is the largest country without an airport. Visitors wishing to travel there by air are advised to fly to Barcelona and take a bus the rest of the way.

★MOST CORRUPT COUNTRY

According to Transparency International's most recent Corruption Perceptions Index, in 2009 Somalia scored 1.1 on its 10-point corruption scale. By contrast, New Zealand rated as the **least corrupt country** with a score of 9.4.

★COUNTRY WITH MOST POLITICAL ARMED GROUPS

On 7 January 2010, an independent commission in the Philippines began work on disbanding politicians' private armies. According to the Philippines' Defence Secretary Norberto Gonzales, there are 132 armed groups, many led by politicians, totalling some 10,000 armed individuals spread throughout the country. Such private armies are typically used to assist the official security forces and to defend communities endangered by communist or Muslim separatist guerrillas, but are also often used to maintain local politicians in power by intimidating rivals, voters and journalists.

★LEAST STABLE STATE

Somalia has lacked an effective central government since 1991, when the previous president was overthrown. Since Ethiopian troops left Somalia in January 2009, its stability rating has fallen further according to *Jane's Intelligence Review*.

SEOUL, SOUTH KOREA

The **first cloned dog to survive birth** was Snuppy, an Afghan hound puppy, created by Hwang Woo-Suk (South Korea) and his team of scientists at Seoul National University (SNU) in South Korea, and born by Caesarean section on 25 April 2005.

★COUNTRIES MOST THREATENED BY INUNDATION

The collection of reef islands and atolls (such as Funafuti Atoll, above) that constitute the low-lying nations of Tuvalu and the Maldives are under imminent threat of disappearing under the waves due to a combination of factors including rising sea levels due to global warming. At their highest elevations, Tuvalu and the Maldives are 5 m (16 ft 3 in) and 2.4 m (8 ft) above sea level respectively.

★LARGEST MARCH AGAINST ILLEGAL DRUGS

The "Grand BIDA March" against illegal drugs included 332,963 people and was held in Manila in the Philippines, on 21 March 2009.

★LARGEST OPIUM PRODUCER

Despite a reduction in recent years, Afghanistan still had the largest opium harvest in 2008, according to United Nations statistics, with a 7,700-tonne (8,480-ton) crop, worth $3.4 billion (£2.3 billion) in the illegal heroin trade.

★LARGEST OPIUM SEIZURE

According to the 2009 report of the United Nations Office on Drugs and Crime (UNODC), Afghanistan's eastern neighbour, Iran seized 427,147 kg (941,698 lb) of opium in 2007, a figure that constitutes 84% of all opium seizures worldwide in that year.

Iran also registered the largest seizures of heroin and morphine in 2007 with 25,580 kg (56,394 lb) – 28% of the global total.

★LARGEST DONOR OF FOREIGN AID

The USA donated $21.7 billion (£10.8 billion) worth of aid to foreign countries in 2007, according to figures published by *The Economist*. The ★**largest recipient of foreign aid** in 2007 was Iraq, which received $9.1 billion (£4.5 billion).

★MOST HUMAN RIGHTS ACTIVISTS KILLED

The 2010 Human Rights Watch World Report revealed that eight murders were perpetrated against human rights supporters in Russia during 2009.

★HIGHEST NATURAL POPULATION INCREASE

The population of the East African state of Niger is currently estimated to grow 3.73% between 2010 and 2015, largely thanks to the country's high fertility rate. It's estimated that there will be 6.86 children for each woman of child-bearing age over the same period.

★LAST SPEAKER OF BO

Bo, the tongue of the Bo tribe of the Andaman Islands in the Bay of Bengal, is said to have emerged 10,000 years ago. In January 2010, it ceased to be a living language when its last native speaker, Boa Sr (pictured above), died.

QUEEN... THE LONGEST-REIGNING LIVING QUEEN IS HER MAJESTY QUEEN ELIZABETH II (B. 21 APRIL 1926), WHO SUCCEEDED TO THE THRONE ON 6 FEBRUARY 1952.

...VIC THE LONGEST-REIGNING QUEEN EVER IS VICTORIA (UK), QUEEN OF GREAT BRITAIN FROM 1837 TO 1901 AND EMPRESS OF INDIA FROM 1876, WHO REIGNED FOR 63 YEARS 216 DAYS.

DID YOU KNOW?

THE LARGEST COUNTRY IN TERMS OF SIZE IS RUSSIA, WHOSE 17,098,242-KM² (6,601,668-MILE²) AREA STRETCHES OVER THE CONTINENTS OF EUROPE AND ASIA.

According to the CIA World Factbook, China has a record population of 1.3 billion citizens.

TRIVIA

LONGEST-REIGNING LIVING MONARCH

Born on 5 December 1927, King Bhumibol Adulyadej, King Rama IX of the Chakri dynasty, of Thailand ascended to the throne on 9 June 1946 following the death of his older brother. His formal coronation did not take place until 5 May 1950, and has since reigned without interruption for over 63 years.

HUMAN SOCIETY
CONFLICT

National Union of Journalists of the Philippines

★ LARGEST CONTRIBUTOR TO UN PEACEKEEPING FORCES

As of 28 February 2010, Bangladesh is the largest contributor of uniformed personnel to UN peacekeeping missions, with a total of 10,852 blue-hatted personnel deployed worldwide.

★ MOST DANGEROUS COUNTRY FOR THE MEDIA

According to the International Federation of Journalists, 74 journalists have been killed in the Philippines since 2002, with 36 being killed in 2009, in the ongoing bloody conflict between the Moro Islamic Liberation Front (MILF) separatists and government forces.

★ LARGEST ARMY

According to 2008 estimates published in the CIA World Factbook, the manpower available for military service in China is 375,009,345 people, with 218,459,000 active military personnel.

★ LARGEST SCUTTLING OF SHIPS

On 27 November 1942, the French fleet in Toulon, France, was scuttled on the orders of the French Admiralty to avoid their capture by German forces. Of the 73 ships sunk in the action, 57 were major vessels, including two battleships, two battle cruisers, four heavy cruisers, two light cruisers, an aircraft transporter, 30 destroyers and 16 submarines. Three submarines escaped Toulon to join up with the Allies, however. Many support vessels were also scuttled in the action.

★ YOUNGEST SERVICEMAN TO DIE IN WORLD WAR II

On 5 February 2010, on what would have been his 83rd birthday, Reginald Earnshaw (UK) was named by the Commonwealth War Graves Commission as the youngest serviceman to have been killed in World War II. He lied about his age in order to join the British Royal Navy, claiming to be 15 years old, and went on to serve as a cabin boy. Reginald was killed on 6 July 1941 at the age of 14 years and 152 days, just five months after joining up, when his ship, the *SS Devon*, was attacked by a German aircraft.

REBELS
BURMESE GOVERNMENT FORCES AREN'T ALONE IN RECRUITING VERY YOUNG ARMY PERSONNEL. THEIR REBEL OPPONENTS ALSO EMPLOY CHILD SOLDIERS, SUCH AS THE ONE PICTURED HERE, IN THEIR STRUGGLE.

★ MOST CHILD SOLDIERS

Under international law, the recruitment of children under the age of 15 to serve in armed forces is a war crime. Consequently it is difficult to collect data on the use of child soldiers. That said, a 2001 report issued by Human Rights Watch suggested that of the 350,000 soldiers serving in Burma's armed forces, 70,000 were estimated to be under 18.

★ SMALLEST ARMY

The smallest and **oldest standing army** is the Pontifical Swiss Guard in the Vatican City, which was created in its current form on 21 January 1506 and had 110 active guards as of 2006. Swiss Guardsmen must be single, Swiss-Catholic men over 1.7 m (5 ft 8 in) tall.

★ OLDEST LIVING WORLD WAR I VETERAN

Frank Woodruff Buckles was born in Harrison County, Missouri, USA, on 1 February 1901 and became the oldest surviving World War I veteran on 18 July 2009, aged 108 years 168 days. Mr Buckles served as an ambulance driver in the Army from 1917 to 1919; he is also the last of 4.7 million Americans who served during the conflict.

★ MOST PEOPLE KILLED BY FRIENDLY FIRE

During their 1788 campaign against the Turks, the Austrian Army crossed a bridge at Karansebes, Turkey. An advance guard of cavalrymen stopped to buy alcohol from local peasants. The infantrymen bringing up the rear wanted a share of the booze. When the cavalry refused, the infantry tried to frighten them, firing their rifles in the air. The surrounding Austrian forces were confused by this and opened fire on their colleagues, causing the utility horses at the rear to stampede. The fighting raged for hours, resulting in over 10,000 dead and injured Austrians.

★ NEW RECORD
★ UPDATED RECORD

★ LARGEST CONTRIBUTOR TO THE UN PEACEKEEPING BUDGET

The UN's Peacekeeping budget between 1 July 2009 and 30 June 2010 is $7.9 billion (£5.2 billion). The largest single contributor to this figure is the USA, which donates 27.17% of the total; the next largest donor is Japan, which provides 12.53% of the total peacekeeping budget.

★ MOST PEOPLE DEPLOYED IN PEACEKEEPING OPERATIONS

According to the Stockholm International Peace Research Institute (SIPRI), a total of 187,586 people were deployed on peacekeeping missions in 2008. Military forces accounted for 166,146 of those deployed. The largest peace operation occurred in Afghanistan.

★ HIGHEST AWARD FOR ANIMAL GALLANTRY

Introduced in 1943 by Maria Dickin, the founder of the People's Dispensary for Sick Animals (PDSA), the Dickin Medal is the highest honour for animals serving in a military conflict. On 24 February 2010, an eight-year-old black Labrador named Treo became the latest animal to be awarded the medal in recognition of the numerous lives he had saved in Afghanistan sniffing out and locating roadside bombs.

★ MOST LAND-MINED COUNTRY

According to the United Nations, Afghanistan now shares with Iraq the record for the most mined country in the world with an estimated total of 10,000,000 mines each. In Afghanistan, more than 60 Afghans fall victim to land mines every month.

LONG...
THE LONGEST WAR THAT COULD BE DESCRIBED AS CONTINUOUS WAS THE THIRTY YEARS WAR FOUGHT BETWEEN THE HOLY ROMAN EMPIRE AND VARIOUS EUROPEAN COUNTRIES FROM 1618 TO 1648.

...SHORT
THE SHORTEST WAR WAS FOUGHT BETWEEN BRITAIN AND ZANZIBAR (NOW PART OF MODERN TANZANIA). IT LASTED FROM 9:00 A.M. TO 9:45 A.M. ON 27 AUGUST 1896 AND ENDED IN A SWIFT BRITISH VICTORY.

OSAKA, JAPAN
The **longest monorail** is the Osaka Monorail, in Osaka, Japan, which has a total length of 22.2 km (13.8 miles). Fully operational since August 1997, its main line runs between Osaka International Airport and Hankyu Railway Minami Ibaraki Station.

34°40'N 135°30'E

CRIME

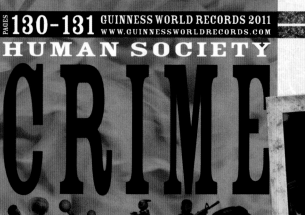

★WORST WAR CRIMINAL CONVICTED IN THE 21ST CENTURY

Kang Kek Ieu, or "Comrade Duch", ran the Tuol Sleng prison in Cambodia, south-east Asia, when the country was under the control of Pol Pot's regime. Between 1977 and 1979, of the 15,000 people who entered the prison, only around 15 emerged alive. This figure makes Kang Kek Ieu the worst war criminal convicted in the 21st century.

★LARGEST SPEEDING FINE

In January 2010, an unnamed Swiss millionaire was given a record fine by the regional court in St Gallen, Switzerland, of 307,496 Swiss Francs (£180,000; $290,000) for speeding. He was caught driving his red Ferrari Testarossa 57 km/h (35 mph) faster than the legal speed limit allowed. The huge fine was based on the driver's wealth, which was assessed at 24 million Swiss Francs (£14.1 million; $22.7 million), and the fact that he was a repeat traffic offender.

★HIGHEST PRISON RIOT DEATH TOLL

The war for supremacy between different drug cartels in Mexico, which saw over 5,400 people killed in 2008, has been carried into Mexican jails. At least 83 prisoners were killed and many more injured in a number of riots during a six-month period covering part of 2008 and part of 2009. The trend appears to have continued into 2010, with the latest riot on 20 January 2010, when at least 23 inmates of rival drug trafficking gangs in a prison in the northern Mexican state of Durango were killed.

★MOST MURDERS

According to the 10th United Nations Survey of Crime Trends and Operations of Criminal Justice Systems, covering the period 2005–06, India has the greatest number of murders of any of the 86 countries listed in the report. It had a total of 32,481 in 2006.

★LARGEST BACKLOG OF COURT CASES

According to an annual report for the Delhi High Court, India, by Chief Justice A P Shah, there is such a backlog of cases that it could take the court 466 years to clear. The court hears cases in an average time of 4 min 55 sec, but has 700,000 cases waiting to be heard out of a national backlog reported by the United Nations Development Programme to be in the order of 20 million. The court has 629 civil cases and around 17 criminal cases pending that are over 20 years old.

★MOST PRISONERS ON DEATH ROW

According to Amnesty International's Annual Report 2009, the country with the most prisoners awaiting execution in 2008 is Pakistan, with over 7,000 – almost one third of the estimated 24,000 on Death Row around the world. In the same year, Pakistan executed at least 36 people and reportedly sentenced 236 to death.

★LARGEST PASSPORT FORGERY

On 8 May 2009, Mandip Sharma (India) and Brando Sibayan (Philippines) received jail terms of four years each from a UK court for running the largest known passport forgery factory. On searching a property in Leicester, UK, officers from the Border Agency found up to 4,000 counterfeit passports for several EU countries.

WORST PHOTOFIT...?

A contender for worst photofit was considered in early 2010, but was rejected by GWR as it actually achieved its purpose. The extremely basic picture of an alleged murderer – drawn for Bolivian police by a neighbour of the victim, Rafael Vargas, who was stabbed seven times – has led to two arrests so far.

EXTRA! FOR THE LATEST DEFENCE TECHNOLOGY, SHOOT TO PP.208-209.

★OLDEST CRIMINAL GANG (AVERAGE AGE)

In March 2009, a group of British criminals with an average age of 57 (the oldest being 83) pleaded guilty to counterfeiting charges and were sentenced to a total of 13 years. They had been able to produce a finished batch of notes worth £800 ($1,136) in just half an hour.

★OLDEST PERSON ACCUSED OF MURDER (FEMALE)

A post mortem examination determined that Elizabeth Barrow (USA), aged 100, had been strangled in her nursing home in Massachusetts, USA, on 24 September 2009. The accused is Laura Lundquist (USA), the victim's roommate, who is 98 years old and a dementia sufferer.

★FIRST JUDICIAL SINGLE-DRUG EXECUTION

On 8 December 2009, convicted murderer Kenneth Biros was executed in Ohio, USA, using a single, large injection of anaesthetic. It is the first time that a single injection has been used in a legal, judicial execution in a democratic state. Normally, a mixture of three drugs is used.

★MOST PRISONERS

According to data from the International Centre for Prison Studies, King's College, London, UK, the USA has 2.3 million prisoners behind bars, of whom 1,610,446 were sentenced prisoners at the end of 2008. China, with four times the population of the USA, has 1.6 million prisoners. The ★country with least prisoners, out of a list of 218 countries for which data was available, was San Marino, with only one.

★LARGEST FINE

In September 2009, US pharmaceutical giant Pfizer Inc. and its subsidiary Pharmacia & Upjohn Company Inc. agreed to pay $2.3 billion (£1.4 billion), the largest-ever health-care fraud settlement, to resolve criminal and civil liability arising from the illegal promotion of certain pharmaceutical products. Of the total, Pfizer will pay a $1.195 billion (£0.75 billion) fine – the largest criminal fine in US history.

★HIGHEST BAIL SET

In New York, USA, on 16 October 2009, bail for the billion-dollar hedge fund owner Raj Rajaratnam (Sri Lanka) was set at a record $100 million (£61.9 million) after his arrest on criminal charges for alleged insider trading.

★LONGEST JURY DELIBERATION

In a 1992 lawsuit in Long Beach, California, USA, which took 11 years and 6 months to reach trial, Shirley and Jason McClure (USA) accused city officials of violating the US Fair Housing Act by conspiring to prevent them from opening a chain of residential homes. The jury deliberated for four-and-a-half months and eventually awarded McClure $25.5 million (£16.8 million) in damages.

DID YOU KNOW?
FROM THE 1997 ELECTION TO *GWR 2011* GOING TO PRESS IN 2010, THE THEN UK LABOUR GOVERNMENT HAD INTRODUCED 4,289 NEW CRIMINAL OFFENCES.

As UK PM, Gordon Brown introduced an average of 33 new offences per month.

TRIVIA

LARGEST PRISON

Housing about 5,000 inmates but with a total capacity of 6,750, the Twin Towers Correctional Facility in Los Angeles, USA, has a 140,000-m² (1.5 million-ft²) floor area and is situated on a 4-ha (10-acre) site. In 2004, it cost around $50 million (£25.9 million) a year to run – $61.21 (£31,77) a day for each inmate.

★ NEW RECORD
★ UPDATED RECORD

QUIZ!
HOW OLD WAS THE OLDEST PERSON TO BE ACCUSED OF MURDER?
SEE P.278 FOR THE ANSWER.

IN...
THE PRISON OPENED IN 1997 BUT THERE WAS NO BUDGET TO RUN IT SO IT REMAINED EMPTY. THE GUARDS EMPLOYED THERE ACTUALLY HAD TO STOP PEOPLE BREAKING IN!

...OUT
INMATE KEVIN PULLUM WALKED OUT OF A TWIN TOWERS EMPLOYEE EXIT ON 6 JULY 2001, TWO HOURS AFTER BEING CONVICTED OF ATTEMPTED MURDER. HE WAS RE-CAPTURED 18 DAYS LATER.

LOS ANGELES COUNTY SHERIFF'S DEPARTMENT
TWIN TOWERS CORRECTIONAL FACILITY
INMATE RECEPTION CENTER • MEDICAL SERVICES

YOKOHAMA, JAPAN
The world's **tallest lighthouse** is the steel "Marine Tower" at Yamashita Park in Yokohama, Japan, at 106 m (348 ft) high. It has a visibility range of 32 km (20 miles) and an observatory located 100 m (328 ft) above ground.

35°27'N
139°38'E

HUMAN SOCIETY
WEALTH & COMMERCE

★ LARGEST LOTTERY PRIZE FUND

Spain's Christmas lottery, nicknamed "El Gordo" (Fat One), is a Christmas tradition in the country and is the world's biggest lottery in terms of the total sum paid out. The 2009 lottery showered €2.3 billion ($3.3 billion; £2.1 billion) on its winners. The top prize went to the 1,950 lucky ticket holders who won €300,000 ($430,797; £269,694) each.

★ LARGEST FIND OF ANGLO-SAXON TREASURE

Metal detectorist Terry Herbert (UK) found more than 1,500 gold and silver pieces, estimated to date from the 7th century, in a farmer's field in Staffordshire, UK. The find, which was announced on 24 September 2009, included at least 650 items of gold, weighing more than 5 kg (11 lb), and 530 silver objects weighing over 1 kg (2.2 lb).

OOH! THE ORAPA DIAMOND MINE, BOTSWANA, IS THE WORLD'S LARGEST BY AREA. IT COVERS 1.18 KM² (0.45 MILES²) AND IN 2003 PRODUCED 16.3 MILLION CARATS (3,260 KG) OF DIAMONDS.

★ RICHEST PERSON (PRESENT DAY)

Mexico's Carlos Slim Helú's estimated worth of $53.5 billion (£35.23 billion) sees him top the 2010 *Forbes* list of the World's Billionaires.

Slim has amassed a fortune that includes fixed-line telephone assets and a construction conglomerate, plus stakes in financial group Inbursa, Bronco Drilling, Independent News & Media, Saks and New York Times Co. He increased his wealth by $18.5 billion (£11.6 billion) in 2009, which helped knock Bill Gates (USA) off the top spot.

★ RICHEST WOMAN

Christy Walton (USA), former daughter-in-law of deceased Wal-Mart founder Sam Walton, has a fortune put by *Forbes* at $22.5 billion (£15 billion). Her sister-in-law Alice Walton (USA) is runner-up, with $19.5 billion (£13.8 billion).

LARGEST PRIVATELY OWNED YACHT

The *Eclipse*, which is owned by Chelsea Football Club (UK) owner Roman Abramovich (Russia), measures 170 m (560 ft) long and was constructed by German shipbuilding company Blohm + Voss. The price of the yacht is estimated at £302 million ($485 million). It is equipped with two helicopter pads, 11 guest cabins, a mini-submarine and its own missile-defence system.

OW! IN THE FINANCIAL YEAR ENDING 2009, THE WORLD'S 1,125 BILLIONAIRES LOST AN ESTIMATED $1.4 TRILLION (£878 BILLION) BETWEEN THEM.

QUIZ! WHO DID CARLOS SLIM HELÚ REPLACE AS THE WORLD'S RICHEST MAN?
SEE P.278 FOR THE ANSWER.

KAWASAKI, JAPAN
35°81'N 139°42'E
The world's **shortest escalator** is the moving walkway at Okadaya More's Shopping Mall at Kawasaki-shi, Japan, which has a vertical height of 83.4 cm (2 ft 8 in). The escalator was installed by Hitachi Ltd.

CASH: The word "cash" comes from the French word "caisse", meaning "money box".

★LARGEST LOSS OF PERSONAL FORTUNE

The collapse of the world's economy saw a decline in many fortunes, but none more dramatic than that of Anil Ambani (India). By March 2009, he had lost an estimated $32 billion (£22.5 billion) – 76% of his fortune – owing to the crumbling value of shares in his companies Reliance Power, Reliance Communications and Reliance Capital.

★LARGEST DECLINE IN BILLIONAIRES IN ONE YEAR

The financial year ending 2009 saw billionaires melting away like snow in spring. According to *Forbes'* annual list, the world lost 332 billionaires, leaving just 793 of these rare creatures compared to 1,125 in the previous year.

★WEALTHIEST UNIVERSITY

Harvard University, located in Cambridge, Massachusetts, is America's oldest university (established 1636) and is also the world's wealthiest. When assessed in June 2009, Harvard's endowment was $26 billion (£15.85 billion), down from $36.9 billion (£22.4 billion) the previous year.

★LARGEST DEPOSIT LOST

In 2008, Mikhail Prokhorov (Russia) agreed to pay €390 million ($528.9 million; £353.8 million) for the villa *Leopolda de Villefranche-sur-Mer*, owned by heiress Lily Safra (Brazil), and located outside Nice, France. Prokhorov withdrew from the sale in 2009, losing his €40-million ($54.2-million; £36.2-million) deposit in the process.

LARGEST LIFE ASSURANCE POLICY

July 2010 marked the 20th anniversary of Peter Rosengard's (UK) record insurance sale. In 1990, he sold the largest ever single life assurance policy for $100 million (£62.7 million) on the life of a well-known US entertainment industry figure. Incredibly, he made the sale during a cold call from a public telephone box!

INSTANT EXPERT

⊗ THE WORLD'S ★FIRST DOLLAR BILLIONAIRE WAS JOHN D ROCKEFELLER (USA, 1839-1937). HE MADE HIS FORTUNE IN THE OIL BUSINESS AND WAS WORTH AN ESTIMATED $1.4 BILLION (£0.28 BILLION).

⊗ IT IS ESTIMATED THAT ROCKEFELLER'S WEALTH WOULD BE THE EQUIVALENT OF $210 BILLION (£140.6 BILLION) TODAY (MEASURED AS A PERCENTAGE OF GDP), WHICH WOULD MAKE HIM, ARGUABLY, THE RICHEST PERSON EVER.

⊗ ROCKEFELLER GAVE AWAY THE VAST MAJORITY OF HIS WEALTH TO WORTHY CAUSES.

★LARGEST CORPORATE BANKRUPTCY

On 15 September 2008, US investment bank Lehman Brothers Holdings Inc. filed for bankruptcy to the tune of $613 billion (£380 billion), having succumbed to the subprime mortgage crisis that started the worldwide recession in 2008.

DID YOU KNOW?

IN 2009, NEW YORK CITY, USA, REGAINED THE TITLE OF ★CITY WITH THE MOST BILLIONAIRES FROM MOSCOW, RUSSIA. THERE ARE CURRENTLY 55 MEMBERS OF THE BIG APPLE BILLIONAIRES CLUB.

TRIVIA

The world's highest average net income in relation to cost of living is earned by the citizens of Zürich, Switzerland.

FULD
PICTURED IS RICHARD FULD – CHAIRMAN AND CHIEF EXEC OF LEHMAN BROTHERS HOLDINGS – WITH PROTESTORS IN WASHINGTON, DC, USA, ON 6 OCTOBER 2008.

The Tower Belcon is a concrete-conveying robot that was completed in 1998. It is the world's **largest robot**, measuring 70.5 m (231 ft) high, with a 76.5-m (250-ft) boom, and can deliver 180 m³ (6,356 ft³) of concrete an hour. It was designed and manufactured by Mitsubishi Heavy Industries, Tokyo, Japan.

HUMAN SOCIETY

CONSUMPTION & WASTE

EXTRA! FOR A DIFFERENT KIND OF CONSUMPTION, LOOK AT EXTREME CUISINE ON P.138.

★ NEW RECORD
★ UPDATED RECORD

LONGEST-SURVIVING GREENHOUSE GAS

Of all the gases emitted by mankind that add to global warming, the longest lived is the refrigerant gas tetrafluoromethane. It can last for 50,000 years in the atmosphere.

★ LARGEST CONSUMER OF ENERGY

The country that consumes more energy than any other is the USA, which was shown to have used 2,321 Mtoe (million tonnes of oil equivalent) in 2006, the latest year for which records exist.

★ LARGEST PRODUCER OF ENERGY (COUNTRY)

China produces more energy annually than any other nation, with 1,749 Mtoe (million tonnes of oil equivalent) as of 2006.

★ LARGEST CONSUMPTION OF ENERGY PER HEAD

The people of Qatar each consumed an average of 22,057 kg (48,627 lb) in 2006. Iceland was in second place with 14,237 kg (31,387 lb) per head, while the USA, which is the greatest annual consumer of energy, is 10th on the list with 7,768 kg (17,125 lb).

★ HIGHEST CARBON DIOXIDE EMISSIONS PER CAPITA

Citizens of Kuwait emitted 36.9 tonnes (40.6 tons) of carbon dioxide per person in 2005.

★ FIRST CLIMIGRATION

In 2009, Alaskan human rights lawyer Robin Bronen coined the word "climigration" to describe the forced migration of people resulting from climate-induced ecological changes in a community's environment.

Bronen used the term in a report on Alaskan indigenous communities who were having to relocate due to climate change. The Intergovernmental Panel on Climate Change (IPCC) has estimated that there will be 150 million such "climate refugees" seeking new homes by 2050.

★ LARGEST PRODUCER OF CARBON DIOXIDE EMISSIONS (COUNTRY)

According to a report compiled by the Netherlands Environmental Assessment Agency, as of 2006 the country responsible for the greatest carbon dioxide emissions is China, which produced 6,200 million tonnes of CO_2 compared with 5,800 million tonnes produced by the USA. By comparison, the UK produced 600 million tonnes.

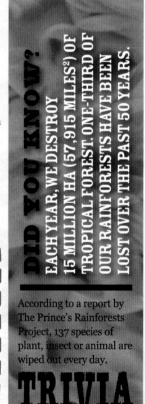

DID YOU KNOW? EACH YEAR, WE DESTROY 15 MILLION HA (57,915 MILES²) OF TROPICAL FOREST. ONE-THIRD OF OUR RAINFORESTS HAVE BEEN LOST OVER THE PAST 50 YEARS.

According to a report by The Prince's Rainforests Project, 137 species of plant, insect or animal are wiped out every day.

TRIVIA

43°00'N 141°21'E **SAPPORO, JAPAN**
The **most consecutive league games scoring hat-tricks** by a football player in a national top division is four by Masashi Nakayama (Japan) for Jubilo Iwata in the Japanese League – First Stage between 15 and 29 April 1998.

MOST TREES PLANTED IN AN HOUR (TEAM)

A team of 100 people planted 26,422 trees at Gransha Park, Derry, UK, on 5 December 2009. BBC Breathing Places achieved the feat in partnership with Conservation Volunteers NI, Western Health & Social Care Trust, Northern Ireland EA and Derry City Council.

★LARGEST ISLAND EVACUATION AS A RESULT OF CLIMATE CHANGE

In 1995, more than 500,000 inhabitants of Bhola Island, Bangladesh, were forced to evacuate when rising seas, attributed to climate change, threatened to flood the island.

★GREENEST CITY

Masdar City in Abu Dhabi, UAE, designed by the British architect firm Foster and Partners, is the world's first city designed to be zero-carbon and zero-waste. All of its power is generated from renewable resources, and all waste material is recycled. Cars are banned in favour of electric, driverless, underground vehicles, so the city's projected 50,000 citizens should leave no carbon footprint.

★MOST STEEL CANS COLLECTED IN ONE MONTH

South African recycling venture Collect-a-Can collected 2,122,238 steel cans weighing 66,319.95 kg (146,210 lb 7 oz) from schools across South Africa between 1 and 31 October 2009, in an initiative to promote the recycling of cans in the country.

★LARGEST COLLECTION OF CLOTHES TO RECYCLE

On 12 August 2009 at Union Station, Washington, DC, USA, *National Geographic Kids* magazine announced that it had collected 33,088 pairs of jeans for recycling through its denim drive event.

All the denim collected will be donated to the organization COTTON. FROM BLUE TO GREEN, which recycles jeans into UltraTouch Natural Cotton Fiber Insulation, a product that is used to help build houses in places that have been damaged by hurricanes and other natural disasters.

It takes about 500 pairs of jeans to recycle enough denim to insulate one average-size house.

MOST BOTTLES RECYCLED BY A DOG

A Labrador called Tubby owned by Sandra Gilmore, of Pontnewydd, Torfaen, UK, has helped recycle an estimated 26,000 plastic bottles over the past six years by collecting them on his daily walks, crushing them and passing them to his owner.

★LARGEST PLASTIC BAG SCULPTURE

A sculpture of a globe made of 17,773 plastic bags measuring 11 m (36 ft 1 in) in circumference was revealed at the Ministerio de Medio Ambiente in Madrid, Spain, by the charity InspirAction to promote recycling and environmental issues on 12 December 2009.

I ♥ CO2 INSPIRACTION

OUCH! ACCORDING TO A REPORT BY THE GARTNER GROUP AND HEWLETT-PACKARD, THE AVERAGE INTERNET USER PRINTS 28 PAGES EVERY DAY.

OH! THE ENERGY NEEDED TO MELT RECYCLED GLASS IS 30% LESS THAN THAT NEEDED TO MELT RAW MATERIALS USED TO MAKE NEW JARS AND BOTTLES.

MELBOURNE, AUSTRALIA

37°48'S 144°57'E

The **most expensive cricket bat** was Sir Donald Bradman's bat, used in his debut Test, which sold for A$145,000 ($121,945; £66,000) at Leski Auctions, Melbourne, Australia, on 24 September 2008. The bat was only used in Bradman's debut Test match in the 1928–29 Ashes series.

GUINNESS WORLD RECORDS

HUMAN SOCIETY
MOST EXPENSIVE

★ SCULPTURE SOLD AT AUCTION

Alberto Giacometti's (Switzerland) bronze sculpture entitled *Walking Man I* (1960) sold to an anonymous bidder at Sotheby's in London, UK, for a record £65,000,000 ($104,300,000) on 3 February 2010. The sculpture stands 1.82 m (6 ft) tall.

DOLLAR: From the Low German "Thal"/"Thaler" meaning "valley". In the 15th century, silver was mined in a place called Joachim's Thal; the coins minted from this silver were known as Thalers.

★ DRAWING BY AN OLD MASTER

Head of a Muse by Raphael (Italy, 1483–1520) sold for £29,200,000 ($46,700,000) at Christie's, London, UK, on 9 December 2009.

COST! TEN YEARS AGO, ANOTHER GIACOMETTI HELD THE MOST EXPENSIVE SCULPTURE RECORD – HIS *GRANDE FEMME DEBOUT 1* SOLD AT CHRISTIE'S FOR $14 MILLION.

ICE-CREAM MAKER

The G Series ice-cream makers launched by NitroCream (USA) are customized and signed by the artists Robert Kennedy and Ward Goodell and sell for $75,000 (£54,484). The G Series uses liquid nitrogen to create desserts almost instantly by mixing the cold nitrogen – which turns into gas at -196°C (-321°F) – directly with the ice-cream or sorbet mixture.

MUSIC SINGLE

A rare seven-inch copy of the unreleased 1965 single "Do I Love You (Indeed I Do)" by Frank Wilson (USA) sold for £25,742 ($39,294) in April 2009 to a buyer who wishes to remain anonymous.

EXTRA! TO FIND OUT MORE ABOUT THE WORLD'S RICHEST AND POOREST, FLICK BACK TO P. 132.

★ BED

The K.mooi Crystal Noir Limited Edition bed created by Maxxa International Limited (China) is covered with 802,903 CRYSTALIZED™ Swarovski crystals and is on sale for RMB 3,000,000 ($440,000; £270,000). It was first unveiled at the 100% Design show in Shanghai, China, on 15 October 2009.

★ CHOCOLATE BAR

A Wispa Gold bar covered in edible gold leaf was created by Cadbury's (UK) in 2009 to celebrate its comeback after six years. The chocolate treat – which usually sells for 55p (82¢) – is available to buy from Selfridges in London, UK, for £961.48 ($1,441).

★ CITY COMMUTE

Based upon an average commuter journey into a city centre by the most popular public means, London is the most expensive city for commuters, averaging £2.62 ($4.33) per single journey. The results were drawn from Mercer's Worldwide Cost of Living 2009.

★ **NEW RECORD**
★ **UPDATED RECORD**

42°5'S
147°19'E
HOBART, TASMANIA, AUSTRALIA

In the **longest debating marathon**, 725 people from the Rostrum Clubs of Tasmania and members of the Tasmanian community debated the motion "Tasmania's greatest asset is its people" for 29 days 4 hr 3 min 20 sec from 2 November to 1 December 1996 on the lawns of Hobart's Parliament House in Tasmania, Australia.

★ DIAMOND PER CARAT

A 7.03-carat fancy vivid-blue modified rectangular brilliant-cut diamond sold at Sotheby's in Geneva, Switzerland, for a record per-carat price of $1,375,938 (£854,705) on 12 May 2009.

LETTER

A letter written by George Washington in 1787 to his nephew Bushrod Washington, urging adoption of the country's new constitution, sold for $3,200,000 (£1,900,000) on 5 December 2009 at Christie's, New York, USA – the highest price ever paid for a single signed letter.

day of Madeleine's disappearance, and the calendar – which was bought by Duncan Mackay (UK) – featured drawings made by Madeleine and her siblings Sean and Amelie.

★ HOTEL SUITE

The Royal Penthouse Suite at the President Wilson hotel in Geneva, Switzerland, costs $65,000 (£41,676) per day, although for that price you do get access to 1,670 m² (18,000 ft²) of space plus views of Mont Blanc (through 6-cm-thick [2-in] bullet-proof windows), a private cocktail lounge, a jacuzzi and fitness centre and a conference room.

★ SPA PACKAGE

On sale at the Vitality Show in London's Earls Court, UK, in March 2010: spa therapy for £5,000 ($7,560). Included was a hot-rock spinal massage using diamonds; a 24-carat-gold facial wrap; a chocolate body wrap; and a caviar-and-coffee hair wash.

★ SUIT

It took Alexander Amosu (UK) over 80 hours – and 5,000 stitches – to create a suit from gold thread and the wool of Himalayan pashmina goats, Arctic musk oxen and Peruvian vicuñas. The suit, finished with nine 18-carat-gold-and-pavé-set-diamond buttons, sold for £70,000 ($113,000) in April 2009 and was delivered to the buyer in an armoured Land Rover.

★ ROUGH DIAMOND

Petra Diamonds Ltd (UK) sold a 507.9-carat rough diamond – the 19th largest gem ever discovered – for $35.5 million (£25.8 million) to the Chow Tai Fook Jewellery Co., Ltd (Hong Kong) on 26 February 2010.

The stone, named the Petra Heritage, weighed just over 100 g (3.3 oz) and is as big as a chicken's egg. It was found in September 2009 in South Africa's Cullinan mine.

★ WALL CALENDAR

A wall calendar entitled *Still Missing Still Missed* was sold for £20,000 ($30,000) at an auction held on 27 January 2010 in London, UK. The auction was in aid of three charities: Missing Children Europe; Missing People; and Madeleine's Fund: Leaving No Stone Unturned, the charity established to find Madeleine McCann (UK), who went missing during a family holiday in Portugal on 3 May 2007. The fund-raiser was held on the 1,000th

The ★ **most expensive man-made object** is the International Space Station – its final cost will be over $100 billion!

TRIVIA

★ FOOTBALLER

The highest transfer fee for a player is a reported €80 million ($131.86 million; £92.27 million) for Cristiano Ronaldo (Portugal) by Real Madrid to English club Manchester United on 1 July 2009. According to Spanish newspaper *El Mundo*, Ronaldo cost Real Madrid 57 times his own weight in gold!

MOVE
IN 2003, RONALDO MOVED FROM SPORTING LISBON (PORTUGAL) TO MANCHESTER UNITED (ENGLAND) FOR A MODEST c12.2 MILLION ($15.3 MILLION; £8.6 MILLION).

MOVIES
RONALDO – AKA CRISTIANO RONALDO DOS SANTOS AVEIRO – WAS NAMED AFTER US PRESIDENT RONALD REAGAN, HIS FATHER'S FAVOURITE FILM ACTOR!

SYDNEY, AUSTRALIA
The Panasonic IMAX Theatre at Darling Harbour in Sydney, Australia, holds the **largest fixed projection screen** in the world, measuring 35.72 x 29.57 m (117 x 97 ft). It opened in September 1996 and can seat 540 people.

33°51'S
151°12'E

HUMAN SOCIETY

EXTREME CUISINE

★ ★ ★ ★ ★ ★ ★ ★ ★ ★ ★ ★ ★

MOST EXPENSIVE...

★**Fish fingers**: In 2004, Barry Coutts' Bistro in Aberdeen, UK, added to their menu haute cuisine fish fingers – made with smoked halibut, king scallops, crayfish, monkfish and Beluga caviar – at a cost of £100 ($167.58) each.

★**Bottle**: Tequila Ley .925 sold a Platinum & White Gold Tequila bottle to a private collector in Mexico City, Mexico, on 20 July 2006 for $225,000 (£120,000).

★**Cherries**: In October 2007, Nick Moraitis (Australia) paid A$35,000 ($31,771; £20,056) to Variety, the children's charity of New South Wales, for a box of cherries sold by Sydney Markets, Australia.

★**Cognac**: A 1788 bottle of Vieux Cognac sold at auction by the Tour D'Argent restaurant (France) in December 2009 raised €25,000 (£21,650; $35,364).

★LARGEST SERVING OF HUMMUS

On 10 May 2010, 300 Lebanese chefs prepared a serving of hummus that weighed 23,130 kg (59,992 lb) in Ain Saadeh, northeast of Beirut. The dish, which beat the previous effort from neighbouring Israel, required 10 tons (22,046 lb) of chickpeas.

MOST PIZZA ROLLS

The **most continuous pizza rolls across the shoulders in 30 seconds** using 567 g (20 oz) of dough is 37 by Tony Gemignani (USA) at the Mall of America, Minneapolis, Minnesota, USA, on 20 April 2006 for the Food Network channel.

QUIZ!
ON 2 MAY 2007, LUP FUN YAU SET A NEW RECORD FOR THE MOST JAM DOUGHNUTS EATEN IN THREE MINUTES. BUT HOW MANY DID HE EAT?
SEE P.278 FOR THE ANSWER.

THE CHOMP-IONS

FOOD	MOST EATEN IN 1 MIN	WHO
After Eights (no hands)	8	Ashrita Furman (USA) James Graham Boyd (UK)
Bananas (peeled & eaten)	6	Robert Godfrey (USA)
Brussels sprouts	31	Linus Urbanec (Sweden)
Garlic cloves	22	Ashrita Furman (USA)
Cockroaches	5	Alexis Chambon (France)
Ferrero Rocher (chocolates)	8	Chris Vollmershausen (Canada)
Jaffa cakes	8	Gustav Schulz (Germany)
Jalapeño chillies	16	Alfredo Hernandes (USA)
Jelly	455 g (16 oz)	Ashrita Furman (USA)
M&Ms (with chopsticks)	42	Fero Andersen (Germany)
Meatballs	27	Nick Marshall (UK)
Sausages	8	Stefan Paladin (NZ)

FOOD	MOST EATEN IN 3 MIN	WHO
Doughnuts (jam)	6	Lup Fun Yau (UK)
Doughnuts (powdered)	5	Christopher "Big Black" Boykin (USA)
Grapes (with teaspoon)	151	Ashrita Furman (USA)
Hot dogs	6	Takeru Kobayashi (Japan)
Oysters	233	Colin Shirlow (UK)
Sweetcorn (with cocktail stick)	236	Ian Richard Purvis (UK)

BANANA: They don't grow on trees – the banana plant is actually one of the world's biggest herbs!

★ MOST BANANAS SNAPPED (ONE MINUTE)

Graheme Celledoni (Australia) snapped a total of 96 bananas in half, using only his hands, at the Innisfail Society Show in Queensland, Australia, on 9 July 2009.

★ MOST ICE-CREAM SCOOPS STACKED ON ONE CONE

Terry Morris (New Zealand) balanced 25 scoops of ice-cream on a single cone on the set of *NZ Smashes Guinness World Records* at Sylvia Park shopping mall, Auckland, New Zealand, on 20 September 2009.

★ MOST NAAN BREAD MADE (ONE HOUR)

A team of five from the Indian Ocean Restaurant in Ashton-under-Lyne, UK, made 640 naan breads on 29 September 2009.

★ FIRST COCKTAIL

In September 2005, archaeochemist Patrick McGovern from Pennsylvania University, USA, announced the discovery of 5,000-year-old earthenware from the banks of the Tigris, between Iran and Iraq, containing traces of tartaric acid, honey, apple juice and barley.

★ LARGEST PIE FIGHT

Shaw Floors in Grapevine, Texas, USA, organized a pie fight between 434 employees on 7 January 2010. The flan fighters flung a total of 1,200 chocolate, apple and cherry pies at a sales meeting to demonstrate the stain resistance of a premium nylon carpet.

FASTEST TIME TO...

★**Carve a turkey**: Paul Kelly (UK) carved a turkey in 3 min 19.47 sec at Little Claydon Farm, Essex, UK, on 3 June 2009.

Pluck a turkey: Vincent Pilkington (Ireland) plucked a turkey in 1 min 30 sec on 17 November 1980.

★ MOST CUSTARD-PIES IN THE FACE

James Kerley "pied" Damien Bignell (both Australia) with 46 custard-pies in a minute on the set of *Australia Smashes Guinness World Records* at the Warringah Mall in Sydney, Australia, on 15 January 2010.

★ MOST PANCAKES MADE (EIGHT HOURS)

A total of 175 volunteers from Batter Blaster (USA) used 37 griddles to prepare a record 76,382 pancakes on 9 May 2009 – and serve them to 20,000 people for breakfast – on the Great Lawn of the Centennial Olympic Park in Atlanta, Georgia, USA. Each recipient paid $1 towards two charities: Homeless and Hosea Feed the Hungry.

★ LARGEST DISPLAY OF TEQUILA

The Tequila Regulatory Council of Mexico displayed a record 1,201 varieties of tequila at Hospicio Cabañas, Guadalajara, Mexico, on 6 November 2009.

TALLEST...

★**Poppadom stack**: A freestanding tower of 1,052 poppadoms (thin and crispy Indian flatbreads) measured 1.51 m (4 ft 11 in) at the Curry Lounge in Nottingham, UK, on 22 July 2009.

★**Sugar cube tower**: Paul Van den Nieuwenhof (Belgium) took 2 hr 12 min to build a record-breaking 1.9-m-tall (6-ft 2-in) tower from 1,753 sugar cubes on 12 November 2009.

★ MOST EGGS HELD IN ONE HAND

Zachery George (USA) held 24 eggs in one hand at the Subway restaurant in Parsons, West Virginia, USA, on 21 March 2009. As stipulated in the guidelines, Zachery had 30 seconds to position all the eggs in his hand and then held them there for 10 seconds.

★ **NEW RECORD**
★ **UPDATED RECORD**

Don't try this at home!

COCO... THE FASTEST TIME TO CLIMB A 9-M (29-FT 6-IN) COCONUT TREE IS 4.88 SECONDS, BY FUATAI SOLO (FIJI) ON 22 AUGUST 1980.

NUTS! A RECORD COCONUT ENSEMBLE OF 5,877 PEOPLE KNOCKED THEIR NUTS TOGETHER TO THE TUNE OF MONTY PYTHON'S "ALWAYS LOOK ON THE BRIGHT SIDE OF LIFE" IN LONDON, UK, ON 23 APRIL 2007.

★ MOST COCONUTS SMASHED WITH ONE HAND IN ONE MINUTE

Nut cracker Muhamed Kahrimanovic (Germany, pictured) crushed 82 coconuts by hand during the Vienna Recordia event in Vienna, Austria, on 27 September 2009. In a similar event held in Malaysia on 21 June 2009, Ho Eng Hui (Malaysia) pierced four coconuts with his right index finger – the ★**most coconuts pierced by finger in one minute.**

INVERCARGILL, NEW ZEALAND

Despite his Hungarian (and therefore landlocked) ancestry, Mike Rácz set the record for the **fastest time to open 100 oysters**, taking just 2 min 20.07 sec – a rate of one oyster every 1.4 seconds – at Invercargill, New Zealand, on 16 July 1990.

46°25'S 168°18'E

HUMAN SOCIETY

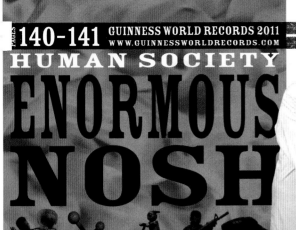

ENORMOUS NOSH

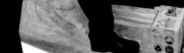

★ LARGEST CUPCAKE

★ LARGEST CUPCAKE

A colossal cupcake weighing 596.47 kg (1,315 lb) was made by Global TV Concepts (USA) during the second annual THINK PINK ROCKS charity concert at Mizner Park in Boca Raton, Florida, USA, on 3 October 2009.

★ HALVA

A halva – a Middle East dessert – weighing 3,811 kg (8,402 lb) was created by the Nazareth Halva Factory in Israel on 14 October 2009. It contained an estimated 20 million calories!

FANTASTIC FEASTS

LARGEST…	RECORD	ORGANIZER/ VENUE	DATE
★Birth feast	819	Council of Utrecht/ Vinkenburgstraat, the Netherlands	24 Jan 09
Breakfast (cooked)	18,941	The Cowboy Breakfast Foundation, San Antonio, USA	26 Jan 01
Breakfast (non-cooked)	27,854 in 1 hr	Nutella/Arena AufSchalke, Gelsenkirchen, Germany	29 May 05
Coffee morning (multi-venue)	576,157	Macmillan Cancer Relief (UK)	26 Sep 03
Picnic (single-venue) (see also p.101)	22,232	Modelo/Parque da Bela Vista, Lisbon, Portugal	20 Jun 09
Tea party (multi-venue)	280,246	The Cancer Council/ 6,062 locations across Australia	26 May 05

★ **NEW RECORD**   **UPDATED RECORD**

LARGEST…

★ CRAB CAKE

The largest crab cake on record weighed 114.75 kg (253 lb) and was made by Special Olympics Maryland in conjunction with Handy International and Graul's Market (all USA) in Hampden, Maryland, USA, on 13 June 2009.

★ FISH FINGER

A 2-m-long (6-ft 6-in) fish finger weighing 136 kg (299 lb 13 oz) was prepared by Michael Gorich (Germany) in Bremerhaven, Germany, on 22 January 2009.

★ FUDGE

On 29 June 2009, William Nicklosovich and Peppermint Jim Crosby (both USA) made a slab of fudge weighing 2.35 tonnes (5,200 lb) at Lansing Community College West Campus, Delta Township, Michigan, USA.

★ HAGGIS

The national dish of Scotland, haggis is a sausage of minced offal with oatmeal, beef suet and spices. The largest ever weighed 560 kg (1,234 lb 9 oz) – about the same as a Jersey cow – and was made by the Mauchline Burns Club in Ayrshire, UK, in May 2009.

★ LOLLIPOP

On 27 August 2009, Ashrita Furman (USA) and members of the New York Sri Chinmoy Centre created a 7.62-m-tall (25-ft) lollipop weighing 2.95 tonnes (6,514 lb) – equal to 165,070 regular lollies!

LARGEST DISH OF MUSSELS

A mussels dish weighing 3,692 kg (4.07 tons) was prepared for the public in the streets of Taranto, Italy, on 1 August 2009.

WHAT?
MUSSELS: 3,300 KG
RED TOMATOES: 300 KG
GARLIC: 30 KG
SALT: 3 KG
OLIVE OIL: 150 KG
PEPPER: 20 KG
PARSLEY: 20 KG
WINE: 150 LITRES
BREAD CROUTONS: 300 KG

WHO?
THE FISHY DISH WAS ORGANIZED BY THE SHOPPING CENTRE MONGOLFIERA AND COOP ESTENSE AND THE "SOCIETA" SVILUPPO COMMERCIALE IN TARANTO, ITALY.

★ LARGEST "FULL ENGLISH" BREAKFAST

A "full English" on the menu at Mario's Cafe Bar in Bolton, Lancashire, UK, weighs on average 2.9 kg (6 lb 7 oz) and costs £10.95 ($17.87). The melee of bacon, sausages, eggs, bread, mushrooms, black pudding, beans and tomatoes is free if eaten within 20 minutes.

★ PORRIDGE

The largest bowl of porridge weighed 171.9 kg (378 lb 15 oz) and was prepared by Mornflake Oats (UK) at the Lowry Theatre, Salford, UK, on 10 September 2009. The 25 kg (55 lb 1 oz) of porridge oats and 150 litres (32.9 gal) of water was sufficient to cater for 830 individual servings.

★ SOUP

DENK Communicatie prepared a 26,658-litre (5,863-gal) vegetable soup in Poeldijk, the Netherlands, on 16 May 2009.

LONGEST...

★ GARLIC BREAD

A garlic bread measuring 3.81 m (12 ft 6 in) was baked by Cole's Quality Foods in Muskegon, Michigan, USA, on 12 June 2009.

★ SAUSAGE CHAIN

On 28 June 2009, at Gelsenkirchen, Germany, more than 10,000 Fleischwurst sausages were linked in a 1,500-m-long (4,921-ft 3-in) chain. The **fastest man to run 1,500 m** – Hicham El Guerrouj (Morocco) – would take 3 min 26 sec to run from end to end!

★ RICE NOODLE

A 548.7-m (1,800-ft 2-in) noodle – as long as five US football fields – was unveiled at Taipei County Hakka Museum, Taiwan, on 28 December 2008.

★ MEATBALL

A meatball weighing 100.92 kg (222 lb 8 oz) was created by Nonni's Italian Eatery in Concord, New Hampshire, USA, on 1 November 2009.

★ MEAT STEW

A 2,328.2-kg (5,132-lb 15-oz) stew containing 1,294.6 kg (2,854 lb) of lamb meat (from an estimated 75 lambs) was cooked in Badajoz, Spain, on 25 October 2009.

★ MOJITO

The largest glass of mojito – a Cuban cocktail of rum, sugar, mint and lime juice – contained 713 litres (156 gal) and measured 1.34 m (4 ft 4 in) tall and 1.25 m (4 ft 1 in) at its widest. It was made by the bar-ristorante Sirio in Spotorno, Savona, Italy, on 28 August 2009, and required at least 90 kg (200 lb) of limes.

LARGEST CHOCOLATE RABBIT

A chocolate rabbit weighing in at 2,800 kg (6,172 lb 15 oz) was made by Supermercados Imperatriz Ltda and Nestlé FoodServices (both Brazil) in São José, Santa Catarina, Brazil, on 30 March 2009.

LONGEST BAR

The longest permanent, continuous bar is the 123.7-m (405-ft 10-in) counter in the Beer Barrel Saloon at Put-in-Bay, South Bass Island, Ohio, USA. The bar has 56 beer taps and features 160 bar stools.

HIGH! IF STOOD ON ITS SIDE, THE BEER BARREL BAR WOULD BE TALLER THAN THE STATUE OF LIBERTY (INCLUDING HER CONCRETE PLINTH)!

DRY! ROBERT BEGLEY (USA) HAS THE GUINNESS WORLD RECORD FOR THE LARGEST COLLECTION OF BAR TOWELS – HE OWNS 2,372 TOWELS FROM 27 COUNTRIES.

WELLINGTON, NZ

Wellington, North Island, New Zealand, with a population of 179,436, is the **most southerly capital city** of an independent country.

41°17'S 174°46'E

HUMAN SOCIETY
COLLECTORS' ITEMS

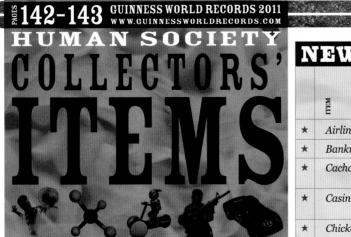

★ ★ ★ ★ ★ ★ ★ ★ ★ ★ ★ ★

★ BOTTLED WATER LABELS

Lorenzo Pescini of Florence, Italy, had a collection of 8,650 different bottled water labels from 185 different countries of 1,683 different springs, as of 12 January 2009. He started his collection in 1992.

★ BUS TICKETS

Ladislav Šejnoha (Czech Republic) had 200,000 bus tickets from 36 countries as of 30 September 2008.

★ CALENDARS

Yakov L Kofman (USA) had put together a collection of 16,552 different calendars as of 26 October 2008. His collection began in 1945.

★ FILM CAMERAS

Since 1960, Richard LaRiviere (USA) has built up a collection of 894 movie cameras. The oldest is a 1907 Darling with hand crank.

★ HEARTS

Dr Diana Reser (Switzerland) has collected 775 heart-shaped motifs and items since becoming a cardiac surgeon in 2006.

★ TROLLS

Sophie Marie Cross (UK) began collecting trolls in 2003 and, as of 3 December 2009, had amassed a set of 633 unique items.

NEW COLLECTIONS

ITEM	COLLECTOR	QUANTITY	DATE ACHIEVED
★ Airline boarding passes	Miguel Fernandez (Spain)	1,020	Aug 2009
★ Banknotes	Anil Bohora (India)	10,025	Jan 2009
★ Cachaça bottles	Messias Soares Cavalcante (Brazil)	12,800	Aug 2009
★ Casino chips and tokens	Bruce and Sue Wunder (both USA)	554	May 2009
★ Chicken memorabilia	Cecil and Joann Dixon (both USA)	6,505	Jun 2006
★ Christmas brooches	Adam Wide (UK)	1,329	Jun 2009
★ Cow memorabilia	Denise Tubangui (USA)	2,261	Oct 2009
★ Hedgehog memorabilia	Bengt W Johansson (Sweden)	468	Nov 2009
★ Joker playing cards	Tony De Santis (Italy)	8,520	Mar 2009
★ Kappa (Japanese river sprite) memorabilia	Tatsuo Kitano (Japan)	7,845	Jun 2009
★ Millstones	He Hengde (China)	39,052	Jul 2009
★ Oil lamps	Gerd Bonk (Germany)	356	Nov 2009
★ Panda memorabilia	Miranda Middleton (USA)	1,175	Jan 2009
★ Stamps (first-day covers)	Joshua Steinberg (UK)	6,037	Nov 2004
★ Sugar packets	Pavlina Yotkova (Bulgaria)	3,384	Apr 2009
★ Surfboards	Donald Dettloff (USA)	647	Nov 2009
★ Tea-bag holders	Mimi Wilfong (USA)	116	Jun 2009

D'OH!
CAMERON GIBBS (AUSTRALIA) HAD AMASSED A TOTAL OF 2,580 DIFFERENT SIMPSONS ITEMS, AS OF 20 MARCH 2008.

★ SMURF MEMORABILIA

Stephen Parkes (UK) began collecting Smurfs as a child, when they were sold by a chain of garages across the UK, and has never stopped! As of 28 January 2010, his collection totals 1,061 and includes Christmas Smurfs, Easter Smurfs, Smurfs dressed as historical figures and Smurfs doing almost every occupation you can imagine. And he's still collecting...

★ NEW RECORD
★ UPDATED RECORD

AUCKLAND, NEW ZEALAND

36°51'S 174°47'E

On 19 February 1998, the four main power cables to the city centre of Auckland, New Zealand, broke down, in the **longest peacetime blackout**. The disruption lasted for 66 days, affected 7,500 business and residential customers and cost businesses some NZ$300 million (US $156 million; £105 million).

CLASSIC COLLECTIONS

ITEM	COLLECTOR	QUANTITY	DATE ACHIEVED
Airline sick-bags	Niek Vermeulen (Netherlands)	6,016	Jan 2010
Barbie dolls	Bettina Dorfmann (Germany)	7,246	Feb 2010
Bells	Myrtle B Eldridge (USA)	9,638	Mar 2005
Board games	Brian Arnett (USA)	1,345	Feb 2007
Bookmarks	Frank Divendal (Netherlands)	103,009	Feb 2010
Candles	Véronique Salmont (France)	2,119	Jun 2009
Clocks	Jack Schoff (USA)	1,509	Feb 2010
Coffee pots	Robert Dahl (Germany)	13,267	Sep 2009
Coloured vinyl records	Alessandro Benedetti (Italy)	1,507	Mar 2010
"Do Not Disturb" signs	Jean-François Vernetti (Switzerland)	10,000	Jun 2009
Hats	Roger Buckey Legried (USA)	100,336	Mar 2010
Ladybird memorabilia	Carine Roosen (Belgium)	3,531	Sep 2009
Magic sets	Manfred Klaghofer (Austria)	2,401	Feb 2010
Masks	Gerold Weschenmoser (Germany)	5,385	Mar 2010
Mobile phones	Carsten Tews (Germany)	1,563	Feb 2010
Model cars	Nabil Karam (Lebanon)	22,222	Nov 2009
Number (license) plates	Shahin Ebrahim Mohajer (Oman)	561	May 2009
Pencils	Vladimir Jindra (Czech Rep.)	11,068	Nov 2009
Rubber ducks	Charlotte Lee (USA)	5,429	Feb 2010
Santa Claus memorabilia	Jean-Guy Laquerre (Canada)	23,947	Feb 2010
Sports mascots	Adina and Falk Hinneberg (both Germany)	874	Feb 2010
Stickers for bumpers	Bill Heermann (USA)	4,131	Apr 2009
Teapots	Tang Yu (China)	30,000	Oct 2008
Toothbrushes	Grigori Fleicher (Russia)	1,320	Nov 2008
Yo-yos	John "Lucky" Meisenheimer (USA)	4,586	Feb 2010

★SOAPS

Carol Vaughan (UK) has collected 1,331 individual bars of soap since 1991. She is always on the lookout for new, unusual soaps – though, of course, she never uses items in her collection to wash with...

MICKEY MOUSE MEMORABILIA

As of 11 December 2008, Janet Esteves (USA) had collected 2,760 different Mickey Mouse items. Janet started her collection in 1960, when she was a child. Her father made regular business trips to California and would bring back Disney products for her.

QUACK! AS OF 28 MAY 2008, MARY BROOKS (USA) HAD 1,285 ITEMS OF DONALD DUCK MEMORABILIA. SHE HAS BEEN COLLECTING FOR OVER 30 YEARS.

HONOLULU, HI, USA
A 4,434-m (14,550-ft) paper flower lei was made by local citizens at the Hyatt Regency Waikiki, Honolulu, Hawaii, USA, on 19 December 1992 – the **largest artificial garland** ever made.

21°18'N
157°49'W

HUMAN SOCIETY

GARDEN GIANTS

★ ★ ★ ★ ★ ★ ★ ★ ★ ★

★ HEAVIEST SWEDE

A swede presented by Scott Robb (USA) at the Alaska State Fair, USA, on 2 September 2009 weighed 37.6 kg (82 lb 14 oz). Scott previously held this record back in 1999, with a 34.35-kg (75-lb 11-oz) specimen.

EXTRA! FOR MORE OUTSIZED FOOD, FLICK BACK TO P.140.

HEAVIEST FRUIT & VEG

FRUIT/VEG	WEIGHT	GROWER	DATE
Apple	1.849 kg (4 lb 1 oz)	Chisato Iwasaki (Japan)	Oct 2005
★ Blueberry	11.28 g (0.4 oz)	Polana SP. Zo.o (Poland)	Aug 2008
Brussels sprout	8.3 kg (18 lb 3 oz)	Bernard Lavery (UK)	Oct 1992
Cabbage	57.61 kg (127 lb)	Steven Hubacek (USA)	4 Sep 2009
Carrot	8.61 kg (18 lb 13 oz)	John Evans (USA)	1998
Cauliflower	24.6 kg (54 lb 3 oz)	Alan Hattersley (UK)	6 Aug 1999
Celery	28.7 kg (63 lb 4.8 oz)	Scott & Mardie Robb (USA)	27 Aug 2003
Courgette	29.25 kg (64 lb 8 oz)	Bernard Lavery (UK)	1990
Cucumber	12.4 kg (27 lb 5.3 oz)	Alfred J Cobb (UK)	5 Sep 2003
Gooseberry	62.01 g (2.19 oz)	Bryan Nellist (UK)	4 Aug 2009
Gourd	42.8 kg (94 lb 5.7 oz)	Robert Weber (Australia)	7 Apr 2001
Grapefruit	3.210 kg (7 lb 12 oz)	Cloy Dias Dutra (Brazil)	9 Nov 2006
Leek	8.1 kg (17 lb 13 oz)	Fred Charlton (UK)	6 Sep 2002
Lemon	5.265 kg (11 lb 9.7 oz)	Aharon Shemoel (Israel)	8 Jan 2003
Marrow	93.7 kg (206.5 lb)	B Wursten (Netherlands)	26 Sep 2009
Nectarine	360 g (12 oz)	Tony Slattery (NZ)	Jan 1998
Onion	7.495 kg (16.52 lb)	John Sifford (UK)	16 Sep 2005
Parsnip	5.90 kg (13 lb)	Peter Glazebrook (UK)	4 Sep 2009
Peach	725 g (25 oz)	Paul Friday (USA)	23 Aug 2002
Pear	2.1 kg (4 lb 8 oz)	Warren Yeoman (Australia)	6 May 1999
Pineapple	8.06 kg (17 lb 12 oz)	E Kamuk (Papua New Guinea)	1994
Pomegranate	1.85 kg (4.08 lb)	Ningyi Li (China)	4 Sep 2009
Potato	3.5 kg (7 lb 11 oz)	K Sloane (UK)	1994
Pumpkin	782.45 kg (1,725 lb)	Christy Harp (USA)	3 Oct 2009
Radish	31.1 kg (68 lb 9 oz)	Manabu Oono (Japan)	9 Feb 2003
Squash	559.73 kg (1,234 lb)	Bradley Wursten (N'lands)	21 Sep 2007
Strawberry	231 g (8 oz)	G Andersen (UK)	1983
Tomato	3.51 kg (7 lb 12 oz)	G Graham (USA)	1986
Watermelon	121.93 kg (268 lb 12 oz)	Lloyd Bright (USA)	Sep 2005

LONGEST CUCUMBER

Frank Dimmock (UK) grew a 104.78-cm-long (41.25-in) cucumber inside a length of gutter pipe in the greenhouse at his home in Thame, Oxfordshire, UK. He had it officially measured on 18 September 2008.

★ HEAVIEST MANGO

Sergio and Maria Socorro Bodiongan (Philippines) presented this Florida Keitt mango – weighing 3.43 kg (7 lb 9 oz) – on 27 August 2009.

GO! MARIA'S MANGO – GROWN IN HER FRONT YARD – MEASURED 30.48 CM (12 IN) IN LENGTH, AND 49.53 CM (19.5 IN) IN CIRCUMFERENCE.

61°13'N 149°53'W

ANCHORAGE, AL, USA

The **fastest-moving major glacier** is the Columbia Glacier, between Anchorage and Valdez in Alaska, USA. In 1999, its average rate of flow was measured at 35 m (115 ft) per day.

★ HEAVIEST AVOCADO

The avocado of Central and South America is the world's **most calorific fruit**, and this particular specimen – grown by avocado enthusiast Gabriel Ramirez Nahim (Venezuela) – is the most calorific of all, tipping the scales at a whopping 2.19 kg (4 lb 13 oz). It was weighed on 28 January 2009 in Caracas, Venezuela.

ACTUAL SIZE

ACTUAL SIZE

NAME
THE WORD "AVOCADO" COMES FROM THE NAHUATL (AZTECAN) FOR "TESTICLE"; OTHER WORDS FROM THE LANGUAGE INCLUDE "CHOCOLATE" AND "CHILLI".

HEAVIEST GOOSEBERRY

Bryan Nellist (UK) of Egton Bridge, North Yorkshire, UK, grew a gooseberry that was weighed at 62.01 g (2.19 oz) on 4 August 2009.

BEET!
PETER GLAZEBROOK (UK) GREW THE LONGEST BEETROOT IN 2008; AT 6.405 M (21 FT), IT'S ABOUT TWICE AS LONG AS A MINI COOPER!

SAUCE!
THE LARGEST SACHET OF KETCHUP MEASURED 1.21 x 2.43 M (4 x 8 FT); IT WAS MADE BY PASTOR DAVID AMSDEN (USA) AND CONTAINED 127 GALLONS OF SAUCE.

TALLEST PLANTS

PLANT	HEIGHT	GROWER	DATE
Amaranthus	8.48 m (27 ft 10 in)	Jesse Eldrid (USA)	25 Oct 2007
Aubergine/brinjal	5.5 m (18 ft 0.5 in)	Abdul Masfoor (India)	Sep 1998
Bean plant	14.1 m (46 ft 3 in)	Staton Rorie (USA)	7 Nov 2003
Brussels sprout	2.8 m (9 ft 3 in)	Patrice & Steve Allison (USA)	17 Nov 2001
Cactus (homegrown)	21.3 m (70 ft)	Pandit S Munji (India)	1 Jan 2004
Celery	2.74 m (9 ft)	Joan Priednieks (UK)	1998
Chrysanthemum	4.34 m (14 ft 3 in)	Bernard Lavery (UK)	1995
Coleus	2.5 m (8 ft 4 in)	Nancy Lee Spilove (USA)	31 Oct 2004
Collard	4.06 m (13 ft 4 in)	Woodrow Wilson Granger (USA)	24 May 2007
Cosmos	3.75 m (12 ft 3 in)	Cosmos Executive Committee (Japan)	17 Oct 2003
Cotton	9.24 m (30 ft 4 in)	D M Williams (USA)	23 Oct 2009
Daffodil	1.55 m (5 ft 1 in)	M Lowe (UK)	1979
Dandelion	1.28 m (4 ft 2 in)	Jeppe, Elise & Simon Hvelplund (Denmark)	1991
Fuchsia (climbing)	11.4 m (37 ft 5 in)	Reinhard Biehler (Germany)	13 Jun 2005
Herba cistanches	1.95 m (6 ft 4 in)	Yongmao Chen (China)	15 Aug 2006
Papaya tree	13.4 m (44 ft)	Prasanta Mal (India)	2 Sep 2003
Parsley	2.37 m (7 ft 9 in)	David Brenner (USA)	10 Jun 2009
Pepper	4.87 m (16 ft)	Laura Liang (USA)	1999
Periwinkle	2.19 m (7 ft 2 in)	Arvind, Rekha, Ashish & Rashmi Nema (India)	10 Dec 2003
Petunia	5.8 m (19 ft 1 in)	Bernard Lavery (UK)	1994
Rose (climbing)	27.7 m (91 ft)	Anne & Charles Grant (USA)	1 Aug 2004
Rose bush (supported)	5.66 m (18 ft 7 in)	Robert Bendel (USA)	12 Oct 2009
Sugar cane	9.5 m (31 ft)	M Venkatesh Gowda (India)	21 Feb 2005
Sunflower	8.03 m (26 ft 4 in)	Hans-Peter Schiffer (Germany)	17 Aug 2009
Sweetcorn (maize)	9.4 m (31 ft)	D Radda (USA)	1946
Tomato	19.8 m (65 ft)	Nutriculture Ltd (UK)	11 May 2000
Zinnia	3.86 m (12 ft 8 in)	Everett W Wallace, Jr & Melody Wagner (both USA)	23 Oct 2008

★ **NEW RECORD**
☆ **UPDATED RECORD**

FAIRBANKS, AL, USA
64°50'N 147°42'W

The Pan-American Highway, the **longest motorable road**, starts at Fairbanks, Alaska, USA, and stretches to Santiago, Chile; it then turns eastwards to Buenos Aires, Argentina, and terminates in Brasilia, Brazil – a distance of more than 24,140 km (15,000 miles).

HUMAN SOCIETY
TOYS & GAMES

★ ★ ★ ★ ★ ★

LARGEST PARTY GAMES

★ OLD MacDONALD HAD A FARM
A record 332 people played the largest game of Old MacDonald Had a Farm on the set of *Lo Show dei Record*, in Milan, Italy, on 25 April 2009.

★ MOST SIMULTANEOUS CHESS GAMES
Morteza Mahjoob (Iran) played 500 games of chess simultaneously against different opponents at the Engelab Sports Complex in Tehran, Iran, on 13–14 August 2009. Only 13 of his opponents beat him.

★ FASTEST JENGA TOWER
Mitchell Bettell (UK) built 10 levels on a Jenga tower in 43.94 seconds at the GWR Live! event held at Butlins, Bognor Regis, UK, on 26 August 2009.

★ HEAD, SHOULDERS, KNEES AND TOES
A mammoth 1,461 participants from Gladesmore Community School and Crowland Primary School got together to play the largest game of Head, Shoulders, Knees and Toes at Markfield Park, Tottenham, London, UK, on 23 October 2009.

IF YOU'RE HAPPY AND YOU KNOW IT
During the SkyFest family festival held in Edinburgh, UK, on 6 September 2009, 755 people took part in the largest-ever game of the children's favourite If You're Happy and You Know It.

★ MUSICAL STATUES
A record 987 people tried to keep very still when the music stopped as they took part in the largest game of musical statues at an event organized by Sir Thomas Boteler Church of England High School in Latchford, Warrington, UK, on 10 July 2009.

★ MUSICAL BUMPS
On 15 July 2009, 348 people gathered at St Thomas of Aquin's High School in Edinburgh, UK, to play the largest-ever game of musical bumps.

MUSICAL CHAIRS
On 5 August 1989, the largest game of musical chairs began with 8,238 participants at the Anglo-Chinese School in Singapore. Three-and-a-half hours later, 15-year-old Xu Chong Wei (Singapore) was left sitting on the last chair.

STACK!
THE LARGEST NUMBER OF DOMINOES STACKED ON ONE SINGLE PIECE WAS 1,002, ACHIEVED BY MAXIMILIAN POSER (GERMANY) IN BERLIN, GERMANY, ON 6 FEBRUARY 2009.

SPIRAL!
THE LARGEST NUMBER OF DOMINOES TOPPLED IN A SPIRAL WAS 28,800, BY MAXIMILIAN POSER (GERMANY) IN BERLIN, GERMANY, ON 14 APRIL 2009.

★ LARGEST GAME OF DODGEBALL
San Diego State University (USA) organized a game of dodgeball for 450 participants at the Aztec Recreation Center in San Diego, California, USA, on 5 September 2009.

DID YOU KNOW?
THE FARTHEST A PAPER AIRPLANE HAS FLOWN IS 63.19 M (207 FT 4 IN).

A record 12,672 paper planes were launched at once on 2 November 2009.

TRIVIA

57°03'N 135°19'W

SITKA, ALASKA, USA
Guy German of Sitka, Alaska, USA, climbed up a 30.5-m (100-ft) fir spar pole and back down to the ground in 24.82 seconds – the **fastest fir tree climb** – at the World Championship Timber Carnival in Albany, Oregon, USA, on 3 July 1988.

LEGO: The name LEGO is an abbreviation of the two Danish words "leg godt", meaning "play well".

★ NEW RECORD
★ UPDATED RECORD

★ GREATEST DISTANCE TRAVELLED BY A RADIO-CONTROLLED MODEL VEHICLE ON A SET OF BATTERIES

A battery-operated radio-controlled model vehicle in the shape of a robot pedalling a three-wheeled cycle covered 23.726 km (14.742 miles), using just one set of Panasonic Evolta batteries, in Le Mans, France, from 5 to 6 August 2009.

EXTRA! FOR VIDEOGAME RECORDS, TAKE A LOOK AT P.160.

SCHOOL FAVES

★ LONGEST HOPSCOTCH GAME

A hopscotch game measuring 4,804.55 m (15,762 ft) – equal in length to about 45 football pitches – was created by Victory Baptist Church in co-operation with Toms Shoes (both USA) in Ladd Landing, Kingston, Tennessee, USA, on 26 September 2009.

★ LARGEST LEGO HOUSE

A full-scale LEGO house measuring 4.69 m (15 ft 4 in) high, 9.39 m (30 ft 9 in) long and 5.75 m (18 ft 10 in) wide was built by 1,200 volunteers and television presenter James May (UK) for the programme *James May's Toy Stories* in Dorking, UK, on 17 September 2009. In all, 2.4 million LEGO bricks were used in the construction.

★ FASTEST GAME OF HOPSCOTCH

Ashrita Furman (USA) completed a game of hopscotch in 1 min 8 sec in New York City, USA, on 29 December 2009.

★ LARGEST GAME OF TAG

On 29 April 2009, 465 people took part in a game of tag at an event organized by Marcia LeVatte (Canada) in Sherwood Park, Canada.

★ LARGEST GAME OF HE LOVES ME, HE LOVES ME NOT

On the set of *Lo Show dei Record*, in Milan, Italy, on 18 April 2009, 331 people picked petals off daisies in a game of He Loves Me, He Loves Me Not.

CLASSIC TOYS

★ LONGEST SLOT CAR TRACK

A fully working slot car track measuring 4.752 km (2.953 miles) was built by James May (UK) and 300 volunteers at Brooklands, UK, on 16 August 2009.

★ MOST RUBIK'S CUBES SOLVED UNDERWATER

David Calvo (Spain) solved four Rubik's Cubes while holding his breath underwater in Madrid, Spain, on 16 January 2009.

★ LONGEST MODEL TRAIN

An HO (that is, 1:87.1) scale model train measuring 271.97 m (892 ft 3 in) made up of eight locomotives and 2,212 carriages was constructed by Miniature Wunderland in Hamburg, Germany, on 25 July 2008.

★ LARGEST SIMULTANEOUS YO-YO

On 13 March 2009, a group of 662 people "yo-yo'd" together at an event organized by CTC Kingshurst Academy in Birmingham, UK.

LARGEST MARIONETTE

A marionette measuring 17.82 m (58 ft 5.5 in) in height was presented by the Villa Marconi Long-Term Care Centre as the mascot to the annual Ital-Fest in Ottawa, Canada, on 6 September 2008.

WHITEHORSE, YT, CANADA

On 22 October 2000, in the city of Whitehorse in the Yukon Territory of Canada, 210 dogs pulled a sled attached to a weight of 65,910 kg (145,302 lb), **the heaviest weight pulled by a dog sled team**. The ... achieved a top ... d of 15 km/h (9 mph) and travelled a distance of six blocks.

60°43'N 135°03'W

ANIMAL MAGIC

★ NEW RECORD
★ UPDATED RECORD

LONGEST TONGUE ON A DOG

The longest recorded canine tongue measures 11.43 cm (4.5 in) and belongs to Puggy, a nine year old male Pekingese owned by Becky Stanford (USA). The record-breaking muscle was measured in Texas, USA, on 8 May 2009.

JUNEAU, AK, USA

58°21'N
134°30'W

Isabel Bush (USA) skipped a record 151,036 jumps of a rope in 24 hours in Juneau, Alaska, USA, on 20–21 July 2005 – the **most skips in 24 hours**.

GUINNESS WORLD RECORDS 2011

CONTENTS

ACTUAL SIZE

EXTRA!
FOR MORE CANINE
CHAMPIONS, SIMPLY
TURN THE PAGE…

VANCOUVER, BC, CANADA
The world's **largest orchestra** consisted of 6,452 musicians from the Vancouver Symphony
Orchestra and music students from throughout British Columbia playing "Ten Minutes
of Nine" for 9 min 44 sec at BC Place Stadium, Vancouver, Canada, on 15 May 2000.

49°15'N
123°06'W

ANIMAL MAGIC
BARKING MAD

★ ★ ★ ★ ★ ★ ★ ★ ★ ★ ★ ★ ★ ★

★ MOST DOGS IN FANCY DRESS

A total of 123 dogs took to the catwalk – or should that be "dogwalk"? -- for the "101 Chihuahua Fashion Show" at the city centre of Oosterhout, the Netherlands, on 3 May 2009. To qualify for this record, each dog had to be dressed for the occasion and walk at least one length of the platform with their owner by their side, as per Guinness World Records guidelines.

★ NEW RECORD
★ UPDATED RECORD

★ FIRST PLANE CRASH CAUSED BY A DOG

At 2:20 p.m. on 29 November 1976, an unrestrained German shepherd dog on board a Piper 32-300 Air Taxi operated by Grand Canyon Air interfered with the controls, causing the plane to crash. The dog perished along with the pilot and lone passenger.

This is the first and, to date, only known accident in which a pet has caused the crash of an aircraft.

LOUDEST BARK

The loudest bark by a dog measured 108 dB and was produced by a white German shepherd dog named Daz, owned by Peter Lucken (UK), in Finsbury Park, London, UK, on 15 June 2009.

★ MOST EXPENSIVE KENNEL

In 2008, UK architect Andy Ramus designed a £250,000 ($384,623) kennel – nicknamed Barkingham Palace – complete with high-tech gadgets such as a plasma TV and a retina-controlled dog flap.

FASTEST CANINE RAT CATCHER

In the 1820s, an 11.8-kg (26-lb) "bull and terrier" dog named Billy killed 4,000 rats in 17 hours, a remarkable achievement considering that he was blind in one eye. His most notable feat was the killing of 100 rats in 5 min 30 sec at the Cockpit in Tufton Street, London, UK, on 23 April 1825. He died on 23 February 1829 at the age of 13 years.

DEEPEST SCUBA DIVE BY A DOG

You've heard about the doggy paddle, but what happens when you take this to an extreme? Dwane Folsom (USA) regularly takes his dog, Shadow, scuba diving off the coast of Grand Cayman Island, going as deep as 4 m (13 ft). Shadow wears a diving suit comprising a helmet, weighted dog jacket and breathing tube connected to his owner's air tank.

★ MOST FRISBEES CAUGHT AND HELD

Edward Watson's (USA) dog Rose can catch seven flying discs, thrown one at a time, and hold them all in her mouth at once!

LOW! THE SHORTEST DOG LIVING MEASURES JUST 10.16 CM (4 IN) TALL. TURN THE PAGE TO FIND OUT MORE ABOUT THIS PINT-SIZED POOCH!

LOWER! THE SMALLEST DOG EVER WAS A FIST-SIZED, DWARF YORKSHIRE TERRIER OWNED BY ARTHUR MARPLES (UK). FULL GROWN, IT STOOD 7.11 CM (2.8 IN) TALL.

45°31'N
122°40'W

PORTLAND, OR, USA
The world's **smallest park** is Mill Ends Park on a safety island on SW Front Avenue, Portland, Oregon, USA. The park is a circle of 60.96 cm (24 in) in diameter, which is an area of 2,917.15 cm² (452.16 in²).

POODLE: From the German *Pudelhund* (*pudeln* means "to splash"). These dogs were first bred to hunt ducks and catch fish!

EXTRA! FIND MORE PECULIAR PETS ON P.152 AND P.154.

★ FASTEST SPEED ON A SKATEBOARD BY A DOG

Meet Tillman, the skateboarding, body-boarding, surfing action dog. The California-based bulldog loves to board, and set a new Guinness World Record -- at X Games 15 in Los Angeles, no less -- as the fastest skateboarding dog! Tillman's average time across a two-way 100-m stretch in a car park was 19.678 seconds.

INSTANT EXPERT

★ ACCORDING TO BIOLOGIST DR RAYMOND COPPINGER, THERE ARE AN ESTIMATED 400 MILLION DOGS IN THE WORLD!

★ DOGS WERE THE FIRST ANIMALS TO BE DOMESTICATED.

★ THE SCIENTIFIC NAME FOR DOG IS *CANIS LUPUS FAMILIARIS*, REFERRING TO A DOMESTICATED FORM OF GREY WOLF.

★ IN SOME COUNTRIES, DOG MEAT IS ACCEPTABLE FARE, WITH *ANIMAL PEOPLE* NEWSPAPER ESTIMATING THAT A TOTAL OF 13-16 MILLION DOGS ARE EATEN IN ASIA EVERY YEAR.

LONGEST TIME ON DEATH ROW FOR A DOG

A dog named Word was held on doggy death row for a total of eight years and 190 days. Word, a Lhasa apso owned by Wilton Rabon of Seattle, Washington, USA, was initially incarcerated at the Seattle Animal Control Shelter, USA, on 4 May 1993 following two biting incidents. He was later released on 10 November 2001 and transported to the Pigs Peace Sanctuary in Washington, USA. Word ended his days as a seeing dog to a visually impaired pot-bellied pig!

LARGEST DOG WEDDING

The record for the largest dog "wedding" ceremony was achieved by 178 dog couples who sealed their marriage at the Bow Wow Vows event at the Aspen Grove Lifestyle Center in Littleton, USA, on 19 May 2007.

HARDIEST DOG

On 15 April 2003, a mixed-breed named Dosha slipped out of her home in Clearlake, California, USA, only to be run over by a truck. A concerned police officer decided to end her pain and shot her in the head; she was then sealed in a bag and placed in a freezer at an animal centre. Two hours later, staff at the clinic looked inside the freezer – and found Dosha alive and sitting up!

LARGEST SOLID OBJECT SWALLOWED BY A DOG

Kyle, a collie/Staffordshire bull terrier, who was 45.7 cm (18 in) long at the time, swallowed a 38-cm (15-in) bread knife in December 2000. The knife was stuck in his stomach, pointing towards his throat. The dog was taken to the People's Dispensary for Sick Animals in Leeds, UK, where Dr Ann Draper carefully removed the knife.

Kyle now lives a normal life back at home with owner Eva Oliver (UK). Let's hope he sticks to a more sensible diet from now on!

LONGEST JOURNEY HOME BY A LOST DOG

The farthest distance a lost pet dog has walked in order to find his way home is 3,218 km (2,000 miles).

Jimpa, a Labrador/boxer cross, turned up at his old home in Pimpinio, Victoria, Australia, after walking across the entire country. His owner, Warren Dumesney (Australia), had taken the dog with him 14 months earlier, but lost him when he worked on a farm at Nyabing, Western Australia. During Jimpa's trek, the dog negotiated the almost waterless Nullarbor Plain.

DID YOU KNOW? • A DOG'S NOSEPRINT IS AS UNIQUE AS A HUMAN FINGERPRINT! • HUMANS HAVE 5 MILLION SMELL (OLFACTORY) CELLS; DOGS HAVE 220 MILLION!

Dogs sweat in just one place: between their paw pads. When they need to cool down, they hang out their tongues!

TRIVIA

FASTEST TIME TO POP 100 BALLOONS BY A DOG

The fastest time to pop 100 balloons by a dog is 44.49 seconds by Anastasia (a Jack Russell terrier), owned by Doree Sitterly (USA), on the set of *Live with Regis and Kelly* in Los Angeles, USA, on 24 February 2008.

TACOMA, WA, USA
The **largest school reunion** involved 3,299 former pupils of Stadium High School, Tacoma, Washington, USA, who attended the centennial event on 16 September 2006.

47°14'N 122°26'W

ANIMAL MAGIC
PETS

★ NEW RECORD
☆ UPDATED RECORD

SMALLEST LIVING DOG

The smallest dog living, in terms of height, is a long-haired female Chihuahua called Boo Boo, who measured 10.16 cm (4 in) tall on 12 May 2007. Boo Boo is owned by Lana Elswick of Raceland, Kentucky, USA.

★EARLIEST DOMESTICATED CAT

The oldest archaeological evidence of the domestication of the cat dates back 9,500 years. The bones of a cat were discovered in the neolithic village of Shillourokambos on Cyprus.

MOST INTELLIGENT DOG BREED

Research by Stanley Coren (USA), Professor of Psychology at the University of British Columbia – and the polling of professional dog obedience judges – reveals the smartest dog breed to be the Border collie, followed by the poodle and German shepherd.

★FARTHEST JUMP BY A GUINEA PIG

The longest leap by a guinea pig was achieved by Diesel (above), who cleared a gap of 20.5 cm (8.07 in) in London, UK, on 27 July 2009. The **highest jump by a guinea pig** was achieved by Puckel Martin, who jumped 20 cm (7.8 in) on 16 March 2003.

★LONGEST JUMP BY A RABBIT

The world record for the longest rabbit jump is 3 m (9 ft 9.6 in) and was achieved by Yabo, handled by Maria Brunn Jensen (Denmark), on 12 June 1999 in Horsens, Denmark. That's some bunny hop...

☆HIGHEST RATE OF PET OWNERSHIP (COUNTRY)

The country with the highest rate of pet ownership per household as of 2010 is Australia, with over 60% of households having at least one animal as a companion (typically a cat or dog) and 83% of Australians having owned a pet at some point in their life.

LONGEST EARS ON A RABBIT

Nipper's Geronimo, an English lop owned by Waymon and Margaret Nipper (USA), has ears that were measured at 79 cm (31.125 in) in a complete span on 1 November 2003 at the American Rabbit Breeders Association National Show in Wichita, Kansas, USA.

★NEWEST BREED OF CAT

Finally recognized as an official cat breed in 2002, though reported in Toronto, Canada, in the mid-20th century, the hairless sphynx cat can trace its origin to a number of cats with a recessive gene that causes hairlessness.

FUR! THE SPHYNX CAT DOES NOT HAVE ANY FUR, BUT ITS SKIN HAS THE SAME COLOURATION AS FUR AND ALSO FEATURES THE USUAL CAT MARKING PATTERNS, SUCH AS SOLID, TABBY OR TORTIE!

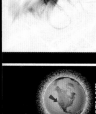

OLDEST CAT EVER

Born on 3 August 1967, Creme Puff lived with her owner, Jake Perry, in Austin, Texas, USA, until 6 August 2005 – an amazing 38 years 3 days!

OLDEST GOLDFISH EVER

In 1956, seven-year-old Peter Hand of Carlton Minniot, North Yorkshire, UK, won a goldfish (which he named Tish) at a fairground stall. For the next 43 years, Peter's parents, Hilda and Gordon, cared for Tish until the fish died in 1999.

OLDEST CAGED GERBIL

A Mongolian gerbil called Sahara, born in May 1973 and belonging to Aaron Milstone of Lathrup Village, Michigan, USA, died on 4 October 1981 aged eight years and four-and-a-half months old.

SMALLEST BREED OF DOMESTIC HAMSTER

The Roborovski (*Phodopus roborovskii*) typically grows to a length of 4–5 cm (1.5–2 in). These hamsters originate from Mongolia and northern China.

PURR!
THE F1 SAVANNAH IS A FIRST-GENERATION SERVAL (WILD CAT)/ DOMESTIC CAT HYBRID, WHICH IS CONSIDERED A DOMESTICATED CAT BY THE INTERNATIONAL CAT ASSOCIATION (TICA).

MOST TOES ON A CAT

Jake, a male ginger tabby cat owned by Michelle and Paul Contant (both Canada), had 28 toes – seven per paw – with each toe having its own claw, pad and bone structure, on 24 September 2002.

★ TALLEST DOMESTIC CAT

Scarlett's Magic, an F1 Savannah cross owned by Kimberly and Lee Draper (USA), measured 41.87 cm (16.48 in) tall on 17 December 2009.

★ LONGEST RABBIT

Darius, a Flemish giant rabbit owned by Annette Edwards (UK, pictured with her big bunny), was found to be 129 cm (4 ft 3 in) long when measured for an article in the UK's *Daily Mail* newspaper on 6 April 2010.

SMALLEST RABBIT

Both the Netherlandish and Polish dwarf breeds of rabbit have a weight range of 0.9–1.13 kg (2–2 lb 7 oz). In 1975, Jacques Bouloc (France) announced a new hybrid of these two breeds that weighed just 396 g (13.9 oz).

OLDEST DOG EVER

The greatest recorded age for a dog is 29 years 5 months for an Australian cattle-dog named Bluey, owned by Les Hall (Australia). Bluey was obtained as a puppy in 1910 and lived until 14 November 1939.

TALLEST LIVING DOG

Giant George is a Great Dane who measured 1.092 m (43 in) tall on 15 February 2010. The huge hound weighs 111 kg (245 lb) and is owned by David Nasser of Tucson, Arizona, USA.

ANIMAL MAGIC
ZOOS & SANCTUARIES

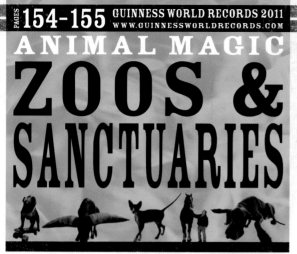

★ ★ ★ ★ ★ ★ ★ ★ ★ ★ ★ ★ ★

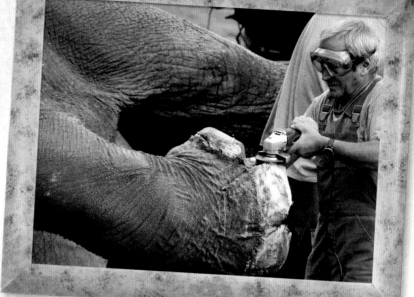

LONGEST SNAKE IN CAPTIVITY

Fluffy, a reticulated python (*Python reticulatus*), lives in Columbus Zoo and Aquarium in Powell, Ohio, USA. When measured in 2009, she was found to be over 7.3 m (24 ft) long.

The **longest snake ever** was found in Indonesia in 1912 and measured 10 m (32 ft 9.5 in).

OLDEST ZOO

The **earliest known collection of animals** was established at modern-day Puzurish, Iraq, by Shulgi, a 3rd-dynasty ruler of Ur from 2097 BC to 2094 BC. In the early 13th century, English monarch King John began the most extensive animal collection of the medieval era, which was housed in the Tower of London.

The ★**oldest continuously operating zoo** is the Tiergarten Schönbrunn, part of the Schönbrunn Palace in Vienna, Austria. Created in 1752 by order of Holy Roman Emperor Francis I, initially as a crown menagerie, it was first opened to the public in 1779. The first elephant born in captivity was born here in 1906.

★LARGEST PEDICURES

Elephants in captivity are the largest animals to receive pedicures. Pictured above is a (sedated) 39-year-old Asian elephant named Boy, receiving a pedicure from a German vet on 23 May 2009, in Kiev Zoo, Ukraine.

LARGEST ZOO

In terms of numbers of different species in captivity, the largest zoo is the Zoologischer Garten Berlin (Berlin zoological garden), also the first zoo in Germany, which opened on 1 August 1844. The 35-ha (86-acre) site currently houses 14,000 animals from 1,500 different species, and receives on average 2.6 million visitors each year.

AQUARIUMS

Sea Life in Brighton, East Sussex, UK, is the world's ★**oldest aquarium**, dating back to 1872. Combining Victorian architecture with modern-day, high-tech exhibits, it contains more than 150 species of marine life, which are exhibited in 57 separate displays.

In terms of water volume, the Georgia Aquarium in Atlanta, Georgia, USA, is

the **largest aquarium**, with 30.28 million litres (8 million gal) of fresh and salt water. The attraction opened in November 2005, covers 51,096 m² (500,000 ft²) and contains 120,000 fish and animals from 500 species. It has 60 different habitats, the largest of which contains 23.47 million litres (6.2 million gal) and was designed to house whale sharks.

EXTRA!
GWR'S TOUR AROUND OUR INCREDIBLE LIVING PLANET STARTS ON P.46.

37°49'N 122°16'W **OAKLAND, CA, USA**

On 11 January 1935, Amelia Earhart (USA) made the **first successful solo flight from Hawaii to North America**, setting off from Wheeler Field, Honolulu, Hawaii, USA, to Oakland Airport, California, USA. The flight lasted 18 hours and covered 3,860 km (2,400 miles).

DID YOU KNOW?

THE LARGEST LION WAS SIMBA, A BLACK-MANED MALE 1.11 M (44 IN) AT THE SHOULDER, WHO LIVED AT ZOOS IN COLCHESTER AND KNARESBOROUGH, UK.

TRIVIA

The largest of the "big cats" is the tiger. Size apart, "big cats" are also distinguished from other cats by their ability to roar.

★ MOST GIRAFFE OFFSPRING BORN IN CAPTIVITY

Denisa, a female giraffe living in the Safari Park zoo in Ramat Gan, Israel, has given birth to a record 11 offspring. She is pictured with her latest, in July 2009.

LARGEST LITTER OF TIGERS

On 15 April 1979, eight tigers were born at Marine World Africa USA, Redwood City, California, USA, to a Bengal tiger (*Panthera tigris tigris*) named Baghdad. This is the greatest recorded number of tigers born in captivity.

★ LARGEST WALK-IN AVIARY

Part of Singapore's Jurong Bird Park – the world's largest bird park, containing 8,000 birds – the world's largest walk-in aviary is the African Waterfall Aviary, containing more than 1,500 free-flying birds belonging to over 50 different species.

OLDEST GORILLA IN CAPTIVITY

Colo (b. 22 December 1956), the first gorilla ever born in captivity, currently lives in Columbus Zoo in Powell, Ohio, USA. She has now reached the grand old age of 53 years.

★ NEW RECORD
★ UPDATED RECORD

GORILLA
THE LARGEST MAMMAL TO BUILD A NEST IS THE AFRICAN GORILLA (*GORILLA GORILLA*), WHICH GROWS UP TO 1.8 M (6 FT) TALL AND WEIGHS UP TO 227 KG (500 LB).

GORILLA
THE GREATEST HEIGHT RECORDED FOR A PRIMATE IN THE WILD IS 1.95 M (6 FT 5 IN) FOR A MOUNTAIN BULL GORILLA FOUND IN THE EASTERN CONGO IN MAY 1938.

SACRAMENTO, CA, USA
The **longest table tennis doubles marathon** lasted 101 hr 1 min 11 sec and was contested by Lance, Phil and Mark Warren and Bill Weir (all USA) in Sacramento, California, USA, on 9–13 April 1979.

38°33'N
121°28'W

ANIMAL MAGIC
DOWN ON THE FARM

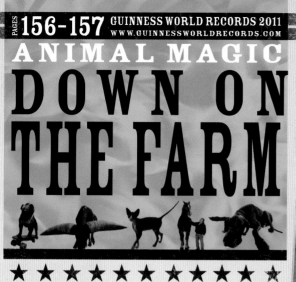

MENTAL! A "MANTLE" OF BEES IS A GIANT CLUSTER OF BEES THAT FORMS A PROTECTIVE LAYER AROUND THE QUEEN. BY WEARING THE QUEEN IN A LOCKET, AN INDIVIDUAL CAN ENCOURAGE A MANTLE OF BEES TO FORM AROUND THEMSELVES!

★ SMALLEST COW

Swallow, a Dexter cow owned by Martyn and Caroline Ryder (both UK) – pictured here with Freddie, a full-size British shorthorn – was measured at 85 cm (33.5 in), from rear foot to hind, at Pike End Farm, Rishworth, Halifax, UK, on 22 July 2009.

**★ NEW RECORD
★ UPDATED RECORD**

★ HEAVIEST MANTLE OF BEES

On 9 March 2009, at the Indian Agriculture Research Institute in New Delhi, India, Vipin Seth (India) was covered by a mantle of bees weighing 61.4 kg (136 lb 4 oz) and comprising an estimated 613,500 bees.

LARGEST FARM

The farm owned by Laucídio Coelho (Brazil) in Mato Grosso, Brazil, covered 8,700 km² (3,360 miles²) and supported 250,000 cattle at the time of Coelho's death in 1975. The smallest US state, Rhode Island, would fit into the farm three times.

★ FIRST MOOSE FARM

The first farm devoted to the domestication and rearing of the moose (*Alces alces*) – the world's **largest species of deer** – is the Kostroma Moose Farm (established 1963) in Kostroma Oblast, Russia. It includes 10 to 15 milk-producing moose cows, with over 800 moose having lived on the farm during its existence.

★ LARGEST ANT FARM

An ant farm measuring 1.2 x 0.9 x 0.08 m (3 ft 11 in x 2 ft 11 in x 3 in) and housing between 200 and 300 ants was unveiled on 28 December 2008 by Colgate Palmolive Ltd as part of a toothpaste advert on the side of a bus stop in Singapore.

MOST HORNS ON A SHEEP

Both ewes and rams of the Jacob sheep – a rare breed produced in both the USA and UK – typically grow two or four horns; however, some six-horned specimens have been recorded.

Vincent also killed 100 turkeys in 7 hr 32 min on 15 December 1978 – an average of one every four-and-a-half minutes!

TRIVIA

34°03′N 118°15′W **LOS ANGELES, CA, USA**
The **first movie shot in Hollywood** was *In Old California* (USA, 1910), which was filmed in Los Angeles in 1907 by a Chicago production that had moved to California to take advantage of the state's sunnier weather.

LARGEST HORN CIRCUMFERENCE

The African ankole watusi breed of cattle are famed for their thick horns. For **steers**, (castrated bulls) Lurch (pictured) is the record holder, with a horn 95.25 cm (37.5 in) in circumference. For **bulls**, C T Woodie takes the title with a 103.5-cm (40.75-in) horn.

FAST!
THE FASTEST TIME TO SHEAR A SINGLE MERINO LAMB IS 53.88 SECONDS BY DWAYNE BLACK (AUSTRALIA) IN BEIJING, CHINA, ON 20 SEPTEMBER 2007.

FASTER!
THE FASTEST TIME TO SHEAR A SINGLE SHEEP IS 45.41 SECONDS ALSO BY DWAYNE BLACK (AUSTRALIA) IN SYDNEY, NEW SOUTH WALES, AUSTRALIA, ON 17 APRIL 2005.

★MOST PROLIFIC CHICKEN

The highest authenticated rate of egg-laying is 371 eggs in 364 days, laid by a White Leghorn (No. 2988) in an official test conducted by Prof. Harold V Biellier and ending on 29 August 1979 at the College of Agriculture, University of Missouri, USA.

★OLDEST LIVING SHEEP

Lucky, a Dorset cross owned by Delrae and Frank Westgarth (Australia) of Lake Bolac, Australia, was born on 25 April 1986.

OLDEST LIVING PIG

The oldest pig is Oscar, who turned 20 years old on 29 October 2009. He lives with his owner, Stacy Leigh Kimbell (USA), in Dallas, Texas, USA.

MOST EXPENSIVE...

Cow: A Friesian fetched $1.3 million (£914,000) at auction in East Montpelier, Vermont, USA, in 1985.
Goat: An Angora buck bred by Waitangi Angoras of Waitangi, New Zealand, was sold to Elliott Brown Ltd of Waipu, New Zealand, for NZ$140,000 ($82,600; £46,200) on 25 January 1985.
Horse: The highest price paid for a thoroughbred at public auction is $16 million (£9.1 million) for a two-year-old colt who had yet to even race. He was bought at an auction held at Calder Race Course, Florida, USA, on 28 February 2006.
★**Pig:** E A Bud Olson and Phil Bonzio paid $56,000 (£37,000) to Jeffrey Roemisch of Texas, USA, for Bud, a cross-bred barrow (a castrated pig), on 5 March 1983.
★**Sheep:** Jimmy Douglas paid £231,000 ($369,000) for an eight-month-old Texel tup (uncastrated ram) in Lanark, Scotland, UK, in August 2009. This valuable sheep was purchased for breeding purposes.

★TALLEST HORSE

Big Jake, a nine-year-old Belgian gelding (castrated) horse, measured 20 hands 2.75 in (210.19 cm; 82.75 in), without shoes, at Smokey Hollow Farms in Poynette, Wisconsin, USA, on 19 January 2010.

EXTRA!
WANT EVEN MORE TALL TALES? WHY NOT TRY PP.76-77 ON FOR SIZE.

SPOKANE, WA, USA

On 17 April 2001, James David (USA) performed a continuous 130-m (425-ft 3-in) skid on his bicycle on a flat surface at the Spokane Raceway Park, Washington, USA – the **longest continuous skid on a bicycle**.

47°39′N 117°25′W

POPULAR CULTURE

NEW RECORD
★ UPDATED RECORD

CONTENTS

HIGHEST BOX-OFFICE FILM GROSS

James Cameron's (Canada) sci-fi extravaganza *Avatar* (USA/UK, 2009) sailed past his own *Titanic* (USA, 1997) to become the biggest movie ever in box-office history, grossing $2.69 billion (£1.80 billion) worldwide as of March 2010. *Avatar* – starring Sam Worthington (UK) and Zoe Saldana (USA), pictured below – is the ★**first movie to gross over $2 billion** and makes Cameron the director of the ★**most movies to gross over $1 billion**. It also claims the title for the ★**fastest-selling Blu-ray disc**, with 2.7 million copies purchased in its first four days on sale in North America alone. For more *Avatar* achievements, see below.

AVATAR RECORDS

RECORD	NOTES	DATE
★ *Highest grossing movie*	Beating *Titanic* (USA, 1997)	26 Jan 2010
★ *Fastest to $500 million*	Achieved in 32 days; *Titanic* took 45 days	19 Jan 2010
★ *Highest grossing PG-13*	Beating *Titanic* (USA, 1997)	1 Mar 2010
★ *Highest grossing 3D movie*	Beating *Up* (USA, 2009, now in 3rd place) and staying ahead of *Alice in Wonderland* (USA, 2010, in 2nd place)	1 Mar 2010
★ *Highest grossing sci-fi movie*	$2.69 billion (£1.80 billion)	1 Mar 2010
★ *Highest grossing New Year's Day*	Took $25.2 million (£16.8 million)	1 Jan 2010
★ *Largest motion-capture project*	Three years of motion-capture by Giant Studios (Los Angeles, USA)	NA
★ *Largest area to be motion-captured*	The Kong stage (Wellington, NZ): 45 x 24 x 12 m (150 x 80 x 40 ft)	NA
★ *Most actors motion-captured for a movie*	Giant Studios captured 80 people	NA
★ *First 3D movie to win Best Cinematography Oscar*	*Avatar* (USA, 2010)	7 Mar 2010

SLOW!
AVATAR WAS IN PRODUCTION FOR SO MANY YEARS THAT EACH FRAME OF THE MOVIE (1/24TH OF A SECOND) TOOK AN AVERAGE OF 47 HOURS TO FILM!

FAST!
THE MOVIE CROSSED THE $1 BILLION MARK IN A RECORD 17 DAYS – A VAST IMPROVEMENT ON THE 197 DAYS THAT IT TOOK THE DARK KNIGHT TO ACHIEVE THE SAME GROSS.

TIJUANA, MEXICO

The world's **largest Caesar salad** was prepared by Canirac – the Tijuana Restaurateurs Chamber of Commerce – on 20 October 2007. A team of 160 people prepared the 3,387-tonne (7,346-lb) salad, which was unveiled in Tijuana, Baja California, Mexico.

32°31'N
117°02'W

POPULAR CULTURE
VIDEO GAMES

HIGHEST REVENUE GENERATED BY AN ENTERTAINMENT PRODUCT IN 24 HOURS

Call of Duty: Modern Warfare 2 (Activision, 2009) generated $401 million (£239 million) in sales within the first 24 hours of its worldwide launch on 11 November 2009. This is the greatest amount ever generated on a first day of sale by an entertainment product, outstripping any film, music or previous videogame launch.

BEST-SELLING VIDEOGAME

With lifetime sales of 45.7 million copies between its launch in 2006 and May 2009, the best-selling videogame of all time is Nintendo's *Wii Sports*, which came bundled with the Wii console.

★BEST-SELLING RHYTHM GAME SERIES

Guitar Hero (RedOctane, 2005) had seen total sales of over 32 million units between November 2005 and June 2009.

★BEST-SELLING CONSOLE REAL-TIME STRATEGY GAME

Of the current generation of consoles, the best-selling Real-Time Strategy game is *Halo Wars* (Microsoft, 2009), which had notched up global sales of 1.21 million as of May 2009.

★HIGHEST CASH PRIZE AWARDED IN A FAN MOD TOURNAMENT

The Sendi Mutiara Multimedia Grand National DotA Tournament, which took place in Kuala Lumpur, Malaysia, on 22–23 November 2008, had a prize fund of 120,000 Malaysian ringgits (£21,000; $35,000). The tournament saw competitors from seven countries compete on the *Warcraft III* mod "Defense of the Ancients". Team Ehome from China emerged as champions, pocketing RM36,000 (£6,500; $10,500) in cash along with other prizes.

★MOST DETAILED VIDEOGAME CHARACTER

With a character model that consists of 32,816 rendered polygons during gameplay, the most detailed videogame character is Lara Croft in her *Tomb Raider: Underworld* (Eidos Interactive, 2008) incarnation.

World Record attempt 24 hour football gaming marathon

★LONGEST FOOTBALL GAME MARATHON

A group of gamers, supported by online gaming leagues website Stryxa.com, recorded the longest marathon playing a football videogame when they played *FIFA 10* (EA Sports, 2009) for 24 hours at Victoria Station, London, UK, from 27 to 28 January 2009.

★FASTEST-SELLING MULTI-PLATFORM ROLE-PLAYING GAME (RPG)

Bethesda's multi-platform RPG *Fallout 3* sold over 4.7 million copies in its first week on sale from 28 October to 4 November 2008.

★FASTEST-SELLING PC GAME

Released on 13 November 2008, *World of Warcraft* expansion pack *Wrath of the Lich King* (Activision Blizzard) sold 2.8 million copies within 24 hours, and 4 million copies in the month following its release.

★MOST POWERFUL FLIGHT SIMULATOR

Described as "a next generation military simulation synthetic environment", the *Simusphere HD World*, produced by Link Simulation and Training (USA) for clients including the United States Air Force (USAF), is the most powerful flight simulation system in the world. The USAF version simulates an F-16 fighter jet and runs on 120 dual core PCs, each of which contains a $400 (£250) graphics card, allowing for 10,000 onscreen objects to be displayed simultaneously.

★FIRST CONCERT HELD IN A REAL AND A VIRTUAL SPACE SIMULTANEOUSLY

On 2 June 2009, US punk-pop band The Dares (Ben Peterson, Matt Peterson and Martin Lascano) performed the first music concert to take place in both the real world and in a virtual space. The gig was held on a stage at E3 2009 in the Los Angeles Convention Center, California, USA, and simultaneously online in *Free Realms* (Sony, 2009). The Dares' set list included the *Free Realms* theme "It's Your World".

★LONGEST DRAW DISTANCE IN A RACING GAME

Codemasters' *FUEL* boasts a draw distance of 40 km (24.8 miles), the longest in a simulation racing game. *FUEL*'s racing environment is inspired by the North American wilderness. The landscape, which is modelled from satellite data and rendered by the game engine, is battered by weather effects including blizzards, tsunamis and tornadoes.

★LARGEST POKÉMON COLLECTION

Lisa Courtney (UK) was found to have 12,113 different items of Pokémon memorabilia when Guinness World Records examined her collection on 13 June 2009.

★LONGEST RACING GAME MARATHON

Rolf Loraas, Hans Moe, Alexander Moerk, Lars-Christian Klingstroem, Per Helge Fagermoen, Benny Charles Fredstad, Benjamin Ward, Jan Dalan and Joachim Olsen (all Norway) played *Need for Speed Shift* (EA, 2009) for 25 hours at Oslo City, Oslo, Norway, from 18 to 19 September 2009.

DRAW DISTANCE: The distance in a 3D scene that is still drawn by the game engine.

LONG! SARA LHADI (NETHERLANDS) SPENT A RECORD 16,799 HOURS PLAYING THE MMORPG *RUNESCAPE* BETWEEN NOVEMBER 2004 AND OCTOBER 2009.

SHORT! JUSTIN TOWELL (UK) COMPLETED EMERALD HILL, ZONE 1, ON *SONIC THE HEDGEHOG 2* ON XBOX LIVE ARCADE, IN A RECORD-BREAKING 21 SECONDS ON 30 OCTOBER 2009.

MEXICALI, MEXICO

The **largest flour taco** in the world weighed 750 kg (1,654 lb) and was made by the city of Mexicali and Cocinex SA de CV, in Mexicali, Mexico, on 8 March 2003.

32°40'N 115°28'W

POPULAR CULTURE
PUBLISHING

★ ★ ★ ★ ★ ★ ★ ★ ★ ★ ★ ★ ★ ★

★ NEW RECORD
★ UPDATED RECORD

★ LARGEST SINGLE-VOLUME BIOGRAPHY

Between 1996 and 2007, Dr A V S Raju (India) wrote a biography chronicling the life of Sri Sathya Sai Baba (India), a popular religious figure and spiritual teacher. The single bound book consists of 32 volumes.

★ MOST BANNED BOOK OF THE YEAR

The book most frequently reported to the American Library Association's (ALA) Office for Intellectual Freedom in 2008 – and each year since 2006 – is *And Tango Makes Three* by Justin Richardson and Peter Parnell (both USA). The award-winning book – which recounts the true tale of two male penguins who raise a baby penguin – attracted the most complaints from parents and school officials for its promotion of a "homosexual lifestyle".

★ LARGEST POP-UP BOOK

The largest pop-up book measures 1.13 m (3 ft 8 in) by 92 cm (3 ft) and weighs 19 kg (42 lb). It is an outsized version of *The Pop-Up Story of Delray Beach* by Roger Culberston (USA) and illustrated by Al Margolis. The book contains six pop-up spreads illustrating the experiences of residents and visitors to the city of Delray Beach, Florida, USA.

MOST NOBEL PRIZES FOR LITERATURE (COUNTRY)

The country that claims the most outright or shared Nobel prizes awarded for literature is France, with 13.

★ YOUNGEST RECIPIENT OF THE NOBEL PRIZE FOR LITERATURE

Poet and author Rudyard Kipling (UK, 1865–1936) won the Nobel prize for literature in 1907 at the age of 42, in recognition of his "power of observation, originality of imagination, virility of ideas".

★ FIRST WOMAN TO WIN THE NOBEL PRIZE FOR LITERATURE

Selma Lagerlöf (Sweden, 1858–1940) was awarded the Nobel prize for literature in 1909 for the "lofty idealism, vivid imagination and spiritual perception that characterize her writings".

★ MOST AUDIO BOOKS PUBLISHED FOR ONE AUTHOR

L Ron Hubbard (USA) has had 185 audio books published as of 21 April 2009.

★ HIGHEST DAILY ENGLISH-LANGUAGE NEWSPAPER CIRCULATION

The Times of India, owned by the Sahu Jain family (India), has an average daily circulation of 3,146,000 according to the latest figures from the World Association of Newspapers and the Audit Bureau of Circulations.

THICKEST BOOK

The entire collection of Agatha Christie's (UK) *Miss Marple* detective stories – a grand total of 12 novels and 20 short stories – was published as one single volume by HarperCollins on 20 May 2009. The capacious compendium is 322 mm (12.67 in) thick.

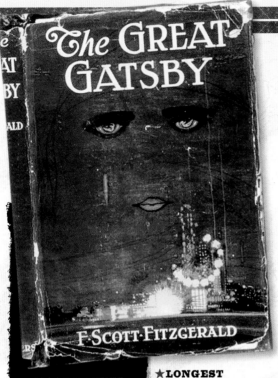

THE GREAT GATSBY

F·SCOTT·FITZGERALD

★ OLDEST PLAYBOY MODEL

Model and presenter Patricia Paay (Netherlands, b. 7 April 1949) posed for the Christmas edition of *Playboy Netherlands* on 10 December 2009 at the age of 60.

★ OLDEST PRINTING AND PUBLISHING HOUSE

Cambridge University Press is the oldest printing and publishing house in the world. It was founded on a royal charter granted to the University by Henry VIII in 1534 and has been operating continuously as a printer and publisher since the first Press book was printed in 1584.

★ RICHEST AUTHOR

According to *Forbes*, J K Rowling (UK), author of the Harry Potter series, has grossed over $1 billion (£627 million) for her novels and from related earnings. Rowling is one of only five self-made female billionaires, and the ★**first billion-dollar author**. The seven Potter books have sold 400 million copies around the world and are published in 55 languages, including Latin and ancient Greek.

★ MOST BOOKS TYPED BACKWARDS

Using a computer and four blank keyboards, and without looking at the screen, Michele Santelia (Italy) has typed backwards 68 books (3,663,324 words; 20,680,060 characters; 24,154 pages; 266,741 paragraphs; 516,498 lines) in their original languages including *The Odyssey*, *Macbeth*, The Vulgate Bible, *Guinness World Records 2002* and the Dead Sea scrolls (in Ancient Hebrew).

Santelia's most recent book typed backwards and in the English language is the *Life of Abraham Lincoln* (956 pages; 160,311 words; 919,124 characters; 2,810 paragraphs; 16,944 lines). He started typing it on 20 January 2009 and finished it on 16 June 2009.

★ LARGEST ATLAS

The 350-year-old Klencke Atlas was presented to Charles II, King of England, on his restoration in 1660. Created by Dutch merchant Yohannes Klencke, the atlas features 41 maps on 39 sheets, and is 1.78 m (5 ft 10 in) tall, 1.05 m (3 ft 5 in) wide and 11 cm (4 in) thick.

MOST BANNED CLASSIC NOVEL

Topping the American Library Association's list of most banned or "challenged" classic novels is *The Great Gatsby* (1924) by F Scott Fitzgerald. The Baptist College in Charleston, South Carolina, USA, challenged the book because of "language and sexual references" as recently as 1987.

★ LONGEST AUDIO BOOK

Published on 1 August 2008 by Tokyo Shigesato Itoi Office K K (Japan), the audio book *50 Lectures* by Takaaki Yoshimoto (Japan) has a running time of 115 hr 43 min.

LONGEST NOVEL

A la recherche du temps perdu by Marcel Proust (France) contains around 9,609,000 characters (each letter counts as a character; so do spaces). The title translates as *In Search of Lost Time* and the first of seven volumes appeared in 1913.

DID YOU KNOW? THE KLENCKE ATLAS WAS GIVEN TO CHARLES II TO WIN HIS FAVOUR. CENTURIES AGO, MAPS WERE OFTEN DESIGNED TO INFLUENCE OR FLATTER POWERFUL PEOPLE.

Unseen by the public for 350 years, the pages of the Klencke Atlas went on show at the British Library, London, UK, in 2010.

TRIVIA

NOVA DESCRITTIONE D'ITALIA DI GIOANN. ANTONIO MAGINO.

EXTRA! FOR ONLINE FACTS, STATS AND WORLD RECORDS, TURN TO P.216.

CALGARY, AB, CANADA

The **longest journey of the Olympic torch within one country** was for the XV Winter Olympic Games in Canada in 1988. The torch arrived from Greece at St Johns, Newfoundland, Canada, on ... November 1987 and was transported a total distance of 18,060 km (11,222 miles)

51°02'N 114°03'W

POPULAR CULTURE
COMICS & GRAPHIC NOVELS

* NEW RECORD *UPDATED RECORD

POPULAR CULTURE

WHAT'S ON TV

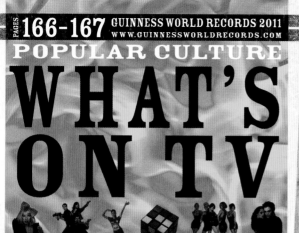

★ ★ ★ ★ ★ ★ ★ ★ ★ ★ ★ ★ ★ ★

★ MOST WATCHED TV SERIES (2009)

Global: The most popular TV show continues to be the medical drama *House* (Fox). According to ratings agency Eurodata TV Worldwide, the show – starring Hugh Laurie (UK) as the unconventional, maverick Dr Gregory House – was seen by more than 81.8 million viewers in 66 countries.

UK: The final of *Britain's Got Talent* was seen by nearly 18 million viewers.

Europe: The *Eurovision Song Contest* 2009 clocked up an impressive 122 million viewers.

USA: *NCIS* (NBC) season 7 episode "Reunion" averaged 21.37 million viewers.

MAD
PICTURED ARE *MAD MEN'S* DON AND BETTY DRAPER (JON HAMM AND JANUARY JONES, BOTH USA). THE SHOW FOLLOWS THE RUTHLESSLY COMPETITIVE WORLD OF ADVERTISING IN THE 1960S.

★ LONGEST-RUNNING MEDICAL DRAMA

Casualty (BBC, 1986–present) is the world's most enduring primetime medical drama series. Only the hospital-based soap opera *General Hospital* (ABC, 1963–present) – now the world's ★ **longest-running daytime soap opera** with the demise of *As the World Turns* (CBS, 1956–2010) – has been broadcast for a longer period.

★ MOST WATCHED TV

2009: The funeral of Michael Jackson (USA) on 7 July 2009 was watched by a global audience of 2–3 billion.

Sports event: According to the BBC, English Premier League football games are broadcast to over 600 million homes in 202 countries.

★ MOST TIME-SHIFTED TV SHOW

According to 2009 figures from Nielsen, the most "time-shifted" primetime show of the year was *Battlestar Galactica* (SYFY), enjoying a 59.4% increase in viewing figures as a result. Time-shifting involves recording TV shows on digital video recorders (DVRs) or storing them via premium TV services such as Sky+ or BT Vision.

★ LONGEST RUNNING SOAP OPERA ON TV

It was announced in 2009 that *As the World Turns* (CBS, 1956–) would be cancelled by September 2010, meaning that the UK's *Coronation Street* (ITV, 1960–) would become the world's longest-running soap opera. Actor William Roache (UK) would then become the ★ **longest-serving soap actor**, having debuted as Ken Barlow in episode 1.

★ HIGHEST-RATED TV SHOWS (CURRENT)

Three shows can boast to be the most critically acclaimed series currently on TV. The third season of *Mad Men* (Lionsgate/AMC, pictured left), *Sons of Anarchy* (FX) and *Modern Family* (ABC) all scored 86/100 on the critical aggregation site metacritic.com.

75 YEARS OF BROADCAST TV

Although experimental services had operated across the world from the 1920s, the television broadcasting age as we recognize it began at 3 p.m. on 2 November 1936 in London, UK, when the BBC launched the world's **first regular television broadcasts**.

"Good afternoon, ladies and gentle-men. It is with great pleasure that I introduce you to the magic of television..."

Leslie Mitchell, first words spoken on TV

1936: First TV announcer
Radio personality Leslie Mitchell is the first of three TV presenters that includes Jasmine Bligh and Elizabeth Cowell (all UK), the **first female TV announcers**.

1936: First black performers
Buck and Bubbles (USA), an energetic, vaudeville comedy dance act, are guests on *Variety* (UK), one of the shows broadcast on the first day of service.

1936: First magazine show
Picture Page (UK), a variety and chat show, runs daily from day one, hosted by Joan Millar (Canada), who becomes the world's **first TV star**.

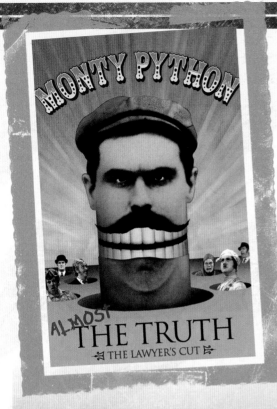

EMMY AWARDS

★ MOST WINS
The televised Oscars (Academy Awards) ceremony has been nominated for 195 Primetime Emmy awards, winning a record 46 times.

★ MOST WINS FOR A VARIETY, MUSIC OR COMEDY SERIES
The Daily Show with Jon Stewart (Comedy Central) has won the Emmy for Outstanding Variety, Music or Comedy series for a record seven consecutive years.

★ YOUNGEST ACTRESS TO WIN A LEAD ACTING EMMY
In 2007, at the age of 23, America Ferrara (USA, b. 18 April 1984) was voted the Outstanding Lead Actress in a Comedy Series for her portrayal of Betty Suarez in *Ugly Betty* (ABC) – the youngest person to win a lead acting Emmy award.

★ HIGHEST-EARNING CELEBRITY
Between June 2009 and June 2010, Oprah Winfrey (USA) earned an estimated $275 million (£186 million) thanks to her magazine, her radio contract, her production company Harpo and the debut of the Oprah Winfrey Network.

★ NOMINATIONS – MOST IN ONE YEAR
Variety show: *Saturday Night Live* (NBC) – 13 nominations in 2009.
Comedy show: *30 Rock* (NBC) – 22 nominations in 2009.
Drama: *NYPD Blue* (ABC) – 27 nominations in 1994.
Mini-series: *Roots* (ABC) – 37 nominations in 1977.

★ MOST DAYTIME EMMYS WON
The Public Broadcasting Service's *Sesame Street* has won a record 122 Daytime Emmys since 1984.

> *"The only people who never tumble are those who never mount the high wire."*
> **Oprah Winfrey**

★ HIGHEST-RATED TV DOCUMENTARY (2009)
Monty Python: Almost the Truth (IFC) enjoyed an average reviewer rating of 84/100, making the six-part series the most critically acclaimed documentary of 2009.

★ HIGHEST PAID
Actor: Charlie Sheen (USA) was estimated to earn $800,000 (£519,295) per episode of *Two and a Half Men* (CBS, 2003–present).

Actress: Katherine Heigl (USA) – Izzie Stevens in *Grey's Anatomy* (ABC, 2005–present) – earned $200,000 (£129,823) per show.

★ HIGHEST-EARNING PRIMETIME TV STARS
While Oprah reigns supreme as the **highest-earning TV personality** (see above), the Forbes Celebrity 100 list identifies Simon Cowell (UK) and Tyra Banks (USA) as the highest-earning *primetime* celebrities. In the 12 months between June 2009 and June 2010, talent judge Cowell earned an estimated $75 million (£48.8 million), while supermodel-turned-host Banks made $30 million (£19.5 million).

IDOL
COWELL PRODUCED THE "GOT TALENT" AND "X FACTOR" FRANCHISES – TWO OF THE FASTEST-SELLING TV FORMATS EVER. "TALENT" WAS THE ONLY SHOW TO BE NO.1 IN THE UK AND USA AT THE SAME TIME.

1936: First TV drama
On day five, excerpts from the West End play *Marigold* by L Allen Harker and F R Pryor (both UK) are broadcast.

1937: First children's series
For the Children (UK) debuts at 3 p.m. on April 24 and runs until 1950 (with a break for World War II); episodes last 10 minutes.

1937: First regular TV chef
Marcel Boulestin (France, left) begins hosting *Dish of the Month* (UK) on 15 October.

1938: First TV sci-fi aired – an adaptation of *R.U.R.* (*Rossum's Universal Robots*), a play in the Czech language by Karel Čapek; also the world's **first depiction of robots**.

1939: First regular US programming
Franklin D Roosevelt (USA) opens the 1939 New York's World Fair (30 April), relayed to the nation via a high-definition telecast.

1939–46: BBC TV suspended for the duration of World War II.

1940: First ice hockey (25 February) and **first basketball game** (28 February) aired.

1941: First TV advert
NBC's WNBT station (USA) promotes a Bulova watch on 27 June.

1949: First Emmy Awards
The TV equivalent of the Oscars is first aired on 25 January.

POPULAR CULTURE
COP & CRIME SHOWS

★ **FIRST ARMCHAIR DETECTIVE SERIES**
The first time the police used TV to appeal for help in a murder case was in Germany in 1938, and the first "missing person" appeal was made on 3 October 1943 by New York police. The first regular series to enlist the help of the public to solve real-life crimes was *Police 5* (LWT, 1962–92), hosted by Shaw Taylor (UK).

★ **FIRST CRIME SHOW ON TV**
Telecrime (BBC, 1938–39) – later known as *Telecrimes* (1946) – challenged TV viewers to unravel crimes before the police and featured the ★**first TV police detective**, Inspector Holt (played by J B Rowe, UK). He was assisted by Sgt Carter (Richard George, UK), ★**TV's first cop sidekick**.

★ **LONGEST-RUNNING COP SHOW (BY DATE)**
Germany's *Der Alte* ("The Old Fox") has run on ZDF since 1977. The UK's longest-running cop shows are ITV's *Taggart* and *The Bill*, which have been running since 1983. The USA's longest-running cop show is *Law & Order* (NBC), which began in 1990.

★ **MOST SUCCESSFUL COP SHOW FRANCHISE**
The Bill (see right) gave rise to a total of three spin-off series. They were:

★ **LONGEST-RUNNING COP SHOW (BY EPISODE)**
At the time of going to press (April 2010), *The Bill* (ITV, 1983–2010) had an episode count of 2,389, with the date of 30 September 2010 slated for its final episode. Despite its various incarnations, *The Bill* is fundamentally a hybrid crime/soap opera, hence the inflated number of episodes.

FRANK COLUMBO
Peter Falk (USA) is the ★**most enduring cop actor**, having portrayed the shambling detective Lieutenant Columbo from *Prescription Murder* (NBC, 1968) to 2003's *Columbo Likes the Nightlife* (ABC).

JANE MARPLE
The ★**most TV depictions of Miss Marple**, Agatha Christie's silver sleuth, is 12, shared by Brit actresses Joan Hickson (*Miss Marple*, BBC, 1984–92, pictured below right) and Geraldine McEwan (*Marple*, ITV, 2004–09, below left).

GEORGE DIXON
The ★**most prolific TV cop** was PC George Dixon (Jack Warner, UK) in *Dixon of Dock Green* (BBC, 1955–76), who appeared in 431 episodes.

FRANK
WHENEVER ASKED FOR HIS FIRST NAME, COLUMBO WOULD ANSWER "LIEUTENANT". BUT LOOK CLOSELY AT HIS WARRANT CARD AND BADGE AND YOU'LL SEE HIS NAME: FRANK!

FIELDS
THE FIRST ACTRESS TO PORTRAY MISS MARPLE WAS THE UK'S GRACIE FIELDS IN THE NBC (USA) *GOODYEAR TV PLAYHOUSE: A MURDER IS ANNOUNCED* IN 1956.

1951: First regular colour broadcast
On 25 June, CBS broadcast the first colour images from five stations on the US east coast... to a virtually non-existent audience, as so few colour TV sets exist!

1951: First use of TV detector vans in the UK to trace TV licence evaders.

1952: Longest-running soap opera Procter & Gamble Productions' *Guiding Light* (CBS, USA) first airs on 30 June, and is the world's longest-lived soap until it finishes in 2009.

1953: The CBS system fails; RCA's system adopted as industry standard in the USA.

1954: First coast-to-coast colour transmission (USA)
RCA's broadcasting wing (NBC) airs first countrywide colour transmission on 1 January 1954 with The Tournament of Roses Parade from Pasadena, California.

1954: First network series regularly shown in colour: NBC sitcom *The Marriage* debuts.

1954: First in-vision weather report is shown with presenter George Cowling (UK) standing in front of a projected map.

1957: *The Sky at Night* (BBC) introduces us to the monocled Patrick Moore (UK, left), who will continue to host the show to the present day, making him the **most enduring TV host**.

TUCSON, AR, USA
Dayton C Fouts of Tucson, Arizona, had the **longest career as Santa Claus**, having played the role every year from 1937 until 1997. He first appeared as Santa for 55 years in Harvey, Illinois, and continued the tradition in Tucson, with his last event at a Tucson Boys Chorus concert.

★FIRST FEMALE TV COP STAR

Decoy (aka *Police Woman: Decoy*), a US series syndicated in 1957–58, starred Beverly Garland (USA) as undercover policewoman Patricia "Casey" Jones. Britain's first female-led cop show was *The Gentle Touch* (ITV, 1980–84), starring Jill Gascoigne as Detective Inspector Maggie Forbes (pictured left).

Burnside, 2000; *Beech is Back*, 2001; and *MIT: Murder Investigation Team*, 2003–05), giving a combined episode count of 2,413 (as of April 2010).

The **most successful non-soap cop show** ever was *Z-Cars* (BBC, 1962–78), which eventually ran to 799 episodes. With its spin-offs *Softly Softly* (1966–69), *Softly Softly: Task Force*

(1969–76), *Barlow at Large* (1971–73), *Barlow* (1974–75), *Jack the Ripper* (1973) and *Second Verdict* (1974), it had a combined episode count of over 1,100. The **most successful non-soap cop show (current)** is *Law & Order* (see right).

★HIGHEST-RATED COP SHOW

According to metacritic.com, *The Sopranos* remains

the most popular "crime" show among TV reviewers, garnering a score of 96/100; *The Wire*, which could be considered more truly a "cop" show – being more about police than criminals – comes in at second place with a metascore of 89/100.

The cop/crime show that most wowed reviewers in 2009 was the FBI-based *White Collar* (USA Network/Fox) with a score of 78/100.

★MOST SUCCESSFUL COP FRANCHISE (CURRENT)

While *Z-Cars* holds the absolute record, in terms of shows currently on air, the franchise winner is *Law & Order* (NBC, 1990–current) – which includes *Criminal Intent*, *Special Victims Unit* (pictured are stars Mariska Hargitay and Ice-T, both USA) and the now defunct *Trial by Jury* and *Conviction*) – with over 915 episodes to date.

HERCULE POIROT

The ★**most depictions of Hercule Poirot on TV** is 60 and counting by David Suchet (UK), who has gone on record saying he hopes to film the entire canon (84 stories) by his 65th birthday in May 2011.

PERRY MASON

The ★**most murders solved on TV** is at least 297 by the defence attorney Perry Mason (Raymond Burr, USA, 1917–93) in *Perry Mason* (CBS, 1957–66) and the *Perry Mason TV Movies* (NBC, 1985–93).

SHERLOCK HOLMES

The **most depictions of Sherlock Holmes on TV** is 41 by Jeremy Brett (UK, pictured) in the ITV series that ran from 1984 to 1994. The **first Holmes TV series** – *Sherlock Holmes* (BBC, 1951) – starred Alan Wheatley (UK).

'ELLO
THE FIRST ACTOR TO PLAY HERCULE POIROT ON TV WAS JAMES L SULLIVAN (UK) IN THE FIRST AGATHA CHRISTIE TV ADAPTATION: *THE WASP'S NEST* (BBC, 1937).

LAW
PERRY MASON WAS THE CREATION OF REAL-LIFE LAWYER ERLE STANLEY GARDNER (USA, 1889–1970), WHO FEATURED HIS FICTIONAL ATTORNEY IN AROUND 80 NOVELS.

ORDER
PERRY MASON HAS APPEARED IN NOVELS, SHORT STORIES, RADIO SERIALS, COMIC BOOKS, TV SERIES, TV MOVIES, DAYTIME SOAPS AND EVEN A BOOK OF POETRY!

TELE-MENTARY
THE FIRST ACTOR TO PORTRAY SHERLOCK HOLMES ON TV WAS LOUIS HECTOR (USA) IN AN EXPERIMENTAL NBC (USA) PRODUCTION IN 1937.

1958: First actor to die on live TV is Gareth Jones (UK) during an ITV production of *Armchair Theatre*.

1958: *Blue Peter*, the **longest-running children's magazine programme**, debuts on BBC1.

1960: Debut of record-breaking soap *Coronation Street* (see p.166).

1963: First murder on live TV takes place as John F Kennedy's assassin, Lee Harvey Oswald (USA), is shot and killed by Jack Ruby (USA).

1963: Longest-running sci-fi show – *Doctor Who* – receives its first airing on 12 November.

1965: First use of the f– word on TV is on 13 November 1965 by literary agent Kenneth Tynan (UK) during a satirical discussion show entitled *BBC3*.

1969: The first Moon landing becomes the **most watched live TV event**, drawing a fifth of 600 million viewers – a fifth of the world population at the time.

1973: First fly-on-the-wall documentary series, *An American Family*, airs to 10 million viewers.

1975: BBC introduces its now classic weather symbols.

POPULAR CULTURE
SCI-FI & FANTASY TV

★ MOST SUCCESSFUL SCI-FI TV ADAPTATION

Paramount's (USA) 2009 movie "re-booting" of the *Star Trek* TV show (NBC, USA, 1966–69, above right) took $385,494,555 (£238,324,000) globally – the biggest box-office gross for a live-action TV adaptation.

★ FIRST SCI-FI SERIAL

The first regular sci-fi serial on TV was *Captain Video and His Video Rangers* (Dumont, USA, June 1949–April 1955). Set in the year 2254, it followed the exploits of Captain Video (played by Richard Coogan, USA), an inventor and "Master of Science". It aired nightly – live – at 7 p.m.

★ FIRST RECORDED SCI-FI TV SHOW

While early TV shows were broadcast live (see *Captain Video,* above), the first sci-fi series to be pre-recorded was *Rocky Jones, Space Ranger* (USA, syndicated, 1953). Recorded shows made for better sets and effects – particularly important for the science-fiction genre.

LONGEST-RUNNING TV SCI-FI

See Doctor Who, pp.172–173, and Smallville, opposite.

★ FIRST SCI-FI SITCOM ON TV

The primetime animated series *The Jetsons* (ABC, USA)

debuted in 1962 as the space-age equivalent of *The Flintstones.* Set in 2062, it depicted modern America as projected into the future.

The ★ **first live-action sci-fi sitcom** was *My Favorite Martian* (CBS, USA, 1963–66), which followed the exploits of a Martian who crash-lands on Earth and is rescued by a newspaper reporter who tries to pass him off as a relative.

★ HIGHEST-RATED SCI-FI MINI-SERIES

"Children of Earth" (UK, 2009), the third season of the BBC's sci-fi mini-series *Torchwood* (UK) received a review score of 80/100 on metacritic.com. This made it the highest rated sci-fi mini-series of 2009, ahead of the reimagined version of *The Prisoner* (AMC/ITV, UK).

WOOD
THE TORCHWOOD INSTITUTE INVESTIGATES EXTRATERRESTRIAL ACTIVITY ON EARTH AND IS SET IN THE CARDIFF, UK, BRANCH OF THE ORGANIZATION.

TORCH
TORCHWOOD (AN ANAGRAM OF DOCTOR WHO) IS A SPIN-OFF SHOW STARRING JOHN BARROWMAN (UK, PICTURED FRONT) AS CAPTAIN JACK HARKNESS.

1976: *The Muppet Show* airs in the UK on 5 September, then in the USA on 27 September; goes on to become the world's **most popular show**, watched by 300 million viewers in 103 countries.

1976: The BBC formally launches its CEEFAX teletext service.

1977: First "gaffe" show *It'll Be Alright on the Night* (ITV, UK) features host Denis Norden (UK) revealing the gaffes or "bloopers" filmed while making television shows.

1979: First use of satellite data for TV weather reports.

1981: MTV launches in the USA.

1983: Largest TV audience (USA) The final episode of *M*A*S*H* (CBS, left) is transmitted on 28 February 1983 to 60.3% of all households in the USA; it is watched by some 125 million people.

1985: Live Aid takes place in London, UK, and Philadelphia, PA, USA, and is watched by

1.5 billion TV viewers worldwide, making it the world's **largest simultaneous charity rock concert** in terms of viewers.

1986: Over 30 million people tune in as Den divorces Angie in *EastEnders* (BBC, UK) on Christmas Day – the **highest ever viewing figures for a series in the UK.**

35°06'N 106°36'W

ALBUQUERQUE, NM, USA

The **first Hot-air Balloon World Championships** were held in Albuquerque, New Mexico, USA, from 10 to 17 February 1973.

CLONE WARS
Star Wars: The Clone Wars (Lucasfilm Animation/Warner Bros TV, 2008–present) is the ★**highest-rated sci-fi animation on TV**, with an average review of 64/100 on metacritic.com on its release. The CGI series has expanded the scope of the "galaxy far, far away" and taken the *Star Wars* story in new directions down darker, more mature paths.

★**FIRST FANTASY SITCOM**
Topper (CBS, then ABC, later NBC; all USA) ran from 1953 to 1956. It was based on Thorne Smith's novels (previously made into films) about the rather staid Cosmo Topper, whose life takes an unexpectedly lively turn after he is haunted by a fun-loving couple who had lived in his house before their deaths.

★**FIRST SUPER HERO ON TV**
Superman was the first comicbook super hero to appear in his own television series. *The Adventures of Superman* (USA, syndicated, 1952) starred George Reeves (USA) as the Man of Steel and was sponsored by Kellogg's.

★**MOST PROLIFIC SCI-FI TV WRITERS**
Rodman "Rod" Serling (USA) – creator and narrator of *The Twilight Zone* (CBS, USA, 1959–64) – wrote 92 episodes (out of 156) of the successful sci-fi anthology show.
Babylon 5 (PTEN) creator Joe Straczynski (USA) also wrote 92 (out of 110) episodes of his CGI-heavy sci-fi show.

★**MOST SCI-FI TV SPIN-OFFS**
The Japanese series *Ultraman* (United Artists/Tokyo Broadcasting System, 1966–67) spawned 30 spin-off series and several movies. Unlike *King Kong* (USA, 1933), which used stop-motion animation, *Ultraman* was made using miniature buildings and an actor wearing a monster costume who moved around the diminutive set, creating havoc.
The technique subsequently became a standard for Japanese monster movies (*kaiju*).

★**LONGEST-RUNNING SCI-FI TV SHOW (CURRENT)**
Smallville (The WB, USA, 2001–), based on the DC Comics character Superman, has aired continuously since 16 October 2001. The last sci-fi show to reach its 10th anniversary was *Stargate SG-1* (Sony/MGM, Canada/USA, 1997–2007).
The original run of *Doctor Who* (BBC, 1963–89) has the absolute record for **most consecutive sci-fi episodes ever**. (For more details, see pp.172–173.)

MOST EXPENSIVE COSTUME FROM A TV SERIES SOLD AT AUCTION
The Superman suit from the 1955 series *The Adventures of Superman* (USA) sold for $129,800 (£81,307) at the Profiles in History auction in Los Angeles, USA, on 31 July 2003. It was one of two costumes from the series worn by George Reeves (USA).

HIGHEST-RATED FANTASY/SCI-FI SHOW
Being Human (BBC) – the tale of a werewolf, vampire and ghost living together in suburban Britain – was the most critically acclaimed sci-fi show of 2009, according to an average of review scores on metacritic.com.

BEING
A DARK COMEDY SERIES BY THE BBC, *BEING HUMAN* ACHIEVED A RATING OF 79/100 ON THE REVIEW AGGREGATION SITE METACRITIC.COM.

HUMAN
THE HIT 2009 SHOW STARS RUSSELL TOVEY, AIDAN TURNER AND LEONORA CRICHLOW (PICTURED LEFT TO RIGHT) AS A WEREWOLF, VAMPIRE AND GHOST RESPECTIVELY.

★ **NEW RECORD**
★ **UPDATED RECORD**

1993: The **first computer-generated 3D models** on TV were the spacecraft conceived for *Babylon 5* (PTEN, USA).

1996: At its peak of popularity, *Baywatch* (NBC, USA) becomes the **most widely viewed TV series** ever, with an estimated weekly audience of more than 1.1 billion in 142 countries in 1996.

1999: Helen Hunt, the star of *Mad About You* (NBC, USA), becomes the **highest-paid TV actress**, with an estimated salary of $31 million (£18.7 million).

2000: Darva Conger (USA) and Rick Rockwell (USA) celebrate the **first reality TV marriage** on *Who Wants to Marry a Multimillionaire?* (Fox, USA).

2004: A four-minute feature film made by director Baz Lurhmann (Australia) advertising Chanel No. 5 perfume is the world's **most expensive TV advertisement** costing $33 million (£18 million) to produce. It starred Nicole Kidman (Australia) as a Marilyn Monroe-style actress who is pursued by the paparazzi.

2006: The **most watched live sporting event on television** is the 2006 FIFA World Cup held in Germany. FIFA claimed that the tournament was seen by 30 billion (non-unique) viewers.

2009: The **most hours on US television** is 16,343 by presenter Regis Philbin (USA), whose career spans 50 years.

2010: According to *Forbes*, the ★**most powerful person in television** is Oprah Winfrey (USA). Winfrey is also the ★**highest-paid TV personality**, having earned $275 million (£183 million) in 2008–09 thanks to her media empire. The philanthropist/actress/producer is arguably the most influential woman in the world.

FEATURE DOCTOR WHO

FREE! WIN!
DOCTOR WHO
MAGAZINE
NEW DOCTOR!
NEW DANGER!

★ LONGEST-RUNNING TV TIE-IN

Doctor Who Magazine launched (as *Doctor Who Weekly*) on 11 October 1979, and went monthly at issue 44. The magazine's tenure is all the more remarkable for the fact that for 16 years of its 31-year run there was no TV series in production!

★★★★★★★★★★★★★

★ LONGEST-RUNNING SCI-FI TV SHOW

Doctor Who (BBC, UK) has chalked up 769 episodes as of June 2010, encompassing 212 storylines including a full-length TV movie. This total does not include spoofs, spin-offs or webisodes.

★ MOST SUCCESSFUL SCI-FI TV SHOW

Based on longevity, DVD sales, views on BBC's iPlayer and publishing spin-offs, *Doctor Who* is the most successful science-fiction programme on TV. This eclipses the original

Star Trek series, which has had numerous spin-offs (such as *The Next Generation* and *Voyager*) that are not a genuine continuation of the same show.

★ MOST PROLIFIC DOCTOR

In terms of the **TV shows**, Tom Baker (UK) starred in 173 episodes (seasons 12–18), more than any other actor. A former monk, Baker was working on a building site when he received the call from the BBC. Famous for his Doctor's lengthy scarf and wild hair, he revitalized the series and lasted seven years.

In terms of **total output** – including audiobooks, TV shows, DVDs, novels and comics – the busiest Doctor was the tenth (David Tennant, UK), with over 342 appearances.

TV's ★least prolific Doctor was the eighth (Paul McGann, UK), who appeared just once, in a 1996 TV movie. Across all media, the fewest appearances to date were made by the ninth Doctor (Christopher Eccleston, UK), with only 25 outings.

★ YOUNGEST DOCTOR

The latest incarnation of the Doctor is Matt Smith (UK, b. 28 October 1982), who was 26 when he filmed his first scenes as the Time Lord.

The ★**oldest Doctor** was William Hartnell (UK), who played the part from the age of 55 to 57. He last reprised the role in 1973, aged 65.

★ DEAREST DALEK

The most money paid for a Dalek prop at auction was £36,000 ($61,934) by the now-defunct company Indeprod in 2005 for this "Dalek Supreme", first seen on screen in the 1970s.

WHO? PICTURED WITH THE DALEK SUPREME IS JUNE HUDSON (UK), WHO PROVIDED COSTUMES FOR SEVERAL EPISODES OF *DOCTOR WHO* IN THE 1980s.

★ NEW RECORD ★ UPDATED RECORD

DID YOU KNOW? THE DOCTOR WHO APPRECIATION SOCIETY, WHICH BEGAN IN MAY 1976, IS THE LONGEST-RUNNING DOCTOR WHO FANCLUB.

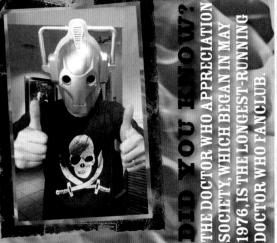

WHO'S WHO IN DOCTOR WHO?

WILLIAM HARTNELL (1963–66)

PATRICK TROUGHTON (1966–69)

JON PERTWEE (1970–74)

TOM BAKER (1974–81)

PETER DAVISON (1981–84)

TARDIS: The Doctor's means of travel.
Stands for: Time And Relative Dimension(s) In Space.

In *Doctor Who Magazine* polls for **most popular Doctor**, Tom Baker has only lost out three times!

TRIVIA

★MOST POPULAR STORY

"The Caves of Androzani" (1984) received an average user review of 9.3/10 on imdb.com, and was voted by readers of *Doctor Who Magazine* as the best ever story. The epic tale recounts the last days of the fifth Doctor (Peter Davison, UK), who, by the end of the serial, is poisoned and forced to regenerate – into the sixth Doctor (Colin Baker, UK) – to save his life. The classic four-parter narrowly beat the 2007 episode "Blink", starring tenth Doctor, David Tennant.

★HUGO AWARDS

The Hugo Awards are presented annually by the World Science Fiction Convention for science fiction and fantasy work (*statue pictured left*). In the category of Best Dramatic Presentation, Short Form – which includes dramatic productions of 90 minutes or less – *Doctor Who* storylines have been nominated 10 times – the ★**most Hugo Award nominations for Best Dramatic Presentation, Short Form**.

In addition, writer Steven Moffat has won a record three awards for his *Doctor Who* stories "The Empty Child"/"The Doctor Dances" (2006), "The Girl in the Fireplace" (2007) and "Blink" (2008). Moffat's three consecutive wins is also a record in this category.

★LARGEST FICTION SERIES

The official *Doctor Who* books – including novels, novelizations of TV episodes and "quick reads" – represent the longest licensed fictional series based on one principal character. Some 472 titles have appeared since the mid-1960s.

★LONGEST-SERVING ASSISTANT

James Robert McCrimmon (played principally by Frazer Hines, UK), companion of the second Doctor, appeared in 115 episodes between 1966 and 1969, making him the longest continually serving assistant on screen. The only character to make more appearances other than a Doctor was Brigadier Sir Alistair Gordon Lethbridge-Stewart, portrayed by actor Nicholas Courtney (UK).

INTERVIEW MATT SMITH – THE ELEVENTH DOCTOR...

Guinness World Records entered the TARDIS for a chat with the new Doctor and asked how he felt being cast as the eleventh Time Lord.

How does it feel to be the eleventh Doctor?
It's a real privilege to join such a successful show; it's a bit like joining Man Utd. It's good to be part of something strong and long may it continue. Plus, I couldn't have inherited the role from a nicer man. I guess it's like anything really – the more you do something the less daunting and intimidating it becomes.

Was there a defining moment during filming when it finally sunk in that you are THE DOCTOR?
I don't know. The Doctor has such a wealth of cultural history and carries such a depth of emotion and duty; initially I didn't know how to digest it all. I just got on with the nuts and bolts of what I had to do... There was a scene when I was standing on the roof in the first episode shouting "I am the Doctor!"...

New Doctor, new TARDIS. What's it like?
It's like a Ferrari, Lamborghini and Porsche all moulded into one! I am quite clumsy though so I kept breaking parts of the console and the poor production team had to keep fixing it. The TARDIS is a magic concept and it provides a constant source of adventure for both the Doctor and the viewers.

Where would you like the TARDIS to take you if you could go anywhere?
I would definitely travel back in time to see the dinosaurs and then I'd get the TARDIS to take me to the bottom of the sea to the lost city of Atlantis.

FACT: THE 11 DOCTORS HAVE ALL BEEN PORTRAYED BY BRITISH ACTORS...

COLIN BAKER (1984–86)

SYLVESTER McCOY (1987–89, 1996)

PAUL McGANN (1996)

CHRISTOPHER ECCLESTON (2005)

DAVID TENNANT (2005–10)

MATT SMITH (2010–)

TOONS & ANIMATION

UP!
YOU WOULD NEED 13 MILLION HELIUM BALLOONS TO LIFT THE AVERAGE 150-M² (1,600-FT²) HOME OFF THE GROUND! IN THE MOVIE, CARL USES JUST 20,622 BALLOONS.

★ HIGHEST-GROSSING 3D ANIMATION

Disney/Pixar's *Up* (USA, 2009) has earned over $507 million (£318 million) at the global box office from its opening on 29 May 2009. The animated feature tells the story of an old man's dream to visit South America – which he does by tethering thousands of helium balloons to his home and flying there!

FIRST...

ANIMATED MOVIE

The first film to use the stop-motion technique – to give the illusion of movement to inanimate objects – was Vitagraph's *The Humpty Dumpty Circus* (USA, 1897). Albert E Smith (USA) borrowed his daughter's toy circus and succeeded in animating acrobat and animal figurines by shooting them in barely changed positions one frame at a time.

The ★**first 2D animation** was J Stuart Blackton's (USA, b. UK) *Humorous Phases of Funny Faces* (USA, 1906), a series of caricatures drawn in white chalk on a blackboard, shot one frame at a time, then wiped clean and redrawn.

FULL-LENGTH FEATURE CARTOON

El Apóstol (Argentina, 1917), a political satire by Quirino Cristiani (Argentina), comprised 58,000 drawings and ran for 70 minutes.

CARTOON "TALKIE"

Max Fleischer's (Austria) animated short *Come Take a Trip in My Airship* (USA, 1924), based on the song of the same name and directed by his brother Dave Fleischer (USA), opened with the animated figure of a woman speaking some patter as the lead-in to the song.

★ FULL-COLOUR CARTOON

The first Technicolor cartoon to be commercially released was Disney's *Flowers and Trees* (USA, 1932), a "Silly Symphonies" short that became the ★**first cartoon to win an Oscar**.

CG IMAGES

The Disney movie *Tron* (USA, 1982) was the first major motion feature to fully utilize computer-generated (CG) animation. The movie's setting, inside a videogame, was ideal inspiration for computer animators.

CG CHARACTER

The first character in a full-length feature film to be entirely computer generated was a stained-glass knight that comes to life and steps down from a window in *Young Sherlock Holmes* (USA/UK, 1985). It was designed by John Lasseter (USA), who would later go on to establish Pixar.

★ FEATURE-LENGTH ANIMATED MOVIE

In 1996, animator John Lasseter received a Special Achievement Academy Award for his "inspired leadership of the Pixar *Toy Story* (USA, 1995) team resulting in the first feature-length computer animated film".

FIRST PRIME-TIME ANIMATION

The Flintstones (ABC, USA, 1960–66) – a cartoon about a "modern Stone Age family" – premiered on the evening of 30 September 1960. The show was designed to appeal to the entire family, not just children.

> *["I would rather entertain and hope that people learned something than educate people and hope they were entertained."]*
> **Walt Disney**

BED
THE FLINTSTONES WAS THE FIRST PRIME-TIME ANIMATED TV SHOW TO DEPICT TWO PEOPLE OF THE OPPOSITE SEX SLEEPING TOGETHER IN THE SAME BED!

TIME
UNTIL *THE FLINTSTONES*, CARTOONS COULD ONLY BE FOUND IN THE CHILDREN'S SCHEDULES – THIS SHOW FIRST AIRED AT 8:30 P.M., SIGNALLING THAT ITS TARGET AUDIENCE WAS BROADER.

★ LONGEST-RUNNING SIT-COM

The longest-running sit-com by episode count – and the ★**longest-running animation series** – is *The Simpsons* (Fox, USA), at 452 episodes and counting. It first aired on 17 December 1989 and, during its 20th season (2008–09), overtook the 435 episodes of former record holder *The Adventures of Ozzie and Harriet* (ABC, USA, 1952–66).

ANIME TO WIN AN OSCAR

Sen to Chihiro no Kamikakushi, aka *Spirited Away* (Japan, 2001), is the first anime to win an Oscar, for Best Animated Feature, in 2003. At 124 minutes, Hayao Miyazaki's (Japan) film is also the longest movie to win in this category.

ANIMATION TO BE NOMINATED FOR BEST FOREIGN LANGUAGE FILM

Vals Im Bashir, aka *Waltz with Bashir* (Israel/Germany/France/USA, 2008), was nominated for Best Foreign Language Film at the 2009 Academy Awards.

The movie, directed by Ari Folman (Israel), tells the story of an ex-soldier piecing together his memories of an Israeli Army mission in the first Lebanon war, which began in June 1982.

HIGHEST-GROSSING...

ANIMATION

Shrek 2 (USA, 2004) took $920.6 million (£464.7 million) at the global box office, making it the fourth biggest movie of all time. The *Shrek* franchise is also the most successful animated movie series ever.

The **highest-grossing animation adjusted for inflation** is *Snow White and the Seven Dwarfs* (USA, 1937), which took $184.9 million (then £37.3 million) at the global box office, equivalent to $1.6 billion (£1.02 billion) in today's money.

★ OPENING WEEKEND

Shrek the Third (USA, 2007) grossed $322,719,944 (£206.2 million) at the domestic box office over its opening weekend beginning on 18 May 2007.

Of this total, $47,077,497 (£30 million) was grossed on Saturday, 19 May – the **highest-grossing day** for an **animation** – and $38,426,991 (£24.5 million) was earned on the Friday – the **highest-grossing opening day for an animation.**

★ STOP-MOTION MOVIE

Aardman Animations' *Chicken Run* (UK, 2000) cost £42 million ($67 million) to make, but recouped $224.8 million (£143.6 million) at the international box office.

INSTANT EXPERT

⭐ AARDMAN ANIMATIONS' *WALLACE & GROMIT: THE CURSE OF THE WERE-RABBIT* (UK, 2005) USED 2.84 TONNES (6,272 LB) OF PLASTICINE!

⭐ *SNOW WHITE AND THE SEVEN DWARFS* (USA, 1937) WAS THE <u>FIRST MOVIE WITH AN OFFICIAL SOUNDTRACK</u>.

⭐ THE JAPANESE ANIME *SOREIKE! ANPANMAN*, WRITTEN BY TAKASHI YANASE (JAPAN), BOASTS THE ★<u>MOST CHARACTERS IN AN ANIMATION SERIES</u>, WITH 1,768 DIFFERENT CHARACTERS AS OF JUNE 2009.

⭐ *THE JUNGLE BOOK* (USA, 1967) WAS THE LAST MOVIE WALT DISNEY PERSONALLY OVERSAW.

★ MOST "ANNIE" NOMINATIONS

The Annie Awards have been presented by the International Animated Film Association in Los Angeles, California, USA, since 1972 and celebrate the best in animation. Three movies have had a record 16 nominations, each winning 10 awards: *The Incredibles* (USA, 2004), *Wallace & Gromit: The Curse of the Were-Rabbit* (UK, 2005), and *Kung Fu Panda* (USA, 2008).

MONTERREY, MEXICO

The **longest hot dog** measured 114.32 m (375.06 ft) and was made by Empacadora Ponderosa (Mexico) in Monterrey, Mexico, on 27 September 2008.

25°40'N
100°18'W

POPULAR CULTURE

BLOCK BUSTERS

CINEMA: Short for "cinématographe", derived from the Greek for "movement" and "record". The term was coined by Louis and Auguste Lumière (both France) for their newly invented combined camera and projector – and also the parlour in which their pictures were watched.

*All box-office figures refer to the US domestic market, unless otherwise indicated

SHERLOCK HOLMES

Guy Ritchie's (UK) *Sherlock Holmes* (USA/Germany, 2009) set a new US box-office record for ★**highest-grossing Christmas Day movie**, earning $24.6 million (£15.3 million)* on Friday, 25 December 2009.

THE DARK KNIGHT

Despite losing almost all of its records to *Avatar* (see p.180), *The Dark Knight* (USA, 2008) is still the ★**highest-grossing movie in its opening weekend**, having taken $158 million (£79 million) from Friday, 18 to Sunday, 20 July 2008.

THE TWILIGHT SAGA: NEW MOON

In November 2009, the *Twilight* sequel *New Moon* (USA, 2009) eclipsed *The Dark Knight* to achieve the ★**highest opening-day gross** of $72.7 million (£43.5 million) in the USA.

AVATAR

Now officially the ★**most successful movie** in history – at least in terms of box-office takings – James Cameron's (Canada) *Avatar*

MEXICO CITY, MEXICO

A total of 18,000 people volunteered to collectively pose naked in the Zocalo Square, Mexico City, Mexico, for photographer Spencer Tunick (USA) on 6 May 2007 – **the largest nude photoshoot**.

"*I think the Smurfs thing is funny, personally. Jar Jar is a bit of a low blow.*"

Director James Cameron on comparisons between the blue-skinned Na'vi of *Avatar* and Smurfs and Jar Jar Binks

HOLMES
SHERLOCK HOLMES IS THE ★MOST FREQUENTLY RECURRING CHARACTER ON SCREEN. HE HAS BEEN PORTRAYED BY SOME 81 ACTORS IN OVER 217 FILMS.

HORROR
WITH A BOX-OFFICE GROSS OF $296,596,319 (£197,192,000) TO 24 MARCH 2010, *NEW MOON* (SEE BELOW LEFT) IS THE MOST SUCCESSFUL MOVIE IN BOTH VAMPIRE AND WEREWOLF GENRES.

★ **NEW RECORD**
★ **UPDATED RECORD**

TAR

SOME GUYS JUST CAN'T HANDLE VEGAS

HANGOVER THE

FEEL IT JUNE 5

SAW III

OPENING WIDE THIS HALLOWEEN

DARK SECRETS REVEALED

JULY 15
WWW.HARRYPOTTER.COM

(USA/UK, 2010) achieved the box-office triple, topping first the foreign chart (23 January 2010), then the world chart (25 January 2010) and finally the domestic (2 February 2010).

THE HANGOVER

The surprise hit of 2009 was Todd Phillips' (USA) road movie *The Hangover* (USA, 2009), which quickly became the ★**highest-grossing R-rated comedy**, grossing $467.3 million (£293.3 million) at the global box office.

SAW III

The ★**highest-grossing Halloween** movie is *Saw III*, the third instalment of the Jigsaw Killer franchise, which had taken $33.6 million (£17.6 million) by 31 October 2006. Globally, the threequel was the most successful of the series.

HARRY POTTER VI

The Half-Blood Prince (UK/USA, 2009) had the ★**highest-grossing worldwide opening**, raking in $394 million (£241 million) up to the end of its first domestic weekend in July 2009.

POPULAR CULTURE
AT THE MOVIES

★ ★ ★ ★ ★ ★ ★ ★ ★ ★ ★ ★ ★ ★

★ LARGEST CINEMA SCREEN (DRIVE-IN)

The famous outdoor water-filming facility at Pinewood Studios in Middlesex, UK, was, in 2009, converted into a giant drive-in theatre with a screen measuring a record 73.1 x 18.3 m (240 x 60 ft). The screen opened on Halloween 2009 with a series of horror flicks.

★ HIGHEST-GROSSING...

Director: Topping the list of Hollywood's highest-grossing directors is Steven Spielberg (USA), whose motion pictures have earned a whopping $3.76 billion (£2.44 billion) in box office receipts.

★ FIRST BEST ACTRESS OSCAR WON FOR DEPICTING A BEST ACTRESS

Cate Blanchett (Australia, pictured) won the 2005 Best Actress Oscar for depicting Best Actress Academy Award winner Katherine Hepburn (USA) in *Aviator* (2004).

As a producer, Spielberg is responsible for generating $5.03 billion (£3.27 billion), making him the ★ **highest-grossing producer** too. ★ **Screenwriter:** The 15 movies written by George Lucas (USA) have grossed a lifetime combined total of $3.33 billion (£2.16 billion).

★ HIGHEST EARNER IN HOLLYWOOD

Michael Bay, director of *Transformers: Revenge of the Fallen* (USA, 2009), earned an estimated $125 million (£78 million) in 2009 thanks to his blockbuster movie release, a share of the merchandising and DVD rights, and a few back-end production deals.

★ LEAST BANKABLE ACTOR

Thanks to flop *Land of the Lost* (USA, 2009), Will Ferrell (USA) floats to the top of the list of most overpaid actors. The movie cost $100 million (£62 million) to make but made just $65 million (£40 million) and is the latest in a run of bad luck for Ferrell. On average, for every $1 (62p) he is paid, he returns just $3.29 (£2) at the box office, according to *Forbes*.

★ LEAST BANKABLE ACTRESS

In the same list is Drew Barrymore (USA), whose $1 fee will see a return of $7.43 (£4.66) – the lowest return on investment for an actress.

★ FIRST WINNER OF A BEST ACTRESS OSCAR AND A WORST ACTRESS RAZZIE IN THE SAME YEAR

Sandra Bullock (USA) won Worst Actress at the 2009 Golden Raspberry Awards for *All About Steve* (USA, 2009) and turned up in person to accept the trophy the day before she won the Academy Award for Best Actress in *The Blind Side* (USA, 2009).

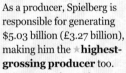

RAZZIES: The Golden Raspberry Awards, set up in 1981 by John Wilson (USA) to "salute the worst that Hollywood has to offer". The anti-Oscars!

★ MOST BANKABLE STARS

The Hollywood actor giving the best value for money is Shia LaBeouf (USA); in 2009, the star of *Transformers* and *Indiana Jones 4* made $160 (£100) for every $1 he was paid. The most bankable actress, according to *Forbes*, is *King Kong* star Naomi Watts (UK), who made $44 (£27) per $1 paid.

DID YOU KNOW?

THERE ARE 11 CATEGORIES IN THE GOLDEN RASPBERRY AWARDS (RAZZIES), INCLUDING WORST PICTURE AND WORST NEW STAR.

Bill Cosby (USA) became the ★ **first Razzie winner to collect the prize in person** in 1987.

TRIVIA

★ **NEW RECORD**
★ **UPDATED RECORD**

AUSTIN, TX, USA

Rob Williams of Austin, Texas, USA, made a Bologna, cheese and lettuce sandwich, complete with olives on cocktail sticks, in 1 min 57 sec on the set of *Guinness World Records: Primetime* on 10 November 2000. His record? The **fastest time to make a sandwich... using just the feet!**

QUIZ!
WHO IS *HURT LOCKER* DIRECTOR KATHRYN BIGELOW'S FAMOUS EX?
SEE P.278 FOR THE ANSWER.

★FIRST FICTIONAL CHARACTER TO BE OSCAR NOMINATED

Donald Kaufman, a fictitious character in Spike Jonze's (USA) *Adaptation* (USA, 2002), was nonetheless nominated for Best Adapted Screenplay along with his (real) "brother" Charlie Kaufman (USA) at the 2003 Oscars. Both characters appeared in the movie – both played by Nicolas Cage (USA) – and both are credited as writers, yet only Charlie exists!

HIGHEST-EARNING MOVIE STARS

Once again, *Harry Potter* leads Daniel Radcliffe and Emma Watson top the chart of Hollywood's highest-earning stars. Emma earned $10 million apiece for the last two Potter movies, while Daniel secured $20 million per film plus a $1 million bonus for licensing and royalties.

★HIGHEST-GROSSING SERIES

The Harry Potter franchise has, in only six movies, earned $5.39 billion (£3.50 billion) at the worldwide box office, ahead of Star Wars ($4.32 billion; £2.81 billion) and James Bond ($4.82 billion; £3.13 billion). The last movie in the series -- *Deathly Hallows* -- will be delivered in two instalments.

OSCARS

★MOST ACTING NOMINATIONS

With a nomination for her role as cook Julia Child in *Julia & Julie* (USA, 2009), Meryl Streep notched up her 16th Oscars nod (having won two).

WORST OSCAR PERCENTAGE

Sound mixer Kevin O'Connell (USA) has had 20 Oscar nominations without a win – the longest losing streak in Oscars history.

★BEST OSCARS PERCENTAGE

Sound editor Mark Berger (USA) has the best "score" at the Oscars with 100% – he has had four wins from four nominations: *Apocalyse Now*, (USA, 1979), *The Right Stuff* (USA, 1983), *Amadeus* (USA 1984) and *The English Patient* (USA, 1996).

★MOST MULTI-DISCIPLINE TECHNICAL OSCARS

Richard Taylor (NZ), effects supervisor at Weta Workshops in Wellington, New Zealand, has won technical Oscars across a record three disciplines: Visual Effects for *King Kong* (NZ/USA/Ger, 2005), and Costume Design and Make-up for *The Return of the King* (USA/NZ/Ger, 2003).

★FIRST FEMALE TO WIN A BEST PICTURE ACADEMY AWARD

When Kathryn Bigelow's (USA, below) *Hurt Locker* (USA, 2008, below right) won Best Picture at the 2010 Academy Awards ceremony, it marked the first time that a female director had won an Oscar in this category. "There should be more women directing," said Bigelow. "There's just not the awareness that it's really possible. It is."

EXES
THE 2009 OSCARS CEREMONY WAS KNOWN AS THE BATTLE OF THE EXES, AS KATHRYN BIGELOW WAS UP AGAINST EX-HUSBAND JAMES CAMERON FOR BEST DIRECTOR.

SEXIST?
BIGELOW WAS ALSO THE FIRST WOMAN TO BE AWARDED THE DIRECTORS GUILD OF AMERICA AWARD FOR OUTSTANDING ACHIEVEMENT IN FEATURE FILM.

OKLAHOMA CITY, OK, USA

The **longest chain of pipe cleaners** measured 3,188 m (10,459 ft) and was achieved by Oklahoma Children's Cancer Association at the Children's Hospital OU Medical Center in Oklahoma City, USA, on 14 February 2007.

35°28'N
97°32'W

3D CINEMA

QUIZ!
WHICH ANIMATED MOVIE WAS THE FIRST TO BE PRODUCED IN STEREOSCOPIC 3D?
FIND OUT THE ANSWER ON p.278.

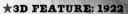

FIRST...

★DEMONSTRATION OF 3D FILM: 1915

An audience at the Astor Theater in New York City, USA, donned red and green glasses for the first time to view test reels of 3D footage.

Produced by Edwin S Porter and William E Waddell (both USA), the footage depicted, among other things, dancing girls and the Niagara Falls -- the first images seen using the anaglyph 3D process.

TRIVIA

DID YOU KNOW?
IN 1894, WILLIAM FRIESE-GREENE (UK) BECAME THE FIRST TO FILE A PATENT FOR A VIEWING DEVICE THAT COMBINES TWO SEPARATE PICTURES INTO ONE 3D IMAGE.

★MOST ANIMATED 3D FEATURES RELEASED IN A SINGLE YEAR

Hollywood embraced 3D cinema in a big way in 2009, with the major studios releasing a grand total of 10 animated 3D features during the year. While most of these animations were new, *Toy Story 3D* (USA, 2009) was a double feature of the first two movies remastered to be a 3D experience.

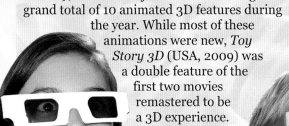

SPEX
THE RED-AND-BLUE-LENS 3D GLASSES ARE NOW A THING OF THE PAST. INSTEAD, TODAY'S "POLARIZED" FILTERS SPLIT THE IMAGE INTO HORIZONTAL AND VERTICAL STRIPS.

★3D FEATURE: 1922

Harry K Fairhall and Robert F Elder (both USA) used two cameras and two projectors – "set at a distance from each other equal to the average distance between the human eyes" – to premiere Nat Deverich's (USA) stereoscopic movie *The Power of Love* (USA, 1922) in front of an invited audience at the Ambassador Hotel Theater in Los Angeles, USA, on 27 September 1922. It was the first and only feature-length application of Fairhall and Elder's new technology. The movie is now lost, sadly.

★3D SCREENING TO A PAYING AUDIENCE: 1922

Research by historian Daniel L Symmes suggests that the documentary short *Movies of the Future* (USA, 1922), directed by William Van Doren Kelley (USA), was the first

stereoscopic print shown to a paying audience. The 14-minute movie explored this nascent film technology and was shown at the Rivoli Theater in New York City, USA, in 1922.

★3D MOVIE TO BE NOMINATED FOR AN OSCAR: 1936

A short experimental movie entitled *Audioscopiks* (USA, 1935), filmed using the Norling-Leventhal 3-Dimensions process – an anaglyph technique devised by John Norling and Jacob Leventhal (both USA) – received Academy Award recognition in the category "Best Short Subject, Novelty".

The eight-minute reel showcased the 3D effect with a ladder being pushed out of a window, a sliding trombone, a woman on a swing and someone throwing a baseball.

★MOST EXPENSIVE 3D ANIMATION

The 2009 3D performance-capture version of *A Christmas Carol* (USA), directed by Robert Zemeckis (USA), cost $200 million (£128 million) to produce. One of the first of the new wave of 3D blockbusters, it went on to gross $323,555,899 (£207 million) globally.

45.6 MILLION:
Computing hours required to make *Monsters Vs. Aliens* (that's 1.9 million complete days, or 5,205 years!).

3D TALKIE: 1936

Sante Bonaldo's production *Nozze Vagabonde* (*Beggar's Wedding*, Italy, 1936), starring Italians Leda Gloria and Ermes Zacconi, was the first movie to offer 3D polarizing glasses and a synchronized soundtrack.

3D MOVIE IN COLOUR: 1952

Bwana Devil (USA, 1952), written and directed by Arch Oboler (USA), promised viewers "The Miracle of the Age!!! A LION in your lap. A LOVER in your arms!". Audiences – who had to wear coloured filter glasses – flocked to the cinema to witness the spectacular tale of two man-eating lions.

37°41'N 97°20'W

WICHITA, KS, USA
The **largest stitched teddy bear** measures 16.86 m (55 ft 4 in) in length and was constructed by Dana Warren (USA). The bear was completed on 6 June 2008 and displayed at the Exploration Place in Wichita, Kansas, USA.

4D: The fourth dimension — in moviespeak, this refers to the use of water, vibrations, smells, etc., to further enhance your viewing sensation!

★ **NEW RECORD**
★ **UPDATED RECORD**

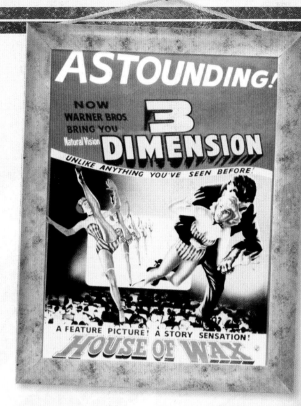

★ FIRST 3D MOVIE WITH STEREO SOUND

Warner Bros., the second major Hollywood studio to enter the 3D market and the first to do so in full colour, released *House of Wax* (1953) with stereo sound.

TOP 10

	MOVIE	WORLDWIDE GROSS TO FEB 2010 (MILLIONS)*	DATE RELEASED
1	*Avatar* (Fox)	$2,376 m	2010
2	*Ice Age: Dawn of the Dinosaurs* (Fox, above)	$884 m	2009
3	*Up* (Buena Vista)	$723 m	2009
4	*Alice in Wonderland* (Walt Disney Pictures)	$660 m	2010
5	*Monsters Vs. Aliens* (Paramount/DreamWorks)	$381 m	2009
6	*A Christmas Carol* (Buena Vista)	$323 m	2009
7	*Chicken Little* (Buena Vista)	$314 m	2005
8	*Bolt* (Buena Vista)	$308 m	2009
9	*G-Force* (Buena Vista)	$285 m	2009
10	*Journey to the Center of the Earth* (Warner Bros./New Line)	$241 m	2009

Source: boxofficemojo.com   *figures as of 3 May 2010

Despite a poor critical reception, the movie grossed $95,000 in its first week from just two theatres.

★ 3D FILM BY A MAJOR STUDIO: 1953

Columbia Pictures became the first big studio to venture into the 3D movie market with their release of *Man in the Dark* (USA, 1953) on 9 April 1953. The movie -- a remake of the 1936 film noir *The Man Who Lived Twice* (USA) – was rushed out to capitalize on the 3D craze, and wowed audiences with scenes in which spiders, fists and dead bodies loomed out of the screen.

★ 3D MOVIE...

In French (1953): *Soirs de Paris* (France, 1953), directed by Jean Laviron (France), ran for 85 minutes.

In Japanese (1953): *Tobidashita Nichi Yôbi*, aka *Runaway Sunday* (Japan, 1953), a supporting movie lasting just 11 minutes.

In Indian (1983): *Chhota Chetan* (India, 1983, aka *My Dear Kuttichathan*), a children's fantasy movie.

MISCELLANY

★ HIGHEST BUDGET-TO-BOX-OFFICE RATIO FOR A 3D MOVIE

To date, the most successful 3D movie in terms of its profitability is *The Stewardesses* (USA, 1969), directed by Al Silliman (USA). A pioneering, single-camera 3D system was devised to keep the total budget just over $100,000. An adult movie, it grossed upwards of $30 million at the box office.

★ BIGGEST 3D OPENING WEEKEND

Tim Burton's (USA) *Alice in Wonderland* (USA, 2010) grossed $116.1 million (£76.6 million) in the USA on 5–7 March. Its nearest 3D rival, *Avatar* (USA, 2009) took £77 million (£47 million) in its opening weekend.

★ FIRST ANIMATED FEATURE PRODUCED IN STEREOSCOPIC 3D

Until *Monsters Vs. Aliens* (USA, 2009), animated movies were converted to 3D after completion; *MvA*, however, was "shot" in a stereoscopic format from the beginning, an expensive "premium" process that added $15 million (£9.4 million) to the budget.

WINNIPEG, MB, CANADA

The **longest recorded heart stoppage** is a minimum of 3 hr 40 min in the case of Jean Jawbone (Canada), who at the age of 20 was revived by a team of 26 using peritoneal dialysis in the Health Sciences Centre, Winnipeg, Manitoba, Canada, on 8 January 1977.

49°54'N 97°08'W

★ **NEW RECORD**
☆ **UPDATED RECORD**

FEATURE
THAT'S SHOWBIZ

★★★★★★★★★★★

Here at *Guinness World Records*, our researchers don't just stick to scientific journals and research papers for record-worthy content – it's also our responsibility to trawl through the thousands of pages of celebrity fashion mags to bring you the most up-to-date showbiz records.

So, what have we discovered this year? Well, Johnny Depp (USA) topped the *People* magazine poll of ★**sexiest men alive** for the second time this year, while the magazine revealed the ★**most beautiful person** to be actress Christina Applegate (USA).

In the power stakes, Brad Pitt (USA) returns as the ★**most powerful actor**, thanks in part to his Oscar-nominated role in *Benjamin Button* (USA, 2008), but largely to endless tabloid news of his family life and stories about his humanitarian activities.

No surprise, then, that 2009's ★**most powerful actress** was Pitt's partner Angelina Jolie (USA)!

The ★**richest fashion designer** is Giorgio Armani (Italy, below). Clothes, watches, perfumes, homeware and hotels all bear his name... an incredible achievement for a medical school drop-out who's now worth a record $5.3 billion (£3.3 billion)!

> { *"I've changed the way people look, definitely."* }
> **Giorgio Armani – currently the world's richest fashion designer – reflects on the impact of his work**

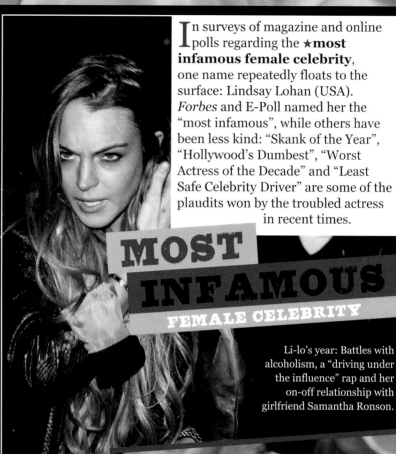

In surveys of magazine and online polls regarding the ★**most infamous female celebrity**, one name repeatedly floats to the surface: Lindsay Lohan (USA). *Forbes* and E-Poll named her the "most infamous", while others have been less kind: "Skank of the Year", "Hollywood's Dumbest", "Worst Actress of the Decade" and "Least Safe Celebrity Driver" are some of the plaudits won by the troubled actress in recent times.

MOST INFAMOUS
FEMALE CELEBRITY

Li-lo's year: Battles with alcoholism, a "driving under the influence" rap and her on-off relationship with girlfriend Samantha Ronson.

... AND MALE CELEBRITY

Alex Rodriguez (USA) has had better years. Since his revelations about drug abuse during the 2000s, the New York Yankees No.13 – and multiple world-record holder – has had a bad press. "Slugger turned tabloid tragedy", said *Forbes*, who listed A-Rod as their No.1 ☆**most infamous male celebrity** thanks to his steroid use, his high-profile divorce and higher-profile affair with Madonna!

PLUS...
A-ROD: THE MANY LIVES OF ALEX RODRIGUEZ, AN UNAUTHORIZED BIOGRAPHY, ALSO ACCUSES THE STAR OF CHEATING DURING BALL GAMES.

POWER COUPLES

	COUPLE	COMBINED EARNINGS (1 JUNE 2008– 1 JUNE 2009)
1	Shawn "Jay-Z" Carter & Beyoncé Knowles (both USA, right)	$122m
2	Harrison Ford & Calista Flockhart (both USA)	$69m
3	Brad Pitt & Angelina Jolie (both USA)	$55m
4	Will & Jada Pinkett Smith (both USA)	$48m
5	David & Victoria Beckham (both UK, below)	$46m
6	Ellen DeGeneres & Portia de Rossi (both USA)	$36m
7	Tom Hanks & Rita Wilson (both USA)	$35.5m
8	Jim Carrey & Jenny McCarthy (both USA)	$34m
9	Tom Cruise & Katie Holmes (both USA)	$33.5m
10	Chris Martin (UK) & Gwyneth Paltrow (USA)	$22m

Source: Forbes

EXTRA!
WHO ARE THE BIGGEST RECORD-BREAKERS IN THE MUSIC INDUSTRY? FIND OUT ON PP.184-187.

EXTRA!
FOR MORE ONLINE STATS, FACTS AND WORLD RECORDS, TURN TO P.216.

☆MOST TRUSTED CELEBRITY

In a survey conducted by E-Poll Market Research for business magazine *Forbes*, respondents were asked to rate the "trustworthiness, awareness and appeal" of celebrities. Top of the list was actor James Earl Jones (USA) – the velvety voice behind NBC's Olympic coverage and the CNN tagline (and *Star Wars*' less-than-trustworthy Darth Vader!).

POSH & THE DOSH

☆MOST SEARCHED-FOR FEMALE

Singer Lady Gaga (USA, aka Stefani Joanne Angelina Germanotta) – was the most searched-for female online in 2009, according to Google, the **largest search engine**.

Did you know: Lady Gaga adapted her stage name from the Queen hit song "Radio Ga Ga".

☆MOST SEARCHED-FOR MALE

The untimely death of Michael Jackson (USA, 1958–2009) – first announced virally – sent you online in your millions, making him the most searched-for male in 2009.

Did you know: Jackson achieved more world records *after* his death than he did when he was alive! See p.187 for more of his posthumous record-breaking feats.

☆HIGHEST-EARNING PRIMETIME TV STAR

From 1 June 2008 to 1 June 2009, *X Factor* and *American Idol* judge Simon Cowell (UK) earned $75 million (£33 million).

☆MOST POWERFUL SPORTS STAR

Despite the shameful end to his year, golfing legend Tiger Woods (USA) earned $103 million (£67 million) in 2009, and topped the 2010 *BusinessWeek* Sports Power 100 list.

☆MOST SEARCHED-FOR CELEBRITY WEDDING

The wedding of the year – if Google's hit tracker is anything to go by – was that of reality TV star Khloé Kardashian and the LA Lakers' Lamar Odom (both USA) on 27 September 2009. It ranked the highest on the Google Zeitgeist list of celeb weddings.

PLUS...
THE REALITY TV SHOW *KEEPING UP WITH THE KARDASHIANS* DEBUTED IN THE USA IN OCTOBER 2007 AND FOLLOWS THE LIVES OF LOS ANGELES SOCIALITES.

CELEBRITY TWEEPS*

Actor Ashton Kutcher (USA, below right) is ahead in the celeb Twitter battle, as the ☆**first tweep with over 1 million followers**. The ☆**most searched-for tweep of 2009**? Singer/actress Miley Cyrus (USA, below left), according to Google.

234,901 FOLLOWERS

4,649,421 FOLLOWERS

*TWEEPS: PEOPLE (PEEPS) WHO USE TWITTER

The **largest baseball bat** measures 4.08 m (13 ft 5 in) with a circumference of 101.6 cm (40 in). Known as "Big Bruce", it is made from white ash – the same material as Major League Baseball bats – and is owned by the Fargo-Moorhead RedHawks baseball club (Fargo Baseball LLC) of Fargo, North Dakota, USA.

POPULAR CULTURE
MUSIC

★ ★ ★ ★ ★ ★ ★ ★ ★ ★ ★ ★ ★ ★ ★

CHART-TOPPERS

★MOST SIMULTANEOUS US HOT 100 HITS BY A FEMALE

On 14 November 2009, 19-year-old US country singer Taylor Swift became the first female artist to have eight tracks simultaneously on the US Hot 100. On that chart she also became the first artist to have five tracks simultaneously enter the Top 30.

★21st CENTURY'S TOP-SELLING ALBUM ACT (USA)

Rapper Eminem (USA) was the biggest-selling album act in the US in the first 10 years of the century, with sales of 32,241,000.

★MOST NEW ENTRIES ON UK ALBUM CHART

On the 19 September 2009 chart, 16 albums by The Beatles (UK) entered the UK Top 75. This included four in the Top 10 – a record for a group.

★MOST SUCCESSIVE WEEKS AT TOP OF US HOT 100

The Black Eyed Peas (USA) spent 26 successive weeks at No.1 on the US Hot 100 in 2009. After 12 weeks at the summit their "Boom Boom Pow" was replaced by "I Gotta Feeling", which stayed at the top for 14 weeks.

★MOST CHARTED TEENAGER (USA)

The 16-year-old singer/actor Miley Cyrus (USA) scored her 29th US Hot 100 chart entry on 7 November 2009 with "Party in the USA". She has had hits under her own name and as Hannah Montana.

MOST SUCCESSFUL FIRST WEEK UK ALBUM SALE

Released on 23 November 2009, Susan Boyle's (UK) *I Dreamed a Dream* sold 411,820 copies in its first week in the UK (133,599 on the first day) – the biggest weekly UK sale by any solo singer's album.

★MOST SUCCESSIVE ALBUM ENTRIES AT NO.1 (USA)

On 6 June 2009, Eminem's (USA) album *Relapse* gave him his fifth successive US album chart entry at No.1. This equalled the record set between 1998 and 2003 by fellow rapper DMX (USA).

★FEMALE WITH MOST ALBUM NO.1s (UK)

Madonna (USA) has had 11 UK No.1 albums. Her latest chart-topper came with *Celebration* on 3 October 2009. She is also the **biggest-selling female album act of the 21st century (UK)**, with sales of 6.68 million to October 2009.

★FEMALE WITH MOST ALBUM NO.1s (USA)

Barbra Streisand (USA) had her ninth No.1 album in the USA on 17 October 2009, aged 67. She is also the first artist to have a No.1 album in five different decades.

Madonna Louise Ciccone was born on 16 August 1958 in Bay City, Michigan, USA. Her first album was *Madonna*, in 1983.

TRIVIA

★MOST WEEKS ON UK CHART IN ANY YEAR

In 2009, Lady Gaga (USA) clocked up 154 chart weeks in the UK Top 75 (with 90 of these in the Top 40), mainly thanks to her hits "Just Dance", "Poker Face", "Paparazzi" and "Bad Romance".

★ BIGGEST JUMP TO NO.1 (UK)

Pixie Lott's (UK) single "Boys and Girls" broke the record for a jump within the Top 75 to the No.1 spot in the UK on 19 September 2009, when it climbed there from No.73.

★ BIGGEST-SELLING DIGITAL ALBUM ACT (USA)

In July 2009, British band Coldplay became the first act to sell over a million digital albums in the USA.

★ MOST SIMULTANEOUS TOP 20 ENTRIES ON US DIGITAL CHART

On 14 November 2009, Taylor Swift (USA) became the first act to have five tracks ("Jump Then Fall", "Untouchable", "Other Side of the Door", "Superstar" and "Come in with the Rain") chart simultaneously.

★ FIRST 3D BROADCAST ON THE INTERNET

British rock trio Keane were the first act to make a 3D broadcast on the Internet. They sang five songs in a 20-minute set from Studio Two at Abbey Road, London, UK. Keane also released the **first USB stick single**, "Nothing in My Way", in 2006.

★ MOST SIMULTANEOUS HITS ON UK SINGLES CHART DEBUT

On the chart dated 23 January 2010, the cast of the US TV series *Glee* (USA) made their UK chart debut with five tracks simultaneously entering the UK Top 75.

ALBUM
SUSAN BOYLE WAS AGED 48 WHEN HER ALBUM *I DREAMED A DREAM* DEBUTED AT NO.1 IN THE US AND UK. SHE IS THE OLDEST ARTIST TO REACH NO.1 ON THESE CHARTS WITH A DEBUT.

★ FASTEST-SELLING ALBUM BY A FEMALE (UK)

Susan Boyle's (UK) debut album *I Dreamed a Dream*, released in November 2009, sold more than a million copies in just 21 days. It was the biggest-selling album in the UK in 2009, and a clip of her singing the title song for the first time on UK TV's *Britain's Got Talent* was the most watched YouTube clip in 2009.

DIGITAL HITS

★ MOST DOWNLOADED ACTS IN A YEAR (USA)

In 2009, Lady Gaga (USA) broke the record for female acts by selling 11.1 million downloads in the USA. The Black Eyed Peas (USA) broke the record for a group, with 10.3 million downloads.

★ FASTEST-SELLING DIGITAL TRACK (UK)

Californian alternative hard rock band Rage Against the Machine's 1993 recording "Killing in the Name" entered the UK singles chart at No.1 on 26 December 2009. It was only available as a download, and in its first week sold 502,672 copies.

★ NEW RECORD
UPDATED RECORD

HOUSTON, TX, USA
The **largest audience to attend a film premiere** was 23,930 people at the opening of *Brewster McCloud* (USA, 1970) at the Houston Astrodome in Houston, Texas, USA, on 5 December 1970.

29°45'N
95°22'W

POPULAR CULTURE
MUSIC

★★★★★★★★★★★★★★★

"It's a great honour to visit the Guinness World Records offices. I love the book."

Michael Jackson, 14 October 2006

DID YOU KNOW?

NO ALBUM HAS SPENT LONGER AT NO.1 IN THE UK THIS CENTURY THAN *THE ESSENTIAL MICHAEL JACKSON*, WHICH HELD THE POSITION FOR SEVEN STRAIGHT WEEKS IN 2009.

Michael Jackson scored 13 US chart-topping singles as a solo star. The **most US No.1 singles** to date is 20, by The Beatles (UK).

TRIVIA

week earlier, it had entered the UK chart at No.24 – it sold there for £172.

★ MOST SINGLES SOLD IN A YEAR (UK)

In 2009, an unprecedented 152.7 million "singles" were sold in the UK, with a record 98% of them being downloaded tracks. It was the first year since 1967 that more singles were sold in the UK than albums.

TOP EARNERS

★ MOST SUCCESSFUL TOUR (SOLO ARTIST)

Madonna's (USA) Sticky & Sweet tour (23 August 2008–2 September 2009) grossed $408 million (£269 million).

★ TOP-SELLING FEMALE RECORDING ARTIST

Madonna (USA) holds the record for album sales up to December 2009 of 75 million in the USA and 200 million abroad.

★ TOP-GROSSING COUNTRY ACT

Kenny Chesney (USA) is the top-grossing country music performer of the 21st century. Since 2002, he has sold seven million tickets to his shows and grossed almost $500 million (£330 million).

★ BIGGEST AND MOST EXPENSIVE TOP 40 BOX SET (US & UK)

The 16-CD box set *The Beatles in Stereo*, which sold for $243.98, entered the US album chart at No.15 on 26 September 2009. One

HIGHEST ANNUAL EARNINGS EVER FOR A POP STAR

In 1989, Michael Jackson (USA) topped the Forbes list as the highest paid entertainer, with annual earnings of $125 million (£76,298,602). This record is still unbroken 21 years later.

YOUNG & OLD

★ OLDEST NO.1 SINGLES ACT (UK)

Sir Tom Jones (UK) was 68 years 9 months old when he sang on "Barry Islands in the Stream" with Vanessa Jenkins, Bryn West and Robin Gibb (all UK).

★ MOST SUCCESSFUL REALITY TV GIRL GROUP

Girls Aloud (UK/Ireland) formed for reality TV show *Popstars: The Rivals* in 2002, and have gone on to have 20 Top 10 singles as of January 2009, including a female record 17 consecutive Top 10 hits from December 2002 to December 2007.

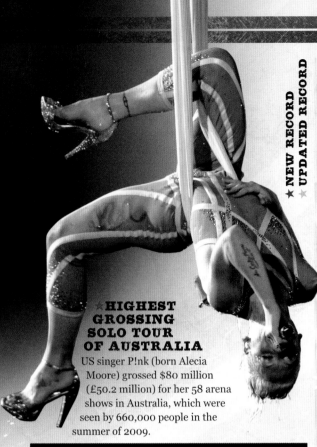

★ **NEW RECORD**
★ **UPDATED RECORD**

★ HIGHEST GROSSING SOLO TOUR OF AUSTRALIA

US singer P!nk (born Alecia Moore) grossed $80 million (£50.2 million) for her 58 arena shows in Australia, which were seen by 660,000 people in the summer of 2009.

A charity single, the track topped the UK chart on 21 March 2009.

★ YOUNGEST COUNTRY "ENTERTAINER OF THE YEAR"

In 2009, 19-year-old Taylor Swift (USA) became the youngest artist to receive the Country Music Association's (CMA) highest award, Entertainer of the Year. In

that year, her 43 shows took $23.7 million (£18 million) gross and her album *Fearless* outsold all others in the USA.

★ OLDEST UK CHART-TOPPER AND RECORD SPANS OF NO.1s

On 9 May 2009, Bob Dylan (USA) topped the UK album chart with *Together Through Life*, which made the 67-year-old the oldest act to top the UK chart with

a newly recorded album. It was his first No.1 for 38 years 7 months and increased his span of studio-recorded No.1 albums to 44 years and 1 month – also both records.

MICHAEL JACKSON, 1958–2009

Before his untimely death on 25 June 2009 at the age of 50, Michael Joseph Jackson (USA) was probably the most famous living human being on the planet. A multiple Guinness World Record holder – he received eight in his lifetime for his chart achievements, album sales, earnings and charity donations – Michael's contribution to the arts was immeasureable. And remarkably, the record breaking continued after his passing.

In the year of his death, a record **11.3 million tracks** by the artist were downloaded in the USA, and **2.8 million albums** were sold in the UK. From his death to the end of November 2009, he sold **7 million albums, 10.2 million downloaded tracks** and **1.3 million DVDs** in the USA. The first morning after his death saw over **1 million YouTube plays of "Beat It"**, and in the first week **2.6 million Michael Jackson downloads** were sold in the USA.

VISIT! PICTURED IS MICHAEL JACKSON DURING A VISIT TO THE GWR OFFICES IN OCTOBER 2006 TO COLLECT HIS CERTIFICATES IN PERSON! HE WAS A LIFE-LONG FAN OF THE BOOK!

CERTIFICATE
The most successful entertainer of all time is Michael Jackson (USA), who in 1989 alone earned $125 million from single and album sales
GUINNESS WORLD RECORDS LTD

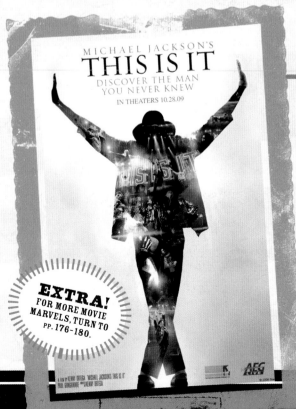

MICHAEL JACKSON'S
THIS IS IT
DISCOVER THE MAN YOU NEVER KNEW
IN THEATERS 10.28.09

EXTRA! FOR MORE MOVIE MARVELS, TURN TO PP. 176-180.

★ HIGHEST-GROSSING CONCERT FILM

The release of Michael Jackson's rehearsals for the This Is It tour on 28 October 2009 grossed $250 million (£165 million). It opened simultaneously in 250,000 theatres around the world and took $200 million (£132 million) in its first two weeks.

CERTIFICATE
The first entertainer to have officially ratified sales of more than 100 million albums outside the USA is Michael Jackson (USA)
GUINNESS WORLD RECORDS LTD

CERTIFICATE
The biggest-selling album of all time, with sales of over 104 million, is Michael Jackson's *Thriller* (1982).
It remained in the Billboard 200 Top 10 for 80 consecutive weeks
GUINNESS WORLD RECORDS LTD

SPRINGFIELD, MO, USA
The **longest distance cycled backwards on a unicycle** was set by Steve Gordon (USA), who covered a distance of 109.4 km (68 miles) in Springfield, Missouri, USA, on 24 June 1999.

177 **W.17°11.98** **N.17°11.98**

POPULAR CULTURE
THEATRE & CLASSICAL ARTS

★★★★★★★★★★★★★★

★MOST PROLIFIC THEATRE PRODUCER

Theatre impresario Howard E Pechet (Canada) produced 485 plays at 10 different venues across Canada, between January 1975 and July 2008.

★MOST FLAMENCO TAPS IN A MINUTE (MALE)

José Miguel Fernández Pintado (Spain) performed 814 flamenco taps in one minute on the set of *Lo Show dei Record* in Rome, Italy, on 1 April 2010.

FASTEST PANTOMIME HORSE (FEMALE)

Samantha Kavanagh and Melissa Archer (both UK, front and rear, respectively) ran 100 m (328 ft) in 18.13 seconds as a pantomime horse at an event organized by the advertising agency Claydon Heeley Jones Mason at Harrow School, Middlesex, UK, on 18 August 2005.

The record for the ★fastest pantomime horse (male) is held by Shane Crawford and Adrian

SMALLEST PROFESSIONAL THEATRE

Founded in 2004, The Theatre Lilli Chapeau, in Miltenberg, Germany, has a maximum capacity of 27 seats. The theatre performs around 70 shows per year and the only performer to have graced its stage is Lilli Chapeau, aka Celine Bauer (pictured above right).

Mott (both Australia), who ran 100 m in 12.045 seconds outside the set of *The Footy Show* in Melbourne, Victoria, Australia, on 30 July 2009.

The ★fastest pantomime horse (mixed) – Nafi Baram and Kathleen Rice (both UK, front and rear, respectively) – ran 100 m in 16.37 seconds at the Battersea Millennium Arena, London, UK, on 30 November 2006.

★MOST TONYS FOR A PLAY

The Coast of Utopia by playwright Tom Stoppard (UK) won a record seven Tony Awards in 2007. A trilogy of plays – *Voyage*, *Shipwreck* and *Salvage* – lasting nine hours in total and embracing a 33-year timespan, *The Coast of Utopia* explores the subject of change as experienced by a huge cast of around 70 real-life Russian writers, politicians, philosophers and journalists.

> "You can't stop my happiness, 'cuz I like the way I am! And you just can't stop my knife and fork when I see a Christmas ham!"
>
> **Edna Turnblad in Hairspray**

EXTRA!
TURN BACK TO PP.182-183 FOR ALL THE TOP SHOWBIZ RECORDS.

★MOST TONY AWARDS FOR PLAYING THE OPPOSITE SEX

Only two actors have ever won a Tony Award for playing someone of the opposite sex: Mary Martin (USA) for playing the title role in *Peter Pan* in 1956 and Harvey Fierstein (USA, left) for his depiction of Edna Turnblad in *Hairspray* in 2003.

MINNEAPOLIS, MN, USA

44°58'N 93°15'W

The **quietest place** in the world is the Anechoic Test Chamber at Orfield Laboratories, Minneapolis, Minnesota, USA. Ultra-sensitive tests performed on 21 January 2004 gave the lab a background noise reading of -9.4 dBA (decibels, A-weighted).

★MOST TONY AWARDS WON FOR BEST ACTRESS IN A MUSICAL

Angela Lansbury (UK, above left) has won four Tony Awards (out of four nominations) in the category of Best Performance by a Leading Actress in a Musical for *Mame* (1966), *Dear World* (1969), *Gypsy* (1975) and *Sweeney Todd* (1979). The ★**most Tony awards for a male actor in a musical** is three, by Hinton Battle (USA, above right), who won for *Sophisticated Ladies* (1981), *The Tapdance Kid* (1984) and *Miss Saigon* (1991), all in the category of Featured Role in a Musical.

★LARGEST SIMULTANEOUS PERFORMANCE OF ONE SHOW

The most widespread simultaneous performance of a show was organized by Stagecoach Theatre Arts and comprised 66 performances of *Glad Rags* in the UK, Ireland and Germany at 4:15 p.m. on 6 December 2008.

★MOST BALLET DANCERS "EN POINTE"

A total of 220 ballet dancers successfully stood "en pointe" (meaning on the tips of their toes) for a minute at the Youth America Grand Prix (USA) 10th Anniversary Gala at New York City Center in Manhattan, New York City, USA, on 22 April 2009.

★LONGEST-RUNNING PLAY

The longest continuously run show in the world is *The Mousetrap* by Dame Agatha Christie (UK, 1890–1976), with 23,940 performances as of 10 May 2010 at St Martin's Theatre in London, UK. The play opened on 25 November 1952 at the Ambassadors Theatre, London, and moved after 8,862 performances to the St Martin's Theatre next door on 25 March 1974. Pictured below is the cast from the 58th annual performance.

FASTEST THEATRICAL PRODUCTION

The cast and crew of Dundee University Musical Society in association with Apex Productions produced and performed *Seven Brides for Seven Brothers* at the Gardyne Theatre, Dundee, UK, at 7:30 p.m. on 27 September 2003 – 23 hr 30 min after first receiving the script. The production time included all auditions, casting, rehearsals, publicity, rigging, stage and set design and construction time.

★LARGEST AUDIENCE FOR A COMEDIAN

German comedian Mario Barth performed in front of an audience of 67,733 people at the Olympiastadion, Berlin, Germany, on 12 July 2008.

★MOST THEATRICAL APPEARANCES ON A SINGLE NIGHT

Pendem Krishna Kumar (India) appeared in nine different scripted roles in nine different theatre productions in Suryapet, India, on 9 July 2009.

POPULAR CULTURE
ART & SCULPTURE

★ LARGEST SAND ART

The largest artwork created from sand – and the ★**largest freehand drawing** – is 4.86 km (3.02 miles) in diameter and contains 1,000 individual circles. Jim Denevan (USA, inset) made the artwork in the Black Rock Desert, Nevada, USA, in May 2009 in seven days, etching the sand with a rake and using chains dragged behind a vehicle.

★ LARGEST RUBIK'S CUBE MOSAIC

Five artists from the art collective Cube Works Studio in Toronto, Canada, re-created *The Last Supper* by Leonardo da Vinci... from 4,050 Rubik's cubes! The miraculous "cube-ist" mosaic measures 5.18 m (17 ft) by 2.59 m (8 ft 6 in), weighs 500 kg (1,102 lb) and was completed on 23 October 2009.

★ **NEW RECORD**
★ **UPDATED RECORD**

LARGEST...

★ DRAWING

The largest pencil drawing by one artist – *My journey of life, where I meet people of different color, birds, trees, etc... and the life goes on* – is 457.2 m (1,500 ft) long and 50.8 cm (20 in) wide, and has an overall surface area of 231.33 m² (2,490 ft²). It was completed by Jainthan Francis (USA) and measured in Sayreville, USA, on 21 June 2009.

ANAMORPHIC:

A work of art that seems distorted from most angles, but will appear normal when seen from a particular viewpoint.

★ ANAMORPHIC PAVEMENT ART

To mark the launch of *Ice Age 3* on DVD in the UK in November 2009, Twentieth Century Fox Home Entertainment asked German artist Edgar Mueller to paint a 318-m² (3,423-ft²) anamorphic reproduction of the movie's poster on the pavement outside London's Westfield Shopping Centre. In the USA, Fox promoted the movie with an ice statue of the character Scrat. Its height made it, briefly, a record-holder, but today the world's ★**tallest ice sculpture** is a 16.22-m-tall (53-ft 2.58-in) piece created by the People's Government of Yichun city, China, on 19 January 2010.

★ FINGER PAINTING

A finger painting measuring 2,101.43 m² (22,619.51 ft²) was created by 3,242 students in Hong Kong, China, on 26 November 2009.

★ SHUTTLECOCK MOSAIC

A shuttlecock mosaic measuring 30.375 m² (326.95 ft²) was created by Fuqiang Zhao (China) on 2 August 2009. It comprised 5,236 individual shuttlecocks and depicted two interlaced hearts and the words "Show the love with shuttlecocks, be together forever".

★ BEAD MOSAIC

The largest bead mosaic measures 6.72 m² (72.33 ft²) and was realized by Cao Zhitao (China) at an event organized by the Fuxin Municipal Government in Fuxin City, Liaoning Province, China, on 25 October 2009. The mosaic contained more than 30,000 agate beads.

★ PAINTING BY NUMBERS

The largest painting by numbers measures 2,461.3 m² (26,493 ft²) and was created by 960 students from Mingren Primary School in Tongliao City, Inner Mongolia, China, on 30 September 2009.

★ GROUND-BASED DIGITAL LUNAR MOSAIC

On 4 April 2009, 11 amateur astronomers (all UK) used a telescope owned by broadcaster Patrick Moore (UK) to capture 288 images of the Moon. These were then digitally stitched together to make a lunar mosaic 87.4 megapixels in size.

LONGEST PAINTING BY NUMBERS

The world's longest painting by numbers measures 959.35 m (3,147 ft 5 in) long and is entitled *Birds and Wetlands*. It was created by 2,041 participants in an event organized by the Hong Kong Wetland Park at their premises in Hong Kong, China, on 17 October 2009.

★LARGEST INFLATABLE SCULPTURE

Gulliver has a volume of 1,791.11 m³ (63,252.45 ft³) and measures 60 x 20 x 7 m (196 ft 10 in x 65 ft 7 in x 22 ft 11 in) in size. It was presented and measured in Taipei, Taiwan, on 20 July 2009.

EXTRA! FOR MORE OUTSIZED ENDEAVOURS, TURN TO P.202.

★PAVEMENT ART

Chalk pavement art measuring 5,600 m (18,372 ft 8 in) long and 2 m (6 ft 6 in) wide was created by 5,000 students from Jena, Germany, on 5 June 2009.

★CARTOON STRIP

The students, teachers and members of Vasavi Vidhyalaya Matriculation School, Trichy, India, created a continuous 601-m (1,971-ft 8-in) cartoon strip. It was measured in Tamil Nadu, India, on 25 January 2010.

MISCELLANY

★LEAST VALUABLE ART COLLECTION IN A PUBLIC MUSEUM

The Museum of Bad Art's (MOBA) collection in Boston, Massachusetts, USA, has the lowest value of any public museum's art collection. Its 573 works are worth a total of just $1,197.35 (£734).

ACTUAL SIZE

★OLDEST FIGURATIVE SCULPTURE

The *Venus of Hohle Fels* is the name given to a female figurine carved from a mammoth tusk and dated to *c.* 33,000 BC. It was discovered in the Hohle Fels ("Hollow Rock") cave near Ulm in Baden-Württemberg, Germany, in September 2008 by Nicolas Conard and a team from the University of Tübingen, Germany.

★LARGEST MODELLING BALLOON SCULPTURE

John Cassidy (USA) used 434 modelling balloons to make a biplane that measured 490 cm (192 in) wide and 375 cm (147 in) long on 25 September 2009.

★CONFETTI MOSAIC

Nikki Douthwaite (UK) made a mosaic consisting of 587,000 hole-punched dots measuring 3.07 x 2.08 m (10 ft 1 in x 6 ft 10 in) between February and June 2008.

★MURAL (SOLO)

Ernesto Espiridion Rios Rocha (Mexico) singlehandedly created a mural covering 1,678 m² (18,066 ft²) in Mazatlán, Mexico, on 6 October 2009.

LONGEST...

★PAINTING

The longest painting measures 4,955 m (16,256 ft 6 in) long and was created by 8,000 students from local schools (all Bahrain) at an event organized by the Ministry of Education in Manama, Bahrain, on 13 December 2009. The theme of the painting was "life in Bahrain".

★OLDEST PAINTING ON A WALL

In October 2006, the French archaeological mission at Dja'de al-Mughara – a Neolithic settlement on the Euphrates river near Aleppo, Syria – identified walls of a house that bore a series of geometric paintings. Measuring 2 m² (25.1 ft²), the wall paintings date from *c.* 9,000 BC.

NEW ORLEANS, LA, USA

The **longest recorded boxing fight** with gloves was between Andy Bowen and Jack Burke (both USA) at New Orleans, Louisiana, USA, on 6–7 April 1893. It lasted 110 rounds, 7 hr 19 min (9:15 p.m.–4:34 a.m.) and was declared a "no contest" (later changed to a draw).

29°58'N
90°0.4'W

ENGINEERING AND TECHNOLOGY

★ ★ ★ ★ ★ ★ ★ ★ ★ ★ ★ ★ ★ ★

HEAVIEST LIMOUSINE

The Midnight Rider is a tractor trailer limousine that weighs 22,933 kg (50,560 lb), is 21.3 m (70 ft) long and 4.1 m (13 ft 8 in) high. This mighty motor features three lounges and a separate bar, and can accommodate 40 passengers served by a crew of four. It was designed by Michael Machado and Pamela Bartholemew (both USA) in California, USA, and began operation on 3 September 2004.

CAR
THE PLUSH INTERIOR DÉCOR IS BASED ON THE DAYS OF THE RAILROAD PULLMAN CARS, WHICH WERE POPULAR FROM THE MID-19TH CENTURY.

BAR
THE BAR CONTAINS AIR-SUSPENSION SEATING FOR A SMOOTH RIDE, SATELLITE TV AND LARGE MOVIE SCREENS, AND AN INTERNAL PHONE SYSTEM WITH FOUR OUTSIDE LINES!

MEMPHIS, TN, USA

The letter M installed on the Great Mississippi River Bridge in Memphis, Tennessee, USA, is 550 m (1,800 ft) long – making it the **longest neon sign**. It comprises 200 high-intensity lamps.

GUINNESS WORLD RECORDS 2011

EXTRA!
TURN TO PP. 210–211
FOR MORE VEHICLE
RECORDS.

CONTENTS

THUNDER BAY, ON, CANADA

Despite having an artificial leg, Terry Fox (Canada, 1958–81) managed to raise Can$24.7 million (US$20.7 million; £9.1 million) on a charity run from St John's, Newfoundland, to Thunder Bay, Ontario. This represents the **largest amount of money raised** in a charity walk or run. He finished in 143 days, from 12 April to 1 September 1980, and covered 5,373 km (3,339 miles).

48°22'N
89°14'W

ENGINEERING AND TECHNOLOGY

ARCHI-TECTURE

★ NEW RECORD ★ UPDATED RECORD

★ LARGEST SHOPPING CENTRE

The Dubai Mall in Dubai, UAE, has an internal floor area of 548,127 m² (5.9 million ft²) over four levels. It houses 1,200 retail outlets and more than 160 food and drink outlets, and opened on 4 November 2008.

LARGEST HOTEL LOBBY

The lobby at the Hyatt Regency in San Francisco, California, USA, is 107 m (350 ft) long, 49 m (160 ft) wide and, at 52 m (170 ft), is the height of a 15-storey building. The lobby has 300,000 cascading lights and features trees, a stream and a fountain.

★ HIGHEST OBSERVATION DECK

A glass observation deck 477.96 m (1,568 ft 1 in) above street level is located on the 100th floor of the Shanghai World Financial Center in Pudong, China. The mixed-use skyscraper also houses the world's ★**highest hotel** – the Park Hyatt Shanghai occupies floors 79 to 93.

★ LARGEST REINFORCED CONCRETE CEMENT FLAT ROOF SPAN

The Satsang Hall within the Govind Devji's Temple in Jaipur, India, has a reinforced concrete cement flat roof with a single span of 36.27 m (119 ft). It was designed by N M Roof Designers Ltd, and the hall was dedicated to the public on 23 July 2009.

★ LARGEST REVOLVING RESTAURANT

Bellini is an Italian and international cuisine restaurant located on the 45th floor of Mexico City's World Trade Center. The establishment opened in 1994 and has an area of 1,044.66 m² (11,244.58 ft²).

★ TALLEST BUILDING

The Burj Khalifa (formally Burj Dubai) opened on 17 January 2009 in Dubai, UAE. It topped out at a record-breaking 828 m (2,717 ft), making it not only the tallest man-made structure on Earth but also the ★**tallest building ever**.

HIGH!
THE RECORD-BREAKING BURJ KHALIFA ALSO HOLDS THE TITLE FOR THE ★BUILDING WITH THE MOST FLOORS, AT 160 STOREYS!

RISE!
DUBAI IS HOME TO A RANGE OF OTHER IMPRESSIVE STRUCTURES, INCLUDING THE ROSE RAYHAAN, THE ★TALLEST HOTEL, STANDING AT 333 M (1,092 FT 6 IN).

47°03'N 87°57'W

MILWAUKEE, WI, USA

Detective Lieutenant Andrew F Anewenter (USA, b. 12 January 1916) holds the record for the **longest-serving police officer**. He worked for the Milwaukee (Wisconsin) Police Department for 61 years, from 1 June 1942 until his retirement on 15 May 2003.

★ LARGEST STEEL STRUCTURE

Designed by Swiss architects Herzog & de Meuron, the Beijing Olympic Stadium, also known as the Bird's Nest, cost $423 million (£265 million) to construct and has a floor space of 258,000 m² (2,777,088 ft²) on a 21-ha (51-acre) site. The main body of the stadium is a saddle-shaped elliptic steel structure weighing 38,100 tonnes (42,000 tons).

LARGEST AIRPORT PASSENGER TERMINAL

The Hong Kong International Airport passenger terminal building is 1.3 km (0.8 miles) long and covers 550,000 m² (5,920,150 ft²). It has a capacity of 45 million passengers a year, arriving on 460 flights every day, and cost $20 billion (£12 billion) to build. The baggage hall alone is as big as the Yankee Stadium in New York, USA.

★ TALLEST STEEL STRUCTURE

Willis Tower (formerly Sears Tower) in Chicago, Illinois, USA, is a 442-m-tall (1,451-ft), 108-storey office skyscraper constructed from steel. The building's design includes nine steel-unit square tubes in a 3 x 3 arrangement, with a 22 x 22 m (75 x 75 ft) footprint. Completed in 1974, it has floor area of 423,637 m² (4.56 million ft²).

★ TALLEST CONCRETE STRUCTURE

Completed in 2009, the 92-storey Trump International Hotel & Tower in Chicago, Illinois, USA, tops out at 360 m (1,170 ft), or 423 m (1,389 ft) including the building's spire. Designed by Skidmore, Owings and Merrill, the complex features 486 residential apartments and a 339-room hotel, and is the world's tallest formwork concrete structure.

HIGHEST CONCENTRATION OF THEME HOTELS

There are more than 16 theme hotels on the Strip in Las Vegas, Nevada, USA. Themes include the skyline of Paris and New York, Treasure Island and Venetian. Las Vegas boasts an incredible 120,000 hotel rooms, nearly one for every four of its inhabitants.

LARGEST RETRACTABLE STADIUM ROOF

Completed in June 1989, the roof of the SkyDome, home of the Toronto Blue Jays baseball team located near the CN Tower in Toronto, Canada, covers 3.2 ha (8 acres), spans 209 m (685 ft) at its widest, and rises to 86 m (282 ft). It weighs 11,000 tonnes (12,125 tons) and takes 20 minutes to open fully. When retracted, the entire field and 91% of the seats are uncovered.

LARGEST RESIDENTIAL PALACE

The palace (Istana Nurul Iman) of HM the Sultan of Brunei in the capital Bandar Seri Begawan is the largest residence in the world, with a floorspace of 200,000 m² (2,152,780 ft²), 1,788 rooms and 257 lavatories.

The Council on Tall Buildings and Urban Habitat provide official guidelines on big structures.

TRIVIA

"In China, a bird's nest is very expensive, something you eat on special occasions."
Architect Li Xinggang explains the origins of the stadium's nickname

★ LARGEST DEPARTMENT STORE

Built by Shinsegae Co. Ltd and opened on 26 June 2009, the Shinsegae ("New World") Centum City Department Store in Busan, South Korea, covers an area of 293,905 m² (3.16 million ft²), beating the previous record holder, the famous Macy's store in New York City, USA, by over 95,000 m² (1.022 million ft²).

ENGINEERING AND TECHNOLOGY
ROLLER COASTERS

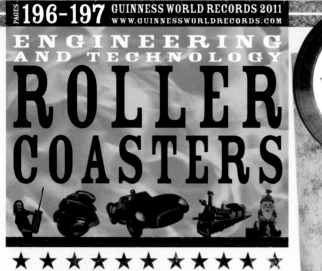

★ ★ ★ ★ ★ ★ ★ ★ ★ ★ ★ ★ ★ ★ ★

★ FASTEST (ABSOLUTE)

The *ring°racer* Formula One-themed coaster at the Nürburgring race track in Nürburg, Germany, features a pneumatic launch system that blasts riders to 216.9 km/h (134.8 mph) in a breathtaking 2.5 seconds – twice as fast as a Formula One car.

★ MOST TRACK INVERSIONS

Colossus at Thorpe Park, Chertsey, Surrey, UK, turns riders upside down a total of 10 times during each 850-m (2,789-ft) run. The ride has a maximum height of 30 m (98 ft) and a top speed of 65 km/h (40 mph). The inversions include a vertical loop, a twin cobra roll, a twin corkscrew and five heart rolls. The *Tenth Ring Roller Coaster* of Chimelong Paradise in Guangzhou, China, also holds the record, but is a duplicate of *Colossus*.

FASTEST

★ ABSOLUTE
See *ring°racer*, left.

★ 4TH DIMENSION
This type of coaster features cars that sit either side of the track and spin about a horizontal axis. The ★**first 4th dimension coaster** was *X* at Six Flags Magic Mountain, in 2002, but the ★**fastest** is *Eejanaika* at Fuji-Q Highland in Fujiyoshida, Yamanashi, Japan, which reaches 126 km/h (78.3 mph).

FLYING
Tatsu at Six Flags Magic Mountain in Valencia, California, USA, is the fastest flying coaster – that is, its riders travel with their backs parallel to the track to give the impression of flight. It reaches speeds of 99.7 km/h (62 mph). At 51.8 m (170 ft) high, it is also the world's **tallest flying coaster**.

SHUTTLE
A shuttle coaster is one that does not complete a full circuit and must therefore travel out and back. The speed record for this category of coaster is shared by *Superman the Escape* at Six Flags Magic Mountain, Valencia, California, USA, and *Tower of Terror* at Dreamworld, Gold Coast, Australia. Both opened in 1997 and both register a top speed of 161 km/h (100 mph).

★ MOST EXPENSIVE

Expedition Everest was opened by Disney for $100 million (£51 million) in 2006 after six years of research and construction. The concept is a train journey through the Himalayas that uses a shortcut via Forbidden Mountain, wherein lies the fearsome Yeti – an enormous 6.7-m-tall (22-ft) audio-animatronic beast controlled by 19 actuators and covered in 93 m² (1,000 ft²) of fur.

36°10'N 86°47'W

NASHVILLE, TN, USA
Dan Runte (USA) reached the **fastest speed for a monster truck** – of 111.5 km/h (69.3 mph) – in *Bigfoot 14* on 11 September 1999 at Symrna Airport, Nashville, Tennessee, USA. The speed was recorded during the run-up to the **longest ever monster truck jump** of 61.57 m (202 ft)

TOP 10 FASTEST

	SPEED	COASTER	PARK	LOCATION	DATE
*	134.8 mph	*ring°racer*	Nürburgring	Nürburg, Germany	2009
1	128 mph	*Kingda Ka*	Six Flags Great Adventure	Jackson, New Jersey, USA	2005
2	120 mph	*Top Thrill Dragster*	Cedar Point	Sandusky, Ohio, USA	2003
3	106.9 mph	*Dodonp*	Fuji-Q Highland	Fujiyoshida, Yamanashi, Japan	2001
4	100 mph	*Superman the Escape*	Six Flags Magic Mountain	Valencia, California, USA	1997
		Tower of Terror	Dreamworld	Coomera, Australia	1997
5	95 mph	*Steel Dragon 2000*	Nagashima Spa Land	Nagashima, Kuwana Mie, Japan	2000
6	93 mph	*Millennium Force*	Cedar Point	Sandusky, Ohio, USA	2000
*	90 mph	*Intimidator 305* (above)	Kings Dominion	Doswell, Virginia, USA	2010
7	85 mph	*Goliath*	Six Flags Magic Mountain	Valencia, California, USA	2000
		Phantom's Revenge	Kennywood	West Mifflin, Pennsylvania, USA	1991
		Titan	Six Flags Over Texas	Arlington, Texas, USA	2001
8	83.9 mph	*Furius Baco*	PortAventura Park	Salou, Tarragona, Spain	2007
9	82 mph	*Xcelerator*	Knott's Berry Farm	Buena Park, California, USA	2002
10	80.8 mph	*Fujiyama*	Fuji-Q Highland	Fujiyoshida, Yamanashi, Japan	1996
		Thunder Dolphin	Tokyo Dome City	Bunkyo Tokyo, Japan	2003

Source: Roller Coaster Database   * Unopened at time of going to press

DID YOU KNOW?
THE ★CONTINENT WITH THE MOST ROLLER COASTERS IS ASIA, WITH 828; NORTH AMERICA IS NEXT, WITH 731.

The ★**longest roller coaster** of all is *Steel Dragon 2000*: 2,478.9 m (8,133 ft 2 in) long, it opened on 1 August 2000.

TRIVIA

★ NEW RECORD   ★ UPDATED RECORD

★SUSPENDED

The speed record for suspended coasters – in which the riders hang from the track and pivot from side to side, emphasizing the track's banks and turns – is shared between *Vortex* at Canada's Wonderland in Vaughan, Ontario, Canada, and *Ninja* at Six Flags Magic Mountain in Valencia, California, USA. Both can reach 88.5 km/h (55 mph).

FASTEST (WOODEN)

Colossos at Heide-Park Soltau in Lower Saxony, Germany, reaches a peak speed of 120 km/h (74.6 mph). It is also the **tallest operating wooden coaster** at 60 m (196 ft 10 in).

TALLEST

ABSOLUTE
Kingda Ka, see *Tallest absolute* (right).

★4TH DIMENSION
At 76 m (249 ft 4 in) tall, *Eejanaika* at Fuji-Q Highland in Yamanashi Prefecture, Japan, is the loftiest of the 4th dimension coasters. The 2-min 10-sec ride opened at a cost of just over Y3.5 billion ($35 million; £24 million).

FLYING
Tatsu, see *Fastest flying coaster*, opposite page.

SHUTTLE
Superman the Escape at Six Flags Magic Mountain, Valencia, California, USA, opened in 1997 at a height of 126.5 m (415 ft).

★SUSPENDED
Vortex at Wonderland in Vaughan, Ontario, Canada, reaches a peak of 27.7 m (91 ft), making it the world's tallest suspended ride.

STEEPEST

★ABSOLUTE
Mumbo Jumbo at Flamingo Land Theme Park & Zoo in Malton, UK, has an angle of descent of 112°. The 30-m-tall (98-ft) ride was opened on 4 July 2009 at a cost of £4 million ($6.3 million). The extreme drop exerts a maximum force of 4 g.

WOODEN
El Toro at Six Flags Great Adventure, New Jersey, USA, has a drop of 76°. The 1,341-m (4,400-ft) ride lasts 1 min 43 sec, reaching speeds of 120 km/h (75 mph). It towers 57.3 m (188 ft) above the theme park at its tallest point.

★SHUTTLE
The steepest angle of descent on a shuttle-style coaster is 90°, a record currently held by at least 14 different rides. The most recent shuttle-style coaster to open was the 60-m (196-ft) *Aftershock* at the Silverwood Theme Park in Athol, Idaho, USA, which had relocated from Six Flags Great America in Gurnee, Illinois, USA.

TALLEST (ABSOLUTE)
Kingda Ka at Six Flags Great Adventure in New Jersey, USA, reaches a height of 139 m (456 ft). It opened in spring 2005 and at the time was the world's fastest coaster.

ENGINEERING AND TECHNOLOGY
BIG ENGINEERING

★ ★ ★ ★ ★ ★ ★ ★ ★ ★ ★ ★ ★

★ LARGEST FLOOD DEFENCE

The Delta Works off the coast of Holland is a huge series of dams, locks, sluices, storm surge barriers and dykes designed to protect low-lying areas of the country from the sea. Construction began in 1950 and ended in 1997 with the completion of the Maeslantkering and the Hartelkering barriers. The Delta Works contain some 16,495 km (10,250 miles) of dykes and around 300 structures.

★ LARGEST MAN-MADE EXCAVATION

The Bingham Canyon Copper Mine near Salt Lake City, Utah, USA, is the world's largest man-made excavation. More than 5.4 billion tonnes (5.9 billion tons) of rock have been excavated from it since 1906. Visible from space, it measures 4 km (2.5 miles) across and 1.2 km (0.75 miles) deep and has been called "the richest hole on Earth".

As of 2004, more than 15.4 million tonnes (16.9 million tons) of copper have been produced from the mine, as well as 652 million g (23 million oz) of gold and 5.3 billion g (190 million oz) of silver.

★ HEAVIEST WEIGHT LIFTED BY CRANE

A barge, ballasted with water and weighing a hefty 20,133 tonnes (44,385,667 lb), was lifted by the "Taisun" crane at Yantai Raffles Shipyard, Yantai, China, on 18 April 2008.

★ LONGEST DRILLED OIL WELL

The world's longest drilled oil well is BD-04-A, with a total length of 12,289 m (40,320 ft). It was completed in May 2008 by Maersk Oil Qatar and Qatar Petroleum, in the Al-Shaheen offshore oil field off the coast of Qatar. The well includes a horizontal section measuring 10,902 m (35,770 ft).

★ LARGEST EXCAVATION BY HAND

The Jagersfontein Mine near Jagersfontein, South Africa, is an open-pit mine that has provided some of the largest diamonds ever discovered. It operated as a mine from 1888 until 1971, first as an open mine and then as an underground mine. The Jagersfontein Mine was dug by hand to a depth of 201 m (660 ft) between 1888 and 1911. The area of the opening measures 19.65 ha (48.55 acres).

★ FARTHEST MAN-MADE LEANING TOWER

The "Capital Gate" has an inclination of 18 degrees and is 160 m (524 ft 11 in) high. It was designed by Global Architects RMJM (Dubai) and was completed in Abu Dhabi, United Arab Emirates, on 4 January 2010.

TALLEST BRIDGE

The 2,460-m-long (8,070-ft) Millau Viaduct across the Tarn Valley, France, is supported by seven concrete piers, the tallest of which measures 333.88 m (1,095 ft 4.8 in) from the ground to its highest point.

★ NEW RECORD
★ UPDATED RECORD

MIGHTY
THE PROJECT WAS FINISHED AFTER ALMOST 50 YEARS IN 1997 WITH THE COMPLETION OF THE MAESLANTKERING AND HARTELKERING BARRIERS.

HIGH
THE DELTA WORKS HAS BEEN DECLARED ONE OF THE SEVEN WONDERS OF THE MODERN WORLD BY THE AMERICAN SOCIETY OF CIVIL ENGINEERS.

MS *Allure of the Seas*, sister ship to the *Oasis*, is due to launch in 2010.

TRIVIA

★ LARGEST LAKE CREATED BY A NUCLEAR EXPLOSION

On 15 January 1965, the Soviet Union detonated a 140-kiloton nuclear device underneath a dry bed of the Chagan River, Kazakhstan. Part of the Soviets' Nuclear Explosions for the National Economy programme, the raised rim of the resulting crater dammed the river, allowing the creation of a reservoir, now known as Lake Chagan. It has a volume of around 100,000 m^3 (3,531,000 ft^3).

TALLEST HOSPITAL

Guy's Tower at Guy's Hospital in London, UK, is 142.6 m (468 ft) tall. It was completed in 1974 and has 34 floors.

TALLEST BOAT LIFT

The Strépy-Thieu boat lift on the Canal du Centre, Hainaut, Belgium, uses a counterweight system to carry boats a vertical distance of 73.15 m (240 ft) from its upstream and downstream sections. The two boxes, or caissons, that each boat enters are 112 x 12 m (367 x 39 ft), and weigh between 7,200 and 8,400 tonnes (7,936–9,259 tons), depending on the current water level. It takes seven minutes for the vertical journey to be completed.

★ TALLEST ELECTRICITY PYLON

At Jiangyin, Jiangsu Province, China, two electricity transmission pylons stand on opposite banks of the Yangtze River at 346.5 m (1,137 ft) tall. Their height allows the power lines to span the river, which is 2,303 m (7,556 ft) wide at this point. Another pylon, on the Damaoshan Mountain in Zhoushan city, China, will be 370 m (1,213 ft) tall when it is completed in 2010.

★ WIDEST CANAL

The Cape Cod Canal, which crosses the land that connects Cape Cod to mainland Massachusetts, USA, was constructed between 1909 and 1916. It is 28 km (17.4 miles) long and 164.6 m (540 ft) wide. It is a segment of the Atlantic Intracoastal Waterway, which runs for 4,800 km (3,000 miles) along the American east coast.

MOST EXPENSIVE OBJECT ON EARTH

The Itaipu hydroelectric dam on the Paraná River between Brazil and Paraguay cost $27 billion (£20.2 billion) to build in 1984 ($35.93 billion, or £25.53 billion today), which makes it the priciest object on Earth. Only the International Space Station (ISS) has cost more as a single project.

★ TALLEST CHIMNEY DEMOLISHED BY EXPLOSIVES

The Westerholt Power Station in Gelsenkirchen-Westerholt, Germany, was a coal power station constructed in the 1960s and decommissioned in 2005. Its chimney, or smokestack, was constructed in 1997 and was 337 m (1,104 ft) high – the tallest in Germany at that time. It was demolished using explosives on 3 December 2006.

★ LARGEST AUTOCLAVE

An autoclave is typically used to sterilize medical or laboratory instruments. In August 2006, ASC Process Systems (USA) announced it had built an autoclave with an internal volume of 2,321 m^3 (82,000 ft^3). It is designed to process components of the Boeing 787 Dreamliner passenger aircraft by subjecting them to temperatures of up to 232°C (450°F) and pressures of up to 10.2 bar.

MOST SPACIOUS BUILDING

The Boeing Company's main assembly plant in Everett, Washington, USA, has a volume of 13.4 million m^3 (472 million ft^3) and a floor area of 39.8 ha (98.3 acres). Boeing's 747, 767 and 777 aircraft are assembled there.

EXTRA!
FOR MORE AERONAUTICAL RECORDS, TURN BACK TO PP.116–117.

ENGINEERING AND TECHNOLOGY

ROAD & RAIL

★ ★ ★ ★ ★ ★ ★ ★ ★ ★ ★ ★ ★

"*I don't have to be a potty mouth, chew tobacco and be 300 pounds to drive a truck.*"

Lisa Kelly, ice road trucker

★LONGEST ICE ROAD

Canada's Tibbitt to Contwoyto Winter Road was first used in 1982 to supply mines in the Northwest Territories. Open from January to the end of March, the ice road is rebuilt annually. It is 568 km (353 miles) long, 495 km (308 miles) of which traverses frozen lakes.

★LONGEST UNDERWATER ROAD TUNNEL

The Tokyo Bay Aqua-Line is a combination of bridge and tunnel that spans Tokyo Bay, Japan. The tunnel section is 9,583 m (31,440 ft) long and was opened in 1997.

★LARGEST NATIONAL ROAD NETWORK

The USA has 6,465,799 km (4,017,661 miles) of roads, of which 4,209,835 km (2,615,870 miles) are paved. China is in second place with 3,583,715 km (2,226,817 miles) of roads.

★OLDEST "MAGIC ROUNDABOUT"

Ring junctions were first designed by the Road Research Laboratory (UK) in order to ease traffic congestion at busy junctions. The first opened in Swindon, UK, in 1972. Nicknamed the "Magic Roundabout", it consists of five mini-roundabouts connected together in a circle, allowing traffic to move in both directions around the main central island.

★FASTEST JET-POWERED TRAIN

The M-497 was a prototype experimental train powered by two General Electric J47-19 jet engines. It was developed and tested in 1966 in the USA and was able to reach a top speed of 296 km/h (183 mph).

★HIGHEST RAILWAY STATION

The Tanggula Railway Station in Tibet is the highest in the world at 5,068 m (16,627 ft) above sea level. The unstaffed station on the Qingzang railway opened on 1 July 2006 and has a 1.25-km-long (0.77-mile) platform.

ROAD

DEADLIEST PLACE TO TRAVEL BY ROAD

According to findings from its first report on global road safety, the World Health Organization states that Eritrea, in Africa, is the deadliest place to travel by road in terms of deaths caused by road traffic accidents. There were 48 deaths per 100,000 people in 2007.

39°08'N
84°30'W

CINCINNATI, OH, USA

The **largest gathering of scarecrows in one location** is 3,311. All were on display at the Cincinnati Horticultural Society's Cincinnati Flower and Farm Fest on Coney Island, Cincinnati, Ohio, USA, on 12 October 2003.

★ OLDEST STACK INTERCHANGE

The Four Level Interchange in Los Angeles, California, USA, features, as its name suggests, four layers of multi-lane road and was first opened to the public in 1953. The interchange links US Route 101 to State Route 110 using a free flowing design to help minimize LA's notorious congestion.

★ OLDEST SUBWAY TUNNEL

The Atlantic Avenue Tunnel beneath Brooklyn, USA, was built over a period of seven months in 1844. Running for 767 m (2,517 ft), it is 6.4 m (21 ft) wide and 5.2 m (17 ft) high. The tunnel was the first in the world built underground in order to improve urban congestion, public safety and rail operations. It operated until 1861, when the ends were sealed off, and was rediscovered in 1981.

RAIL

★ LONGEST METRO BY TOTAL LENGTH

The London Underground, London, UK, has a combined length of around 400 km (250 miles) of track, as well as 270 stations. Some 45% of it is underground. With its first section opening in 1863, the London Underground is also the **oldest metro system** in the world.

★ LARGEST NATIONAL RAIL NETWORK

The USA has some 226,427 km (140,695 miles) of rail. Second place belongs to Russia, with 87,157 km (54,156 miles) of track.

SMALLEST ARMOURED TRAIN

During World War II, the 381-mm-gauge (15-in) Romney, Hythe & Dymchurch Railway, which runs between Hythe and Dungeness along the coast of Kent, UK, was requisitioned by the British government for use in the war effort. Roughly a quarter of the size of UK standard-gauge trains, a steam locomotive and several carriages were given steel armour for wartime use.

FASTEST STEAM LOCOMOTIVE

The London North Eastern Railway "Class A4" No. 4468 *Mallard* hauled seven coaches at a speed of 201 km/h (125 mph) between Grantham, Lincolnshire, and Peterborough, Cambridgeshire, UK, on 3 July 1938.

HEAVIEST HAUL RAILWAY

On 8 April 2008, the Fortescue Metals Group (Australia) completed 250 km (155 miles) of single track railway line capable of running 2.5-km-long (1.53-mile) trains carrying a gross load of 38,400 tonnes (42,328 tons) of ore.

OLDEST STEAM LOCOMOTIVE IN USE

The *Fairy Queen* was built in 1855 by Kitson Thompson Hewitson of Leeds, UK. Brought back into service in October 1997 hauling a twin coach train between Delhi Cantonment, Delhi, and Alwar, Rajasthan, India, the train now provides a popular service to tourists.

★ NEW RECORD
★ UPDATED RECORD

CHUFF! THE OFFICIAL SPEED OF THE *FAIRY QUEEN* IS 40 KM/H (25 MPH), ALTHOUGH IT IS CAPABLE OF GOING MUCH FASTER THAN THIS.

CHUFF! THE *FAIRY QUEEN* WAS RESTORED AND MADE FULLY FUNCTIONAL IN 1966. WHEN NOT IN USE, IT IS KEPT AT THE INDIAN NATIONAL RAILWAY MUSEUM IN NEW DELHI.

ATLANTA, GA, USA
33°45'N 84°23'W
Willie Jones (USA) was admitted to Grady Memorial Hospital, Atlanta, Georgia, USA, on 10 July 1980 with heatstroke on a day when the temperature reached 32.2°C (90°F) with 44% humidity. His temperature was found to be 46.5°C (115.7°F) – the **highest known body temperature**.

ENGINEERING AND TECHNOLOGY
BIG STUFF

★ ★ ★ ★ ★ ★ ★ ★ ★ ★ ★ ★ ★

★LARGEST...

★BACKPACK/ RUCKSACK

A backpack/rucksack 3 m (9 ft 10 in) tall and 2.95 m (9 ft 8 in) wide, adorned with the character Lulu Caty, was manufactured by Lulu Caty (Rainbow Max Co., China) and unveiled in Dubai, UAE, on 10 October 2009.

★CHRISTMAS STAR ORNAMENT

Measuring 31.59 m (103 ft 8 in) tall, the largest Christmas star ornament was constructed by Apple A Day Properties (India) and unveiled in Kochi, Kerala, India, on 31 December 2009. The giant festive decoration was created to celebrate the building of a new music academy in the city.

★LARGEST SCREWDRIVER

Thomas Blackthorne (UK) owns the world's largest screwdriver. It has an acrylic handle that measures 19.5 cm (7.6 in) at its widest point and is 50 cm (19.6 in) long. The steel shaft is 25 mm (1 in) thick and projects a further 51 cm (20 in), making the overall length 101 cm (39.7 in).

EXTRA! CAN'T GET ENOUGH BIG STUFF? NO PROBLEM – JUST TURN THE PAGE TO FIND MORE SCALED-UP RECORDS.

★LARGEST SPORTS SHOE

A sports shoe measuring 4 m (13 ft 1 in) long, 1.6 m (5 ft 2 in) wide and 1.7 m (5 ft 6 in) high was created by Launch Group (UK) in Cardiff, UK, in March 2009. It was made on behalf of supermarket chain Tesco's support for Cancer Research UK's Race for Life.

★CUP OF TEA

Mercy Health Center of Fort Scott, Kansas, USA, made a cup of tea measuring 2.41 m (7.92 ft) in diameter, 0.6 m (1.96 ft) in height and with a volume of 3,000 litres (660 gallons). The giant cuppa was unveiled on 26 September 2009.

★FAN

A fan measuring 8.48 m (27 ft 10 in) long and 5.18 m (17 ft) in height when fully opened was created by Goods of Desire (G.O.D.) and was unveiled at the G.O.D. Peak Galleria store in Hong Kong, China, on 20 August 2009. The fan was made from wood and paper and operated just like a standard-size fan of that construction.

★GLASS OF SPRITZER

A spritzer with a volume of 500 litres (109 gal) was created by the Hungarian Wine Marketing Agency in Budapest, Hungary, on 20 June 2009. It was made by combining 250 litres (54 gal) each of Neszmely Rose wine and soda water.

★LONGEST USABLE GOLF CLUB

Measuring 4.09 m (13 ft 5 in) in length, the longest usable golf club was created by Denmark's Karsten Maas. The club was used to drive a ball a distance of 123 m (403 ft 6 in) on a Trackman device at the Bella Centre, Copenhagen, Denmark, on 24 January 2009.

★GOLF TEE

Students of Jerry Havill's Team Problem Solving Course at Bay de Noc Community College in Escanaba, Michigan, USA, built a giant golf tee that measured 8.13 m (26 ft 8 in) long with a head diameter of 88.9 cm (35 in) and a shaft width of 35.24 cm (13.87 in). It was unveiled on 23 July 2009.

★POM-POM

A pom-pom measuring 91.4 cm (3 ft) high and 320 cm (10 ft 5 in) across was created by the creative arts department at Self Unlimited in Kent, UK, on 30 June 2009.

LARGEST WARDROBE

Jan Bilý (Czech Republic) and his company Art-Style created a wardrobe that measures 6.06 m (19 ft 10 in) high, 4.07 m (13 ft 4 in) wide and 1.5 m (4 ft 11 in) deep. The wardrobe, which has two doors, was presented and measured in Prague, Czech Republic, on 10 September 2009.

★ POSTER

A 42.6 x 63.1-m (139-ft 9-in x 207-ft) poster was created by Alpiq (Switzerland) and presented and measured at the Cleuson Dam near Nendaz, Switzerland, on 8 February 2010. The poster is a greeting to Swiss athletes at the Winter Olympics in Vancouver, Canada.

★ SANTA HAT

Measuring a whopping 15.47 m (50 ft 9 in) long and 8.23 m (27 ft) wide, the largest Santa hat was created by children from

★ LARGEST BEACH BALL

An inflatable beach ball measuring 12.59 m (41 ft 3 in) in diameter was made by Westtoer (Belgium) and was displayed in Liège, Belgium, on 8 August 2009.

the Chill Youth Club (all Norway). The festive headgear, which took a total of three months to construct, was presented in Fredrikstad, Norway, on 9 December 2008.

★ TRUMPET

Benny J Mamoto (Indonesia) built a playable trumpet measuring 32 m (104 ft 11.8 in) long with a bell of 5.20 m (17 ft) in diameter and 6.8 m (22 ft 3.7 in) in circumference. It was displayed in Tondano, North Sulawesi, Indonesia, on 31 October 2009.

LONGEST...

★ ABACUS

An abacus measuring 13.11 m (43 ft 0.14 in) was presented at an event organized by the Development & Reform Commission of Fuxin Municipal Government in Fuxin city, Liaoning province, China, on 25 October 2009.

★ SOFA

Fancy a nice long sit down? You could do worse than choose the world's longest sofa, which was measured at 890.25 m (2,920 ft 9 in) in Sykkylven, Norway, on 14 June 2009. The super-size sofa, which was manufactured by 20 local furniture factories, was put together and displayed across the span of the Sykkylven bridge.

★ TABLE CLOTH

A table cloth measuring 1,151.2 m (3,776 ft 10 in) long and 1.6 m (5 ft 3 in) wide was made by Green Development Ltd (Poland) and unveiled in Żyrardów, Poland, on 13 June 2009.

★ WALK-THROUGH HORROR HOUSE

The Cutting Edge Haunted House in Fort Worth Texas, USA, had a walk-through measured at 689.17 m (2,261 ft 0.9 in) long on 12 September 2009.

★ WEDDING DRESS TRAIN

Watters Inc. (USA) created a wedding dress train 2,386.44 m (7,829 ft 6 in) long. It was measured in Round Mountain, Texas, USA, on 19 December 2009.

★ WOODEN CHAIN

Markley B Noel (USA) created a wooden chain measuring 148.59 m (487 ft 6 in) long in Kalamazoo, Michigan, USA, on 2 October 2009.

★ LONGEST RIDEABLE SURFBOARD

A surfboard measuring 9.42 m (30 ft 10 in) long was successfully ridden by Rico De Souza (Brazil, pictured) at Solemar Beach, Espirito Santo, Brazil, on 12 June 2009.

The **largest surfboard ever** was made by Nev Hyman (Australia) and is 12 m (39 ft 4 in) long, 3 m (9 ft 10 in) wide and 30 cm (11.8 in) thick. It was launched in Queensland, Australia, on 5 March 2005.

TRASH

A RECORD 7.13-M-TALL (23-FT 4-IN), 4.76-M-WIDE (15-FT 7-IN) LITTER BIN WAS CREATED BY REALIZAR IMPACT MARKETING AND MODELO (PORTUGAL) IN JUNE 2009.

BRUSH

A WORLD-BEATING PAINT BRUSH MEASURING 4.35 M (14 FT 3 IN) IN LENGTH WAS CREATED BY PRIMARIA MUNICIPIULUI CAMPINA (ROMANIA) IN SEPTEMBER 2009.

ENGINEERING AND TECHNOLOGY
BIG STUFF

★LARGEST HIGH DEFINITION TV SCREEN

A Diamond Vision High Definition LED television screen measuring 10.88 x 107.52 m (35 ft 8.4 in x 352 ft 9 in) was unveiled on 28 January 2010 at Meydan Racecourse, Dubai, UAE. The world-beating screen, which has a total surface area of 1,169.82 m² (12 591.83 ft²), was created by the Mitsubishi Electric Corporation (Japan) for the Meydan City Corporation, which is based in Dubai.

★LONGEST BALLOON CHAIN

A balloon chain measuring 4.77 km (2.92 miles) long was constructed by customers of the shopping centre Belforte (Italy). The chain, which used 42,000 balloons, was displayed and measured in Serravalle, Italy, on 12 July 2009.

★LONGEST CHAIN OF FIRE HOSES

Verband Bernischer Gemeiden and Gebäudeversicherung Bern organized the connection of the longest chain of fire hoses, which carried water a distance of 56 km (34.8 miles) between Frutigen and Bern, Switzerland, on 19 September 2003.

LARGEST...

OBJECT	DIMENSIONS	RECORD HOLDER	DATE ACHIEVED
★ Ball point pen	3.63 m (11 ft 11 in) long	Biswaroop Roy Chowdhury (India)	29 March 2009
★ Canned food structure	115,527 cans	Disney VoluntEARS (USA)	11 February 2010
★ Cardboard box	6.12 m (20 ft 1.2 in) wide; 14.05 m (46 ft 1.2 in) long; 2.75 m (9 ft 0.3 in) tall	Chegg.com (USA)	19 September 2009
★ Ceramic plate	2,870 kg (6,327 lb 4 oz) in weight; 5.8 m (19 ft) in diameter	Joe Kabalan and the Association of Lebanese Industrialists (both Lebanon)	24 October 2009
★ Chair	30 m (98 ft 5 in) tall	XXXLutz and Holzleimbauwerk Wiehag GmbH (both Austria)	9 February 2009
★ Chess set	Board: 5.89 m (19 ft 4 in) on each side King: 119 cm (47 in) tall; 37.4 cm (1 ft 2 in) wide	Medicine Hat Chess Club (Canada)	27 May 2009
★ Chinowa	11 m (36 ft 1 in) in diameter	Aichiken Gokokujinjya (Japan)	28 June 2009
★ Chopsticks	8.4 m (27 ft 6 in)	Wakasa Chopsticks Industry Cooperative (Japan)	22 March 2009
★ Cup of hot chocolate	318.23 litres (70 gal; 84.07 US gal)	City of St Thomas (Canada)	22 December 2009
★ Cup of soft drink	4,593.7 litres (1,010.47 gal; 1,213.5 US gal)	People's Government of Jiagedaqi District, China	6 August 2009
★ Cushion	10.08 x 10.08 m (33 ft 0.8 in x 33 ft 0.8 in)	Shanghai Konglong Textile Ornaments Co., Ltd (China)	29 May 2009
★ Dog biscuit	105 kg (231 lb 7 oz)	Warner Bros Entertainment UK and the Canine Cookie Company (both UK)	5 October 2009
★ Flag (draped)	43,404.95 m² (467,206.99 ft²)	Grace Galindez-Gupana (Philippines)	11 April 2009
★ Flute	3.25 m (10 ft 7 in) long; 5 cm (1.97 in) in diameter	Fushun Youth and Children Palace (China)	14 July 2009
★ Football shirt	71.35 x 79.15 m (234 ft 1 in x 259 ft 8 in)	AVEA (Turkey)	5 April 2009
★ Fresh flower garland	2.2 km (1.3 miles) long	The people of Peiting (Germany)	19 July 2009

★ NEW RECORD   ★ UPDATED RECORD

★LARGEST CARD STRUCTURE

Bryan Berg (USA) completed a playing card structure measuring 10.39 m (34 ft 1.05 in) long, 2.88 m (9 ft 5.39 in) tall and 3.54 m (11 ft 7.37 in) deep at the Venetian Macao-Resort-Hotel in Macau, China, on 10 March 2010. The structure, which was made of 218,792 cards, was a replica of the Macau skyline.

LARGEST... CONT'D

OBJECT	DIMENSIONS	RECORD HOLDER	DATE ACHIEVED
★ Glowstick	3 m (9 ft 10 in) tall; 20 cm (7.87 in) in diameter	KNIXS GmbH (Germany)	29 June 2009
☆ Hand-woven carpet	955 m² (10,279 ft²)	Samovar Carpets & Antiques (Kuwait)	1 November 2009
★ Horseshoe	56 cm (1 ft 10 in) long; 61.5 cm (2 ft) wide	Caritas Tagesstätte Krumbach (Austria)	21 June 2008
★ Impossible bottle	60 litres (13.1 gal; 15.8 US gal)	Aidano Dallafiora (Italy)	24 August 2009
☆ Inflatable sofa	20.5 m (67 ft 3 in) long; 8.10 m (26 ft 9 in) wide; 8.1 m (26 ft 5 in) tall	Jacobs Krönung (Germany)	14 April 2009
★ Javelin	28.83 m (94 ft 7 in) long; 30 cm (11 in) diameter	Vattenfall (Germany)	31 July 2009
★ Model aircraft by wing-span	15 m (49 ft 2 in) wing-span	Markus Stadelmann (Switzerland)	8 May 2009
☆ Postcard	48.75 m² (524.74 ft²)	Deutsche Post (Germany) and Toyota Cars (Japan)	10 August 2009
☆ Punch bag	6.97 m (22 ft 10 in) tall; 98 cm (3 ft 2 in) wide; 800 kg (1,763 lb) in weight	Helio Dipp, Jr and Cintia Schmitt (both Brazil)	28 March 2009
☆ Scissors	2.31 m (7 ft 7 in) from tip to handle	Neerja Roy Chowdhury (India)	16 August 2009
☆ Sheet of handmade paper	13.9 x 6.9 m (45 ft 7 in x 22 ft 7 in)	Made for Masaki Takahashi and Kazuki Maeda (both Japan)	19 August 2009
☆ Shopping bag (made from paper)	4.18 m x 6.62 m x 1.79 m (13 ft 8 in x 21 ft 8 in x 5 ft 10 in)	Kaufland (Romania)	18 May 2009
☆ Shower	30.48 m (100 ft) long; 12.19 m (40 ft) wide; 3.04 m (10 ft) tall	PertPlus and Chicago firefighters (both USA)	9 July 2009
★ Sky lantern	11.68 m (38 ft 3 in) high; 10 m (32 ft 9 in) wide; 9.3 m (30 ft 6 in) deep; 1,086.24 m³ (38,360.2 ft³) volume	Jhon Freddy Daza, Eyder Burbano and Rene Muñoz (all Colombia)	11 January 2009
★ Ten Commandments tablet	65.04 m² (700.08 ft²)	Grace Galindez-Gupana (Philippines)	11 April 2009
★ Trousers	12.19 m (40 ft) long; 7.92 m (26 ft) waist	Rishi S. Thobhani from R.S.T. International Limited (UK)	23 May 2009

★LARGEST SANDAL
Created in December 2003 by Nelson Jimenez Florez (Colombia), the largest sandal measures 6.6 m (21 ft 7 in) long, 2 m (6 ft 6 in) wide and 3.5 m (11 ft 5 in) high and was designed on behalf of Diseos Ruddy, Bucaramanga, Colombia.

★LARGEST HANDBAG
A handbag created by Picard and Klar in Offenbach, Germany, measured 5 m (16 ft 4 in) tall, 6.5 m (21 ft 3 in) long and 2.5 m (8 ft 2 in) deep in June 2001.

★LARGEST PACKAGED PRODUCT DISPLAY
A display of promotional Kleenex tissue boxes measuring 289.64 m³ (10,228.54 ft³) was constructed by Al-Mansouriya Consumers Trading Co. and Olayan Kimberly-Clark (both Kuwait) at The Sultan Center, Kuwait, on 7 March 2010.

★LONGEST WOODEN BENCH
A 613.13-m-long (2,011-ft 6-in) bench was built by a group of people from Osieczna (Poland) and unveiled in Szlachta, Poland, on 27 August 2005.

★LARGEST GARDEN SPADE
An 3.61-m-tall (11-ft 10-in) spade with a 59.8-cm-wide (1-ft 11-in) blade was manufactured by Rollins Bulldog Tools Ltd (UK) and presented in Wigan, UK, on 7 December 2009.

★LARGEST BUTTON-DOWN SHIRT
On 25 June 2009, Walbusch (Germany) presented a button-down shirt 65.39 m (214 ft 6 in) long, with a chest of 52.72 m (172 ft 11 in) and sleeves of 23.98 m x 15.64 m (78 ft 8 in x 51 ft 3 in). The gargantuan garment was measured at the LTU Arena, in Düsseldorf, Germany.

MITT
THE LARGEST BASEBALL MITT MEASURES 8 M (26 FT) HIGH, 9.7 M (32 FT) WIDE, 3.6 M (12 FT) DEEP AND WEIGHS 9,070 KG (20,000 LB).

★LARGEST GARDEN GNOME
A giant garden gnome measuring 5.41 m (17 ft 8 in) tall was made by the company PHU MALPOL (Poland) and presented in Nowa Sol, Poland, on 2 June 2009. It was built from fibreglass-covered polystyrene.

MATS
USING 70,000 BEERMATS, SVEN GOEBEL (GERMANY) BUILT A STRUCTURE MEASURING 3 M (9 FT 10 IN) TALL AND 5 M (16 FT 4 IN) WIDE IN GERMANY ON 16 AUGUST 2004.

COLUMBUS, OH, USA
39°59'N 82°59'W

Working on the basis that a joke must have a beginning, a middle and an end, the **longest joke-telling marathon** was achieved by Mike Hessman of Columbus, Ohio, USA, who told 12,682 jokes in 24 hours on 16–17 November 1992.

ENGINEERING AND TECHNOLOGY
ALTERNATIVE ENERGIES

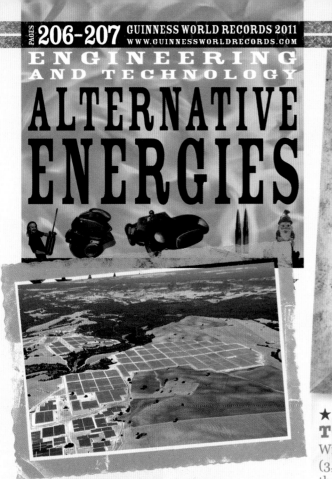

★LARGEST TOKAMAK

With a radius of 2.96 m (9 ft 8.5 in) and a plasma volume of 100 m³ (3,500 ft³), the Joint European Torus in Culham, Oxfordshire, UK, is the largest operating tokamak in the world. Tokamaks use a magnetic field to confine plasma and are used for experiments in nuclear fusion.

★LARGEST PHOTOVOLTAIC POWER STATION

The Olmedilla Photovoltaic Park in Olmedilla, Spain, uses around 162,000 solar panels to generate a maximum of 60 megawatts on a sunny day. Completed in September 2008, it can provide enough electricity to power around 40,000 homes.

★ **NEW RECORD**
UPDATED RECORD

★OLDEST ALTERNATIVE FUEL

In medieval Europe, c. 1500, the overuse of wood for burning led to general shortages and deforestation. Around this time, Europeans began to burn coal instead of wood, the first time in history that an alternative fuel was adopted because of shortages of conventional fuel.

★LARGEST HYDROELECTRIC WAVE-POWER DEVICE

In November 2009, Aquamarine Power (UK) launched Oyster, a 194-tonne (213-ton) device bolted to the sea floor off the Orkney Islands, UK. It consists of a simple mechanical hinged flap that, at 10 m (33 ft) below the sea's surface, oscillates with passing waves and drives hydraulic pistons that power a turbine. This demonstration model is designed to supply around 315 kilowatts of power.

Hydro power remains the **largest contributor to renewable energy**, reaching a capacity of 770 gigawatts in 2007.

★HIGHEST ALTITUDE WIND GENERATOR

In December 2007, a wind generator designed to supply power to a gold mine became operational in the Veladero mine in San Juan, in the Andes mountain range, Argentina. Built by DeWind (Germany) and owned by Barrick (Canada), the hub of the generator is 4,110 m (13,484 ft) above sea level.

On 11 March 2009, strong winds across Spain allowed the country's wind power infrastructure to generate some 11,180 megawatts, 40% of all of its national electricity requirements – the **★highest percentage of power generated by wind**.

★LARGEST SOLAR-POWERED BUILDING

In December 2009, China unveiled an office building in Dezhou, Shangdong province, that meets almost all of its energy needs with its solar-panelled roof. The building covers 75,000 m² (807,000 ft²) and contains research facilities, display areas and a hotel.

Altamont Pas, California, USA, is the **largest wind farm**, with a record 7,300 turbines.

TRIVIA

★ MOST ELECTRICITY PRODUCED FROM A KITE

In 2008, scientists at Delft University of Technology, the Netherlands, successfully tested a kite-powered electricity-generating system known as Laddermill. The concept involves a kite being raised upwards by the wind, with the strings of the kite attached to a generator on the ground. The test involved a single kite with an area of 10 m² (107 ft²) that was able to generate 10 kw of electricity while in flight – enough to power approximately 10 homes. The researchers believe that in time they could generate 100 megawatts of electricity

★ FIRST CLEAN COAL POWER STATION

In September 2008, a new prototype power plant went online at The Schwarze Pumpe power station, Spremberg, Germany. It is the first in the world to use the CCS technique – carbon capture and storage, which means it captures the CO_2 emissions produced from burning coal, preventing them from entering the atmosphere.

In this prototype power station, the two liquids used are salt water from the sea and fresh water from run-off into the sea. The station's initial capacity is around 4 kilowatts, enough to heat a large kettle, but scientists hope that this can be increased to 25 megawatts by 2015.

★ FASTEST CAR POWERED BY BIOGAS

Jürgen Hohenester (Germany) hit 364.6 km/h (226.55 mph) in a biogas-powered car at the ATP testing facilities in Papenburg, Germany, on 3 April 2009. The technology was developed by TÜV Rheinland's Competence Centre for Alternative Fuels (Germany).

this way, enough for up to 100,000 homes.

★ LARGEST SOURCE OF HELIUM 3

Helium 3 is an isotope of helium that is a strong candidate as fuel for nuclear fusion. It is produced by the Sun and streams off into space as part of the solar wind. Helium 3 exists only as a trace on Earth but, on the Moon, with its lack of atmosphere and magnetic field, the solar Helium 3 atoms directly strike and embed themselves into the lunar soil. The isotope was discovered on the Moon by Apollo astronauts and scientists estimate there could be 1 million tonnes of it spread across the lunar surface – enough to power the whole world's energy needs for thousands of years.

★ FIRST OSMOTIC POWER STATION

In November 2009, a prototype osmotic power station went online on the banks of the Oslo fjord in Norway. It generates power using osmosis, which occurs naturally when two solutions of different concentrations meet each other at a semi-permeable membrane. The pressure difference generated as one liquid passes through the membrane can be converted to electricity.

★ LARGEST OFFSHORE WIND FARM

The Horns Rev 2 offshore wind farm was officially inaugurated on 17 September 2009. Located in a shallow region of the North Sea, off the coast of Denmark, it comprises 91 turbines, each with a maximum capacity of 2.3 megawatts, giving a total of 209 megawatts at peak production.

POWER
THE USA IS THE GREATEST PRODUCER OF WIND POWER, WITH ABOUT 2% OF ITS ELECTRICITY PRODUCED IN THIS WAY. IT IS HOPED THAT THIS FIGURE WILL RISE TO 20% BY 2030.

WIND
THE WORLD'S FIRST WIND FARM WAS BUILT IN 1980, AND LOCATED ON CROTCHED MOUNTAIN, NEW HAMPSHIRE, USA. ITS 20 TURBINES COULD PRODUCE 30 KILOWATTS EACH.

GREENVILLE, SC, USA
The **largest group of carol singers** consisted of 7,514 participants and took place at the Bob Jones University, South Carolina, USA, on 3 December 2004.

34°50'N
82°23'W

ENGINEERING AND TECHNOLOGY
DEFENCE TECHNOLOGY

★ LARGEST AIRCRAFT "GRAVEYARD"

The 309th Aerospace Maintenance and Regeneration Group (aka "The Boneyard", above) is a US Air Force storage facility, where old planes are salvaged for parts or made ready for service again. Located on the Davis-Monthan Air Force Base in Tucson, Arizona, USA, the 10.3-km² (4-mile²) site accommodates around 4,000 aircraft.

★ NEW RECORD ★ UPDATED RECORD

★ LONGEST CONFIRMED SNIPER KILL

Confirmed by GPS, Craig Harrison (UK) of the UK's Household Cavalry killed two Taliban insurgents from a distance of 2,474 m/2.47 km (8,120 ft, or 1.54 miles) in November 2009. It took the 8.59 mm rounds almost three seconds to hit their targets, which were 914 m (3,000 ft) beyond the L115A3 sniper rifle's recommended range. A third shot took out the insurgent's machine gun.

RECORD-BREAKING C-5M SUPER GALAXY

The largest aircraft in the US Air Force, the Lockheed Martin C-5M Super Galaxy, set 41 aviation records on 13 September 2009 in a flight from Dover Air Force Base, Delaware, USA. Of these, 33 were new records and eight were updates of existing records. The principle flight record set was a world altitude record of 12,554 m (41,188 ft) obtained in 23 min 59 sec while carrying a 80,108 kg (176,610 lb) payload.

★ FIRST USE OF PLAYSTATIONS AS MILITARY TRAINING EQUIPMENT

The British Royal Navy is the first service organization to use Sony PlayStations for military use. Marine engineering technicians have been provided with the PlayStations to enable them to use study packages produced by the Maritime Warfare School at HMS Collingwood, Fareham, UK. So far, the school has bought 230 consoles, in recognition of the arrival of a generation that no longer naturally studies from books.

★ DEADLIEST UAV

The Predator C Avenger Unmanned Aerial Vehicle is capable of 740 km/h (460 mph) at 18,288 m (60,000 ft) for up to 20 hours. The ability to carry 1,360 kg (3,000 lb) of weapons and its stealthy design – there are no sharp angles between surfaces in order to reduce its radar signature – make it the world's deadliest UAV to date. Its first flight was on 4 April 2009.

★ MOST ADVANCED ROBOTIC SNAKE FOR MILITARY OPERATIONS

The Israeli Defence Ministry has developed a 1.8-m (6-ft) robotic snake that can be fitted with video and audio equipment, operated from a laptop. It is used to advance on the ground into hostile environments to collect information. It also has applications for locating survivors in disaster areas or after terrorist attacks.

★ SMALLEST ROBOTIC MINESWEEPER

Engineers at the Massachusetts Institute of Technology (MIT) in Massachusetts, USA, have designed small robots, smaller than a cigarette lighter, based on the Atlantic razor clam (*Ensis directus*). The clam is one of nature's best diggers, able to burrow about 1 cm (0.3 in) per second. Used in conjunction with seabed-penetrating sonar to locate sea mines, the robotic clam can be deposited next to the mine in order to detonate it.

DID YOU KNOW?

THE L115A3 LONG RANGE RIFLE (BELOW) IS DESIGNED TO ACHIEVE A FIRST-ROUND HIT AT 600 M (1,968 FT) AND HARASSING FIRE OUT TO 1,100 M (3,608 FT).

The rifle's heavy 8.59 mm bullets are less likely to be deflected in flight.

TRIVIA

★ SMALLEST FLIGHT-DECK PRINTER

The world's smallest flight-deck printer is the ToughWriter 5, used to print in-flight text and graphics. It is 185 mm (7.3 in) deep and weighs less than 4 kg (9 lb).

EXTRA! FOR MORE MILITARY HARDWARE RECORDS, TURN BACK TO PP.128-129.

EXTRA! FOR EPIC-SCALE ENGINEERING RECORDS, TURN BACK TO pp.198-199.

★MOST NUCLEAR WEAPONS

As of May 2010, Russia had 4,650 operational warheads out of a stockpile of 12,000, according to the Federation of American Scientists. Pictured above is a Topol-M intercontinental ballistic missile, displayed in Moscow's Victory Day Parade in May 2009.

★OLDEST SERVING MILITARY WARSHIP

Built in the Netherlands, the VMF *Kommuna* is a 2,267-tonne (2,500-ton) catamaran salvage vessel that entered service in 1915 and is still serving in the Russian Navy today, employed to recover small submarines and submersibles. It is considered more cost effective to keep the ship operational than to fund and build a replacement.

★LARGEST AIRSHIP

Built by Zeppelin Luftschifftechnik GmbH Germany and owned by the US company Airship Ventures Inc., *Eureka* has a length of 75 m (246 ft). Airships are used nowadays for surveillance, research, sightseeing and advertising. Plans are underway to make a geostationary airship platform for military intelligence and reconnaissance applications.

★LONGEST FLIGHT BY SOLAR-POWERED SPYPLANE

Between 28 and 31 July 2008, *Zephyr*, a solar-powered, high-altitude, long-endurance (HALE) unmanned aerial system (UAS), achieved a record flight of 82 hr 37 min. *Zephyr* is launched by hand, and flies on solar power generated by amorphous silicon arrays that cover the 22.8-m (75-ft) wings. By night, it is powered by a lithium-sulphur battery that is charged during the day. Made of carbon fibre weighing less than 30 kg (100 lb), it is designed to carry military surveillance payloads and operate at altitudes of 18,288 m (60,000 ft) at speeds of up to 112 km/h (70 mph).

★FIRST USE OF QUAD BIKES IN COMBAT

A total of 200 upgraded quad bikes have been ordered for UK forces in Afghanistan. They will be used to deliver vital combat supplies and are fitted with dual stretchers to evacuate two casualties at a time, thereby speeding up emergency treatment.

★NEWEST LITTORAL COMBAT SHIP

The US Navy commissioned the USS *Independence* littoral ("close-to-shore") combat ship, LCS-2, into service on 16 January 2010. Although it is the second vessel in the LCS class, it is the first of a new type of ship based on a three-hulled design and built of aluminium. Manufactured by General Dynamics and Austal (USA), it can carry a crew of 75 and accommodate two MH-60S Seahawk helicopters. It is 115.5 m (379 ft) long and has a top speed of around 44 knots (81.4 km/h; 50.6 mph).

★MOST EXPENSIVE SINGLE WEAPON SYSTEM

The USS *Ronald Reagan*, the CVN 76 class, nuclear-powered aircraft carrier is, with its crew, armament, 85 aircraft and other defence and communication systems, the most costly operational weapon system in the world. Its total cost was around $4.5 billion (£3.1 billion).

★SUBMARINE WITH BIGGEST "EARS"

HMS *Astute* is a nuclear-powered attack submarine currently undergoing sea trials for the UK's Royal Navy. It has the biggest "ears" of any sonar system in service today. The Type 2076 sonar is reported to be able to detect ships leaving New York harbour while lying in the English Channel, 5,556 km (3,452 miles) away.

DOWN HMS *ASTUTE* CAN PURIFY WATER AND AIR, AND IS THEREFORE ABLE TO CIRCUMNAVIGATE THE GLOBE WITHOUT RESURFACING.

DOWN THE SUBMARINE'S NUCLEAR REACTOR WILL NOT NEED TO BE REFUELLED DURING ITS EXPECTED 25-YEAR SERVICE.

ENGINEERING AND TECHNOLOGY
MEGA MOTORS

★ ★ ★ ★ ★ ★ ★ ★ ★ ★ ★ ★

SMALLEST AND LOWEST CARS

The ★smallest car is 104.14 cm (41 in) high and 66.04 cm (26 in) wide and was measured in Wingrave, UK, on 8 May 2009.

The ★lowest car measures 48.26 cm (19 in) from the ground. Both cars were created by Perry Watkins (UK).

★FASTEST 0–60MPH ACCELERATION BY A FOUR-SEATER PRODUCTION CAR

A Nissan GT-R achieved an acceleration of 0–60 mph (0–100 km) in 3.5 seconds while completing a lap of the Nürburgring circuit in Nürburg, Germany, on 17 April 2008.

★HIGHEST VEHICLE MILEAGE

A 1966 Volvo P-1800S owned by Irvin Gordon of East Patchogue, New York, USA, had covered in excess of 4,379,033.78 km (2,721,000 miles) by August 2009. The car is still driven on a daily basis and

★HIGHEST AVERAGE SPEED IN A STEAM CAR

On 26 August 2009, Don Wales (UK) achieved a Fédération Internationale de l'Automobile (FIA) approved average speed of 225.05 km/h (139.84 mph) over two consecutive one-kilometre runs in the British Steam Car's *Inspiration Streamliner* at Edwards Air Force Base in California, USA.

covers over 160,000 km (100,000 miles) per year, thanks in part to being driven to car shows and events in Europe and the USA.

★MOST EXPENSIVE CAR

The greatest confirmed price paid for a car is $17,275,000 (£12,000,000) for a red vintage 1963 Ferrari 250 GT, of which only 36 were ever made. It was sold to DJ and TV presenter Chris Evans (UK) on 14 May 2010.

★MOST EXPENSIVE "VETERAN" CAR

The highest amount paid for a London to Brighton Run veteran (i.e., pre-1905) car is £3,521,500 ($7,242,916) for the oldest surviving Rolls-Royce, numbered 20154. The two-seater, 10-hp car, manufactured by the Rolls-Royce factory in Manchester, UK, in 1904, was sold to an anonymous British collector in London, UK, on 3 December 2007.

FASTEST PRODUCTION MOTORCYCLE

The Suzuki GSX1300R Hayabusa is reported to reach speeds of 312 km/h (194 mph), making it the fastest production bike in the world. Named after a Japanese peregrine falcon, the 215-kg (474-lb) Hayabusa is powered by a 1,298 cc (72.2 cu in) engine with four valves per cylinder.

HORSEPOWER: A measurement of power, originally to compare the output of steam engines against the power of draft (heavy labour) horses.

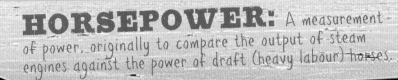

DID YOU KNOW?

IN JULY 2009, DIVERS RECOVERED A 1925 BUGATTI THAT HAD BEEN SITTING ON THE BOTTOM OF LAKE MAGGIORE, ITALY, FOR 73 YEARS. IT COULD FETCH MORE THAN $129,500 (£80,000) AT AUCTION.

The Bugatti was dumped in the water in 1936 by a frustrated Swiss official. The owner had abandoned it still owing import tax.

TRIVIA

★ MOST EXPENSIVE POST-WAR CAR

The highest amount of money paid for a post-war car is £8,000,000 ($12,390,000) for a two-seat 1957 Ferrari 250 Testa Rossa. This rare racing car is one of only 22 built and was sold at Ferrari's factory and test circuit at Maranelo, Italy, on 17 May 2009.

★ FASTEST ELECTRIC CAR

The highest average speed achieved for an electric vehicle is 487.672 km/h (303.025 mph) over a two-way flying kilometre by *Buckeye Bullet 2*, designed and built by engineering students at The Ohio State University at the university's Center for Automotive Research (CAR) and driven by Roger Schroer (USA) at the Bonneville Salt Flats, Utah, USA, on 25 September 2009. The hydrogen fuel cell streamliner is nicknamed "La Jamais Contente" in tribute to the first vehicle to go faster than 100 km/h (60 mph) in 1899.

FASTEST CARAVAN TOW BY A PRODUCTION CAR

A Mercedes Benz S600 driven by Eugene Herbert (South Africa) reached a speed of 223.881 km/h (139.113 mph) towing a standard caravan at Hoedspruit Air Force Base, adjacent to the Kruger National Park, South Africa, on 24 October 2003.

FASTEST PRODUCTION CAR

The Ultimate Aero TT Super Car, made by Shelby Supercars (USA), achieved two-way timed speeds in excess of 412 km/h (256.14 mph) on Highway 221, Washington, USA, on 13 September 2007. It can go from 0 to 60 mph in just 2.78 seconds.

LIGHTEST CAR

Louis Borsi (UK) has built and driven a 9.5-kg (21-lb) car with a 2.5 cc engine. It is capable of 25 km/h (15 mph) at top speed.

★ FASTEST AMPHIBIOUS CAR

With an engine based on the LS Corvette power train, the WaterCar Python is the fastest amphibious vehicle in the world. It has a top speed of 96 km (60 mph; 52 knots) on water and can perform a 0–60 mph acceleration in 4.5 seconds on land. The Python is hand-built to order; prices start from $200,000 (£123,000).

FUEL BB2 IS THE FIRST HYDROGEN FUEL CELL STREAMLINER. IT IS DRIVEN BY A 700-HP ELECTRIC MOTOR FUELLED BY ONBOARD HYDROGEN AND OXYGEN.

COOL A RADIATOR WOULD CAUSE TOO MUCH DRAG TRAVELLING AT OVER 480 KM (300 MPH), SO AN ICE BATH WAS USED TO KEEP THE FUEL CELLS COOL.

★ NEW RECORD
UPDATED RECORD

SAVANNAH, GA, USA

The **highest speed recorded on an aquabike** (PWC) is 122.79 km/h (76.172 mph) over a measured kilometre by Forrest Smith (USA) on a modified Yamaha GP1200R at Savannah, Georgia, USA, on 5 July 2002.

32°04'N 81°05'W

ENGINEERING AND TECHNOLOGY

TOP TECH

ACTUAL SIZE

EXTRA! EXPERIENCE THE CUTTING-EDGE OF SCIENCE ON PP. 214-215.

★THINNEST x10 ZOOM DIGITAL CAMERA

Casio's 12.1-megapixel Exilim EX-H10 digital camera is, at 24.3 mm (just under 1 in) thick, the slimmest digital camera with a x10 optical telephoto zoom. At just 164 g (5.78 oz), it is also among the lightest. It can take 100 pictures a day for 10 days without needing to be charged.

★ NEW RECORD
★ UPDATED RECORD

★MOST SECURE MOUSE

The Fujitsu PalmSecure mouse may look like a regular three-button optical mouse, but it features a CIA-level security device to prevent unauthorized use: a palm-vein biometric sensor. As you place your hand over the mouse, the sensor reads the unique pattern of veins on your palm and, if there is a match, grants you access to the cursor. It retails for Y20,500 ($220; £130).

★LIGHTEST TOUCHSCREEN MOBILE PHONE

The modu-t (right), which weighs a mere 55.1 g (1.94 oz), is manufactured by modu Ltd (Israel) and was launched at the Mobile World Congress in Barcelona, Spain, on 15 February 2010. The phone is 46.5 x 75 x 11 mm (1.83 x 2.95 x 0.43 in) in size.

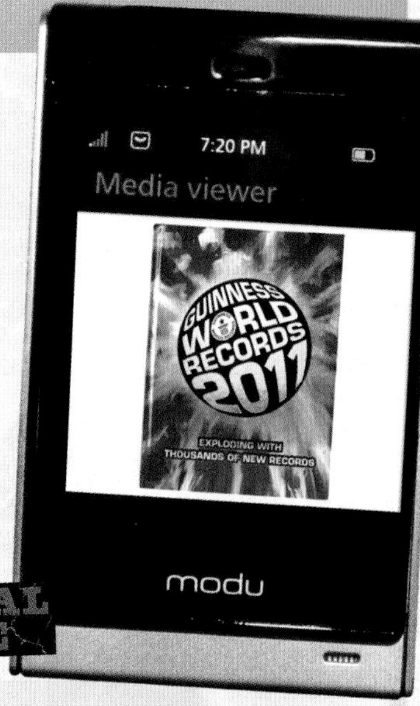

Media viewer
7:20 PM
GUINNESS WORLD RECORDS 2011 EXPLODING WITH THOUSANDS OF NEW RECORDS
modu

ACTUAL SIZE

★MOST EXPENSIVE TELEVISION

The PrestigeHD Supreme Rose TV, made from 28 kg (61 lb) of 18-carat rose gold inset with 72 brilliant 1-carat flawless diamonds, costs £1.5 million ($2,250,000).

BLING! THE SUPREME ROSE TV WAS DESIGNED BY STUART HUGHES (UK) AND HAS ALLIGATOR SKIN HAND-SEWN INTO THE INNER SCREEN LAYER.

★THINNEST LCD TV

LG Korea has created a fully hi-def (1,920 x 1,080 pixel) liquid-crystal display panel that is a mere 2.6 mm (0.10 in) thick – thinner than a UK £1 coin. The 106-cm (42-in) screen uses an ultraslim LED backlighting system, and the entire unit weighs just 4.2 kg (9 lb 4 oz).

THIN IN MAY 2009, LG KOREA PRODUCED A 5.9-MM (0.2-IN) LCD PANEL – THEN THE WORLD'S THINNEST. JUST SEVEN MONTHS LATER, THIS NEW PANEL SMASHED THEIR OWN RECORD.

★ FIRST 3D CAMCORDER

On 7 January 2010, Panasonic unveiled the world's first professional-use 3D camcorder, equipped with double lenses that can record high-definition movies on an SD memory card. The twin-lens camera was demonstrated during a press preview at the company's plant in Amagasaki city in Hyogo prefecture, western Japan. The retail price? $21,000 (£13,800).

FIRST USB PROSTHETIC

In May 2008, Finnish computer programmer Jerry Jalava lost part of a finger in a motorcycle accident. Instead of a regular fingertip prosthetic, Jalava had a 2-GB USB memory stick made, allowing him to carry data around with him constantly.

★ SMALLEST MP3 PLAYER

No bigger than a couple of sugar cubes, the Micro Sport MP3 player (right) boasts a 4-GB memory, full stereo sound through its two ear-buds and a rechargeable battery.

ACTUAL SIZE

★ MOST POWERFUL VACUUM CLEANER

The handheld Dyson DC31 vacuum cleaner is powered by a digital motor that spins at 104,000 rpm. That's five times faster than the engine of a Formula One racing car, and ten times faster than a standard commercial airliner!

★ FASTEST SMS

Sonja Kristiansen (Norway) wrote a 160-character text message in 37.28 seconds at Oslo City Shopping Centre in Oslo, Norway, on 14 November 2009.

★ BEST-SELLING iPAD APP

At the time of going to press (April 2010), Apple had just launched their much-anticipated iPad. This tablet computer sold at least 300,000 units on its first day (although some early estimates place this figure as high as 700,000), with 1 million apps downloaded.

To date, the biggest-selling paid-for app is Pages, which is a word-processing program.

The most downloaded free app for the iPad as of April 2010 is iBooks – an ebook reader and shopfront with which the user can browse for (and download) tens of thousands of books, many of them free. *Be sure to look out for* **Guinness World Records: At Your Fingertips**, *a free iPad lite app that showcases record-breaking achievements.*

★ MOST COMPACT ELECTRIC BIKE

Weighing in at 10 kg (22 lb), and folding down to just 15 x 60 x 60 cm (6 x 23.5 x 23.5 in) – smaller than most folding bicycles – the YikeBike is the most compact folding electric bicycle on the market. The "mini-farthing" design is based on the "penny farthing" bicycle of c.1870.

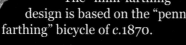

The **first brain-cell transplant** was performed at the University of Pittsburgh Medical Center on 23 June 1998. The operation aimed to reverse the stroke damage suffered by 62-year-old Alma Cerasini (USA), who had experienced some speech loss and paralysis.

ENGINEERING AND TECHNOLOGY
CUTTING-EDGE SCIENCE

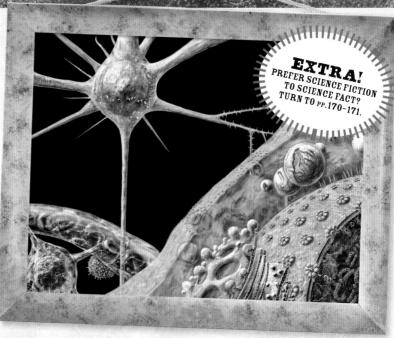

EXTRA!
PREFER SCIENCE FICTION TO SCIENCE FACT? TURN TO PP.170-171.

MOST WATER-REPELLENT MAN-MADE MATERIAL

In February 2010, scientists at the University of Florida, USA, announced that they had created an almost perfect water-repellent, or hydrophobic, surface. They used sheets of polypropylene and a mould to create tiny irregular "hairs" on the surface of the sheets, which resemble the microscopic structure of hairs on some water-walking arthropods.

★ **NEW RECORD**
★ **UPDATED RECORD**

★ HIGHEST LASER ENERGY SHONE ON TO A SINGLE TARGET

In June 2009, scientists at the National Ignition Facility at Lawrence Livermore National Laboratory in California, USA, began operating the array of 192 powerful lasers designed to research nuclear fusion. The lasers are focused on a fingernail-sized container known as a hohlraum that will eventually contain a pellet of hydrogen fuel for fusion experiments. On 27 January 2010, researchers fired the laser array for a few billionths of a second and delivered one megajoule of energy on to the target. This is equivalent to the explosion caused by 0.2 kg (0.44 lb) of TNT.

★ FIRST EVIDENCE OF EVOLUTION WITHOUT DNA

In January 2010, scientists at the Scripps Research Institute, California, USA, reported that they had witnessed evidence of evolution occurring in the lifeless, DNA-less proteins known as prions (artwork shown above). They exhibited signs of adapting to new evironments and following the rules of natural selection. Prions are associated with 20 different diseases of the brain in humans and animals.

★ DEEPEST UNDERGROUND LAB

SNOLAB, 2 km (1.2 miles) below ground in Sudbury, Ontario, Canada, is best known for housing the Sudbury Neutrino Observatory. The observatory was created to study neutrinos – weakly interacting particles – using the rock above it to filter out cosmic radiation. This ensured that only neutrinos, which easily penetrate matter, were observed.

★ LARGEST KNOWN PRIME NUMBER

The latest giant number discovered by the Great Internet Mersenne Prime Search project was announced on 23 August 2008. It is a Mersenne prime, which means it can be written as 2^n-1, where "n" is a power; $2^{43112609}-1$ contains some 12,978,189 digits. As a prime number, it can only be divided by itself and 1.

★ FASTEST COMPUTER

The Jaguar supercomputer at the Oak Ridge National Laboratory in Oak Ridge, Tennessee, USA, became the world's fastest in November 2009 following an upgrade. Built by Cray Inc. (USA), it is capable of 1.759 petaflops (quadrillion floating point operations per second).

DID YOU KNOW?
THE JAGUAR SUPERCOMPUTER COULD BE USED TO INVESTIGATE NEW ENERGY SOURCES OR DISSECT THE DYNAMICS OF CLIMATE CHANGE.

Aircraft manufacturer Boeing has used the Jaguar supercomputer to test airplane designs.

TRIVIA

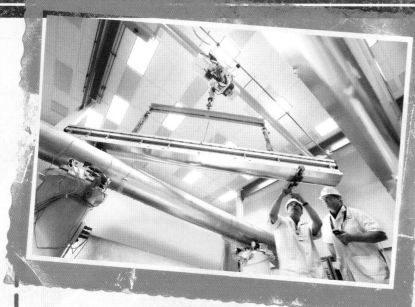

★SHORTEST-WAVELENGTH LASER

The Linac Coherent Light Source (LCLS) at the SLAC National Accelerator Laboratory, Stanford, California, USA, is an X-ray laser capable of producing X-ray laser radiation at a wavelength of just 0.15 nanometres. Visible light that the human eye can see ranges from around 390 to 750 nanometres.

★HIGHEST ENERGY OPERATIONAL ACCELERATOR

On 19 March 2010, scientists at the Large Hadron Collider in Geneva, Switzerland, announced that they had used the particle accelerator to produce two beams of protons, each with energies of 3.5 tera electron volts. (One electron volt equals the kinetic energy gained by an electron when it is accelerated by one volt. "Tera" means "trillion".)

★SLOWEST LIGHT

In January 2010, a team of US scientists reported that they had "frozen" light to a standstill for 1.5 seconds using a form of supercold matter known as a Bose–Einstein condensate.

★HIGHEST MAN-MADE TEMPERATURE

In February 2010, scientists at Brookhaven National Laboratory's Relativistic Heavy Ion Collider on Long Island, New York, USA, announced that they had smashed together gold ions at nearly the speed of light, briefly forming an exotic state of matter known as a quark-gluon plasma. This substance is believed to have filled the universe just a few microseconds after the Big Bang. During the experiment the plasma reached temperatures of around 4 trillion°C, some 250,000 times hotter than the centre of the Sun.

LOWEST MAN-MADE TEMPERATURE

A team of scientists at the Massachusetts Institute of Technology (MIT), Cambridge, Massachusetts, USA, led by Professor Aaron E Leanhardt, managed to produce a temperature of 450 picokelvin above absolute zero by cooling down a Bose–Einstein condensate. Details of their research first appeared in *Science* magazine on 12 September 2003.

★FIRST HOMOGENEOUS SELF-RIGHTING SHAPE

The Gömböc is a mathematical shape first theorized in 1996 and proven in 2006 by Hungarian scientists Péter Várkonyi and Gábor Domokos. It is a three-dimensional shape that is mono-monostatic, convex and homogeneous, i.e. with equal density throughout. It is characterized by its properties of balance in that it has two equilibria, one stable and one unstable.

★FIRST VIRUS-POWERED BATTERY

In April 2009, scientists at MIT in Massachusetts, USA, announced that they had used genetically engineered viruses to build the positive and negative ends of a lithium ion battery. In tests, the new battery technology can be charged up more than 100 times before deteriorating.

★HEAVIEST ELEMENT

Copernicium, with an atomic number of 112, is the heaviest element officially recognized to date. It was first created on 9 February 1996 at the Gesellschaft für Schwerionenforschung (GSI, right) in Darmstadt, Germany, and officially named copernicium on 19 February 2010.

LONG COPERNICIUM WAS CREATED USING GSI'S LINEAR ACCELERATOR, PICTURED RIGHT. THIS DEVICE HAS A TOTAL LENGTH OF 120 M (393 FT 8 IN).

FAST THIS TYPE OF PARTICLE ACCELERATOR GREATLY INCREASES THE VELOCITY OF CHARGED SUBATOMIC PARTICLES.

PANAMA CITY, PANAMA

The **longest ever journey on an aquabike** is 17,266.69 km (10,729 miles), by Adriaan Marais and Marinus du Plessis (both South Africa), who arrived in Panama City, Panama, after 95 days of navigation, on 19 September 2006.

8°59'N 79°31'W

ENGINEERING AND TECHNOLOGY
INTERNET

★ ★ ★ ★ ★ ★ ★ ★ ★ ★ ★ ★ ★ ★ ★

★ OLDEST .COM

Symbolics.com was registered by computer manufacturer Symbolics Inc. (USA) on 15 March 1985, making it the world's oldest .com url. Symbolics.com is still registered and active today, and was bought by XF.com in 2009.

★ FIRST TWEET

Twitter was invented by Jack Dorsey (USA) in 2006. Users can post messages ("tweets") of up to 140 characters, which are sent to their subscribers. The first tweet was posted by Dorsey at 9:50 p.m. PST on 21 March 2006, and read "just setting up my twittr".

★ FIRST TWEET FROM SPACE

On 21 October 2009, US astronauts Nicola Stott and Jeff Williams took part in a live "tweetup" from the International Space Station with around 35 members of the public at NASA Headquarters, Washington, DC, USA.

★ LARGEST BOTNET

In December 2009, an operation by Spanish police and the FBI closed down a network of more than 13 million PCs that had been infected with viruses. This so-called "Mariposa botnet" was designed to steal credit card data, passwords and account information. It had infected machines in 190 countries, spreading via USB sticks, spammed links and a vulnerability in Internet Explorer.

★ FASTEST-SELLING TOP-LEVEL DOMAIN

The .me domain is the Internet country code for Montenegro, located in south-eastern Europe, which first became an independent state in June 2006. Registration for .me domains was made available on 16 July 2008. By January 2010, more than 320,000 .me domains had been sold, making it the fastest-selling top-level domain in the history of the Internet. The suffix is popular due to its attractiveness for social networking websites.

DID YOU KNOW?

WIKIPEDIA IS THE LARGEST ONLINE ENCYCLOPEDIA. IT CONTAINED 19,878,548 PAGES IN NUMEROUS LANGUAGES AS OF 31 MARCH 2010, AND HAS UNDERGONE 377,162,709 PAGE EDITS SINCE ITS LAUNCH ON 15 JANUARY 2000.

★ GREATEST MEMES

According to MSNBC, the top internet meme (see left) of 2009 was Kanye West's antics during the MTV Video Music Awards in New York City, USA, on 13 September, when he grabbed the mic from award-winner Taylor Swift, announcing Beyoncé should have won. West's outburst led to the "Ima let you finish" meme. In second place was the "Crasher Squirrel", in which Melissa Brandts and her husband Jackson were taking a photo of themselves using a timer. During the shot, a squirrel popped up in front of the camera.

MEME
AN IDEA THAT POSSESSES SOME QUALITY THAT MAKES PEOPLE WANT TO SHARE IT WITH EACH OTHER – SUCH AS A JOKE, OR A YOUTUBE VIDEO. ON THE INTERNET, MEMES ARE SAID TO GROW AND BE TRANSMITTED "VIRALLY".

WIKIPEDIA
The Free Encyclopedia

TORONTO, ON, CANADA
The **tallest free-standing tower** (as opposed to a guyed mast) in the world is the $63-million (£28-million) CN Tower in Toronto, Canada, which rises to 553.34 m (1,815 ft 5 in). Excavation began on 12 February 1973 and the tower topped out on 2 April 1975.

TOP 10 MOST VIEWED (2009)

	ARTIST, SONG TITLE/ FILM	FORMAT	VIEWS
1	Soulja Boy Tellem: "Crank Dat (Soulja Boy)"	Music Video	722,438,268
2	*Twilight Saga: New Moon* (preview)	Film	639,966,996
3	Beyoncé: "Single Ladies (Put a Ring on it)"	Music Video	522,039,429
4	Michael Jackson: "Thriller"	Music Video	443,535,722
5	"The Gummy Bear Song"	Music Video	394,327,606
6	Lady Gaga: "Poker Face"	Music Video	374,606,128
7	Lady Gaga: "Bad Romance"	Music Video	360,020,327
8	Timbaland: "Apologize" (feat. OneRepublic)	Music Video	355,404,824
9	Susan Boyle: *Britain's Got Talent*	TV	347,670,927
10	*Twilight* (preview)	Film	343,969,063

Source: Visible Measures Internet Research Company

★MOST SONGS DOWNLOADED FROM ONE COMPANY

On 25 February 2010, the 10 billionth song was downloaded from iTunes, Apple's online music store: "Guess Things Happen That Way", a 1958 hit by Johnny Cash. To mark the event, the lucky downloader, Louie Sulcer (USA), received a $10,000 iTunes gift card from Apple.

★LARGEST INTERNET EXCHANGE

Of the exchanges that make their data public, the largest by traffic is the Deutscher Commercial Internet Exchange in Frankfurt, Germany. As of March 2010, it had a maximum throughput of 1,994 gigabits/ sec. (The term "Throughput" refers to the amount of work processed in a given time.)

★FIRST FLASHMOB

"Flashmobs" are sudden gatherings of people in a public place at a set time to engage in a brief and usually pointless activity. The first notable flashmob, organized by Bill Wasik (USA), occurred in May 2003 in New York City, USA, though police had received a tip-off. The second attempt, also by Wasik, was more successful: on 3 June 2003, nearly 100 people gathered at a $10,000 (£5,620) rug at Macy's department store in New York (below).

★MOST INTERNET USERS (COUNTRY)

According to www.internet worldstats.com, China had approximately 360,000,000 Internet users by September 2009, 26.9% of its population.

★MOST VIEWED ONLINE VIDEO AD

As of 19 August 2009, the advertisement for Evian Roller Babies had been watched 25,687,416 times via online video sites.

★LARGEST ONLINE QUIZ

Five hundred employees of DKV Seguros, Spain, took part in an online quiz in Saragoza, Spain, on 9 September 2009.

★LONGEST LAN PARTY

From 11 to 12 April 2009, a non-stop local area network (LAN) party lasting 40 hours was completed by 274 gamers during Cyber Fusion 2009 at the Multimedia University in Cyberjaya, Malaysia.

★LARGEST AUDIENCE FOR AN INTERNET CONCERT

On 25 October 2009, U2's set at the Rose Bowl, Pasadena, USA, was streamed live on YouTube. It was watched over the web by nearly 10 million people.

IN SPACE
DURING THE EUROPEAN LEG OF U2'S 360° TOUR THERE WAS A LIVE VIDEO LINK-UP WITH THE CREW OF THE INTERNATIONAL SPACE STATION!

AWARD
U2 (IRELAND) HAVE WON A RECORD 22 GRAMMYS, THE MOST FOR ANY GROUP. THEY HAVE ALSO WON SEVEN BRIT AWARDS, MORE THAN ANY OTHER GROUP.

★ NEW RECORD
★ UPDATED RECORD

HUNTINGDON, WV, USA   40°3.0'N 78°1.0'W

The record for the **longest interval between the birth of twins** is held by Peggy Lynn (USA), of Huntingdon, West Virginia, USA, who gave birth to a baby girl, Hanna, on 11 November 1995. She did not deliver the other twin, Eric, until 2 February 1996, 84 days later, at the Geisinger Medical Center, Danville, Pennsylvania, USA.

SPORTS

CONTENTS

ROCHESTER, NY, USA

43°09'N
77°41'W

On 16 October 1976, Kathy Wafler (USA) peeled an apple in 11 hr 30 min, resulting in a peel length of 52.51 m (172 ft 4 in) – the **longest unbroken apple peel**, at Long Ridge Mall, Rochester, New York, USA.

GRAND!
THE FOUR TENNIS GRAND SLAM TOURNAMENTS ARE THE AUSTRALIAN OPEN, THE FRENCH OPEN, WIMBLEDON AND THE US OPEN.

SLAM!
SIX PEOPLE HAVE WON ALL FOUR GRAND SLAM TITLES IN THEIR CAREER: FRED PERRY, DON BUDGE, ROD LAVER, ROY EMERSON, ANDRE AGASSI AND ROGER FEDERER.

★ MOST GRAND SLAM TITLES

When Roger Federer (Switzerland, pictured) clinched his fourth Australian Open title by defeating Andy Murray (UK) 6-3 6-4 7-6 (13-11) on 31 January 2010, he recorded his 16th Grand Slam singles title, the **greatest number of Grand Slam singles tennis titles won by a man**. Federer's first Grand Slam win had come at Wimbledon: he triumphed over Mark Philippoussis (Australia) at the London, UK, tournament on 6 July 2003.

As well as six Wimbledon grass court Slam victories, Federer has won four Australian Open titles, five US Open titles and, in 2009, won his first French Open title, beating Robin Söderling (Sweden) in the final.

NASSAU, BAHAMAS
Sir Etienne Dupuch of Nassau, Bahamas, was editor-in-chief of *The Tribune* from 1919 to 1972 and contributing editor until his death on 23 August 1991, a total of 72 years. His is the **longest editorship** on record.

25°03′ N
77°20′ W

SPORTS
ACTION SPORTS

★ NEW RECORD
★ UPDATED RECORD

EXTRA! FOR MORE FABULOUS FEATS AND DARING DEEDS, DON'T FORGET STUNTS ON P.88.

ON A WING AND A PRAYER

With an impressive six titles to his name between 1985 and 1999, Jerzy Makula (Poland) has the ★**most wins of the World Glider Aerobatic Championships**, a competition organized by the Gliding Commission of the Fédération Aéronautique Internationale (FAI).

★FARTHEST DYNO WALL CLIMB

Dynamic ("dyno") moves involve climbers flinging themselves from one handhold to the next. Nicky de Leeuw (Netherlands) achieved a distance of 2.80 m (9 ft 2 in) in Eindhoven, the Netherlands, on 14 June 2009. The ★**farthest distance by a woman in Dyno climbing** is 1.98 m (6 ft 5 in) by Anne-Laure Chevrier (France) on the set of *Lo Show dei Record* in Milan, Italy, on 17 April 2009.

AQUABIKE

• On 11 October 1996, Cory A Wimpheimer (USA) recorded a time of 17.76 seconds to complete an International Jet Sports Boating Association (IJSBA) Pro Runabout 785 slalom course on Lake Havasu, Arizona, USA. This represents the ★**fastest time** in which this course has been completed.
• The ★**most wins of the IJSBA Pro Runabout 1200 World Championships** is five by Chris MacClugage (USA) who claimed titles in 1999, 2001–02, 2004 and 2005.

• Based in Monaco, the Union Internationale Motonautique (UIM) is the governing body for the sports of powerboating and aquabiking. Gimmi Bosio (Italy) holds the record for the ★**most wins of the UIM Aquabike Pro Runabout 1200 World Championship**, with two titles, in 2001–02. The ★**most wins of the UIM Pro Ski World Championship** is also two, with Kevin Laigle (France) claiming the top spot in 2002 and 2004.

PARA-GLIDING

• Nicole Fedele (Italy) paraglided 164.6 km (102.2 miles) from Sorica, Slovenia, to Piombada, Italy, and back on 19 August 2009, to secure the record for the ★**farthest paragliding out-and-return distance (female)**.

• The record for the ★**farthest paragliding out-and-return distance (male)** is held by Aljaz Valic, who flew 259.7 km (161.3 miles), departing from and returning to Soriska Planina, in his Slovenian homeland, on 20 July 2006.
• The team of Toby Colombe and Cefn Hoile (both UK) achieved a distance of 167.3 km (104 miles) in setting the record for the ★**farthest paragliding out-and-return distance by a team** when gliding from Sorica in Slovenia and back on 26 July 2009.
• The ★**farthest flight by a paraglider (male)** was made by Nevil Hulett (South Africa) who paraglided a distance of 502.9 km (312.5 miles) from Copperton, South Africa, on 14 December 2008.

BUNGEE

• The ★**highest bungee dive into water** was recorded by action sports enthusiast Zhang Di (China), who performed a dive into water from a height of 50 m (164 ft) in Quindao city, Shandong province, China, on 15 November 2006.
• The **highest bungee jump from a building** is 199 m (652 ft 10 in) by A J Hackett (New Zealand), who leaped off a platform at 233 m (764 ft 5 in) on the Macau Tower, Macau, China, on 17 December 2006. This meant that Hackett came within 34 m (111 ft 6 in) of the ground at the lowest point of his jump.

AWESOME AQUA-BATICS!

L... Stone (UK, right) and Alessander Lenzi (Brazil) share the honour of the ★**most wins of the Union Internationale Motonautique (UIM) Aquabike Pro Freestyle Class World Championship**, with three wins apiece. Lenzi won the title from 2003 to 2005 and Stone took the top spot from 2006 to 2008.

38°53'N 77°02'W

WASHINGTON, DC, USA

Founded on 24 April 1800, the Library of Congress in Washington, DC, USA, contains over 128 million items, including approximately 29 million books, 2.7 million recordings, 12 million photographs, 4 million maps and 57 million manuscripts. It is the world's **largest library.**

★LONGEST MOUNTAINBOARD RACE

With a course that stretches 11.18 km (6.95 miles) down Palomar Mountain, San Diego County, California, USA, the annual Nate Harrison Grade Race is a true mountainboard endurance test. Four victories over the event's six-year history makes Kris Kidwell (USA) the king of the mountain.

The **farthest distance covered on a jet ski in 24 hours** is 1,641.43 km (1,019.94 miles) by Ivan Otulic (Croatia).

TRIVIA

WAKE-BOARDING

• The ★**longest wakeboarding ramp jump (male)** is a 15-m (49-ft 2-in) attempt by Jérôme Macquart (France), which was filmed as part of *L'Été De Tous Les Records*, in Argelès-Gazost, France, on 14 July 2004.
• In wakeboarding, the term "superman" describes the situation when boarders are completely lifted off the surface of the water, higher than head height, and assume a stretched pose (with the wakeboard attached to their feet). Jérôme Macquart performed an unprecedented five "supermans" in 30 seconds at Biscarrosse, France, on 14 July 2005. This feat represents the ★**most wakeboarding "supermans" in 30 seconds**.
• Aged 63 years 227 days when she competed in the Battle of Bull Run Wakeboard Tournament at Smith Mountain Lake, Virginia, USA, on 25 July 2009, Linda Brown (USA, b. 10 December 1945) is the ★**oldest competitive wakeboarder**.

AERO-BATICS

• Daredevil pilot Joann Osterud (Canada) flew upside down for 4 hr 38 min 10 sec on a flight from Vancouver to Vanderhoof, Canada, on 24 July 1991, to record the **longest inverted flight (aerobatics)**.
• Svetlana Kapanina (Russia) has recorded the ★**most wins of the women's Aerobatics World Championships**, having won the women's overall competition an unprecedented six times, in 1996, 1998, 2001, 2003, 2005 and 2007.
• No single male pilot has dominated the World Championships in quite the way that Svetlana Kapanina has in the women's event. The ★**most wins of the men's Aerobatics World Championships** is two, achieved by two pilots, Petr Jirmus (Czechoslovakia) in 1984 and 1986; and Sergei Rakhmanin (Russia) in 2003 and 2005.

★MOST KITE SURFING CHAMPIONSHIPS (FEMALE)

When it comes to kite surfing, few can compare to Kristin Boese (Germany, above). Between 2005 and 2008, she won nine kite surfing world championship titles!

KITE SURFING

• The ★**longest journey kite surfing (male)** is 178.50 nautical miles (330.58 km; 205.41 miles) by Steen Carstens (Denmark), who travelled from Sprogo, Denmark, to Lysekil, Sweden, on 17 August 2009. The **longest continuous kite surfing journey (female)** was 115.4 nautical miles (213.72 km; 132.80 miles) by Andreya Wharry (UK) between Watergate Bay, UK, and Dungarven, Ireland, on 7 September 2005.
• The **youngest kite surfing world champion (female)** is Gisela Pulido (Spain, b. 14 January 1994) who won her first Kiteboard Pro World Tour (KPWT) world title on 4 November 2004 aged 10 years 294 days.

AIR IAN METCHER (AUSTRALIA) WAS 85 YEARS OLD WHEN HE WON AN AEROBATICS TITLE IN 2001, MAKING HIM THE OLDEST COMPETITIVE AEROBATIC PILOT.

WATER NUNO GOMES (SOUTH AFRICA) PERFORMED A RECORD 318.25-M-DEEP (1,044-FT) SCUBA DIVE IN THE RED SEA OFF DAHAB, EGYPT, ON 10 JUNE 2005.

★MOST SURFERS ON A WAVE

A total of 110 surfers rode a single wave at the Earthwave Beach Festival, Muizenberg Beach, Cape Town, South Africa, on 4 October 2009 at an event to raise awareness of climate change.

SPORTS
ATHLETICS

★ NEW RECORD
✩ UPDATED RECORD

MOST IAAF WORLD ATHLETE OF THE YEAR AWARDS

The IAAF World Athlete of the Year Award is organized by the International Association of Athletics Federations and given annually to the most outstanding global track and field athlete. The ★most Men's IAAF World Athlete of the Year Trophies won is three by Hicham El Guerrouj (Morocco), each year from 2001 to 2003. The ★most Women's IAAF World Athlete of the Year Trophies won is also three, by Yelena Isinbayeva (Russia) in 2004–05 and 2008.

HIGHEST POLE VAULT (FEMALE)

Despite missing out in the 2009 World Championships, Yelena Isinbayeva (Russia) has continued to break records in women's pole-vaulting over the past year, both indoors and outdoors.

The **highest pole vault (female) (indoors)** now stands at 5.00 m (16 ft 4 in) and was set in Donetsk, Ukraine, on 15 February 2009. On 29 August 2009, in Zurich, Switzerland, Isinbayeva extended the record for ★ **highest pole vault (female) (outdoors)** to 5.06 m (16 ft 7 in) on her first attempt at the height at the Zurich Weltklasse event.

FASTEST MAN

Usain Bolt's (Jamaica) incredible career continues, quite literally, apace. In 2009, he broke the following sprint records: ★**fastest run 100 m (male)** in 9.58 seconds in Berlin, Germany, on 16 August; ★**fastest run 150 m (male)** – a distance not monitored by the IAAF – in 14.35 seconds in Manchester, UK, on 17 May; and ★**fastest run 200 m (male)** in 19.19 seconds in Berlin, Germany, on 20 August.

FAST
THE FASTEST 400 M EVER RUN IS 43.18 SECONDS BY MICHAEL JOHNSON (USA) IN SEVILLE, SPAIN, ON 26 AUGUST 1999. USAIN BOLT'S FASTEST 400 M IS 45.28 SECONDS, SO FAR...

VAST
ARVIND PANDYA (INDIA) RAN BACKWARDS ACROSS THE USA FROM LOS ANGELES TO NEW YORK CITY IN 107 DAYS IN 1984.

SEIKO NEW WR
SEIKO 9.58

DID YOU KNOW?

ON 15 NOVEMBER 2009, TIRUNESH DIBABA (ETHIOPIA) COMPLETED A 15-KM (9.3-MILE) ROAD RUN IN 46 MIN 28 SEC AT THE ZEVENHEUVELENLOOP EVENT IN NIJMEGEN, THE NETHERLANDS.

TRIVIA

Eleanor Robinson (UK) ran 1,000 km (620 miles) in 7 days 1 hr 28 min 29 sec on 11–18 March 1998.

KINGSTON, JAMAICA
The **highest maiden Test century** is 365 not out by Sir Garfield St Aubrun Sobers (Barbados) for the West Indies against Pakistan at Kingston, Jamaica, on 27–28 February and 1 March 1958.

★FARTHEST HAMMER THROW (FEMALE)

Poland's Anita Wlodarczyk threw the hammer a record 77.96 m (255 ft 9 in) to win the gold medal at the 12th IAAF World Championships in Berlin, Germany, on 22 August 2009.

★FASTEST RUN 5,000 M (FEMALE) (INDOORS)

Meseret Defar (Ethiopia) ran 5,000 m in 14 min 24.37 sec at the GE Galan Meeting in Stockholm, Sweden, on 18 February 2009.

★FASTEST RELAY RUNNING 100 MILES BY A TEAM OF 10

The fastest time to complete 100 miles (160.9 km) by a team of 10 runners in relay is 8 hr 19 min 53 sec by members of the ECU Cross-Country Alumni (USA). The record-breaking relay took place at Ada High School Track, Ada, Oklahoma, USA, on 31 December 2009.

★FASTEST RELAY 100 X 10 KILOMETRES

The record for the fastest 100 x 10-km (6.2-mile) relay is 77 hr 17 min 25 sec and was set by the Florida Striders Track Club (USA) at Bishop John J Snyder High School, Jacksonville, Florida, USA, from 3 to 6 December 2009.

FASTEST 100 KM ULTRA DISTANCE TRACK (WOMEN)

Norimi Sakurai (Japan) ran 100 km in 7 hr 14 min 6 sec in Verona, Italy, on 27 September 2003.

MOST MOUNTAIN RUNNING TITLES

The ★most wins of the Mountain Running World Championship (male) is six by Jonathan Wyatt (New Zealand), who was victorious in 1998, 2000, 2002, 2004–05 and 2008.

The ★most wins of the Mountain Running World Championship (female) is four, and has been achieved by two runners: Isabelle Guillot (France) in 1989, 1991, 1993 and 1997; and Gudrun Pfluger (Austria) in 1992, 1994, 1995 and 1996.

MOST EUROPEAN ATHLETE OF THE YEAR AWARDS

The ★most Men's European Athlete of the Year Trophies won by an individual athlete is two, by three different athletes: Jonathan Edwards (UK) in 1995 and 1998; Jan Železný (Czech Republic) in 1996 and 2000; and Christian Olsson (Sweden) in 2003–04.

The ★most Women's European Athlete of the Year Trophies won by an individual athlete is also two, by Carolina Klüft (Sweden) in 2003 and 2006; and Yelena Isinbayeva (Russia) in 2005 and 2008. This annual award is decided by votes from members of the European Athletic Association, media and fans.

LONGEST TRIPLE JUMP (MALE) (INDOORS)

Teddy Tamgho (France) jumped 17.9 m (58 ft 9 in) in Doha, Qatar, on 14 March 2010. Tamgho set the mark on his last jump of the competition to surpass the record of 17.83 m (58 ft 5.96 in) held jointly by Aliecer Urrutia (Cuba) and Christian Olsson (Sweden).

EXTRA! FOR MORE EXCEPTIONAL ATHLETICS RECORDS, SEE THE SPORTS REFERENCE SECTION, STARTING ON P.268.

★FASTEST RUN 4 X 1,500 M RELAY

On 4 September 2009, in Brussels, Belgium, William Biwott Tanui, Gideon Gathimba, Geoffrey Kipkoech Rono and Augustine Kiprono Choge, representing Kenya, ran the 4 x 1,500 m relay in 14 min 36.23 sec. The time was almost two seconds better than the previous best set by West Germany in 1977.

The **largest naturally frozen ice rink** is the Rideau Canal Skateway in Ottawa, Canada. It is 7.8 km (4.8 miles) long and has a total maintained surface area of 165,621 m² (1.782 million ft²).

SPORTS
AUTO-SPORTS

BRO'!
MICHAEL SCHUMACHER (PICTURED) AND HIS YOUNGER BROTHER, RALPH, ARE THE ONLY BROTHERS IN FORMULA ONE HISTORY TO HAVE BOTH WON F1 RACES.

★MOST FORMULA ONE GRANDS PRIX

The greatest number of Formula One (F1) Grand Prix wins by a driver is 91, by Michael Schumacher (Germany) between 30 August 1992 and 1 October 2006. Schumacher also holds the record for the ★**most points scored in a Formula One career**: he amassed 1,377 points from races between 25 August 1991 and 14 March 2010.

★MOST NASCAR TRUCK SERIES CHAMPIONSHIPS

Ron Hornaday, Jr (USA) has been National Association for Stock Car Auto Racing (NASCAR) Truck Series champion four times, 1996–2009.

CARS

DAKAR RALLY

The ★**most consecutive Dakar rallies completed** is 20, by Yoshimasa Sugawara (Japan), from 1983 to 2009.

He also holds a record for the ★**most consecutive Dakar rallies raced**, having entered 26 competitions during the same time period.

★MOST F1 FASTEST LAPS IN A CAREER

The greatest number of fastest laps achieved by one driver in a Formula One career is 76 by Michael Schumacher (Germany) between 25 August 1991 and 22 October 2006.

The ★**most fastest laps by one driver in a Formula One season** is 10, by Michael Schumacher in 2004 and Kimi Raikkonen (Finland) in 2005 and 2008.

MOST F1 POLE POSITIONS

The prolific Michael Schumacher also holds the record for the ★**most Formula One pole positions**: 68, achieved while he was driving for the Benetton and Ferrari teams between 1991 and 2006.

The ★**most consecutive Formula One pole positions** is eight, by Ayrton Senna (Brazil) for McLaren between the 1988 Spanish Grand Prix and the 1989 USA Grand Prix.

★MOST F1 WINS BY A MANUFACTURER

Ferrari (Italy) won 210 Formula One Grands Prix between 1961 and 2010, the greatest number of Grand Prix wins by a manufacturer.

Ferrari has also achieved the ★**most Formula One Constructors' World Championship titles**, with 16, in 1961, 1964, 1975–77, 1979, 1982–83, 1999–2004 and 2007–08.

★MOST F1 GRAND PRIX STARTS

Rubens Barrichello (Brazil) had 284 Formula One Grand Prix starts from 1993 to 2009.

★YOUNGEST DRIVER TO FINISH AN F1 RACE

Jaime Alguersuari (Spain, b. 23 March 1990) was aged just 19 years 125 days when he completed the Hungarian Grand Prix in Budapest, Hungary, on 26 July 2009.

WORLD RALLY CHAMPIONSHIPS

The ★**most FIA World Rallying Championship title wins** is six and was achieved by Sebastien Loeb (France) in 2004–09. This achievement also gives Loeb the record for the ★**most consecutive FIA World Rally Championship titles**, with six titles between 2004 and 2009. He won his sixth title on 25 October 2009 by just one point (93 points to 92) over his Finnish rival Mikko Hirvonen.

The ★**most World Rally Championship race wins** is 53 and was achieved – yes, you've guessed it – by Sebastien Loeb, in 2002–09.

★MOST MOTO GRAND PRIX CHAMPIONSHIPS

Valentino Rossi (Italy) has won six Moto Grand Prix championships, in 2002–05 and 2008–09. Racing for the FIAT Yamaha Team, he acquired 306 points, winning six of the 17 races he took part in. The Moto GP was instituted in 2002, replacing the World Motorcycling Championship 500 cc Grand Prix.

F1!
THE TERM "FORMULA ONE" REFERS TO RULES (THE "FORMULA") TO WHICH ALL DRIVERS AND MANUFACTURERS TAKING PART IN THE RACE MUST AGREE.

★ MOST E1 CLASS ENDURO WORLD CHAMPIONSHIPS

Two riders have won the E1 class Enduro World Championships on two occasions: Ivan Cervantes (Spain), in 2005–06, and Mika Ahola (Finland, pictured above), in 2008–09.

QUIZ!
MICHAEL SCHUMACHER IS AN F1 LEGEND, BUT HE IS NOT THE YOUNGEST DRIVER TO FINISH AN F1 RACE. WHO IS?

SEE p.278 FOR THE ANSWER.

BIKES

★ MOST WINS AT THE LE MANS 24-HOUR RACE

The greatest number of wins by a driver at the Le Mans 24-hour race is eight, by Tom Kristensen (Denmark), in 1997, 2000–05 and 2008.

★ MOST CONSECUTIVE SPRINT CUP SERIES CHAMPIONSHIPS

Jimmie Johnson (USA) won four consecutive National Association for Stock Car Racing (NASCAR) Sprint Cup Series championships, from 2006 to 2009.

SUPERBIKE CHAMPIONSHIPS

The ★most American Motorcyclist Association (AMA) Superbike titles won by an individual rider is seven, by Matt Mladin (Australia), in 1999–2001, 2003–05 and 2009.

Between 1979 and 2009, Suzuki and Kawasaki (both Japan) won the championship 13 times, the most AMA Superbike titles won by a manufacturer.

The most Superbike world championship manufacturer's titles won is 16 by Ducati, in 1991–96, 1998–2004, 2006 and 2008–09.

ISLE OF MAN TT RACES

The ★fastest average speed by a rider at the Isle of Man TT is 211.754 km/h (131.578 mph) by John McGuinness (UK) on a Honda CBR1000RR in 2009.

The ★fastest lap recorded by a rider at the Isle of Man TT in the Superbike TT class is 17 min 21.29 sec, also by John McGuinness, on a Honda CBR1000RR, in 2009.

John McGuinness also recorded the ★fastest time by a rider in an Isle of Man TT Superbike race (six laps). Riding a 1000 HM Plant Honda, he registered a time of 1 hr 46 min 7.16 sec in 2009.

★ MOST WORLD TOURING CAR CHAMPIONSHIPS BY A DRIVER

Guernsey-born racer Andy Priaulx has won three World Touring Car Championships driving for BMW Team UK, from 2005 to 2007.

The ★fastest lap by a woman on the 60.75-km (37.73-mile) Isle of Man TT course is 19 min 22.6 sec at an average speed of 188.02 km/h (116.83 mph) and was achieved by Jenny Tinmouth (UK) on 12 June 2009.

★ MOST MOTOCROSS DES NATIONS WINS

The Motorcross des Nations, also known as the "Olympics of Motocross", has been contested annually since 1947. The national team with the greatest number of wins is the USA, with 20 between 1981 and 2009.

DID YOU KNOW?

THE ★MOST F1 RACES DRIVEN BEFORE A WIN IS 129, BY MARK WEBBER (AUSTRALIA), WHO WON AT LAST AT THE GERMAN GRAND PRIX ON 12 JULY 2009. IT'S NOT A RECORD HE'S LIKELY TO BRAG ABOUT…

★ NEW RECORD ★ UPDATED RECORD

TRIVIA

André Lagache and René Léonard (both France) won the first Le Mans race, staged in 1923.

Dorothy Allison, from Jersey City, New Jersey, USA, assisted police in over 5,000 cases, the most crime cases worked on by a psychic. Allison, who did not receive any payment, was able to describe the face of David Berkowitz, the "Son of Sam" serial killer who terrorized New York in 1977, to a police sketch artist

SPORTS
BALL SPORTS

★ MOST POINTS IN A PRO BEACH VOLLEYBALL MATCH

When Larissa Franca and Juliana Felisberta Silva (Brazil, pictured) defeated Misty May-Treanor and Kerri Walsh (USA) 28-26, 40-42, 15-13 in Acapulco, Mexico, on 30 October 2005, the two teams clocked up a record 164 points in the match.

MOST ALL-IRELAND FINAL WINS

Kerry (Ireland) have won Gaelic football's All-Ireland Senior Football Championships, the sport's premier knockout competition, 36 times between 1903 and 2009.

AUSSIE RULES

★ MOST LEIGH MATTHEWS TROPHIES

Gary Ablett, Jr (Australia) has been awarded a record three Leigh Matthews Trophies, the highly coveted award presented to the most valuable player in the Australian Football League over a season. Ablett earned the awards playing for Geelong in 2007–09.

★ MOST PLAYERS USED IN AN AFL SEASON

In 1911, St Kilda used 62 players over the course of the season, a record for the Australian Football League (then Victorian Football League).

CANADIAN FOOTBALL

★ LARGEST GREY CUP TV AUDIENCE

The Canadian Football League's (CFL) Grey Cup is the biggest TV sports event in Canada. A total of 6.1 million viewers watched the Grey Cup match between the Montreal Alouettes and Saskatchewan Roughriders at Calgary, Canada, on 29 November 2009. The Alouettes won the game 28-27.

EXTRA! PREFER BATS TO BALLS? CHECK OUT TENNIS & RACKET SPORTS ON P.254.

★ MOST VOLLEYBALL GRAND PRIX WINS

Brazil's female volleyball team has won the Grand Prix event eight times: in 1994, 1996, 1998, 2004–06 and 2008–09.

CASH! MISTY MAY-TREANOR (USA) HAS WON A RECORD $1,833,658 (£1,120,191) IN BEACH VOLLEYBALL EARNINGS THROUGH TO THE END OF THE 2009 SEASON.

40°43'N 74°00'W

NEW YORK CITY, NY, USA

The **underground system with the most stations** is the New York City subway, with 468 stations (277 of which are underground) in a network that covers 370 km (230 miles). It serves an estimated 4.5 million passengers per day.

★MOST NETBALL GOALS SCORED IN ONE HOUR (TEAM)

A record 257 netball goals were scored in one hour at an event organized by The Co-operative World Netball Series, at Piccadilly Gardens, Manchester, UK, on 16 September 2009.

HURLING

★MOST WINS OF ALL-IRELAND FINALS

Between 1904 and 2009, Kilkenny won a total of 32 All-Ireland Hurling Championships, the most wins by one team.

Part of Kilkenny's success included the **greatest number of successive wins in the All-Ireland Hurling Final**, with four in a row from 2006 to 2009, equalling Cork's run from 1941 to 1944.

KORFBALL

★MOST INDOOR EUROPEAN CUPS

Dutch korfball club Papendrechtse have won the indoor Korfball European Cup five times, in 1985, 1990, 1999–2000 and 2002.

★MOST WORLD GAMES WINS

The Netherlands holds the record for the most wins of the korfball tournament at the World Games with seven victories, in 1985, 1989, 1993, 1997, 2001, 2005 and 2009.

VOLLEY-BALL

★MOST WOMEN'S BEACH VOLLEYBALL WORLD CHAMPIONSHIPS

The world championships were first staged for both men and women in 1997. The USA women's pair has won the title four times, in 2003, 2005, 2007 and 2009.

★MOST MEN'S WORLD LEAGUE TITLES

Two national sides have each won eight gold medals in the World League: Italy were victorious in 1990–92, 1994–95, 1997 and 1999–2000, while Brazil won in 1993, 2001, 2003–07 and 2009.

CUP!
THE LARGEST BEACH VOLLEYBALL TOURNAMENT, THE HOSVI CUP, FEATURED 1,448 PARTICIPANTS AT THE HOSVI BEACH RESORT, ITALY, ON 24 MAY 2009.

★MOST TOUCHDOWN PASSES IN A CFL SEASON (BY A QUARTERBACK)

Doug Flutie (USA) threw 48 touchdown passes playing for the Calgary Stampeders in the Canadian Football League in 1995.

HANDBALL

★HIGHEST COMBINED SCORE IN A WORLD CHAMPIONSHIP FINAL

The 2005 Men's Handball World Championship final between Spain and Croatia saw an aggregate of 74 points scored. Spain won 40-34.

★The **highest combined score recorded in a Women's Handball World Championship final** is 61 points, in the match between France and Hungary in 2003. France won the match 32-29.

★FIRST NETBALL WORLD SERIES WINNERS

The inaugural Netball World Series was played in 2009 at Manchester, UK, and was won by New Zealand. This international competition features modified rules and will be played every year by the top six teams in the world.

DID YOU KNOW?

THE MOST CONSECUTIVE VOLLEYBALL PASSES IS 92 AND WAS SET BY SV BAYER WUPPERTAL (GERMANY) IN THE BAYERHALL, WUPPERTAL, GERMANY, ON 25 NOVEMBER 2006.

The Brazil men's pair has won the beach volleyball World Championships title four times, in 1997, 1999, 2003 and 2005.

TRIVIA

SPORTS
BASEBALL

★ ★ ★ ★ ★ ★ ★ ★ ★ ★ ★ ★ ★

WORLD SERIES

★MOST GAMES PITCHED IN THE WORLD SERIES (CAREER)

Mariano Rivera (Panama) of the New York Yankees (USA) pitched a record 24 games in World Series play in 1996, 1998, 1999, 2000, 2001, 2003 and 2009. The right-handed relief pitcher has won five World Series with the Yankees (1996, 1998, 1999, 2000 and 2009).

MOST HOME RUNS IN A WORLD SERIES GAME

Two batters have hit three home runs in a World Series game: Reggie Jackson (USA) of the New York Yankees (USA) in Game 6 of the 1977 World Series against the Los Angeles Dodgers (USA) on 18 October 1977; and Babe Ruth (USA) of the New York Yankees in Game 4 of the 1926 World Series against the St Louis Cardinals (USA) on 6 October 1926 and in Game 4 of the 1928 World Series, also against the St Louis Cardinals, on 9 October 1928.

★MOST STRIKEOUTS BY A BATTER IN A SINGLE WORLD SERIES

Ryan Howard of the Philadelphia Phillies (both USA) holds the unfortunate record for the most strikeouts by a batter in a World Series, with 13 in the 2009 World Series against the New York Yankees (USA).

★MOST RUNS BATTED IN A WORLD SERIES GAME

Hideki Matsui (Japan) equalled the record for most runs batted in a World Series game when he hit six, playing for the New York Yankees against the Philadelphia Phillies (both USA) in Game 6 of the 2009 World Series on 4 November 2009. Matsui equalled the record of Robert C Richardson (USA) of the New York Yankees against the Pittsburgh Pirates (USA) in Game 3 of the 1960 World Series on 8 October 1960.

★LARGEST TELEVISION AUDIENCE FOR A WORLD SERIES

The highest average viewing figures per game for a baseball World Series is 44,278,950 viewers for the 1978 World Series between the New York Yankees and the LA Dodgers (both USA), between 10 and 17 October 1978. The games were broadcast on NBC and averaged a 56% share, meaning that they reached around 24.5 million homes.

★MOST WINS OF THE WORLD SERIES

The New York Yankees (USA) have won the World Series on 27 occasions: 1923, 1927–28, 1932, 1936–39, 1941, 1943, 1947, 1949–53, 1956, 1958, 1961–62, 1977–78, 1996, 1998–2000 and 2009.

WOW!
LAWRENCE PETER "YOGI" BERRA (USA) PLAYED IN A RECORD 14 WORLD SERIES FOR THE NEW YORK YANKEES (USA) BETWEEN 1947 AND 1963.

MOST HOME RUNS IN A SINGLE WORLD SERIES

Chase Utley of the Philadelphia Phillies (both USA) hit five home runs in the 2009 World Series against the New York Yankees (USA), equalling the record set by Reggie Jackson (USA) of the New York Yankees in the 1977 World Series against the Los Angeles Dodgers (USA).

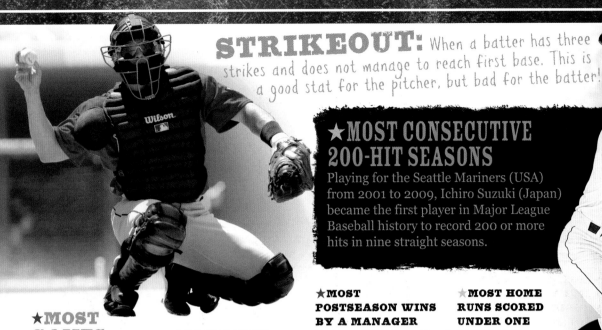

STRIKEOUT:
When a batter has three strikes and does not manage to reach first base. This is a good stat for the pitcher, but bad for the batter!

★ MOST CONSECUTIVE 200-HIT SEASONS

Playing for the Seattle Mariners (USA) from 2001 to 2009, Ichiro Suzuki (Japan) became the first player in Major League Baseball history to record 200 or more hits in nine straight seasons.

OWW!
GUS WEYHING (USA) HIT A RECORD 277 BATSMEN DURING HIS CAREER AS A PITCHER BETWEEN 1887 AND 1901. DESPITE THIS, HE WAS KNOWN AS A DECENT PITCHER!

★ MOST GAMES PLAYED AT CATCHER

In 2009, Ivan Rodriguez (Puerto Rico) celebrated his 2,288th career game as catcher with the Texas Rangers, Florida Marlins, Detroit Tigers, New York Yankees and Houston Astros (all USA) since he made his Major League debut on 20 June 1991.

MLB CAREER RECORDS

★ MOST EJECTIONS FROM A GAME

Robert J Cox (USA) has been ejected from an MLB game 150 times while managing the Toronto Blue Jays (Canada) and Atlanta Braves (USA) from 1978 to 2009.

★ MOST ASSISTS BY A FIRST BASEMAN IN A SEASON

Albert Pujols (Dominican Republic) achieved 185 assists as first baseman for the St Louis Cardinals (USA) during the 2009 season.

★ MOST GAMES PLAYED AT SHORTSTOP

Omar Vizquel (Venezuela) set a Major League Baseball record by playing 2,681 games in the shortstop position. Since 1989, he has played for the Seattle Mariners, Cleveland Indians, San Francisco Giants, Texas Rangers and Chicago White Sox (all USA).

The venerable Vizquel also tops the list for ★**most double-plays by a shortstop**, having participated in a record 1,720 double-plays during a 20-year career in which he has received 11 Gold Glove awards in recognition of his fielding expertise.

★ MOST POSTSEASON WINS BY A MANAGER

Joe Torre (USA) has achieved a record 84 postseason wins as a manager while at the helm of the Atlanta Braves, New York Yankees and Los Angeles Dodgers (all USA) from 1982 to 2009.

★ MOST HOME RUNS IN POSTSEASON

The Dominican Republic's Manny Ramirez has hit a record 29 postseason home runs playing for the Cleveland Indians, Boston Red Sox and Los Angeles Dodgers (all USA) from 1995 to 2009.

★ MOST HOME RUNS SCORED UNDER ONE MANAGER

Chipper Jones (USA) has hit 426 home runs playing for the Atlanta Braves under manager Robert J Cox (both USA) from 1993 to 2009.

★ MOST STRIKEOUTS BY A LEFT-HANDED PITCHER

Left-handed pitcher Randy Johnson (USA) has recorded 4,875 strikeouts playing for the Montreal Expos (Canada), Seattle Mariners, Houston Astros, Arizona Diamondbacks and New York Yankees (all USA) from 1988 to 2009.

★ MOST COMBINED WINS AND SAVES

Andy Pettitte (USA) and Mariano Rivera (Panama) have combined for a win and a save on 59 occasions pitching for the New York Yankees (USA) from 1996 to 2009. Pettitte and Rivera surpassed the previous mark of 57 by Bob Welch and Dennis Eckersley (both USA) playing for the Oakland Athletics (USA) in the 1980s and 1990s.

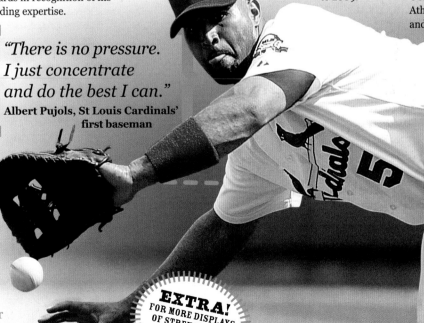

> "There is no pressure. I just concentrate and do the best I can."
> **Albert Pujols, St Louis Cardinals' first baseman**

EXTRA!
FOR MORE DISPLAYS OF STRENGTH AND BALANCE, PITCH INTO P.90.

★ NEW RECORD
UPDATED RECORD

PROVIDENCE, RI, USA

Ashrita Furman (USA) simultaneously balanced 700 eggs vertically on one end at the Rhode Island School of Design in Providence, Rhode Island, USA, on 29 October 2006 – the **most eggs balanced by an individual**.

41°49'N
71°25'W

SPORTS
BASKETBALL

NBA

★HIGHEST MARGIN OF VICTORY IN A PLAY-OFF GAME

On 27 April 2009, the Denver Nuggets (USA) beat the New Orleans Hornets (USA) by 58 points, in a play-off game that they won 121-63, matching the Minneapolis Lakers' (USA) 133-75 win over the St Louis Hawks (USA) in 1956.

★HIGHEST 3-POINT FIELD GOAL PERCENTAGE (CAREER)

Steve Kerr (USA) recorded a 3-point field goal percentage of .454 playing for six different teams from 1988–89 to 2002–03.

HIGH
EPIPHANNY PRINCE (USA), FROM MURRY BERGTRAUM HIGH SCHOOL IN NEW YORK CITY, USA, SCORED A HIGH SCHOOL RECORD 113 POINTS AGAINST BRANDEIS HIGH IN 2006.

SCHOOL
THE MOST FREE THROWS IN ONE MINUTE IS 50 BY BOB J. FISHER (USA) AT VALLEY HEIGHTS HIGH SCHOOL, BLUE RAPIDS, KANSAS, USA, ON 9 JANUARY 2010.

QUIZ!
HOW MANY COUNTRIES HAVE THE HARLEM GLOBETROTTERS PLAYED IN TO DATE?
SEE P.278 FOR THE ANSWER.

★YOUNGEST INDIVIDUAL TO SCORE 25,000 POINTS IN AN NBA CAREER

Kobe Bryant (USA, b. 23 August 1978) was 31 years 151 days old when he reached the landmark of 25,000 National Basketball Association (NBA) career points. He achieved this feat playing for the Los Angeles Lakers (USA) on 21 January 2010.

★YOUNGEST INDIVIDUAL TO SCORE 12,000 POINTS IN A CAREER

At 24 years 35 days, Lebron James (USA, b. 30 December 1984) is the youngest player in NBA history to score 12,000 career points. James reached the mark playing for the Cleveland Cavaliers (USA) on 3 February 2009.

★MOST PLAY-OFF GAMES WON BY A COACH

As coach of the Chicago Bulls (USA) between 1989 and 1997 and the Los Angeles Lakers (USA) during two stints in charge, 1999–2003 and 2005–10, Phil Jackson (USA) won a record 219 play-off games.

★MOST ASSISTS IN ONE QUARTER

Steve Blake (USA) of the Portland Trail Blazers (USA) recorded 14 assists in the first quarter of a game against the Los Angeles Clippers (USA) on 22 February 2009. Blake matched the mark set by John Lucas (USA) of the San Antonio Spurs (USA) during the second quarter of a game against the Denver Nuggets (USA) on 15 April 1984.

★MOST CONSECUTIVE LOSSES TO START A SEASON

The New Jersey Nets (USA) started the 2009–10 season with a record 18 defeats in a row from 28 October to 3 December 2009.

★ NEW RECORD
★ UPDATED RECORD

★MOST BLOCKED SHOTS IN AN NBA FINALS GAME

Dwight Howard (USA) holds the record for the most blocked shots in an NBA Finals game with nine, playing for the Orlando Magic (USA) in Game 4 of the NBA Finals against the Los Angeles Lakers (USA) on 11 June 2009.

46°48'N 71°13'W
QUEBEC CITY, CANADA

The **most goals scored by an individual in a National Hockey League (NHL) game** is seven by Joe Malone for the Quebec Bulldogs in their game against the Toronto St Patricks in Quebec City, Canada, on 31 January 1920.

★HIGHEST 3-POINT FIELD GOAL PERCENTAGE (WNBA)

The highest 3-point field goal percentage (minimum 100 attempts) in Women's National Basketball Association (WNBA) games is .458 by Jennifer Azzi (USA) for the Detroit Shock (1999), the Utah Starzz (2000 –02) and the San Antonio Silver Stars (all USA) in the 2003 season.

★MOST FIELD GOALS IN A CAREER

Lisa Leslie (USA) scored 2,332 field goals in a 12-year career playing for the Los Angeles Sparks (USA) between 1997 and 2009.

WNBA

★HIGHEST FREE THROW PERCENTAGE

Eva Nemcova (Czech Republic) made a free throw percentage of .897 playing for the Cleveland Rockers (USA) from 1997 to 2001.

★HIGHEST REBOUNDS PER GAME AVERAGE

Cheryl Ford (USA) averaged 9.7 rebounds per game playing for the Detroit Shock (USA) since 2003.

★MOST CONSECUTIVE LOSSES BY AN NBA TEAM

The National Basketball Association (NBA) record for most consecutive losses by a team is 24 by the Cleveland Cavaliers (USA). The Cavaliers' record stretched over two seasons, 1981–82 and 1982–83.

MOST NBA CHAMPIONSHIP TITLES WON BY A COACH

In 2009, Phil Jackson (USA) won his 10th NBA title as head coach, surpassing Red Auerbach's (USA) nine titles. Jackson won six NBA titles with the Chicago Bulls (USA) in 1991–93 and 1996–98, and four with the Los Angeles Lakers (USA) in 2000–02 and 2009.

★HIGHEST POINT-SCORING AVERAGE IN A CAREER

Seimone Augustus (USA) has scored 2,230 points in 105 games for the Minnesota Lynx (USA) since 2006, giving her a record point-scoring average of 21.2.

SKILLS

★MOST BASKETBALL BOUNCES IN ONE MINUTE

Kiran Harpal (Netherlands) made 384 bounces of a basketball in one minute at the Hiernasst Youth Centre in Wijchen, the Netherlands, on Guinness World Records Day, 12 November 2009.

★FARTHEST SLAM DUNK USING A TRAMPOLINE

Jordan Ramos (UK) set the record for the farthest slam dunk from a trampoline with a 7.15-m (23-ft 5-in) effort on the set of *Blue Peter*, at BBC Television Studios, UK, on 30 March 2010.

★MOST FREE THROWS IN ONE HOUR

Perry Dissmore (USA) made an incredible 1,926 basketball free throws in one hour at Chipola College's Milton Johnson Health Center in Marianna, Florida, USA, on 9 October 2009.

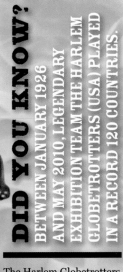

EXTRA!
WANT TO FIND OUT ABOUT THE NBA ALL-STAR JAM SESSION? TAKE A TRIP TO P.248.

DID YOU KNOW?

BETWEEN JANUARY 1926 AND MAY 2010, LEGENDARY EXHIBITION TEAM THE HARLEM GLOBETROTTERS (USA) PLAYED IN A RECORD 120 COUNTRIES.

The Harlem Globetrotters claim to have played more than 25,000 games in their 84-year history.

TRIVIA

BOSTON, MA, USA

The **first telephone call** was made in March 1876 in Boston, Massachusetts, USA, when Alexander Graham Bell (UK) phoned his assistant in a nearby room and said "Come here, Watson, I want you."

SPORTS
COMBAT SPORTS

LONG
BOXERS BOB ITZSIMMONS (UK, 1863-1917) AND JACK JOHNSON (USA, 1878-1946) SHARE THE LONGEST BOXING CAREER TITLE, WITH 31 YEARS IN THE RING EACH.

★ OLDEST FEMALE PRO BOXER

Kazumi Izaki (Japan, b. 2 March 1963) was 46 years 304 days old when she fought Naoko Fujioka (Japan) in a flyweight bout in Tokyo, Japan, on 30 November 2009, although she was defeated by her younger opponent with a Technical Knockout (TKO) in round two.

★ MOST FULL-CONTACT KICKS IN AN HOUR BY A TEAM

A team of 36 members of the Cobh Martial Arts Academy performed a total of 12,428 contact kicks in one hour in Cobh, Cork, Ireland, on 22 April 2009.

★ MOST WRESTLING CHOKESLAMS IN ONE MINUTE

A chokeslam is a move in which a wrestler grasps an opponent's neck and slams him or her down. Italian wrestlers Nury Ayachi (aka Kaio), Carlo Lenzoni (aka Charlie Kid) and Mariel Shehi performed 34 chokeslams in a minute on the set of *Lo Show dei Record* in Rome, Italy, on 25 February 2010.

★ MOST COMPETITIVE FULL-CONTACT ROUNDS

Between February 1993 and 12 November 2009, Paddy Doyle (UK) achieved 6,324 competitive full contact rounds in boxing and other martial arts.

★ MOST MARTIAL ARTS KICKS IN ONE MINUTE, ONE LEG (FEMALE)

Chloe Bruce (UK) performed 212 martial arts kicks in a minute using just her right leg on the set of *Zheng Da Zong Yi – Guinness World Records Special* in Beijing, China, on 19 June 2009. Chloe's kicks were so swift that slow-motion footage was required to verify her feat.

★ MOST MARTIAL ARTS THROWS IN ONE MINUTE

Veteran television comedian Joe Pasquale (UK) performed 29 martial arts throws in one minute on the set of *Guinness World Records – Smashed* at Pinewood Studios, UK, on 15 April 2009.

SHORT
TONY CANZONERI (USA, 1908-59) WAS WORLD LIGHT-WELTERWEIGHT BOXING CHAMPION FOR JUST 33 DAYS, FROM 21 MAY TO 23 JUNE 1933. STILL, AT LEAST IT GIVES HIM A GWR RECORD!

★ NEW RECORD
★ UPDATED RECORD

QUIZ!
WHO WROTE THE MARQUESS OF QUEENSBURY RULES?
SEE P.278 FOR THE ANSWER.

★ MOST UFC MIDDLEWEIGHT CHAMPIONSHIP WINS

Lean, keen fighting machine Anderson Silva (Brazil) won a total of seven Ultimate Fighting Championship (UFC) Middleweight Championship bouts between 2006 and 2009.

DID YOU KNOW?

ON 13 MAY 2000, *RIKISHI ASANOKIRI* LOST HIS SUMO BOUT DURING A TOURNAMENT AT THE KOKUGIKAN, SUMIDA-KU, TOKYO, JAPAN, BECAUSE HIS BELT FELL OFF DURING THE CONTEST

John Ozuna (USA) threw a record-breaking 69.6-km/h (43.3-mph) martial arts punch at KO Kung Fu Karate, San Jose, California, USA, in 2008.

TRIVIA

★MOST CONSECUTIVE SOLO OLYMPIC GOLDS IN FOIL FENCING (FEMALE)

Foil fencer Valentina Vezzali (Italy) cut out a niche for herself in the world of fencing with three consecutive individual Olympic gold medals in foil fencing to her name, achieved in 2000, 2004 and 2008.

MOST BOXING WORLD TITLES IN DIFFERENT WEIGHT DIVISIONS

Two men have held boxing titles at five different weight divisions. Thomas Hearns (USA) established his record between 1980 and 1988 while Manny Pacquiao (Philippines, pictured) recently equalled the feat with titles in the WBO Welterweight, WBC Lightweight, WBC Super Featherweight, IBF Super Bantamweight and WBC Flyweight divisions.

★MOST PUNCHES LANDED IN A CHAMPIONSHIP BOXING MATCH

Troy Dorsey (USA) landed a bone-shaking 620 punches during the course of a 12-round IBF Featherweight title match against Jorge Paez (Mexico) in Las Vegas, Nevada, USA, on 4 February 1990. Perhaps surprisingly, this feat of fast-flying fists didn't result in Dorsey's victory. He eventually lost the fight in a split decision, despite the fact that Paez landed only 340 punches in reply.

★MOST PUNCHES THROWN IN A CHAMPIONSHIP BOXING MATCH

Antonio Margarito (Mexico) threw 1,675 punches in a 12-round WBO Welterweight title match victory against Joshua Clottey (Ghana) in Atlantic City, New Jersey, USA, on 2 December 2006.

★MOST MARTIAL ARTS THROWS OF THE SAME PERSON IN ONE MINUTE

Martial artist Vito Zaccaria (Italy) performed a total of 30 martial arts throws on his fellow countryman Michele Vallieri in one minute on the set of *Lo Show dei Record* in Milan, Italy, on 25 April 2009.

★MOST SUMO TOP DIVISION WINS

The most Makunouchi wins in Sumo wrestling by an individual *rikishi* is 815 by Kaio (Japan, born Hiroyuki Koga) from 1993 to 2010.

★TALLEST UFC FIGHTER

In the world of UFC fighting there is no one taller than Stefan Struve (Netherlands), who measures 2.11 m (6 ft 11 in). The ★shortest UFC fighters are the 1.65-m (5-ft 6-in) Manny Gamburyan, Tyson Griffin, Matt Serra and Sean Sherk (all USA).

MOST JUDO WORLD CHAMPIONSHIP WINS

Ryoko Tani (Japan) won a record seven women's World Judo Championship titles in the 48 kg (105 lb) category between 1993 and 2007 – her first win came when she was just 18 years and 27 days old.

INSTANT EXPERT

⊗ THERE ARE FOUR OFFICIAL SANCTIONING BODIES FOR THE SPORT OF BOXING – THE WORLD BOXING ASSOCIATION (WBA), THE WORLD BOXING COUNCIL (WBC), THE INTERNATIONAL BOXING FEDERATION (IBF) AND THE WORLD BOXING ORGANIZATION (WBO).

⊗ DESPITE BEING NAMED AFTER THE NINTH MARQUESS OF QUEENSBURY, THE FAMOUS RULES THAT BEAR HIS NAME WERE ACTUALLY WRITTEN BY WELSHMAN JOHN GRAHAM CHAMBERS.

⊗ BOXING FIRST BECAME AN OLYMPIC SPORT AT THE 1904 OLYMPIC GAMES HELD IN ST LOUIS, MISSOURI, USA.

EXTRA! FOR MORE PEOPLE WHO AIM TO PLEASE, CHECK OUT TARGET SPORTS ON p.252.

RIKISHI: The Japanese word for a professional Sumo wrestler.

LA PAZ, BOLIVIA

La Paz, the administrative and de facto capital of Bolivia, stands at an altitude of 3,631 m (11,913 ft) above sea level, making it the **highest capital city**. Its airport, El Alto, is at 4,080 m (13,385 ft). Sucre, the legal capital of Bolivia, stands at 2,824 m (9,301 ft) above sea level.

SPORTS
CRICKET

★ ★ ★ ★ ★ ★ ★ ★ ★ ★ ★ ★ ★

★FIRST PLAYER TO SCORE 200 IN A 50-OVER INTERNATIONAL

Sachin Tendulkar (India) smashed 200 not out off 147 balls, including 25 fours and three sixes, playing for India against South Africa in Gwalior, India, on 24 February 2010.

★FIRST PLAYER TO SCORE A CENTURY IN ONE-DAY INTERNATIONALS FOR TWO TEAMS

On 4 February 2007, aged 20 years 147 days, Dubliner Eoin Morgan scored 115 for Ireland against Canada in the ICC World Cricket League at Jaffery Sports Club Ground, Nairobi, Kenya. On 2 March 2010, Morgan recorded an unbeaten 110 for England against Bangladesh in Mirpur, Bangladesh.

★HIGHEST SUCCESSFUL RUN CHASE IN FIRST-CLASS CRICKET

India's West Zone amassed 541-7 against South Zone (India) in the Duleep Trophy Final on 10 February 2010.

★MOST SUCCESSFUL CAPTAIN IN TEST MATCH HISTORY

Ricky Ponting (Australia) won his 42nd Test match in charge of Australia in the First Test against Pakistan in Melbourne, Australia, on 29 December 2009.

★FASTEST TWENTY20 CENTURY

Andrew Symonds (Australia) hit the fastest century in Twenty20 cricket when he cracked 100 runs off 34 balls playing for Kent against Middlesex at Maidstone, Kent, UK, on 2 July 2004. Symonds went on to make 112 off 43 balls in a knock that featured 18 fours and three sixes.

★MOST TEST CATCHES BY A WICKET-KEEPER

Mark Boucher (South Africa) made 472 catches in 131 Tests playing for South Africa between 17 October 1997 and 9 February 2010.

Bob Taylor (UK) made 1,473 catches playing for Derbyshire (UK) and England between 1960 and 1988, the ★most catches by a wicket-keeper in first-class cricket.

MOST WINS

★FRIENDS PROVIDENT TROPHY

Lancashire (UK) have won the Friends Provident Trophy a total of seven times, in 1970–72, 1975, 1990, 1996 and 1998. The Friends Provident Trophy is the current incarnation of the premier one-day cup competition in English county cricket.

★MOST ASIA CUP WINS

The Asia Cup, a One-Day International tournament, was instituted in 1984. The most wins of the Asia Cup is four, by India in 1984, 1988, 1991 and 1995, and Sri Lanka in 1986, 1997, 2004 and 2008 (pictured).

★MOST SIXES SCORED IN AN IPL INNINGS

Brendan McCullum (New Zealand) hit 13 sixes playing for Kolkata Knight Riders against Royal Challengers Bangalore in the very first Indian Premier League (IPL) match at Bangalore, India, on 18 April 2008.

EXTRA!
PREFER BATMAN TO BATSMAN? CHECK OUT COMICS & GRAPHIC NOVELS ON P.164.

CARACAS, VENEZUELA
10°30′ N
66°55′ W

The **longest regularly scheduled bus route**, known as the "Liberator's Route", is 9,660 km (6,003 miles) long and links Caracas, Venezuela and Buenos Aires, Argentina, passing through the capitals of six South American countries.

LONG
THE LONGEST INDIVIDUAL NET SESSION LASTED FOR 24 HOURS AND WAS COMPLETED BY STEPHEN SPEAK (USA) ON 28–29 APRIL 2001.

GONG
IN 2010, ENGLAND BATSMAN CLAIRE TAYLOR BECAME THE ★FIRST WOMAN TO BE NAMED AMONG WISDEN'S FIVE "CRICKETERS OF THE YEAR" IN THE 120-YEAR HISTORY OF THE AWARD.

GOOCH'S GLORY

The **most runs scored by one player in a Test match** is 456 by Graham Gooch (England) in the first Test against India at Lord's, Middlesex, UK, between 26 and 31 July 1990. Gooch, who was England captain at the time, scored 333 in the first innings and 123 in the second.

★FORD RANGER ONE-DAY CUP

The Ford Ranger One-Day Cup is the current name of Australia's premier domestic one-day cricket competition. Western Australia have won the competition 11 times, from 1970–71 to 2003–04.

MOST WICKETS TAKEN

INTERNATIONAL MATCHES

Muttiah Muralitharan (Sri Lanka) has taken a grand total of 1,315 wickets playing for Sri Lanka, the ICC XI and the Asia XI between 1992 and 2009. This overall figure comprises 792 Test wickets, the ★**most wickets taken in a Test career**, 512 One-Day International wickets, the **most wickets taken in a One-Day International career**, and 11 wickets in Twenty20 international matches.

TEST INNINGS

Two bowlers have taken all 10 wickets in a Test match innings. Jim Laker took 10-53 for England v. Australia at Old Trafford, UK, on 31 July 1956; and Anil Kumble (India) took 10-74 for India v. Pakistan in New Delhi, India, on 7 February 1999.

TWENTY20 MATCHES

Yasir Arafat (Pakistan) has taken 90 wickets in 69 Twenty20 matches between 2006 and 2010.

★MOST TWENTY20 INTERNATIONAL WICKETS IN A CAREER

Umar Gul (Pakistan) has taken 43 wickets in Twenty20 internationals, playing for Pakistan between 2007 and 2010. Gul's wickets have come at an average of one every 13 balls bowled.

DID YOU KNOW?

THE HIGHEST SCORE IN THE WOMEN'S CRICKET WORLD CUP IS 229 N.O. BY BELINDA CLARK FOR AUSTRALIA V. DENMARK IN MUMBAI, INDIA, ON 16 DECEMBER 1997.

The **most wickets taken in women's Cricket World Cup matches** is 39, by Lyn Fullston (Australia).

TRIVIA

SACHIN'S SUCCESS

Indian legend Sachin Tendulkar seems to break batting records wherever he goes. Here are four of his latest:

Most runs in an ODI career, with 17,598 runs, and **most centuries in ODI matches**, with 46 centuries between 18 December 1989 and 24 February 2010. **Most runs in Test cricket**, with 13,447 runs, and **most centuries in Test cricket**, with 47 tons in a Test career that began on 15 November 1989.

He has also achieved the **highest partnership in One-Day International matches** – 331 runs with Rahul Dravid (India) against New Zealand in Hyderabad, India, on 8 November 1999.

Wilfred Benitez (Puerto Rico) was 17 years 176 days old when he won the WBA light welterweight title in San Juan, Puerto Rico, on 6 March 1976 to become the **youngest boxing world champion**.

SPORTS
CYCLING

FASTEST 3 KM TEAM PURSUIT (WOMEN'S TEAM)
The Great Britain trio of Elizabeth Armitstead, Wendy Houvenagel and Joanna Rowsell set a new record for the women's 3 km team pursuit of 3 min 21.875 sec in Manchester, UK, on 1 November 2009.

LONG!
THE LONGEST RACE IN TOUR DE FRANCE HISTORY WAS THE 1926 RACE, WHICH COVERED A TOTAL OF 5,795 KM (3,600 MILES).

MOST WINS...

★ UCI TIME TRIAL WORLD CHAMPIONSHIPS (FEMALE)
France's Jeannie Longo-Ciprelli has won four Time Trial World Championships, in 1995–97 and 2001.
She also holds the record for the ★ **most UCI Road Race World Championships won by a female**, with five wins in 1985–87, 1989 and 1995.

UCI TIME TRIAL WORLD CHAMPIONSHIPS (MALE)
Two men have won the Time Trial World Championships on three occasions: Michael Rogers (Australia) triumphed in 2003–05, and Fabian Cancellara (Switzerland) in 2006–07 and 2009.

★ TRIALS CYCLING WORLD CHAMPIONSHIPS (TEAM)
Spain is the only team to have won the Trials Cycling World Championships twice, in 2008 and 2009.

★ UCI PROTOUR
Spain's Alejandro Valverde is the only rider to have won the UCI ProTour on two occasions, in 2006 and 2008.

★ UCI WOMEN'S ROAD WORLD CUPS
Four women have won the UCI Road World Cup on two occasions: Diana Ziliute (Lithuania), in 1998 and 2000; Nicole Cooke (UK), in 2003 and 2006; Oenone Wood (Australia), in 2004 and 2005; and Marianne Vos (Netherlands), in 2007 and 2009.

TRIALS CYCLING WORLD CHAMPIONSHIPS – ELITE CLASS (MALE)
Benito Ros Charral (Spain) has won the Elite Men's Trials World Championships a record six times, in 2003–05 and 2007–09.

★ UCI TRIALS CYCLING WORLD CHAMPIONSHIPS (FEMALE)
Switzerland's Karin Moor has won the Trials Cycling World Championships title on eight occasions, in consecutive years from 2001 to 2007 and again in 2009.

★ MOUNTAIN BIKE WORLD CHAMPIONSHIPS (MARATHON, MALE)
Only two male riders have secured the UCI Mountain Bike Marathon World Championships on two occasions: Thomas Frischknecht (Switzerland) in 2003 and 2005, and Roel Paulissen (Belgium) in 2008–09.
The most wins of the **Mountain Bike World Championships (Marathon) by a female rider** is four by Gunn-Rita Dahle Flesjå (Norway) in 2004–06 and 2008.

MOUNTAIN BIKE WORLD CUPS (FOUR-CROSS, FEMALE)
Anneke Beerten (Netherlands) has won the women's Four-Cross Mountain Bike World Cup on three occasions, in 2007–09.
Brian Lopes (USA) has won three Four-Cross World Cups, in 2002, 2005 and 2007, the greatest number by a male rider.

★ NEW RECORD
★ UPDATED RECORD

MOST MOUNTAIN BIKE CROSS-COUNTRY WORLD CUPS (MALE)
Julien Absalon (France) has won more mountain bike cross-country World Cup titles than any other man. His record five victories came in 2003 and from 2006 to 2009. Absalon has also won two Olympic gold medals in the discipline, in 2004 and 2008.

SHORT!
THE SHORTEST TOURS DE FRANCE WERE HELD IN 1903 AND 1904, WHEN THE RACES COVERED A TOTAL OF 2,428 KM (1,508 MILES).

"It's about winning gold medals and I'd rather have one gold than three silvers."
Sir Chris Hoy displays the mentality of a winner

DID YOU KNOW?

THE UNION CYCLISTE INTERNATIONALE (UCI) IS THE WORLD GOVERNING BODY FOR THE SPORT OF CYCLING.

The ★greatest distance cycled on a static bike in a minute is 2.04 km (1.27 miles), by Miguel Angel Castro (Spain).

TRIVIA

★MOST GIRO D'ITALIA FEMMINILE WINS

Fabiana Luperini (Italy) has won the Tour of Italy women's race (Giro d'Italia Femminile) on five occasions, consecutively from 1995 to 1998 and again in 2008.

FASTEST...

★UNPACED 500 M, STANDING START (WOMEN'S TEAM)

The Australia team of Kaarle McCulloch and Anna Meares set the team record for the women's unpaced 500 m cycle from a standing start with a time of 33.149 seconds at Pruszkow, Poland, on 26 March 2009.

The day before, Simona Krupeckaite (Lithuania) had set the individual female fastest time for the discipline, with 33.296 seconds at the same event in Poland.

★UNPACED 750 M, STANDING START (MEN'S TEAM)

The Great Britain team of Chris Hoy, Jason Kenny and Jamie Staff recorded a time of 42.950 seconds for the unpaced 750 m cycle from a standing start at Beijing, China, on 15 August 2008. The time came en route to the trio winning the team sprint gold medal at the Beijing Olympic Games, in which they beat France in the final in a time of 43.128 seconds.

LAND'S END TO JOHN O'GROATS

A classic cycling challenge, the 1,407-km (874-mile) route from Land's End in Cornwall, England, UK, to John O'Groats in Caithness, Scotland, UK, requires riders to travel the length of Great Britain between its two most distant mainland points.

The ★fastest time by a male rider to cycle from

Land's End to John O'Groats is 44 hr 4 min 19 sec, by Gethin Butler (UK) in September 2001.

The ★fastest time by a female rider to cycle from Land's End to John O'Groats is 52 hr 45 min 11 sec, set by Lynne Taylor (UK) on 3 October 2002.

Lynne is also the co-holder of the ★fastest time to cycle from Land's End to John O'Groats on a tandem (mixed team), having achieved a time of 51 hr 19 min 23 sec with Andy Wilkinson (UK) in 2000.

★MOST UCI MEN'S ROAD WORLD CUPS

Paolo Bettini (Italy) has won the UCI Road World Cup three times, which is a record for a male rider. The wins came in 2002–04. This competition was replaced by the UCI ProTour in 2005.

★UNPACED 200 M FLYING START (MALE)

Kevin Sireau (France) set a new record of 9.572 seconds for the unpaced 200 m flying start sprint in Moscow, Russia, on 30 May 2009.

PORT OF SPAIN, TRINIDAD AND TOBAGO

10°40'N 61°31'W

India scored 413-5 to beat Bermuda (156 all out) by 257 runs at Queen's Park Oval, Port of Spain, Trinidad and Tobago, on 19 March 2007, the highest margin of victory in a cricket World Cup match

SPORTS
FOOTBALL

MOST WINS OF THE BEACH SOCCER WORLD CUP

Brazil have won the FIFA Beach Soccer World Cup on four of the five occasions it has been held (2006–09). Before it became officially recognized by FIFA in 2005, a version of the Beach Soccer World Cup had been running since 1995, and Brazil had won nine out of the 10 events.

★ **LOWEST GOAL AVERAGE IN FIFA WORLD CUP FINALS**

The goal average at the 1990 FIFA World Cup Finals in Italy was just 2.21 per game, the lowest since the competition began in 1930. The overall average for the 18 World Cup Finals to Germany 2006 is 2.91 goals per match.

★ **MOST FIFA FAIR PLAY TROPHY WINS**

Brazil have won the FIFA Fair Play Trophy four times, in 1982, 1986, 1994 and 2006. The trophy is awarded to the team with the best record of fair play during a World Cup Final.

★ **LONGEST UNBEATEN RUN IN INTERNATIONAL FOOTBALL**

Two international football teams have achieved unbeaten runs stretching to the 35-game mark: Brazil were the first team to set the record, between 16 December 1993 and 18 January 1996, and Spain from 11 October 2006 until 20 June 2009.

In this period, Brazil won the 1994 World Cup, reached the 1995 Copa America final and reached the final of the 1996 Gold Cup. Their run was ended with a 2-0 defeat in the Gold Cup final to Mexico. During the 35-game run Brazil did lose one game by penalty shoot-out (the 1995 Copa America final to hosts Uruguay), but were still unbeaten after extra-time.

Spain's undefeated sequence, meanwhile, saw them win the 2008 European Championships and reach the semi-finals of the 2009 Confederations Cup before losing to the USA.

★ **MOST GOALS SCORED IN A WORLD CUP FINALS**

A record 171 goals were scored by the 32 teams in the FIFA World Cup Finals held in France in 1998.

★ **MOST GOALS SCORED IN A FIFA BEACH SOCCER WORLD CUP CAREER**

Madjer (Portugal) is the most prolific goalscorer in FIFA Beach Soccer World Cups, with 67 goals between 2005 and 2009. Madjer also has the **most FIFA Beach Soccer World Cup Golden Shoe awards**, having won three times.

MOST WINS OF THE CONFEDERATIONS CUP

When Brazil came back from a 0-2 half-time deficit to beat the USA 3-2 in the final of the 2009 Confederations Cup in South Africa on 28 June 2009, it saw the South American country register its third victory in the competition. Previous wins had occurred in 1997 and 2005.

EXTRA!
TURN TO P.136 TO FIND OUT WHO'S THE MOST EXPENSIVE FOOTBALLER OF ALL TIME.

SOCCER:

It is widely believed that the word "soccer" is a contraction of "Association" from "Association Football"

MOST AFRICA CUP OF NATIONS WON BY A PLAYER

Ahmed Hassan has played in eight Africa Cup of Nations tournaments for Egypt between 1996 and 2010. During that period he has been on the winning side a record four times, in 1998, 2006, 2008 and 2010.

MOST GOALS SCORED IN FIFA WOMEN'S WORLD CUP MATCHES

Brigit Prinz (Germany) has scored a total of 14 goals in FIFA Women's World Cup matches. Her latest goal was scored in the FIFA World Cup Final at the Hongkou Stadium in Shanghai, China, on 30 September 2007.

on 16 February 2000. Nakayama netted on 1 min, 2 min and 3 min 15 sec, beating the 62-year-old mark set by George William Hall (England), who scored three goals in 3 min 30 sec against Ireland at Old Trafford, Manchester, UK, on 16 November 1938.

HIS
THE MOST INTERNATIONAL CAPS WON BY A MALE FOOTBALLER IS 181 BY MOHAMED AL-DEAYEA FOR SAUDI ARABIA BETWEEN 1990 AND 2006.

AFRICA CUP OF NATIONS

The ★**most consecutive matches played in Africa Cup of Nations tournaments** is 34, by Rigobert Song (Cameroon) between 1996 and 2010. During his run, Song was part of the victorious Cameroon teams of 2000 and 2002.

★ MOST GOALS SCORED IN AFRICA CUP OF NATIONS

Cameroon's Samuel Eto'o has scored a total of 18 goals in Africa Cup of Nations tournaments from 1996 to 2010. He has also won the African Footballer of the Year award three times, a record he shares with Abedi Pelé (Ghana) and George Weah (Liberia).

FASTEST HAT-TRICK IN INTERNATIONAL FOOTBALL

Japanese international Masashi "Gon" Nakayama scored a hat-trick in 3 min 15 sec against Brunei during an Asian Cup qualifying match played

MOST GOALS SCORED IN A COPA AMERICA TOURNAMENT

Three footballers have scored nine goals in a single Copa America tournament: Jair Rosa Pinto (Brazil) in 1949; and Humberto Maschio (Argentina) and Javier Ambrois (Uruguay), both in 1957.

MOST APPEARANCES AS CAPTAIN IN FIFA WORLD CUP FINALS

Argentina's Diego Maradona captained his country in 16 World Cup Finals matches between 1982 and 1994. Maradona's tenure as captain included leading his country to World Cup victory in the 1986 final against West Germany.

MOST GOALS SCORED IN INTERNATIONAL FOOTBALL (MALE OR FEMALE)

The record for most career international goals scored, by a man or woman, is 158 by Mia Hamm (USA) from 1987 to 2004. Hamm's stellar career included 275 appearances for the USA national team and two Women's World Cup titles, in 1991 and 1999.

★ **NEW RECORD**
★ **UPDATED RECORD**

★ MOST CONSECUTIVE WINS IN INTERNATIONALS

Between 26 June 2008 and 20 June 2009, Spain won 15 consecutive international football matches. The sequence began when they beat Russia 3-0 in the semi-finals of the 2008 European Championships. Their 15th consecutive win came with a 2-0 victory over South Africa in their final group game in the 2009 Confederations Cup.

HERS
THE MOST INTERNATIONAL CAPS WON BY A FEMALE FOOTBALLER IS 342 BY KRISTINE LILLY FOR THE USA IN A CAREER THAT BEGAN IN 1987.

SPORTS
FOOTBALL

EXTRA!
PREFER TO PLAY FOOTBALL
WITH A CONTROLLER
IN YOUR HAND?
GO TO VIDEOGAMES
ON P.160.

PREMIER LEAGUE BAD BOYS

The ★**most yellow cards received by a player in the English Premier League** is 93 by Lee Bowyer (UK, above right) between 1996 and 2010. The **most red cards received by a player in the English Premier League** is eight, by three players: Richard Dunne (Ireland, above left) between 1996 and 2008; Duncan Ferguson (UK) between 1994 and 2006; and Patrick Vieira (France) between 1996 and 2005.

★MOST WINS OF BUNDESLIGA BY A PLAYER

Two players have won Germany's Bundesliga title on eight occasions: Mehmet Scholl (Germany, pictured) in 1994, 1997, 1999–2001, 2003 and 2005–06; and Oliver Kahn (Germany) in 1997, 1999–2001, 2003, 2005–06 and 2008. Both players were part of the Bayern Munich team.

> "I don't try to favour the foreign players."
> **Arsenal manager Arsène Wenger (France)**

★YOUNGEST FOOTBALL PLAYER IN A TOP DIVISION

Mauricio Baldivieso (Bolivia) was aged 12 years 362 days when he represented Aurora FC against La Paz in the Clausura competition of the Liga de Fútbol Profesional Boliviano at Estadio Hernando Siles, La Paz, Bolivia, on 19 July 2009.

★YOUNGEST GOALSCORER IN LA LIGA

The youngest goalscorer in the top division of Spanish football is Iker Muniain (Spain), who was 16 years 289 days old when he scored for Athletico Bilbao in a 2-2 draw with Real Valladolid, in Valladolid, Spain, on 4 October 2009.

★MOST BUNDESLIGA TITLES WON BY A COACH

Udo Lattek (Poland) secured eight Bundesliga titles in his career as a football coach. Six titles came in his two spells as coach of Bayern Munich, winning in 1972–74 and 1985–87, and two with the Borussia Monchengladbach team in 1976–77.

★FIRST ALL-FOREIGN PREMIER LEAGUE MATCH SQUAD

The squad selected by Arsenal (UK) for the match against Crystal Palace (UK) on 14 February 2005 was the first all-foreign line-up to play in an English Premier League match. The squad consisted of: Jens Lehmann (Germany); Lauren (Cameroon); Kolo Touré (Ivory Coast); Pascal Cygan, Gaël Clichy, Robert Pirès, Patrick Vieira and Thierry Henry (all France); Edu (Brazil); Jose-Antonio Reyes (Spain); and Dennis Bergkamp (Netherlands). Subs: Manuel Almunia and Cesc Fàbregas (both Spain); Philippe Senderos (Switzerland); Mathieu Flamini (France); and Robin van Persie (Netherlands). Arsenal won 5-1.

TOP! THE ★**MOST DOMESTIC LEAGUE TITLES WON BY A FOOTBALL CLUB** IS 53, BY RANGERS FC (UK), IN THE SCOTTISH DIVISION 1 AND PREMIER DIVISION BETWEEN 1891 AND 2010.

RICH! THE **HIGHEST ANNUAL REVENUE FOR A FOOTBALL CLUB** IS 401,400,000 EUROS (£363,645,271, $544,699,707) BY REAL MADRID (SPAIN) IN 2008-09.

GEORGETOWN, GUYANA
6°48'N 58°10'W

The **most successful lawyer** is Sir Lionel Luckhoo (Guyana), senior partner of Luckhoo and Luckhoo of Georgetown, Guyana, who succeeded in getting 245 successive murder-charge acquittals between 1940 and 1985.

LONGEST HOME UNBEATEN STREAKS IN THE TOP DIVISION OF THE LEADING DOMESTIC LEAGUES

SOURCE: INFOSTRADA SPORTS

NUMBER	CLUB	START DATE	END DATE	WON	DRAWN	LEAGUE
121	Real Madrid	17 February 1957	21 February 1965	112	9	La Liga (SPA)
93	PSV	17 February 1983	4 March 1989	77	16	Eredivisie (NED)
92	FC Nantes	4 June 1976	14 March 1981	80	12	Ligue 1 (FRA)
88	Torino	31 January 1943	23 October 1949	78	10	Série A (ITA)
86	Chelsea	20 March 2004	5 October 2008	62	24	Premier League (ENG)
73	Bayern Munich	11 April 1970	14 September 1974	62	11	Bundesliga (GER)
68	Palmeiras*	23 February 1986	2 September 1990	45	23	Série A (ITA)
49	Banfield**	7 May 1950	24 May 1953	35	14	Primera División (ARG)
25	Urawa Red Diamonds	24 September 2005	7 April 2007	22	3	J-League (JPN)
25	Gamba Osaka	29 March 2006	11 August 2007	20	5	J-League (JPN)
24	Columbus Crew	28 June 2008	26 September 2009	18	6	MLS (USA)

Notes:

*Palmeiras streak also includes São Paulo Championship (Paulista);

**Banfield streak does not include 1951 championship decider against Racing, which was played on a neutral pitch.

DID YOU KNOW?

STEVE RALSTON (USA) HAS PLAYED A RECORD 33,143 MINUTES IN HIS MAJOR LEAGUE SOCCER (MLS) CAREER (1996–2009).

Jeff Cunningham (USA) has scored a record 36 match-winning goals in his MLS career.

TRIVIA

★ MOST COPPA ITALIA WINS

Two teams have won the Coppa Italia, the premier cup competition in Italian football, on a record nine occasions: Juventus in 1938, 1942, 1959–60, 1965, 1979, 1983, 1990, 1995; and Roma in 1964, 1969, 1980–81, 1984, 1986, 1991, 2007–08.

★ MOST WINS OF THE TIPPELIGAEN

The Tippeligaen is the top division of league football competition in Norway. The most successful team in the league, in terms of titles won, is Rosenborg, who have been league champions a record 21 times between 1967, when they won their first title, and 2009, when they won their latest.

★ MOST GOALS SCORED IN A PREMIER LEAGUE MATCH BY AN INDIVIDUAL PLAYER

Three players have scored five goals in a single English Premier League match: Andy Cole (UK) for Manchester United versus Ipswich at Old Trafford, Manchester, UK, on 4 March 1995; Alan Shearer (UK) for Newcastle United versus Sheffield Wednesday at St James' Park, Newcastle, UK, on 19 September 1999; and most recently Jermain Defoe (UK) for Tottenham Hotspur versus Wigan Athletic at White Hart Lane, London, UK, on 22 November 2009.

★ MOST DURABLE FOOTBALL REFEREE

Hungary's Csernyi Géza (b. 25 March 1932) has been an active football referee for 57 years. Géza gained his refereeing qualification on 7 June 1950 and officiated his last match in Hungary in February 2007.

★ MOST FOOTBALL MANAGEMENT REJECTION LETTERS

Between 2000 and 2010, Patrick Rielly (UK) has received 46 rejection letters from football clubs to whom he has applied to be manager. His first rejection came from Millwall FC, others include Celtic, Manchester City and West Ham United (all UK).

FASTEST SPOT KICK

Francisco Javier Galan Màrin (Spain, above) spot-kicked a football at 129 km/h (80.1 mph) for *El Show de los Récords* in Madrid, Spain, on 29 October 2001. The **fastest known shot on goal** was by David Hirst (UK) for Sheffield Wednesday v. Arsenal (both UK) on 16 September 1996. It clocked in at 183 km/h (114 mph) – but hit the bar!

★ NEW RECORD ★ UPDATED RECORD

The **first player to score a hat-trick** (three goals in a match) in a FIFA World Cup finals is Bert Patenaude (USA) playing for the USA in a match against Paraguay at the 1930 World Cup in Estadio Gran Parque Central, Montevideo, Uruguay, on 17 July 1930.

34°53'S
56°10'W

SPORTS
GOLF

"Records are made to be broken. Could somebody make 10 [birdies] in a row? Sure."

Birdie king Mark Calcavecchia (USA)

★ MOST BIRDIES RECORDED IN A US MASTERS ROUND

Anthony Kim (USA) scored 11 birdies in his second round at The Masters tournament at Augusta National, Augusta, Georgia, USA, on 10 April 2009. The previous record of 10 birdies had been set by Nick Price (Zimbabwe) in 1986.

EXTRA! FOR A DIFFERENT KIND OF BIRDIE, SPREAD YOUR WINGS AND FLY OVER TO P.64.

★ NEW RECORD
★ UPDATED RECORD

★ LOWEST SCORE BELOW PAR IN 72 HOLES IN A PGA TOUR EVENT

Ernie Els (South Africa) had a score of -31 (31 under par) after 72 holes of the 2003 Mercedes Championships, Maui, Hawaii, USA, from 9 to 12 January 2003.

★ HIGHEST PRIZE MONEY FOR A GOLF TOURNAMENT

The Professional Golfer's Association (PGA) tour Players Championships contested at Sawgrass, Florida, USA, in 2008 and 2009 had a total prize pool of $9,500,000 (£6,614,445) each year – with $1,710,000 (£1,190,814) going to the winner.

★ HIGHEST COMBINED PRIZE MONEY FOR THE WGC MATCH PLAY CHAMPIONSHIP

The World Golf Championships (WGC) Match Play Championship played at the Ritz-Carlton Golf Club, Marana, Arizona, USA, in 2009 had a total prize pool of $8,500,000 (£5,251,523).

★ LOWEST SCORE IN 72 HOLES IN A PGA TOUR EVENT

Tommy Armour III (USA) posted a four-round score of 254 (26 strokes under par) at the 2003 Valero Texas Open, San Antonio, Texas, USA, from 25 to 28 September 2003.

★ MOST BIRDIES IN A 72-HOLE GOLF PGA TOUR EVENT

Mark Calcavecchia (USA) hit 32 birdies in 72 holes at the 2001 Phoenix Open in Phoenix, USA, from 25 to 28 January 2001. The feat was equalled by Paul Gow (Australia) at the 2001

★ MOST CONSECUTIVE BIRDIES IN A PGA TOUR EVENT

Playing "preferred lies" on a rain-sodden course, US PGA tour veteran Mark Calcavecchia (USA) scored nine consecutive birdies in the third round of the Canadian Open at Oakville, Ontario, Canada, on 25 July 2009.

B.C. Open, in New York, USA, from 19 to 22 July 2001.

★ MOST CONSECUTIVE US AMATEUR GOLF TITLES

Before embarking on a stellar professional career, Tiger Woods (USA) recorded three consecutive US Amateur Championship wins between 1994 and 1996.

MOST CURTIS CUP APPEARANCES

Carole Semple-Thompson (USA) played in 12 ties and won a record 18 matches from 1974 to 2002.

★ MOST SOLHEIM CUP APPEARANCES

Laura Davies (UK) has played for Europe in every Solheim Cup from 1990 to 2009, making 11 appearances.

MORE! A RECORD 632 PEOPLE TOOK PART IN A GOLF LESSON TAUGHT BY ZHANG LIANWEI (CHINA) IN HAINAN PROVINCE, CHINA, ON 11 DECEMBER 2009.

FORE! IN FEBRUARY 1971, ASTRONAUT ALAN SHEPARD (USA) STRUCK TWO GOLF BALLS ON THE SURFACE OF THE MOON. THE MOST REMOTE GOLF SHOT EVER.

★ LONGEST SEATED GOLF SHOT

Dale Sheppard (Australia) hit a golf ball 113.55 m (372 ft 6 in), while seated, on the Moonah Links Golf Club's Open Course 11th hole in Mornington Peninsula, Victoria, Australia, on 27 November 2009.

PARAMARIBO, SURINAME

5°52'N
55°10'W

Suriname, with a population of 436,494, has only one cinema, which can be found in the capital Paramaribo – the **fewest cinemas per head of population**. In 1997, this cinema saw a total of 103,626 admissions.

★LONGEST 19TH HOLE

The "Extreme 19th" at the Legend Golf and Safari Resort, South Africa, measures 400 m (1,312 ft 4 in) in horizontal distance, with the tee and hole separated by a 430-m (1,410-ft 9-in) drop. The tee is located on Hanglip Mountain.

★MOST SOLHEIM CUP POINTS SCORED

Sweden's Annika Sorenstam scored 24 Solheim Cup points playing for the Europe team in the biennial event from 1994 to 2007.

Sorenstam also holds the record for the **highest career earnings on the US LPGA Tour**, with $22,573,192 (£17,292,700) between 1993 and 2009.

★MOST HOLES PLAYED BY A PAIR IN 12 HOURS (CART)

Using a golf cart to speed their progress, Jason Casserly and Chris Woods (both Australia) played 189 holes of golf in 12 hours at Grafton District Golf Club, Grafton, Australia, on 26 April 2009. The golfers used foursome rules (taking alternate shots), starting at 5:30 a.m., just before sunrise, and finishing just

before sunset at 5:30 p.m. They were raising money for the Grafton Oncology Ward. The final score after 10-and-a-half rounds was 952 (206 over par).

★MOST HOLES PLAYED BY FOURBALL TEAMS IN 24 HOURS

In an event organized by PGA Design Consulting Ltd, MBC ESPN and AHA Golf Inc. at Gunsan Country Club, South Korea, 93 fourball teams played 6,974 holes of golf in 24 hours on 28 June 2009.

★OLDEST GOLFER TO WIN A CLUB CHAMPIONSHIP

Tom S Bennett (USA, b. 26 January 1934) won the Valencia Golf and Country Club championship aged 75 years 56 days in Naples, Florida, USA, on 23 March 2009.

★FEWEST STROKES TO COMPLETE A MARATHON DISTANCE

Jake Sand (USA) took 494 strokes to complete the marathon distance of 26 miles 385 yd (42.195 km) playing golf at Desert Mountain Golf Resort, Arizona, USA, on 28 May 2009. Sand averaged a very creditable 93.4 yd (85.4 m) per shot and completed the marathon distance in a time of 9 hr 57 min 25.14 sec.

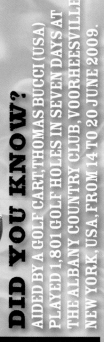

YOUNGEST WINNER ON THE PGA EUROPEAN TOUR

Danny Lee (New Zealand, b. 24 July 1990) was aged just 18 years 213 days when he won the Johnnie Walker Classic at The Vines Resort and Country Club, Perth, Australia, on 22 February 2009.

★LARGEST ONE-DAY GOLF TOURNAMENT

A one-day golf tournament featuring 1,019 participants was held by Golfers512 Fund Raising Campaign (China) at Mission Hills Golf Club in Shenzhen, China, on 12 June 2009.

★MOST 18-HOLE GOLF COURSES PLAYED IN ONE YEAR

Cathie and Jonathan Weaver (both Canada) played a total of 449 different 18-hole golf courses in one year. Their golfing bonanza was staged at a variety of locations across Canada and the USA, from 1 April 2008 to 31 March 2009.

★HIGHEST WINNING US MASTERS SCORE

The highest score recorded by a golfer to win The Masters golf tournament is 289, by three golfers: Sam Snead (USA) in 1954, Jack Burke, Jr (USA) in 1956 and Zach Johnson (USA, far left) in 2007.

DID YOU KNOW?

AIDED BY A GOLF CART, THOMAS BUCCI (USA) PLAYED 1,801 GOLF HOLES IN SEVEN DAYS AT THE ALBANY COUNTRY CLUB, VOORHEESVILLE, NEW YORK, USA, FROM 14 TO 20 JUNE 2009.

The longest golf course in British Open history was Carnoustie, Scotland, which measured 7,421 yd (6,785 m) in 2007.

TRIVIA

SPORTS
ICE HOCKEY

★ EXTRA!
FOR WARMER, MORE
RELAXING PASTIMES,
TRY OUT SOME TOYS &
GAMES ON P.146.

★ **NEW RECORD**
★ **UPDATED RECORD**

★ MOST REGULAR-SEASON GOALS CONCEDED BY A GOALTENDER

Gilles Meloche (Canada) has allowed more regular-season goals in his career than any other NHL goaltender, having conceded 2,756 goals playing for the Chicago Black Hawks, California Golden Seals, Cleveland Barons, Minnesota North Stars and Pittsburgh Penguins (all USA) from the 1970–71 season to 1987–88.

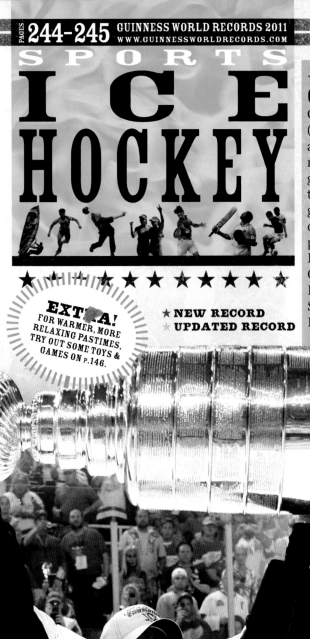

GOALIES

★ MOST MATCHES WON BY AN NHL GOALTENDER

Martin Brodeur is no stranger to these pages, but as the Canadian netminder's career goes on and on, the records just keep tumbling. Brodeur has now recorded 598 regular-season wins in his career playing for the New Jersey Devils (USA) since the 1993–94 season to January 2010.

• Brodeur also holds the NHL record for ★ **most regular-season games played by a goaltender**, having played 1,069 times for the Devils in his career.

• Such career longevity has seen Brodeur take the records for ★ **most regular-season minutes played**, with 63,091, and also the ★ **most regular-season shutouts by a goaltender**, with 108 career clean sheets.

★ MOST STANLEY CUP PLAYOFF GAMES PLAYED BY A GOALTENDER

Retired goaltending great Patrick Roy (Canada) still holds the NHL record for most games played by a goaltender in the Stanley Cup playoffs, having featured in 247 matches playing for the Montreal Canadiens (Canada) and Colorado Rockies (USA) from 1985–86 to 2002–03.

• Having played in so many playoff games for two exceptional teams, it's perhaps no surprise that Roy, dubbed "St Patrick" by fans, holds the NHL record for **most wins by a goaltender in the Stanley Cup playoffs** with 151 career victories.

• Roy is the **only player to have won the Conn Smythe Trophy on three occasions**, in 1986, 1993 and 2001. The prestigious trophy is awarded each year to the Most Valuable Player in the Stanley Cup playoffs.

★ MOST REGULAR SEASON LOSSES BY A GOALTENDER

In a career that stretched from 1989 to 2009, Curtis Joseph (Canada) tied the unfortunate record for most regular-season career losses by an NHL goaltender, which had been set by Lorne "Gump" Worsley (Canada) between 1952 and 1974. Both long-playing netminders have experienced 352 defeats.

Per Olsen (Denmark) hit the **fastest goal**, 2 seconds into a game in the Danish First Division on 14 January 1990.

TRIVIA

★ YOUNGEST CAPTAIN OF A STANLEY CUP-WINNING TEAM

At 21 years 10 months 5 days, Sidney Crosby (Canada, b. 7 August 1987) became the youngest captain of a Stanley Cup-winning team when the Pittsburgh Penguins defeated the Detroit Red Wings (both USA) in the 2009 finals.

NUUK, GREENLAND

64°10'N
51°45'W

The Ameralik Span is the **longest span of an electrical overhead powerline** in the world. It is situated near Nuuk on Greenland and crosses Ameralik fjord with a span width of 5.37 km (3.34 miles).

(Canada), for the New York Islanders against the Boston Bruins (both USA) at Boston, USA, on 22 March 1984; and Alexander Mogilny (Russia), for the Buffalo Sabres (USA) against the Toronto Maple Leafs (Canada) at Toronto, Ontario, Canada, on 21 December 1991.

★FIRST TEAM TO WIN 3,000 REGULAR-SEASON GAMES

The Montreal Canadiens (Canada) beat the Florida Panthers (USA) 5-2 on 29 December 2008 in Sunrise, Florida, USA – their 3,000th regular-season victory. The Canadiens are the first team in NHL history to achieve the feat.

SCORING

FASTEST GOALS SCORED IN AN NHL MATCH

The quickest goals in an NHL match came five seconds after the opening whistle.

ONLY PLAYERS TO SCORE IN THEIR FIRST SIX GAMES

Three players – Joe Malone, Newsy Lalonde and Cy Denneny (all Canada) – each scored in their first six games during the NHL's inaugural season back in 1917–18.

On 1 November 2006, Evgeni Malkin (Russia) became the first NHL player in 89 years to score in his first six games while playing for the Pittsburgh Penguins (USA). His scoring streak began on 18 October 2006.

This record is held jointly by three players. Doug Smail (Canada), for the Winnipeg Jets (Canada) against the St Louis Blues (USA) at Winnipeg, Manitoba, Canada, on 20 December 1981; Bryan John Trottier

★MOST TRADED PLAYERS

Mike Sillinger (right) and Brent Ashton (both Canada) have each been traded (sold to another team) a record nine times during their careers playing in the NHL.

★MOST SHOOTOUT GOALS

As of March 2010, Vyacheslav Kozlov (Russia) has scored 27 NHL ice hockey shootout goals in his career, playing for the Detroit Red Wings, Buffalo Sabres and Atlanta Thrashers, from 1991 to 2010.

★MOST CONSECUTIVE SEASONS SCORING OVER 100 POINTS

The Detroit Red Wings (USA) became the first team in the history of the NHL to top 100 points in 10 straight seasons, from 1999–2000 to 2009–10.

★MOST CONSECUTIVE GAMES IN WHICH AN NHL DEFENCEMAN HAS SCORED

Mike Green (Canada) set a record for defencemen by scoring a goal in eight consecutive games for the Washington Capitals (USA) during the 2008–09 season, his last goal coming in a 5-1 win over the Tampa Bay Lightning (USA) on 14 February 2009.

"Try to just carry a positive attitude and try to be a good teammate every day."

Mike Sillinger on playing for a number of teams (see left)

OLD! THE OLDEST REGULAR ICE HOCKEY PLAYER IS KLAUS SIMON (GERMANY), WHO CURRENTLY PLAYS FOR CLUB OSTERODE (GERMANY) AGED 69.

YOUNG! ON 12 NOVEMBER 1942, AGED 16 YEARS 11 MONTHS, BEP GUIDOLIN (CANADA) BECAME THE YOUNGEST NHL PLAYER WHEN HE PLAYED FOR THE BOSTON BRUINS (USA).

The **shortest married couple** – Douglas Maistre Breger da Silva and Claudia Pereira Rocha (both Brazil) – measured 90 cm (35 in) and 93 cm (36 in) respectively when married on 27 October 1998, in Curitiba, Brazil.

SPORTS
MARATHONS

AMAZING AUSSIE

The ★most wins of the wheelchair event at the New York Marathon by a male athlete is four by Kurt Fearnley (Australia) in 2006–09. Kurt also holds the record for the ★fastest time to complete the London Marathon by a male wheelchair athlete with 1 hr 28 min 57 sec on 26 April 2009.

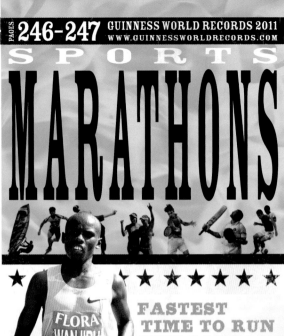

★ NEW RECORD
★ UPDATED RECORD

FASTEST TIME TO RUN THE LONDON MARATHON (MALE)

Kenya's Samuel Wanjiru recorded the fastest time to complete the London Marathon by a male athlete when he finished the 26-mile 385-yard (42.195-km) course, which winds through the streets of London, UK, in 2 hr 5 min 10 sec on 26 April 2009.

★FASTEST MARATHON ON CRUTCHES (ONE LEG)

Simon Baker (UK) completed the fastest marathon on crutches using one leg when he crossed the finish line at the 2008 Dublin City Marathon in Dublin, Ireland, in 6 hr 42 min 47 sec on 27 October 2008.

★FASTEST MARATHON BY A RELAY TEAM

The fastest time in which a relay team has completed a marathon is 2 hr 10 min 50 sec, by the Team Jack & Adam's Bicycles/Zapata Roadrunners (USA), formed by Rueben Ondari, Stephen Ariga, Kibet Cherop, Scott Kimbell and Derek Yorek (Kenya/USA), in the Silicon Laboratories Austin Marathon Relay, at Auditorium Shores in Austin, Texas, USA, on 27 September 2009.

FAST
THE FASTEST TIME TO COMPLETE THE LONDON MARATHON BY A FEMALE WHEELCHAIR ATHLETE IS 1 HR 48 MIN 4 SEC BY SANDRA GRAF (SWITZERLAND) IN 2008.

★FASTEST MARATHON WEARING ARMOUR

On 21 September 2008, Peter Pedersen (Denmark) completed the HC Andersen Marathon in Odense, Denmark, in 6 hr 46 min 59 sec wearing a full suit of armour for the entire run.

★MOST SIBLINGS TO COMPLETE A MARATHON

A total of 16 siblings from the Kapral family – Chris, Vince, Steve, Tony, Joe, Doug, Angela, Allison, Theresa, Phil, Michelle, Mary, Nick, Mike, David and Sarah (all USA) – ran the Community First Fox City Marathon, Appleton, Wisconsin, USA, on 20 September 2009.

DID YOU KNOW?

HAILE GEBRSELASSIE (ETHIOPIA) RAN THE FASTEST MARATHON EVER – IN A TIME OF 2 HR 3 MIN 59 SEC – IN BERLIN, GERMANY, ON 28 SEPTEMBER 2008.

Haile Gebrselassie's marathon world record run had an average speed of 20.4 km/h (12.6 mph).

TRIVIA

BRASÍLIA, BRAZIL

15°48'S 47°54'W

The **widest road** in the world is the Monumental Axis, a 2.4-km-long (1.8-mile), six-lane boulevard in Brasília, the capital of Brazil. The road, which was opened in April 1960, is 250 m (820 ft 2 in) wide.

VIRGIN LONDON MARATHON 2010

On 25 April 2010, an incredible 36,549 runners completed the Virgin London Marathon (UK), a record for this great city marathon, which was celebrating its 30th anniversary. Once again Guinness World Records was proud to be involved, with 75 runners competing in 27 record categories and an astounding 19 new Guinness World Records awarded on the day. Well done everyone!

LONDON MARATHON RECORDS

	RECORD TITLE	RECORD RESULT & RUNNER		RECORD TITLE	RECORD RESULT & RUNNER		RECORD TITLE	RECORD RESULT & RUNNER
	★Fastest marathon carrying a 60-lb pack	5 hr 28 min 53 sec by Benjamin Harrop (UK)		★Fastest marathon in a fireman's uniform	5 hr 32 min 55 sec by Nigel Addison-Evans (UK)		★Fastest marathon in school uniform (female)	4 hr 14 min 46 sec by Louise Winstanley (UK)
	★Fastest marathon in an animal costume (male)	3 hr 30 min 10 sec by Kevin Robins (UK) dressed as a tiger		★Fastest marathon dressed as a golfer (male)	3 hr 43 min 20 sec by Bertrand Bodson (Belgium)		★Fastest marathon in a superhero costume (female)	3 hr 8 min 55 sec by Jill Christie (UK)
	★Fastest marathon dressed as a baby	3 hr 13 min 30 sec by Tony Audenshaw (UK)		★Fastest marathon dressed as a jester	3 hr 33 min 55 sec by David Smith (UK)		★Fastest marathon dressed as a television character (male)	4 hr 1 min 40 sec by Paul Franks (UK) dressed as a dalek
	★Fastest marathon dressed as a bottle (female)	4 hr 54 min 36 sec by Gill Begnor (UK)		★Fastest marathon dressed as a leprechaun	3 hr 9 min 40 sec by Ben Afforselles (UK)	See picture, right	★Tallest costume worn running in a marathon	7.04 m (23 ft 1 in) by Jean Paul Delacy (UK)
	★Longest crochet chain whilst running a marathon	77.4 m (253 ft) by Susie Hewer (UK)		★Fastest marathon in a martial arts suit	3 hr 39 min 20 sec by Peter Kelly (UK)		★Fastest marathon dressed as a cartoon character	3 hr 7 min 34 sec by David Ross (UK) dressed as Fred Flintstone
	★Fastest marathon dressed as a doctor (male)	4 hr 21 min 9 sec by Tom Solomon (UK)		★Fastest marathon in a nurse's uniform (male)	3 hr 46 min 27 sec by Andrew White (UK)		★Fastest marathon dressed as a book character	4 hr 1 min 47 sec by Ian Young (UK) dressed as Sherlock Holmes

TEAM CATERPILLAR

The ★**most runners linked to complete a marathon** is 34, by Team Caterpillar at the Virgin London Marathon, London, UK, on 25 April 2010. The team, organized by Phil Nevin (UK), included Princess Beatrice (UK), the first royal to run the London Marathon, and Virgin boss Richard Branson (UK) and finished in a time of 5 hr 13 m 3 sec.

SPORTS
NBA JAM

★LARGEST SPORTS TRADING CARD

At the NBA All-Star Jam Session in Dallas, Texas, USA, on 13 February 2010, a sports trading card measuring 151 x 213 cm (59.75 x 84 in) was unveiled by Panini (USA). The colossal card featured LA Lakers star Kobe Bryant (USA).

★MOST POINTS SCORED AS KOBE BRYANT ON THE NBA 2K10 VIDEOGAME

At the NBA All-Star Jam Session, fans and players get the chance to show off their skills on the latest NBA videogame. On 13 February 2010, Chico Kora (USA) scored 29 points playing as Kobe Bryant on 2K Sports *NBA 2K10* (playing a four-minute game, with one minute per quarter).

Several other videogame records were set at the NBA All-Star Jam Session.

The ★**most steals on 2K Sports NBA 2K10 (playing a four-minute game, with one minute per quarter)** is seven by Wesley Parker (USA), on 10 February 2010.

The ★**most assists**, within the same parameters, is 16 by Andrew Frost and J R Wildly (both USA), on 11 February 2010.

★MOST FREE THROWS MADE IN TWO MINUTES WHILE ALTERNATING HANDS

Jeff Harris (USA) made 44 basketball free throws in two minutes using alternate hands at the NBA All-Star Jam Session in Dallas, Texas, USA, on 10 February 2010.

The ★**most points scored in the first half of a 2K Sports NBA 2K10 videogame**, within the same parameters, is 17 by Cody Redrick and Brandon McJunlain (both USA), on 12 February 2010.

HIGHEST SLAM DUNK WITH A BACKFLIP

Jerry Burrell (USA) made a slam dunk having performed a backflip from a 4.67-m-tall (15-ft 4-in) platform. Burrell achieved the feat during the NBA All-Star Jam Session in Phoenix, Arizona, USA, on 16 February 2009.

ALL THE RECORD FOR THE MOST CONSECUTIVE ALL-STAR GAME SELECTIONS IS 14, JOINTLY HELD BY SHAQUILLE O'NEAL, JERRY WEST AND KARL MALONE (ALL USA).

★FARTHEST SHOT MADE WHILE SITTING ON COURT

Orlando Magic (USA) centre Dwight Howard (USA) made a shot measured at 15.99 m (52 ft 6 in) while sitting on the court at the NBA All-Star Jam Session in Dallas, Texas, USA, on 13 February 2010.

STAR MICHAEL JORDAN (USA) SCORED 262 POINTS IN NBA ALL-STAR GAMES, INCLUDING 20 POINTS IN HIS 14TH AND FINAL GAME IN ATLANTA, GEORGIA, USA, ON 9 FEBRUARY 2003.

DID YOU KNOW?

THE ★FARTHEST SIX-PERSON TANDEM BEFORE A DUNK USING A TRAMPOLINE IS 6 M (20 FT) AND WAS ACHIEVED BY TEAM ACRODUNK (USA).

The **most consecutive three-pointers scored** on *NBA 2K9* is eight by Marcus Platt (USA).

TRIVIA

SANTOS, BRAZIL

23°58'S 46°20'W

The **tallest cemetery** is the Memorial Necrópole Ecumônica in Santos, near São Paulo, Brazil. The cemetery is 10 storeys high and occupies an area of 1.8 ha (4.4 acres). Its first burial was on 28 July 1984.

★ FARTHEST HOOK SHOT

Special K Daley (USA) of the Harlem Globetrotters recorded a hook shot measured at 14.15 m (46 ft 6 in) at the NBA All-Star Jam Session, Dallas, Texas, USA, on 13 February 2010.

108,713

★ LARGEST ATTENDANCE FOR A BASKETBALL GAME

The NBA All-Star Game played at Cowboys Stadium in Arlington, Texas, USA, on 14 February 2010 was watched by 108,713 fans, the largest ever basketball crowd. The game saw the East beat the West 141–139.

Baker achieved the record by spinning one ball on top of the other.

At the same event, Baker also performed the **most headers while spinning two basketballs**, with 40 bounces of the ball on his forehead.

LONGEST TIME SPINNING TWO BASKETBALLS USING ONE HAND

During the NBA All-Star Jam Session held in Phoenix, Arizona, USA, on 14 February 2009, professional basketball freestyler Tommy Baker (UK) spun two basketballs using one hand for 32.88 seconds.

LONGEST TIME SPINNING A BASKETBALL ON ONE TOE

Jack Ryan (USA) spun a basketball on his toe for 9.53 seconds at the NBA All-Star Jam Session in New Orleans, Louisiana, USA, on 13 February 2008.

LONGEST TIME SPINNING A BASKETBALL ON ONE FINGER

Joseph Odhiambo (USA) spun a basketball continuously for 4 hr 15 min on 19 February 2006 in Houston, Texas, USA.

MOST FREE THROWS

At the NBA All-Star Jam Session in New Orleans, Louisiana, USA, on 16 February 2008, Becky Hammon of the San Antonio Silver Stars (both USA) made the **most free throws in one minute by a female player**: 38.

At the same event three days earlier, NBA Hall of Famer Rick Barry (USA) had recorded the **most underhanded free throws in one minute**: 24. National Wheelchair

Basketball Association (NWBA) player Jeff Griffin (USA) scored the **most consecutive free throws from a wheelchair**, with three successful throws in a row, on 12 February 2009 at the NBA All-Star Jam Session in Phoenix, Arizona, USA.

MOST THREE-POINTERS IN TWO MINUTES

On 17 February 2008, Jason Kapono (USA) of the Toronto Raptors (Canada) scored 43 three-pointers in two minutes at the NBA All-Star Jam Session in New Orleans, Louisiana, USA.

★ LONGEST TIME SPINNING A BASKETBALL ON THE NOSE

Harlem Globetrotter Scooter Christensen (USA) kept a ball spinning on his nose for 5.1 seconds during the NBA All-Star Jam Session in Dallas, Texas, USA, on 13 February 2010.

MOST UNDERHANDED HALF-COURT SHOTS IN ONE MINUTE

Only two people have achieved two underhanded half-court shots in one minute: Jason Kidd (USA) of the Dallas Mavericks (USA) and Bucket Blades (USA, pictured) of the Harlem Globetrotters. Kidd set the record during the NBA All-Star Jam Session in New Orleans, Louisiana, USA, on 16 February 2008 and Blades equalled it during the NBA All-Star Jam Session in Dallas, Texas, USA, on 13 February 2010.

EXTRA! FOR MORE ALL-COURT ACTION, TRACK BACK TO THE BASKETBALL SPREAD ON PP.230–231.

★ NEW RECORD
★ UPDATED RECORD

RIO DE JANEIRO, BRAZIL
Rio de Janeiro's annual carnival, normally held during the first week of March, is the **largest carnival** in the world, attracting approximately 2 million people each day.

22°54'S
43°14'W

SPORTS
RUGBY

EXTRA!
FOR GENERAL
BALL SPORTS
RECORDS, TURN
TO PP.226-227.

★MOST CONSECUTIVE SUPER LEAGUE TITLES

Leeds Rhinos (UK) achieved a record three consecutive rugby league Super League titles between 2007 and 2009. On each occasion, the Rhinos defeated St Helens (UK) in the final of the competition.

RUGBY LEAGUE

★MOST POINTS SCORED IN A SUPER LEAGUE MATCH

Playing for Leeds Rhinos against Huddersfield Giants (both UK) in a Super League match on 16 July 1999, Iestyn Harris (UK) scored an incredible 42 points, the most by an individual in a Super League match.

★MOST TRIES SCORED IN A SUPER LEAGUE CAREER

With 169 touchdowns, Keith Senior (UK) has scored more tries in Super League matches than any other player, playing between 1996 and 2009 for Sheffield Eagles and Leeds Rhinos (both UK).

★MOST TRIES IN A SUPER LEAGUE SEASON

Lesley Vainikolo (New Zealand) scored 36 tries playing for Bradford in the Super League in 2004.

★MOST WINS OF THE STATE OF ORIGIN SERIES

The State of Origin series, a yearly three-match rugby league competition between the Australian states of Queensland and New South Wales has been won by Queensland on a record 18 occasions since 1980.

★MOST SIBLINGS TO PLAY IN AN INTERNATIONAL MATCH

Four brothers – Kristian, Markus, Nick and James Keinhorst (all Germany) – represented Germany against the Czech Republic in the European Rugby League Shield Competition in Prague, Czech Republic, on 4 August 2007.

★MOST POINTS SCORED IN A NATIONAL RUGBY LEAGUE CAREER

In a 13-year career (1996 to 2009) playing for the Canterbury Bulldogs (New Zealand), Hazem El Masri (Lebanon) has scored 2,418 points playing in National Rugby League matches, the greatest number of points scored by an individual player in the history of the competition. Masri also holds the record for **most points scored by an individual player in a National Rugby League season**, with 342.

MOST TRI-NATIONS/FOUR NATIONS TITLES

The Rugby League Tri-Nations was won a record three times by Australia, in 1999, 2004 and 2006. In 2009, the Rugby League Four Nations replaced the Tri-Nations, with Australia once again running out victors.

OLD! THE OLDEST PLAYER TO REPRESENT THE BRITISH & IRISH LIONS IN A TEST MATCH IS NEIL BACK (UK). HE WAS 36 YEARS AND 160 DAYS OLD AT THE TIME.

YOUNG! NINIAN JAMIESON FINLAY (1858–1936) AND CHARLES REID (1864–1909) WERE BOTH 17 YEARS 36 DAYS OLD WHEN THEY DEBUTED FOR SCOTLAND.

TRY: In rugby's early days, crossing the goal line with the ball was known as "running in"; the ball was then kicked back to another player, who could "try" to score a goal. The word "try" was first used in the laws of rugby in 1877.

★YOUNGEST REFEREE

Harry Goodhew (UK, b. 10 April 1997) became the youngest Rugby Union referee when he refereed two U12s matches at Dulwich College, London, UK, on 30 November 2008 aged 11 years 234 days. Harry completed the RFU Entry Level Referee Award Stages 1 and 2 on 7 September 2008.

★MOST POINTS IN A FIVE AND SIX NATIONS CHAMPIONSHIP CAREER

Jonny Wilkinson (UK) scored 529 points in Five and Six Nations matches between 1998 and 2010.

★MOST POINTS IN A TRI-NATIONS CAREER

Dan Carter (New Zealand) scored 363 points playing for the All Blacks in Tri-Nations matches between 2003 and 2009.

★HIGHEST ATTENDANCE FOR A GUINNESS PREMIERSHIP MATCH

The largest paying attendance for a single Guinness Premiership regular season match to date is 76,716 for Harlequins versus London Wasps at Twickenham Stadium, London, UK, on 27 December 2009. Harlequins usually play their home games at Twickenham Stoop, London, UK, which has a rather more modest seating capacity of 14,816.

RUGBY UNION

★MOST APPEARANCES IN A SUPER RUGBY CAREER

Sean Hardman (Australia) made 137 appearances in Super Rugby matches playing for the Queensland Reds between 1999 and 2009.

★HIGHEST SCORE IN A SUPER RUGBY MATCH (TEAM)

In defeating the Waratahs (Australia) by 96 points to 16 at Jade Stadium, Christchurch, New Zealand, on 11 May 2009, the Crusaders (New Zealand) recorded the highest team score in a Super Rugby game.

★MOST CAPS WON AS CAPTAIN

John Smit (South Africa) was awarded a total of 67 caps as captain of his national team. He won his caps playing between 2003 and 2009.

★MOST DROP GOALS SCORED IN AN INTERNATIONAL MATCH (INDIVIDUAL)

Jannie de Beer (South Africa) scored five drop goals playing for South Africa against England in the 1999 IRB World Cup Quarter Finals at Stade de France, Paris, France, on 24 October 1999. The Springboks won the game 44-21.

★MOST DROP GOALS SCORED IN AN INTERNATIONAL CAREER (INDIVIDUAL)

Jonny Wilkinson (UK) scored 33 drop goals playing for England and the British & Irish Lions, between 1998 and 2010. He won the 2003 World Cup for England against Australia with a drop goal in extra time.

MOST BRITISH & IRISH LIONS TESTS WITHOUT A WIN

The lengthiest winless streak played by the British & Irish Lions lasted for eight tests, between 2001 and 2009. The run was finally brought to an end by the Lions' 28-9 victory against South Africa in Johannesburg on 4 July 2009.

★ NEW RECORD
UPDATED RECORD

DID YOU KNOW?

THE MOST RUGBY CONVERSIONS SCORED IN ONE HOUR IS 408. THE RECORD WAS ACHIEVED BY THAT TO HEATH CRUSADERS UNDER 12s IN ST HELENS, UK, ON 17 MAY 2009, AT AN EVENT IN AID OF THE TEENAGE CANCER TRUST.

TRIVIA

In 1886, the first point-scoring system was introduced in Rugby Union. In those days, a goal = 3 points and a try = 1 point.

DAKAR, SENEGAL
14°41'N
17°26'W

Ari Vatanen (Finland) has won the Dakar Rally four times, first in 1987 and then on three more occasions from 1989 to 1991 inclusively – the **most Dakar Rally wins**.

SPORT
TARGET SPORTS

★ ★ ★ ★ ★ ★ ★ ★ ★ ★ ★ ★ ★

ARCHERY

★ LARGEST ARCHERY TOURNAMENT

On 22 August 2009, 332 participants took part in an archery contest in Xinbaerhuyou County, Inner Mongolia Autonomous Region, China. The event was organized by the Archery Association of Xinbaerhuyou County.

★ MOST POINTS IN A FITA ROUND OUTDOOR COMPOUND (FEMALE)

Jamie Van Natta (USA) scored 1,412 points from a possible 1,440 in a single International Archery Federation (FITA) round outdoor compound at East Lansing, Michigan, USA, on 21 September 2007.

MOST BULL'S-EYES IN 90 SECONDS

The speed-shooting record for the greatest number of bull's-eyes shot in 90 seconds is three and was set by Jeremie Masson (France) on 15 July 2004. The archer was standing at a distance of 18 m (59 ft) from the targets.

★ MOST LIGHT-BULBS HIT IN THREE MINUTES

Using recurve bows, Marco Vitale and Oscar De Pellegrin (both Italy) shot a total of 11 light-bulbs in three minutes on the set of *Lo Show Dei Record* in Milan, Italy, on 19 April 2009.

DARTS

★ MOST WORLD CHAMPIONSHIP TITLES

The greatest number of World Championship titles won to date is 15 by Phil Taylor (UK), with the World Darts Organization (WDO) in 1990 and 1992, and the Professional Darts Corporation (PDC) in 1995–2002, 2004–06 and 2009–10.

★ MOST WORLD MATCHPLAY TITLES

Phil Taylor (UK) has won 10 World Matchplay darts titles, in 1995, 1997, 2000–04, 2006 and 2008–09.

147! THE YOUNGEST SNOOKER PLAYER TO SCORE A COMPETITIVE MAXIMUM WAS RONNIE O'SULLIVAN (UK), AGED 15 YEARS 98 DAYS, AT ALDERSHOT, UK, ON 13 MARCH 1991.

★ LARGEST ELECTRONIC DARTS TOURNAMENT

The XVIII Campeonato Nacional de Dardos Electrónicos at Benidorm, Alicante, Spain, from 6 to 9 March 2008, had 8,209 players. It was organized by Federación Española de Dardos Electrónicos (FEDE).

★ MOST PRIZE MONEY WON

Phil Taylor (UK) won £200,000 ($327,590) when he took the 2010 Professional Darts Corporation (PDC) World Championship at Alexandra Palace, London, UK, on 3 January 2010.

POOL

MOST WORLD TITLES

Ralph Greenleaf (USA) won the world professional pool title a record 19 times between 1919 and 1937.

WEBER CUP:
Tenpin bowling's "Ryder Cup": Bowlers from the USA and Europe compete against each other over three days.

The **most Weber Cup** wins is six, by the USA, in 2000–02 and 2006–08. (The USA's Tommy Jones is pictured in 2008.) The ★**widest margin of victory** in the contest is seven points and occurred twice: in 2000, when the USA beat Europe 18-11 in Warsaw, Poland; and in 2004, when the USA beat Europe 18-11 in Manchester, UK.

MOST WORLD CHAMPIONSHIPS

Earl Strickland (USA) has won a total of three pool World Championships, in 1990–91 and 2002.

YOUNGEST WORLD CHAMPIONSHIP WINNER

The youngest player to win a pool World Championship is Chia-ching Wu (Taiwan, b. 9 February 1989). He was aged 16 years 121 days when he won the title at Kaohsiung, Taiwan, on 10 June 2005.

★ MOST 147 BREAKS IN SNOOKER WORLD CHAMPIONSHIP MATCHES

Ronnie O'Sullivan (UK) has made three maximum (147) breaks in snooker World Championships, the most by any player. His record-breaking scores came at the Crucible Theatre, Sheffield, UK, in 1997, 2003 and 2008.

DID YOU KNOW?
IN 1366, KING EDWARD III OF ENGLAND BANNED HIS TROOPS FROM BOWLING BECAUSE IT STOPPED THEM FROM PRACTISING THEIR ARCHERY!

In 1841, ninepin bowling was banned in Connecticut, USA, as it was encouraging gambling. To beat the ban, bowlers added another pin. Tenpin bowling was born.

TRIVIA

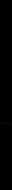
NEW RECORD
UPDATED RECORD

FASTEST MAXIMUM BREAK

The speediest 147 in a professional tournament took 5 min 20 sec, and was achieved by Ronnie O'Sullivan (UK) during the World Championships at Sheffield, UK, on 21 April 1997.

LONGEST UNBEATEN RUN

From 17 March 1990 to his defeat on 13 January 1991 by Jimmy White (UK), Stephen Hendry (UK) won five successive titles and 36 consecutive matches in ranking tournaments.

★ MOST POINTS IN A FITA ROUND OUTDOOR COMPOUND (MALE)

Peter Elzinga (Netherlands) scored 1,419 points from a possible 1,440 in an International Archery Federation (FITA) round outdoor compound at Almere, the Netherlands, on 17 May 2009.

MOSCONI CUP

The Mosconi Cup is a nine-ball pool tournament fought every year between two teams from the USA and Europe. Earl Strickland (USA) shares the record for the ★most appearances in the Mosconi

Cup for the USA, having played 13 times from 1996 to 2008. Johnny Archer (USA) also appeared 13 times, in 1997–2009.

The ★most wins of the Mosconi Cup by a team is 12, by the USA. They were victorious in 1994, 1996–2001, 2003–06 and 2009.

SNOOKER

★ LONGEST FRAME IN A PROFESSIONAL SNOOKER MATCH

A frame lasting 93 min 12 sec took place in a first-round match between Shaun Murphy and Dave Harold (both UK) at the 2008 China Open, Beijing Student University Stadium, Beijing, China, on 24 March 2008.

SNOOKER WORLD CHAMPIONSHIP

The ★longest frame in a World Championship match lasted 75 minutes exactly. It was the second frame of a last 16 match between Stephen Maguire and Mark King (both UK) at the Crucible in Sheffield, UK, on 26 April 2009.

The ★greatest number of appearances at the snooker World Championship by an individual player is 29, by Steve Davis (UK) from 1979 to 2009.

★ MOST CENTURY BREAKS

Stephen Hendry (UK) recorded 740 breaks of 100 or more during his professional snooker career between 1985 and 2009.

TENPIN BOWLING

★ MOST PBA TITLES

The greatest number of Professional Bowlers Association (PBA) tenpin bowling titles won by an individual is 46 and was achieved by Walter Ray Williams, Jr (USA) between 8 March 1986 and 5 September 2009.

HIGH EARNERS

The ★most money won by an individual bowler in their rookie PBA season is $84,811 (£52,697) by Rhino Page (USA) in 2008.

★ MOST MOSCONI CUP APPEARANCES FOR EUROPE

Ralf Souquet (Germany) appeared in pool's Mosconi Cup playing for Europe a record 15 times. Souquet's appearances came in tournaments staged between 1994 and 2009.

The ★most money won by an individual bowler in a PBA season is $419,700 (£260,784) by Walter Ray Williams, Jr (USA) in 2002–03.

The ★most money earned in a PBA career is $3,960,702 (£2,467,722), also by Walter Ray Williams, Jr, between 1980 and 2009.

EXTRA! FOR BALL SPORTS OF ALL SORTS, GET YOUR KICKS ON P.226.

★ MOST WINS OF DARTS WORLD GRANDS PRIX

The greatest number of World Grands Prix titles won by an individual darts player is nine by Phil Taylor (UK), in 1998–2000, 2002–03, 2005–06 and 2008–09.

PORTO, PORTUGAL
The **largest patchwork quilt** measured 25,100 m² (270,174 ft²). The project was carried out by Realizar – Eventos Especiais, Lda of Parque da Cidade, Porto, Portugal, and completed on 18 June 2000.

SPORTS
TENNIS & RACKET SPORTS

★ NEW RECORD
★ UPDATED RECORD

TENNIS

★ MOST ACES SERVED IN A DAVIS CUP MATCH

Ivo Karlovic (Croatia) served 78 aces against Radek Stepanek (Czech Republic) in the semi-final of the Davis Cup, held at Porec, Croatia, on 18 September 2009. Sadly, Karlovic's serving power was not enough to grant him victory – he lost the match 7-6, 6-7, 6-7, 7-6, 14-16.

★ MOST CONSECUTIVE GRAND SLAM TOURNAMENTS PLAYED

From her first appearance at Wimbledon on 20 June 1994 to her first match at the 2009 US Open on 31 August 2009, Ai Sugiyama (Japan) played 62 consecutive Grand Slam tournaments.

★ LARGEST SINGLE-DAY ATTENDANCE AT WIMBLEDON

A total of 45,955 people watched the second day of the Wimbledon tournament, at London, UK, on 23 June 2009.

MOST TENNIS CLUB CHAMPIONSHIPS (MALE)

Stuart Foster (UK) has secured 55 championships at Leverstock Green Lawn Tennis Club in Hemel Hempstead, Hertfordshire, UK, from 1985 to 2009.

Stuart also holds the record for the ★ **most tennis club men's doubles championships with multiple partners**, with 24 titles won from 1985 to 2009 at the same club.

★ HIGHEST EARNINGS IN A SEASON (FEMALE)

Serena Williams (USA) earned a whopping $6,545,586 (£4,185,692) in 2009. This is just a small chunk of the $30,491,460 (£19,498,312) she earned in her career between 1997 and 2009. While this gives her the record for the ★ **highest earnings in a professional career (female)**, her wealth is a fraction of the $55,350,788 (£36,864,300) Roger Federer (Switzerland) won between 1998 and 2010 – the ★ **highest earnings in a tennis career (male)**.

★ TALLEST GRAND SLAM WINNER

Juan Martín Del Potro (Argentina) measured 198 cm (6 ft 6 in) when he won the 2009 US Open in Flushing Meadows, New York City, USA, on 14 September 2009.

DID YOU KNOW?

ALTHOUGH PLAGUED BY INJURY, MARIA SHARAPOVA (RUSSIA) REMAINS THE HIGHEST ANNUAL EARNING FEMALE IN TENNIS – SHE MADE $22 MILLION IN 2008-09!

The goal for top tennis players is to get a "Grand Slam" – victories in all four Majors (see p.219). An even harder feat is to win all four in one year!

TRIVIA

EXTRA! FOR MORE OF ROGER FEDERER'S TENNIS RECORDS, TURN TO PP.218-219.

★ MOST GAMES IN A WIMBLEDON FINAL

The Wimbledon final held on 5 July 2009 was a particularly punishing affair, with Andy Roddick (USA) forcing Roger Federer (Switzerland) to play 77 games before the Swiss tennis legend finally claimed a 5-7, 7-6, 7-6, 3-6, 16-14 victory.

CORK, IRELAND

51°53'N 8°28'W

The **largest attendance at a hurling match** was 84,865 for the All-Ireland final between Cork and Wexford at Croke Park, Dublin, Ireland, in 1954.

THE BODY-SLAMMING BRYANS

Twins Bob and Mike Bryan (both USA, aka "the Bryans") scored the ★most wins of the International Tennis Federation Men's Doubles World Championship by the same pair with six, in 2003–07 and 2009.

RACQUET-BALL

★MOST MEN'S TEAM WINS AT THE WORLD RACQUETBALL CHAMPIONSHIPS

Instituted in 1984 and based on the US game of racquetball, the World Racquetball Championships has been won a total of eight times by the US men's team, between 1984 and 2008.

The achievements of the men's team pale in comparison to those of the US women's team, however, which has won the competition on 13 occasions, the record for the ★most women's team wins at the World Racquetball Championships.

TABLE TENNIS

★MOST MEN'S TEAM EUROPEAN TABLE TENNIS CHAMPIONSHIPS

Sweden's table tennis team won a total of 14 European Table Tennis Championship team titles between 1964 and 2002.

BADMINTON WORLD CHAMPIONSHIPS

In the struggle for the ★most Badminton World Championships men's singles titles, Lin Dan (China) takes the honours, with wins in 2006, 2007 and 2009. His latest victory saw Lin finally take the record from his fellow countryman, Yang Yang.

BADMINTON

★MOST WORLD TEAM BADMINTON CHAMPIONSHIP APPEARANCES

The men's team from Denmark has put in 25 appearances at the final stage of the World Team Badminton Championships, otherwise known as the Thomas Cup, between 1949 and 2008.

★LONGEST BADMINTON DOUBLES MARATHON

Dedicated sportsmen Joost Berkelmans, Rick Blok, Thijs Maassen and Steven van Puffelen (all Netherlands) played an extended doubles badminton marathon lasting 27 hours at De Toekomstgroep badminton sports hall, Almere, the Netherlands, from 27 to 28 February 2009.

POWER PLAYER

Squash maestro Jonathon Power (Canada) claimed the record for the ★most wins of the Professional Squash Association Masters singles tournament with a total of three victories, in 2001–02 and 2005. Shortly after his last win, Jonathon announced his retirement from the sport.

OUT! ALTHOUGH HE WAS THE FIRST MAN TO WIN A GRAND SLAM (ALL FOUR MAJORS), FRED PERRY (UK) NEVER MANAGED THE FEAT IN A SINGLE YEAR.

IN! AUSTRALIAN ROD LAVER WAS THE FIRST MAN TO WIN TWO SINGLE-SEASON GRAND SLAMS, FIRST AS AN AMATEUR IN 1962, AND THEN AS A PRO IN 1969.

SPORTS
WACKY WORLD CHAMPIONSHIPS

★ NEW RECORD
☆ UPDATED RECORD

FASTEST SNAIL

The annual World Snail Racing Championships is held in July outside St Andrews Church in Congham, Norfolk, UK. Races are conducted on a 33-cm (13-in) circular course, on which the snails race from the centre to the perimeter. The all-time record holder is a snail named Archie, trained by Carl Bramham (UK), who "sprinted" to the winning post in 2 min 20 sec in 1995.

OLDEST SHIN-KICKING CHAMPIONSHIPS

Competitive shin-kicking is known to have been taking place since 1636 as part of Robert Dover's Cotswold Olimpicks, held in England since 1612. These Olimpicks were hosted continually until 1644, then again from 1660 to 1852, revived in 1951 and then held annually from 1965. Competitors must wear soft shoes and can protect their shins with straw.

FIRST REDNECK GAMES

In 1996, radio DJ Mac Davis (USA) of station Y-96 of East Dublin, Georgia, USA, conceived the Redneck Games as an antidote to that year's Olympic Games in nearby Atlanta. "The media kept saying that the Olympics were going to be run by a bunch of rednecks," said Davis, "so we figured if that's what the world expects, we'll give it to them." The Games feature events such as the cigarette flip, bobbing for pig's trotters and the mud-pit belly-flop.

LARGEST AUDIENCE AT A CAMEL WRESTLING FESTIVAL

At the 1994 Camel Wrestling Festival, a crowd of 20,000 people watched 120 dromedaries wrestle in a 2,000-year-old stadium in the city of Ephesus in Selçuk, Turkey.

☆ MOST WORMS CHARMED

Sophie Smith (UK) charmed a record 567 worms in 30 minutes from a 3-m² (9.84-ft²) plot at the 2009 World Worm Charming Championships, held in Willaston, Cheshire, UK, on 27 June 2009.

MOST ELEPHANT POLO WORLD CHAMPIONSHIPS

The Tiger Top Tuskers team (Nepal) have won the World Elephant Polo Association Championships in Nepal on eight occasions, in 1983–85, 1987, 1992, 1998, 2000 and 2003.

SPLASH!
IN THE MUD-PIT BELLY-FLOP AT THE REDNECK GAMES, POINTS ARE AWARDED FOR BEAUTY OF FORM AND THE SIZE OF THE SPLASH.

CRUSH!
WINNERS OF EVENTS AT THE REDNECK GAMES WIN A HIGHLY COVETED TROPHY – A HALF-CRUSHED, EMPTY, MOUNTED BEER CAN!

MOST TIDDLY-WINKS TITLES

Larry Khan (USA) won 19 singles titles at the Tiddlywinks World Championships between 1983 and 2003. He also won 10 pairs titles between 1978 and 1998.

(UK) in 1971–73, Mike Fordham (UK) in 1983–85 and David Hollis (UK) in 1999–2001. Hollis was also the **youngest World Pea Shooting champion** when he took the title in 1999 aged 13 years old.

FASTEST WIFE CARRYING

Margo Uusarj and Sandra Kullas (both Estonia) completed the 253.5-m (831-ft 8-in) obstacle course at the World Wife-Carrying Championships, held annually in Sonkajärvi, Finland, in 56.9 seconds on 1 July 2006. This is the fastest time achieved since the rule for a minimum wife weight of 49 kg (108 lb) was introduced in 2002.

★MOST HORSESHOE PITCHING WORLD CHAMPIONSHIPS (MALE)

Alan Francis (USA) has won a record 15 Horseshoe Pitching

World Championships in the Men's category, in 1989, 1993, 1995–99, 2001 and 2003–09. Historically the championships have been played at irregular intervals since their inception in 1909.

MOST CONSECUTIVE WORLD PEA SHOOTING CHAMPIONSHIPS

Three people have won the World Pea Shooting Championships, held annually in Witcham, Cambridgeshire, UK, on three consecutive occasions: Dennis Minett

★MOST WINS OF THE SAUNA WORLD CHAMPIONSHIPS

The Sauna World Championships is held in Heinola, Finland, each year. The title is awarded to the person who stays in the sauna for the longest time. Timo Kaukonen (Finland) has won the event five times, in 2003, 2005–07 and 2009.

MOST WORLD CONKER CHAMPIONSHIPS WON (MALE)

Two men have won the World Conker Championship in Ashton, Northamptonshire, UK, on three occasions: P Midlane (UK) in 1969, 1973 and 1985 and J Marsh (UK) in 1974, 1975 and 1994.

QUIZ!
WHAT NUMBER DO YOU GET IF YOU ADD TOGETHER THE MOST WORMS CHARMED AND THE MOST HORSESHOE PITCHING TITLES WON?
SEE P.278 FOR THE ANSWER.

SEE P.278 FOR THE ANSWER.

DID YOU KNOW?

DAVID JONES (UK) CARRIED A RECORD 50-KG (110-LB) BAG OF COAL OVER A 1,012.5-M (3,321-FT 9-IN) COURSE IN 4 MIN 6 SEC AT THE COAL CARRYING CHAMPIONSHIP RACE AT GAWTHORPE, UK, ON 1 APRIL 1991.

In tiddlywinks, the large disc, which is used to flip the smaller discs into the air, is called a "squidger".

TRIVIA

SPORT STACKING

Sport stacking involves stacking plastic cups in specific sequences in the fastest time possible. The current master of sport stacking is Steven Purugganan (USA), who holds many world records including:

• The ★**fastest sport stacking individual cycle stack**, in 5.93 seconds on 3 January 2009.

• On 19 April 2009 at the WSSA World Sport Stacking Championships in Denver, Colorado, USA, Team USA (comprising Purugganan along with Joel Brown, Luke Myers and Alex Schumann, all USA) completed the ★**fastest sport stacking 3-6-3 timed relay** in 12.72 seconds.

• At the same event, Steven Purugganan and his brother Andrew Purugganan (USA) completed the ★**fastest sport stacking doubles cycle stack** in 7.58 seconds.

SPORTS

WATER-SPORTS

★ ★ ★ ★ ★ ★ ★ ★ ★ ★ ★ ★ ★ ★

DIVING

★ MOST GOLD MEDALS WON AT A SINGLE EUROPEAN CHAMPIONSHIP

Tania Cagnotto (Italy) won an impressive three golds at the 2009 European Diving Championships in Turin, Italy, on 5 April 2009.

★ MOST WORLD CHAMPIONSHIPS

Jingjing Guo (China) won a grand total of 10 FINA diving world titles, in the women's 3 m springboard, individual and synchronized categories in 2001, 2003, 2005, 2007 and 2009.

CANOEING

★ OLDEST OLYMPIC MEDALLIST (FEMALE)

Josefa Idem (Italy, b. 23 September 1964) was aged 43 years 335 days when she won silver in the K1 class 500 m flatwater event at the 2008 Olympic Games in Beijing, China, on 23 August 2008.

GREATEST DISTANCE ON FLOWING WATER IN 24 HOURS

Ian Adamson (USA) paddled 421 km (261.6 miles) down the Yukon River, Canada, from 20 to 21 June 2004.

★ FASTEST LONG COURSE 100 M FREESTYLE (MALE)

Brazilian Cesar Cielo Filho completed the 100 m freestyle event in 46.91 seconds on 30 July 2009 at the Fédération Internationale de Natation (FINA) World Championships in Rome, Italy. The event was the last before FINA's new guidelines on swimsuits came into effect in January 2010.

FASTEST LONG COURSE 100 M BACKSTROKE (FEMALE)

Gemma Spofforth (UK) claimed her first World Championship title, and a world record into the bargain, with her 58.12-second swim in Rome, Italy, on 28 July 2009.

SCUBA DIVING

★ LONGEST DIVE IN AN ENCLOSED ENVIRONMENT

Cem Karabay (Turkey) spent 135 hr 2 min 19 sec inside a water tank, breathing via scuba equipment, at the Beylikduzu Migros Shopping Mall in Istanbul, Turkey, from 30 August to 5 September 2009.

SWIMMING

The Marathon Swimming World Cup was an endurance swimming event organized by FINA and held between 1993 and 2006. Petar Stoychev (Bulgaria) holds the record for the ★ **most men's Marathon Swimming World Cups**, with six wins from 2001 to 2006.

The ★ **most women's Marathon Swimming World Cups** is the three wins racked up by Edith van Dijk (Netherlands) in 2000–01 and 2005.

In 2007, the event was superseded by the FINA 10 km Marathon Swimming World Cup. Three swimmers share the record for the ★ **most FINA 10 km Marathon Swimming World Cups (male)** – Vladimir Dyatchin (Russia), Valerio Cleri (Italy) and Thomas Lurz (Germany) for their respective victories in 2007, 2008 and 2009.

EXTRA!
FOR MORE SWIMMING RECORDS, DIVE INTO OUR SPORTS REFERENCE SECTION, STARTING ON P.268.

BRILLIANT BJÖRN

World-beating windsurfer Björn Dunkerbeck (Switzerland) has the ★**most Professional Windsurfers Association (PWA) World Championship titles**, with 33 wins between 1988 and 2001, including a PWA Freestyle World Championship victory in 1998 and a PWA Speed World Championship title in 1994.

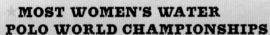

MOST WOMEN'S WATER POLO WORLD CHAMPIONSHIPS

Since the introduction of the women's Water Polo World Championships in 1986, the USA women's team has won the event three times, in 2003, 2007 and 2009.

Angela Maurer (Germany) has earned the distinction of winning the **most FINA 10 km Marathon Swimming World Cups (female)**, with a total of two victories, in 2007 and 2008.

★LARGEST RACE (OPEN WATER)

A total of 13,755 participants swam the 2009 Midmar Mile at Midmar Dam, Howick, near Pietermaritzburg, South Africa, from 7 to 8 February 2009.

UNIVERSITY BOAT RACE

The annual Boat Race held each spring between teams from the UK universities of Oxford and Cambridge was inaugurated on 10 June 1829 with a race from Hambledon Lock to Henley Bridge on the River Thames; Oxford won. Outrigged eights boats were first used in 1846 and have since been adopted as the standard vessel for the event.

In the 156 races to 2010, Cambridge has won a total of 80 times, Oxford 75 times and there was a dead heat on 24 March 1877, handing Cambridge the record for the ★**most wins**.

Cambridge also hold the record for the **most consecutive wins**, with a series of 13 victories from 1924 to 1936.

The **oldest rower** was Mike Wherley (USA, Oxford) at 36 years 14 days, in the 2008 race, although cox Andrew Probert (UK, Cambridge) was aged 38 years 3 months for the 1992 race.

Finally, the **lightest individual oarsman** was Alfred Higgins (UK), who weighed 60.1 kg (132 lb 6 oz) for the 1 April 1882 race.

WIND
BJÖRN DUNKERBECK ALSO HOLDS THE RECORDS FOR ★MOST WAVE WINDSURFING TITLES (SEVEN WINS) AND ★MOST RACE WINDSURFING TITLES (12 WINS).

★FASTEST 2,000 M ROWING SINGLE SCULLS (MEN)

New Zealand rower Mahe Drysdale completed the 2,000 m course in the men's sculls in 6 min 33.35 sec at Poznań, Poland, on 29 August 2009.

BAGGED
IN THE COURSE OF HIS WINDSURFING CAREER, BJÖRN HAS PICKED UP AN IMPRESSIVE TOTAL OF SIX GUINNESS WORLD RECORDS ACHIEVEMENTS.

SPORTS
WHEEL SKILLS

MISTY FLIP:
Front flip with a 180° twist. The skater (or rider) either goes off the jump backwards or lands backwards.

★MOST 180° JUMPS (SWITCHES) ON A BICYCLE IN ONE MINUTE

Kenny Belaey (Belgium) performed 35 jumps of 180° at the Safety Jogger Classic bike festival held in Belgium, on 20 September 2009.

BICYCLE

• Xavi Casas (Andorra) recorded the ★**most people stepped over by bicycle in two minutes** when he cleared 97 people on the set of *Guinness World Records*, Madrid, Spain, on 14 January 2009.
• Benito Ros Charral (Spain) recorded the ★**highest bunny hop on a bicycle**, achieving a hop of 1.42 m (4 ft 8 in) at the 2009 Bike the Rock festival in Heubach, Germany, on 17 May 2009.
• Charral has also accomplished the ★**fastest time to bunny hop 15 hurdles on a trials bicycle**, with a time of 26.08 seconds on the set of *Zheng Da Zong Yi – Guinness World Records Special* in Beijing, China, on 20 November 2009.

• Also on the set of *Zheng Da Zong Yi – Guinness World Records Special*, the UK's Ben Wallace recorded the ★**highest bicycle backflip** with a flip of 2.60 m (8 ft 6 in).
• Austria's Thomas Öhler completed the ★**highest bicycle wall climb** with a 2.89-m (9-ft 5.9-in) climb at the MTB Freestyle night, Kaprun, Austria, on 7 August 2009.
• Lance Trappe (USA) executed the ★**most continuous front wheel hops on a bicycle**, with 108 hops at Lake Buena Vista, Florida, USA, on 16 June 2009.

INLINE SKATES

• Steve Swain (UK) completed the ★**highest misty flip on inline skates** with a 2.08-m (6-ft 10-in) attempt in London, UK, on 23 April 2009.

★MOST WORLD UNICYCLE HOCKEY TITLES

UNICON, the world championships of unicycling, has been held biennially since 1984. Unicycle hockey was added to the programme of events in 1994, since when nine tournaments have been contested. The Swiss Power Team (Switzerland) has won the title a record three times, in 2004, 2006 and 2010 (pictured, in red).

• The ★**highest ramp jump on inline skates** is 4.7 m (15 ft 5 in) and was achieved by Zhang Baoxiang (China) in Beijing, China, on 5 November 2009.
• Paul Randles (UK) completed the ★**fastest 20-cone backwards slalom on inline skates** in 5.62 seconds on the set of *Guinness World Records* in Madrid, Spain, on 23 January 2009.

> "Our goal is to make this as authentic as possible... Just a full-on, old-school stunt."
> **Travis Pastrana keeps rally-car-jumping real**

FES, MOROCCO
The **oldest existing, and continually operating educational institution** in the world is the University of Karueein, founded in 859 AD in Fez, Morocco. The University of Bologna, Italy, was founded in 1088 and is the oldest university in Europe.

QUIZ!
JUST HOW HIGH IS THE HIGHEST WALL CLIMB ON A BICYCLE?
SEE P.278 FOR THE ANSWER.

★MOST DOWNHILL SKATEBOARD CHAMPIONSHIPS (FEMALE)

Three women have won the International Gravity Sports Association Women's Downhill Championships on two occasions: Angelina Nobre (Switzerland) in 2004–05, Jolanda Vogler (Switzerland) in 2006–07 and Brianne Davies (Canada, pictured) in 2008–09.

★FASTEST INLINE SPEED SKATER OVER 300 M

On 19 September 2009, Joey Mantia (USA) set the fastest track 300 m by an individual male inline speed skater, as ratified by the sport's governing body, the Fédération Internationale de Roller Sports, when he recorded a time of 24.25 seconds in Haining, China.

MOTOR-BIKE

• The **longest motorcycle ramp jump** is 106.98 m (351 ft) and was achieved by Robbie Maddison (Australia) at the Crusty Demons Night of World Records in Melbourne, Victoria, Australia, on 29 March 2008.
• Ricardo Piedras (Spain) set the ★**longest jump with a backflip performed on a minimoto** with his 12.72-m (41-ft 9-in) jump in Milan, Italy, on 11 April 2009.

★LONGEST JUMP IN A RALLY CAR

On 31 December 2009 in Long Beach, California, USA, Travis Pastrana (USA) made a record leap of 81.9 m (269 ft) in his Subaru rally car. The ramp-to-ramp jump was made off the Pine Street Pier on to a floating barge anchored in Long Beach's Rainbow Harbor as part of the "RedBull: New Year. No Limits" event.

• Michele Pradelli (Italy) performed the **longest standing jump on a motorcycle** (4.26 m; 13 ft 11 in) in Milan, Italy, on 25 April 2009.
• The record for the **most jumps between containers on trial bikes in 2 minutes** (35), set in Rome, Italy, on 11 March 2010, is shared by David Cobos (Spain) and Luca Cotone (Italy) .

SKATE-BOARD

• The UK's Alex DeCunha recorded the ★**most skateboarding no-comply flips in one minute** by achieving 56 flips in 60 seconds on the set of *Guinness World Records Smashed* at Pinewood Studios, UK, on 15 April 2009.
• Rob Dyrdek (USA) recorded the ★**most skateboard 720 kick flips in one minute** – a total of seven – on MTV's *The Rob & Big Show* in Los Angeles, California, USA, on 17 September 2007.

• On the same show, Dyrdek recorded the ★**most heel-flip shove-its in one minute** with 10.
• With an effort of 1.5 m (4 ft 11 in), Terence Bougdour (France) set the record for the **highest skateboard 540 McTwist off a halfpipe** on the set of *L'Été De Tous Les Records* in La Tranche Sur Mer, France, on 27 July 2005.

WOW!
STEFAN AKESSON (SWEDEN) SKATEBOARD WHEELIED FOR A RECORD 68.54 M (224 FT 10 IN) IN STOCKHOLM, SWEDEN, ON 2 NOVEMBER 2007.

LOW!
THE LOWEST MOTORCYCLE BACKFLIP EVER WAS 91 CM (3 FT) OFF THE GROUND, ACHIEVED BY TRAVIS PASTRANA (USA) ON 17 NOVEMBER 2008.

EXTRA!
FOR MORE FUN ON WHEELS, TAKE A LONG RUN UP AND JUMP OVER TO AUTOSPORTS ON P.224.

RedBull
new year
No LIMITS

DOUGLAS, ISLE OF MAN
The **oldest trams in revenue service** are cars 1 and 2 of the Manx Electric Railway, dating from 1893. These run regularly on the 28.5-km (17.7-mile) railway between Douglas and Ramsey, Isle of Man, UK.

54°08'N
4°29'W

SPORTS
WORLD OF SPORTS

★ ★ ★ ★ ★ ★ ★ ☆ ★ ★ ★ ★ ★ ☆

★MOST ASIAN GAMES MEN'S TEAM SEPAK TAKRAW WINS

Sepak Takraw is a game similar to volleyball that uses a small rattan ball, where players are allowed to kick, knee, head and chest the ball. Thailand have won the Sepak Takraw men's team event at the Asian Games on three occasions, in 1998, 2002 and 2006.

FISTBALL

Fistball is a game of European origin that dates back to Roman times. It is similar to volleyball, but only the fists or arms may be used to make contact with the ball, which is allowed to bounce.

The ★most wins of the Fistball Men's World Championship is seven by West Germany, who won in 1968, 1972, 1976, 1979, 1982, 1986 and 1990.

The ★most wins of the Fistball Women's World Championship is three by Germany, who came first in 1994, 1998 and 2006.

TUG OF WAR

Tug of War is a classic test of strength in which two teams of eight pull against each other from each end of a rope, the winners being the team that manages to pull the other over a centre line. To ensure sides are evenly matched, teams are placed in weight categories.

The ★most wins of the men's -640 kg outdoor Tug of War event at the World Games is four by Switzerland, who were crowned champions in 1989, 1993, 2005 and 2009.

The ★most wins of the women's -520 kg indoor Tug of War event at the World Games is two by Chinese Taipei, who were victorious in 2005 and 2009.

PESÄPALLO

Pesäpallo is often known as Finnish Baseball, and is a fast-moving sport similar to baseball and rounders.

The ★first ever Pesäpallo World Cup was held in Helsinki, Finland, in 1992, with seven nations competing; Finland, Sweden, Australia, Estonia, Germany, Lithuania and Japan.

TCHOUKBALL

Tchoukball is a modern team sport developed in Western Europe. It is similar to netball and handball and is played indoors by two teams of nine players.

The ★most wins of the men's Tchoukball World Championship is six by China in 1984, 1987, 1989, 1990, 2000 and 2002.

The ★most wins of the women's Tchoukball World Championship is seven by China in 1984, 1987, 1989, 1990, 2000, 2002 and 2004.

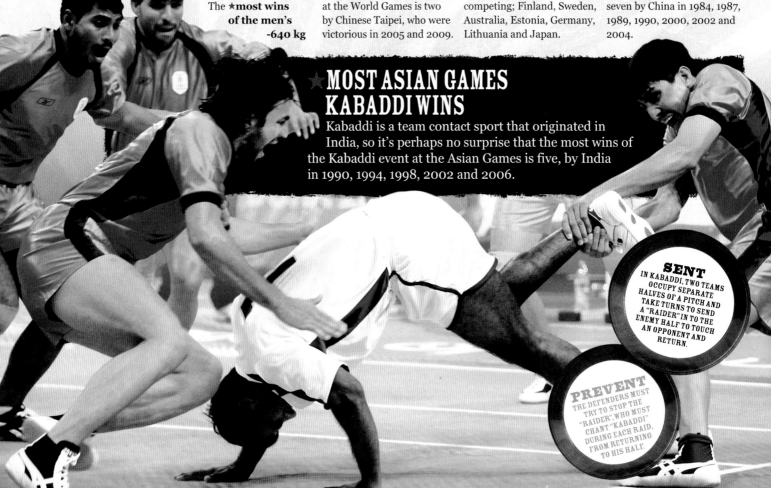

★ MOST ASIAN GAMES KABADDI WINS

Kabaddi is a team contact sport that originated in India, so it's perhaps no surprise that the most wins of the Kabaddi event at the Asian Games is five, by India in 1990, 1994, 1998, 2002 and 2006.

SENT
IN KABADDI, TWO TEAMS OCCUPY SEPARATE HALVES OF A PITCH AND TAKE TURNS TO SEND A "RAIDER" IN TO THE ENEMY HALF TO TOUCH AN OPPONENT AND RETURN.

PREVENT
THE DEFENDERS MUST TRY TO STOP THE "RAIDER", WHO MUST CHANT "KABADDI" DURING EACH RAID, FROM RETURNING TO HIS HALF.

N 36°43' W 4°25'W

MALAGA, SPAIN

Robert Lantsoght of Malaga, Spain, has the **largest collection of golf clubs** – 4,393 individual clubs – which he has amassed since 1992. He displays them in his golf-themed restaurant on the Costa del Sol.

WOODBALL

★MOST POINTS FOR ENDURANCE BOOMERANG THROWING

The greatest number of points in the Endurance event, as recognized by the International Federation of Boomerang Associations, is 61 by Switzerland's Manuel Schütz in Milan, Italy, on 2 October 2005. Points are awarded in the Endurance event for the number of catches in five minutes.

★MOST WINS OF THE WOODBALL WORLD CUP

Woodball is a sport popular in south-east Asia, similar to golf and croquet, where mallets are used to hit balls through gates. The ★**most wins of the men's Woodball World Cup** is two, by Malaysia in 2006 and 2008. The ★**most wins of the women's Woodball World Cup** is three, by Taiwan in 2004, 2006 and 2008.

AUSTRALIAN ROUND BOOMERANG THROWING

Australian Round is considered to be the most exacting, and therefore most difficult, boomerang discipline. Competitors must throw their boomerangs at least 50 m (164 ft) and make them return to the same place. Points are awarded on distance, accuracy and catch. The ★**most points scored boomerang throwing in an Australian Round**, as recognized by the International Federation of Boomerang Associations, is 99 points by Fridolin Frost (Germany) in Viareggio, Italy, on 27 October 2007.

HURLING

A popular pursuit in Ireland, the Gaelic sport of hurling bears some superficial resemblance to hockey. In hurling, players form two teams of 15 and use sticks, called hurleys, to hit a ball, called a sliotar, into or over a goal that resembles the ones used in football, but with posts that extend far higher than the bar. Under the bar is a goal and is worth three points, over the bar, only one.

The **highest individual hurling score** was by Nick Rackard of Wexford, Ireland, who scored 7 goals and 7 points against Antrim in the 1954 All-Ireland semi-final. Meanwhile, the **highest team score in an All-Ireland final** is 41 by Tipperary (4 goals, 29 points) when they beat Antrim (3 goals, 9 points) at Croke Park, Dublin, Ireland, in 1989.

EXTRA! FOR MORE HURLING RECORDS, HEAD OVER TO BALL SPORTS ON P.226, AND HAVE YOUR HURLEY READY!

CAMOGIE

While only men play hurling, there is a variation of the sport for women called camogie. The ★**highest team score in a Senior Camogie Championship final** is 39 (11 goals, 6 points) set by Dublin against Mayo (1 goal, 3 points) at Croke Park, Dublin, Ireland, on 13 September 1959.

The ★**most All-Ireland Senior Camogie Championships won by one team** is 26 by Dublin, between 1932 and 1984.

The **longest camogie marathon** lasted 24 hr 7 min and was achieved by Croydon Camogie Club (UK) at Emerald GAA Grounds, Ruislip, UK, from 23 to 24 August 2008.

★FIRST PATO WORLD CHAMPIONSHIPS

Pato is the national sport of Argentina and is similar to polo. The players do not use mallets, though, and the ball is larger and has handles. The inaugural Pato World Championships was held in Buenos Aires, Argentina, in 2006 and was won by Portugal.

★ NEW RECORD
★ UPDATED RECORD

GLASGOW, UK

55°51'N
4°15'W

The **tallest cinema complex** in the world is the Cineworld Cinema, Glasgow, UK, with an overall height of 62 m (203.41 ft), which is 12 storeys high, holds 18 screens and has a seating capacity of 4,277.

SPORTS
X GAMES

★ ★ ★ ★ ★ ★ ★ ★ ★ ★ ★ ★

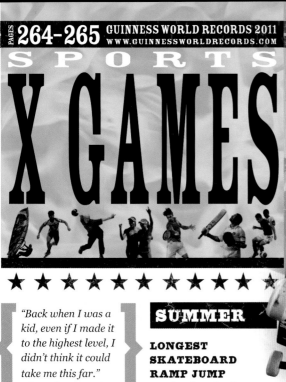

> "Back when I was a kid, even if I made it to the highest level, I didn't think it could take me this far."
> **X Games icon Dave Mirra**

★ FIRST AMPUTEE TO WIN A SUMMER X GAMES GOLD MEDAL

Riding a 2009 Suzuki RMZ450F, Chris Ridgway (USA) won gold in the X Games adaptive Moto X class at X Games 15 in Los Angeles, California, USA, on 31 July 2009.

SUMMER

LONGEST SKATEBOARD RAMP JUMP

Pro skateboarder Danny Way (USA) performed a skateboard ramp jump with a 24-m (79-ft) 360 air on his Mega Ramp at X Games 10 in Los Angeles, California, USA, on 8 August 2004.

YOUNGEST X GAMES GOLD MEDALLIST

On 17 August 2003, Ryan Sheckler (USA, b. 30 December 1989) won the Skateboard Park gold medal at ESPN X Games 9 in Los Angeles, California, USA. He was 13 years 230 days old at the time.

Lyn-z Adams Hawkins (USA, b. 1 September 1989) became the **youngest female to win a gold medal at the X Games** in any discipline when she won the Skateboard Vert competition aged 14 years 321 days at X Games 10, Los Angeles, California, USA, on 7 August 2004.

★ MOST MEDALS

Dave Mirra (USA), who competes in BMX Freestyle, has won a total of 24 ESPN X Games medals. Mirra also holds the record for the ★**most BMX Freestyle**

YOUNGEST X GAMES ATHLETE

Nyjah Huston (USA, b. 30 November 1994) was 11 years 246 days old when he made his debut at X Games 12 (3–6 August 2006). He competed in the Men's Skateboard Street event.

★ MOST SUMMER X GAMES SKATE MEDALS

The greatest number of ESPN Summer X Games Skateboard medals is 19 and was achieved by Andy Macdonald (USA) between 1999 and 2009.

medals, with 23. Fourteen of those are gold, giving Mirra another record for the **most ESPN Summer X Games gold medals won**.

MOST MOTO X MEDALS AT SUMMER X GAMES

As of ESPN Summer X Games 12, held in 2006, Travis Pastrana (USA) had won 11 Moto X medals, including seven gold.

GREATEST ATTENDANCE FOR A SUMMER ACTION SPORTS EVENT

ESPN Summer X Games Five, held in San Francisco, California, USA, were attended by 268,390 visitors over its 10-day duration

EXTRA! FOR WORLD CHAMPIONSHIP GAMES OF A TRULY WACKY NATURE, FLIP BACK TO P.256.

DID YOU KNOW?

X GAMES KNOWS NO AGE LIMIT. OLDEST MEDALLIST ANGELIKA CASTENEDA (USA) WAS 53 YEARS OLD WHEN SHE WON GOLD IN 1996 FOR THE X VENTURE RACE.

X GAMES

LONGEST MOTO X DIRT-TO-DIRT BACKFLIP

Jeremy Stenberg, pictured, and Nate Adams (both USA) completed a Moto X dirt-to-dirt backflip of 30.48 m (100 ft) during the Moto X Freestyle Finals at X Games 11 in Los Angeles, California, USA, on 6 August 2005.

Winter X Games 11 in Aspen/Snowmass, Colorado, USA, on 28 January 2007.

Aleisha Cline (Canada), Magdalena Jonsson (Sweden) and Ophélie David (France) have all won five medals for Skier X, the ★**most Skier X Women's medals**. Out of that total, both Cline and David have won four golds.

★MOST SKIING MEDALS

Tanner Hall (USA) has won 11 ESPN Winter X Games medals in skiing disciplines, as of the ESPN Winter X Games 11 in Aspen/Snowmass, Colorado, USA, between 28 and 31 January 2007. Hall has won a gold for Big Air, three golds and one silver for Slopestyle and three golds and three silvers for SuperPipe Men's.

Jon Olsson (Sweden) holds the record for the ★**most skiing Slopestyle medals**, with five: bronze in 2002–05 and 2008.

★MOST SNOCROSS MEDALS

Tucker Hibbert (USA) has won nine SnoCross medals since 1999, comprising five golds, three silvers and one bronze.

Hibbert also holds the record for the ★**most consecutive gold medals won in Winter X Games snowmobile SnoCross**, with four. He won his last gold at Winter X Games 14 in 2010. It was the first "four-peat" (four gold medals) in snowmobile history.

GREATEST ATTENDANCE FOR A WINTER ACTION SPORTS EVENT

A total of 85,100 spectators attended Winter X Games 5 in 2001 at Mount Snow, Vermont, USA.

WINTER OLLIE DAYS

Phil Smage (USA) is ollie royalty! He holds records for the **highest ollie** (70.5 cm; 27.75 in), **longest ollie** (3.45 m; 11 ft 4 in) and **most ollies** (14) on a snowskate board.

..INTER

WINTER

★MOST GOLD MEDALS

Shaun White (USA) has won 10 ESPN Winter X Games gold medals. White's tally of gold medals all come from the snowboard Superpipe and Slopestyle disciplines. He won his 10th gold medal at Winter X Games 14 in 2010.

★MOST MEDALS

Prolific X Games star Shaun White also holds the record for the most ESPN Winter X Games medals won, with 15. His 15th medal came at Winter X Games 14 in 2010.

MOST SKIER X MEDALS

The largest medal haul for Skier X Men's is six by Enak Gavaggio (France). He took gold in 1999, four bronze in 2001–04 and a fifth at ESPN

SUMMER THE FIRST X GAMES WAS HOSTED IN RHODE ISLAND, USA, IN 1995. THEN, AS NOW, THE SPONSOR WAS AMERICAN SPORTS BROADCASTER ESPN.

WINTER TWO YEARS AFTER THE INAUGURAL SUMMER X GAMES, THE WINTER EQUIVALENT KICKED OFF AT MOUNTAIN RESORT IN CALIFORNIA'S BIG BEAR LAKE.

★MOST SNOWSKATE KICK FLIPS IN 30 SECONDS

Max Hilty (USA) completed a total of 14 kick flips on his snowskate board in 30 seconds at Winter X Games 14 in Aspen, Colorado, USA, on 29 January 2010.

★ NEW RECORD
★ UPDATED RECORD

SPORTS
X GAMES

★ ★ ★ ★ ★ ★ ★ ★ ★ ★ ★ ★ ★ ★

★MOST BMX WHEELIE HOPS

Manuel Torres (USA) performed 62 wheelie hops in 30 seconds at X Games 15 in Los Angeles, California, USA, on 30 July 2009. A wheelie hop consists of lifting only the front wheel of a bike off the ground.

★MOST HEELFLIPS AND NOLLIES IN 30 SECONDS

Ivan Sebastian Cordova (USA) performed a record nine skateboard heelflips in 30 seconds at X Games 15 in Los Angeles, California, USA, on 1 August 2009. At the same event, Ivan performed the ★most nollies in 30 seconds: 15.

EXTRA! ARE YOU MAD FOR MEGAMOTORS? THEN PUT YOUR FOOT DOWN AND HEAD FOR P.210.

total of 16 rock and rolls in 30 seconds at X Games 15 in Los Angeles, California, USA, on 31 July 2009.

★MOST 360 FRONTSIDE SPINS IN 30 SECONDS

Lunati Hamilton (USA) performed six 360 frontside spins in 30 seconds at X Games 15 in Los Angeles, California, USA, on 30 July 2009.

★HIGHEST OLLIE ON A SNOWSKATE BOARD

Phil Smage (USA) achieved a 72.4-cm (28.5-in) ollie on a snowskate board at Winter X Games 14 in Aspen, Colorado, USA, on 29 January 2010.

★HIGHEST AIR ON SKIS ON A SUPERPIPE

At Winter X Games 14 in Aspen, Colorado, USA, on 31 January 2010, Peter Olenick (USA) managed a 7.58-m (24-ft 11-in) air on skis on a superpipe.

SKATEBOARD

★MOST BACKSIDE GRINDS IN 30 SECONDS

On 31 July 2009, Terrance Covington (USA) achieved 17 backside grinds in 30 seconds at X Games 15 in Los Angeles, California, USA.

★MOST ROCK AND ROLLS IN 30 SECONDS

Terrance Covington and Dalton Price (both USA) achieved a

SNOWBOARD

★HIGHEST AIR ON A SNOWBOARD IN A SUPERPIPE

On 30 January 2010, at Winter X Games 14 in Aspen, Colorado, USA, Shaun White (USA) performed a 7-m (23-ft) air on a snowboard in a superpipe.

★MOST GOLD MEDALS IN WOMEN'S SKIER X

Ophelie David (France) has won a record four individual Winter X Games women's Skier X medals, a feat that represents the first four-peat in Winter X Games skiing history.

★MOST SKATEBOARD SHOVE-ITS IN 30 SECONDS

The greatest number of skateboard shove-its achieved in 30 seconds is 14 by Eddie Davis (USA), at X Games 15 in Los Angeles, California, USA, on 30 July 2009.

GAMES

★ NEW RECORD
★ UPDATED RECORD

OLLIE: A no-hands aerial skateboard trick, named after skateboard legend Alan "Ollie" Gelfand.

★ MOST OLLIES IN 30 SECONDS

Sten Carr (USA) performed a total of 34 ollies in 30 seconds at X Games 15 in Los Angeles, California, USA, on 2 August 2009.

★MOST CONSECUTIVE SNOWBOARDER X GOLD MEDALS

Nate Holland (USA) had won five consecutive gold medals at the Winter X Games Snowboarder X competition as of January 2010. Holland won his fifth gold medal (an achievement known as the "five-peat") – the first in the history of the tournament – at Winter X Games 14 in 2010.

★MOST SNOWBOARDER X MEDALS

Seth Wescott (USA) has won an unprecedented seven medals for Snowboarder X Men's: he picked up four silvers in 2002, 2004, 2005 and 2010 and three bronzes in 1998, 2001 and 2007.

The ★**most medals for Snowboarder X Women's** won at Winter X Games competitions is seven by Lindsey Jacobellis (USA), who won six golds in 2003–05 and 2008–10 and silver at Winter X Games 11 in Aspen/Snowmass, Colorado, USA, in January 2007.

★MOST SLOPESTYLE MEDALS

Shaun White (USA) has picked up an unprecedented eight snowboard Slopestyle Winter X Games medals. He won five golds in 2003–06 and 2009, a silver in 2002 and two bronze medals in 2007–08.

The ★**most women's snowboard Slopestyle medals** won at the Winter X Games is six by Janna Meyen-Weatherby (USA). She collected four gold medals in 2003–06, a silver medal in 2002 and a bronze medal in 2010.

★MOST SUPERPIPE MEDALS

Shaun White (USA) has seven medals in the men's snowboard SuperPipe at the Winter X Games: five gold medals (2003, 2006 and 2008–10) and two silver (2002 and 2007).

He has also won the most ★**medals overall** (14) and the ★**most gold medals** (10) in Winter X Games history.

Kelly Clark (USA) has won the ★**most women's snowboard SuperPipe medals**, with seven: gold in 2002 and 2006, silver in 2003–04 and 2009–10 and bronze in 2008.

★HIGHEST HIPPY JUMP ON A SNOWSKATE

Kyle Williams (USA) achieved a 47-cm (18.5-in) hippy jump on a snowskate at Winter X Games 14 in Aspen, Colorado, USA, on 31 January 2010.

WINTER WINNERS

GWR truly established a presence at Winter X Games 14 in January 2010, carrying out a host of record attempts with skating, biking, snowboarding kids. Pictured below are some of those who set new records.

HIGH! DANNY WAY (USA) PERFORMED THE HIGHEST SKATEBOARD AIR OFF A QUARTERPIPE – 7.1 M (23 FT 6 IN) – OFF AN 8.2-M (27-FT) RAMP ON 19 JUNE 2003.

HIGHER! THE HIGHEST AIR ON A BMX BIKE IS 8.07 M (26 FT 6 IN) BY MAT HOFFMAN (USA), ON 20 MARCH 2001. HE WAS TOWED BY A MOTORCYCLE IN THE RUN-UP.

CARDIFF, UK
On 29 November 2005, scientists at Cardiff University in Wales, UK, announced the development of machinery that can drill holes just 22 microns (0.022 mm) across, making them the smallest holes ever drilled

WIN.8
512X6N.8

SPORTS

SPORTS REFERENCE

MEN'S OUTDOOR 1,500 M

In a record that has stood for more than 12 years, Hicham El Guerrouj (Morocco) won the 1,500 m event at the IAAF Golden League Golden Gala in Rome, Italy, in a time of 3 min 26 sec on 14 July 1998. He also holds the world records for the mile and the 2,000 m.

★ **NEW RECORD**
⚡ **UPDATED RECORD**

ATHLETICS – OUTDOOR TRACK EVENTS

MEN	TIME/DISTANCE	NAME & NATIONALITY	LOCATION	DATE
★100 m	9.58	Usain Bolt (Jamaica)	Berlin, Germany	16 Aug 2009
★200 m	19.19	Usain Bolt (Jamaica)	Berlin, Germany	20 Aug 2009
400 m	43.18	Michael Johnson (USA)	Seville, Spain	26 Aug 1999
800 m	1:41.11	Wilson Kipketer (Denmark)	Cologne, Germany	24 Aug 1997
1,000 m	2:11.96	Noah Ngeny (Kenya)	Rieti, Italy	5 Sep 1999
1,500 m	3:26.00	Hicham El Guerrouj (Morocco)	Rome, Italy	14 Jul 1998
1 mile	3:43.13	Hicham El Guerrouj (Morocco)	Rome, Italy	7 Jul 1999
2,000 m	4:44.79	Hicham El Guerrouj (Morocco)	Berlin, Germany	7 Sep 1999
3,000 m	7:20.67	Daniel Komen (Kenya)	Rieti, Italy	1 Sep 1996
5,000 m	12:37.35	Kenenisa Bekele (Ethiopia)	Hengelo, the Netherlands	31 May 2004
10,000 m	26:17.53	Kenenisa Bekele (Ethiopia)	Brussels, Belgium	26 Aug 2005
20,000 m	56:26.00	Haile Gebrselassie (Ethiopia)	Ostrava, Czech Rep	26 Jun 2007
1 hour	21,285 m	Haile Gebrselassie (Ethiopia)	Ostrava, Czech Rep	27 Jun 2007
25,000 m	1:13:55.80	Toshihiko Seko (Japan)	Christchurch, NZ	22 Mar 1981
30,000 m	1:29:18.80	Toshihiko Seko (Japan)	Christchurch, NZ	22 Mar 1981
3,000 m steeplechase	7:53.63	Saif Saaeed Shaheen (Qatar)	Brussels, Belgium	3 Sep 2004
110 m hurdles	12.87	Dayron Robles (Cuba)	Ostrava, Czech Rep	12 Jun 2008
400 m hurdles	46.78	Kevin Young (USA)	Barcelona, Spain	6 Aug 1992
4 x 100 m relay	37.10	Jamaica (Asafa Powell, Nesta Carter, Michael Frater, Usain Bolt)	Beijing, China	22 Aug 2008
4 x 200 m relay	1:18.68	Santa Monica Track Club, USA (Michael Marsh, Leroy Burrell, Floyd Heard, Carl Lewis)	Walnut, USA	17 Apr 1994
4 x 400 m relay	2:54.29	USA (Andrew Valmon, Quincy Watts, Harry Reynolds, Michael Johnson)	Stuttgart, Germany	22 Aug 1993
4 x 800 m relay	7:02.43	Kenya (Joseph Mutua, William Yiampoy, Ismael Kombich, Wilfred Bungei)	Brussels, Belgium	25 Aug 2006
★4 x 1,500 m relay	14:36.23	Kenya (Geoffrey Kipkoech Rono, Augustine Kiprono Choge, William Biwott Tanui, Gideon Gathimba)	Brussels, Belgium	4 Sep 2009

WOMEN	TIME/DISTANCE	NAME & NATIONALITY	LOCATION	DATE
100 m	10.49	Florence Griffith-Joyner (USA)	Indianapolis, USA	16 Jul 1988
200 m	21.34	Florence Griffith-Joyner (USA)	Seoul, South Korea	29 Sep 1988
400 m	47.60	Marita Koch (GDR)	Canberra, Australia	6 Oct 1985
800 m	1:53.28	Jarmila Kratochvílová (Czechoslovakia)	Munich, Germany	26 Jul 1983
1,000 m	2:28.98	Svetlana Masterkova (Russia)	Brussels, Belgium	23 Aug 1996
1,500 m	3:50.46	Qu Yunxia (China)	Beijing, China	11 Sep 1993
1 mile	4:12.56	Svetlana Masterkova (Russia)	Zurich, Switzerland	14 Aug 1996
2,000 m	5:25.36	Sonia O'Sullivan (Ireland)	Edinburgh, UK	8 Jul 1994
3,000 m	8:06.11	Wang Junxia (China)	Beijing, China	13 Sep 1993
5,000 m	14:11.15	Tirunesh Dibaba (Ethiopia)	Oslo, Norway	6 Jun 2008
10,000 m	29:31.78	Wang Junxia (China)	Beijing, China	8 Sep 1993
20,000 m	1:05:26.60	Tegla Loroupe (Kenya)	Borgholzhausen, Germany	3 Sep 2000
1 hour	18,517 m	Dire Tune (Ethiopia)	Ostrava, Czech Republic	12 Jun 2008
25,000 m	1:27:05.90	Tegla Loroupe (Kenya)	Mengerskirchen, Germany	21 Sep 2002
30,000 m	1:45:50.00	Tegla Loroupe (Kenya)	Warstein, Germany	6 Jun 2003
3,000 m steeplechase	8:58.81	Gulnara Samitova-Galkina (Russia)	Beijing, China	17 Aug 2008
100 m hurdles	12.21	Yordanka Donkova (Bulgaria)	Stara Zagora, Bulgaria	20 Aug 1988
400 m hurdles	52.34	Yuliya Pechonkina (Russia)	Tula, Russia	8 Aug 2003
4 x 100 m relay	41.37	GDR (Silke Gladisch, Sabine Rieger, Ingrid Auerswald, Marlies Göhr)	Canberra, Australia	6 Oct 1985
4 x 200 m relay	1:27.46	United States "Blue" (LaTasha Jenkins, LaTasha Colander-Richardson, Nanceen Perry, Marion Jones)	Philadelphia, USA	29 Apr 2000
4 x 400 m relay	3:15.17	USSR (Tatyana Ledovskaya, Olga Nazarova, Maria Pinigina, Olga Bryzgina)	Seoul, South Korea	1 Oct 1988
4 x 800 m relay	7:50.17	USSR (Nadezhda Olizarenko, Lyubov Gurina, Lyudmila Borisova, Irina Podyalovskaya)	Moscow, Russia	5 Aug 1984

OFF THE PACE?
ASIDE FROM USAIN BOLT'S REMARKABLE 100 M AND 200 M RUNS (SEE ABOVE), VERY FEW ATHLETICS RECORDS HAVE BEEN BROKEN THIS YEAR.

EDINBURGH, UK
55°57'N 3°09'W

The world's **largest performing arts festival** is the annual Edinburgh Festival Fringe, instituted in 1947. Between 7 and 31 August 2009, its record year, there were 18,901 artists, 34,265 performances of 2,265 shows and the box office sold no less than 1,859,235 tickets.

ATHLETICS - INDOOR TRACK EVENTS

MEN	TIME/DISTANCE	NAME & NATIONALITY	LOCATION	DATE
50 m	5.56	Donovan Bailey (Canada)	Reno, USA	9 Feb 1996
60 m	6.39	Maurice Greene (USA)	Madrid, Spain	3 Feb 1998
	6.39	Maurice Greene (USA)	Atlanta, USA	3 Mar 2001
200 m	19.92	Frank Fredericks (Namibia)	Liévin, France	18 Feb 1996
400 m	44.57	Kerron Clement (USA)	Fayetteville, USA	12 Mar 2005
800 m	1:42.67	Wilson Kipketer (Denmark)	Paris, France	9 Mar 1997
1,000 m	2:14.96	Wilson Kipketer (Denmark)	Birmingham, UK	20 Feb 2000
1,500 m	3:31.18	Hicham El Guerrouj (Morocco)	Stuttgart, Germany	2 Feb 1997
1 mile	3:48.45	Hicham El Guerrouj (Morocco)	Ghent, Belgium	12 Feb 1997
3,000 m	7:24.90	Daniel Komen (Kenya)	Budapest, Hungary	6 Feb 1998
5,000 m	12:49.60	Kenenisa Bekele (Ethiopia)	Birmingham, UK	20 Feb 2004
50 m hurdles	6.25	Mark McKoy (Canada)	Kobe, Japan	5 Mar 1986
60 m hurdles	7.30	Colin Jackson (GB)	Sindelfingen, Germany	6 Mar 1994
4 x 200 m relay	1:22.11	Great Britain & Northern Ireland (Linford Christie, Darren Braithwaite, Ade Mafe, John Regis)	Glasgow, UK	3 Mar 1991
4 x 400 m relay	3:02.83	USA (Andre Morris, Dameon Johnson, Deon Minor, Milton Campbell)	Maebashi, Japan	7 Mar 1999
4 x 800 m relay	7:13.94	Global Athletics & Marketing, USA (Joey Woody, Karl Paranya, Rich Kenah, David Krummenacker)	Boston, USA	6 Feb 2000
5,000 m walk	18:07.08	Mikhail Shchennikov (Russia)	Moscow, Russia	14 Feb 1995

WOMEN	TIME/DISTANCE	NAME & NATIONALITY	LOCATION	DATE
50 m	5.96	Irina Privalova (Russia)	Madrid, Spain	9 Feb 1995
60 m	6.92	Irina Privalova (Russia)	Madrid, Spain	11 Feb 1993
	6.92	Irina Privalova (Russia)	Madrid, Spain	9 Feb 1995
200 m	21.87	Merlene Ottey (Jamaica)	Liévin, France	13 Feb 1993
400 m	49.59	Jarmila Kratochvílová (Czechoslovakia)	Milan, Italy	7 Mar 1982
800 m	1:55.82	Jolanda Ceplak (Slovenia)	Vienna, Austria	3 Mar 2002
1,000 m	2:30.94	Maria de Lurdes Mutola (Mozambique)	Stockholm, Sweden	25 Feb 1999
1,500 m	3:58.28	Yelena Soboleva (Russia)	Moscow, Russia	18 Feb 2006
1 mile	4:17.14	Doina Melinte (Romania)	East Rutherford, USA	9 Feb 1990
3,000 m	8:23.72	Meseret Defar (Ethiopia)	Stuttgart, Germany	3 Feb 2007
5,000 m	14:24.37	Meseret Defar (Ethiopia)	Stockholm, Sweden	18 Feb 2009
50 m hurdles	6.58	Cornelia Oschkenat (GDR)	Berlin, Germany	20 Feb 1988
60 m hurdles	7.68	Susanna Kallur (Sweden)	Karlsruhe, Germany	10 Feb 2008
4 x 200 m relay	1:32.41	Russia (Yekaterina Kondratyeva, Irina Khabarova, Yuliya Pechonkina, Yulia Gushchina)	Glasgow, UK	29 Jan 2005
4 x 400 m relay	3:23.37	Russia (Yulia Gushchina, Olga Kotlyarova, Olga Zaytseva, Olesya Krasnomovets)	Glasgow, UK	28 Jan 2006
★ 4 x 800 m relay	•8:12.41	Moscow 1 (Tatyana Andrianova, Oksana Sukhachova-Spasovkhodskaya, Elena Kofanova, Yevgeniya Zinurova)	Moscow, Russia	28 Feb 2010
3,000 m walk	11:40.33	Claudia Stef (Romania)	Bucharest, Romania	30 Jan 1999

• Still awaiting ratification at the time of going to press

OFFICIAL WEBSITES
ATHLETICS: WWW.IAAF.ORG
ULTRARUNNING: WWW.IAU.ORG.TW

ATHLETICS - ULTRA LONG DISTANCE (TRACK)

MEN	TIME/DISTANCE	NAME & NATIONALITY	LOCATION	DATE
50 km	2:48.06	Jeff Norman (GB)	Timperley, UK	7 Jun 1980
100 km	6:10.20	Donald Ritchie (GB)	London, UK	28 Oct 1978
100 miles	11:28.03	Oleg Kharitonov (Russia)	London, UK	20 Oct 2002
1,000 km	5 days 16:17.00	Yiannis Kouros (Greece)	Colac, Australia	26 Nov–1 Dec 1984
1,000 miles	11 days 13:54.58	Peter Silkinas (Lithuania)	Nanango, Australia	11–23 Mar 1998
6 hours	97.2 km (60.4 miles)	Donald Ritchie (GB)	London, UK	28 Oct 1978
12 hours	162.4 km (100.91 miles)	Yiannis Kouros (Greece)	Montauban, France	15–16 Mar 1985
24 hours	303.506 km (188.59 miles)	Yiannis Kouros (Greece)	Adelaide, Australia	4–5 Oct 1997
48 hours	473.495 km (294.21 miles)	Yiannis Kouros (Greece)	Surgères, France	3–5 May 1996
6 days	1,038.851 km (645.51 miles)	Yiannis Kouros (Greece)	Colac, Australia	20–26 Nov 2005

WOMEN	TIME/DISTANCE	NAME & NATIONALITY	LOCATION	DATE
50 km	3:18.52	Carolyn Hunter-Rowe (GB)	Barry, UK	3 Mar 1996
100 km	7:14.06	Norimi Sakurai (Japan)	Verona, Italy	27 Sep 2003
100 miles	14:25.45	Edit Berces (Hungary)	Verona, Italy	21–22 Sep 2002
1,000 km	7 days 1:28.29	Eleanor Robinson (GB)	Nanango, Australia	11–18 Mar 1998
1,000 miles	13 days 1:54.02	Eleanor Robinson (GB)	Nanango, Australia	11–23 Mar 1998
6 hours	83.2 km (57.7 miles)	Norimi Sakurai (Japan)	Verona, Italy	27 Sep 2003
12 hours	147.6 km (91.71 miles)	Ann Trason (USA)	Hayward, USA	3–4 Aug 1991
24 hours	250.106 km (155.40 miles)	Edit Berces (Hungary)	Verona, Italy	21–22 Sep 2002
★ 48 hours	385.130 km (239.31 miles)	Mami Kudo (Japan)	Surgères, France	22–24 May 2009
6 days	883.631 km (549.06 miles)	Sandra Barwick (New Zealand)	Campbelltown, Australia	18–24 Nov 1990

INDOOR 5,000 M
Meseret Defar (Ethiopia) is elated after winning the women's 5,000 m in a time of 14 min 24.37 sec at the Stockholm Globe Arena, Sweden, on 18 February 2009.

DUNDEE, UK
Jenny Wood-Allen (b. 1911) from Dundee, UK, is the **oldest female to complete a marathon**. She ran the 2002 London Marathon in 11 hr 34 min, aged 90 years 145 days.

56°28'N 2°59'W

SPORTS
SPORTS REFERENCE

ATHLETICS - ROAD RACE

MEN	TIME	NAME & NATIONALITY	LOCATION	DATE
★10 km	27:01	Micah Kipkemboi Kogo (Kenya)	Brunssum, the Netherlands	29 Mar 2009
15 km	41:29	Felix Limo (Kenya)	Nijmegen, the Netherlands	11 Nov 2001
	41:29	Deriba Merga (Ethiopia)	Ras Al Khaimah, UAE	20 Feb 2009
★20 km	55.21	Zersenay Tadese (Eritrea)	Lisbon, Portugal	21 Mar 2010
★Half marathon	58.23	Zersenay Tadese (Eritrea)	Lisbon, Portugal	21 Mar 2010
★25 km	•1:11:50	Samuel Kiplimo Kosgei (Kenya)	Berlin, Germany	9 May 2010
★30 km	1:27:49	Haile Gebrselassie (Ethiopia)	Berlin, Germany	20 Sep 2009
Marathon	2:03:59	Haile Gebrselassie (Ethiopia)	Berlin, Germany	28 Sep 2008
100 km	6:13:33	Takahiro Sunada (Japan)	Tokoro, Japan	21 Jun 1998
Road relay	1:57:06	Kenya (Josephat Ndambiri, Martin Mathathi, Daniel Mwangi, Mekubo Mogusu, Onesmus Nyerere, John Kariuki)	Chiba, Japan	23 Nov 2005

WOMEN	TIME	NAME & NATIONALITY	LOCATION	DATE
10 km	30:21	Paula Radcliffe (GB)	San Juan, Puerto Rico	23 Feb 2003
★15 km	46:28	Tirunesh Dibaba (Ethiopia)	Nijmegen, the Netherlands	15 Nov 2009
20 km	1:02:57	Lornah Kiplagat (Netherlands)	Udine, Italy	14 Oct 2007
Half marathon	1:06:25	Lornah Kiplagat (Netherlands)	Udine, Italy	14 Oct 2007
25 km	1:22:13	Mizuki Noguchi (Japan)	Berlin, Germany	25 Sep 2005
30 km	1:38:49	Mizuki Noguchi (Japan)	Berlin, Germany	25 Sep 2005
Marathon	2:15:25	Paula Radcliffe (GB)	London, UK	13 Apr 2003
100 km	6:33:11	Tomoe Abe (Japan)	Tokoro, Japan	25 Jun 2000
Road relay	2:11:41	China (Jiang Bo, Dong Yanmei, Zhao Fentgting, Ma Zaijie, Lan Lixin, Li Na)	Beijing, China	28 Feb 1998

• Still awaiting ratification at the time of going to press

ATHLETICS - RACE WALKING

MEN	TIME	NAME & NATIONALITY	LOCATION	DATE
20,000 m	1:17:25.6	Bernardo Segura (Mexico)	Bergen, Norway	7 May 1994
20 km (road)	1:17:16	Vladimir Kanaykin (Russia)	Saransk, Russia	29 Sep 2007
30,000 m	2:01:44.1	Maurizio Damilano (Italy)	Cuneo, Italy	3 Oct 1992
50,000 m	3:40:57.9	Thierry Toutain (France)	Héricourt, France	29 Sep 1996
50 km (road)	3:34:14	Denis Nizhegorodov (Russia)	Cheboksary, Russia	11 May 2008

WOMEN	TIME	NAME & NATIONALITY	LOCATION	DATE
10,000 m	41:56.23	Nadezhda Ryashkina (USSR)	Seattle, USA	24 Jul 1990
20,000 m	1:26:52.3	Olimpiada Ivanova (Russia)	Brisbane, Australia	6 Sep 2001
20 km (road)	1:25:41	Olimpiada Ivanova (Russia)	Helsinki, Finland	7 Aug 2005

ATHLETICS - INDOOR FIELD EVENTS

MEN	RECORD	NAME & NATIONALITY	LOCATION	DATE	
High jump	2.43 m (7 ft 11.66 in)	Javier Sotomayor (Cuba)	Budapest, Hungary	4 Mar 1989	* 60 m 6.71 seconds; long jump 7.73 m; shot 13.12 m; high jump 2.11 m; 60 m hurdles 7.77 seconds; pole vault 5.10 m; 1,000 m 2 min 32.67 sec
Pole vault	6.15 m (20 ft 2.12 in)	Sergei Bubka (Ukraine)	Donetsk, Ukraine	21 Feb 1993	
Long jump	8.79 m (28 ft 10.06 in)	Carl Lewis (USA)	New York City, USA	27 Jan 1984	
★Triple jump	17.90 m (58 ft 9 in)	Teddy Tamgho (France)	Doha, Qatar	14 Mar 2010	
Shot	22.66 m (74 ft 4.12 in)	Randy Barnes (USA)	Los Angeles, USA	20 Jan 1989	
★Heptathlon*	•6,499 points	Ashton Eaton (USA)	Fayetteville, USA	13 Mar 2010	

WOMEN	RECORD	NAME & NATIONALITY	LOCATION	DATE	
High jump	2.08 m (6 ft 9.8 in)	Kajsa Bergqvist (Sweden)	Arnstadt, Germany	4 Feb 2006	† 60 m hurdles 8.22 seconds; high jump 1.93 m; shot 13.25 m; long jump 6.67 m; 800 m 2 min 10.26 sec
Pole vault	5.00 m (16 ft 4 in)	Yelena Isinbayeva (Russia)	Donetsk, Ukraine	15 Feb 2009	
Long jump	7.37 m (24 ft 2.15 in)	Heike Drechsler (GDR)	Vienna, Austria	13 Feb 1988	
Triple jump	15.36 m (50 ft 4.72 in)	Tatyana Lebedeva (Russia)	Budapest, Hungary	6 Mar 2004	
Shot	22.50 m (73 ft 9.82 in)	Helena Fibingerová (Czechoslovakia)	Jablonec, Czechoslovakia	19 Feb 1977	
Pentathlon†	4,991 points	Irina Belova (EUN)	Berlin, Germany	15 Feb 1992	

• Still awaiting ratification at the time of going to press

★ MEN'S HALF MARATHON

On 21 March 2010, Zersenay Tadese (Eritrea) won the 20th Lisbon Half Marathon in Portugal. He did so in a time of 58 min 23 sec, and during the same race ran the 20 km in a record 55 min 21 sec.

★ NEW RECORD
★ UPDATED RECORD

★HEPTATHLON

Ashton Eaton (USA) is shown below during the pole vault competition of the heptathlon in Fayetteville, USA, on 13 March 2010. He set a new mark of 6,499 points, thereby breaking Dan O'Brien's 17-year-old record.

OFFICIAL WEBSITES
ATHLETICS & RACE WALKING:
WWW.IAAF.ORG
CYCLING:
WWW.UCI.CH

ATHLETICS - OUTDOOR FIELD EVENTS

MEN	RECORD	NAME & NATIONALITY	LOCATION	DATE
High jump	2.45 m (8 ft 0.45 in)	Javier Sotomayor (Cuba)	Salamanca, Spain	27 Jul 1993
Pole vault	6.14 m (20 ft 1.73 in)	Sergei Bubka (Ukraine)	Sestriere, Italy	31 Jul 1994
Long jump	8.95 m (29 ft 4.36 in)	Mike Powell (USA)	Tokyo, Japan	30 Aug 1991
Triple jump	18.29 m (60 ft 0.78 in)	Jonathan Edwards (GB)	Gothenburg, Sweden	7 Aug 1995
Shot	23.12 m (75 ft 10.23 in)	Randy Barnes (USA)	Los Angeles, USA	20 May 1990
Discus	74.08 m (243 ft 0.53 in)	Jürgen Schult (USSR)	Neubrandenburg, Germany	6 Jun 1986
Hammer	86.74 m (284 ft 7 in)	Yuriy Sedykh (USSR)	Stuttgart, Germany	30 Aug 1986
Javelin	98.48 m (323 ft 1.16 in)	Jan Železný (Czech Republic)	Jena, Germany	25 May 1996
Decathlon*	9,026 points	Roman Šebrle (Czech Republic)	Götzis, Austria	27 May 2001
WOMEN	**RECORD**	**NAME & NATIONALITY**	**LOCATION**	**DATE**
High jump	2.09 m (6 ft 10.28 in)	Stefka Kostadinova (Bulgaria)	Rome, Italy	30 Aug 1987
★Pole vault	5.06 m (16 ft 7.21 in)	Yelena Isinbayeva (Russia)	Zurich, Switzerland	28 Aug 2009
Long jump	7.52 m (24 ft 8.06 in)	Galina Chistyakova (USSR)	St. Petersburg, Russia	11 Jun 1988
Triple jump	15.50 m (50 ft 10.23 in)	Inessa Kravets (Ukraine)	Gothenburg, Sweden	10 Aug 1995
Shot	22.63 m (74 ft 2.94 in)	Natalya Lisovskaya (USSR)	Moscow, Russia	7 Jun 1987
Discus	76.80 m (252 ft)	Gabriele Reinsch (GDR)	Neubrandenburg, Germany	9 Jul 1988
★Hammer	77.96 m (255 ft 9 in)	Anita Wlodarczyk (Poland)	Berlin, Germany	22 Aug 2009
Javelin	72.28 m (253 ft 6 in)	Barbora Spotáková (Czech Republic)	Stuttgart, Germany	13 Sep 2008
Heptathlon†	7,291 points	Jacqueline Joyner-Kersee (USA)	Seoul, South Korea	24 Sep 1988
Decathlon**	8,358 points	Austra Skujyte (Lithuania)	Columbia, USA	15 Apr 2005

*100 m 10.64 seconds; long jump 8.11 m; shot 15.33 m; high jump 2.12 m; 400 m 47.79 seconds; 110 m hurdles 13.92 seconds; discus 47.92 m; pole vault 4.80 m; javelin 70.16 m; 1,500 m 4 min 21.98 sec

† 100 m hurdles 12.69 seconds; high jump 1.86 m; shot 15.80 m; 200 m 22.56 seconds; long jump 7.27 m; javelin 45.66 m; 800 m 2 min 8.51 sec

** 100 m 12.49 seconds; long jump 6.12 m; shot 16.42 m; high jump 1.78 m; 400 m 57.19 seconds; 100 m hurdles 14.22 seconds; discus 46.19 m; pole vault 3.10 m; javelin 48.78 m; 1,500 m 5 min 15.86 sec

CYCLING - ABSOLUTE TRACK

MEN	TIME/DISTANCE	NAME & NATIONALITY	LOCATION	DATE
★200 m (flying start)	9.572	Kevin Sireau (France)	Moscow Russia	30 May 2009
500 m (flying start)	24.758	Chris Hoy (GB)	La Paz, Bolivia	13 May 2007
1 km (standing start)	58.875	Arnaud Tournant (France)	La Paz, Bolivia	10 Oct 2001
4 km (standing start)	4:11.114	Christopher Boardman (GB)	Manchester, UK	29 Aug 1996
Team 4 km (standing start)	3:53.314	Great Britain (Ed Clancy, Paul Manning, Geraint Thomas, Bradley Wiggins)	Beijing, China	18 Aug 2008
1 hour	*49.7 km	Ondrej Sosenka (Czech Republic)	Moscow, Russia	19 Jul 2005
WOMEN	**TIME/DISTANCE**	**NAME & NATIONALITY**	**LOCATION**	**DATE**
200 m (flying start)	10.831	Olga Slioussareva (Russia)	Moscow, Russia	25 Apr 1993
500 m (flying start)	29.655	Erika Salumäe (USSR)	Moscow, Russia	6 Aug 1987
★500 m (standing start)	33.296	Simona Krupeckaite (Lithuania)	Pruszków, Poland	25 Mar 2009
3 km (standing start)	3:24.537	Sarah Ulmer (New Zealand)	Athens, Greece	22 Aug 2004
1 hour	*46.065 km	Leontien Zijlaard-Van Moorsel (Netherlands)	Mexico City, Mexico	1 Oct 2003

*Some athletes achieved better distances within an hour with bicycles that are no longer allowed by the Union Cycliste Internationale (UCI). The 1-hour records given here are in accordance with the new UCI rules.

MEN'S CYCLING 500 M FLYING START

Chris Hoy (UK) celebrates breaking the world 500 m altitude record at the Alto Irpavi Velodrome, on 13 May 2007 in La Paz, Bolivia. He achieved a time of 24.758 seconds.

TRIVIA

DID YOU KNOW? TRACK RACING DATES BACK TO THE END OF THE 19TH CENTURY. THE FIRST TRACK WORLD CHAMPIONSHIPS WERE HELD IN 1895. CYCLING WAS ALSO INCLUDED AS AN EVENT IN THE FIRST MODERN OLYMPIC GAMES OF 1896.

★WOMEN'S CYCLING 500 M STANDING START

Simona Krupeckaite (Lithuania) rode the women's 500 m in a time of 33.296 seconds at the UCI Track Cycling World Championships held at the BGZ Arena in Pruszków, Poland, on 25 March 2009.

SPORTS
SPORTS
SPORTS REFERENCE

★ ★ ★ ★ ★

★MEN'S STATIC APNEA

On 8 June 2009 in Hyeres, France, freediver Stephane Mifsud (France) held his breath under water in the men's static apnea event, clocking a time of 11 min 35 sec.

FREEDIVING

MEN'S DEPTH DISCIPLINES	DEPTH/TIME	NAME & NATIONALITY	LOCATION	DATE
★Constant weight with fins	•124 m (406 ft 9 in)	Herbert Nitsch (Austria)	The Bahamas	22 Apr 2010
★Constant weight without fins	•95 m (311 ft 8 in)	William Trubridge (New Zealand)	The Bahamas	26 Apr 2010
★Variable weight	142 m (465 ft 10 in)	Herbert Nitsch (Austria)	The Bahamas	7 Dec 2009
No limit	214 m (702 ft)	Herbert Nitsch (Austria)	Spetses, Greece	14 Jun 2007
★Free immersion	•120 m (393 ft 8 in)	Herbert Nitsch (Austria)	The Bahamas	25 Apr 2010
MEN'S DYNAMIC APNEA	**DEPTH/TIME**	**NAME & NATIONALITY**	**LOCATION**	**DATE**
With fins	250 m (800 ft 2 in)	Alexey Molchanov (Russia)	Lignano, Italy	5 Oct 2008
Without fins	213 m (698 ft 9 in) 213 m (698 ft 9 in)	Tom Sietas (Germany) Dave Mullins (New Zealand)	Hamburg, Germany Wellington, New Zealand	2 Jul 2008 12 Aug 2008
MEN'S STATIC APNEA	**DEPTH/TIME**	**NAME & NATIONALITY**	**LOCATION**	**DATE**
★Duration	11 min 35 sec	Stephane Mifsud (France)	Hyères, France	8 Jun 2009
WOMEN'S DEPTH DISCIPLINES	**DEPTH/TIME**	**NAME & NATIONALITY**	**LOCATION**	**DATE**
Constant weight with fins	96 m (314 ft 11 in)	Sara Campbell (UK)	The Bahamas	2 Apr 2009
★Constant weight without fins	62 m (203 ft 5 in)	Natalia Molchanova (Russia)	The Bahamas	3 Dec 2009
Variable weight	122 m (400 ft 3 in)	Tanya Streeter (USA)	Turks and Caicos Islands	19 Jul 2003
No limit	160 m (524 ft 11 in)	Tanya Streeter (USA)	Turks and Caicos Islands	17 Aug 2002
Free immersion	85 m (278 ft 10 in)	Natalia Molchanova (Russia)	Crete, Greece	27 Jul 2008
WOMEN'S DYNAMIC APNEA	**DEPTH/TIME**	**NAME & NATIONALITY**	**LOCATION**	**DATE**
★With fins	225 m (738 ft 2 in)	Natalia Molchanova (Russia)	Moscow, Russia	25 Apr 2010
★Without fins	160 m (524 ft 11 in)	Natalia Molchanova (Russia)	Aarhus, Denmark	20 Aug 2009
WOMEN'S STATIC APNEA	**DEPTH/TIME**	**NAME & NATIONALITY**	**LOCATION**	**DATE**
★Duration	8 min 23 sec	Natalia Molchanova (Russia)	Aarhus, Denmark	21 Aug 2009

ROWING

MEN	TIME	NAME & NATIONALITY	LOCATION	DATE
★Single sculls	6:33.35	Mahe Drysdale (New Zealand)	Poznan, Poland	29 Aug 2009
Double sculls	6:03.25	Jean-Baptiste Macquet, Adrien Hardy (France)	Poznan, Poland	17 Jun 2006
Quadruple sculls	5:36.20	Christopher Morgan, James McRae, Brendan Long, Daniel Noonan (Australia)	Beijing, China	10 Aug 2008
Coxless pairs	6:14.27	Matthew Pinsent, James Cracknell (GB)	Seville, Spain	21 Sep 2002
Coxless fours	5:41.35	Sebastian Thormann, Paul Dienstbach, Philipp Stüer, Bernd Heidicker (Germany)	Seville, Spain	21 Sep 2002
Coxed pairs*	6:42.16	Igor Boraska, Tihomir Frankovic, Milan Razov (Croatia)	Indianapolis, USA	18 Sep 1994
Coxed fours*	5:58.96	Matthias Ungemach, Armin Eichholz, Armin Weyrauch, Bahne Rabe, Jörg Dederding (Germany)	Vienna, Austria	24 Aug 1991
Eights	5:19.85	Deakin, Beery, Hoopman, Volpenhein, Cipollone, Read, Allen, Ahrens, Hansen (USA)	Athens, Greece	15 Aug 2004
LIGHTWEIGHT	**TIME**	**NAME & NATIONALITY**	**LOCATION**	**DATE**
Single sculls*	6:47.82	Zac Purchase (GB)	Eton, UK	26 Aug 2006
Double sculls	6:10.02	Mads Rasmussen, Rasmus Quist (Denmark)	Amsterdam, the Netherlands	23 Jun 2007
Quadruple sculls*	5:45.18	Francesco Esposito, Massimo Lana, Michelangelo Crispi, Massimo Guglielmi (Italy)	Montreal, Canada	Aug 1992
Coxless pairs*	6:26.61	Tony O'Connor, Neville Maxwell (Ireland)	Paris, France	1994
Coxless fours	5:45.60	Thomas Poulsen, Thomas Ebert, Eskild Ebbesen, Victor Feddersen (Denmark)	Lucerne, Switzerland	9 Jul 1999
Eights*	5:30.24	Altena, Dahlke, Kobor, Stomporowski, Melges, März, Buchheit, Von Warburg, Kaska (Germany)	Montreal, Canada	Aug 1992
WOMEN	**TIME**	**NAME & NATIONALITY**	**LOCATION**	**DATE**
Single sculls	7:07.71	Rumyana Neykova (Bulgaria)	Seville, Spain	21 Sep 2002
Double sculls	6:38.78	Georgina and Caroline Evers-Swindell (New Zealand)	Seville, Spain	21 Sep 2002
Quadruple sculls	6:10.80	Kathrin Boron, Katrin Rutschow-Stomporowski, Jana Sorgers, Kerstin Köppen (Germany)	Duisburg, Germany	19 May 1996
Coxless pairs	6:53.80	Georgeta Andrunache, Viorica Susanu (Romania)	Seville, Spain	21 Sep 2002
Coxless fours*	6:25.35	Robyn Selby Smith, Jo Lutz, Amber Bradley, Kate Hornsey (Australia)	Eton, UK	26 Aug 2006
Eights	5:55.50	Mickelson, Whipple, Lind, Goodale, Sickler, Cooke, Shoop, Francia, Davies (USA)	Eton, UK	27 Aug 2006
LIGHTWEIGHT	**TIME**	**NAME & NATIONALITY**	**LOCATION**	**DATE**
Single sculls*	7:28.15	Constanta Pipota (Romania)	Paris, France	19 Jun 1994
Double sculls	6:49.77	Dongxiang Xu, Shimin Yan (China)	Poznan, Poland	17 Jun 2006
Quadruple sculls*	6:23.96	Hua Yu, Haixia Chen, Xuefei Fan, Jing Liu (China)	Eton, UK	27 Aug 2006
Coxless pairs*	7:18.32	Eliza Blair, Justine Joyce (Australia)	Aiguebelette-le-Lac, France	7 Sep 1997

Denotes non-Olympic boat classes

58°28'N
2°14'W

MANCHESTER, UK

Liverpool Road Station in Manchester, UK, is the **oldest railway station.** It was first used on 15 September 1830 and was finally closed on 30 September 1975.

SPEED SKATING - LONG TRACK

MEN	TIME/POINTS	NAME & NATIONALITY	LOCATION	DATE
500 m	34.03	Jeremy Wotherspoon (Canada)	Salt Lake City, USA	9 Nov 2007
2 x 500 m	68.31	Jeremy Wotherspoon (Canada)	Calgary, Canada	15 Mar 2008
1,000 m	1:06.42	Shani Davis (USA)	Salt Lake City, USA	7 Mar 2009
★1,500 m	•1:41.04	Shani Davis (USA)	Salt Lake City, USA	11 Dec 2009
3,000 m	3:37.28	Eskil Ervik (Norway)	Calgary, Canada	5 Nov 2005
5,000 m	6:03.32	Sven Kramer (Netherlands)	Calgary, Canada	17 Nov 2007
10,000 m	12:41.69	Sven Kramer (Netherlands)	Salt Lake City, USA	10 Mar 2007
500/1,000/500/1,000 m	137.230 points	Jeremy Wotherspoon (Canada)	Calgary, Canada	18–19 Jan 2003
500/3,000/1,500/5,000 m	146.365 points	Erben Wennemars (Netherlands)	Calgary, Canada	12–13 Aug 2005
500/5,000/1,500/10,000 m	145.742 points	Shani Davis (USA)	Calgary, Canada	18–19 Mar 2006
Team pursuit (eight laps)	3:37.80	Netherlands (Sven Kramer, Carl Verheijen, Erben Wennemars)	Salt Lake City, USA	11 Mar 2007

WOMEN	TIME/POINTS	NAME & NATIONALITY	LOCATION	DATE
★500 m	•37.00	Jenny Wolf (Germany)	Salt Lake City, USA	11 Dec 2009
2 x 500 m	74.42	Jenny Wolf (Germany)	Salt Lake City, USA	10 Mar 2007
1,000 m	1:13.11	Cindy Klassen (Canada)	Calgary, Canada	25 Mar 2006
1,500 m	1:51.79	Cindy Klassen (Canada)	Salt Lake City, USA	20 Nov 2005
3,000 m	3:53.34	Cindy Klassen (Canada)	Calgary, Canada	18 Mar 2006
5,000 m	6:45.61	Martina Sáblíková (Czech Republic)	Salt Lake City, USA	11 Mar 2007
500/1,000/500/1,000 m	149.305 points 149.305 points	Monique Garbrecht-Enfeldt (Germany) Cindy Klassen (Canada)	Salt Lake City, USA Calgary, Canada	11–12 Jan 2003 24–25 Mar 2006
500/1,500/1,000/3,000 m	155.576 points	Cindy Klassen (Canada)	Calgary, Canada	15–17 Mar 2001
500/3,000/1,500/5,000 m	154.580 points	Cindy Klassen (Canada)	Calgary, Canada	18–19 Mar 2006
★Team pursuit (six laps)	2:55.79	Canada (Kristina Groves, Christine Nesbitt, Brittany Schussler)	Calgary, Canada	6 Dec 2009

•Still awaiting ratification at the time of going to press

SPEED SKATING - SHORT TRACK

MEN	TIME/POINTS	NAME & NATIONALITY	LOCATION	DATE
★500 m	•40.651	Sung Si-Bak (South Korea)	Marquette, USA	14 Nov 2009
1,000 m	1:23.454	Charles Hamelin (Canada)	Montreal, Canada	18 Jan 2009
1,500 m	2:10.639	Ahn Hyun-Soo (South Korea)	Marquette, USA	24 Oct 2003
3,000 m	4:32.646	Ahn Hyun-Soo (South Korea)	Beijing, China	7 Dec 2003
5,000 m relay	6:38.486	South Korea (Kwak Yoon-Gy, Lee Ho-Suk, Lee Jung-Su, Sung Si-Bak)	Salt Lake City, USA	19 Oct 2008

WOMEN	TIME/POINTS	NAME & NATIONALITY	LOCATION	DATE
500 m	42.609	Wang Meng (China)	Beijing, China	29 Nov 2008
★1,000 m	•1:29.049	Zhou Yang (China)	Vancouver, Canada	26 Feb 2010
1,500 m	2:16.729	Zhou Yang (China)	Salt Lake City, USA	9 Feb 2008
3,000 m	4:46.983	Jung Eun-Ju (South Korea)	Harbin, China	15 Mar 2008
★3,000 m relay	•4:06.610	China (Sun Linlin, Wang Meng, Zhang Hui, Zhou Yang)	Vancouver, Canada	24 Feb 2010

•Still awaiting ratification at the time of going to press

★ **NEW RECORD**
★ **UPDATED RECORD**

★WOMEN'S 3,000 M SHORT TRACK RELAY

China's gold medallists Sun Linlin, Wang Meng, Zhang Hui and Zhou Yang (from left to right) attend the medal ceremony at the Vancouver Winter Olympics in Canada. They skated the women's 3,000 m relay in a time of 4 min 6.61 sec on 24 February 2010.

MEN'S 1,500 M LONG TRACK

Shani Davis (USA) skates during the ISU World Cup Speed Skating Championships at the Utah Olympic Oval in Kearns, Salt Lake City, USA. Here he finished the 1,500 m in a time of 1 min 41.04 sec. He holds two more records: the "big combination" (with 145.742 points), which he has held since March 2006, and the 1,000 m (in 1 min 6.42 sec).

OFFICIAL WEBSITES
FREEDIVING:
WWW.AIDA-INTERNATIONAL.ORG
ROWING:
WWW.WORLDROWING.COM
SPEED SKATING:
WWW.ISU.ORG

SPORTS

SPORTS REFERENCE

SWIMMING – LONG COURSE (50 M POOL)

MEN	TIME	NAME & NATIONALITY	LOCATION	DATE
★50 m freestyle	20.91	Cesar Cielo Filho (Brazil)	Sao Paulo, Brazil	18 Dec 2009
★100 m freestyle	46.91	Cesar Cielo Filho (Brazil)	Rome, Italy	30 Jul 2009
★200 m freestyle	1:42.00	Paul Biedermann (Germany)	Rome, Italy	28 Jul 2009
★400 m freestyle	3:40.07	Paul Biedermann (Germany)	Rome, Italy	26 Jul 2009
★800 m freestyle	7:32.12	Zhang Lin (China)	Rome, Italy	29 Jul 2009
1,500 m freestyle	14:34.56	Grant Hackett (Australia)	Fukuoka, Japan	29 Jul 2001
4 x 100 m freestyle relay	3:08.24	USA (Michael Phelps, Garrett Weber-Gale, Cullen Jones, Jason Lezak)	Beijing, China	11 Aug 2008
★4 x 200 m freestyle relay	6:58.55	USA (Michael Phelps, Ricky Berens, David Walters, Ryan Lochte)	Rome, Italy	31 Jul 2009
50 m butterfly	22.43	Rafael Muñoz (Spain)	Malaga, Spain	5 Apr 2009
100 m butterfly	49.82	Michael Phelps (USA)	Rome, Italy	1 Aug 2009
200 m butterfly	1:51.51	Michael Phelps (USA)	Rome, Italy	29 Jul 2009
★50 m backstroke	24.04	Liam Tancock (UK)	Rome, Italy	2 Aug 2009
★100 m backstroke	51.94	Aaron Peirsol (USA)	Indianapolis, USA	8 Jul 2009
★200 m backstroke	1:51.92	Aaron Peirsol (USA)	Rome, Italy	31 Jul 2009
★50 m breaststroke	26.67	Cameron van der Burgh (South Africa)	Rome, Italy	29 Jul 2009
★100 m breaststroke	58.58	Brenton Rickard (Australia)	Rome, Italy	27 Jul 2009
★200 m breaststroke	2:07.31	Christian Sprenger (Australia)	Rome, Italy	30 Jul 2009
★200 m medley	1:54.10	Ryan Lochte (USA)	Rome, Italy	30 Jul 2009
400 m medley	4:03.84	Michael Phelps (USA)	Beijing, China	10 Aug 2008
★4 x 100 m medley relay	3:27.28	USA (Aaron Peirsol, Eric Shanteau, Michael Phelps, David Walters)	Rome, Italy	2 Aug 2009

WOMEN	TIME	NAME & NATIONALITY	LOCATION	DATE
★50 m freestyle	23.73	Britta Steffen (Germany)	Rome, Italy	2 Aug 2009
★100 m freestyle	52.07	Britta Steffen (Germany)	Rome, Italy	31 Jul 2009
★200 m freestyle	1:52.98	Federica Pellegrini (Italy)	Rome, Italy	29 Jul 2009
★400 m freestyle	3:59.15	Federica Pellegrini (Italy)	Rome, Italy	26 Jul 2009
800 m freestyle	8:14.10	Rebecca Adlington (UK)	Beijing, China	16 Aug 2008
1,500 m freestyle	15:42.54	Kate Ziegler (USA)	Mission Viejo, USA	17 Jun 2007
★4 x 100 m freestyle relay	3:31.72	Netherlands (Inge Dekker, Ranomi Kromowidjojo, Femke Heemskerk, Marleen Veldhuis)	Rome, Italy	26 Jul 2009
★4 x 200 m freestyle relay	7:42.08	China (Yang Yu, Zhu Qian Wei, Liu Jing, Pang Jiaying)	Rome, Italy	30 Jul 2009
★50 m butterfly	25.07	Therese Alshammar (Sweden)	Rome, Italy	31 Jul 2009
★100 m butterfly	56.06	Sarah Sjostrom (Sweden)	Rome, Italy	27 Jul 2009
★200 m butterfly	•2:01.81	Liu Zige (China)	Jinan, China	21 Oct 2009
★50 m backstroke	27.06	Zhao Jing (China)	Rome, Italy	30 Jul 2009
★100 m backstroke	58.12	Gemma Spofforth (UK)	Rome, Italy	28 Jul 2009
★200 m backstroke	2:04.81	Kirsty Coventry (Zimbabwe)	Rome, Italy	1 Aug 2009
★50 m breaststroke	29.80	Jessica Hardy (USA)	Federal Way, USA	7 Aug 2009
★100 m breaststroke	1:04.45	Jessica Hardy (USA)	Federal Way, USA	7 Aug 2009
★200 m breaststroke	2:20.12	Annamay Pierse (Canada)	Rome, Italy	30 Jul 2009
★200 m medley	2:06.15	Ariana Kukors (USA)	Rome, Italy	27 Jul 2009
★400 m medley	4:29.45	Stephanie Rice (Australia)	Beijing, China	10 Aug 2008
★4 x 100 m medley relay	3:52.19	China (Zhao Jing, Chen Huijia, Jiao Liuyang, Li Zhesi)	Rome, Italy	1 Aug 2009

• *Still awaiting ratification at the time of going to press*

★ MEN'S 200 M BREASTSTROKE

Christian Sprenger (Australia) competes in the 200 m breaststroke final during the 13th Fédération Internationale de Natation (FINA) World Championships on 30 July 2009 in Rome, Italy. He finished in 2 min 7.31 sec.

★ **NEW RECORD**
★ **UPDATED RECORD**

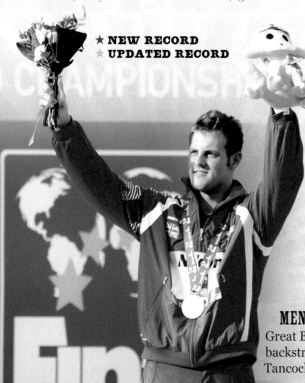

MEN'S 50 M BACKSTROKE

Great Britain's Liam Tancock stands on the podium after winning the 50 m backstroke at the FINA World Championships in Rome, Italy, on 2 August 2009. Tancock won gold and set a new world record of 24.04 seconds.

The **earliest surviving film** is a sensitized 53.9-mm-wide (2.1-in) paper roll that runs at 10 to 12 frames per second. It was shot by Louis Aimé Augustin Le Prince (UK), who filmed the garden of his father-in-law Joseph Whitley, in Roundhay, Leeds, West Yorkshire, UK, in October 1888.

SWIMMING – SHORT COURSE (25 M POOL)

MEN	TIME	NAME & NATIONALITY	LOCATION	DATE
★50 m freestyle	20.30	Roland Schoeman (South Africa)	Pietermaritzburg, South Africa	8 Aug 2009
100 m freestyle	44.94	Amaury Leveaux (France)	Rijeka, Croatia	13 Dec 2008
★200 m freestyle	1:39.37	Paul Biedermann (Germany)	Berlin, Germany	15 Nov 2009
★400 m freestyle	3:32.77	Paul Biedermann (Germany)	Berlin, Germany	14 Nov 2009
800 m freestyle	7:23.42	Grant Hackett (Australia)	Melbourne, Australia	20 Jul 2008
1,500 m freestyle	14:10.10	Grant Hackett (Australia)	Perth, Australia	7 Aug 2001
★4 x 100 m freestyle relay	3:03.30	USA (Nathan Adrian, Matt Greves, Garrett Weber-Gale, Michael Phelps)	Manchester, UK	19 Dec 2009
★4 x 200 m freestyle relay	6:51.05	Canada (Colin Russel, Stefan Hirniak, Brent Hayden, Joel Greenshields)	Leeds, UK	7 Aug 2009
★50 m butterfly	21.80	Steffen Deibler (Germany)	Berlin, Germany	14 Nov 2009
★100 m butterfly	48.48	Evgeny Korotyshkin (Russia)	Berlin, Germany	15 Nov 2009
★200 m butterfly	1:49.11	Kaio Almeida (Brazil)	Stockholm, Sweden	10 Nov 2009
★50 m backstroke	22.61	Peter Marshall (USA)	Singapore, Singapore	22 Nov 2009
★100 m backstroke	48.94	Nick Thoman (USA)	Manchester, UK	18 Dec 2009
★200 m backstroke	1:46.11	Arkady Vyatchanin (Russia)	Berlin, Germany	15 Nov 2009
★50 m breaststroke	25.25	Cameron van der Burgh (South Africa)	Berlin, Germany	14 Nov 2009
★100 m breaststroke	55.61	Cameron van der Burgh (South Africa)	Berlin, Germany	15 Nov 2009
★200 m breaststroke	•2:00.67	Daniel Gyurta (Hungary)	Istanbul, Turkey	13 Dec 2009
★100 m medley	•50.76	Peter Mankoc (Slovenia)	Istanbul, Turkey	12 Dec 2009
★200 m medley	1:51.55	Darian Townsend (South Africa)	Berlin, Germany	15 Nov 2009
★400 m medley	•3:57.27	Laszlo Cseh (Hungary)	Istanbul, Turkey	11 Dec 2009
★4 x 100 m medley relay	3:19.16	Russia (Stanislav Donets, Sergey Geybel, Evgeny Korotyshkin, Danila Izotov)	St Petersburg, Russia	20 Dec 2009

WOMEN	TIME	NAME & NATIONALITY	LOCATION	DATE
50 m freestyle	23.25	Marleen Veldhuis (Netherlands)	Manchester, UK	13 Apr 2008
★100 m freestyle	51.01	Lisbeth Trickett (Australia)	Hobart, Australia	10 Aug 2009
★200 m freestyle	•1:51.17	Federica Pellegrini (Italy)	Istanbul, Turkey	13 Dec 2009
★400 m freestyle	3:54.92	Joanne Jackson (UK)	Leeds, UK	8 Aug 2009
800 m freestyle	8:04.53	Alessia Filippi (Italy)	Rijeka, Croatia	12 Dec 2008
★1,500 m freestyle	15:28.65	Lotte Friis (Denmark)	Birkerod, Denmark	28 Nov 2009
4 x 100 m freestyle relay	3:28.22	Netherlands (Hinkelien Schreuder, Inge Dekker, Ranomi Kromowidjojo, Marleen Veldhuis)	Amsterdam, the Netherlands	19 Dec 2008
4 x 200 m freestyle relay	7:38.90	Netherlands (Inge Dekker, Femke Heemskerk, Marleen Veldhuis, Ranomi Kromowidjojo)	Manchester, UK	9 Apr 2008
★50 m butterfly	24.38	Therese Alshammar (Sweden)	Singapore, Singapore	22 Nov 2009
★100 m butterfly	•55.05	Diane Bui-Duyet (France)	Istanbul, Turkey	12 Dec 2009
★200 m butterfly	2:00.78	Liu Zige (China)	Berlin, Germany	15 Nov 2009
★50 m backstroke	•25.70	Sanja Jovanovic (Croatia)	Istanbul, Turkey	12 Dec 2009
★100 m backstroke	55.23	Sakai Shiho (Japan)	Berlin, Germany	15 Nov 2009
★200 m backstroke	2:00.18	Sakai Shiho (Japan)	Berlin, Germany	14 Nov 2009
★50 m breaststroke	28.80	Jessica Hardy (USA)	Berlin, Germany	15 Nov 2009
★100 m breaststroke	1:02.70	Rebecca Soni (USA)	Manchester, UK	19 Dec 2009
★200 m breaststroke	2:14.57	Rebecca Soni (USA)	Manchester, UK	18 Dec 2009
★100 m medley	57.74	Hinkelien Schreuder (Netherlands)	Berlin, Germany	15 Nov 2009
★200 m medley	2:04.60	Julia Smit (USA)	Manchester, UK	19 Dec 2009
★400 m medley	4:21.04	Julia Smit (USA)	Manchester, UK	18 Dec 2009
★4 x 100 m medley relay	3:47.97	USA (Margaret Hoelzer, Jessica Hardy, Dana Vollmer, Amanda Weir)	Manchester, UK	18 Dec 2009

• *Still awaiting ratification at the time of going to press*

OFFICIAL WEBSITE SWIMMING: WWW.FINA.ORG

★MEN'S 50 M BUTTERFLY

Steffen Deibler (Germany) swims in a men's 50 m butterfly heat at the FINA short course World Cup in Berlin, Germany, on 14 November 2009. He achieved a record 21.80 seconds in the event.

★WOMEN'S 1,500 M FREESTYLE

Lotte Friis (Denmark) swam the women's 1,500 m short course freestyle in a time of 15 min 28.65 sec in Birkerod, Denmark, on 28 November 2009.

EXTRA! FOR TALES OF RECORD-BREAKING ACHIEVEMENTS ON THE WORLD'S OCEANS, TURN TO P.118.

ZARAGOZA, SPAIN
On 18 May 2003, a total of 157 mixed couples performed the folk dance "The Jota of Aragon" for eight minutes in Zaragoza, Spain, making this the **largest castanet dance** ever performed.

41°39'N
0°53'W

SPORTS

SPORTS REFERENCE

★ ★ ★ ★ ★

MEN'S 77 KG SNATCH

Lu Xiaojun (China) lifts 174 kg in the snatch in the men's 77 kg category at the World Weightlifting Championships in Goyang, South Korea, on 24 November 2009. Xiaojun also holds the record for the total, having successfully lifted 378 kg at the same event.

★ WOMEN'S 75+ KG CLEAN & JERK

Jang Mi-Ran (South Korea) celebrates after lifting 187 kg in the clean and jerk in the women's 75+ kg category at the World Weightlifting Championships in Goyang, South Korea, on 28 November 2009. She also holds the records for the snatch and the total in this category.

OFFICIAL WEBSITES
WEIGHTLIFTING:
WWW.IWF.NET

WATERSKIING:
WWW.IWSF.COM

WEIGHTLIFTING

MEN	CATEGORY	WEIGHT	NAME & NATIONALITY	LOCATION	DATE
56 kg	Snatch	138 kg	Halil Mutlu (Turkey)	Antalya, Turkey	4 Nov 2001
	Clean & jerk	168 kg	Halil Mutlu (Turkey)	Trencín, Slovakia	24 Apr 2001
	Total	305 kg	Halil Mutlu (Turkey)	Sydney, Australia	16 Sep 2000
62 kg	Snatch	153 kg	Shi Zhiyong (China)	Izmir, Turkey	28 Jun 2002
	Clean & jerk	182 kg	Le Maosheng (China)	Busan, South Korea	2 Oct 2002
	Total	326 kg	Zhang Jie (China)	Kanazawa, Japan	28 Apr 2008
69 kg	Snatch	165 kg	Georgi Markov (Bulgaria)	Sydney, Australia	20 Sep 2000
	Clean & jerk	197 kg	Zhang Guozheng (China)	Qinhuangdao, China	11 Sep 2003
	Total	357 kg	Galabin Boevski (Bulgaria)	Athens, Greece	24 Nov 1999
77 kg	★ Snatch	174 kg	Lu Xiaojun (China)	Goyang, South Korea	24 Nov 2009
	Clean & jerk	210 kg	Oleg Perepetchenov (Russia)	Trencín, Slovakia	27 Apr 2001
	★ Total	378 kg	Lu Xiaojun (China)	Goyang, South Korea	24 Nov 2009
85 kg	Snatch	187 kg	Andrei Rybakou (Belarus)	Chiang Mai, Thailand	22 Sep 2007
	Clean & jerk	218 kg	Zhang Yong (China)	Ramat Gan, Israel	25 Apr 1998
	Total	394 kg	Andrei Rybakou (Belarus)	Beijing, China	15 Aug 2008
94 kg	Snatch	188 kg	Akakios Kakhiasvilis (Greece)	Athens, Greece	27 Nov 1999
	Clean & jerk	232 kg	Szymon Kolecki (Poland)	Sofia, Bulgaria	29 Apr 2000
	Total	412 kg	Akakios Kakhiasvilis (Greece)	Athens, Greece	27 Nov 1999
105 kg	Snatch	200 kg	Andrei Aramnau (Belarus)	Beijing, China	18 Aug 2008
	Clean & jerk	237 kg	Alan Tsagaev (Bulgaria)	Kiev, Ukraine	25 Apr 2004
	Total	436 kg	Andrei Aramnau (Belarus)	Beijing, China	18 Aug 2008
105+ kg	Snatch	213 kg	Hossein Rezazadeh (Iran)	Qinhuangdao, China	14 Sep 2003
	Clean & jerk	263 kg	Hossein Rezazadeh (Iran)	Athens, Greece	25 Aug 2004
	Total	476 kg	Hossein Rezazadeh (Iran)	Sydney, Australia	26 Sep 2000
WOMEN	CATEGORY	WEIGHT	NAME & NATIONALITY	LOCATION	DATE
48 kg	Snatch	98 kg	Yang Lian (China)	Santo Domingo, Dominican Republic	1 Oct 2006
	Clean & jerk	120 kg	Chen Xiexia (China)	Taian City, China	21 Apr 2007
	Total	217 kg	Yang Lian (China)	Santo Domingo, Dominican Republic	1 Oct 2006
53 kg	Snatch	102 kg	Ri Song-Hui (North Korea)	Busan, South Korea	1 Oct 2002
	Clean & jerk	129 kg	Li Ping (China)	Taian City, China	22 Apr 2007
	Total	226 kg	Qiu Hongxia (China)	Santo Domingo, Dominican Republic	2 Oct 2006
58 kg	Snatch	111 kg	Chen Yanqing (China)	Doha, Qatar	3 Dec 2006
	Clean & jerk	141 kg	Qiu Hongmei (China)	Taian City, China	23 Apr 2007
	Total	251 kg	Chen Yanqing (China)	Doha, Qatar	3 Dec 2006
63 kg	Snatch	116 kg	Pawina Thongsuk (Thailand)	Doha, Qatar	12 Nov 2005
	Clean & jerk	142 kg	Pawina Thongsuk (Thailand)	Doha, Qatar	4 Dec 2006
	Total	257 kg	Liu Haixia (China)	Chiang Mai, Thailand	23 Sep 2007
69 kg	Snatch	128 kg	Liu Chunhong (China)	Beijing, China	13 Aug 2008
	Clean & jerk	158 kg	Liu Chunhong (China)	Beijing, China	13 Aug 2008
	Total	286 kg	Liu Chunhong (China)	Beijing, China	13 Aug 2008
75 kg	★ Snatch	132 kg	Svetlana Podobedova (Kazakhstan)	Goyang, South Korea	28 Nov 2009
	★ Clean & jerk	160 kg	Svetlana Podobedova (Kazakhstan)	Goyang, South Korea	28 Nov 2009
	★ Total	292 kg	Svetlana Podobedova (Kazakhstan)	Goyang, South Korea	28 Nov 2009
75+ kg	Snatch	140 kg	Jang Mi-Ran (South Korea)	Beijing, China	16 Aug 2008
	★ Clean & jerk	187 kg	Jang Mi-Ran (South Korea)	Goyang, South Korea	28 Nov 2009
	Total	326 kg	Jang Mi-Ran (South Korea)	Beijing, China	16 Aug 2008

VALENCIA, SPAIN

On the last Wednesday in August the town of Buñol, near Valencia, Spain, holds its annual tomato festival. At the 2004 Tomatina, 38,000 people spent one hour at the world's **largest food fight** throwing about 125 tonnes (275,500 lb) of tomatoes at each other.

WATERSKIING

MEN	RECORD	NAME & NATIONALITY	LOCATION	DATE
Slalom	1.5 buoy | 9.75-m line | 58 km/h	Chris Parrish (USA)	Trophy Lakes, USA	28 Aug 2005
Barefoot slalom	20.6 crossings of wake in 30 seconds	Keith St Onge (USA)	Bronkhorstspruit, South Africa	6 Jan 2006
Tricks	12,400 points	Nicolas Le Forestier (France)	Lac de Joux, Switzerland	4 Sep 2005
★Barefoot tricks	11,250 points	Keith St Onge (USA)	Maize, USA	15 Aug 2009
★Jump	75.2 m (246 ft 8 in)	Freddy Krueger (USA)	Seffner, USA	2 Nov 2008
Barefoot jump	27.4 m (89 ft 11 in)	David Small (GB)	Mulwala, Australia	8 Feb 2004
Ski fly	91.1 m (298 ft 10 in)	Jaret Llewellyn (Canada)	Orlando, USA	14 May 2000
Overall	2,818.01 points*	Jaret Llewellyn (Canada)	Seffner, USA	29 Sep 2002

WOMEN	RECORD	NAME & NATIONALITY	LOCATION	DATE
Slalom ★	1 buoy | 10.25-m line | 55 km/h	Kristi Overton Johnson (USA) Karina Nowlan (Australia) Regina Jaquess (USA)	West Palm Beach, USA Sacramento, USA Santa Rosa, USA	14 Sep 1996 22 Sep 2008 4 Jul 2009
Barefoot slalom	17.0 crossings of wake in 30 seconds	Nadine de Villiers (South Africa)	Witbank, South Africa	5 Jan 2001
★Tricks	9,080 points	Natallia Berdnikava (Belarus)	Polk City, USA	31 Oct 2009
★Barefoot tricks	4,400 points	Nadine de Villiers (South Africa)	Witbank, South Africa	5 Jan 2001
★Jump	56.6 m (186 ft)	Elena Milakova (Russia)	Rio Linda, USA	21 Jul 2002
Barefoot jump	20.6 m (67 ft 7 in)	Nadine de Villiers (South Africa)	Pretoria, South Africa	4 Mar 2000
Ski fly	69.4 m (227 ft 8.2 in)	Elena Milakova (Russia)	Pine Mountain, USA	26 May 2002
★Overall	2,934.36 points**	Regina Jaquess (USA)	Santa Rosa, USA	17 Jul 2009

*5@11.25 m, 10,730 tricks, 71.7 m jump **4@10.75 m, 8,180 tricks, 52.2 m jump; calculated with the 2006 scoring method

★WOMEN'S OVERALL
Waterskiier Regina Jaquess (USA) in action on 17 July 2009 at Santa Rosa, California, USA. She achieved an overall score of 2,934.36 points.

LONGEST SPORTS MARATHONS

SPORT	TIME	NAME & NATIONALITY	LOCATION	DATE
★Aerobics	26 hours	Dinaz Vervatwala (India)	Secunderabad, India	9–10 Jan 2010
★Baseball	48 hr 9 min 27 sec	Jonny G Foundation Cardinals and Edward Jones Browns (USA)	St Louis, Missouri, USA	9–11 Oct 2009
★Basketball	82 hours	Treverton College (South Africa)	Mooi River, South Africa	7–10 Aug 2009
Basketball (wheelchair)	26 hr 3 min	University of Omaha students and staff (USA)	Omaha, Nebraska, USA	24–25 Sep 2004
Bowling (tenpin)	120 hours	Andy Milne (Canada)	Mississauga, Ontario, Canada	24–29 Oct 2005
Bowls (indoor)	36 hours	Arnos Bowling Club (UK)	Southgate, London, UK	20–21 Apr 2002
★Bowls (outdoor)	170 hr 3 min	Goulburn Railway Bowling Club (Australia)	Goulburn, NSW, Australia	19–26 Jan 2009
★Cricket	67 hr 9 min	New South Wales Police Force officers (Australia)	Bateau Bay, NSW, Australia	8–11 Feb 2009
★Curling	54 hr 1 min	The Burlington Golf and Country Club (Canada)	Burlington, Ontario, Canada	12–14 Mar 2010
★Darts (doubles)	30 hours	Richard Saunders, Lee Hannant, Andrew Brymer, Paul Taylor (UK)	Twyford, Berkshire, UK	9–10 Jan 2009
Darts (singles)	26 hr 42 min	Stephen Wilson and Robert Henderson (UK)	Palnackie, Scotland, UK	20–21 Jun 2008
Floorball	24 hr 15 min	TRM Floorball and Hornets Regio Moosseedorf Worblental (Switzerland)	Zollikofen, Switzerland	27–28 Apr 2007
★Football	37 hours	TSV Mutlangen & FC Raron II (Germany)	Mutlangen, Germany	16–17 Jul 2009
★Football (five-a-side)	27 hr 15 min	Collingwood College Challengers & Radio Basingstoke Bandits (UK)	Camberley, Surrey, UK	17–18 Oct 2009
Hockey (ice)	241 hr 21 min	Brent Saik and friends (Canada)	Strathcona, Alberta, Canada	8–18 Feb 2008
Hockey (indoor)	50 hours	Bert & Macs and Mid-Town Certigard teams (Canada)	Lethbridge, Alberta, Canada	25–27 Mar 2008
Hockey (inline/roller)	24 hours	8K Roller Hockey League (USA)	Eastpointe, Michigan, USA	13–14 Sep 2002
Hockey (street)	105 hr 17 min	Molson Canadian and Canadian Tire teams (Canada)	Lethbridge, Alberta, Canada	20–24 Aug 2008
Korfball	30 hr 2 min	Kingfisher Korfball Club (UK)	Larkfield, Kent, UK	14–15 Jun 2008
Netball	58 hours	Sleaford Netball Club (UK)	Sleaford, Lincolnshire, UK	25–27 Jul 2008
★Pétanque (boules)	52 hours	Gilles de B'Heinsch (Belgium)	Arlon, Belgium	18–20 Sep 2009
Pool (singles)	53 hr 25 min	Brian Lilley and Daniel Maloney (USA)	Spring Lake, North Carolina, USA	10–12 Oct 2008
Skiing	202 hr 1 min	Nick Willey (Australia)	Thredbo, NSW, Australia	2–10 Sep 2005
Snowboarding	180 hr 34 min	Bernhard Mair (Austria)	Bad Kleinkirchheim, Austria	9–16 Jan 2004
Table football	51 hr 52 min	Alexander Gruber, Roman Schelling, Enrico Lechtaler, Christian Nägele (Austria)	Bregenz, Austria	27–29 Jun 2008
Table tennis (doubles)	101 hr 1 min 11 sec	Lance, Phil and Mark Warren, Bill Weir (USA)	Sacramento, California, USA	9–13 Apr 1979
Table tennis (singles)	132 hr 31 min	Danny Price and Randy Nunes (USA)	Cherry Hill, New Jersey, USA	20–26 Aug 1978
Tennis (doubles)	50 hr 0 min 8 sec	Vince Johnson, Bill Geideman, Brad Ansley, Allen Finley (USA)	Hickory, North Carolina, USA	7–9 Nov 2008
★Tennis (singles)	36 hr 36 min 36 sec	Jeroen Wagenaar and Serge Fernando (Netherlands)	Hellevoetsluis, the Netherlands	11–12 Sep 2009
Volleyball (beach)	24 hr 10 min	Krzysztof Garbulski, Michal Fuks, Adam Jankowski, Tomasz Konior (Poland)	Ustka, Poland	27–28 Jun 2008
Volleyball (indoor)	76 hr 30 min	Zespół Szkół Ekonomicznych students (Poland)	Sosnowiec, Poland	4–7 Dec 2009

★ NEW RECORD ★ UPDATED RECORD

LONDON, UK
Davenports in London is the **oldest magic shop**. The family-run business was founded in 1898 by Lewis Davenport (UK) and opened at his home on Ryles Road, Plaistow, London, UK, in 1903.

0°22'N 0°07'W

CREDITS & ACKNOWLEDGEMENTS

★ ★ ★ ★ ★ ★ ★ ★ ★ ★ ★ ★

QUIZ ANSWERS

Q1, p.29
What was the name given to NASA's first space shuttle?
A: *Columbia*

Q2, p.47
How long is the aye aye's tale?
A: 50.5 cm (20 in)

Q3, p.56
To which group do the following belong, mollusc or crustacean?
A: Crab; B: Octopus; C: Slug
A: A) crustacean; B) mollusc; C) mollusc

Q4, p.58
Of all the fish in the sea, which is the largest?
A: whale shark

Q5, p.60
Which classic arcade videogame features an amphibian attempting to cross a road and a river?
A: *Frogger*

Q6, p.80
Which of these measures the most: the longest beard, longest moustache or highest hairstyle?
A: Longest moustache at 4.29 m (14 ft) held by Ram Singh Chauhan (India)

Q7, p.92
Anssi Vanhala solved a Rubik's cube in 36.77 seconds using...?
A: The feet

Q8, p.112
What was the name of the vehicle that first broke the speed of sound on land and who was its pilot?
A: *Thrust SSC*, driven by Andy Green

Q9, p.117
In 1911, Norway's Roald Amundsen became the first man to reach the South Pole. What other polar record did he achieve 15 years later?
A: He made the first aircraft flight over the North Pole, in the airship *Norge*

Q10, p.124
On average, how many graves did Johann Heinrich Karl Thime dig a year in his 50-year career?
A: Over 466 graves – that's more than one a day!

Q11, p.131
How old is the oldest person accused of murder?
A: 98-years-old

Q12, p.132
Who did Carlos Slim Helu replace as the world's richest man?
A: Bill Gates

Q13, p.138
On 2 May 2007, Lup Fun Yau set a new record for the most jam doughnuts eaten in three minutes. But how many did he eat?
A: six

Q14, p.179
Who is *Hurt Locker* director Katheryn Bigelow's famous ex?
A: James Cameron

Q15, p.180
Which animated movie was the first to be made in stereoscopic 3D?
A: *Monsters Vs Aliens*

Q16, p.225
Michael Schumacher is an F1 legend, but he is not the youngest driver to finish an F1 race. Who is?
A: Jaime Alguersuari of Spain

Q17, p.230
How many countries have the Harlem Globetrotters played in to date?
A: 120 countries

Q18, p.232
Who wrote the Marquess of Queensbury rules?
A: No, it wasn't the Marquess of Queensbury – he only endorsed the rules. They were written by Welsh sporting all-rounder John Graham Chambers. We have him to thank for boxing gloves and the ten-count

Q19, p.257
What number do you get if you add together the most worms charmed to the most horseshoe pitching titles won?
A: 582 (567 worms plus 15 horseshoe titles)

Q20, p.261
Which is higher: the highest wall climb on a bicycle... or the highest wall climb by a dog?
A: 2.89 m (9 ft 5.9 in)

Guinness World Records would like to thank the following individuals, companies, groups, websites, societies, schools, colleges and universities for their help in the creation of the 2011 edition:

Academy of Motion Picture Arts & Sciences, Oscar Rogelio Antillon Aceituno, Heather Anderson, Ulla Anlander, Roberta Armani, Arriva London, All at Ascent Media, Astoria Park (Queens, NYC), Ted Batchelor and family, Bender Media Services (Sally Treibel, Susan Bender), Beano Max, British Film Institute, Robert Bierfreund, Oliver Blair (Dyson), Bleedingcool.com (Rich Johnston), Luke and Joseph Boatfield, Brian Bolland, Boostamonte Mountainboarding (Brad Beren), Richard Booth, Olivia and Alexander Boulton, Ceri, Katie, Georgie and Emily Boulton, Alfie Boulton-Fay, Victor Bourdariat, Pete Bouvier, Box Office Mojo, Jason Bradbury, Matthew R I Bradford, Bragster team (Dan Barrett, Andy Dust, Luke Forsythe, Adam Moore, Peter Vandenberk), British Waterways Scotland (Donald Macpherson), Sarah Brown, Vittorio 100% Brumotti, Rachel Buchholz (NGK Magazine), Business Week, Kirk, Beth and Gavin Butterfield, CCTV (Guo Tong, Wang Wei and Tony), Kwang-Sung Chun, Simone Ciancotti, Cinefex, Adam Cloke, Mark Collins, Columbus Zoo, Ohio, USA, Commission for the Geological Map of the World, Connexion Cars (Rob and Tracey), Julia Cottrell, Gerard Danford, Debby DeGroot, Deno's Wonder Wheel Amusement Park, Coney Island, USA, Jose Torres Diaz, Doctor Who (BBC America, Russell T Davies, Stephen Moffat, Matt Smith and David Tennant), Doctor Who Magazine, Electric Sky (Jakki Hart and David Pounds), Louis Epstein, ESPN X Games (Marc Murphy, Dan Gordner, Valerie Benardinelli, Katie Moses Swope, Danny Chi, Crystal Yang and Amy Lupo), Eurodata TV Worldwide, Europroducciones TV, Europroducciones, Europroduzzione and Veralia (Renato Vacatello, Stefano Torrisi, Carlo Boserman, Marco Fernandez De Araoz, Gabriela Ventura, Marco Boserman, Mar Izquierdo, Maria Ligues, Dario Viola, Amato Penasilico and Chiara Duranti), Amelia Ewen, Toby Ewen, Eyeworks Australia & New Zealand (Julie Christie, Joanne Law, Philippa Rennie, Erin Downton, Georgina Sinclair, Marc Ellis and James Kerley), Eyeworks Europe (Wim, Kathe, Oliver and Pian), Molly & Isobel Fay, Finnish Naval Academy (Sr lt Tero Hanski), First News (Serena Lacy, Kelane Henderson and the team), FJT Logistics Limited, Forbes, Formulation Inc, The Gadget Show, Alfons Gidlöf, Vilgot Gidlöf, Karen Gillen, Go' Morgen Danmark/Go' Aften Danmark, Google, Alan Green (International Regulations Commission, International Sailing Federation), Jordan, Ryan and Brandon Greenwood, Victoria Grimsell, Kris Growcott, GXT (Paula, Giuliano and Francesco), Haaga-Helia University of Applied Sciences, Hachette Book Group (Craig Young, Vanessa Vasquez and Todd McGarity), Kari Haering (Zone Living), Dan Hall, Hampshire Sports and Prestige Cars, Ray Harper, Roger Hawkins, Merja Hedman and the Finnish Sauna Society, Stuart Hendry, Gavin Hennessey, Tamsin Holman, Hollywood Press Association, Marsha K Hoover, Alistair Humphreys, ICM (Michael Kagan and Greg Lipstone), I Gri.siani hair salon, Rome, Italy, Infomag (Emin Gorgun and Ipek Hazneci), Infostrada Sports (Philip Hennemann and Erik Kleinpenning), INP Media (Bryn Downing), International Commission on Stratigraphy, Internet Movie Database, The Irish Sun (Helen Morrogh), ITV

Productions (Jeremy Philips, Caz Stuart and Bernard Kelly), Melanie Johnson, Richard Johnston, Andy Jones, Todd Klein, Dr Erwin J.O. Kompanje and family, Sultan and Hasan Kösen, Kathrine Krone, Olaf Kuchenbecker, Josh Kushins (Lucasfilm), Orla and Thea Langton, Jony Levi, Paul Levitz, Carey Low, Jim Lyngvild, Sean Macaulay, Manda, Macmillan Distribution, Norman D Mangawang, Médiamétrie, Melia White House Hotel, London, Clare Merryfield, Mark Messenger, Dan Meyer, Millennium Seed Bank (Sarah Moss), Steven Moffat, Sophie and Joshua Molloy, Monte-Carlo Television Festival, National Geographic Kids, NBA (Gail Hunter, Patrick Sullivan, Jason Lodato and Karen Barberan), David Nelson, New York City Police Department, The Nielson Company, Jan Nielsen, Norddeich (York and Jurgen), Andrea Oddone, Outline Productions (Laura Mansfield, Diana Hunter and Helen Veale), Andres Ostrofsky, Paley Center for Media, New York, USA (Ron Simon), Eddie Palmer, Dan Phillips, Stuart Phillips, POD Worldwide (Christy Chin, Alex Iskandar Liew and Yip Cheong), Rob Pullar, Queen's Head and Artichoke, RCAF Trenton, Ontario, Canada, Ryan Reiter (Hollywood Almost Free Outdoor Cinema), R&G Productions (Stephane Gateau, Jerome Revon, Patrice Parmentier, Vanina Latcheva and Deborah Amar), Martyn Richards Research (Martyn Richards), Ristorante Sant'Eustorgio (Paolo e Filippo Introini), Stephen Rodriguez (MLS), Ian Rollins, Roma Medical (John Pitt and John Dalton), Edward Russell, Eric Sakowski, Scottish Canoe Association (Margaret Winter), The Scottish Sun (Gill Smith and Graeme Donohue), Screecher's Pix (Hayma, Monique and Ryan), Secondskin Makeup Artist, Alex Segura (DC Comics), Victor Hugo Camacho Sedano, Joshua Selinger, Tom Sergeant, SET Japan (Adrian Grey), Dean Shaw (Game Stores Group), Chris Sheedy, The Simpsons (Matt Groening, Antonia Coffman and Art Villanueva), Richard Sisson, Sky 1 (James Townley), Glori Slater (K9 Storm Inc), Carlton J Smith, Matt Smith, Nick Smith, Phee Smith, Sean Sorensen (Motion Theory), Southern California Steampunks, Tom Spilsbury, Ian Starr, Start Licensing (Ian Downes), Daniel Stolar, St Pancras International (Kate Fisher), Nick Steel, Ri Streeter (Weta Workshop), Seyda Subasi-Gemici, The Sultan's Tent restaurant, Toronto, Canada, The Sun (Caroline Iggulden and Dave Masters), Atichart Tavornmard, Charlie Taylor, Holly Taylor, Stephen Taylor, Torfaen County Borough Council (Ben Payne, communications officer), TNR (Claire, Sophie and Tessa), Virgin London Marathon (Natasha Grainger, Nicola Okey and Tiffany Osborne), UCLH (Sharon Spiteri), Maria Vivas, Wandsworth Film Office, Louisa, Jessica, Isabel and Sam Way, Westminster City Council (Francesca Pipe), Adam Wide, Dan Woods, World Health Organization, World Health Statistics, Oz Wright, David Wyatt, X Games, YouTube, Zippy Productions.

IN MEMORIA
Henry Allingham (**oldest living man**), Gertrude Baines (**oldest living woman**), Melvin Boothe (**longest fingernails - male**), Terry Calcott (**fastest motocycle wheelie**), Chanel and Otto (**oldest dogs**), Gibson (**tallest dog**), Michael Jackson (**most successful pop artist**), Lurch (**largest horn circumference - steer**), He Pingping (**shortest living mobile man**), Tomoji Tanabe (**oldest living man**), Helen Wagner (**longest serving soap star**), Don Vesco (**fastest wheel-driven vehicle**)

PICTURE CREDITS
2 Ranald Mackechnie/GWR; Tristan Savatier; Takezo2000 **3** Robert Vos/Photoshot **5** Paul Michael Hughes/GWR **6** NASA; John Wright/GWR; John Wright/GWR **7** Marc Henrie/Getty Images; Paul Michael Hughes/GWR **8** Intro (UK) all John Kirkby **9** Paul Michael Hughes/GWR; Ken McKay/Rex Features **10** Gareth Cattermole/Getty Images **11** Maria Elisa Duque/GWR; Chen Jie/GWR **8** Intro (Int) Graig Abel/Getty Images **9** Ed Oudenaarden/Getty Images; Paul Michael Hughes/GWR **10** Paul Michael Hughes/GWR **11** Maria Elisa Duque/GWR; Chen Jie/GWR; Rafa Rivas/Getty Images; Jasper Juinen/Getty Images **8** Paul Michael Hughes/GWR; Paul Michael Hughes/GWR; Paul Michael Hughes/GWR **9** Charles Eshelman/Getty Images; Richard Bradbury/GWR **10** Joe Murphy/Getty Images Jacob Chinn/Guinness World Records **11** Maria Elisa Duque/GWR; Chen Jie/GWR **8** Jamie Squire/Getty Images; Michael Kappeler/Getty Images; Streeter Lecka/Getty Images; Streeter Lecka/Getty Images **9** Richard Bradbury/GWR **11** Maria Elisa Duque/GWR; Chen Jie/GWR; Richard Bradbury/GWR **12** Paul Michael Hughes/GWR **13** Adam Bouska; Paul Michael Hughes/GWR; Paul Michael Hughes/GWR **14** Paul Michael Hughes/GWR; Getty Images **15** Paul Michael Hughes/GWR; John Wright/GWR **16** Paul Michael Hughes/GWR **17** Paul Michael Hughes/GWR **18** Paul Michael Hughes/GWR **19** Paul Michael Hughes/GWR **20** Tim Anderson/GWR; Yuri Ceschin/GWR; Press Eye **21** Tim Anderson/GWR; Hakan Eijkenboom; Yuri Ceschin/GWR **22** all NASA **24** NASA; Robert Gendler/Science Photo Library **25** Steve A Munsinger/Science Photo Library; NASA/Science Photo Library; David Ducros/Science Photo Library **26** all NASA **27** all NASA **28** Getty Images; NASA **29** Lori Losey/Getty Images; Getty Images; NASA **30** NASA **31** Dorling Kindersley; G Scharmer, L Rouppe van der Voort (KVA)/Reel EFX Inc. **32** Getty Images **33** M Timothy O'Keefe/Alamy **34** Daniel Riordan; Tom Fox/Corbis **35** Corbis; Grant Dixon/Getty Images **36** Alamy; Eitan Simanor/Getty Images **37** Kevin Schafer/Getty Images; Getty Images; John Beatty/Getty Images **38** Paul Nicklen/Getty Images NASA; Stephen Belcher/FLPA **39** Steven Miller/NRL; NOAA/National Science Foundation **40** Reuters; Jeff Hunter/Getty Images

INDEX

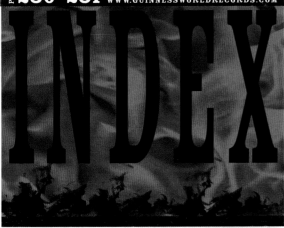

★ ★ ★ ★ ★ ★ ★ ★ ★ ★ ★

This year's index is organized into two parts: by subject and by superlative. Bold entries in the subject index indicate a main entry on a topic, and entries in BOLD CAPITALS indicate an entire chapter. Neither index lists personal names.

INTRODUCTION
STOP PRESS

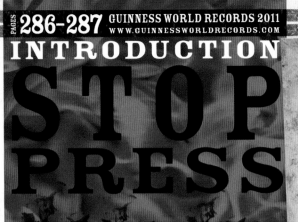

★ ★ ★ ★ ☆

★ FASTEST VIOLIN PLAYER

Ben Lee (UK), of violin duo FUSE, played "Flight of the Bumblebee" in 1 min 4.21 sec in London, UK, on 7 April 2010. The quality of the performance was verified by Rodney Friend, the leader/ concertmaster who has performed with the London Symphony Orchestra, New York Philharmonic Orchestra and the BBC Symphony Orchestra in a career spanning 30 years.

★ OLDEST LIVING PERSON

Just as we were going to press we received this image of Eugénie Blanchard (St Barts, France, b. 16 February 1896), who became the oldest person on the planet upon the death of the previous record holder, Kama Chinen (Japan), on 2 May 2010. Eugénie shares her nationality with the **oldest person ever**; *see p.83 for details.*

★ MOST PORK SCRATCHINGS EATEN

Scott Dustan (UK) ate 27 g (0.95 oz) of deep-fried cured pork rind in one minute at The Union, London, UK, on 30 April 2010. At the same event, Courtney Shapiro (USA/UK) consumed 21 g (0.74 oz) in 30 seconds.

★ FASTEST TIME TO KAYAK/CANOE LOCH NESS

A team of 26 Asda employees and suppliers led by senior meat buyer Jim Viggars (all UK) kayaked the length of Loch Ness, UK, from Fort Augustus to Dores (a distance of 17.9 nautical miles; 33.15 km; 20.59 miles) in 5 hr 19 min 17 sec on 18 May 2010. The record attempt was organized to raise funds for the Tickled Pink breast cancer charity. All of the team members lined up to cross the finish line together and therefore achieved the same time.

★ LARGEST GAME OF MUSICAL STATUES

A total of 1,079 participants took part in a game of musical statues at an event organized by Danone Finland in Helsinki, Finland, on 25 April 2010.

★ GREATEST PRIZE MONEY FOR A HORSE RACE

The largest prize fund for a single horse race is $10 million (£6.71 million), for the Dubai World Cup, held at Meydan Racecourse in Dubai, UAE, on 27 March 2010.

★ SHORTEST PERSON TO PERFORM A WING WALK

The **shortest professional stuntman**, Kiran Shah (UK), stands at 1 m 26.3 cm (4 ft 1.7 in) and performed his first wing walk in Cirencester, Gloucestershire, UK, on 30 April 2010.

LARGEST PASTA BOWL

Buca di Beppo Italian Restaurant (USA) served up a stomach-bulging 6,253-kg (13,786-lb) bowl of pasta at the chain's Anaheim restaurant, Garden Grove, California, USA, on 12 March 2010.

FREE SPAGHETTI MARCH 15

THE ★ LARGEST CAR MOSAIC WAS CREATED WITH 460 VOLKSWAGEN CARS IN AN EVENT ORGANIZED BY VOLKSWAGEN DO BRASIL IN SÃO PAULO, BRAZIL, ON 10 APRIL 2010.

EXTRA!
IS IT ART YOU ARE
LOOKING FOR?
IF SO, TURN TO
PP. 190-191.

APNEA: The suspension of breathing, particularly that practised by divers, from the Greek verb "to breathe".

LARGEST ICE MAZE

The Arctic Glacier Ice Maze (USA) at the Buffalo Powder Keg Festival in Buffalo, New York, USA, featured an ice maze measuring 1,194.33 m² (12,855.68 ft²) on 26 February 2010. The maze was constructed using 2,171 blocks of ice, each weighing 136.08 kg (300 lb).

★ LARGEST SCULPTURE MADE FROM RECYCLED MATERIAL

Under the auspices of RESUR, the local government consortium for the recycling of solid waste materials, a team of students from the Granada School of Architecture in Granada, Spain, designed and built a castle measuring 29 m (95 ft 1.7 in) long, 14.07 m (46 ft 1.9 in) wide and 7 m (22 ft 11.5 in) tall from approximately 50,000 tetra pak milk cartons on 17 May 2010. The cartons were collected by the primary schools in the Granada region in the two weeks before the record attempt took place. The structure had no internal frame and was held together solely with staples and string.

★ MOST CANS CRUSHED WITH A VEHICLE IN THREE MINUTES

Ian Batey crushed 61,106 cans in three minutes driving a 9-tonne (10-ton) monster truck for Burn Energy Drink (UAE) at the Jumeirah Beach Residence, in Dubai, UAE, on 6 March 2010.

★ FREEDIVING/ DYNAMIC APNEA WITH FINS (WOMEN)

Natalia Molchanova (Russia) dived to a depth of 225 m (738 ft 2 in) without an external oxygen supply in Moscow, Russia, on 25 April 2010, breaking her own record.

★ LONGEST BUBBLE CHAIN

Just as we were finishing off this year's book, bubble blower Sam Heath (aka Sam Sam the Bubbleman) popped into the GWR offices in London, UK, where he created a chain of 26 bubbles. Sam used a standard drinking straw and bubble wand to make the chain.

SHAVES
BARBER JOHN McGUIRE (IRELAND) SHAVED A RECORD 60 HEADS IN ONE HOUR ON THE THE RAY D'ARCY SHOW ON TODAY FM IN DUBLIN, IRELAND, ON 18 FEBRUARY 2010.

WAVES
RTÉ'S THE AFTERNOON SHOW ORGANIZED 414 SWIMMING LESSONS ACROSS IRELAND TO CLAIM THE RECORD FOR THE ★LARGEST SWIMMING LESSON OVER MULTIPLE LOCATIONS ON 21 MAY 2010.

★ NEW RECORD
★ UPDATED RECORD

1940

8 MARCH In Finland, Viipuri falls to Red Army, but Stalin refuses an armistice.

9–11 APRIL German troops invade Norway and Denmark. Denmark surrenders. First British troops dispatched to Norway.

10 MAY Hitler launches invasion of the Low Countries and France, engaging French and British forces.

4 JUNE Last British evacuation ship leaves Dunkirk.

4 AUGUST Italians invade British Somaliland in East Africa.

20 SEPTEMBER – 29 OCTOBER Chinese attack Japanese lines, repelling them into Indochina.

25 OCTOBER Hostilities end in German-occupied France.

28 OCTOBER Italian troops invade Greece from occupied Albania.

---

5 APRIL Allies inform Norway and Sweden that they will begin mining Norwegian waters.

10 APRIL Major naval engagements between British and German ships. German cruiser *Königsberg* sunk by British dive-bombing attack.

17 JUNE Japan starts a blockade to stop military supplies reaching China.

3 JULY The Royal Navy attacks French fleet at Oran and Mers-el-Kebir to prevent ships from falling into German hands.

6 JULY First U-boat base in France opens at Lorient on the Atlantic coast.

9 JULY First battle between British and Italian naval forces in Mediterranean.

17–20 OCTOBER U-boats sink 32 ships from convoys SC-7 and HX-79.

---

31 JANUARY RAF Coastal Command planes enter service with ASV (Air to Surface Vessel) radar, which could detect surfaced submarines at a range of up to 36 miles (58km).

11 JUNE Italian aircraft bomb British bases at Malta, Aden and Port Sudan.

30 JULY First phase of Battle of Britain ends.

7 SEPTEMBER London subjected to massive bombing as *Luftwaffe* begins move to night *Blitz* attacks.

14/15 NOVEMBER Air raid on Coventry causes severe damage and marks commencement of heavy attacks on British industrial cities.

4/5 DECEMBER The RAF bombs Turin and Dusseldorf.

---

12 MARCH Peace agreement between USSR and Finland signed in Moscow.

27 APRIL Germany declares war on Norway.

8 MAY Neville Chamberlain resigns as British Prime Minister. Winston Churchill replaces him.

28 MAY King Leopold of Belgium orders his army to surrender to Germany.

10 JUNE Norway surrenders to Germany.

22 JUNE Armistice signed between France and Germany.

16 SEPTEMBER US introduces conscription.

27 SEPTEMBER Japan signs tripartite pact with Germany and Italy.

1941

22 JANUARY Tobruk falls to the British.

7 MARCH British and Commonwealth troops land in Greece. Within two months they have evacuated.

6 APRIL Axis forces invade Yugoslavia.

22 JUNE Germans launch Operation Barbarossa, the invasion of the USSR.

26–27 JUNE Finland and Hungary declare war on the USSR.

4 SEPTEMBER Leningrad comes under German siege.

23 NOVEMBER German troops advance to within 30 miles (48km) of Moscow.

7 DECEMBER Japanese troops invade British Malaya.

15 DECEMBER Japanese troops enter Burma.

---

19 MARCH Churchill forms Battle of the Atlantic Committee to coordinate British efforts against U-boats.

27 MAY First convoy to enjoy protection of continuous escort sails from Canada. *Bismarck* sunk by the battleships *King George V* and *Rodney*.

4 SEPTEMBER A German U-boat is engaged by US destroyer USS *Greer*.

26 SEPTEMBER First Arctic convoy carrying war material to the USSR leaves Britain.

31 OCTOBER Torpedo attack by U-boat sinks destroyer USS *Reuben James*.

10/11 MAY Last night of *Blitz* on Britain sees heaviest attack of the war on London.

1 AUGUST Soviet TB-3 bomber successfully employs dive-bombing technique in attack on German forces in Romania.

14 SEPTEMBER German heavy transport gliders are used for first time in assault on Baltic islands.

07 DECEMBER Japanese aircraft from aircraft carriers attack the US fleet and airfields at Pearl Harbor, Hawaii, destroying hundreds of planes, but failing to sink any aircraft carriers.

10 DECEMBER British warships HMS *Repulse* and *Prince of Wales* sunk by Japanese air attack off the coast of Malaya.

---

13 APRIL Japanese-Soviet non-aggression treaty signed.

17 APRIL Yugoslavia surrenders.

9–12 AUGUST Churchill and Roosevelt produce the Atlantic Charter.

2 SEPTEMBER Through the Lend-Lease Act, the US begins to send aid to the USSR and supplies 50 destroyers to the UK.

13 NOVEMBER USA repeals Neutrality Act.

5 DECEMBER Britain declares war on Finland, Hungary and Romania.

11 DECEMBER Germany declares war on US.

FOR 1942–45 SEE INSIDE BACK COVER

GREAT BATTLES
OF WORLD WAR II

GREAT BATTLES
OF WORLD WAR II

General Editor: Dr. Chris Mann

Bath · New York · Singapore · Hong Kong · Cologne · Delhi · Melbourne

This edition published by Parragon in 2010
Parragon
Queen Street House
4 Queen Street
Bath BA1 1HE, UK

ISBN: 978-1-4454-0834-7

Editorial and design by
Amber Books Ltd
Bradley's Close
74–77 White Lion Street
London N1 9PF
United Kingdom
www.amberbooks.co.uk

Project Editor: Michael Spilling
Design: Graham Beehag
Picture Research: Terry Forshaw
Text: Rupert Butler, Martin J. Dougherty,
Michael E. Haskew, Christer Jorgensen,
Chris Mann and Chris McNab

Printed in China

PICTURE CREDITS

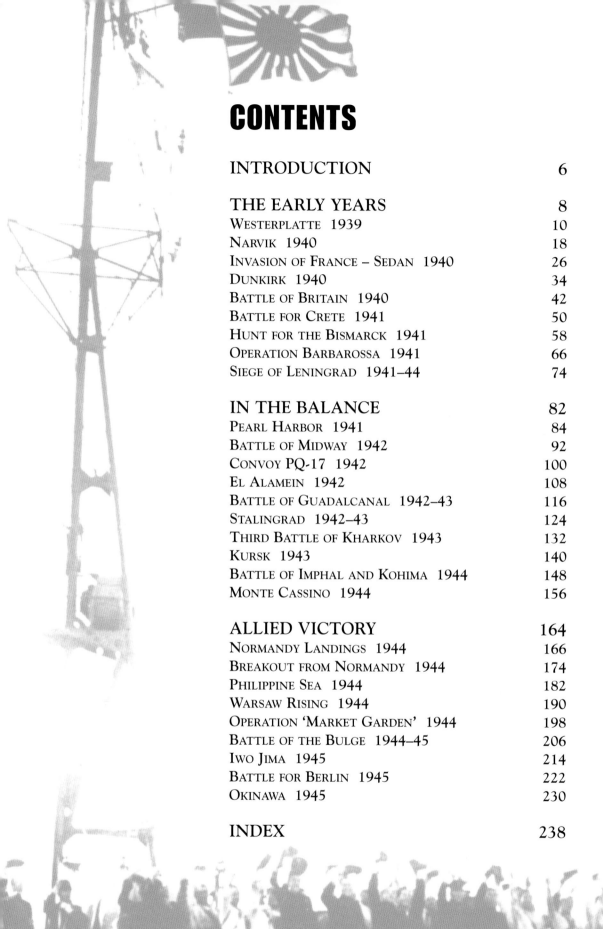

CONTENTS

INTRODUCTION

World War II was the most destructive conflict in human history. We tend to trace its progress through the milestones of the major engagements between the combatants. This is perfectly understandable, as the course of military history is marked by decisive battles.

This conforms to Western military philosophy, as propounded by Carl Von Clausewitz (1780–1831), that it is job of the military commander to seek out and attack that which will defeat the enemy, his 'centre of gravity'. At the operational level, this centre is the army, and thus it is important to bring an opponent to battle and to win decisively.

Yet in the twentieth century's two world wars, decisive victory proved elusive. Many of the battles or campaigns examined in this work were the result of seeking the decisive blow. Pearl Harbor, the Battle of Britain, Operation *Barbarossa*, Monte Cassino and *Market Garden* are good examples. Yet the knock-out blow was rarely achieved. The breakthrough at Sedan is perhaps the only case where a campaign was virtually decided in a single battle. Rather,

LEADERS IN VICTORY: *British Prime Minister Winston Churchill (left), US President Franklin Roosevelt (centre) and Soviet premier Joseph Stalin (right) meet at the Yalta Conference, February 1945. At this tripartite conference, the fate of millions of people was decided by agreements made about the post-war reorganization of Europe.*

these battles mark significant moments or turning points over longer, drawn-out campaigns. The battles were building blocks on the way to final victory or defeat. They moved front lines, wore down the enemy's strength and set up the next major clash. Such was the nature of Total War between industrialized nations.

Thus the battles examined in this collection follow the process as the Allies and Axis sought to impose their will on each over the course of six long years of war. The myth of early German invincibility is challenged by some of the battles from the early period of the war. Whilst Sedan, Dunkirk, Crete and the opening phases of Barbarossa demonstrate the German mastery of combined arms warfare, Westerplatte, Narvik and Leningrad show that the Allies were capable of checking the *Wehrmacht*.

As the prospect of immediate victory faded, the battles of the middle phase of the war took on a more attritional aspect. El Alamein, Stalingrad, Kursk, Imphal and Cassino were all grinding, drawn-out and costly struggles, in which Allied grit and material strength were key to victory. Naval and amphibious warfare was similarly attritional and the battles of Midway and Guadalcanal were more about wearing down Japanese strength than achieving rapid victory. Yet the Germans and Japanese were remarkably skilled and resilient opponents, and even as the tide turned irrevocably they put up extraordinary resistance in Normandy and Arnhem and on the islands of Iwo Jima and Okinawa.

It is the job of armies and their commanders to fight these battles and campaigns. The nature of the political leaderships of the major protagonists goes some way to explain the ferocity and longevity of the conflict. This is particularly the case with regards to the rulers of the totalitarian states, Nazi Germany's Adolf Hitler, the Soviet Union's Joseph Stalin and the military leaders of Japan, whose expansionist goals and uncompromising war aims did much to prolong the fighting. Yet they were also matched in determination by the leaders of democracies, Britain's Winston Churchill and the United States' Franklin Roosevelt.

The determination of the political leaders to fight to the bitter end was made possible only by the efforts of ordinary people. In a long, drawn-out war of attrition, the willingness of the populations to produce the matériel necessary, provide the manpower and endure, for the first time in history, the deliberate, large-scale targeting of civilians by aerial bombardment was absolutely crucial.

Ultimately, the 'Total War' of World War II was brought to a close only by the capture of the German capital, Berlin, and the use of a new and terrible weapon, the atomic bomb, against Japan.

Dr. Chris Mann, General Editor

THREE CHILDREN WAIT *amongst the wreckage of a bomb-damaged street in London following a German air raid, September 1940.*

THE GERMAN FÜHRER *Adolf Hitler shares words with his Italian counterpart, Benito Mussolini, in a cavalcade through Munich, June 1940.*

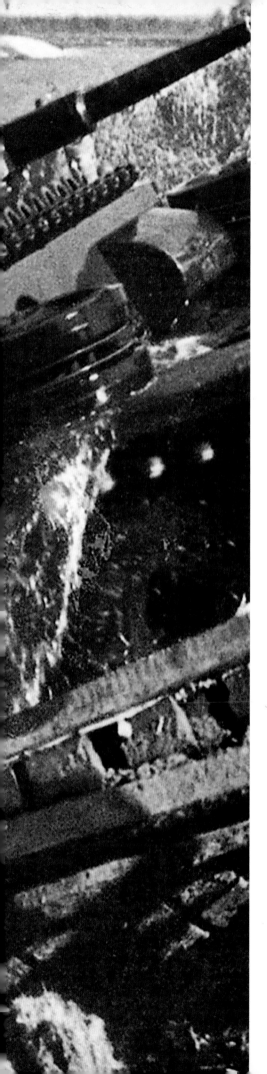

THE EARLY YEARS

The opening campaigns of World War II were marked by German victory after German victory. Superior use of modern weapons systems such as tanks and aircraft, sound doctrine and bold leadership swept aside more minor powers and even lead to impressive victories against broadly numerically, technologically equal and, sometimes, superior powers such as Britain, France and the Soviet Union.

Yet despite the achievements of the German military, the final crushing victory proved elusive and Allied victories in the skies of southern England and outside the gates of Moscow meant Germany was committed to a long-term attritional struggle.

A GERMAN PANZER III *tank crosses a river in Belorussia following the invasion of the Soviet Union in June 1941. German armour proved invincible in the early years of the war, primarily due to superior tactics.*

WESTERPLATTE 1939

Gdansk's Westerplatte peninsula was the site of the official start of World War II. A small forested island separated from Gdansk by the harbour channel, Westerplatte was established as a Polish military outpost during the interwar period.

The Poles were equipped with one 75mm (3in) field gun, two 37mm (1.5in) antitank guns, four mortars and several medium machine guns, but lacked any true fortifications. By the autumn of 1939, the Polish garrison occupying Westerplatte comprised 182 soldiers, who were expected to withstand any attack for 12 hours. The Versailles treaty made the city of Danzig (Gdansk) a free city state under the protection of the League of Nations, where Poland had a post office, special harbour rights and from 1924 the right to have a 'protected' depot. The site of the railway depot was the small, flat sandy peninsula of Westerplatte, which covered about half a square kilometre of land.

When Hitler took power in January 1933, the Poles set out to reinforce their defences at Westerplatte. They built bunkers, officially designated as

WESTERPLATTE FACTS

Who: Major Henryk Sucharski (1898–1946) led the small Polish garrison's resistance during a week of fighting against superior German naval and military police forces under the respective commands of Rear-Admiral Gustav Kleikamp and Police General Friedrich Eberhardt.

What: Westerplatte's unexpectedly fierce resistance delayed the German occupation of the narrow Polish coastline, thereby indirectly saving the Polish Navy and embarrassing the Germans.

Where: The semi-fortified supply depot on the Westerplatte peninsula at the mouth of the Vistula river north of Danzig (Gdaƒsk).

When: 1–7 September 1939

Why: Hitler was determined, despite the existence of a non-aggression pact from 1934, to destroy Poland.

Outcome: The attack on Westerplatte on the morning of 1 September unleashed World War II.

JUST BEFORE THE GERMAN ONSLAUGHT: *Polish troops with a light field piece on army manoeuvres, led by an officer wearing the characteristic four-cornered peaked cap.*

'Guardhouses', while making concrete reinforced shelters at the bottom of the barracks and the NCOs' villa. In addition, the Poles created seven field works (*placówka*), two of which blocked access across the vulnerable land-bridge to the mainland. From March 1939, when Hitler made his demands on Poland, the garrison was on full alert and had completed the construction of the fieldworks by late August. The number of troops was also increased from the stipulated 88 men to 210 by 31 August. The commandant was Henryk Sucharski (1898–1946) and his deputy Captain Dabrowski.

PREPARATIONS

On the German side, the fighting would be done by the *SS-Heimwehr* force of 1500 men led by Police General Friedrich Eberhardt. He had some 225 crack German Marines, under Lieutenant Henningsen, to spearhead any attack on the depot. Overall command would rest with Rear-Admiral Gustav Kleikamp whose flagship *Schleswig-Holstein*, built in 1908, was officially on a courtesy visit in Danzig. It had anchored on the southern embankment of the Harbour canal at Neufahrwasser during the morning of 25 August – only 150m (164 yards) away. Sucharski put his garrison on heightened alert and ordered that all defensive work was to be conducted during the night, since the Germans could use the tall warehouses along the quays to observe the peninsula during daytime. Kleikamp moved his ship further upstream on 26 August, to be in a better position to open fire on Westerplatte.

FRIDAY 1 SEPTEMBER

At 4.48 a.m. on Friday 1 September, the massive guns of the *Schleswig-Holstein* fired eight grenades at the southeast sector of Westerplatte. World War II had erupted and Sucharski radioed to Hel Peninsula, 'SOS: I'm under fire.'

Three large holes had been created in the perimeter wall while warehouses with oil were blazing away. Eight minutes later, Henningsen's marines attacked in formation of three platoons while his pioneers managed to blow up the railway gate in the perimeter fence cutting across the land bridge. But then things went wrong for the Germans.

First the Poles counterattacked, knocking out the machine-gun nest at the German *Schupo* (security police) post, for the loss of three men. Then Polish commander Lieutenant Leon Pajak opened intense howitzer fire on the advancing Germans, who faltered and stopped their attack. Sucharski ordered his artillery to fire on the German sniper machine-gun nests on top of the warehouses across the canal. It had the desired effect: there was no more shooting from that direction. Then the same battery almost knocked out *Schleswig-Holstein*'s command post, but finally the ship's guns managed to knock out the battery.

LEFT: A GERMAN MARINE in full white summer uniform as war breaks out in September 1939.

BELOW: AS THE FIGHTING INTENSIFIES, Westerplatte's oil tanks and buildings burn fiercely in the darkness of the night.

STILL PULLING A FIERCE PUNCH for an old lady: the Schleswig-Holstein opens fire with her main guns.

At 6.22 a.m., the Marines radioed frantically to the ship: '*Verluste zu gross, gehen zurück*' ('Heavy losses, we're leaving'). At the other end of the Westerplatte, the Danzig police had tried to seize control of the harbour but armed civilians and the garrison had defeated this surprise attack. A total of 50 Germans lay dead while the Poles had lost only eight men. Kleikamp, who had expected to take the depot through a lightning strike, now had a real battle on his hands. Reinforced by 60 *SS-Heimwehr* troops, the marines attacked again at 8.55 a.m., led by Henningsen. They got through the perimeter wall, which lay in ruins, but they were halted by mines, fallen trees, barbed wire and intense Polish fire. By noon, the fighting was still continuing, but the demoralized SS men fled. Henningsen was mortally wounded, and half an hour later the marines had had enough as well.

The fighting had cost the Germans 82 lives and Westerplatte was still holding out. The only consolation for the Germans was that they had massacred the Polish defenders of the post office in Danzig city. The German strike against Westerplatte had been an utter fiasco.

THE LULL: 2–5 SEPTEMBER

In the ensuing days, the Germans claimed they were not making any serious moves on the armed depot, while to the tired, hungry and harassed defenders there seemed to be no end to the German attacks.

Eberhardt convinced the German Commander General Fedor von Bock (1880–1945) that a land attack was not possible. Bock agreed, having witnessed the fiasco of 1 September. The following day, the *Luftwaffe* attacked the garrison with 60 bombers, dropping more than 100 bombs. No 5 bunker sustained a direct hit, killing all but three of its occupants while the kitchen, food supplies and the radio station were knocked out.

urged that Westerplatte was to surrender. An angered Dabrowski adamantly opposed such defeatism and stormed out. Sucharski ordered his men to fight on with the same dogged and brave fashion as before.

FIRETRAIN ATTACK: 6 SEPTEMBER

The Germans had no inkling that the Poles were contemplating capitulation. Every day that Westerplatte held out was superb propaganda for Poland and a humiliation for Hitler who fumed at the setbacks. A Polish agent working for the Germans pointed out that Westerplatte had no deep bunker defences.

At 3 a.m. on 6 September, the Germans sent a fire-train against the land-bridge but it was de-coupled too early by the terrified engine driver and failed to reach the oil cistern inside the Polish perimeter. If it had succeeded, it would have set the forest alight and destroyed its valuable cover for the defenders. The blazing wagons gave the

LEFT: TESTED IN SPAIN IN 1938, the Stuka was used to terrorize both military and civilians in dive bombing operations in Poland.

Now the garrison faced hunger, total isolation and the prospect of renewed attacks. Westerplatte had no anti-aircraft (AA) defences at all and this made the aerial attack on 2 September destructive to the troops' plummeting morale.

During the night of 3/4 September, the Germans attacked the Polish outposts but these were repelled. On 4 September, a German torpedo boat (T-196) made a surprise attack on the peninsula from the sea side. At the same time, the forward post of 'Wal' had been abandoned and this seemed to invite a German attack along the northern side of Westerplatte – only the 'Fort' position prevented this. At the same time, there was no hot food and the number of wounded was piling up.

On 5 September, Sucharski called a war council in the food stores where he

RIGHT: FINALLY, AFTER A WEEK of fierce fighting, the German Reichsflagge is raised above Westerplatte following the capture of the outpost.

THE SCHLESWIG-HOLSTEIN

Built between 1905 and 1908, the old battlecruiser was retained in service after 1919, when most of the German Navy was sunk, and modernized in 1925–6, 1930–31 and 1936. She was used as a cadet training ship and a floating battery. Her displacement was 13,454 tonnes (14,830 tons), her dimensions 126m (413ft) long and 22.2m (73ft) broad, while her draught (the depth of water needed in order to float) was 8.25m (27ft). The *Schleswig-Holstein* was armed with four 280mm (11in), ten 150mm (6in) and four 88mm (3.46in) naval guns as well as four 200mm (8in) AA guns. Her crew was reinforced with 225 Marines and 60 AA artillery troops when facing the indomitable Poles of Westerplatte. The ordinary crew numbered 907 men, but with all the troops this had grown to a total of 1197 by 25 August 1939.

Poles a perfect field of fire and the Germans suffered heavy casualties as a consequence. A second fire-train attack came in the afternoon but it failed too.

7 SEPTEMBER: THE LAST ASSAULT

Sucharski held a second council of war in the evening and he had by then made up his mind not to continue fighting. After all, the German Army was now outside Warsaw and the first cases of gangrene had appeared among the wounded.

At 4.30 a.m., the Germans opened intense fire upon Westerplatte, which continued until 7 a.m., when there was a final rolling barrage followed by German storm columns. Despite the use of flamethrowers, the Poles repelled the assault. But Bunker 2 was now destroyed and Numbers 1 and 4 badly damaged.

At 9.45 a.m. the white flag appeared, and at 11.00 a.m. Sucharski surrendered the post to Kleikamp who allowed the valiant commandant to keep his sword. The German troops paraded in full order when the haggard and exhausted Polish garrison marched out of Westerplatte at 11.33 a.m.

The White Eagle of Poland had surrendered at last but not without a truly heroic struggle.

LED BY THEIR OFFICER, Polish soldiers are escorted from the fighting – still erect and proud despite their defeat.

WESTERPLATTE

1 A mere 200 Polish troops sheltering on a shallow riverine peninsula faced the awesome might of the German *Wehrmacht*.

WESTERPLATTE

DANZIG POLICE

2 The first German attack on 1 September against the perimeter wall was a resounding failure, leaving 80 Germans dead.

4 During the night of 3–4 September, a German night attack against Westerplatte's perimeter upset some of the defenders.

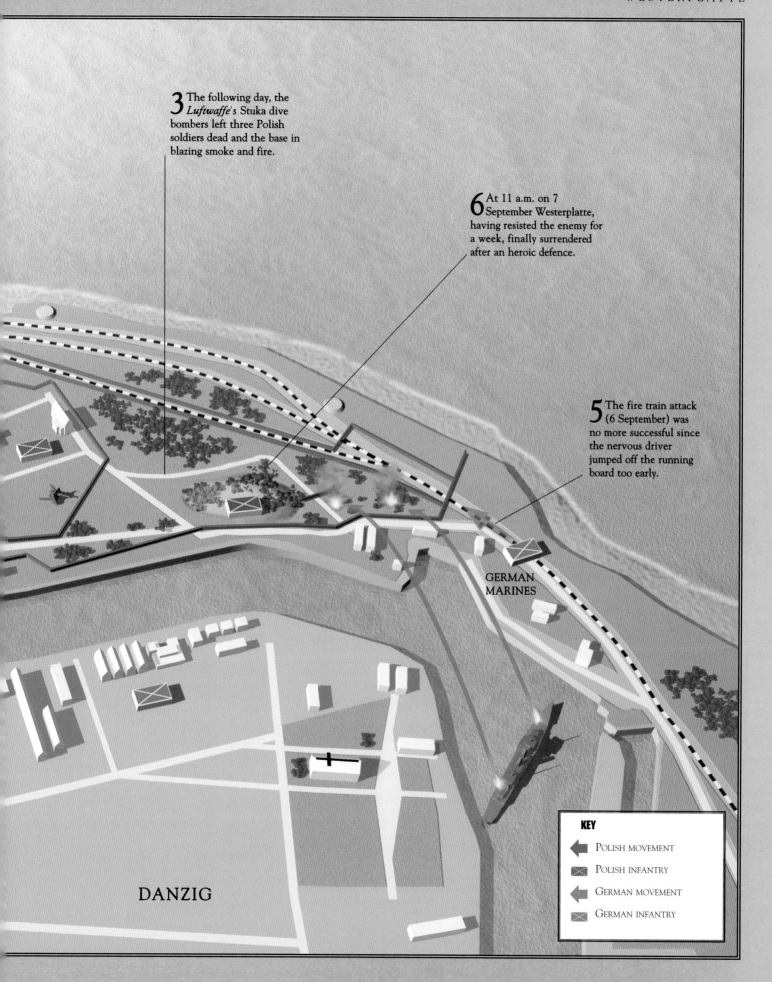

3 The following day, the *Luftwaffe*'s Stuka dive bombers left three Polish soldiers dead and the base in blazing smoke and fire.

6 At 11 a.m. on 7 September Westerplatte, having resisted the enemy for a week, finally surrendered after an heroic defence.

5 The fire train attack (6 September) was no more successful since the nervous driver jumped off the running board too early.

GERMAN MARINES

DANZIG

KEY

◄ POLISH MOVEMENT

✖ POLISH INFANTRY

◄ GERMAN MOVEMENT

✖ GERMAN INFANTRY

NARVIK 1940

In early April 1940, the race was on to see which of the warring powers – Britain or Germany – would be first to seize the strategically vital port of Narvik in northern Norway. General Eduard Dietl, the commander of the German expeditionary force of 2000 mountain troops, made an unopposed landing at Narvik on 9 April.

The Germans' entry onboard 10 modern German cruisers had been blocked by two ancient Norwegian ironclads that were promptly sunk by torpedoes. Berlin had told Dietl and his men that they would be treated as 'liberators' by the Norwegians. To give credence to this fantasy, the local commander Colonel Konrad Sundlo (1881–1965) promptly capitulated. His deputy, Major Spjeldnes, took his 209 troops out of town right under the noses of the puzzled Germans whom he greeted with a cheerful '*Guten Morgen*' (Good Morning). Upon hearing this, Dietl gave orders that all Norwegians were to be disarmed. Otherwise Narvik fell without a shot being fired in anger.

NARVIK FACTS

Who: The German and Austrian mountain troopers were led by Hitler's favourite general, Eduard Dietl (1890–1944). He faced a superior allied force commanded first by General Pierse Mackesy (1883–1956) and general Field-Marshal Claude Auchinleck (1884–1981). The French were under the command of General Antoine Béthouart (1889–1982).

What: Narvik, recaptured by the Allies by 28 May, was Germany's first military defeat in World War II.

Where: The iron-ore port of Narvik in the semi-Arctic north of Norway.

When: 9 April–7 June 1940

Why: Hitler wanted Norway's strategically valuable coastline, ports and airfields in his war against Britain.

Outcome: The belated Allied recapture of Narvik could not change the outcome of the battle for Norway or the catastrophic fortunes of the Allies on the continent after Hitler's invasion of the Low Countries on 10 May 1940.

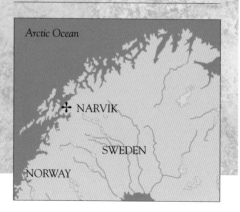

A VILLAGE OUTSIDE NARVIK is swept up in the fighting as it burns after an Allied naval bombardment in May 1940.

LEFT: MERCHANT SHIPS IN NARVIK HARBOUR *in various stages of burning and sinking after the unexpected Allied attack.*

At dawn the following day, four British destroyers led by RN commander Bernard Warburton-Lee (1895–1940) steamed into the port. Lee's ships sank two German destroyers, the captain of one of which was thrown up in the air with the ship but survived. Lee's own ship went straight into a nearby cliff, earning him a posthumous VC.

Three days later, Lee was avenged when the RN returned and sank the remaining eight destroyers. The First Lord of the Admiralty, Churchill, was delighted but in Berlin Hitler was apoplectic at the news. Dietl's force was now completely cut off and Hitler wanted to pull him back.

Dietl had not been idle. He equipped the redundant 2500 sailors with captured Norwegian arms and built a powerful defensive perimeter around Narvik and along the Ofot railway into Sweden. The 'neutral' Swedes were to keep him generously supplied and informed.

LOST OPPORTUNITY

On 16 April, the lacklustre British commander, General Pierse Mackesy (1883–1956), wired London telling the Cabinet that he could not advance on Narvik. The following day, Hitler cancelled the order to evacuate Dietl, and the Allies concentrated on holding southern Norway

BELOW: GERMANS AND AUSTRIANS *served in the Gebirgs or mountain troops, shown here being flown in a German transport plane (Junkers Ju-52) to Narvik.*

instead of throwing Dietl's isolated garrison out of Narvik. Thanks to the 'neutral' Swedes, Dietl received 24 waggon-loads of supplies (including much needed ammunition) and three troops disguised as 'medical' staff.

Nevertheless by late April the Allied Expeditionary Force (AEF) under Admiral Lord Cork (1873–1967) numbered 30,000, including four battalions of *Chasseurs Alpins* (Alpine Hunters) and Polish mountain troops and two battalions of Foreign legionnaires.

FIRST ALLIED OFFENSIVE: 12 MAY

On 28 April, General Antoine Béthouart (1889–1982) landed at Harstad – the Allied GHQ – to be told by Mackesy that Narvik should be taken by a three-pronged attack. Béthouart wanted none of that. His *Chasseurs Alpins*, together with Norwegian ski troops, would seize the Oyjord peninsula as a bridgehead for the final assault upon Narvik.

At midnight on 12 May in brilliant sunshine and glittering snow, the Allied flotilla opened fire on Bjerkvik, north of Narvik and held by the *Windisch* Group. The Foreign legionnaires landed and advanced in the face of heavy enemy fire. Bjerkvik was an inferno, in which the civilian population was massacred in the crossfire. It took two hours to clear the village.

At Meby, the German resistance was crushed by the guns of HMS *Effingham*, two French Renault tanks and the 2nd Battalion of the Legion. By 7.30 a.m., after three hours of intense fighting, the Legion captured Elve-gaardsmoen and a mountain of German supplies, including Dietl's correspondence, fell into French hands. Béthouart sent the Poles and his tanks to chase down the Oyjord peninsula. The Germans fled.

The German army had invaded the Low

ABOVE: A GERMAN NAVAL OFFICER of the Kriegsmarine addresses naval marines and mountain troops on board a German transport ship following operations at Narvik.

LEFT: THE CHASSEURS ALPINS were specially trained and equipped for fighting in mountainous, cold and snowy terrain.

Countries on 10 May, the same day Churchill was made British Prime Minister. They also controlled the whole of Norway south of Mosjoen, with the aim of relieving Dietl at Narvik. Time was not on the Allies' side. On 20 May, Churchill complained that the AEF was tying up much needed resources in a sideshow campaign.

HOLLOW VICTORY

The British commander Field-Marshal Claude Auchinleck (1884–1981) and Béthouart agreed to take Narvik in a four-pronged attack on the Germans.

At 11.45 p.m. on 27 May, the Allied Fleet opened up a withering bombardment of the landing beaches. Shells plastered Narvik town, Ankenes, Fagernes and the entire shoreline until wooden houses along the shore were burning like torches and the coastline was enveloped in thick smoke.

At 12.15 a.m., the legionnaires landed right into the lap of Naval Artillery Company Nöller, numbering 50 troops, and engaged them in savage hand-to-hand fighting. The heavily outnumbered sailors retreated to the railway embankment, closely followed up the slope by the legionnaires who took control of the railway area despite fierce resistance. A German gun was firing out of the nearby tunnel. The legionnaires pulled up by hand a French gun and fired at the mouth of the tunnel until the German battery was silenced for good.

A Norwegian battalion landed at Orneset and combined with the legionnaires to attack Hill 457, where the German *Gebirgsjägers* and sailors had entrenched themselves. They offered heavy resistance and the advancing Allied troops suffered heavy casualties. By four in the morning, the Poles were under heavy German fire at Ankenes while the Legion's 2nd Battalion had not landed across Rombaksfjord.

Half an hour later, German bombers attacked the Allied Fleet, forcing it back and denying the AEF supportive fire.

Two German companies immediately attacked down the slope of Hill 457, forcing the faltering Allies back and putting their precarious bridgehead in peril. At Ankenes, the Polish left flank was under threat. At sea, Béthouart's chief of staff was killed by German fire while two landing craft were sunk. Things were not looking good.

At 6 a.m., British Hurricanes flew over the battlefield, chasing away the *Luftwaffe* while the 2nd Battalion finally landed at Taraldsvik. The legionnaires and the Norwegians drove back the enemy. They gained the upper hand at Hill 457, which was now pockmarked with craters and littered with corpses.

Meanwhile the 2nd Battalion and the Norwegians pushed back the Germans along the Ofoten railway, while on the northern side of Rombaksfjord the *Chasseurs Alpins* and Norwegians drove back the Germans towards Hundal. The 2nd Polish Battalion took Nybord, from where it could fire on Ankenes.

ESCORTED BY A ROYAL NAVY DESTROYER, British troops in life vests are transported to the far north in April 1940.

At Narvik, Major Häussel and his mixed force of 400 sailors and mountain troops had no reserves, were running low on ammunition and had no communications with Dietl's HQ. Häussel decided to evacuate Narvik, taking his force along the still open Beisfjord road. That left small pockets of Germans still fighting at Hill 457 and Fagernes. By the afternoon, the Allied troops led by Béthouart made a triumphant entry into the newly liberated Narvik.

FRENCH TROOPS DISEMBARK somewhere in the vicinity of Narvik, prior to their successful capture of the port.

It did not last. On 7 June, the Allies sailed out of Narvik, taking the Norwegian King and Government to Britain in exile. By 1941, Narvik was supplying the Germans with 612,000 tonnes (674,615 tons) of iron ore. It had all been in vain.

THE NORWEGIAN ARMED FORCES (1940)

On paper, the mobilized Norwegian army was to number 100,000 men organized in six territorial divisions, one of which was to be under the command of General Carl Fleischer (1883–1942) at Harstad. The troops were equipped with green uniforms dating from 1912 and armed with 1894 Krag-Jorgensen rifles.

The army had no tanks, a handful of armoured cars, few heavy machine guns and no real professional core. The tiny Norwegian airforce numbered 76 planes (mostly Gloucester Gladiators) and 940 men – it was knocked out on 9 April. The Navy had 113 vessels including two armoured cruisers, *Eidsvold* and *Norge*.

GLUM NORWEGIAN SOLDIERS surrender to the Germans knowing a harsh occupation awaits their country.

NARVIK

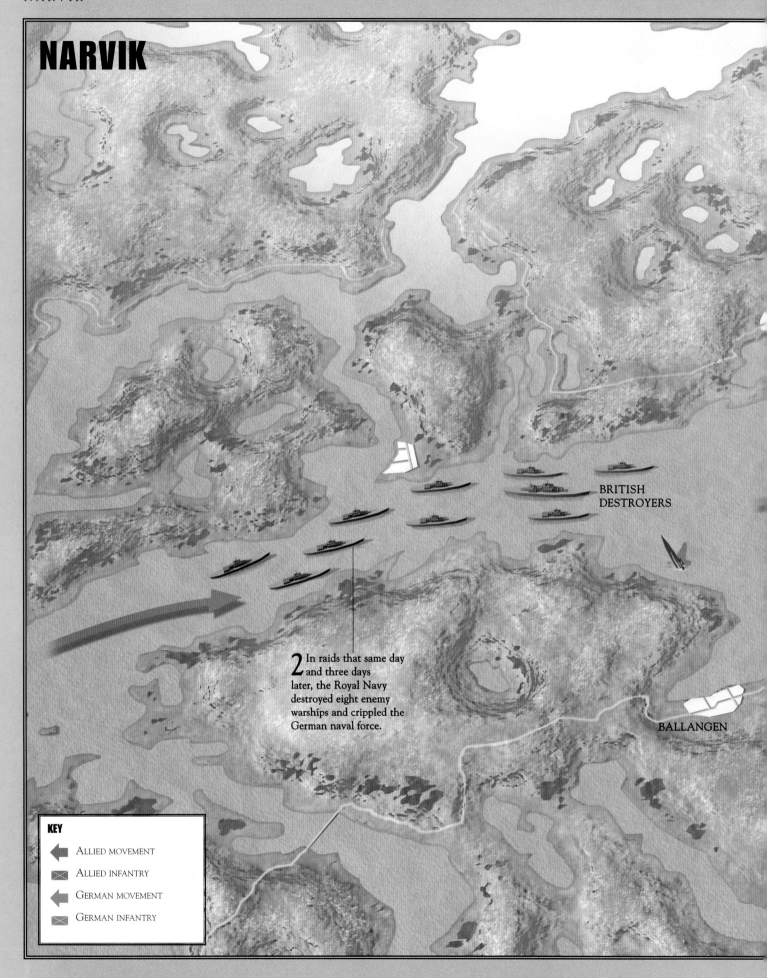

BRITISH
DESTROYERS

2 In raids that same day
and three days
later, the Royal Navy
destroyed eight enemy
warships and crippled the
German naval force.

BALLANGEN

KEY

◄ ALLIED MOVEMENT

✉ ALLIED INFANTRY

◄ GERMAN MOVEMENT

✉ GERMAN INFANTRY

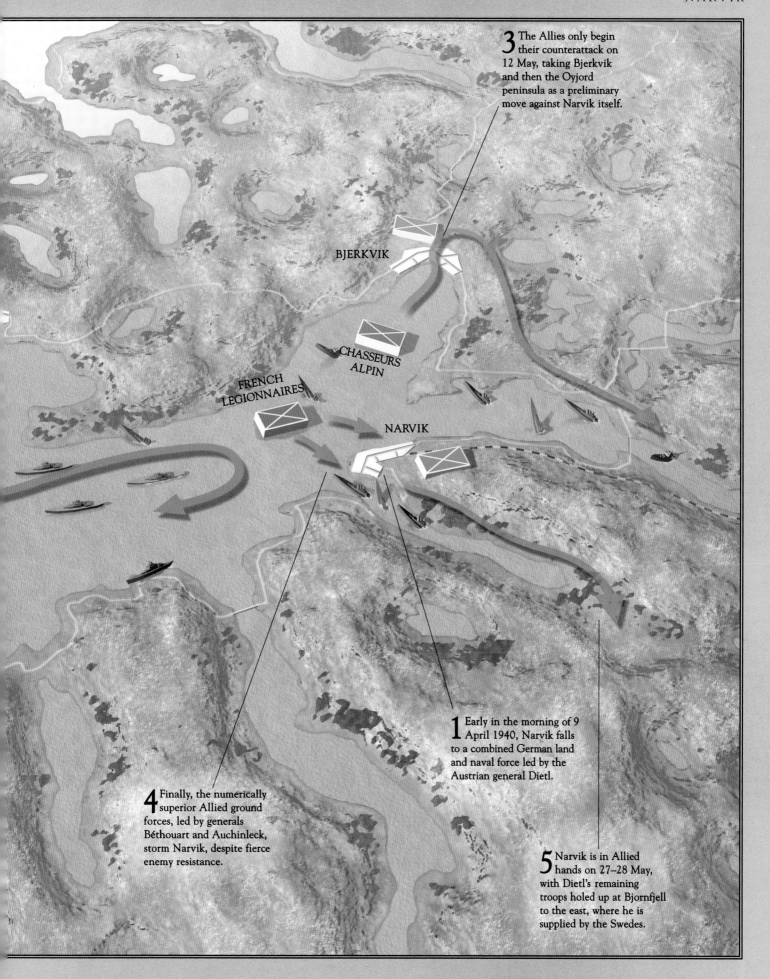

3 The Allies only begin their counterattack on 12 May, taking Bjerkvik and then the Oyjord peninsula as a preliminary move against Narvik itself.

BJERKVIK

CHASSEURS ALPIN

FRENCH LEGIONNAIRES

NARVIK

1 Early in the morning of 9 April 1940, Narvik falls to a combined German land and naval force led by the Austrian general Dietl.

4 Finally, the numerically superior Allied ground forces, led by generals Béthouart and Auchinleck, storm Narvik, despite fierce enemy resistance.

5 Narvik is in Allied hands on 27–28 May, with Dietl's remaining troops holed up at Bjornfjell to the east, where he is supplied by the Swedes.

INVASION OF FRANCE – SEDAN 1940

The conquest of France and the Netherlands during the summer of 1940 was a conspicuous triumph for Germany's Army and Air Force, leading to the defeat of the French, Dutch and Belgian armies. After the successful Polish campaign the previous September, Hitler relished the the triumph of his original Blitzkrieg (Lightning War), codenamed Fall Gelb (Case Yellow), with its emphasis on mobility and fluidity.

However, bad weather, equipment deficiencies and the need for fresh training led to further postponements. Major General Erich von Manstein (1887–1973), Chief-of-Staff in Field-Marshal Gerd von Rundstedt's (1875–1953) Army Group A, urged a giant armoured sweep through the thickly

INVASION OF FRANCE – SEDAN FACTS

Who: Gerd von Rundstedt (1875–1953) and his Chief-of-Staff Erich von Manstein (1887–1973) commanded Army Group A. Heinz Guderian (1888–1954), key in developing the concept of mass tank divisions, versus General Maurice Gamelin (1872–1958), French Commander-in-Chief, and his eventual successor Maxime Weygand (1867–1965).

What: The tactics of *Blitzkrieg* – panzers working in close coordination with artillery and dive bombers (Stukas) – achieved conspicuous successes.

Where: Germany's area of victories extended from the 'impregnable' French Maginot line to Belgium, the edge of the English Channel and the Netherlands to the north.

When: 10–28 May 1940

Why: Hitler wished to turn his attentions to a decisive assault on the Soviet Union.

Outcome: French forces in the Allied line's vital centre were shattered. In the north, Dutch armed forces were all but destroyed.

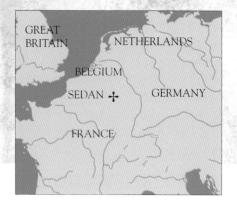

MAY 1940: A GERMAN ARMOURED COLUMN *of Panzer II tanks passes French anti-tank barriers in Sedan, following the evacuation of the town by the French Army.*

A YOUNG GERMAN SOLDIER POSES for the camera in the advance towards Dunkirk. He is armed with a Kar-98 rifle and has a grenade tucked in his belt.

was considered impregnable. The Belgians shared the belief in the Maginot Line, the elaborate system of fortifications running along France's eastern frontier. Fast-moving German armies had no trouble in outflanking it. Seven panzer divisions totalling 2270 tanks, self-propelling guns and armoured vehicles drove unopposed through Luxembourg and into the wooded hills and densely forested plateau of the Belgian Ardennes. The area was only lightly screened by French cavalry, in the belief that the narrow roads of the region could not accommodate a large armoured force.

In the early hours, the tanks of General Erwin Rommel (1891–1944), the recently appointed commander of 7th Panzer Division, crossed the southern end of the Belgian frontier, heading for the Meuse at Dinant 105km (65 miles) away. Simultaneously Hitler's panzers rolled over the Luxembourg frontier.

General Heinz Guderian (1888–1954), the spearhead commander, had spelt out to his men the prime objective – the Channel. His superior, General Ewald von Kleist (1881–1954), had command of the principal panzer forces in the *Sichelschnitt* (Sickle Stroke) plan, scything through the Allied front's centre to the English Channel, trapping the British Expeditionary Force and the First and Seventh French Armies against the sea. A gigantic phalanx of armour and vehicles, enjoying the added protection of the *Luftwaffe*, stretched back for 160km (100 miles), with its rear rank lying 80km (50 miles) east of the Rhine. Due to intelligence disregarded by the *Deuxième Bureau*, all areas were virtually undefended.

PANZER THRUST

French forces, many on leave, were hastily recalled following an order from General Maurice Gamelin (1872–1958), the Commander-in-Chief. Two Corps on the left of the Ninth Army under France's General André Corap (1873–1953) took up positions on the Meuse between

wooded Ardennes, which the French considered impassable. It was planned that the Germans would then cross the river Meuse just north of the French frontier town of Sedan and break out into the open country, with a race to the Channel at Abbeville. After slicing through the French at Sedan, there would be a heading west along the Somme's north bank to the Channel, entrapping the bulk of major Anglo-French forces.

ATTACK ON THE LOW COUNTRIES

As dawn broke on 10 May, a special force of 424 men and a swarm of gliders swooped down to destroy the heavily armoured fort of Eben Emael, a key Belgian defence, which

THE THICK ARMOURED French Char B1 bis tank required costly maintainance and constant refuelling and faced frequent breakdowns.

Namur and Givet, crossing the water to clash with von Rundstedt, approaching through the Ardennes.

On 12 May, Guderian's corps had captured Bouillon in the western part of the Belgian province of Luxembourg, crossing the French frontier just north of Sedan, where the Belgians had left many road blocks undefended. Keen to press his advantage, Guderian persuaded von Kleist to let him unleash his three panzer divisions across the Meuse near Sedan without waiting for rear guard infantry protection. Howling Junkers JU 87 Stuka bombers rained down on the French artillery while high velocity 88mm (3.46in) 'ack-ack' guns

A BREAK ON THE GERMAN advance through the Ardennes – triumphant despite the Allied belief that swift movement was impossible in such terrain.

sprayed the enemy bunkers. Infantry of the crack Infantry regiment *Grossdeutschland*, thrusting through Luxembourg into Belgium towards the Meuse, were ferried over to attack the French positions. Within hours, *Grossdeutschland* gained a river line that the French believed would hold. A gap was smashed between Second and Ninth French armies; Guderian's Panzer Corps, driving through the breach, wheeled and positioned on line direct to the English Channel.

Further German advances revealed insufficient coordination between French tanks and infantry. Nevertheless 6th and 8th Panzer Divisions had to contend with ripostes of machine-gun fire, which also hampered the work of engineers building pontoons across the river at the village of Monthermé, within some of the most rugged territory in the Ardennes. Regrouped German armour secured the position after a fierce engagement. Two French

Divisions, 55th and 71st, faced annihilation. Rommel's 7th Panzer Division had reached the Meuse below the city of Dinant but encountered French heavy artillery shelling and small arms fire from troops on the left bank. Rommel's attention fastened on the plight of his motorized infantry attempting to cross the river in its inflatable boats. To screen the crossings, he ordered buildings on the German side to be set alight. The resulting smoke drifted across the river. Rommel's assault troops were able to establish a bridgehead; French reservists were too stunned to fight back.

At Sedan, the entire 1st Panzer Brigade crossed the Meuse on a hastily constructed pontoon bridge. *Luftwaffe* fighters fended off enemy assaults while to the south Guderian's forces deepened their bridgehead, by evening 48km (30 miles) wide. On 14 May also, Allied forces had their first encounter with the Germans sweeping through Belgium. Guderian's rapid advance caused anxiety in Berlin that, deprived of infantry, he could be cut off by any counterattack. But, in fact, the Allies were in danger of being outflanked.

ROAD TO PARIS

The British Prime Minister Winston Churchill (1874–1965) next day received a despairing telephone call from the French premier Paul Reynaud (1878–1966) declaring, 'We are beaten … The road to Paris is open'. With forces hastily assembled near the town of Montcornet, north of Paris, Colonel Charles de Gaulle (1890–1970) launched three

LEFT: THIS CORPORAL SERVED with 1st Panzer Regiment, one of the many Panzer units involved in the breakthrough at Sedan.

BELOW: AN EFFECTIVE LIGHT medium tank with mounted assault, antitank and anti-aircraft armament, the Pz 38t was Czech manufactured throughout the war. This example fought with the 2nd Panzer Division.

offensive actions, all but reaching Guderian's advanced headquarters, only to be repulsed. A shaky defensive perimeter, to where the British and French could retreat, was assembled around Dunkirk. The situation in Europe deteriorated still further. The concern was how British and French forces could escape annihilation at Dunkirk. Nevertheless on 21 May four battalions clashed with 7th Panzer and the Waffen SS *Totenkopf* Division near Arras, costing the Germans 700 casualties and the loss of 20 tanks. But two days later the German armoured divisions had penetrated to the coast. The BEF was cut off, communications severed and ammunition short. To make matters worse, on 28 May the Belgian army capitulated.

AFTERMATH

Many reasons have been cited for Hitler's order to Guderian to halt his forces at Dunkirk. It might have been advice that the boggy terrain near the coast was unsuitable for tanks, or maybe it was the setback at Arras – or perhaps von Rundstedt's wish to regroup forces for the assault on Paris. Churchill was determined to keep France in the war and sent what reinforcements he could, landing at Cherbourg and Brest, but progress in all areas was hopeless in the face of the panzers and Stukas. On 14 June, the unstoppable juggernaut of the *Wehrmacht* entered the undefended French capital. Within months, Hitler's interest was turning to the east.

ERICH VON MANSTEIN

Erich Von Manstein (1887–1973), the architect of *Blitzkreig*, achieved promotion to general field marshal on 19 July 1940, after France fell. In 1941–42, he conducted Eleventh Army's conquest of the Crimea, while his Caucasian counteroffensive saved Army Group Don from destruction after Germany's devastating defeat at Stalingrad at the end of 1942. He clashed increasingly with Hitler as the military situation on the Eastern Front declined. This served to fuel Hitler's distrust – probably influenced by Manstein's Jewish origins. Hitler sacked him in 1944, but he proved a tough survivor despite a flirtation with the anti-Nazi resistance movement. In 1948, he was arraigned as a war criminal, imprisoned and then released in 1953. He was subsequently consultant to the West German government on military matters, dying near Munich on 1 June 1973, aged 85.

PANZER IIIs AND IVs roll down the main street of a town somewhere in northern France. Notably, Panzer IV was the sturdy warhorse throughout, more than holding its own against Allied opponents.

THE INVASION OF FRANCE – SEDAN

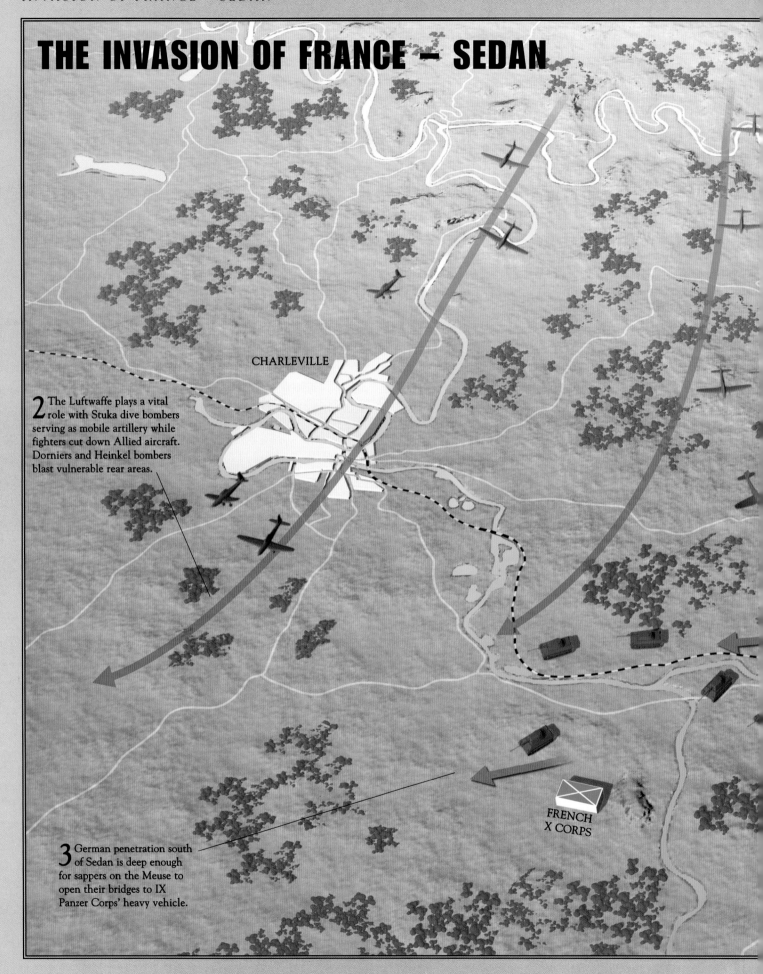

CHARLEVILLE

2 The Luftwaffe plays a vital role with Stuka dive bombers serving as mobile artillery while fighters cut down Allied aircraft. Dorniers and Heinkel bombers blast vulnerable rear areas.

3 German penetration south of Sedan is deep enough for sappers on the Meuse to open their bridges to IX Panzer Corps' heavy vehicle.

FRENCH X CORPS

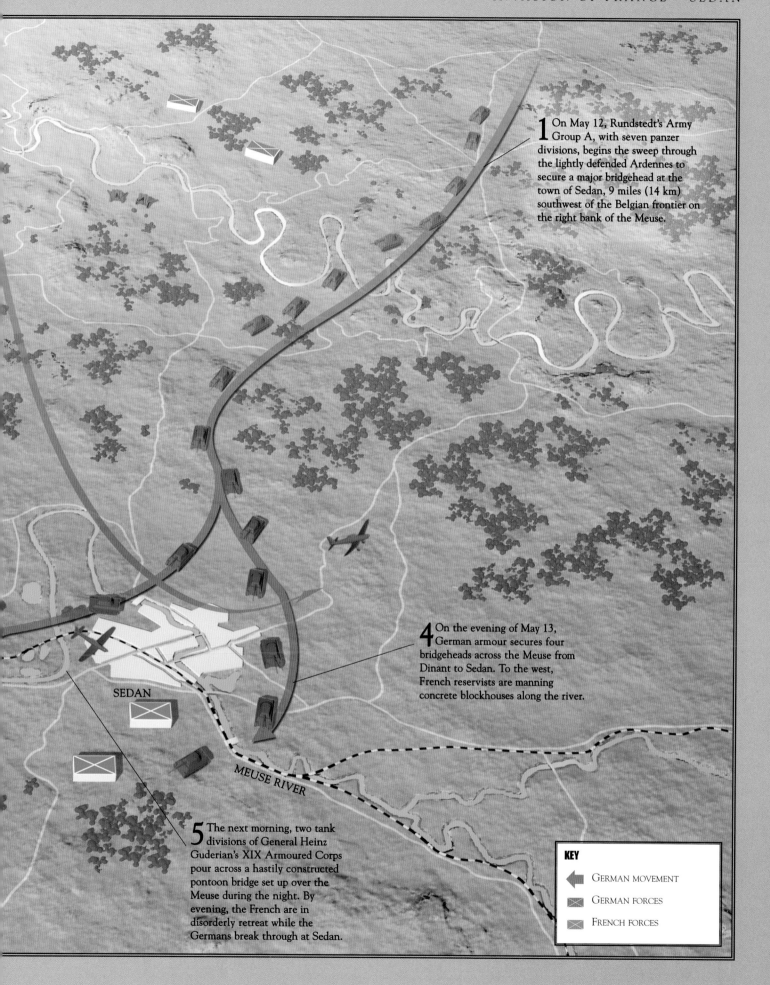

1 On May 12, Rundstedt's Army Group A, with seven panzer divisions, begins the sweep through the lightly defended Ardennes to secure a major bridgehead at the town of Sedan, 9 miles (14 km) southwest of the Belgian frontier on the right bank of the Meuse.

4 On the evening of May 13, German armour secures four bridgeheads across the Meuse from Dinant to Sedan. To the west, French reservists are manning concrete blockhouses along the river.

SEDAN

MEUSE RIVER

5 The next morning, two tank divisions of General Heinz Guderian's XIX Armoured Corps pour across a hastily constructed pontoon bridge set up over the Meuse during the night. By evening, the French are in disorderly retreat while the Germans break through at Sedan.

KEY

← GERMAN MOVEMENT

⊠ GERMAN FORCES

⊠ FRENCH FORCES

DUNKIRK 1940

During the opening weeks of World War II in the West, thousands of soldiers of the British Expeditionary Force and the French First Army, with their backs to the sea, were evacuated from the European continent in nine desperate days of fighting on the coast of the English Channel.

The rescue itself was deemed a 'miracle' as a hastily assembled flotilla of military and civilian vessels of every description ran a gauntlet of air attacks by the German *Luftwaffe* to ferry the troops to safety.

For eight months, the opposing armies had only watched one another warily. Then, on 10 May 1940, the *Sitzkrieg* ('Phoney War') was shattered with the German invasion of France and the Low Countries. In the north, 30 divisions of Army Group B advanced across the frontiers of The Netherlands and Belgium on a 322km (200-mile) front. Further south, 45 divisions of Army Group A slashed through the Ardennes Forest and skirted the defences of the Maginot Line. Led by one of the world's foremost proponents of mobile warfare, General Heinz Guderian

DUNKIRK FACTS

Who: The British Expeditionary Force, French, Belgian and Dutch armed forces, with the British under Field-Marshal John, Lord Gort (1886–1946) versus German Army Group A under General Gerd von Rundstedt (1875–1953).

What: The Germans forced the evacuation of the British and other Allied troops from the European Continent but failed to deliver the devastating blow that might have altered the course of World War II inexorably in their favour.

Where: The port city of Dunkirk and environs on the coast of the English Channel in northwest France.

When: 26 May– 4 June 1940

Why: The Germans sought to occupy Western Europe with the conquest of France and the Low Countries.

Outcome: The Allied forces lost thousands of prisoners along with vast quantities of war matériel; however, 338,226 soldiers were evacuated to England.

WOUNDED BRITISH AND FRENCH *soldiers file from the beach at Dunkirk. Within days of the German offensive launched on 10 May 1940, the British Expeditionary Force and remnants of the French Army were forced to evacuate the European continent.*

(1888–1954), German tanks and motorized infantry swept relentlessly northwest in a great arc, reaching the coast in only 10 days.

BLITZKRIEG

The startling swiftness of the German offensive threatened to trap all Allied troops north of the thrust by Army Group A as Guderian sent three panzer divisions racing towards the Channel ports of Boulogne, Calais and Dunkirk. Three key positions, the French at Lille, Belgian Army units along the Lys river and the British at Calais, offered resistance to the German onslaught. Within 72 hours of reaching Abbeville, the Germans captured both Boulogne and Calais, and elements of the 1st Panzer Division had advanced to within 19km (12 miles) of Dunkirk, the sole remaining avenue of

THE INDOMITABLE 'TOMMY'

His trusty Lee-Enfield rifle slung across his shoulder and the distinctive helmet secured by its sturdy chinstrap, a soldier of the British Expeditionary Force (BEF), affectionately known as a 'Tommy', manages a cheerful expression during the dark days of 1940. As the threat of war with Nazi Germany increased, conscription rapidly raised the strength of the British Army, and in 1939 alone the size of the force grew by a million men.

At the time of the German spring offensive in 1940, the BEF comprised 10 divisions deployed on the European continent. During the evacuation of the BEF from Dunkirk, codenamed Operation *Dynamo*, more than 218,000 British and 120,000 French soldiers were evacuated to safety in Britain by a seaborne effort that included many civilian craft.

escape for Allied forces in northern France and Belgium. Although he had been ordered to mount a counterattack in support of the French, Field-Marshal John, Lord Gort (1886–1946), commander of the British Expeditionary Force, chose instead to concentrate his troops in the vicinity of Dunkirk in order to evacuate as many soldiers as possible to the relative safety of England. The heroic defence of Lille by the French, of Boulogne by the 2nd Battalion Irish Guards and a battalion of the Welsh Guards, and Calais by the British 30th Infantry Brigade, bought precious time for Gort to prepare a defensive perimeter around Dunkirk. But the effort appeared to be in vain as German tank commanders peered at the town's church spires through binoculars.

THE PANZERS PAUSE

Quite unexpectedly, the greatest assistance to the Allied evacuation plan came from Hitler himself. On 24 May the *Führer* visited the headquarters of General Gerd von Rundstedt (1875–1953), commander of Army Group A, at Charleville. Influenced by *Reichsmarschall* Hermann Göring (1893–1946) to allow his *Luftwaffe* to deliver the death blow to the enemy at Dunkirk, Hitler directed Rundstedt to halt the tanks of six panzer divisions along the Aa canal.

ABOVE: THOUSANDS OF ALLIED SOLDIERS waiting for rescue at Dunkirk while German armour and infantry continue to pressure a shrinking perimeter.

Guderian was rendered 'utterly speechless' by the order. For nearly 48 hours the German ground assault abated and the Allied troops around Dunkirk were pummelled by screeching Stukas and strafed by *Luftwaffe* fighters. On 26 May, the ground attack resumed but the reprieve allowed Gort to patch together the tenuous defence of a 48km (30-mile) stretch of beach from Gravelines in the south to Nieuport, Belgium, in the north. Two days later, Belgian King Léopold III (1901–1983) ordered his forces to surrender, and the Allied defensive perimeter continued to contract. Eventually the Allies were squeezed into a pocket only 11km (7 miles) wide.

OPERATION DYNAMO

As early as 20 May, while the Allied debacle on the Continent was unfolding, British Prime Minister Winston Churchill (1874–1965) authorized the preparation of

RIGHT: UNDER CONSTANT THREAT of Luftwaffe air attack, soldiers of the British Expeditionary Force queue up for the next watercraft that will transport them from Dunkirk to safety.

Operation *Dynamo*, the evacuation of the British Expeditionary Force from France.

The hard-pressed Royal Navy could not possibly supply the number of vessels needed for the rescue, and Vice-Admiral Bertram Ramsay (1883–1945) called for boats in excess of 9.3m (30ft) in length to assemble at ports in England. Cabin cruisers, ferries, sailing schooners and their civilian crews joined Royal Navy destroyers in the treacherous 88km (55-mile) journey through a maze of German contact mines sown in the Channel, under continuous air attack and often within range of fire from German heavy artillery.

AIR RAIDS

Luftwaffe bombing had set the town of Dunkirk ablaze and wrecked the port facilities. Rescue vessels were compelled to risk running aground in the shoals along the beaches or to tie up at one of two 'moles' – rocky breakwaters covered with planking wide enough for men to stand three abreast – in order to take soldiers aboard. Countless acts of heroism occurred as vessels made numerous shuttle runs. One 19m

AS A PALL of smoke from a Luftwaffe air strike rises in the background, a British soldier lying on his back takes aim at a low flying German plane.

(60ft) yacht, the *Sundowner*, carried 130 soldiers to safety, while close to a hundred perished aboard the paddlewheel steamer *Fenella* when a German bomb ripped through its deck and detonated. Nearly one-third of the 693 boats involved were destroyed, but from 26 May until the final rescue run in the pre-dawn hours of 4 June, a total of 338,226 Allied soldiers reached England.

When the battered and exhausted Allied troops arrived, they were welcomed as heroes. Townspeople poured out of their homes with food and drink for the famished soldiers. Virtually all of their heavy equipment had been abandoned on the Dunkirk beaches, thousands of their comrades were killed or captured, and the armed forces of Britain and France had suffered one of the greatest military defeats in their history.

Yet these men had survived. Amid the celebration Churchill groused, 'Wars are not won by evacuation.' He later wrote, 'There was a white glow, overpowering, sublime,

RIGHT: THEIR VESSEL SUNK by German aircraft, dazed French soldiers and sailors of the Royal Navy are plucked from the waters of the English Channel during Operation Dynamo.

which ran through our Island from end to end … and the tale of the Dunkirk beaches will shine in whatever records are preserved of our affairs.'

AFTERMATH

Historians have debated Hitler's reasons for halting the panzers. Some assert that the focus of the Germans was already on the complete defeat of France and the capture of Paris. Others say that Hitler was concerned about the marshy terrain in Flanders, which was less than ideal for the manoeuvring of tanks. The tanks themselves had been driven rapidly and engaged for some time. Many of them undoubtedly needed refitting and some of their precious number would have been lost in an all-out attack on the Allied defences. Göring had argued that the *Luftwaffe* was certainly more loyal and fervently Nazi than the leadership of the German Army; therefore, his air arm should be given the honour of annihilating the enemy.

In the end, the *Luftwaffe* had failed to force an Allied capitulation. Thousands of Allied soldiers had escaped death or capture. The miracle of Dunkirk stands as a stirring moment in military history, and Hitler's decision to halt his panzers as one of the great 'what ifs' of World War II.

BELOW: CAPTURED BRITISH AND FRENCH soldiers await disposition following the German occupation of Dunkirk. The Luftwaffe had failed to annihilate the Allied force, and those who were rescued fought another day.

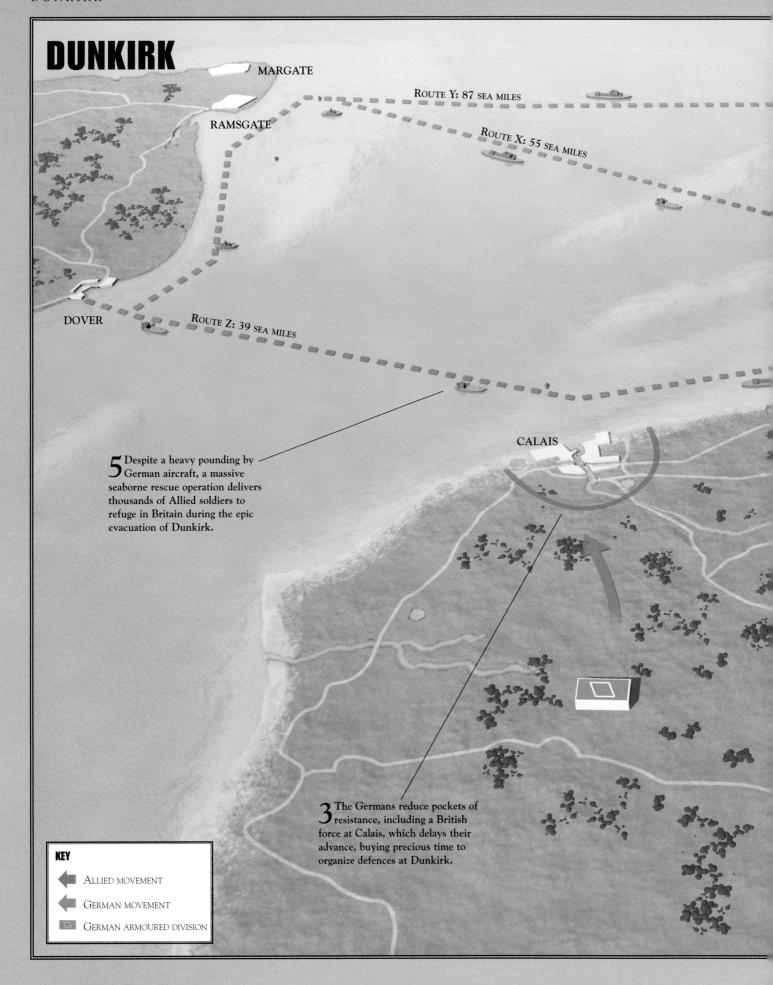

DUNKIRK

MARGATE

RAMSGATE

ROUTE Y: 87 SEA MILES

ROUTE X: 55 SEA MILES

DOVER

ROUTE Z: 39 SEA MILES

CALAIS

5 Despite a heavy pounding by German aircraft, a massive seaborne rescue operation delivers thousands of Allied soldiers to refuge in Britain during the epic evacuation of Dunkirk.

3 The Germans reduce pockets of resistance, including a British force at Calais, which delays their advance, buying precious time to organize defences at Dunkirk.

KEY

← ALLIED MOVEMENT

← GERMAN MOVEMENT

▱ GERMAN ARMOURED DIVISION

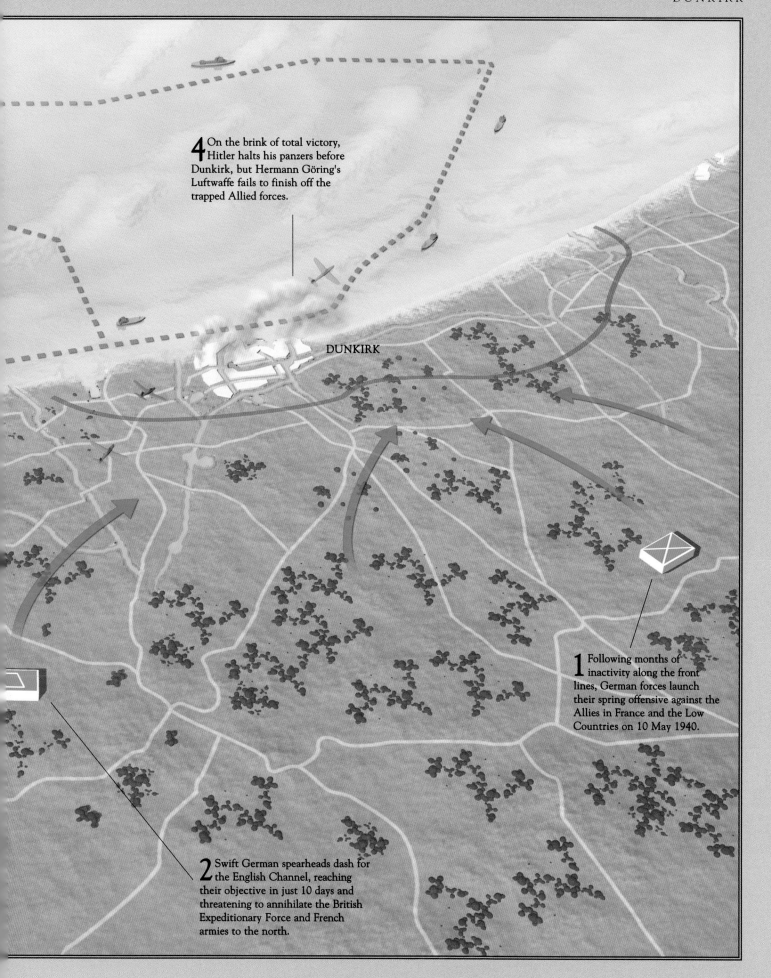

4 On the brink of total victory, Hitler halts his panzers before Dunkirk, but Hermann Göring's Luftwaffe fails to finish off the trapped Allied forces.

DUNKIRK

1 Following months of inactivity along the front lines, German forces launch their spring offensive against the Allies in France and the Low Countries on 10 May 1940.

2 Swift German spearheads dash for the English Channel, reaching their objective in just 10 days and threatening to annihilate the British Expeditionary Force and French armies to the north.

BATTLE OF BRITAIN

1940

The German conquest of France and the Low Countries had been accomplished with astonishing speed. During the opening months of World War II in Europe, Nazi Germany had emerged victorious across the Continent. As German troops paraded down the Champs Elysées, Führer Adolf Hitler and his generals planned for the invasion of Great Britain.

German officers and soldiers had gazed from the French coastline across the 32km (20 miles) of the English Channel which separated them from their enemy. To a man, they knew that the conquest of Great Britain would be their greatest challenge to date. However, they were brimming with confidence.

BATTLE OF BRITAIN FACTS

Who: The German *Luftwaffe* commanded by *Reichsmarschall* Hermann Göring (1893–1946) versus Royal Air Force Fighter Command under Air Chief Marshal Hugh Dowding (1882–1970).

What: The *Luftwaffe* attempted to destroy the Royal Air Force and later to raze British cities.

Where: The skies above Britain and the English Channel.

When: 10 July 1940–10 May 1941

Why: Initially, the Germans needed control of the skies to cover Operation *Sea Lion*, the invasion of Great Britain. Later, the Blitz raids were primarily terror attacks.

Outcome: The *Luftwaffe* failed to subdue the RAF and break the will of the British people. Operation *Sea Lion* was cancelled.

FROM HIS ROOFTOP vantage point, an air raid warden scans the skies above London for Luftwaffe bombers. The dome of St. Paul's Cathedral rises in the background.

ABOVE: *British Prime Minister Winston Churchill visits coastal defences on the southern coast of England, August 1940.*

Operation *Sea Lion*, as the invasion was codenamed, would involve the marshalling of troops and matériel, as well as the rounding up of enough barges suitable for transporting the most formidable fighting machine in the world across the narrow expanse of the Channel. Still, all of the victories thus far, all of the planning and all of the *Führer's* bold rhetoric meant far less without mastery of the skies. Control of the air was a prerequisite to any successful invasion.

KANALKAMPF

Its opening phase was known as *Kanalkampf,* or the Channel Battle, to the Germans. For the rest of the world, the aerial conflict which began on 10 July 1940 and lasted fully 10 months was known collectively as the Battle of Britain. Less than three weeks after the Fall of France, *Reichsmarschall* Hermann Göring (1893–1946) and his *Luftwaffe* began the effort to take control of the skies above Britain. Hitler had initially set the date for the invasion as 15 August, and the German planes were to pound British harbours and shipping.

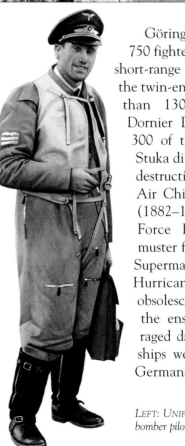

Göring had gathered more than 750 fighters, including the nimble but short-range Messerschmitt Me-109 and the twin-engine Me-110, to escort more than 1300 Heinkel He-111 and Dornier Do-17 bombers along with 300 of the infamous Junkers Ju-87 Stuka dive bombers which had sown destruction in Poland and France. Air Chief Marshal Hugh Dowding (1882–1970), chief of Royal Air Force Fighter Command, could muster few more than 700 frontline Supermarine Spitfire and Hawker Hurricane fighters and other obsolescent types in defence. During the ensuing four weeks, dogfights raged daily, a number of merchant ships were sunk by the marauding Germans and the Royal Navy

LEFT: *Uniformed in his flight suit, a Luftwaffe bomber pilot proceeds to a pre-mission briefing.*

ABOVE: CONCEIVED AS A *commercial airliner, the Heinkel He-111 was easily converted to a bomber.*

relocated most of its ships and personnel to Portsmouth from Dover. The *Luftwaffe* failed, however, to sufficiently erode the strength of the Royal Air Force.

Early in the battle the British came fully to appreciate the value of accurate intelligence and a new early warning device called radar, both of which provided advance notice to them of incoming German air raids. It was also quickly determined that the lumbering Stukas were unfit for air-to-

BELOW: COURAGEOUS MEMBERS OF *the London Fire Brigade wrestle a hose into position to combat a fire ignited by Luftwaffe incendiary bombs.*

air combat, easy prey for RAF fighters. Although they had lost 300 planes, while half that number of British aircraft had fallen, the Germans considered their initial operations sufficiently effective to begin round two of the aerial preparations for invasion.

DER ADLERTAG

Still confident of victory, German airmen often sang a jaunty tune with the lyric, *'Wir fliegen gegen England'* ('We are flying against England'). Göring scheduled *Adlertag*, or

THE MESSERSCHMITT ME-109 was the premiere Luftwaffe fighter aircraft of World War II. It was heavily armed and skilfully piloted, but its limited range allowed only 20 minutes of fighting time in hostile airspace over Britain.

Eagle Day, for 13 August 1940. The second phase of the Battle of Britain was intended to bring the RAF to its knees, through the systematic bombing of its airfields in southern and central England; the destruction of the 93m (300ft) towers and installations which comprised the early warning radar stations strung along the English coastline; and, finally, the elimination of the planes and pilots of Fighter Command.

On Eagle Day, the Germans lost 46 planes, and the RAF 13. However, a week of nearly continuous daylight aerial combat followed. Citizens below could see the swirling vapour trails of the dogfighting planes. Occasionally they saw the puff of an exploding aircraft or the long, black trail of a burning machine as it hurtled towards the ground. At times, it actually seemed to be raining spent cartridges from British and German machine guns and cannon. Though its actual losses may have been fewer than those of the *Luftwaffe*, Fighter Command was being stretched to breaking point. Young pilots were often thrown into combat

with only a few hours of flying time, facilities had been bombed and strafed, and the rigours of combat had taken their toll on the remaining airworthy planes.

A CHANCE REPRIEVE

In concert with daylight raids, Göring also instructed his pilots to fly nocturnal bombing missions against military targets in Britain. Major cities, particularly London, had not been targeted due to the probability of retaliation by RAF bombers against German cities. However, on the night of 24 August 1940 a few *Luftwaffe* bombers strayed off course and dropped their ordnance on the city of London. The next night RAF bombers hit Berlin. Enraged, the *Führer* vowed to lay waste to British cities.

On 7 September 1940, Hitler authorized a change in strategy. The *Luftwaffe* was to bomb London into submission. A week later, however, he postponed Operation Sea Lion indefinitely. On the first night of the Blitz, more than 2000 Londoners were killed or wounded. The sacrifice of the civilian population proved to be the salvation of Fighter Command, which was given time to rest and refit. London was not the only city ravaged by German bombs in the months to come. On the night of 14 November 1940, Coventry was assailed by more than 400 *Luftwaffe* bombers, killing 568 civilians and injuring more than 1200 others. Birmingham, Liverpool and Manchester were hit. But the turning point had come with the change in German strategy and the refusal of the British people to buckle. The last *Luftwaffe* raids of the Blitz struck London on the night of 10 May 1941.

AN EASTWARD GAZE

Hitler's frustration with Göring's failure to destroy the RAF was tempered by his preoccupation with preparations for Operation *Barbarossa*, the invasion of the Soviet Union, which was scheduled for 22 June 1941. Some historians argue that the *Führer* had been reluctant to continue fighting the British, hoping that the fellow Anglo-Saxons might join in the war against the Soviet communists. At any rate, as early as the autumn of 1940 Hitler had concluded that the Battle of Britain could not be won. The opportunity for victory had been squandered and *Luftwaffe* losses continued to mount. British cities burned, but he RAF remained a potent force.

Prime Minister Winston Churchill (1874–1965) hailed the spirit of the British people and called the time of peril and suffering 'their finest hour'. On 20 August 1940, Churchill rose to address the House of Commons, praising the courage of the intrepid Royal Air Force pilots. 'Never in the field of human conflict,' he declared, 'has so much been owed by so many to so few.'

LONDONERS GAZE SKYWARD *for any sign of approaching German aircraft as crews man antiaircraft guns positioned in Hyde Park. Hitler and Luftwaffe chief Hermann Göring believed that the Blitz could bring Great Britain to its knees.*

SUPERMARINE SPITFIRE

Originally conceived in the 1930s by British aircraft designer Reginald Mitchell, the Supermarine Spitfire flew for the first time on 5 March 1936. Production began two years later. Powered by the Rolls-Royce Merlin engine and initially armed with a pair of 20mm (0.78in) cannon and four .303 Browning machine guns, the Spitfire represented the leading edge of technology deployed by the Royal Air Force during the Battle of Britain.

The superior performance of the Spitfire made it a worthy adversary of the German Messerschmitt Me-109. However, it was available in limited numbers compared to the older Hawker Hurricane. Therefore, the RAF instructed Spitfire squadrons to engage the German fighters, while the Hurricanes attacked the slower bomber formations. The aircraft depicted is a Spitfire Mk 1 of No. 66 Squadron.

BATTLE OF BRITAIN

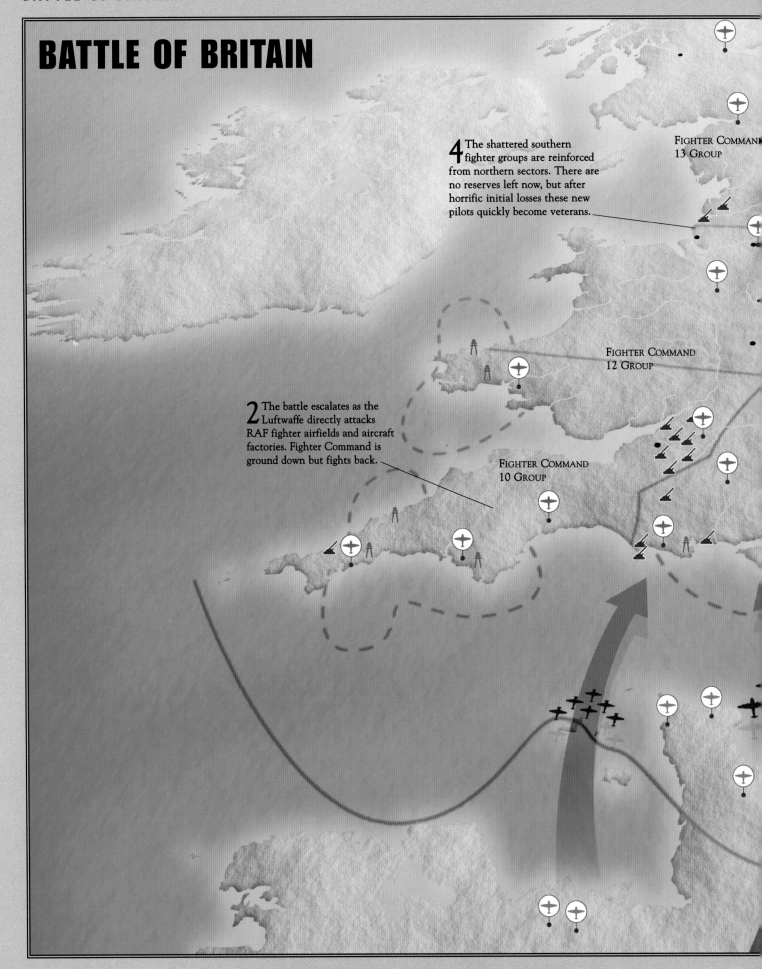

4 The shattered southern fighter groups are reinforced from northern sectors. There are no reserves left now, but after horrific initial losses these new pilots quickly become veterans.

FIGHTER COMMAND
13 GROUP

FIGHTER COMMAND
12 GROUP

2 The battle escalates as the Luftwaffe directly attacks RAF fighter airfields and aircraft factories. Fighter Command is ground down but fights back.

FIGHTER COMMAND
10 GROUP

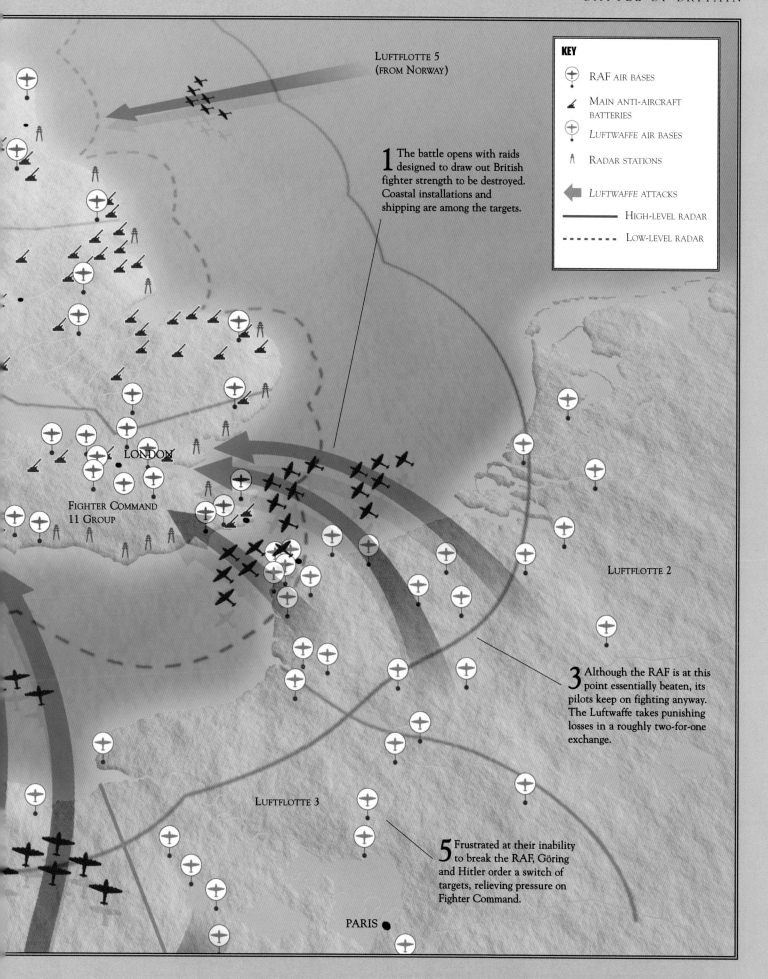

LUFTFLOTTE 5
(FROM NORWAY)

KEY

RAF AIR BASES

MAIN ANTI-AIRCRAFT
BATTERIES

LUFTWAFFE AIR BASES

RADAR STATIONS

LUFTWAFFE ATTACKS

HIGH-LEVEL RADAR

LOW-LEVEL RADAR

1 The battle opens with raids designed to draw out British fighter strength to be destroyed. Coastal installations and shipping are among the targets.

LONDON

FIGHTER COMMAND
11 GROUP

LUFTFLOTTE 2

3 Although the RAF is at this point essentially beaten, its pilots keep on fighting anyway. The Luftwaffe takes punishing losses in a roughly two-for-one exchange.

LUFTFLOTTE 3

5 Frustrated at their inability to break the RAF, Göring and Hitler order a switch of targets, relieving pressure on Fighter Command.

PARIS

BATTLE FOR CRETE

1941

The German airborne assault of Crete, although successful in terms of conquest, came at a terrific cost in lives, and led to the sharp decline of the Luftwaffe's parachute arm as a surprise weapon. German airborne forces were never to launch an operation of this scale again.

Crete, a mountainous island 260km (160-mile) long, some 100km (60 miles) from mainland Greece and lying in the eastern Mediterranean, was from late April 1941 the sole piece of Greek territory left in Allied hands. One of the threats posed by Crete to the Germans was its key resource for the formidable presence of the Royal Navy at Suda Bay, to the east of the then capital, Khania. It was one of the Mediterranean's largest natural harbours and vital as a refuelling centre. British aircraft could also block naval convoys crossing the Mediterranean to supply Rommel's forces in North Africa. In addition, Hitler foresaw Crete as a

BATTLE FOR CRETE FACTS

Who: Overall commander of the 'Creforce' garrison, Major-General Bernard Freyberg VC (1889–1963) versus General Kurt Student (1890–1978), Commander of XI *Flieger* Corps, the *Luftwaffe's* elite airborne troops.

What: The Germans landed in Crete from the Greek mainland and in 10 days of fierce fighting drove out the bulk of Allied troops.

Where: Crete, the largest island in Greece and the second largest in the eastern Mediterranean.

When: The main German attack on Greece took place between 20 May and 2 June 1941.

Why: The Germans urgently sought a free gateway to the East and Crete posed a major threat to their operations, especially

the naval convoys crossing the Mediterranean to replenish Rommel's forces in North Africa.

Outcome: German forces occupied Crete until the end of 1944 when, along with Greece and Albania, the island was abandoned and Hitler ordered a major retreat from the Balkans.

GLIDER-BORNE TROOPS LANDED AS part of the airborne invasion of Crete, enjoy a rest and a meal of wurst.

potentially valuable fortress guarding the Balkan flank of his projected Operation *Barbarossa*, the invasion of the Soviet Union. Hitler ordered the invasion of Crete on 25 April to be designated Operation *Merkur* (Mercury). However, due to logistical problems, the date was postponed to 20 May.

PARATROOP WARFARE

General Kurt Student, begetter of the *Fallschirmjäger* ('Hunters from the sky'), was a strong advocate of aerial warfare and had pressed the case vigorously for an airborne assault on Crete. But Hitler had considered an air campaign too dangerous and had predicted an unacceptably heavy toll of casualties. However, following pressure from the *Luftwaffe* chief Hermann Göring (1893–1946) he had yielded.

In anticipation of invasion, Commonwealth forces in Crete were, in May 1941, organized in five widely separated defence areas along the north coast – around the three airfields at Heraklion, Rethymnon and Maleme, as well as at Suda Bay and the port of Khania. At dawn on 20 May, the island's defence garrison of Anzac (Australian, New

LEFT: ELITE GLIDER-BORNE FORCES of German Gebirgsjäger (mountain troops) from the Greek mainland poised to land on Crete.

BELOW: JU 52S CARRYING AIRBORNE forces landed on key airports on the second day of the invasion, beginning with the capture of Maleme airport.

GENERAL KURT STUDENT

General Kurt Student (1890–1978, pictured right) was a World War I fighter pilot, chosen by Göring in 1938 to form a parachute infantry force, which later expanded to around 4500 men. After the evacuation from Crete, Student's troops fought mainly as infantry. Student received no decoration for his services and his personal access to Hitler came to an end. Though he claimed little interest in Nazism, he was brought before an Allied military tribunal in 1947 on eight charges of war crimes in Crete, including sanctioning the execution of British prisoners of war. He was acquitted on certain counts but sentenced to five years in prison. The Greeks requested his extradition from Germany for war crimes but he was never handed over, and died at the age of 88.

EVERY SURVIVING MEMBER of Student's forces received an Iron Cross, but after such losses, he said: 'Crete was the grave of the German paratroops'.

Zealand), British and local troops was subjected to familiar heavy bombing and the scream of Stukas.

What followed a few hours later was a major invasion by elite airborne forces. The assault was in two waves: the first launched against Maleme and Khania to the west, the second against Rethymnon and Heraklion, further to the east. This consisted of transport and 100 gliders, launched from bases on the Greek mainland. These delivered 6000 paratroopers and airborne infantry on and around Maleme with bombers pounding New Zealand troop positions.

General Student divided his forces into three battle groups: West, Centre and East, concentrating particularly on Khania and the prominent hunk of the Akrotiri peninsula. He would thus be given both an airfield and harbour where the battle line could be reinforced, the main object being the capture of the capital.

With more than 40,000 defenders – ANZAC and British troops, Greek and Cretan irregulars – was the 'Creforce' Commander, Major-General Bernard Freyberg, a VC from World War I. He faced serious problems: tired and demoralized troops, battered tanks from North Africa, no air cover and paucity of communications. But Freyberg was receiving intelligence from deciphered German codes alerting him to Student's intentions. He also had the support of a fiercely loyal local population.

BRIDGEHEADS ESTABLISHED

Although many of the Germans paras presented easy targets as they drifted down over New Zealand positions, many survived to regroup and fight fiercely, on Maleme. A severe

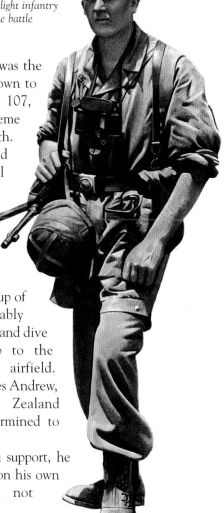

A MEMBER OF 7TH FLIEGER DIVISION (7th Air Division) of the Fallschirmjäger units, consisting of airborne light infantry which made a drop during the battle of Crete.

blow on the first day was the loss of a small hill known to the military as Hill 107, commanding the Maleme airfield from the south. The area around the airfield and hill was made up of 5 square kilometres (2 square miles) of rough territory, much of it giving poor visibility. There was a significant buildup of German forces, notably paratrooper battalions and dive bombers forming up to the southeast of the airfield. Lieutenant-Colonel Les Andrew, the area's New Zealand commander, was determined to go on the offensive.

Receiving no extra support, he attacked the invaders on his own initiative but could not contend with the overwhelming superiority of the paratroopers holding the hill. His small force was soon beaten back and his tanks immobilized. A promise of reinforcements came to nothing and Andrew was given permission to withdraw. Hill 107 was taken unopposed and control of the airfield passed to the Germans.

Student, more determined than ever to consolidate the Maleme bridgehead, flew in over the next two days a total of 3200 mountain troops and paras. He encountered fierce local resistance. But the Germans beat it off and the Stukas went in. On 25 May, the New Zealanders under Colonel Howard Kippenberger had some success with a counterattack near Galatas, lying to the southwest of Khania. But this simply delayed the German advance and Kippenberger had no resources to recover.

FLIMSY CANVAS AND WOOD-BUILT German gliders were vulnerable targets. Many crashed into olive trees or were shattered on landing, their fleeing crews cut down by the defenders.

The remainder of the Maleme position had to be yielded in the face of the presence of 2000 additional German mountain troops. The defenders retreated to Khania, which fell on 27 May. Resistance to the overwhelming air and eventually land power of the Germans became impossible, not least through lack of ammunition which severely weakened the Allied divisions. All was now set for a general evacuation.

Withdrawal from Suda Bay was covered by flown-in British commandos, while between 28 May and 1 June Britain's Mediterranean Fleet took off around 17,000 men, from Sphakia on the island's south coast, mostly from open beaches during a few short hours of darkness. Nine ships were sunk by the *Luftwaffe*. Back on land, 5000 men had to be left behind after being separated from their units. The Germans lost 1990 killed in action, while British and Commonwealth forces lost 1742. For the Allies, the debacle of Crete was complete.

ABOVE: GERMAN PARATROOPERS move forward past the bodies of Allied soldiers after their successful air invasion of Crete.

AFTERMATH

Hitler, severely shaken by figures for casualties in Crete, informed Student that he considered the days of the parachutist over, since its arm was no longer a surprise weapon. During the battle for Crete, over 1700 ANZAC and British troops had died, a similar number were wounded and around 12,000 were taken prisoners. The full extent of German losses differ, one of the highest figures being 3986 killed and missing with about 2000 having perished in the parachute drop alone.

Subsequent airborne operations by the Germans were strictly limited. As it turned out, the occupation of Crete proved a mixed blessing. The Cretans put up unremitting guerrilla resistance, forcing the Germans to garrison more troops than they wished, thereby making them unavailable elsewhere.

LEFT: ALTHOUGH MANY BRITISH 'TOMMIES', such as these on Suda Bay, were forced to surrender, others escaped in small craft or fled into the mountains to fight with partisans.

BATTLE FOR CRETE

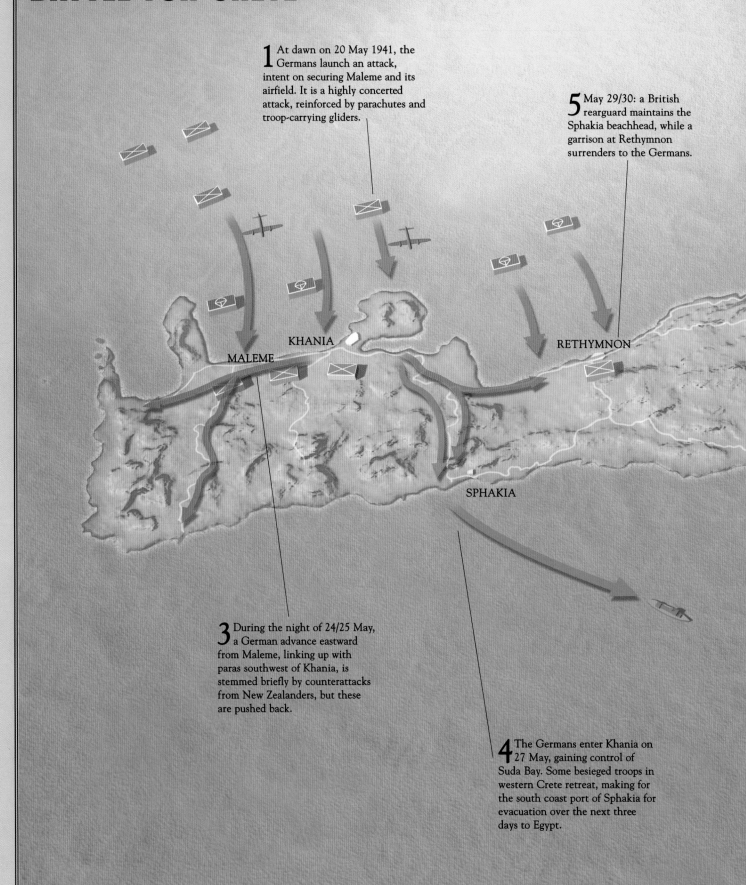

1 At dawn on 20 May 1941, the Germans launch an attack, intent on securing Maleme and its airfield. It is a highly concerted attack, reinforced by parachutes and troop-carrying gliders.

5 May 29/30: a British rearguard maintains the Sphakia beachhead, while a garrison at Rethymnon surrenders to the Germans.

KHANIA

MALEME

RETHYMNON

SPHAKIA

3 During the night of 24/25 May, a German advance eastward from Maleme, linking up with paras southwest of Khania, is stemmed briefly by counterattacks from New Zealanders, but these are pushed back.

4 The Germans enter Khania on 27 May, gaining control of Suda Bay. Some besieged troops in western Crete retreat, making for the south coast port of Sphakia for evacuation over the next three days to Egypt.

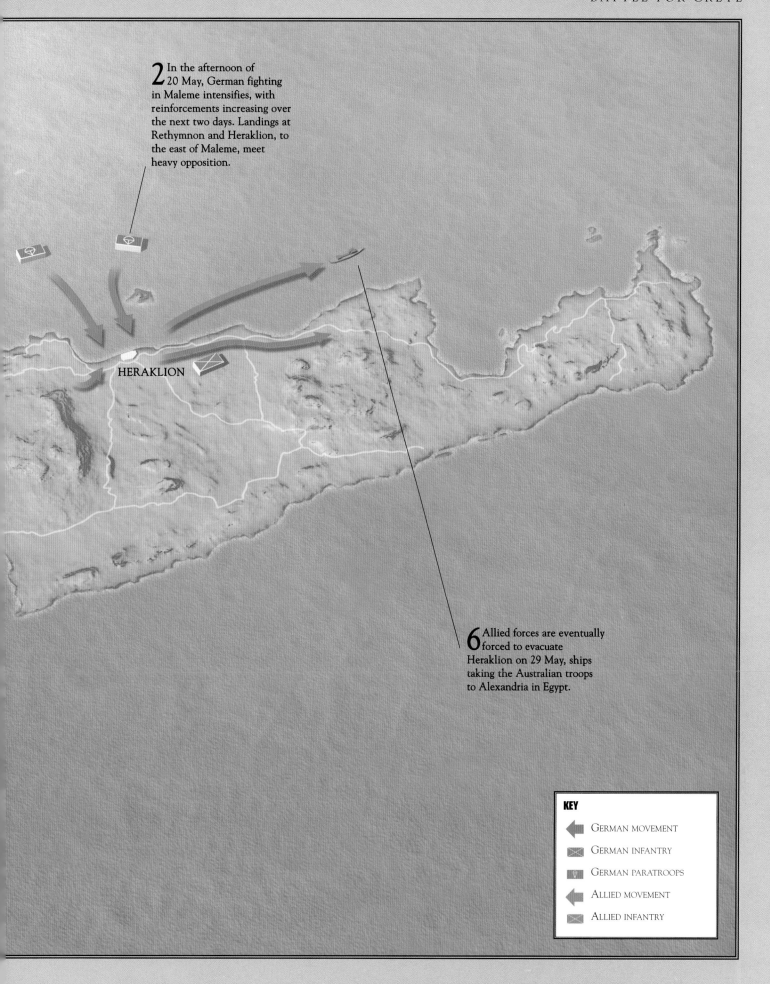

2 In the afternoon of 20 May, German fighting in Maleme intensifies, with reinforcements increasing over the next two days. Landings at Rethymnon and Heraklion, to the east of Maleme, meet heavy opposition.

HERAKLION

6 Allied forces are eventually forced to evacuate Heraklion on 29 May, ships taking the Australian troops to Alexandria in Egypt.

KEY

⬅ GERMAN MOVEMENT

✉ GERMAN INFANTRY

▽ GERMAN PARATROOPS

⬅ ALLIED MOVEMENT

✉ ALLIED INFANTRY

HUNT FOR THE BISMARCK 1941

By the summer of 1941, the Battle of the Atlantic had become a struggle for the survival of Great Britain. Not only were Nazi U-boats ravaging convoys and sinking merchant vessels laden with precious cargoes, but surface raiders of the Kriegsmarine (German Navy) also posed a significant threat.

From January to April, more than 610,000 tonnes (672,410 tons) of Allied shipping were lost. Then in May the worst fears of the British Admiralty were realized. The massive 42,800-tonne (47,200-ton) battleship *Bismarck* had weighed anchor and Operation *Rheinübung* (Rhine Exercise) was under way. In company with the heavy cruiser *Prinz Eugen*, the great battleship might wreak havoc on Allied merchant shipping with its eight 380mm (15in) guns.

HUNT FOR THE BISMARCK FACTS

Who: Elements of the British Royal Navy under Admiral John Tovey (1885–1971) versus the German battleship Bismarck and cruiser *Prinz Eugen*, under Admiral Günther Lütjens (1889–1941).

What: The *Bismarck* and *Prinz Eugen* tried to attack Allied shipping but were confronted by the Royal Navy.

Where: The North Atlantic near Allied convoy routes.

When: 18–27 May 1941

Why: The Germans hoped to inflict substantial losses on Allied merchant shipping, thereby strangling the supply line to Great Britain.

Outcome: During an epic chase, the Royal Navy sank the *Bismarck*. The *Kriegsmarine* mounted no more serious surface threats to Allied shipping in the Atlantic.

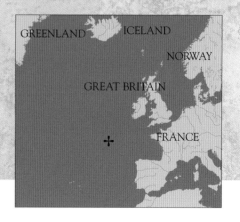

FAIREY SWORDFISH TORPEDO PLANES, *the flying anachronisms that slowed the German battleship* Bismarck, *are lashed to the flight deck of the aircraft carrier HMS* Victorious *amid an angry sea.*

Admiral Günther Lütjens, commander of the Kriegsmarine *task force which included the battleship* Bismarck *and the heavy cruiser* Prinz Eugen, *wearing his Knight's Cross.*

Recognizing the imminent danger, Admiral John Tovey (1885–1971), commander of the British Home Fleet at Scapa Flow, began to marshal his scattered surface assets to find and sink the Bismarck. Meanwhile Admiral Günther Lütjens (1889–1941), at sea aboard the German behemoth, knew that his movements during daylight hours had been observed by the Swedish cruiser *Gotland* and patrol planes from the neutral country. On 21 May, the battleship was photographed by a British reconnaissance aircraft.

BREAKOUT AND PURSUIT

Lütjens was determined to break out into the open sea and chose the Denmark Strait, one of three options, as his avenue of approach. Shadowed by a pair of British cruisers (*Suffolk* and *Norfolk*), the *Bismarck* and *Prinz Eugen* were engaged in the pre-dawn darkness of 24 May by the brand new battleship HMS *Prince of Wales* and the venerable battlecruiser HMS *Hood*. Launched in 1918, the *Hood* was equal in firepower to the *Bismarck* but it was vulnerable to the enemy's heavy guns, its designers having sacrificed armour protection for speed more than 20 years earlier.

Seconds into the fight, a German shell penetrated the *Hood's* thin armour and detonated an ammunition magazine. A gigantic explosion enveloped the warship and the pride of the Royal Navy was gone. Only three of the battle-cruiser's 1421 sailors survived. The *Prince of Wales* was seriously damaged, one German shell wrecking her bridge. Although the *Bismarck* sustained only three hits, one of these gashed her forecastle and tonnes of seawater poured in. Another ruptured a fuel tank and precious oil leaked in a telltale slick. Urged by the *Bismarck's* captain, Ernst Lindemann, to head back to Germany, Lütjens instead dispatched the *Prinz Eugen* to continue prowling for merchantmen and turned his wounded battleship towards the French port of Brest. En route, he hoped that U-boats might offer protection and air cover from planes based in France might soon appear.

THE BISMARCK

Named in honour of the Iron Chancellor of a unified Germany, the battleship *Bismarck* undertook Operation Rhine Exercise on 18 May 1941. Displacing nearly 43,000 tons, the warship posed a major threat to Allied shipping in the Atlantic. The *Bismarck's* main armament consisted of eight 380mm (15in) guns.

Capable of achieving speed in excess of 30 knots, the *Bismarck* was relentlessly pursued by heavy units of the Royal Navy. It was disabled by Swordfish torpedo planes and was eventually sunk on 27 May. However, the battleship and her consort, the heavy cruiser *Prinz Eugen*, had previously achieved a great success: the sinking of the battlecruiser HMS *Hood*, the pride of the Royal Navy.

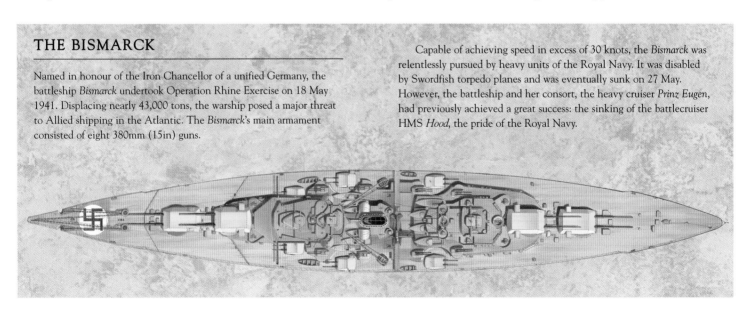

SAILORS OF THE German Navy, or Kriegsmarine, stand at attention during an inspection by officers prior to their departure from an anchorage on the Baltic Sea.

PERSEVERANCE AND LUCK

Devastated by the loss of the *Hood*, the British nevertheless continued their pursuit of the *Bismarck*. The Germans gave the shadowing cruisers the slip on the night of the 24 May after beating back an attack by Fairey Swordfish torpedo lauched planes from the aircraft carrier *Victorious*. Lütjens then inexplicably began to broadcast a lengthy radio message to Berlin, unaware that he had temporarily shaken the British off his trail. The British picked up the signal, corrected a navigational error which had sent them steaming in the wrong direction and locked on to their quarry once again.

On the morning of 26 May, a Consolidated PBY Catalina flying boat spotted the *Bismarck* less than 1300km (800 miles) from the French coast and nearing the range of a protective *Luftwaffe* air umbrella. Several of the Royal Navy warships initially engaged in the chase were obliged to turn for home as fuel ran low. The battleship HMS *King George V*, with Tovey aboard, ploughed ahead. Detached from convoy duty, the battleship HMS *Rodney* joined the pursuit, as did Gibraltar-based Force H, under Admiral James Somerville (1882–1949). The British had lost critical time and distance, though. The *Bismarck* might still escape.

SWORDFISH AT SUNSET

Tovey had one more card to play. The Fairey Swordfish was a flying anachronism, a biplane constructed primarily of wood, canvas and wire. Fifteen of these planes,

SAILING IN LINE ASTERN, the Bismark *as seen from the rear of the* Prinz Eugen *as they head out into the North Atlantic.*

torpedoes slung beneath their bellies, took off from the pitching deck of the Force H aircraft carrier HMS *Ark Royal* on the afternoon of the 26 May. Several mistakenly attacked the cruiser HMS *Sheffield* and luckily did not score a hit.

In the gathering twilight, the remaining 'Stringbags' pressed home their attacks through a curtain of withering anti-aircraft fire. Two torpedoes struck home. One of these hits was inconsequential. The other was catastrophic for the Germans. Flying only 15.5m (50ft) above the water and in gale force winds, Sub-Lieutenant John Moffat released his plane's weapon, which slammed into the *Bismarck's* stern and jammed her rudders 15° to port. As a result, the great ship was able to steer only one course, northwest towards the assembling might of the vengeful Royal Navy.

TORRENT OF SHELLS

Every sailor aboard the *Bismarck* now knew that the fate of their ship was sealed. Lindemann ordered the storage areas open and allowed the men to take what provisions they could. A cable from Hitler – 'The whole of Germany is with you' – seemed a forlorn hope. The Royal Navy would come with morning light and the death struggle would follow.

At 8.47 a.m. on 27 May, the 406mm (16in) guns of the *Rodney* barked from a range of 19km (12 miles). The *King George V* joined in. The crew of the *Bismarck* fought valiantly, but repeated hits seriously damaged her fire control system and disabled her main armament. The British battleships closed to less than 3.2km (2 miles) and bodies of dead and wounded sailors littered the *Bismarck's* decks. By 11 a.m., the ship was still afloat but blazing from bow to stern and unable to fight back. Shortly afterwards, the battleship rolled to port and sank stern first.

LINGERING CONTROVERSY

Three torpedo hits from the cruiser HMS *Dorsetshire* have long been credited with administering the *coup de grâce*. However, survivors of the *Bismarck* have insisted that they opened the vessel's seacocks and scuttled the ship. Exploration of the wreckage tends to support their claim but remains inconclusive. Only 110 of the *Bismarck's* complement of more than 2000 sailors were pulled from the chilly waters of the Atlantic. More might have been rescued, but a U-boat alarm sounded and the British were forced to abandon many sailors to the sea.

ABOVE: FAIREY SWORDFISH BIPLANES, torpedoes slung beneath their fuselages, in flight. Constructed primarily of wood and canvas, the Swordfish proved effective against the Bismarck.

The epic *Bismarck* chase resonates through history as a classic tale of naval warfare. In a practical sense, the loss of the great warship effectively ended the threat of the *Kriegsmarine* surface fleet to Allied merchant shipping in the Atlantic. Hitler simply became unwilling to risk his few capital ships in such an endeavour. Far to the north, German warships, including another giant, the battleship *Tirpitz*, menaced Allied convoys to the ports of Murmansk and Archangel in the Soviet Union. However, the Atlantic was to be the domain of the U-boats until they too were defeated.

BELOW: DAMAGED AND DOWN by the bow, the Bismarck ploughs through the waters of the Atlantic prior to its deadly rendezvous with the Royal Navy, principally the battleships King George V and Rodney.

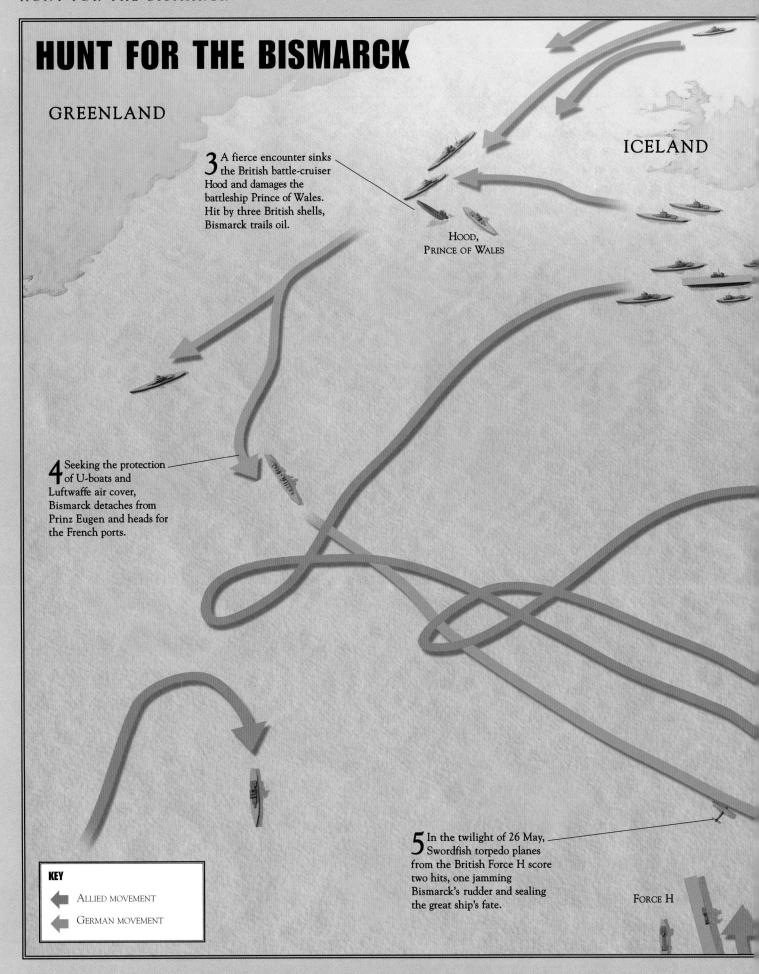

HUNT FOR THE BISMARCK

GREENLAND

ICELAND

3 A fierce encounter sinks the British battle-cruiser Hood and damages the battleship Prince of Wales. Hit by three British shells, Bismarck trails oil.

HOOD,
PRINCE OF WALES

4 Seeking the protection of U-boats and Luftwaffe air cover, Bismarck detaches from Prinz Eugen and heads for the French ports.

5 In the twilight of 26 May, Swordfish torpedo planes from the British Force H score two hits, one jamming Bismarck's rudder and sealing the great ship's fate.

FORCE H

KEY

ALLIED MOVEMENT

GERMAN MOVEMENT

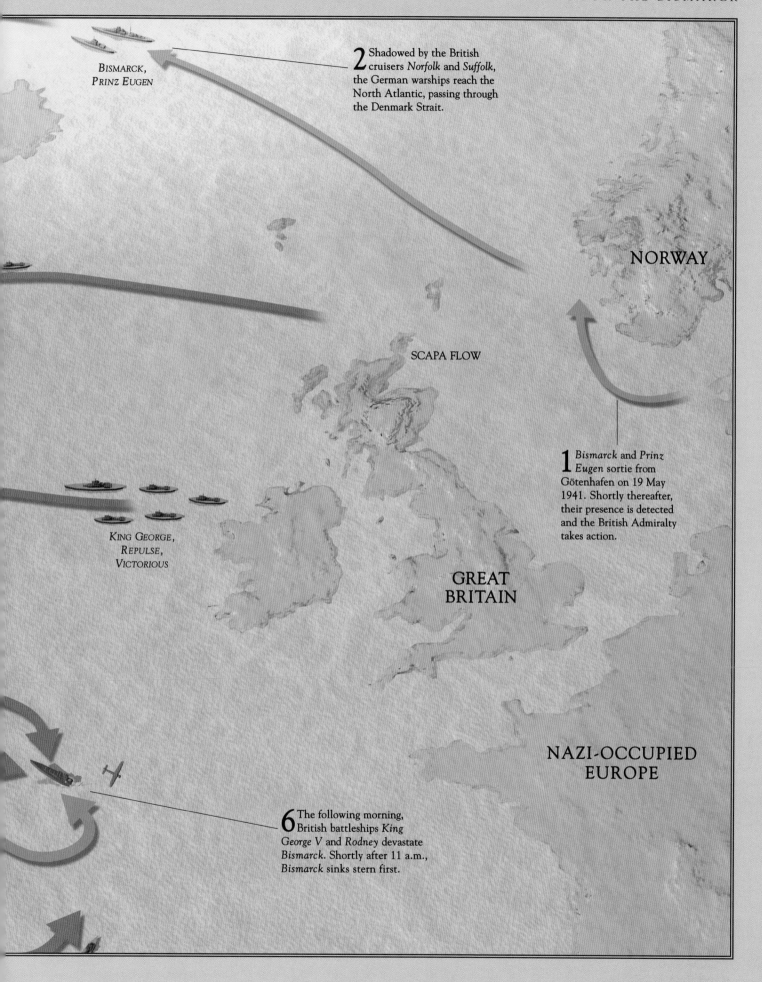

BISMARCK,
PRINZ EUGEN

2 Shadowed by the British cruisers *Norfolk* and *Suffolk*, the German warships reach the North Atlantic, passing through the Denmark Strait.

NORWAY

SCAPA FLOW

1 *Bismarck* and *Prinz Eugen* sortie from Götenhafen on 19 May 1941. Shortly thereafter, their presence is detected and the British Admiralty takes action.

KING GEORGE,
REPULSE,
VICTORIOUS

GREAT
BRITAIN

NAZI-OCCUPIED
EUROPE

6 The following morning, British battleships *King George V* and *Rodney* devastate *Bismarck*. Shortly after 11 a.m., *Bismarck* sinks stern first.

OPERATION BARBAROSSA

1941

A massive German army of 3.3 million men supported by over 3000 tanks and almost as many aircraft invaded the Soviet Union on 22 June 1941. The huge invasion force was to capture Moscow, the Ukraine and Leningrad in short order.

The largest military operation of all time, codenamed *Barbarossa* ('Red Beard'), was under way. It would see the German *Wehrmacht* achieve its most spectacular victories. It did not lead to ultimate victory, however, and the Red Army would storm Berlin four years later.

Hitler had placed the greatest emphasis in his plans for the capture of Leningrad – the USSR's second city and primary naval base – and the clearing of the Baltic States. Yet he had allocated the least number of troops, some 26 divisions to Army Group North under Marshal von Leeb (1876–1956). As a consequence,

OPERATION BARBAROSSA FACTS

Who: Three German Army Groups (North, Centre and South) led respectively by Marshals Ritter von Leeb (1876–1956), Fedor von Bock (1880–1945) and Gerd von Rundstedt (1875–1953) were charged by Hitler to destroy the Red Army in two months.

What: Barbarossa was the decisive turning point of the war. If the Soviet Union survived the German onslaught, Hitler's Reich would face a two-front war.

Where: By July 1941, when Finland had joined the German onslaught in the north, the Eastern Front would eventually stretch from the Black Sea to the Arctic North and the Germans would almost reach the gates of Moscow.

When: 22 June–5 December 1941

Why: Undaunted by his failure to subdue Britain during the summer of 1940, Hitler gambled that his *Wehrmacht* would be able to knock out the Soviet Union before the United States eventually intervened in the war on the side of Britain.

Outcome: Ultimately the outcome of *Barbarossa* would decide the outcome of World War II.

A CZECH-BUILT 35(T) TANK PASSES *a burning manor house in White Russia in early June 1941 as the* blitzkrieg *rips through Soviet territory.*

Leeb's advance was slow and it was not until September that his exhausted troops managed to cut off Leningrad from the rest of the USSR. And instead of a swift capture of the great city, a long and ultimately fatal siege ensued.

UKRAINIAN VICTORIES, ROSTOV SETBACK

Marshal Gerd von Rundstedt's (1875–1953) Army Group South – 41 divisions, including five panzer and 14 Romanian divisions – were entrusted with the vital task of taking the Ukraine. With its abundant grain fields and the industrial might of the Donbass region, it was a prize that was much needed.

Unfortunately for Rundstedt, however, the Southwestern Front, the strongest of the Soviet army groups, offered fierce

HISTORY TENDS TO SEE THE GERMAN ARMY as a fast-moving, motorized force. However, the reality was that a great deal of equipment was moved by horse power – 750,000 horses were used in the invasion of the Soviet Union.

resistance, led ably by its commander General Mikhail Kirponos (1892–1941). As a result, Army Group South was able to advance only slowly and deliberately. Nevertheless, the panzer forces of Army Group Centre intervened, converging on 10 September with those of Rundstedt's panzers east of Kiev.

Three massive Soviet armies (Fifth, Twenty-Sixth and Thirty-Seventh) were now trapped in and around Kiev. Kirponos died trying to escape the German trap and a staggering 665,000 of his men were captured.

THE 'LIBERATOR' SOON turned to savage oppressor: a German landser (infantryman) with a burning Russian cottage in the background.

On 30 September, the 1st Panzer Group attacked and had, by 6 October, trapped much of the Soviet Southern Front in a large pocket in southeast Ukraine. Two armies (the Ninth and Eighteenth) were destroyed, yielding 100,000 prisoners.

The German advance continued towards Rostov on the Don river, which was captured on 20 November. However, the Soviet High Command (*Stavka*) launched a vigorous counterattack with three armies against the by now over-extended German lines. By 29 November, this strategically located city was back in Soviet hands and the Germans had narrowly escaped an early version of Stalingrad.

ADVANCE OF ARMY GROUP CENTRE

When Napoleon had invaded Russia in 1812, he ultimately reached Moscow but still did not achieve victory. Hitler's generals – especially Fedor von Bock (1880–1945), the commander of Army Group Centre – believed that the Soviet Union would collapse if Moscow was captured. Here, as in the south, the Germans scored some major successes. A string of armies were trapped inside the Bialystok salient and in a vast pocket west of Minsk, yielding 300,000 prisoners. Stalin had the Western Front's commander, General Dimitri Pavlov (1897–1941), fired and shot upon his return to Moscow for his failures. His place was taken by Marshal Simeon Timoshenko (1883–1973), an experienced and hard-headed commander.

The Red Army continued to suffer catastrophic reverses, however. Smolensk, the gateway to Moscow, fell on 16 July. Stalin was now determined to block the German advance, and a series of counterattacks were launched by the Western Front armies, costing them yet another 300,000 men and 3000 tanks. Among the Germans, the feeling spread that

GENERAL HEINZ GUDERIAN

Heinz Guderian (1888–1954) was Hitler's most successful tank commander, who combined brilliant brains with outstanding abilities as a practical and hard-headed field commander. He was made head of the 2nd Panzer Division in 1935, took part in the Polish campaign (September 1939) and broke through at Sedan on 14 May 1940. During the *Barbarossa* campaign, Guderian was in command of the 2nd Panzer Group, renamed simply 'Guderian'. He was set to march on Moscow, having taken Smolensk in July when his panzer forces were diverted south. Guderian was called '*Schneller Heinz*' (Hurrying Heinz) by his hard-pressed but admiring troops. During Operation *Typhoon*, Guderian held command of the Second Panzer Army but was fired on 25 December and remained without a command until 1943.

with each success they were no closer to victory and that the Red Army's reserves were inexhaustible.

Hitler, who did not share his generals' views, diverted most of Army Group Centre's panzer divisions to take part in the battle for Kiev. For more than a month, the Central Front of 800km (496 miles) remained unchanged, giving the Red Army invaluable time to prepare its defences. General Andrei Yeremenko (1892–1970) had three armies (30 divisions) at Bryansk, and Timoshenko had six armies with 55 divisions at Vyazma. Incredibly, all these forces had been either wiped out or captured by October.

LEFT: AS RUSSIA FACES yet another savage invasion, these Ukrainians dig antitank ditches during the late summer of 1941.

The march on Moscow, codenamed Operation *Typhoon*, was unleashed early in the morning of 2 October in brilliant sunshine. Army Group Centre numbered a million men in 77 divisions with 1700 tanks and almost a thousand planes.

Five days later, General Höppner's Fourth Panzer Group co-operating with General Hermann Hoth's (1885–1971) Third Panzer Group had trapped Timoshenko's six armies in a massive pocket in and around Vyazma.

THE BATTLE FOR MOSCOW

On 9 October, Hoth and Hoeppner linked up with Guderian's panzer forces, trapping the Third, Thirteenth and Fiftieth Soviet armies north and south of Bryansk. Leaving only a minimum of troops to seal up the pockets at Vyazma and Bryansk, the Army Group's panzer groups aimed for Mozhaiska and Tula. These pockets were eliminated by 14 and 20 October respectively, leaving eight armies destroyed. The yield was as massive as at Kiev – some 673,000 prisoners, more than 1000 tanks and 5000 guns.

Despite torrential rains that turned the roads into quagmires, the Germans had covered two-thirds of the distance to Moscow by the middle of the month. Finally, Soviet morale snapped. On 16 October, law and order collapsed in the capital, a million of its citizens fleeing for their lives in the 'Great Flight'. Only a policy of shooting to kill by the NKVD (Soviet Secret Police) stemmed the panic and prevented further looting and chaos.

In early November, the weather turned colder, enabling the Germans to advance again across frozen and hard roads. But it was soon too cold with temperatures of -21°C (-6°F),

BELOW: A GERMAN PAK-36 team knocks out a light Soviet tank during the fighting of the summer of 1941.

RIGHT: OCTOBER 1941 – *Soviet propaganda trying to show a united nation rallying to the defence of the capital. In reality, there was oppression, corruption and defeatism before the onset of winter.*

and a new commander had appeared on the Soviet side, General Georgi Zhukov (1896–1974), who had already saved Leningrad and was now planning a counterattack against the exhausted Germans. By 18 November, Zhukov had 21 rested, fully equipped and battle-hardened Siberian divisions ready to be unleashed against Bock's army.

The German plan was for a frontal assault with 36 divisions while the three panzer groups encircled the Soviet defenders around Moscow. On 27 November, 2nd Panzer Division was just 22km (14 miles) from the capital and could see the spires of the Kremlin palaces through the haze.

Bock's Army Group now held a front almost 1000km (600 miles) long with a mere 60 divisions. The crawling offensive came to a halt on 5 December when temperatures plunged to a bone-chilling -35°C (-31°F). That same day Zhukov ordered General Ivan Konev's (1897–1973) Kalinin Front to attack, and the following day his own Western Front went on to the offensive.

The attack took the Germans completely by surprise, and over the next two months the Red Army held the initiative on the Central Front. Hitler gave orders that there was to be no retreat and this probably saved Army Group Centre from a complete collapse.

The failure of *Typhoon* spelled the defeat of *Barbarossa*. In the long run, the Soviet counterattack sounded the death-knell to the German Nazi Reich as well. Two days after Zhukov began his offensive, the United States entered the war, and Hitler's defeat was now only a question of time.

ЗАЩИТИМ РОДНУЮ

МОСКВУ

BELOW: THE PANZER MK III (this model belonging to the 2nd Panzer Division) was the sturdy workhorse of the German Panzer forces but was no match for the Soviet T-34.

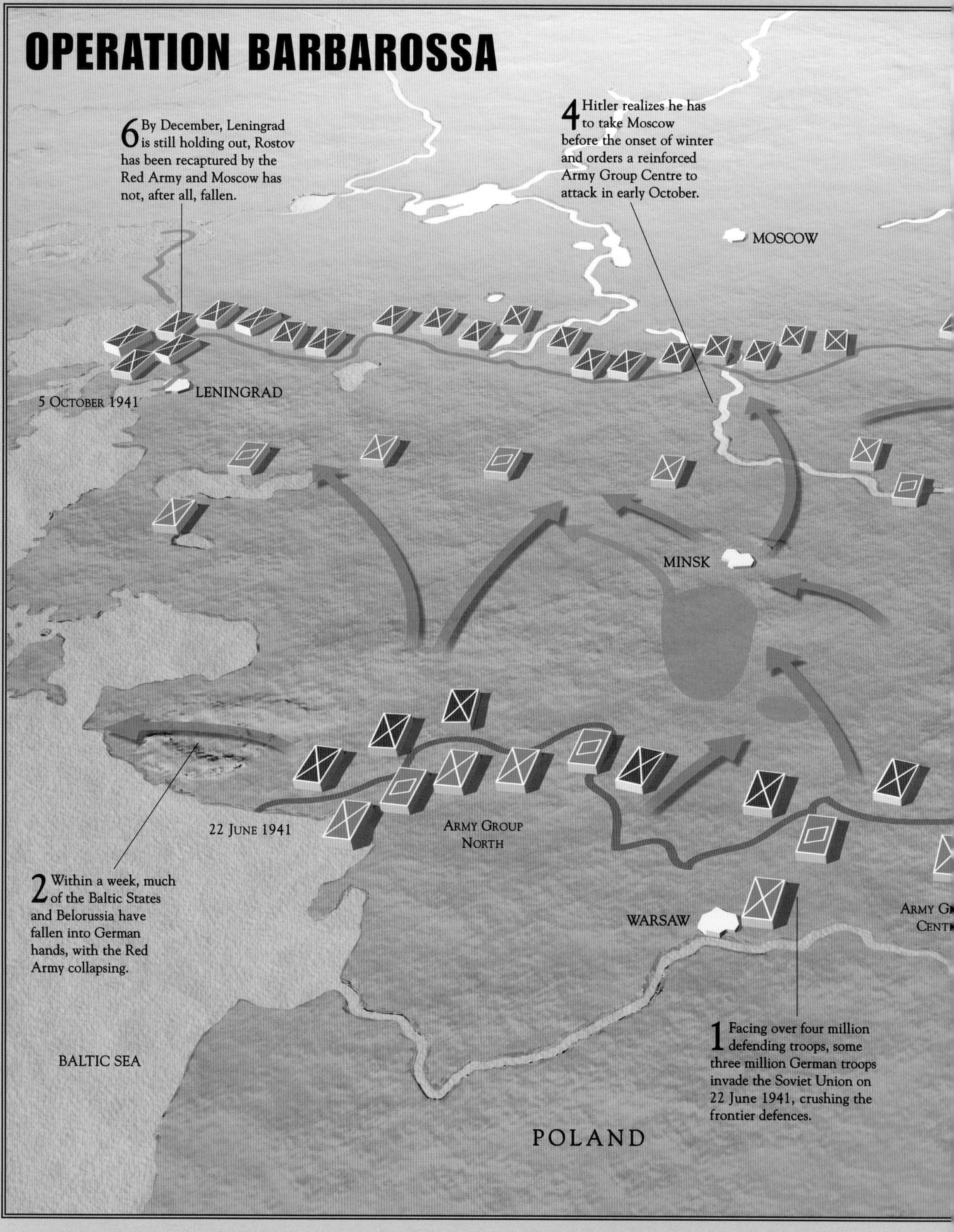

OPERATION BARBAROSSA

6 By December, Leningrad is still holding out, Rostov has been recaptured by the Red Army and Moscow has not, after all, fallen.

4 Hitler realizes he has to take Moscow before the onset of winter and orders a reinforced Army Group Centre to attack in early October.

MOSCOW

5 OCTOBER 1941   LENINGRAD

MINSK

2 Within a week, much of the Baltic States and Belorussia have fallen into German hands, with the Red Army collapsing.

22 JUNE 1941

ARMY GROUP NORTH

WARSAW

ARMY G[R]
CENT[RE]

1 Facing over four million defending troops, some three million German troops invade the Soviet Union on 22 June 1941, crushing the frontier defences.

BALTIC SEA

POLAND

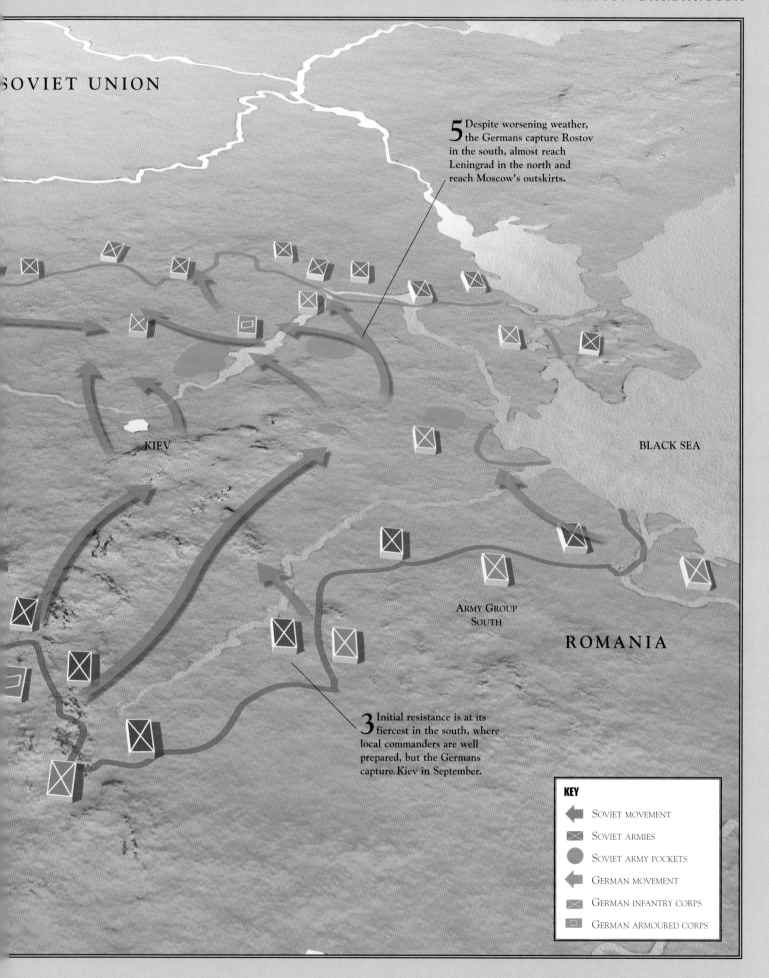

SOVIET UNION

5 Despite worsening weather, the Germans capture Rostov in the south, almost reach Leningrad in the north and reach Moscow's outskirts.

KIEV

BLACK SEA

ARMY GROUP
SOUTH

ROMANIA

3 Initial resistance is at its fiercest in the south, where local commanders are well prepared, but the Germans capture Kiev in September.

KEY

← SOVIET MOVEMENT

⊠ SOVIET ARMIES

● SOVIET ARMY POCKETS

← GERMAN MOVEMENT

⊠ GERMAN INFANTRY CORPS

▱ GERMAN ARMOURED CORPS

SIEGE OF LENINGRAD 1941–44

The siege of Leningrad was a ghastly epic of endurance that cost the lives of up to 1.5 million people, both soldiers and civilians. In total, it ran for nearly 900 days.

On 22 June 1941, German forces surged across the Soviet border in Operation *Barbarossa*. The *Wehrmacht* was split into three major formations – Army Groups North, Centre and South – each with its own objectives. Army Group North under the command of Field-Marshal Wilhelm von Leeb (1876–1956), had Leningrad as its goal, a large urban zone of a million souls located on the Gulf of Finland. Von Leeb's forces, as with the other elements of *Barbarossa*, made vigorous progress, pushing on through the Baltic states and breaking across the Luga river just 120km (75 miles) south of Leningrad on 9 August.

SIEGE OF LENINGRAD FACTS

Who: The German Army Group North under several commanders versus the Soviet Volkhov and Leningrad Fronts, commanded by General Kirill Meretskov (1897–1968) and Marshal Leonid Govorov (1897–1955) respectively.

What: A partial blockade of Leningrad by Army Group North reduced Leningrad to starvation conditions, the blockade being broken only by a succession of Soviet offensives over nearly three years.

Where: Leningrad (now renamed St Petersburg), a city in the far north of Russia, nestling on the Gulf of Finland.

When: The siege effectively ran from September 1941 to January 1944.

Why: Leningrad was an early target of Hitler's Operation *Barbarossa*, but by the end of 1943 the German operations there had little military function besides maintaining the overall German frontline.

Outcome: A million civilians died from starvation, bombing and shelling, but the ultimate defeat of the Germans was a key ingredient in the German Army's defeat on the Eastern Front.

A RED ARMY UNIT *makes a characteristic attack in the Leningrad sector, winter 1943 – a simple charge backed by heavy machine-gun support.*

ABOVE: JU-87 STUKA DIVE-BOMBERS were used intensively as 'flying artillery' to intercept Soviet supply runs into Leningrad from across Lake Ladoga.

SAVED FOR A SIEGE

The fate of the city seemed assured, not least because German-allied Finnish forces were fighting down from the north between Lake Ladoga and the sea. Important road and rail links into Leningrad fell to the Germans one by one – Novgorod on 16 August, Chudovo on the 20th – and by 1 September the German artillery shells were dropping into the city itself. The inhabitants of Leningrad prepared themselves for a battle for survival. From 9 September, the esteemed Soviet General Georgi Zhukov (1896–1974) was in the city, transforming it from a beautiful northern city into a massive fortress ringed by defensive positions, pillboxes and trenches. Yet the direct German assault on Leningrad did not come. On 6 September, Hitler switched the priority of *Barbarossa* to objectives further south and drew off much of von Leeb's panzer strength to support the offensive. Therefore Leningrad would have to be defeated by siege and bombardment.

Throughout September and October, the strategic situation for Leningrad worsened considerably. The major railway stations at Schlisselburg and Mga to the east

fell into German hands, and in October von Leeb began an offensive towards the vital railway centre at Tikhvin, which fell on 8 November. A ring of steel was closing around Leningrad, but the fighting was far from easy for the Germans. The offensive had grossly overstretched an already weakened Army Group North and it faced pressing resistance from the armies of the Volkhov Front commanded by General Kirill Meretskov (1897–1968).

By 10 December 1941, Tikhvin was back in Soviet hands following a huge but crudely handled Red Army offensive and by early January the Germans were forced to re-establish their frontlines further west. Only

LEFT: A WELL-EQUIPPED Red Army infantryman, seen here in the autumn of 1941, armed with the Tokarev SVT-40, an early Soviet semi-automatic rifle.

ABOVE: THE LIFELINE – A TRUCK CONVOY moves across a frozen Lake Ladoga. Under such conditions, up to 400 trucks a day were able to make the journey.

the narrowest of supply corridors, however, remained for Leningrad's already desperate people.

STARVATION AND RESISTANCE

As the German and Soviet armies outside Leningrad battled for dominance, a horrifying battle against starvation was under way within the city itself. In an especially bitter winter, the citizens of Leningrad were beginning to starve in their thousands, their predicament worsened by a collapse in fuel supplies for warmth.

By the end of November, people were trying to survive on a daily ration of less than 250g (9oz) of bread. Bodies littered

RIGHT: GERMAN INFANTRY BATTLE the Russian winter, late 1941. As elsewhere, the harsh Russian climate hampered German mobility on the Leningrad Front.

ABOVE: LENINGRAD CIVILIANS GATHER in a small group to distribute what meagre supplies are available, transporting them across icy streets on sledges.

BELOW: THE T34/76 TANK WAS the primary Soviet armoured fighting vehicle of the Leningrad Front, and its numbers were critical in breaking the German siege in 1944.

every street – people would literally died on their feet or curled up in doorways. On one day alone, 13,500 deaths occurred. Film footage of the period shows old people scraping out refuse bins with spoons and putting what they found into their mouths. Cannibalism became one way of surviving, and disturbing-looking meat appeared on sale by some street vendors. Every animal, wild or domestic, was killed for food, and other items such as linseed oil and tallow candles found their way on to the menu. Against this horrifying backdrop was the constant German air and artillery bombardment.

The main lifeline to the city was Lake Ladoga, though it was hardly adequate. Supplies were moved by land to Tikhvin, then to disembarkation points such as Novaya Ladoga and Lednevo. Small boats of every military and civilian variety sailed the waters in the non-winter months, frequently under heavy German air assault, to dock in Osinovets, northeast of Leningrad. When Lake Ladoga froze over, up to 400 trucks a day shuttled supplies straight across the ice and took back refugees on the return

journey. Conditions for the supply convoys were grim: many truck crews, ship crews and refugees found their graves at the bottom of Ladoga. However, in the spring of 1942 fuel and electricity pipelines were laid across the river, bringing power for cooking and heating. Yet although conditions had improved by the end of 1942 blockade conditions existed for nearly 900 days, during which time about one million people died out of a population of 2.5 million. Some sources put the death toll as high as 1.5 million.

BREAKING THE SIEGE

In 1942, the Soviets looked to make further gains. In January, a large offensive by the Volkhov Front between Novgorod (just north of Lake Ilmen) and Spasskaya Polist made a 60km (37-mile) salient in the German frontline, but the offensive had stalled by March, leaving the Germans to nip out of the salient and completely destroy the Soviet Second Shock Army. Nevertheless, the Soviet attack had alarmed Hitler enough for him to replace von Leeb as commander of the Army Group North (von Leeb had requested a tactical withdrawal in the face of the offensive) with Field-Marshal Georg von Küchler (1881–1968). Küchler himself would go in August 1942 after he resisted Hitler's idea for a general offensive to crush Leningrad, codenamed *Northern Lights*. Manstein then took what was proving to be a poisoned chalice for German commanders.

Between 27 August and 25 September 1942, there was considerable movement around Leningrad. An offensive by Meretskov against the bottleneck was eventually stopped by Manstein, but his counteroffensive also ground to a halt against the Soviet defence. The critical change in fortunes, however, came in January 1943. The Soviet Leningrad Front under Marshal Leonid Govorov (1897–1955), four armies strong, launched a combined offensive with the Volkhov Front against the German forces in the bottleneck. The sheer weight of men and armour was irresistible and Schlisselburg was back in Soviet hands by 19 January. By early February, the Soviets were running direct rail journeys into Leningrad, albeit ones under constant German bombardment – the corridor secured by the Red Army was only 10km (6.2 miles) wide.

SIEGE OVER

The worst of the siege was over but the partial blockade ran until January 1944. The Germans held their lines even as they were weakened by Hitler's redeployment of forces for his 1943 offensives in the Ukraine. On 14 January 1944, an overwhelming Soviet offensive by both Red Army fronts flooded over the German defences and put the *Wehrmacht* troops on the retreat. On 27 January, with the recapture of the Leningrad–Moscow rail line, Stalin officially declared the siege of Leningrad over.

THE BETRAYAL OF LENINGRAD

The siege of Leningrad became iconic in the years following its liberation, with artists, writers, musicians and historians enshrining the resistance in their work. This publicity soon fuelled Stalin's paranoia – he had long suspected that Leningrad (as Russia's second city) could produce a rival power base to his own. In 1946, he acted against the figures behind Leningrad's resistance, arresting them on false charges. The Leningrad Party Organization was purged and some 2000 people were executed, imprisoned or exiled between 1946 and 1950, including Pyotr Popkov, Aleksei Kuznetsov and Nikolai Voznesensky, important players in Leningrad's survival and attempted post-war renaissance.

LOCAL PEOPLE MARK the fiftieth anniversary of the end of the siege of Leningrad at the St Petersburg Cemetery, 1994.

SIEGE OF LENINGRAD

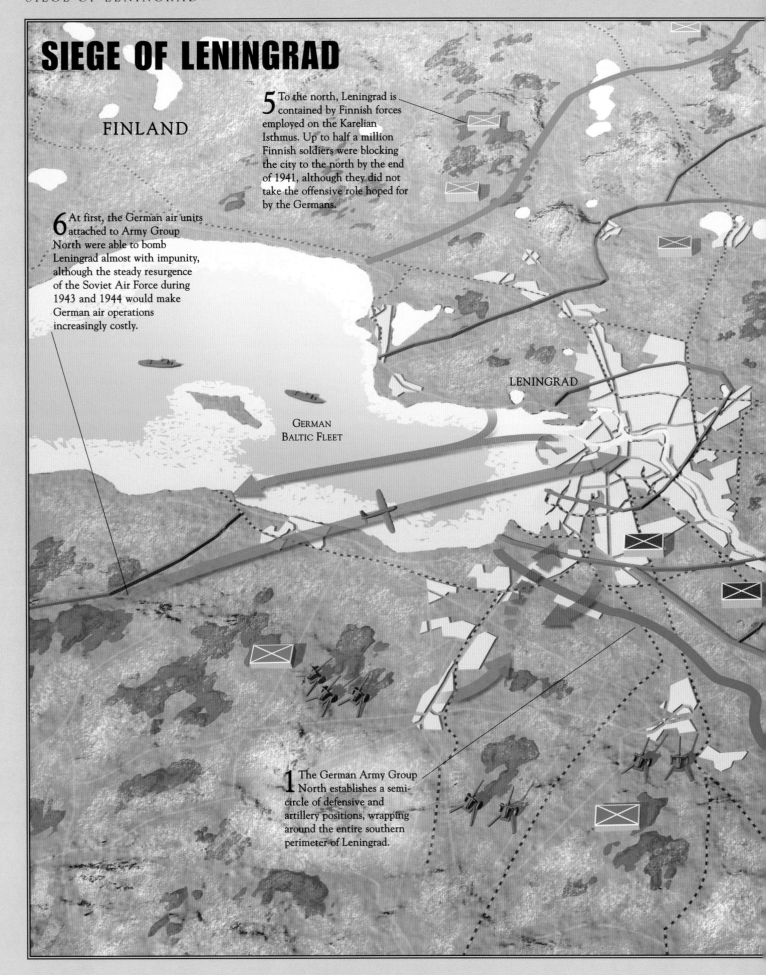

FINLAND

5 To the north, Leningrad is contained by Finnish forces employed on the Karelian Isthmus. Up to half a million Finnish soldiers were blocking the city to the north by the end of 1941, although they did not take the offensive role hoped for by the Germans.

6 At first, the German air units attached to Army Group North were able to bomb Leningrad almost with impunity, although the steady resurgence of the Soviet Air Force during 1943 and 1944 would make German air operations increasingly costly.

GERMAN
BALTIC FLEET

LENINGRAD

1 The German Army Group North establishes a semi-circle of defensive and artillery positions, wrapping around the entire southern perimeter of Leningrad.

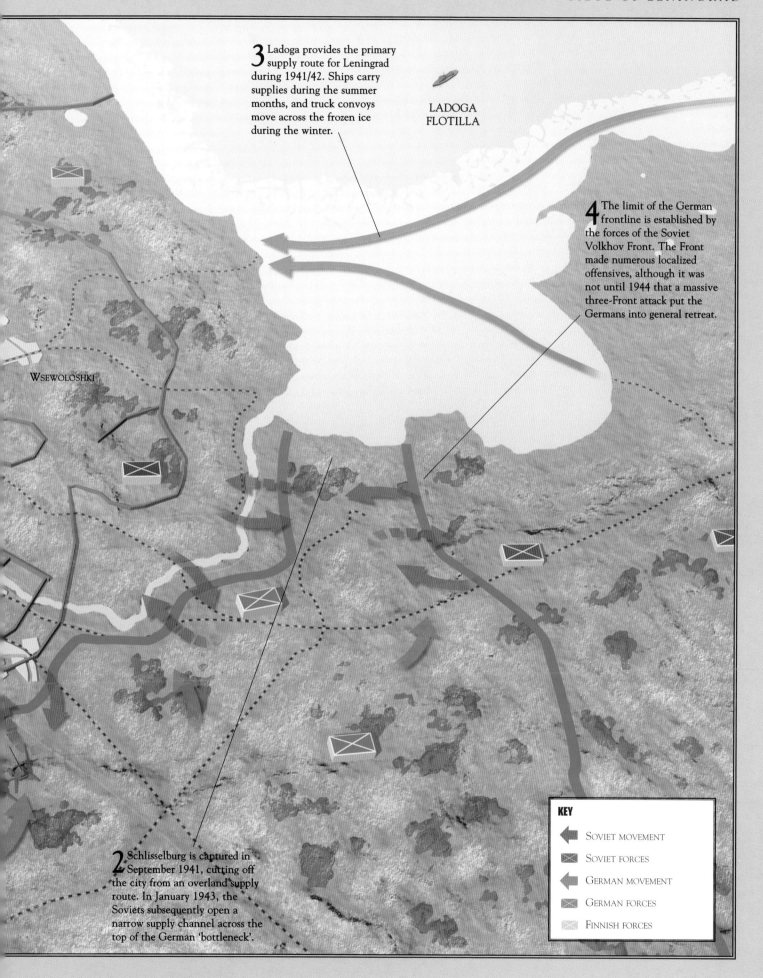

3 Ladoga provides the primary supply route for Leningrad during 1941/42. Ships carry supplies during the summer months, and truck convoys move across the frozen ice during the winter.

LADOGA
FLOTILLA

4 The limit of the German frontline is established by the forces of the Soviet Volkhov Front. The Front made numerous localized offensives, although it was not until 1944 that a massive three-Front attack put the Germans into general retreat.

WSEWOLOSHKI

2 Schlisselburg is captured in September 1941, cutting off the city from an overland supply route. In January 1943, the Soviets subsequently open a narrow supply channel across the top of the German 'bottleneck'.

KEY

← SOVIET MOVEMENT

⊠ SOVIET FORCES

← GERMAN MOVEMENT

⊠ GERMAN FORCES

⊠ FINNISH FORCES

IN THE BALANCE

With the entry of the United States into the war in December 1941, Winston Churchill famously 'slept the sleep of the saved and the thankful' because 'there was no more doubt about the end.' Yet Germany remained ascendent and Japan was rampaging through the Far East. American power would take time to deploy decisively and the war was by no means won.

It took desperate and bloody battles at El Alamein in the Western Desert and on a far greater scale at Stalingrad and Kursk on the Eastern Front to turn the tide against the Germans, and at Midway, Guadalcanal and Imphal to do the same against the Japanese in the Pacific theatre.

US MARINES TAKE COVER *amidst landing operations in the Solomon Islands, 30 June 1943. The crucial battles at Midway and Guadalcanal proved to be the turning point in the war in the Pacific.*

PEARL HARBUR 1941

When Japanese warplanes swept in to attack the US naval base at Pearl Harbor and other installations on the Hawaiian island of Oahu on 7 December 1941, the act was the culmination of years of growing tension between the two countries. Japan, seeking preeminence in Asia and the Pacific, required land and other natural resources to sustain its growing population and fuel its formidable military machine.

In 1931, Japan's army had invaded Manchuria, and a decade of fighting in China followed. By 1941, Japan had occupied all of Indochina. Recognizing the US and the traditional European powers as the chief impediments to the establishment of its 'Greater East Asia Co-Prosperity Sphere', Japan prepared for a war that its militaristic leaders considered inevitable.

In response to the growing threat, President Franklin D. Roosevelt (1882–1945) utilized political and economic pressure to curb Japanese ambitions. In May 1940, he ordered the US Pacific Fleet, already in Hawaiian waters for

PEARL HARBOR FACTS

Who: The Japanese Combined Fleet under strategic command of Admiral Isoroku Yamamoto (1884–1943) and tactical command of Vice-Admiral Chuichi Nagumo (1887–1944) versus the US Pacific Fleet under Admiral Husband Kimmel (1882–1968) and US Army forces under General Walter Short (1880–1949).

What: The Japanese Combined Fleet assembled six fleet carriers to launch an audacious attack on the US Pacific Fleet base of Pearl Harbor 5472km (3400 miles) away.

Where: Pearl Harbor and US military facilities on the Hawaiian island of Oahu.

When: 7 December 1941

Why: In the face of US and British sanctions, Japan needed to neutralize US naval power in the Pacific, at least temporarily, in order to seize British and Dutch resources in the region, especially oil.

Outcome: Tactically Japan caused considerable damage at little cost to itself, but, in the words of Vice-Admiral Nagumo, it managed only 'to awaken a sleeping giant and fill her with a terrible resolve'.

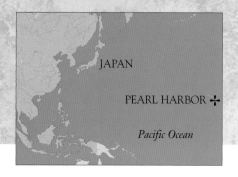

JAPAN

PEARL HARBOR ✛

Pacific Ocean

STRUCK BY SEVERAL JAPANESE *torpedoes, the battleship USS* West Virginia *burns and settles to the shallow bottom of Pearl Harbor. In the foreground, sailors pull a survivor from the water.*

LEFT: JAPANESE PREMIER HIDEKI TOJO led his nation to war with the United States. After the war, Tojo survived a suicide attempt. He was later tried, convicted, and executed for war crimes.

exercises, to remain on station at Pearl Harbor rather than return to its home port of San Pedro, California. In the summer of 1940, he prohibited the export of strategic minerals, chemicals and scrap iron to Japan. On 26 July 1941, in retaliation for Japan's occupation of Indochina, he imposed an embargo on oil, nationalized the Filipino Army and froze Japanese assets in the United States.

WAR WARNINGS

Admiral Isoroku Yamamoto (1884–1943), Commander-in-Chief of the Combined Fleet, was reluctant to go to war with the United States. Nevertheless he became the architect of what was conceived as a crippling blow to American military power in the Pacific, a pre-emptive strike by carrier-based aircraft against the US Pacific Fleet anchored at Pearl Harbor. For months, the Japanese pilots trained in secret. Then, on 26 November 1941, the powerful

BELOW: THE ENGINES OF JAPANESE Mitsubishi Zero fighters roar to life aboard the aircraft carrier Shokaku. The Zeroes provided air cover for the attackers at Pearl Harbor.

armada sailed from Hittokapu Bay in the Kurile islands. Two battleships, three cruisers, nine destroyers and three submarines escorted the heart of the strike force, six aircraft carriers, *Akagi, Kaga, Soryu, Hiryu, Shokaku* and *Zuikaku*.

American military leaders and diplomats acknowledged that war with Japan was imminent. However, they were convinced that the first blow would fall in the Philippines or Southeast Asia. The day after the Japanese fleet sailed, US commanders across the Pacific received a war warning. But the commander of the US Pacific Fleet, Admiral Husband Kimmel (1882–1968), and his Army counterpart, General Walter Short (1880–1949), were preoccupied with safeguarding installations and equipment from sabotage. They also fell victim to a series of communication failures.

EARLY WARNINGS IGNORED

In the pre-dawn hours of 7 December, the Japanese strike force had reached its appointed station 370km (230 miles) north of the island of Oahu. At 3.30 a.m. Pacific time, US cryptanalysts in Washington DC intercepted the last of a 14-part message from Tokyo to its emissaries there. The message seemed to indicate the opening of hostilities by Japan within a matter of hours.

At 3.45 a.m., the minesweeper USS *Condor*, on routine patrol, sighted what appeared to be a submarine periscope in

A JAPANESE PILOT wearing leather headcover, goggles and flight suit, strides towards his waiting aircraft. At the time of Pearl Harbor, many Japanese fliers had combat experience, gained in China.

a restricted area near the entrance to Pearl Harbor. The sighting was probably one of five Japanese midget submarines which were tasked with entering the harbour and firing torpedoes at American warships. Although the submarines failed in their assigned task, their two-man crews were lionized as heroes in Japan – with one notable exception. After his disabled midget submarine was beached, Ensign Kazuo Sakamaki was captured and became the first Japanese prisoner of war in World War II.

As streaks of daylight brightened the eastern sky, 183 Japanese planes of the first attack wave were being launched from the decks of the carriers. At 6.40 a.m., the destroyer USS *Ward*, patrolling the entrance to Pearl Harbour sighted and attacked one of

THE VERSATILE 'VAL'

Designed in 1935 as the Dive Bomber Type 99 Model 11, the Aichi D3A1 was the primary dive bomber of the Imperial Japanese Navy until 1942. Designated the 'Val' by the Allies, this aircraft was utilized in large numbers during the attack on Pearl Harbor, 7 December, 1941.

In the hands of a skilled pilot, the Val proved a highly accurate platform for the delivery of ordnance, achieving a success rate of greater than 80 per cent at its peak. However, following severe losses of veteran airmen, particularly at the battles of the Coral Sea and Midway and during the prolonged actions in the vicinity of the Solomons, the combat efficiency of the Val suffered.

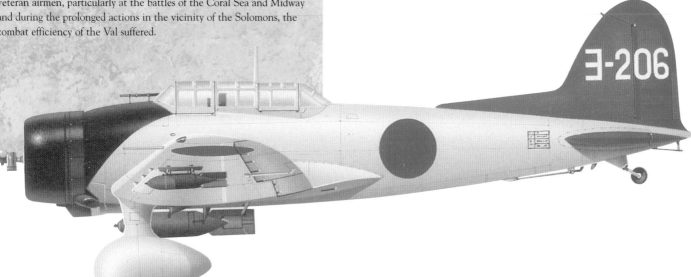

the midget submarines. The destroyer's second 76mm (3in) shell struck the conning tower of the craft, which sank immediately. The *Ward's* message concerning hostile contact was dismissed as another phantom sighting. Just 20 minutes later, the US Army's Opana radar station at Point Kahuku on Oahu picked up and reported an unidentified formation of aircraft. This warning was also discounted. By 7.30 a.m., the 170-planes of the Japanese second wave were airborne.

TORA, TORA, TORA!

Unmolested by US fighters or antiaircraft defences, the bombers of Lieutenant-Commander Mitsuo Fuchida (1902–1976) cleared the mountains west of Pearl Harbor. When it was apparent that the attackers had achieved complete surprise, Fuchida transmitted the message, *'Tora, Tora, Tora!'* to the Japanese fleet. The first bombs fell on Ford Island at 7.55 a.m.; Kaneohe Naval Air Station, Wheeler Field, Bellows Field, Hickam Field and Ewa Marine Corps Air Station came under attack from bombers and strafing fighters, destroying most American aircraft on the ground.

Moored along Battleship Row southeast of Ford Island, the pride of the US Pacific Fleet lay at anchor. Seven battleships – *Nevada, Arizona, West Virginia, Tennessee, Oklahoma, Maryland* and *California* – represented easy targets for screeching dive bombers and torpedo planes, which skimmed the harbour at barely 15.5m (50ft) to launch their deadly weapons. The flagship of the fleet, the battleship USS *Pennsylvania*, lay in a nearby drydock.

ABOVE: EDGY AMERICAN SOLDIERS, *one with a pair of binoculars, scan the skies above Pearl Harbor following the Japanese attack. Their weapons are Browning 7.62mm (0.3in) machine guns.*

BELOW: WITH THE SMOKE *from the effects of the Japanese attack blackening the sky, the USS Shaw explodes with spectacular consequences during the Japanese raid on Pearl Harbor.*

Within minutes, Pearl Harbor was ablaze. Four battleships were sunk. The *West Virginia* was hit by seven torpedoes and two bombs. The *California* took two torpedoes and a bomb. The *Oklahoma* was hit by at least five torpedoes and capsized, trapping many sailors below decks. A bomb fashioned from a modified 355mm (14in) shell originally intended for a naval cannon penetrated the deck of the *Arizona* and ignited a catastrophic explosion that shattered the ship and took the lives of 1177 men. The *Pennsylvania*, *Maryland*, *Nevada* and *Tennessee* were heavily damaged. The cruisers *Helena*, *Raleigh* and *Honolulu*; the destroyers *Cassin*, *Downes* and *Shaw*; the seaplane tender *Curtiss* and the repair ship *Vestal* were damaged, and the target ship *Utah* and minelayer *Oglala* were sunk.

THE WAKES OF JAPANESE torpedoes reach out toward Battleship Row at Pearl Harbor on 7 December 1941, while the shock waves of prior hits and oil haemorrhaging into the harbour are also visible.

STUNNING BLOW

In little more than two hours, Japan had altered the balance of power in the Pacific. The bold attack had taken the lives of 2403 Americans. Eighteen of 96 vessels at Pearl Harbor were sunk or damaged heavily. A total of 165 US aircraft were destroyed and 128 others damaged. In exchange, the Japanese lost 29 aircraft, five midget submarines, one fleet submarine and 185 dead.

Although they had achieved a great victory, the Japanese failed to achieve two major goals. The US aircraft carriers, their primary objective, were at sea and thus spared the attack. The marauding planes had also neglected nearly 23 million litres (5 million gallons) of fuel oil stored in tanks around Pearl Harbor and barely touched repair facilities, which would prove essential to future operations. The day after the attack, President Roosevelt asked a joint session of Congress for a declaration of war and called 7 December 1941 'a date which will live in infamy'.

PEARL HARBOR

3 At 7.55 a.m., 'Kate' torpedo bombers target ships to the northwest of Ford Island. This was where the missing carriers were normally berthed.

MIDDLE LOCH

FORD ISLAND NAVAL AIR STATION

6 The USS Nevada attempted to make for the safety of open water, but was attacked by wave after wave of torpedo and dive bombers.

USS CALIFORNIA

US NAVY YARD

5 Attacked by both the first and second waves, Hickam Field suffers the heaviest damage of Oahu's airbases.

SOUTHEAST LOCH

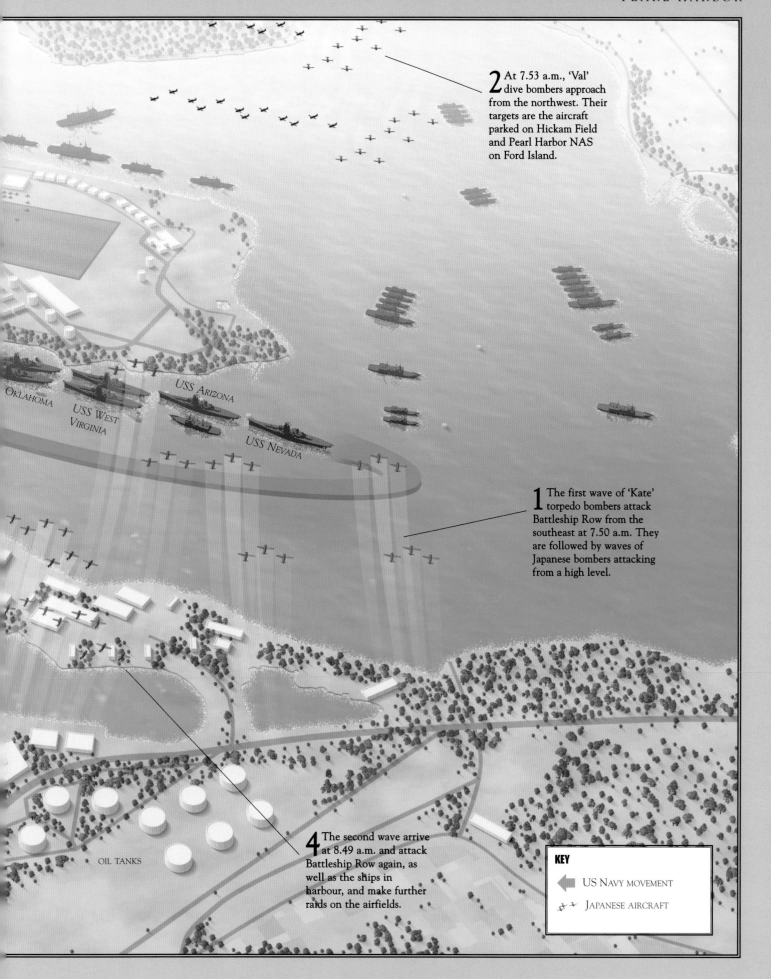

2 At 7.53 a.m., 'Val' dive bombers approach from the northwest. Their targets are the aircraft parked on Hickam Field and Pearl Harbor NAS on Ford Island.

OKLAHOMA

USS WEST VIRGINIA

USS ARIZONA

USS NEVADA

1 The first wave of 'Kate' torpedo bombers attack Battleship Row from the southeast at 7.50 a.m. They are followed by waves of Japanese bombers attacking from a high level.

4 The second wave arrive at 8.49 a.m. and attack Battleship Row again, as well as the ships in harbour, and make further raids on the airfields.

OIL TANKS

KEY

⬅ US NAVY MOVEMENT

✈✈ JAPANESE AIRCRAFT

BATTLE OF MIDWAY 1942

Reluctant to go to war in the first place, Admiral Isoroku Yamamoto (1884–1943), Commander-in-Chief of the Japanese Combined Fleet, had warned prior to the attack on Pearl Harbor, 'For six months, I will run wild in the Pacific. After that, I make no guarantees.'

Yamamoto was familiar with the United States, having attended Harvard University and served as a naval attaché in Washington DC. He recognized the huge industrial might of the United States and was convinced that a series of rapid victories and the destruction of the US Pacific Fleet were Japan's only hope of winning the war.

Although the Pearl Harbor attack had been a success, the American aircraft carriers had been at sea and were not destroyed. Yamamoto realized that he had

BATTLE OF MIDWAY FACTS

Who: Japanese naval forces under Admiral Isoroku Yamamoto (1884–1943) and Admiral Chuichi Nagumo (1887–1944) versus the US Pacific Fleet under Admirals Chester Nimitz (1885–1966), Frank Jack Fletcher (1885–1973) and Raymond Spruance (1886–1969).

What: A Japanese armada of four aircraft carriers carrying 256 aircraft, 11 battleships and numerous smaller vessels opposed an American force that included three aircraft carriers, 234 carrier- and land-based planes, and a variety of smaller craft.

Where: The central Pacific west of Hawaii and the northern Pacific near the Aleutians.

When: 4–7 June 1942

Why: The Japanese attempted to capture Midway atoll and occupied the islands of Attu and Kiska in the Aleutians.

Outcome: A turning point in the Pacific War, the battle was a devastating defeat for Japan. Four aircraft carriers were sunk and the invasion of Midway was cancelled.

CREWMEN ABOARD THE aircraft carrier USS Yorktown *tend planes on the ship's flight deck. Damaged at Coral Sea, the* Yorktown *was repaired within 72 hours of returning to Pearl Harbor.*

ABOVE: THE CREWMEN OF *the American search plane that located the Japanese invasion force headed for Midway atoll pose beside their Consolidated PBY Catalina flying boat.*

unfinished business. It was still necessary to engage the bulk of the US warships in a decisive battle. Despite the setback at Coral Sea in May, he forged ahead in the first week of June 1942 with plans for the capture of Midway, a tiny atoll less than 1930km (1200 miles) west of Hawaii and composed of two small islands, Sand and Eastern. With Midway in Japanese hands, the defensive perimeter of the Empire would be extended considerably. Hawaii itself might be open to invasion. In the process, Yamamoto would annihilate what remained of the US Pacific Fleet.

READING ENEMY MAIL

Yamamoto was unaware, however, that US Navy cryptanalysts based at Pearl Harbor had cracked the Japanese naval code, JN 25, and that Admiral Chester Nimitz (1885–1966), Commander-in-Chief of the US Pacific Fleet, was planning to counter the Midway operation. Nimitz ordered the aircraft carriers USS *Enterprise* and USS *Hornet* and their escorts to join the

LEFT: ADMIRAL CHESTER W. NIMITZ *became the Commander of the Pacific Fleet after Pearl Harbor. Aggressive and willing to take risks, he played decisive roles in the American victories at the battles of Coral Sea and Midway.*

ABOVE: THE GRUMMAN TBF AVENGER *torpedo bomber was also capable in level bombing and anti-submarine roles. A number of these large, multipurpose aircraft were present at Midway.*

USS *Yorktown* – seriously damaged at Coral Sea but returned to service following a Herculean 72-hour repair effort at Pearl Harbor – northeast of Midway, to lie in wait for the Japanese. Admiral Frank Jack Fletcher (1885–1973), aboard the *Yorktown*, was to assume overall command of the American naval force, while Admiral Raymond Spruance (1886–1969) operated with a great deal of autonomy in command of the *Enterprise* and *Hornet*.

Yamamoto, meanwhile, stuck to his penchant for complex operations and formulated a plan that would initially involve a feint against the islands of Attu and Kiska in the Aleutian Islands far to the north. He further divided his forces into a powerful surface fleet formed around the super battleship *Yamato*, an invasion force transporting 500 soldiers to capture Midway and a carrier force consisting of four aircraft carriers, *Akagi*, *Kaga*, *Soryu* and *Hiryu*, which together transported 234 combat aircraft. Yamamoto himself sailed aboard the *Yamato*, while Admiral Chuichi Nagumo (1887–1944) commanded the carrier force.

BELOW: THE DOUGLAS SBD DAUNTLESS *dive bomber was responsible for inflicting the lethal damage against four aircraft carriers of the Imperial Japanese Navy during the Battle of Midway.*

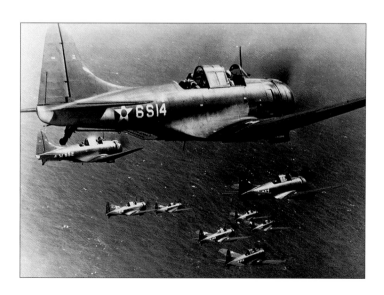

BATTLE JOINED

On the morning of 3 June, a US search plane spotted the Japanese invasion force, but subsequent attacks by aircraft based at Midway failed to achieve any success. The next day, the Japanese carrier force emerged from dense fog and rain as Nagumo launched more than 100 planes to strike Midway

BELOW: THE LAST SURVIVOR *of the Japanese battle fleet at Midway,* Hiryu *was struck by SBD Dauntless dive bombers late on 4 June 1942. Burning fiercely, the carrier was abandoned and scuttled some 12 hours later.*

in an effort to render its airstrip unusable and soften up the atoll's defences.

The attack was only partially effective and Nagumo faced a dilemma. A portion of his aircraft had been retained and armed with torpedoes to hit the American carriers if and when they were sighted. A second attack on Midway would require that these planes have their torpedoes exchanged for bombs, a hazardous and time-consuming process. The need for a second attack on Midway was confirmed by the appearance of American land-based bombers overhead. Although they scored no hits, Nagumo ordered planes not returning from the first Midway raid to be rearmed with bombs.

Moments later, however, Nagumo's resolve was again tested when a Japanese reconnaissance aircraft reported 10 US ships, including a carrier, steaming just over 320km (200 miles) to the northeast. Nagumo considered ordering the planes already rearmed with bombs to take off against Midway while those still carrying torpedoes attacked the American ships.

To complicate matters, the planes returning from the first Midway attack and the Zero fighters flying protective combat air patrol above his ships were low on fuel and needed to land. Finally, Nagumo decided to recover planes that were airborne and to equip with torpedoes the bombers which had been withheld. In their haste to land and refuel

BELOW: BADLY DAMAGED IN A collision with its sister ship, Mogami, and by repeated US air attacks, the Japanese heavy cruiser Mikuma drifts prior to sinking on 6 June 1942.

BELOW: DISPLACING 19,800 TONS and carrying 71 aircraft, the Japanese carrier Soryu (Green Dragon) was a veteran of Pearl Harbor. Hit by three American bombs at Midway, Soryu was turned into a blazing inferno and sunk.

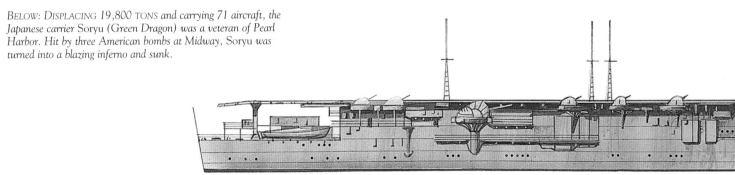

aircraft while rearming others, Japanese crewmen stretched fuel lines across the carrier decks and stacked bombs below without properly securing them. For a dangerously long time, the Japanese aircraft carriers were as vulnerable as they could possibly be. Fletcher and Spruance swung into action when a search plane located the enemy carrier force at about 5.30 a.m. on 4 June. Near the limits of their range, more than 150 dive bombers, torpedo bombers and fighters took off from the *Hornet*, *Enterprise* and *Yorktown*.

FATAL MISCALCULATION

Some of the formations drifted off course and the opportunity for a coordinated attack was lost. In a twist of fate, however, this worked to the advantage of the Americans. The slow, obsolete torpedo bombers found the Japanese first but were decimated by anti-aircraft fire and the covering Zeros.

Nearly every one was lost without scoring a single hit. Shortly after 10 a.m., the Japanese carriers began the launch of their own planes. As the first aircraft roared down the flight decks, lookouts shouted the warning. Unmolested by the fighters, which were off chasing the last of the torpedo planes, 50 American dive bombers pressed home their attacks. In a flash, the course of the Pacific War was changed. Bombs exploded among aircraft waiting to take off and amid the ordnance stacked below decks. *Akagi*, *Kaga* and *Soryu*, engulfed in flames, were doomed.

The lone surviving Japanese carrier, the *Hiryu*, had been steaming in a rain squall some distance away and managed to launch a strike against *Yorktown*, seriously damaging the veteran of the Coral Sea fight. Although damage control parties worked to save the ship, *Yorktown* was spotted by a Japanese submarine and sunk along with the destroyer USS *Hammann* on 7 June. The *Hiryu*, however, did not outlive her sisters for long. US dive bombers scored four hits on the afternoon of 4 June, turning the last Japanese carrier into a blazing hulk.

AN EMPIRE SHATTERED

The action in the waters around Midway on 4 June 1942 turned the tide of World War II in the Pacific. The loss of four aircraft carriers, a cruiser, 332 aircraft and more than

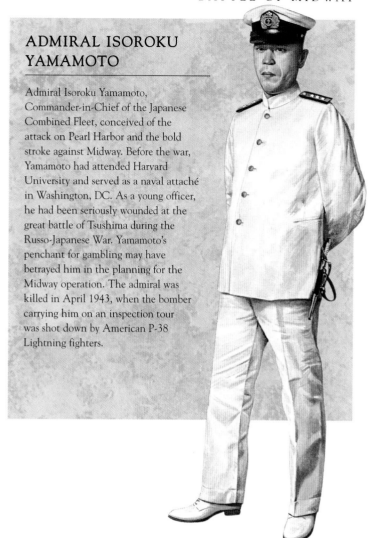

ADMIRAL ISOROKU YAMAMOTO

Admiral Isoroku Yamamoto, Commander-in-Chief of the Japanese Combined Fleet, conceived of the attack on Pearl Harbor and the bold stroke against Midway. Before the war, Yamamoto had attended Harvard University and served as a naval attaché in Washington, DC. As a young officer, he had been seriously wounded at the great battle of Tsushima during the Russo-Japanese War. Yamamoto's penchant for gambling may have betrayed him in the planning for the Midway operation. The admiral was killed in April 1943, when the bomber carrying him on an inspection tour was shot down by American P-38 Lightning fighters.

2000 men was a crippling blow from which the Japanese never recovered. In contrast, the US lost one carrier, a destroyer, 137 planes and 307 men.

Yamamoto briefly entertained the prospect of bringing his overwhelming superiority in battleships and cruisers to bear in a surface engagement against the Americans. Spruance would have none of it. He had recognized a great victory, remembered the admonition of Nimitz to employ the 'principle of calculated risk' and retired out of harm's way. The invasion of Midway was cancelled. The defeated Japanese retreated and for the remainder of the war were obliged to fight defensively.

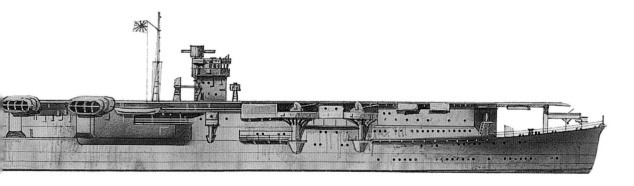

MIDWAY

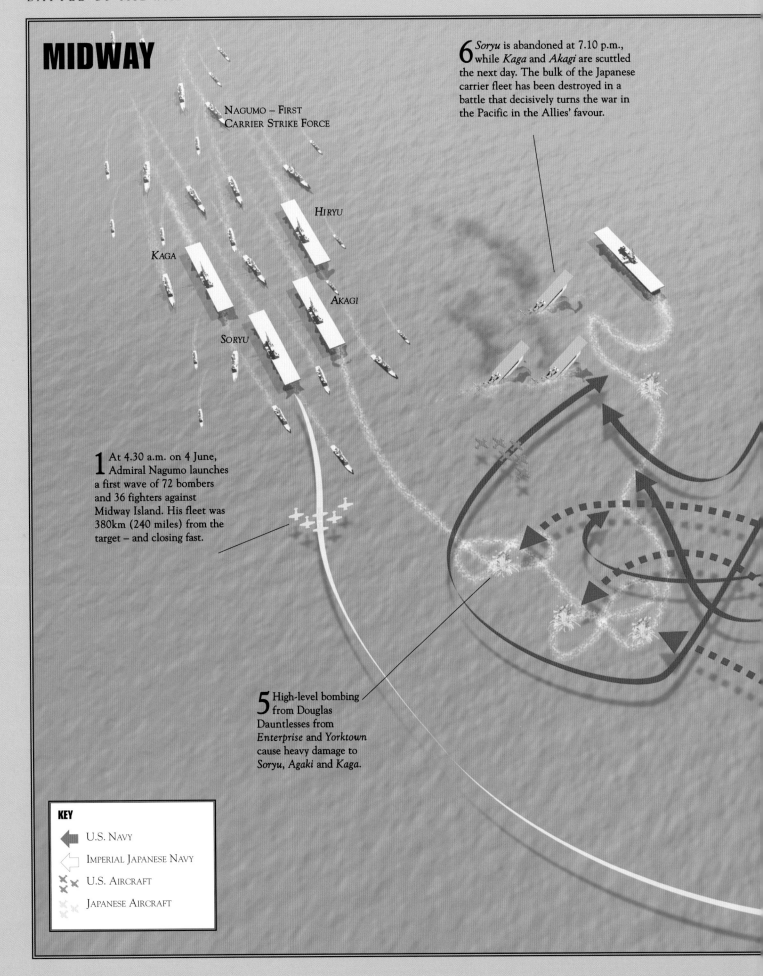

Nagumo – First
Carrier Strike Force

HIRYU

KAGA

AKAGI

SORYU

6 *Soryu* is abandoned at 7.10 p.m., while *Kaga* and *Akagi* are scuttled the next day. The bulk of the Japanese carrier fleet has been destroyed in a battle that decisively turns the war in the Pacific in the Allies' favour.

1 At 4.30 a.m. on 4 June, Admiral Nagumo launches a first wave of 72 bombers and 36 fighters against Midway Island. His fleet was 380km (240 miles) from the target – and closing fast.

5 High-level bombing from Douglas Dauntlesses from *Enterprise* and *Yorktown* cause heavy damage to *Soryu, Agaki* and *Kaga*.

KEY

◄ U.S. Navy

◁ Imperial Japanese Navy

✕ ✕ U.S. Aircraft

✕ ✕ Japanese Aircraft

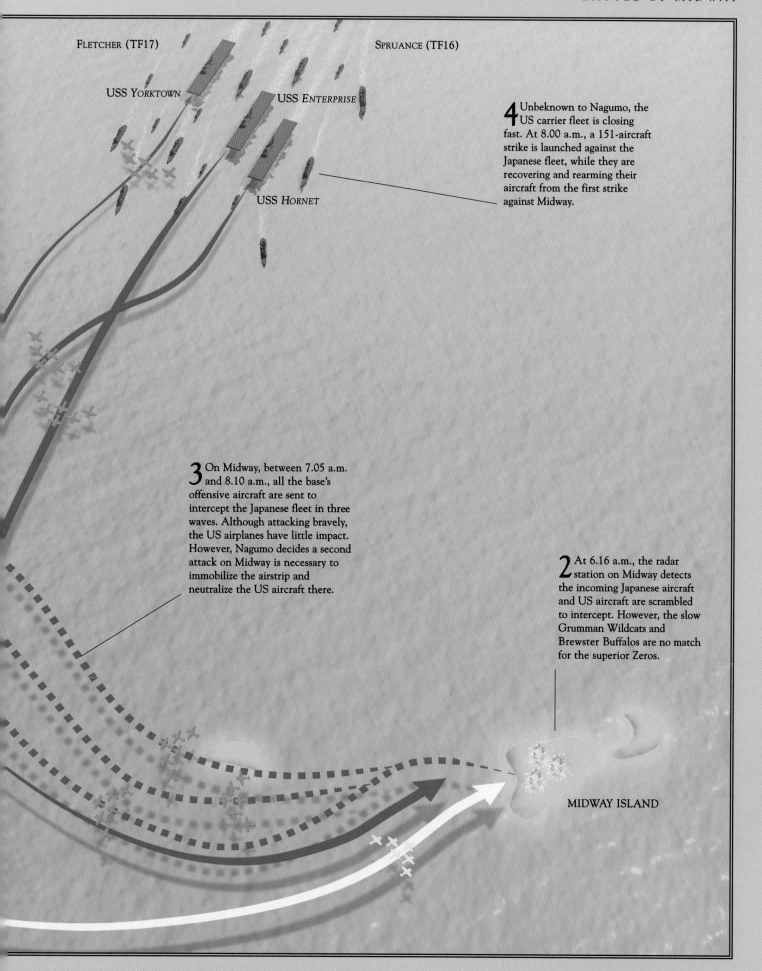

FLETCHER (TF17)

SPRUANCE (TF16)

USS YORKTOWN

USS ENTERPRISE

USS HORNET

4 Unbeknown to Nagumo, the US carrier fleet is closing fast. At 8.00 a.m., a 151-aircraft strike is launched against the Japanese fleet, while they are recovering and rearming their aircraft from the first strike against Midway.

3 On Midway, between 7.05 a.m. and 8.10 a.m., all the base's offensive aircraft are sent to intercept the Japanese fleet in three waves. Although attacking bravely, the US airplanes have little impact. However, Nagumo decides a second attack on Midway is necessary to immobilize the airstrip and neutralize the US aircraft there.

2 At 6.16 a.m., the radar station on Midway detects the incoming Japanese aircraft and US aircraft are scrambled to intercept. However, the slow Grumman Wildcats and Brewster Buffalos are no match for the superior Zeros.

MIDWAY ISLAND

CONVOY PQ-17 1942

Convoy PQ-17 was in some ways a triumph for the heavy surface raiders, even though they played no part in the actual attacks. The threat that a battleship was at large was enough to force the convoy to scatter, at which point its fate was sealed.

At the outbreak of World War II, the *Kriegsmarine* possessed a handful of powerful heavy cruisers and capital ships. These were not enough to threaten the Royal Navy but they did affect the course of the war.

The strategy of a 'fleet in being' meant that rather than coming out to fight a battle that they would certainly lose, the German major units tied down, merely through their existence, large segments of the Allied fleet that could be used elsewhere such as in the Mediterranean or the Pacific.

Traditionally, weaker naval powers have resorted to 'cruiser warfare' – ie, raiding the sea traffic of their enemies. While this is normally the province of cruisers and submarines, a capital ship could swiftly slaughter a convoy and its escorts.

CONVOY PQ-17 FACTS

Who: An Allied convoy of 33 ships with an escort of four cruisers, three destroyers and two Royal Navy submarines sailing to the Soviet Union, versus 10 submarines, aircraft based on the Norwegian mainland and the threat of surface attack.

What: A gradual massacre of the merchant ships and their escorts.

Where: North of Norway in the Arctic Sea, close to the island of Spitzbergen.

When: June–July 1942

Why: The convoy scattered in response to a supposed surface threat.

Outcome: Massive casualties among the Allied merchant ships, with only 11 ships arriving at their destination. Shortly afterwards, the Allies suspended Arctic convoys because of the heavy losses.

DEPTH CHARGES EXPLODE *in the Arctic twilight. Whether or not the submarine was destroyed, aggressive depth-charging could prevent it from making a successful attack while the convoy moved on. The submarines of the period were too slow to catch up with most convoys once they were past.*

THE TYPE IX U-BOAT was capable of long-range operations, though it had to travel mostly on the surface. These boats could strike anywhere on a convoy route and remain at sea for long periods waiting for a suitable target.

The big surface raiders of the German Navy were thus a serious threat to Allied supply lines. Although raiding cruises by the heavy ships had not achieved as much as might have been hoped, an attack on a concentrated high-value target such as a major convoy could achieve results of strategic importance.

Much effort was expended on keeping the major units of the *Kriegsmarine* bottled up, especially when a critical convoy was under way. Some convoys were protected by old battleships or given distant heavy covering forces that could counter a sortie by the major raiders. However, some areas were simply too hazardous for capital ships. One such was the Arctic passage to Murmansk.

The German attack on Russia in 1941 brought the Soviet Union into the war on the side of the Allies and ultimately doomed the Axis to defeat. However, there was a time when the situation in Russia was desperate and the new allies needed to send support. The only practicable way was to ship vast quantities of tanks, vehicles, artillery, aircraft and other war matériel into Russian ports, and the only available route was through the Arctic Ocean, around the north of Norway and into the Kola Inlet on the White Sea.

ARCTIC CONVOYS

Arctic convoys were difficult enough without enemy interference. Ice was a constant hazard – not just in the water but forming on ships. It jammed turrets and winches and, more dangerously, increased topweight so that ships rolled more and could become unstable. Ice clearance was a constant task. The Arctic ocean largely freezes in the

winter; pack ice advances far south. This requires ships making the passage to travel relatively close to the northern coastline of Norway, which was at the time occupied by German forces. Aircraft and submarines based there not only had less far to travel to find the convoy but also a smaller area to search in.

However, winter convoys were at least covered by darkness – that far north, there were months of night in which the sun barely rose above the horizon. In the summer, convoys could take a more northerly route, putting some

distance between the ships and their enemies, but the constant daylight offset this defensive advantage.

Convoys were given a code name and number that indicated, to those who knew the system, their route and sometimes composition or speed. 'Fast' convoys received a different designation to those that could make a relatively low average speed. Each route had its own pair of code

TYPE VIIC U-BOAT

Coming into service in 1941, just as the 'happy time' for U-boats was ending, the Type VIIC was smaller than the Type IX and had a shorter range as well as a smaller torpedo load. It was the mainstay of the German U-boat service for the remainder of the war and several hundred were built.

Although the tide was slowly turning against the U-boats, the Type VIIC was highly successful in combat. Many received *Schnorkels* from 1944 onwards, increasing their underwater endurance. Others were modified into flak boats to counter air attacks near the U-boat bases in the Bay of Biscay.

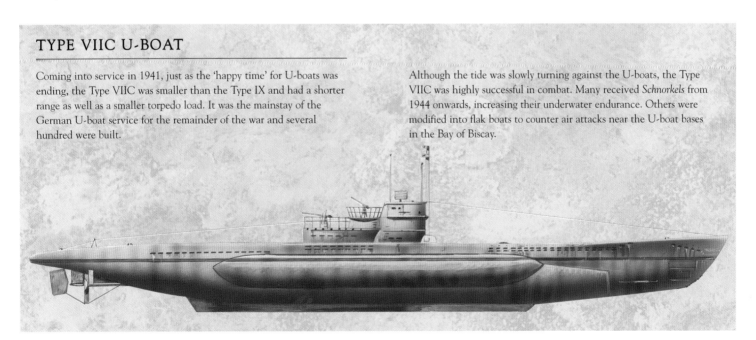

letters. Arctic convoys to Russia were designated PQ, with returning convoys labelled QP.

PQ convoys began with PQ-1, which assembled in Iceland and set sail on 29 September 1941. Only one ship was lost among the 103 that set out before the spring of 1941, but the sinking of a destroyer by a U-boat on January 1942 warned of things to come. Losses mounted, with increasing pressure from air and submarine units. PQ-16 lost five of its 30 merchant ships, four others arriving damaged.

CONVOY PQ-17

It was with the expectation of a tough passage that PQ-17 formed up. It was the largest convoy thus far, with 36 merchant ships. The close escort consisted of four destroyers, 10 lighter craft (mostly armed trawlers) and two anti-aircraft ships. Distant cover was provided by four cruisers and four destroyers. A heavy force containing two battleships, two cruisers and an aircraft carrier was available for the first part of the route but could not be risked past the North Cape.

German high command considered breaking the Arctic convoy route to be of great importance and had made plans for heavy air and submarine attacks plus a possible sortie by heavy

POOR VISIBILITY WAS a mixed blessing for the arctic convoys. It helped them to avoid submarine and air attack but also concealed the U-boats that did find the convoy as they closed in to make their attack.

surface units. The Allies were aware that this was a prospect, though they could not know whether an attack was planned.

The convoy sailed on 27 June 1942. It took a very northerly route, passing close to the Svalbard archipelago, to keep as much distance between it and the enemy's northern bases as possible. This meant struggling through sea ice at times and some ships were damaged. One had to be sent back to join another that had turned back just after leaving Iceland.

Despite this and being spotted first by U-boats and later by aircraft, the convoy suffered no losses until 4 July. Two ships were sunk after three days of intermittent air attack. However, something much more serious happened that day. The Allies received word that the battleship *Tirpitz* was out.

Tirpitz was the most powerful ship in the German fleet. Modern and well-designed, she was quite probably capable of defeating a single Allied battleship if she met one; the convoy escorts and cruisers would stand no chance. *Tirpitz* was fast enough to destroy the escorting cruisers and then chase down the slow merchant ships; if she got into range of the convoy, it would be a massacre. Worse, she was reported as sailing in company with two heavy cruisers and several destroyers. The only chance to save any of the convoy was to scatter it and to hope that the heavy raiders found only some of the ships.

The British intelligence service was subsequently able to establish that this was not a sortie against PQ-17 but merely a redeployment. The damage had been done, though. The order to scatter was sent and the covering force was pulled back. Many of the warship crews were sickened by what they heard on the radio. Unable to help, they heard the scattered merchant ships struggling on under submarine and air attack – vessels calling for help and then going off the air.

Many of the escort crews met a hostile reception in the bars of their home ports. Challenged by other sailors for 'abandoning' PQ-17, they gave vent to their own bitter emotions. There were many fights, and several men were killed. The 'stigma' of PQ-17 took a long time to erase, even though none of what happened was the sailors' fault: the Admiralty ordered the convoy to scatter and the ship captains were bound to obey.

On 5 July, the convoy came under heavy attack from aircraft and lost six ships, while submarines accounted for six more. The remaining close escorts did what they could for nearby vessels, but without an organized convoy the merchants were desperately vulnerable, especially to submarines. With no destroyer force to counter them, U-boats could make their attacks at leisure and consequently were very effective.

Similarly, the *Luftwaffe* was able to press home its attacks with great precision, since there was little anti-aircraft fire.

This, too, increased the effectiveness of the sorties. As a consequence, nine more ships were sunk over the following five days. The survivors began to arrive in Russia on 10 July. Eleven ships straggled in over the next week. More than half the convoy had been destroyed by aircraft and submarines. Some of the ships would have been sunk whether or not the full escort had been available. However, the circumstances leading to the destruction of PQ-17 were brought about just by the threat of attack. The very existence of the 'fleet in being' brought ruin upon the Arctic convoy route.

AFTERMATH

The effect of the 'abandonment' on the psyche of the escort crews is summed up by a statement made by one of the captains involved. During Operation *Pedestal*, a convoy to Malta facing heavy opposition, this officer said: 'I don't care what signals I get from whom, so long as there's a merchant afloat I'm putting my ship alongside her and we're going to Malta.' His was one of three destroyers that rescued the crippled tanker *Ohio* and somehow got her into Grand Harbour, quite probably changing the course of the war.

ABOVE: A ROYAL NAVY OFFICER *dressed for Arctic convoy service. The cold was a deadly enemy; men keeping watch or venturing above decks risked hypothermia, and falling overboard was a death sentence.*

LEFT: CAPTAIN HEINZ BEILFELD of *U-703 is congratulated by a superior officer after the successful raid against convoy PQ-17.*

CONVOY PQ-17

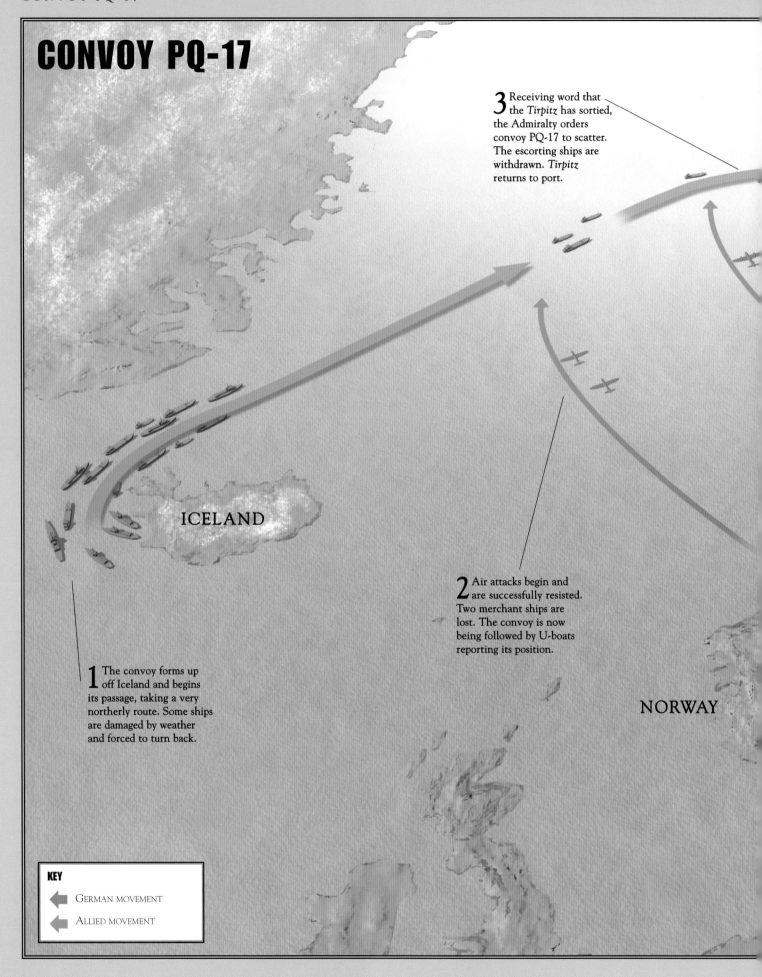

3 Receiving word that the *Tirpitz* has sortied, the Admiralty orders convoy PQ-17 to scatter. The escorting ships are withdrawn. *Tirpitz* returns to port.

ICELAND

2 Air attacks begin and are successfully resisted. Two merchant ships are lost. The convoy is now being followed by U-boats reporting its position.

NORWAY

1 The convoy forms up off Iceland and begins its passage, taking a very northerly route. Some ships are damaged by weather and forced to turn back.

KEY

◀ GERMAN MOVEMENT

◀ ALLIED MOVEMENT

SPITZBERGEN

4 Struggling on independently, the merchant ships are subjected to intense air and submarine attack. Twelve ships are sunk in a single day.

5 The intensity of the attack abates after several days, largely due to the difficulty in finding the scattered ships and the distances involved.

TROMSO

ARCHANGEL

6 The survivors straggle into the White Sea over the course of a week. More than half the convoy has been sunk.

EL ALAMEIN

1942

The Battle of El Alamein, 23 October–4 November 1942, taking its name from an Egyptian railway halt west of Alexander, marked a turning point in the war in North Africa. The British Prime Minister Winston Churchill (1874–1965) claimed that, 'Before Alamein we never had a victory. After Alamein we never had a defeat.'

Although Churchill's pronouncement was something of an exaggeration, the German–Italian army was forced into full-scale retreat and its position worsened considerably after the Allied landings in French North Africa on 8 November. However, for the Commonwealth army the battle also had the psychological effect of finally breaking the myth of German invincibility.

The war in the Western Desert had swung back and forth over the course of nearly two years. Field-Marshal Erwin Rommel's (1891–1944) German–Italian Panzer Army Africa had driven the British back past the Egyptian border, where it

EL ALAMEIN FACTS

Who: The Commonwealth Eighth Army (British, Australian, New Zealand, Indian and South African troops) led by Lieutenant-General Bernard Montgomery (1887–1976) faced Field Marshal Erwin Rommel's (1891–1944) Panzer Army Africa, renamed the German–Italian Panzer Army on 25 October 1942.

What: Operation Lightfoot was a carefully planned and prepared set-piece offensive launched by Montgomery on the Axis forces, who had shifted to the defensive after being defeated at Alam Halfa in September.

Where: El Alamein, a small Egyptian railway halt, 95 kilometres (60 miles) west of Alexandria.

When: 23 October to 4 November 1942

Why: Growing British material strength allowed Montgomery to shift decisively to the offensive against Rommel's over-extended forces and finally ensure the safety of the Suez Canal and the Middle Eastern oil fields.

Outcome: Although Rommel was able to escape with a large proportion of his army, El Alamein marked a clear turning point in the Western Desert Campaign with the initiative shifting decisively to the Allies.

A PROBABLY STAGED photograph of troops of the 51st Highland Division running past a knocked-out German Panzer Mark III at El Alamein.

ABOVE: *FIELD MARSHAL ERWIN ROMMEL, the charismatic, energetic commander of German and Italian forces in the Western Desert.*

BELOW: *BRITISH ARTILLERY BOMBARDS German positions during the buildup to the offensive at El Alamein, Operation* Lightfoot.

was stopped by General Claude Auchinleck's (1884–1981) Eighth Army between 1 and 4 July 1942, at the first battle of El Alamein. By the time Rommel was ready to try again, Auchinleck had been replaced as Army Commander by Lieutenant General Bernard Law Montgomery (1887–1976). Montgomery was a meticulous planner and superb trainer of men, and set about rebuilding the Eighth Army, both in terms of matériel and confidence.

When Rommel attacked in September at Alam Halfa, the British were well prepared and he was soundly defeated. At the end of a long logistical chain, plagued by shortages of fuel and facing an increasingly strong Commonwealth Army, Rommel, debilitated by ill health, shifted to the defensive. The Germans and Italians set about establishing a system of strong points set among deep minefields. Rommel's mobile troops were held back behind his infantry to counter any breakthrough, but the desperate lack of fuel meant they were held closer to the front than normal. In the north, he placed 15th Panzer, 90th Light and the Italian *Littorio* armoured divisions; and in the south, 21st Panzer and *Ariete*.

SET-PIECE BATTLE

Montgomery refused to be pushed by Churchill into attacking before he believed he was ready. He would launch his offensive only when he was sure his men were trained to the peak of perfection and completely in his grip, ready to do exactly what he wanted of them. Unlike so many previous desert battles, Alamein would be a set-piece affair, with both

RIGHT: A PRIVATE FROM THE 9TH Australian Division with his Short Magazine Lee Enfield Rifle. He is well wrapped-up to withstand the rigours of the desert at night.

flanks soundly anchored by the Mediterranean to the north and the impassable Qattara Depression to the south. Montgomery could muster 195,000 men to Rommel's 105,000, of whom 53,000 were German. He fielded 1000 tanks to the enemy's 500 and roughly double the amount of aircraft.

The Commonwealth forces, broadly speaking, held a two-to-one advantage in most weapon systems. Montgomery's plan was that four infantry divisions of Lieutenant-General Oliver Leese's (1884–1978) XXX Corps would clear a path through the German positions in the north to allow the two armoured divisions of Lieutenant-General Herbert Lumsden's (1897–1945) X Corps to push through and take defensive positions in the west. Then the infantry would break up the German line to the north and south – 'crumbling' as Montgomery called it. Brian Horrocks's (1895–1985) XIII Corps would make strong representations to the south.

THE OFFENSIVE OPENS

Operation *Lightfoot*, a codename in somewhat poor taste given the 445,000 German mines, opened with a massive barrage on the evening of 23 October. It took the Germans by surprise and seriously disrupted Axis communications. General George Stumme (1886–1942), commanding in Rommel's absence on sick leave, died of a heart attack going forward to find out what was happening. The battle started well but resistance began to stiffen quickly, particularly in the 51st Highland Division's sector. The northernmost 9th Australian Division took all its objectives, but the armour

RIGHT: A HEAVILY DECORATED GERMAN tanker swigs from his water, standing atop of his Panzer Mark III.

was to advance through the Highlanders and the 2nd New Zealand Division, where more difficulties had been encountered and heavy casualties suffered. The Commonwealth forces had failed to reach their first day objectives. Bitter fighting continued over the next couple of days and, although progress was slow, a couple of serious German counterattacks were repulsed. Rommel returned on 26 October and concentrated what armour he could muster after the attritional fighting of the previous few days to counterattack a salient created by British 1st Armoured Division on the slight rise of Kidney Ridge. Both 21st Panzer and 90th Light Divisions were stopped dead by well-served antitank guns, artillery and air power. Meanwhile, Montgomery's forces slowly reduced the Axis positions, although progress was much slower than expected.

SUPERCHARGE LAUNCHED

The failure to make much headway forced Montgomery to come up with another plan. Operation *Supercharge* shifted the weight of the offensive away from the north to the Kidney Ridge area on the night of 1 November. Led by Lieutenant-General Bernard Freyberg's (1889–1963) New Zealanders, bolstered by three British brigades, *Supercharge*

THE US-BUILT M3 Medium Tank (known to the British as the Lee or Grant) first saw service in the Western Desert in early 1942. Although it had a number of flaws, the British appreciated the fire power provided by its hull-mounted 75mm (2.95in) gun.

penetrated deep into the Axis position and convinced Rommel that the battle was lost.

On 3 November, he began to pull back his armoured forces and ordered the rest of his men to disengage. The New Zealanders and 1st Armoured Division, then 7th Armoured Division threatened to cut off the escape, which was in itself hampered by Hitler ordering Rommel to stand fast. Rommel managed to extricate large numbers of his forces, although 30,000 – about a third of them German – were taken prisoner. The Battle of El Alamein was over and had cost the Allies 13,560 casualties, Major-General Douglas Wimberley's (1896–1983) inexperienced 51st Highland Division taking the brunt, with the other infantry divisions also suffering heavily.

PURSUIT AND DEFENCE

Montgomery was hesitant in the pursuit and Rommel was able to retreat westwards about 1000km (620 miles) before turning to make a serious stand in January 1943. By then, the strategic situation had worsened even further for the Axis, as on 8 November US and British forces landed in French North Africa seriously threatening Rommel's rear. The remorseless logic of a two-front campaign doomed the Axis presence in Africa.

GENERAL BERNARD MONTGOMERY

Bernard Montgomery combined undeniable charisma and flair for showmanship with a single-minded dedication to the profession of arms. He proved to be a superb trainer of men and meticulous planner, who did much to banish the myth of German invincibility. He was seriously wounded in World War I, but by the outbreak of World War II he commanded 3rd Division, which he led with distinction through the French campaign of 1940.

Corps and Area commands in Britain followed. Then, in August 1942, the death of Lieutenant-General William Gott, Churchill's first choice as commander for the Eighth Army, gave Montgomery his opportunity.

ABOVE: A GERMAN TANK MAN surrenders to Commonwealth infantry in another probably staged photo from the period.

El Alamein was the climax of the campaign in the Western Desert and the turning point in the war in North Africa. Montgomery had approached the battle with determination and a hard-headed will to succeed. He had also proved flexible enough – although he would never admit it – to change his plan midway through the battle. More importantly, he had proved himself to be a general capable of defeating the Germans. This was vital for the morale of the Eighth Army, vital for Churchill, who was under political pressure at home, and vital for the British nation as a whole.

LEFT: THE MARK II MATILDA had been a mainstay of British tanks forces in the early part of the desert war, but by El Alamein it was obsolescent.

EL ALAMEIN

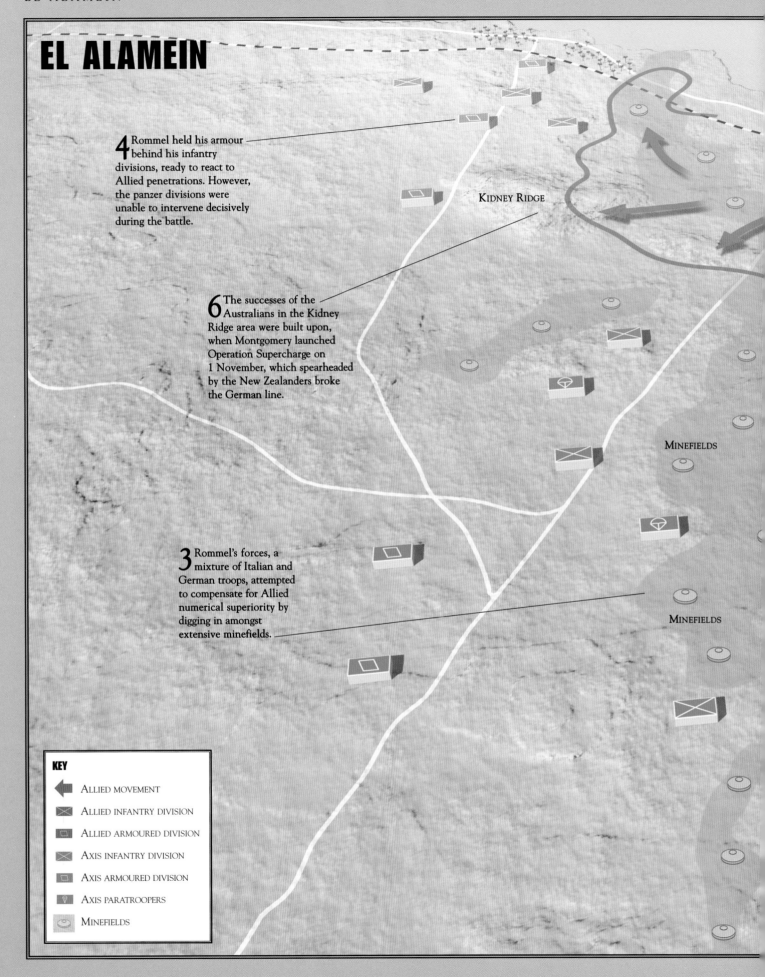

4 Rommel held his armour behind his infantry divisions, ready to react to Allied penetrations. However, the panzer divisions were unable to intervene decisively during the battle.

KIDNEY RIDGE

6 The successes of the Australians in the Kidney Ridge area were built upon, when Montgomery launched Operation Supercharge on 1 November, which spearheaded by the New Zealanders broke the German line.

MINEFIELDS

3 Rommel's forces, a mixture of Italian and German troops, attempted to compensate for Allied numerical superiority by digging in amongst extensive minefields.

MINEFIELDS

KEY

- ← ALLIED MOVEMENT
- ⊠ ALLIED INFANTRY DIVISION
- ▭ ALLIED ARMOURED DIVISION
- ⊠ AXIS INFANTRY DIVISION
- ▭ AXIS ARMOURED DIVISION
- ▽ AXIS PARATROOPERS
- ◯ MINEFIELDS

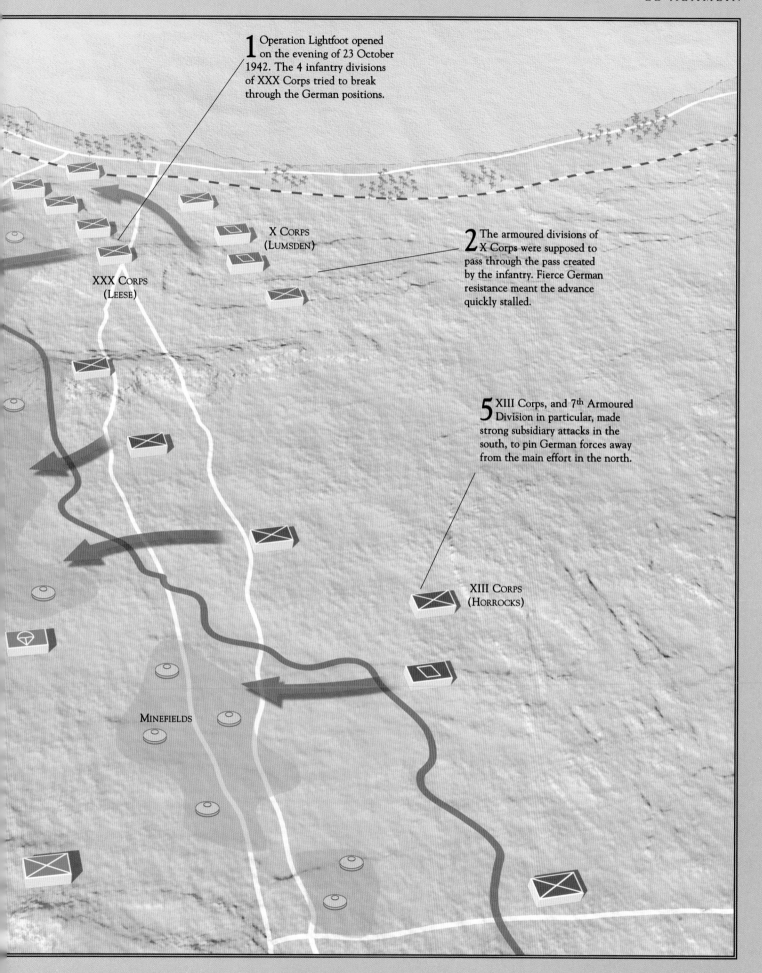

1 Operation Lightfoot opened on the evening of 23 October 1942. The 4 infantry divisions of XXX Corps tried to break through the German positions.

X CORPS
(LUMSDEN)

2 The armoured divisions of X Corps were supposed to pass through the pass created by the infantry. Fierce German resistance meant the advance quickly stalled.

XXX CORPS
(LEESE)

5 XIII Corps, and 7th Armoured Division in particular, made strong subsidiary attacks in the south, to pin German forces away from the main effort in the north.

XIII CORPS
(HORROCKS)

MINEFIELDS

BATTLE OF GUADALCANAL 1942–3

After defeating the Imperial Japanese Navy at the Battle of Midway in June 1942, the Allies set about clearing Japanese bases from the Solomon Islands. This required amphibious operations against several islands – including Tulagi, where a seaplane base needed removing, and Guadalcanal, where a major airbase was being constructed.

The Allies assembled an invasion force at Fiji under US Vice-Admiral Frank Fletcher (1885–1973), with ground forces led by Major-General Alexander Vandegrift (1887–1973), commander of the US 1st Marine Division, which provided most of the ground forces.

BATTLE OF GUADALCANAL FACTS

Who: Allied forces from the United States, Australia and New Zealand versus Japanese ground, air and naval forces.

What: The battle of Guadalcanal was a drawn-out fight lasting several months and involving land, naval and air forces. Allied forces captured the island and held it against determined attack.

Where: Guadalcanal in the Solomon Islands, in the South Pacific.

When: August 1942–February 1943

Why: The island was important to both sides as a base for future operations.

Outcome: With its eventual success, the Allies won their first major ground victory against the Japanese. Despite heavy losses on both sides, the island was held by the Allies and used as a forward base.

US MARINES GO ASHORE in August 1942. There was little opposition to the initial landings on Guadalcanal, though later the island was bitterly contested until the Japanese finally gave up.

This was met by carrier-based fighters, with casualties on both sides. Some attacks got through and caused damage to transport ships not yet unloaded. Soon afterwards, the carrier force had to withdraw for lack of fuel.

An attack by a powerful Japanese cruiser force under Vice-Admiral Gunichi Mikawa (1888–1981) resulted in heavy losses to Allied cruisers off Savo island, and the decision was taken to withdraw the surviving naval vessels from the area. This meant it became necessary to pull the half-unloaded transports out as well – they were too vulnerable to air attack without carrier cover and surface ships without cruisers to protect them.

The forces ashore on Guadalcanal at this point comprised some 11,000 marines, but much of their heavy equipment was still aboard the transports steaming away towards safety. Nevertheless they proceeded with the plan and finished building the airfield the Japanese had started, naming it Henderson Field.

Approaching under cover of bad weather, the assault force went ashore on 7 August 1942. The main objective was the capture of Guadalcanal itself and the airbase there. Other forces were tasked with capturing Tulagi and other smaller islands in the group.

On Guadalcanal itself, things went very well. The terrain, which was mostly jungle, proved more of a problem than enemy resistance for the first day, and by the end of the second the airfield was in Allied hands, along with stores, supplies and construction equipment abandoned there.

Although heavily outnumbered, the Japanese troops on the other islands put up a stiff fight and had to be eliminated almost to a man. This sort of fanatical resistance became familiar as the war went on and resulted in heavy casualties for the Allies, even when dealing with quite small outposts.

Meanwhile, the Allies came under attack from aircraft out of Rabaul on the island of New Britain in New Guinea.

SECURING THE ISLAND

Some Japanese forces had dispersed around the island after the Allied landings, and these were reinforced by a small number landed by destroyer. Patrols and expeditions were launched to locate and remove these holdouts, and though success was mixed the enemy was largely kept away from the airfield, which received its first aircraft – a mix of fighters and dive bombers.

The island was harassed by air attacks more or less constantly, but the Japanese commanders were not satisfied: they wanted the Allies driven off Guadalcanal and the rest of the Solomons, and so planned an

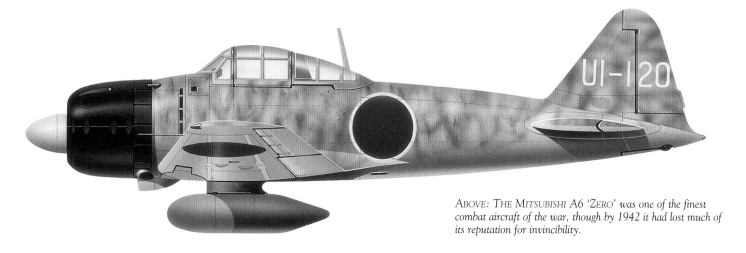

ABOVE: THE MITSUBISHI A6 'ZERO' was one of the finest combat aircraft of the war, though by 1942 it had lost much of its reputation for invincibility.

ABOVE: US MARINE GENERAL VANDERGRIFT and US Navy Admiral Kelly were in command of the land and naval components of the operation respectively. Amphibious operations of this kind required close cooperation between services.

amphibious attack of their own. The task fell to Seventeenth Army, which was already heavily committed to the battles for New Guinea.

Some elements of Seventeenth Army were available for an operation against Guadalcanal but they arrived in piecemeal fashion. The first assault force was a contingent of about 1000 men of the 28th Infantry Regiment under Colonel Kiyonao Ichiki (1892–1942). This inadequate force was landed from destroyers and immediately moved west to engage the defenders.

Although it was outnumbered more than ten to one Ichiki's force attacked towards Henderson Field under cover of darkness. Japanese casualties were extremely high and the attack achieved nothing. A subsequent marine counterattack scattered the survivors after Ichiki himself was killed.

A second force, about 2000 strong, was also on its way and its approach was covered by Japanese naval forces, including three carriers. This resulted in the Battle of the Eastern Solomons as the Allied carrier forces engaged the Japanese fleet. Amid this action, aircraft out of Henderson field attacked the Japanese troop transports and caused heavy casualties. The survivors were eventually landed from destroyers.

During this period, the Allied forces on Guadalcanal were reinforced with additional aircraft, steadily increasing the strength of the island's air group despite losses in combat. Guadalcanal became a big threat to Japanese intentions in the area and both sides knew that a major operation to eliminate Henderson Field and its air group was going to be launched.

General Vandergrift set his marines, now reinforced, to improving their positions. Units were redeployed to create a better overall defence while minor operations were undertaken against the increasing Japanese forces on the island. Dysentery was a serious problem for the garrison, with as much as 20 per cent of the force down at any given time, and the island's terrain also made offensive operations difficult.

THE TOKYO EXPRESS

After losing many transports to air attack, Japanese commanders decided that a traditional amphibious operation was not feasible and instead implemented what became known as the Tokyo Express, whereby destroyers and light cruisers dashed in under cover of night to land relatively small forces and re-supply them.

The Tokyo Express was a clever solution to the problem of getting troops on to Guadalcanal, but it had its limitations. Small warships could not carry heavy equipment or artillery and ships engaged in these operations were not available for war-fighting missions elsewhere. Nevertheless the Tokyo Express ran several thousand Japanese troops into Guadalcanal over the next few weeks until sufficient forces had been built up for an attack.

RIGHT: THE JAPANESE DEPLOYED large numbers of naval infantry personnel to defend the Pacific islands. Marines by any other name, these troops put up a determined fight on Guadalcanal and elsewhere.

THE M3 STUART was too light for anything but reconnaissance duty in the European theatre, but in the Pacific island terrain the light tank really came into its own.

On 31 August, General Kawaguchi arrived to take command of all Japanese forces on Guadalcanal, and on 7 September he gave the order for an assault on Henderson Field. A raid by US Marines hit the supply base of one of these groups the next day, giving an indication that a large force was on the island and an attack was imminent.

JAPANESE ATTACKS

The Japanese plan was to attack at night, in three groups from the east, west and south. However, the Allies were forewarned and had posted troops on a rise to the south of Henderson Field. This later became known as Edson's Ridge after Lieutenant-Colonel Merritt Edson (1897–1955), who led the defence. They were right in the path of the main Japanese force when the attack went in on 12 September.

Fighting on the ridge was heavy and the defenders, who were outnumbered more than three to one, were eventually pushed on to a central high point. There they resisted several assaults, but were unable to prevent other Japanese troops bypassing them. Those who got past Edson's Ridge ran into other defenders, who were able to hold and eventually repel them. Attacks in other sectors were likewise halted. Finally, after two days of intense fighting, the Japanese pulled back to regroup.

Both sides rebuilt their forces and defences as best they could. More Allied troops were brought in, although the sea routes were hotly contested. The US carrier *Wasp* was sunk during this operation. General Vandergrift reorganized his forces and promoted some men, including Edson.

After a period of bad weather, the air battle resumed on 27 September, with even greater intensity as both sides had been reinforced. On the ground, more Japanese troops arrived while US forces tried to drive the scattered survivors of previous attacks away from their defences and prevent the new arrivals from establishing themselves close to the airfield. The result was several clashes in late September and early October which disrupted Japanese offensive preparations.

However, the island's defenders were under pressure from the air and the Japanese buildup was causing concern. Reinforcements were requested and in due course set sail.

The timing was fortuitous. US naval units covering the reinforcement convoy ran into a major Japanese force shipment that included vessels tasked to bombard Henderson Field. In the resulting Battle of Cape Esperance, the US vessels inflicted a heavy defeat on the Japanese navy, though the associated Tokyo Express convoy got through and unloaded on Guadalcanal.

Another bombardment was ordered for 13 October while yet more troops were brought in. This time, the attack included two battleships and did major damage to the airfield, which nevertheless was restored to minimal function in time to launch strikes against the Japanese troop transports.

By the middle of October, the Japanese had brought several thousand troops on to Guadalcanal and had repeatedly shelled the airfield. Ground forces began to move into position for the assault. Some 20,000 Japanese troops were available, the main attack coming in from the south with additional flanking operations. The attack was dislocated by delays in preparation, and communication problems meant that some forces attacked on 23 October and some the day after. The assault was sustained, and in

DESPITE GREAT DETERMINATION, many of the Japanese attacks on US positions were ill-advised given the tactical situation. Heavy casualties were inevitable.

some places the Japanese got through the outer defences despite heavy casualties. A handful of tanks were used but were easily disabled by the defenders.

Although under pressure, the defenders held out on the ground while the air forces fought off air and naval attacks. Repeated frontal charges were cut up by infantry weapons and artillery firing over open sights. Finally, on 26 October, the assault was called off, and the Japanese retreated.

ENDGAME

Land warfare in the Pacific was heavily influenced by the situation at sea. Whichever side had sea control could bring in supplies and reinforcements, tipping the balance of the land engagement. Thus the naval actions off Guadalcanal were vital to the land campaign. Several battles were fought at sea in the vicinity of Guadalcanal, including the Battles of Savo Island and Cape Esperance. On 13 November 1942, a Japanese force attempting to bring reinforcements to the islands and to bombard Henderson Field clashed with US ships in a close-range brawl that cost both sides dearly and left the US Navy very short of ships to defend Guadalcanal when the Japanese Navy came back to try again.

Further Japanese attempts to reinforce their presence on the island were unsuccessful and US forces began taking the offensive, pushing the enemy away from the airfield. Cut off from re-supply and being ground down, the remaining Japanese forces were evacuated in early February, ending the campaign. Guadalcanal was the first clear-cut land victory over the Japanese and did much to restore Allied confidence. It also deprived the Japanese of an important forward base. The battle had a wider significance too.

After the failure of the first big attack, Japanese commanders realized that the struggle for Guadalcanal was a battle of real strategic significance and gave it great prominence. One consequence of this was that forces advancing on Port Moresby in New Guinea were pulled back and denied reinforcements. Thus the fighting on Guadalcanal indirectly assisted the Allied cause elsewhere.

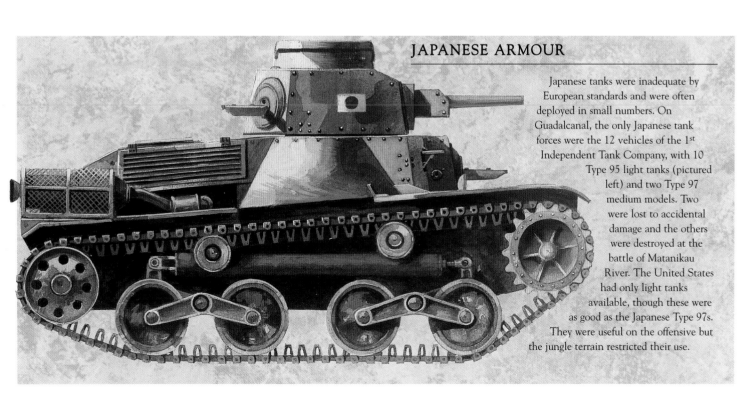

JAPANESE ARMOUR

Japanese tanks were inadequate by European standards and were often deployed in small numbers. On Guadalcanal, the only Japanese tank forces were the 12 vehicles of the 1st Independent Tank Company, with 10 Type 95 light tanks (pictured left) and two Type 97 medium models. Two were lost to accidental damage and the others were destroyed at the battle of Matanikau River. The United States had only light tanks available, though these were as good as the Japanese Type 97s. They were useful on the offensive but the jungle terrain restricted their use.

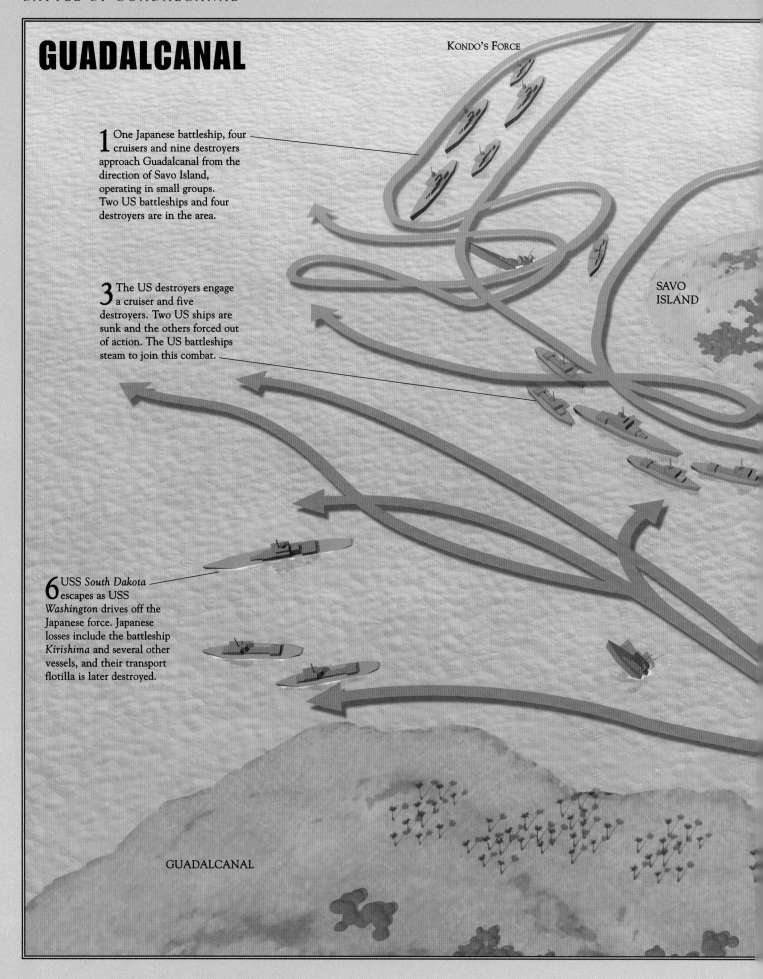

GUADALCANAL

KONDO'S FORCE

1 One Japanese battleship, four cruisers and nine destroyers approach Guadalcanal from the direction of Savo Island, operating in small groups. Two US battleships and four destroyers are in the area.

3 The US destroyers engage a cruiser and five destroyers. Two US ships are sunk and the others forced out of action. The US battleships steam to join this combat.

SAVO ISLAND

6 USS *South Dakota* escapes as USS *Washington* drives off the Japanese force. Japanese losses include the battleship *Kirishima* and several other vessels, and their transport flotilla is later destroyed.

GUADALCANAL

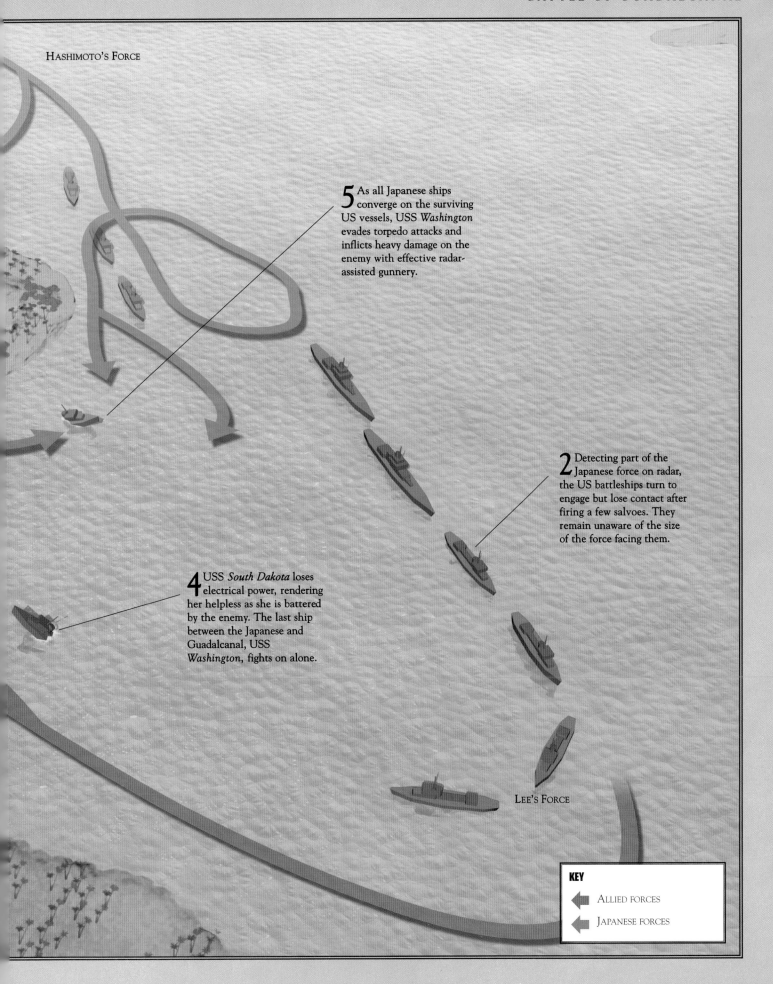

HASHIMOTO'S FORCE

5 As all Japanese ships converge on the surviving US vessels, USS *Washington* evades torpedo attacks and inflicts heavy damage on the enemy with effective radar-assisted gunnery.

2 Detecting part of the Japanese force on radar, the US battleships turn to engage but lose contact after firing a few salvoes. They remain unaware of the size of the force facing them.

4 USS *South Dakota* loses electrical power, rendering her helpless as she is battered by the enemy. The last ship between the Japanese and Guadalcanal, USS *Washington*, fights on alone.

LEE'S FORCE

KEY

◀ ALLIED FORCES

◀ JAPANESE FORCES

STALINGRAD 1942–43

Stalingrad changed the face of World War II. In a cataclysmic struggle, the Wehrmacht *experienced its first major army-sized defeat and the strategic advantage on the Eastern Front began to shift to the Red Army.*

As the crushing Russian winter of 1941–42 ran its course, Adolf Hitler was faced with a critical strategic decision. His *Barbarossa* campaign to smash the Soviet Union, which began in June 1941, had stalled before Moscow and was even put into temporary retreat by a Soviet counteroffensive on 5–6 December. Only the late spring would return the *Wehrmacht* to mobility and Hitler decided to apply this mobility in a new direction. Instead of renewing the Moscow offensive, much as the Soviets expected, Hitler ordered Operation *Blue* – a massive offensive by his Army Group South through the Ukraine and into the Crimea towards the Caucasus. The ultimate objective was to capture the Soviet oilfields of the Caucasus, oilfields upon which Germany relied to power its war machine.

STALINGRAD FACTS

Who: The German Sixth Army under General Friedrich Paulus (1890–1957), along with elements of the Fourth Panzer Army under General Hermann Hoth (1885–1971), versus the Red Army's Stalingrad Front, principally the Sixty-Second Army under Major-General Vasily Chuikov (1900–1982).

What: German forces nearly succeeded in conquering Stalingrad, but with massive losses. A Soviet counteroffensive trapped 250,000 Germans within the city. About 100,000 of these men were killed and 110,000 went to almost certain death in Soviet captivity.

Where: The city of Stalingrad, set on the Volga river.

When: 14 September 1942 to 2 February 1943

Why: The Stalingrad battle was part of a German campaign to occupy the Soviet Union's southern oilfields in the Caucasus. Stalingrad needed securing to protect the German left flank.

Outcome: Stalingrad marked the beginning of the German defeat on the Eastern Front, with the Red Army maintaining an offensive drive for the rest of the war.

AMIDST THE DEVASTATION OF STALINGRAD, *a heavily armed German platoon prepares to make yet another assault on Soviet positions.*

A TWO-MAN GERMAN MG34 *machine-gun team occupies a shell-hole in the ruined Stalingrad suburbs, September 1942.*

Operation *Blue* began on 28 June, consisting of 1.3 million men (including 300,000 German allies, principally Romanians and Italians) and 1500 aircraft. Army Group South was divided into Army Groups A and B, and the plan was for both groups to converge on the city of Stalingrad on the banks of the Volga, at which point Army Group B would remain on the Don and Volga rivers to provide flank protection for Army Group A's assault into the Caucasus. As with the *Wehrmacht* operations of the previous spring/summer, the Germans made good headway, and by mid-July the Sixth Army under General Friedrich Paulus (1890–1957) – the main component of Army Group B – was closing in on Stalingrad.

On 23 July, Hitler gave the order to take the city itself. General Hermann Hoth's (1885–1971) Fourth Panzer Army was deployed south of Stalingrad to assist in the assault. On the same day, Stalin issued his own directive stating that Stalingrad

RIGHT: GENERAL VASILY CHUIKOV, commander of the Soviet Sixty-Second Army, seen here (centre) in his command post at Stalingrad.

would be defended to the last. Soviet forces in the newly designated Stalingrad Front consisted of the Sixty-Second, Sixty-Third and Sixty-Fourth Armies. Although Stalingrad was an important industrial centre, the fact that it bore Stalin's name gave the Soviet leader a definite psychological imperative to see that it did not fall.

STREET BATTLE

The prelude to fighting within the city was a heavy air bombardment by *Luftlotte* 4, which reduced much of the city to rubble and killed more than 30,000 people. By 12 September, German troops were already pushing into the city's suburbs, where they faced a defence of almost psychotic vigour from the troops of Chuikov's Sixty-Second Army within the city. Chuikov, a rough-edged commander in contrast to the urbane Paulus, had a numerical disadvantage within the city compared to the Germans (roughly 54,000 Soviets to 100,000 Germans).

Yet the battle for Stalingrad was to be pure street fighting, a form of warfare depriving the Germans of the mobility that was their accustomed route to success in battle. Moreover, Chuikov deliberately pushed his troops into extreme close-quarters battle, ordering them to 'hug' the German troops and thus limit enemy use of air bombardment and heavy artillery fire, both of which would

risk the danger of 'friendly fire' casualties. The effect was that every building, and every room in every building, became a battleground, the Germans paying for each yard with blood.

By the end of September, Paulus and Hoth had taken around two-thirds of Stalingrad. An offensive launched on 14 September by LI Corps penetrated deep inside the city, taking the Mamayev Kurgan heights (a salient feature of the

BELOW: ALL AVAILABLE SOVIET personnel were used in the defence of Stalingrad – this group includes sailors and civilians.

ABOVE: TROOPS AND ARMOUR of the Soviet Twenty-First Army advance during Operation Uranus, the two-pronged offensive designed to trap German forces in Stalingrad.

city) and driving through towards the No 1 Railway station. The aim was to reach the Volga and destroy the Soviet landing stages, which were receiving resupply and reinforcements boated across the river (a harrowing experience for boat crews and passengers, who were bombed remorselessly by German attack aircraft). However, last-

BELOW: THE ITALIAN EIGHTH ARMY begins its long retreat from positions on the left flank of the German Sixth Army, December 1942.

minute reinforcements from Major-General Aleksandr Rodimtsev's (1905–1977) 13th Guards Division meant that the station changed hands 15 times before it finally fell to the Germans. Hoth's Fourth Panzers coming up from the south had a similar harrowing experience but made better progress, reaching the river by 13 October.

Between mid-October and mid-November, the Germans slowly squeezed the Soviets back, battling through the factory district at appalling cost (major battlegrounds were the Barrikady, Krasny Oktyabr and Tractor factories). Stalingrad was by now utterly destroyed, but the rubble created by German firepower actually made a convoluted landscape that was easier to defend and harder to attack. By 18 November, the Soviets held only a thin broken strip of territory on the Volga, little more than 10 per cent of the city. Winter was beginning, however, and the Germans were shattered and depleted from the last weeks of fighting.

THE SOVIET OFFENSIVE

On 19 November, Soviet forces around Stalingrad played their masterstroke, a counteroffensive planned by General Georgy Zhukov (1896–1974). North of Stalingrad, the Soviet Southwest Front and Don Front launched a six-army push southwards across the Don, smashing weak Romanian resistance. The next day, the Stalingrad Front attacked north from positions south of Stalingrad, once again overcoming weak German flank protection. On 23 November, the two

A YAK 1B *of the 37th Guards IAP. The Soviets had a total of about 1400 aircraft at Stalingrad, flying about 500 sorties a day.*

'pincers' met behind Stalingrad, trapping the Sixth Army and much of the Fourth Army – more than 250,000 men – within the city. A German disaster was unfolding.

In the early days of the offensive, a German breakout was possible but it was refused by Hitler. Instead, he opted for one of Hermann Göring's wildly optimistic aerial resupply plans, which was never realistic, and then for a relief offensive by Manstein's Eleventh Army. This offensive – Operation *Winter Storm* – was launched on 12 December and made some progress but was eventually battered to a standstill 48km (30 miles) from Stalingrad. Two weeks later, Manstein's forces were in retreat from fresh Soviet offensives, leaving the German soldiers in Stalingrad to a ghastly fate.

Horrific fighting continued in Stalingrad for over a month as the Soviets steadily crushed the German occupiers. Although 34,000 Germans were evacuated by air before the final airfield fell on 25 January, more than 100,000 *Wehrmacht* troops were killed in this period. Finally, between 31 January and 2 February, Paulus and some 110,000 German survivors surrendered, destined for Soviet labour camps from which only 5000 men would emerge alive.

THE BEGINNING OF THE END

The German defeat at Stalingrad tilted the balance of the war both strategically and psychologically. Strategically, it put paid to Operation *Blue* and began, in effect, the German retreat that would end in Berlin in 1945. Psychologically it gave the Soviets an enormous boost of confidence and showed that they could compete with the Germans on both tactical and strategic levels. For the Germans, it was an undeniable sign that they could be defeated – the glory days of 1939–40 were now forgotten.

FIELD-MARSHAL FRIEDRICH PAULUS

Friedrich Paulus (1890–1957) cut his military teeth as an army captain during World War I and showed the ability and ambition that enabled him to rise to the rank of general by 1939. He subsequently served as deputy to General Franz Halder, the German Chief of Staff, before taking his most infamous command, that of the Sixth Army, in 1941. Paulus was an urbane 'old school' officer whose loyalty to the military led him, initially, to obey Hitler's ludicrous 'to the last man' defence orders at Stalingrad. On 31 January 1942, Hitler made Paulus a field-marshal, knowing that no field-marshal in German history had ever surrendered or been captured alive. (Hitler was in effect requesting his suicide.) At this point, however, Paulus chose to ignore the precedent and surrendered, going on to be a vocal critic of the Nazi regime while in captivity. His last career posting was as an adviser to the East German Army in the mid-1950s.

FIELD-MARSHAL PAULUS *(left) and his chief-of-staff Arthur Schmidt (right) seen after their surrender in early 1943.*

STALINGRAD

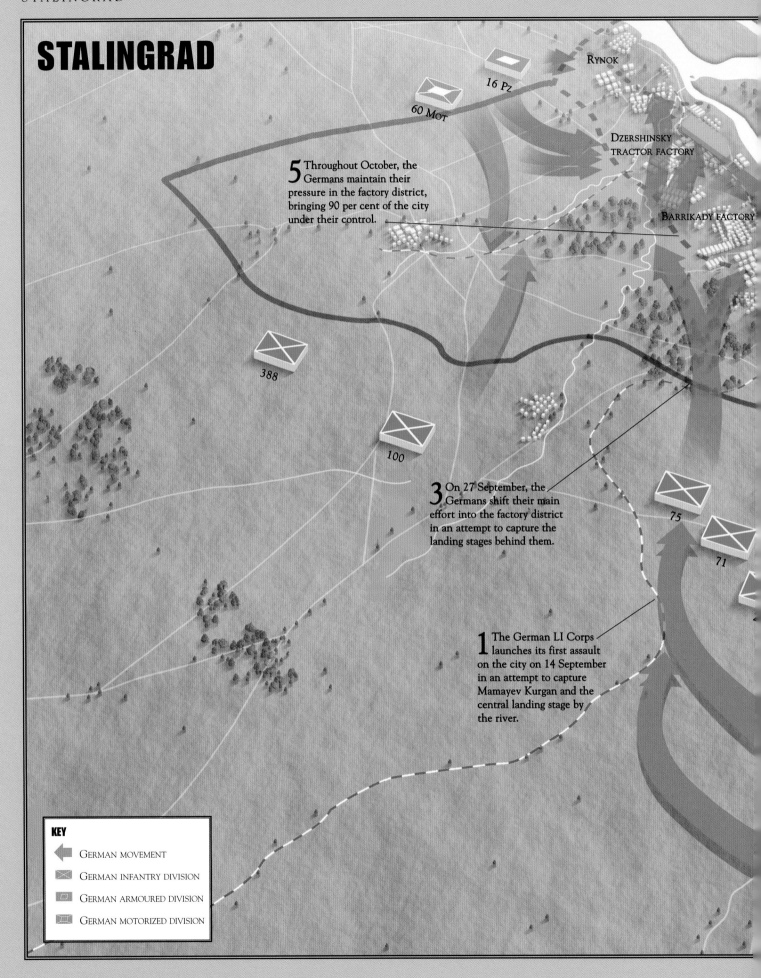

RYNOK

16 Pz

60 Mot

DZERSHINSKY
TRACTOR FACTORY

5 Throughout October, the Germans maintain their pressure in the factory district, bringing 90 per cent of the city under their control.

BARRIKADY FACTORY

388

100

3 On 27 September, the Germans shift their main effort into the factory district in an attempt to capture the landing stages behind them.

75

71

1 The German LI Corps launches its first assault on the city on 14 September in an attempt to capture Mamayev Kurgan and the central landing stage by the river.

KEY

⬅ GERMAN MOVEMENT

◨ GERMAN INFANTRY DIVISION

▭ GERMAN ARMOURED DIVISION

▥ GERMAN MOTORIZED DIVISION

6 The last major German attack begins on 11 November. Eight days later, the Soviets launch Operation Uranus, cutting off the Sixth Army in the city.

4 The Soviets managed to maintain their supply lines across the Volga, providing the Sixty-Second Army with just enough men and matériel to hang on to their foothold in the city.

RED OCTOBER
FACTORY

MAMAYEV
KURGAN

GRAIN SILO

KRASNAYA
SLOBODA

RIVER VOLGA

14 PZ

94

24 PZ

29 MOT

2 The Fourth Panzer Army attacks in support in the south of the city, but is held up by fanatical resistance around the grain silo.

THIRD BATTLE OF KHARKOV 1943

The Third Battle of Kharkov is generally considered to be the last German victory on the Eastern Front. It stands as a classic example of armoured manoeuvre tactics executed under difficult conditions against a well-prepared and numerically superior enemy.

When Hitler ordered the invasion of the Soviet Union in 1941, he did not envisage a long war. There was a time when a knockout blow might have been achieved, but the Soviets averted defeat long enough for the weather to close in. This granted some time to prepare and allowed renewed German offensives to be halted.

The German army tried again in 1942 and then 1943, but decisive victory proved elusive and all the time Soviet strength was increasing. The odds became

THIRD BATTLE OF KHARKOV FACTS

Who: 160,000 German troops led by Field Marshal Erich von Manstein (1887–1973) versus approximately 300,000 Soviet troops of the Bryansk, Volkhov and South Western Fronts led by generals Golikov and Vatutin (1901–1944).

What: Committed to the operation by the Red Army were the Bryansk, Voronezh and the South Western Fronts. These included the Fortieth, Sixty-Ninth and Third Tank armies. The Germans' counteroffensive was led by the Fourth Panzer Army and included the II SS Panzer Corps, comprising the *Leibstandarte Adolf Hitler* and *Das Reich* divisions.

Where: The city of Kharkov in the Ukraine.

When: February–March 1943

Why: The city was important politically and as a transport nexus.

Outcome: The city was captured by the Germans but was lost again in August to a Soviet offensive.

PANZERGRENADIERS OF THE SS DIVISION Das Reich ride into Kharkov on the engine deck of a Panzer III. Early 1943 was the last period in which the war on the Eastern Front was winnable for Germany.

slimmer each year, but there was no choice: Germany had to attack and defeat the enemy its leader had chosen.

By the beginning of 1943, the tide was turning against Germany. Defeats in North Africa had dealt a serious blow to German prestige. Her allies were reconsidering their position and there seemed little prospect of persuading others – such as Turkey – to join the fight. Meanwhile at home there were economic problems and social unrest.

SOVIET SUCCESSES

The fall of Stalingrad after months of bitter fighting was a serious blow to German morale and prestige while their opponents were riding a wave of success. The Red Army began advancing, urged on by a jubilant Stalin, who believed that he could sweep the invaders out of Russia with a headlong offensive. Leningrad was relieved and the threat to Moscow greatly diminished. In the south, Soviet troops were making gains against the tired and depleted Germans.

There was a danger that the German Army Group South might be cut off and forced to surrender and matters were not helped by a catastrophic defeat in Stalingrad. However, the German commander Field-Marshal Von Manstein (1887–1973) ignored his orders to die in place and organized a fighting retreat that not only got his army out

T-34 TANKS IN Dzerzhinsky Square, Kharkov. After the fall of Stalingrad, it seemed that the Germans could be swiftly pushed out of Soviet Russia, but their recapture of Kharkov challenged that assumption.

of the trap in condition to fight on but also bought time for reinforcements to arrive.

The Soviets were running ahead of their logistics capability and beginning to falter, but were forced to push on by Stalin's urgings. The Soviet high command did not believe that the battered German army could do anything but retreat westwards, putting up local resistance. A counterattack was obviously out of the question.

REINFORCEMENTS ARRIVE

In fact, the German army did possess the capability to counterattack. Reinforcements had begun to arrive. In some cases, these were damaged units pushed back into the line after receiving some replacement personnel and equipment and were in little better shape than the line formations. However, some very powerful units were placed at Manstein's disposal.

Most significantly Manstein was given control of I SS Panzer Corps. This comprised the SS *Totenkopf*, *Liebstandarte* and *Das Reich* divisions, all of which had been

THESE WAFFEN-SS SOLDIERS show the benefits of their period of rest and refitting. Their good morale and better supply situation enabled them to defeat a larger number of Soviet troops in the battle for Kharkov.

refitting and were well rested. More importantly perhaps, they were equipped with the new Panzer VI Tiger tank armed with a formidable 88mm (3.46in) gun. Much of the divisions' tank strength was made up of lesser vehicles but the Tigers made a potent spearhead.

The first arrivals were formed into a battle group and pushed into the line to halt the Soviet advance. Remnants of German and Italian units retreated past them, but despite heavy Soviet attacks the battle group was able more or less to hold its positions. A period of repositioning then followed as the German army tried to establish defences that would prevent the strategic city of Kharkov being encircled.

Although the Soviets were suffering severe ammunition shortages and were becoming disorganized, they pushed forward faster than expected. It became obvious that an attack on Kharkov could not be prevented by defensive measures. The SS troops were ordered to attack.

The Soviet advance on Kharkov took the form of a pincer movement, in which the southern arm was much more powerful. The advancing Soviets were hit from the flank with armoured units and dive-bombers savaging their rear echelon support units before falling on the disorganized combat formations.

The attack was a success and halted the advance for a time. However, the Soviets were still able to drive forwards and despite inflicting heavy casualties the SS troops were pushed back. Again the German force was threatened with encirclement. The SS commander Paul Hausser (1880–1972) asked for permission to retreat.

Although Hitler himself refused permission to retreat and commanded the SS troops to hold at all costs, Hausser decided to ignore this order. He launched a local counter-

T-34/76: THE GREATEST TANK OF WORLD WAR II?

The T-34 was among the most important weapons systems in the Red Army in World War II. At the time it was first fielded in 1940, it was easily the finest tank design in the world. Individually, T-34s were workmanlike rather than excellent combat vehicles. They were well protected, mobile, and possessed a good gun that could knock out enemy tanks at a respectable range. However, they were also prone to mechanical problems, especially with the transmission.

One for one, German tanks were generally better, but the phrase 'all things being equal' never applies in warfare. Tanks did not fight one on one but as part of a military/technical/industrial partnership in which the fighting capabilities of the vehicle were only one aspect. The ability to repair or replace breakdowns and get tanks back into the fight was also critical, as was the capacity to manufacture them in large enough numbers to make a difference. It was in this context that the T-34 was a world-beater.

attack with tanks to blunt the Soviet offensive and pulled his force back on 15 February. Disregarding renewed orders to stand his ground, Hausser was able to bring his force out in reasonably good order despite large Soviet forces entering the city.

Hitler was enraged and ordered Manstein to use Hausser's command as the spearhead of an attack to retake the city of Kharkov. This suited Manstein. A deep salient had appeared in the battle front where the Soviets had pushed forwards. This created an ideal opportunity for a double envelopment against the shoulders of the salient, pincering off and encircling the advancing Soviets for destruction.

Plans were made while the SS troops reorganized themselves, amalgamating their depleted tanks and other assets into scratch battalions. This method of creating effective battle groups from the remains of heavily damaged units was a hallmark of the German forces during World War II and allowed the shrinking formations to go on fighting long after the individual units they were created from had ceased to be useful.

ABOVE: A MACHINE-GUN TEAM *of the SS Division* Liebstandarte. *In close-quarters urban fighting, the observer's submachinegun and grenade might prove more useful than the support weapon.*

ABOVE: GENERAL PAUL HAUSSER *defied Hitler's orders to fight to the last and instead pulled his troops out of a bad position, creating the opportunity for a successful counterattack.*

MANSTEIN'S COUNTERATTACK

Manstein's counterattack went in on 19 February 1943. The SS formations spearheaded the northern half of the pincer attack while regular Panzer units led the southern arm. Despite minefields and foul weather that included both snow and fog, the SS troops advanced to contact and hit the enemy flank. Early successes included cutting the main road link to the River Dnieper, hampering Soviet movements.

Renewing the advance, the SS force fought several small but sharp encounter battles with Soviet units moving up to the front, capturing the town of Pavlograd on 24 February.

Elsewhere, the flanking movements had thrown the Soviets into confusion and their advance to the Dnieper was brought to a halt then pushed back. The way to Kharkov was now open and the *Das Reich* division led the way towards the city. The Soviet high command issued 'hold at all costs' orders. Reinforcements were rushed into Kharkov and attacks made elsewhere to try to divert German resources. This measure failed. The strategic rail junctions at Lasovaya were taken by the *Das Reich* and *Totenkopf* divisions.

Still Soviet reinforcements continued to arrive. The Third Tank Army (equivalent to a Panzer corps) managed to get between the *Das Reich* and *Liebstandarte* divisions. This was a perilous situation – or a great opportunity to smash it from both sides, depending on your viewpoint.

Hausser took the latter view and launched an attack that became a three-day slogging match. Despite appalling weather, the landscape rapidly turning into a sea of mud and critical supply shortages, the SS troops gradually came out on top. By the time it was over, three Soviet tank brigades, three infantry divisions and an entire corps of cavalry were shattered or captured.

Under this punishing onslaught, the Soviet forces pulled back in some areas, and on 11 March a battle group of SS troops established itself within the city limits. On 12 March, the battle for the city began. Despite extremely stubborn resistance, notably around the railway station and the industrial district, the Soviets were gradually pushed out of the city.

By now, the Soviets were in a state of confusion and thoroughly demoralized. Driving ever eastwards, the SS divisions, though heavily depleted, smashed up two Guards Tank Corps and four infantry divisions. The last organized resistance was around a tractor factory outside the city. Once this was taken, Kharkov was firmly in German hands.

Subsequent operations cleared Soviet forces out of the immediate area and stabilized the front before the spring

BELOW: COSSACK CAVALRY WERE more often used for scouting operations, but if they achieved surprise and got in among enemy infantry, their sabres and pistols were highly effective.

RIGHT: AN NCO OF THE SS DAS REICH division bundled up warmly against the cold. Heavy gloves could interfere with operating a weapon, so some troops sawed the trigger guard off.

thaw turned everything to mud and brought a halt to offensive operations on both sides.

AFTERMATH

Hitler remained angry at Hausser for ignoring his orders and refused to decorate him even though his troops had performed brilliantly in the battle for the city. His command did receive considerable replacements and much of its artillery was upgraded to self-propelled guns. The formation was re-designated II SS Panzer Corps.

In the wake of the victory at Kharkov, plans were formulated to launch a new offensive in the summer. Codenamed Operation *Citadel*, it would smash the Soviet forces facing Army Group South and tip the balance of the war back in the direction of Germany – if it succeeded. The stage was thus set for the Battle of Kursk; the greatest armoured clash of all time.

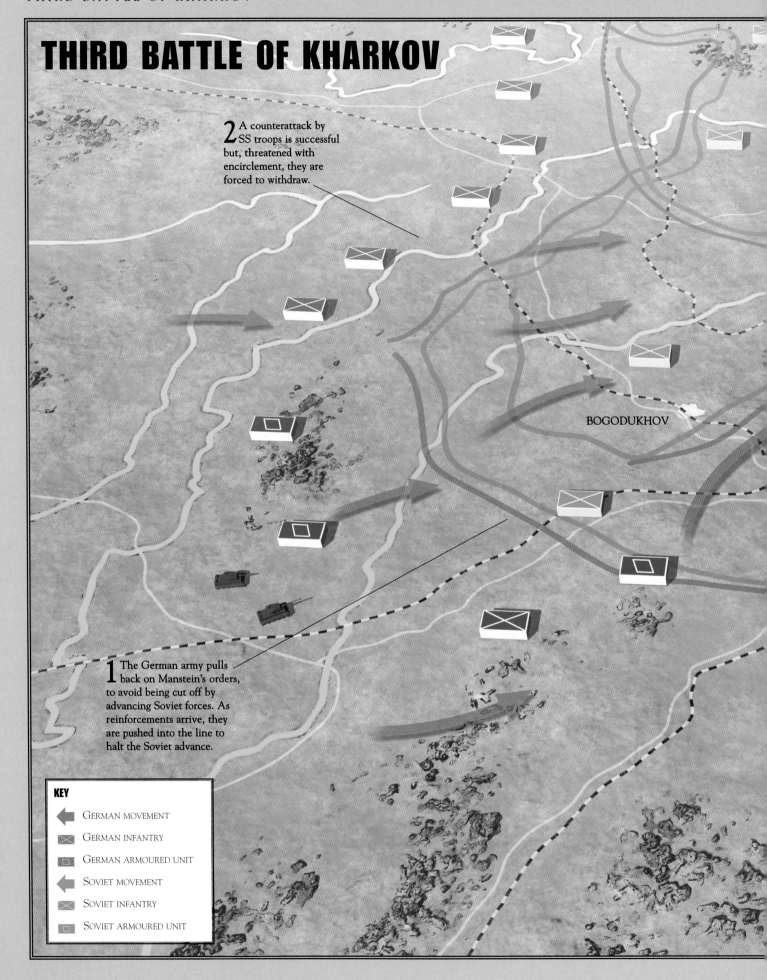

THIRD BATTLE OF KHARKOV

2 A counterattack by SS troops is successful but, threatened with encirclement, they are forced to withdraw.

BOGODUKHOV

1 The German army pulls back on Manstein's orders, to avoid being cut off by advancing Soviet forces. As reinforcements arrive, they are pushed into the line to halt the Soviet advance.

KEY

- GERMAN MOVEMENT
- GERMAN INFANTRY
- GERMAN ARMOURED UNIT
- SOVIET MOVEMENT
- SOVIET INFANTRY
- SOVIET ARMOURED UNIT

5 The Soviet forces disintegrate and are pursued eastwards, suffering heavy casualties in the process. Kharkov remains in German hands for the time being.

FRONT LINE, 23 MARCH

KHARKOV

4 After heavy fighting, SS troops manage to gain a foothold in Kharkov itself and begin clearing the city.

FRONT LINE, 28 FEBRUARY

3 Manstein launches a double-envelopment attack. The northern pincer is spearheaded by SS panzer troops, the southern by regulars.

KURSK 1943

The July 1943 Battle of Kursk was the greatest clash of armoured forces yet seen in warfare. The origins of this German offensive – Operation Citadel – lay in the disastrous start to 1943, when Soviet counterattacks not only destroyed the Sixth Army in Stalingrad but also imperilled Field-Marshal Erich von Manstein's Army Group Don.

However, between 18 February and 18 March von Manstein's effective counteroffensive destroyed the Soviet spearheads and subsequently a pause descended over the Eastern Front as the exhausted combatants rebuilt their shattered forces for the looming summer campaign. These battles left a large Soviet-held salient jutting west into the German lines around Kursk. Hitler ordered his forces to launch a double-pincer attack across the base of this salient to surround and destroy the sizable Soviet force trapped within. Such an offensive would accomplish this encirclement within a restricted geographical area, a sensible plan that reflected the *Wehrmacht's* dwindling operational mobility. For

KURSK FACTS

Who: Elements of Field Marshal Günther von Kluge's (1882–1944) Army Group Centre and Field Marshal Erich von Manstein's (1887–1973) Army Group South faced Marshal Konstantin Rokossovsky's (1896–1968) Central Front and Marshal Nikolai Vatutin's (1901–1944) Voronezh Front under the direction of Supreme Commander-in-Chief Marshal Georgi Zhukov (1896–1974).

What: The German strategic offensive of 1943, aimed at eliminating the Soviet salient centred around Kursk.

Where: The area around Kursk in the Ukraine, an important rail junction 800km (497 miles) south of Moscow.

When: 4 to 13 July 1943

Why: Only having resources for a limited offensive in the east and needing a victory to reassure wavering allies, the Kursk salient provided the Germans with an apparently manageable strategic objective.

Outcome: The German offensive failed and the Soviet counterattack provided a launching point for further Soviet operations in 1943. The strategic balance in the East had shifted in favour of the Soviets for good.

A RARE PHOTOGRAPH of a Churchill tank from Fifth Guards Army, a unit equipped with a number of Lend-Lease vehicles from the Western Allies. It is passing a knocked-out German Sd Kfz 232.

ABOVE: A HEAVY PANZER BATTALION, *equipped with Tiger Mark Is, deploys prior to the Battle of Kursk. Much hope was placed by the Germans on their new generation of armour.*

Citadel, therefore, the Germans achieved a massive concentration of force by assembling 17 panzer/panzergrenadier divisions across a total attack frontage of just 164km (102 miles).

BELOW: FIELD MARSHAL MODEL *(centre, with goggles on cap) addresses some of his soldiers in the build-up to the battle of Kursk.*

DELAYS AND POSTPONEMENTS

The Germans set *Citadel* to begin in early May, but Hitler repeatedly postponed the offensive so that small numbers of Germany's latest weapons could reach the front. Hitler believed that with these 340 new 'war-winning' weapons – 250 Panther medium and 90 Tiger heavy tanks – the massive German forces committed to *Citadel* could smash any resistance the Soviets offered, however powerful. Yet the Germans proved unable to exploit their concentration of

PANZER V 'PANTHER' TANK

The Panther was built as a direct response to encountering the Soviet T-34 during 1941. The T-34 outclassed the current generation of German tanks and thus a counter was required. The MAN-produced Panther owed its sloping armour to the Soviet design, but maintained the German tradition of superbly designed, expensive and complex engineering. Its high velocity 75mm (2.95in) gun had excellent armour-piercing capabilities and proved very well protected.

A prototype was ready by September 1942 and the first production models by December. It was deployed for the first time at Kursk, although these early models were plagued with automotive problems.

force. The obvious German preparations for *Citadel* cast aside any element of surprise while Hitler's repeated postponements gave the Soviets sufficient time to construct the most powerful defensive system yet seen in the war. The Germans remained partially ignorant of the strength of these Soviet defences, thanks to the latter's skill at concealment and deception. Either that or they dismissed this strength; all it would mean was a bigger 'prize' when the German offensive successfully encircled the salient. Indeed, when *Citadel*

commenced on 4/5 July the Germans were outnumbered by the Soviets – astonishing given that the offensive was of the Germans' choosing in timing, location and method.

PINCER MOVEMENT

The Germans deployed two main groupings for *Citadel*: in the north, elements of Field-Marshal Günther von Kluge's (1882–1944) Army Group Centre; and in the south, forces from von Manstein's Army Group South. In the north,

SOVIET INFANTRYMEN deploy their 14.5mm (0.57in) Simov PTRS Rifle. By 1943, the antitank rifle was obsolescent and would struggle to pierce German armour from most angles, but it remained in service due to lack of anything else.

ABOVE: MARSHAL KONSTANTIN ROKOSSOVSKY *was one of the new breed of successful Soviet commanders coming to the fore after the disasters of 1941–42. He commanded the Central Front at Kursk.*

General Walter Model's (1891–1945) Ninth Army had at its disposal six panzer/panzergrenadier and 14 infantry divisions. In the south, Colonel-General Hermann Hoth's (1885–1971) Fourth Panzer Army and General Franz Kempf's (1886–1964) Army Detachment put into the field 11 panzer/ panzergrenadier and 10 infantry divisions. The offensive commenced on 4 July, when von Manstein's forces initiated preliminary attacks from the salient's southern shoulder. At dawn the next day, 10 of Model's divisions assaulted the first Soviet defence line. By evening Model's forces had only managed painfully slow advances – at most, 10km (six miles) along a front some 40km (25 miles) long.

Meanwhile that same day, Hoth and Kempf's forces initiated their main assaults along the southern shoulder. By dusk, Hoth's forces had advanced only 10km (six miles) south to penetrate the first Soviet defensive line. Further east, Kempf's forces failed even to smash through the first Soviet defensive line. During the next day, Model's forces in the north attacked the Soviet second defence line, aiming to capture the Olkhovtka Ridge, from where they could surge through the open plain to the south. Though the repeated German attacks made some progress, intense Soviet counterattacks prevented the capture of Ponyri.

Between 7 and 9 July, both sides threw in their reserves as Model repeatedly attempted to capture this village in the face of fanatical resistance that included powerful counterattacks. Finally, between 10 and 11 July, these Soviet counterattacks halted Model's advance. The northern German thrust had proven a dismal failure: despite a week of intense and costly attacks, it had managed to advance just 15km (9 miles).

In the south, on 6 July, Hoth's XXXXVIII Panzer Corps pushed north towards the second Soviet defence line near Oboyan despite counterattacks by fresh Soviet armoured reserves. Further east, II SS Panzer Corps drove the defenders north towards the village of Prokhorovka. Over the next four days, these two panzer corps inched their way north towards Oboyan and Prokhorovka in the face of bitter Soviet resistance sustained by freshly arrived reserves. Between 10 and 11 July, German forces successfully pierced the third Soviet defensive line in an attempt to outflank the Soviet units located further west around Oboyan. Sensing the danger in this success, the Soviets redeployed the Fifth Guards Tank Army to the area north of Prokhorovka.

THE GREATEST TANK BATTLE

On 12 July, the climax to *Citadel* occurred – the titanic clash of armour at Prokhorovka, into which the Soviets committed Fifth Guards Tank Army. With 800 Soviet tanks engaging 600 panzers, this action was the largest armoured battle of the war. For eight hours, the battle raged back and forth with the tanks throwing up vast clouds of dust that limited visibility to just a few yards.

The Soviets exploited these conditions, closing the range so that the Germans could not benefit from their lethal long-range guns. Tactically the battle was a draw, but strategically it was a German disaster: the Germans spent their armoured strength – whereas sizable Soviet armoured reserves remained available – and lost the initiative to the Red Army, an opportunity the latter then ruthlessly exploited.

Prokhorovka convinced Hitler that *Citadel* could not succeed and on 13 July he cancelled the offensive. Between 15 and 25 July, the German assault forces conducted a slow fighting withdrawal back to their starting positions in the face of ferocious Soviet attacks. On 12 July, moreover, the Soviets had also launched an offensive against the German units that protected the northern flank of Model's forces. Catching the Germans by surprise, the Soviets gradually drove them back 120km (80 miles).

Then, on 3 August, the Soviets attacked the German forces concentrated along the southern shoulder of the erstwhile Kursk salient. This new Soviet attack swiftly eliminated the German-held bulge to the south of the former salient. After securing rapid success with these two counterattacks, the Soviets escalated their operations into a general strategic counteroffensive across the entire centre and south of the Eastern Front. During the remainder of 1943, this general counteroffensive west drove the Germans back to the river Dnieper and beyond.

AFTERMATH

All things considered, *Citadel* was a dire German strategic defeat. Despite their huge concentration of force, all the Germans gained was an advance never deeper than 40km (25 miles) and through insignificant terrain, for the heavy price of 52,000 casualties and 850 AFVs. Indeed, all *Citadel* accomplished was to shatter the German strategic armoured reserves, thus making it easier for the Soviets to achieve rapid operational successes with their counterattacks. In fact, Kursk – rather than Stalingrad – was probably the key turning point of the war, which ensured Germany would be defeated in 1945.

THE CREW OF A SOVIET T-34 tank surrender to an SS soldier, presumably during the fighting on the southern side of the Kursk salient.

KURSK

1 The Battle of Kursk climaxed on 12 July, when the Soviets committed the Fifth Guards Tank Army against II SS Panzer Corps near the village of Prokhorovka in the south of the Kursk Salient.

FRONT LINE, 5 JULY

FRONT LINE, 13 JULY

3 SS Pz Div
TOTENKOPF

1 SS
LEIBSTA

2 II SS Panzer Corps had made reasonable progress in the opening days of the battle. Its progress in the Prokhorovka threatened the Soviet position in the south of the Salient.

2 SS Pz Div
DAS REICH

6 The setbacks at Prokhorovka convinced Hitler that Operation Citadel would fail and he cancelled the offensive on 13 July. It was a major strategic victory for the Soviets.

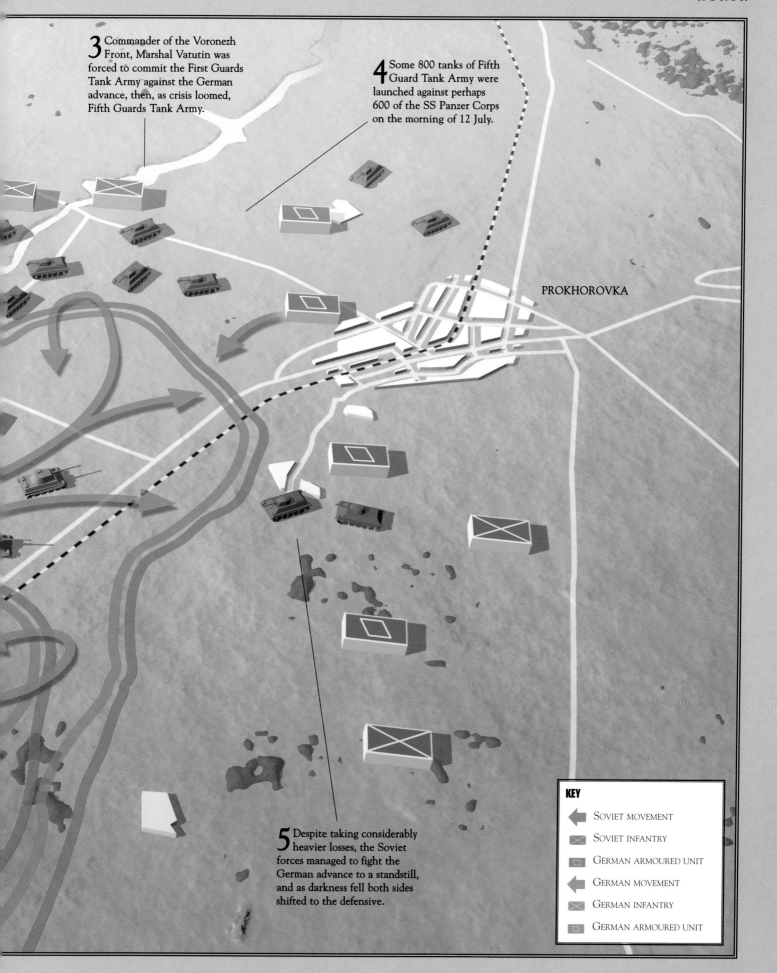

3 Commander of the Voronezh Front, Marshal Vatutin was forced to commit the First Guards Tank Army against the German advance, then, as crisis loomed, Fifth Guards Tank Army.

4 Some 800 tanks of Fifth Guard Tank Army were launched against perhaps 600 of the SS Panzer Corps on the morning of 12 July.

PROKHOROVKA

5 Despite taking considerably heavier losses, the Soviet forces managed to fight the German advance to a standstill, and as darkness fell both sides shifted to the defensive.

KEY

← SOVIET MOVEMENT

⬚ SOVIET INFANTRY

▭ GERMAN ARMOURED UNIT

← GERMAN MOVEMENT

⬚ GERMAN INFANTRY

▭ GERMAN ARMOURED UNIT

BATTLE OF IMPHAL AND KOHIMA 1944

The Battle of Imphal and the action at Kohima represented the high water mark of Japanese aspirations in Burma and India. However, after some initial successes, the defeated Japanese fell back into Burma and were subsequently driven back the way they had come.

The Japanese advance in the early months of World War II seemed unstoppable. Allied forces were driven down the Malay Peninsula to the 'fortress island' of Singapore and forced to surrender there. Other formations were pushed back through Burma towards India. A determined rearguard action slowed the Japanese advance and the monsoon brought it to a halt.

This gave the Allies a chance to regroup and mount a defence, which the terrain favoured. The jungle and hills of the Burmese–Indian border region would

BATTLE OF IMPHAL FACTS

Who: British and Indian troops opposed by Japanese forces and elements of the anti-British Indian National Army.

What: Japanese forces encircled the city of Imphal but were driven off and then counterattacked.

Where: The city of Imphal, the capital of the state of Manipur in northeast India.

When: 8 March–3 July 1944

Why: The Japanese wished to invade India and 'liberate' it from the British. This was their last chance of launching a major land invasion against British India, since their military resources were being rapidly used up against the United States in the Pacific.

Outcome: The Japanese were decisively defeated and never again threatened British India with invasion.

THE WIDE IRRAWADDY RIVER *was a serious obstacle to the logistics services of armies operating in the region. This makeshift barge turns a disadvantage into an asset, using the river to transport a truck.*

LIGHT UTILITY VEHICLES like these British Universal Carriers (Bren Carriers) were invaluable in keeping the supply lines open. As the name suggests, they could carry almost anything over rough terrain or on roads.

funnel an advance into corridors that could be defended with relative ease. The city of Imphal provided a base and logistics centre for the allies while the Japanese would have to operate at the end of a long supply line that ran through difficult terrain.

Breaking the Allied positions around Imphal would be a major undertaking, requiring resources that might be better used elsewhere. Thus the pressure dropped off considerably, allowing the Allies to build up their strength for an offensive back into Burma. Raids, including the famous exploits of the Chindits, were launched into Japanese territory.

This required some kind of countermeasure, and Japanese commanders decided that since it would require as much manpower to mount a proper defence of Burma as to drive the Allies out of Imphal, the offensive option was the most suitable.

THE JAPANESE ATTACK AT IMPHAL

Japanese forces in the region gained a new and aggressive commander, Lieutenant-General Masakazu Kawabe (1886–1965), who thought an attack on Imphal was practicable. There were several benefits to a victory there. As well as countering the Chindit raids, elimination of the logistics base at Imphal would cut off Allied supplies going

to Chinese Nationalist forces that were still fighting the Japanese to the North. More importantly, it would open the way to attack India.

India was extremely important to the British Empire, supplying large numbers of troops to the Imperial forces. However, there was a movement towards independence and the Japanese believed that India might be induced to break away, depriving the Allies of a vast amount of manpower. For this reason, the coming offensive was to include elements of the Indian National Army, a force raised from Indian prisoners taken by the Japanese during the Malaya campaign and who were willing to fight against the British in the name of Indian independence.

The Allies had occupied several forward positions in preparation for their own offensive into Burma. The Japanese plan was to encircle and eliminate these quickly before advancing on Imphal and driving off the defenders. This was by no means as easy as it sounded, since the attack would have to be made through difficult country at the end of a long supply chain. Some of the senior officers involved had grave doubts about the plan, especially the logistical elements.

Nevertheless the campaign opened on 8 March 1944, at which point the Allies began to withdraw their forward units. Some managed this without undue difficulty, but others had to fight their way out with the aid of the few available reserves. By the beginning of April, the Allies had pulled back to the Imphal plain and were receiving reinforcements by air.

Japanese troops then converged on Imphal along several roads. They were travelling light, having left much of their artillery and heavy equipment behind. One reason for this was the conviction that the terrain was unsuitable for tanks and so antitank weapons would not be needed. Ironically, it was exactly the same misconception that allowed Japanese tanks to do so much damage to the Allies in Malaya at the beginning of the war.

The Allies were using US-supplied M3 Lee light tanks, which could cope with the difficult terrain. Although far too light for anything

EXPECTING TO FIGHT ONLY INFANTRY, the Japanese forces brought along anti-personnel support weapons like this light machinegun but left most of their antitank weaponry behind as they advanced on Imphal.

but armoured reconnaissance elsewhere in the world, the Lees were more than capable of cutting up infantry, with little in the way of antitank equipment.

There were other serious problems too. The Japanese needed to capture Allied supplies or at least airfields suitable to fly them into before their supplies ran out. Inventive solutions, such as bringing herds of buffalo along behind the combat formations as rations 'on the hoof', had failed, and the situation was becoming serious. Foraging parties were able to obtain some supplies at a cost of diluting the combat effectiveness of the units involved.

Repeated attacks were put in against Imphal, but they grew steadily weaker and never really had a chance of success. Conversely, although the Allies were themselves getting short of supplies and ammunition their defence became increasingly aggressive, launching local counterattacks to harass the Japanese positions.

MERILL'S MARAUDERS

Named after its commander, Brigadier-General Frank Merrill (1903–55), the 5307th Composite Unit (Provisional) became better known as Merrill's Marauders during its long-range raiding exploits in the China-Burma theatre.

After training with the highly successful Chindits, the all-volunteer Marauders embarked on a campaign of harassment deep within Japanese territory. Despite heavy casualties and sickness caused by the harsh jungle conditions, they were able to cut Japanese supply lines and inflict serious losses on their opponents in dozens of actions.

At the end of the war, every member of the Marauders was awarded the Bronze Star and the unit was honoured with a Distinguished Unit Citation for its contribution to the Burma campaign.

The Allies were able to fly supplies into Imphal, as they had during the battle of the Admin Box a few months earlier. Where similar attempts had failed, such as the German 'air bridge' at Stalingrad, the position at Imphal was such that the besieging Japanese forces ran short before the Allies did.

OPERATIONS AGAINST KOHIMA

Meanwhile, the Japanese had tried for two weeks in early April to capture the Kohima ridge, which would allow them to control the main supply route into Imphal. The ridge was to have been seized early in the campaign, but stubborn defence by Allied troops encountered in the advance delayed the arrival of the Japanese at their objective. This bought time for a defence to be put in place.

The defenders at Kohima came under increasing pressure due to heavy shelling interspersed with infantry assaults. They held out in a shrinking perimeter, and by 17 April the situation was desperate. However, the position was relieved the next day by troops moving up from India. The attacks continued unabated, but the chances of success were ever decreasing.

By early May, more Allied troops had joined the fight at Kohima, and the Japanese, now very short of supplies, came under air attack as well as increasing bombardment. The ridge was partially cleared of Japanese defenders after a very stubborn fight, but as late as mid-May some high points were still stubbornly held.

However, with Allied troops across their supply line and almost out of ammunition, the starving Japanese were forced to pull back and leave the ridge to the Allies. Not that there was much left of it or the villages there – Kohima has been referred to as the Stalingrad of the East, and with good reason.

ABOVE: THE ROUGH TERRAIN of the Imphal region could in many places be crossed only on foot, and slowly at that. This severely restricted the offensive capabilities of both sides.

BELOW: WHERE THE TERRAIN was more open, light vehicles and tanks such as these Lee-Grants were able to operate. Lacking antitank weapons, the Japanese could do little about them.

ABOVE: COOPERATION BETWEEN BRITISH *and Indian formations allowed the Allies to go over to the offensive after the Imphal-Kohima road was reopened. Field conferences like this one were essential to maintain coordination.*

At the end of May, the Japanese pulled back from Kohima entirely. Many units broke up, straggling east and south in search of food. They were unable to play any further part in the campaign. Meanwhile, with the road now open, the British began to push through to Imphal.

THE ALLIES COUNTERATTACK AT IMPHAL

Japanese attacks on Imphal itself wound down by 1 May. A siege continued, but there was no longer any real chance of a successful assault. As the Japanese supply situation worsened, the Allies were re-supplied by airdrops at both Imphal and Kohima. This was a difficult and hazardous undertaking, especially at Kohima, but it enabled the Allies to establish superiority over their weakening opponents.

This took time due to poor weather and the stubbornness of the Japanese troops. Even desperately short of food and ammunition, they were difficult to shift from their positions. Although the Japanese commanders on the spot knew they could not win this battle, a final effort was ordered. A few reinforcements had arrived and these allowed the assault to achieve some limited success. Nevertheless by 22 June the road through to Kohima was opened and the siege was effectively over.

The Japanese divisions around Imphal were at the end of their tether and more or less ignored orders from above to make a new assault. Bowing to the inevitable, the order was given for a retreat and on 3 July the divisions began pulling back. Many of these formations were debilitated by disease and starvation and were able to do little more than shamble eastwards, leaving their remaining heavy equipment and artillery behind.

AFTERMATH

The ill-advised advance on Imphal was the turning point of the campaign. From then on the Japanese were on the defensive and were steadily pushed back. For the Allies, the dark days of shambolic retreat were long over and they returned to Burma confident that they could take on and beat the Imperial Japanese Army.

ABOVE: INDIAN TROOPS WAIT IN A CLEARING. *The thick vegetation was a serious obstacle to troop movements and tended to funnel units into predictable lines of advance.*

BATTLE OF IMPHAL AND KOHIMA

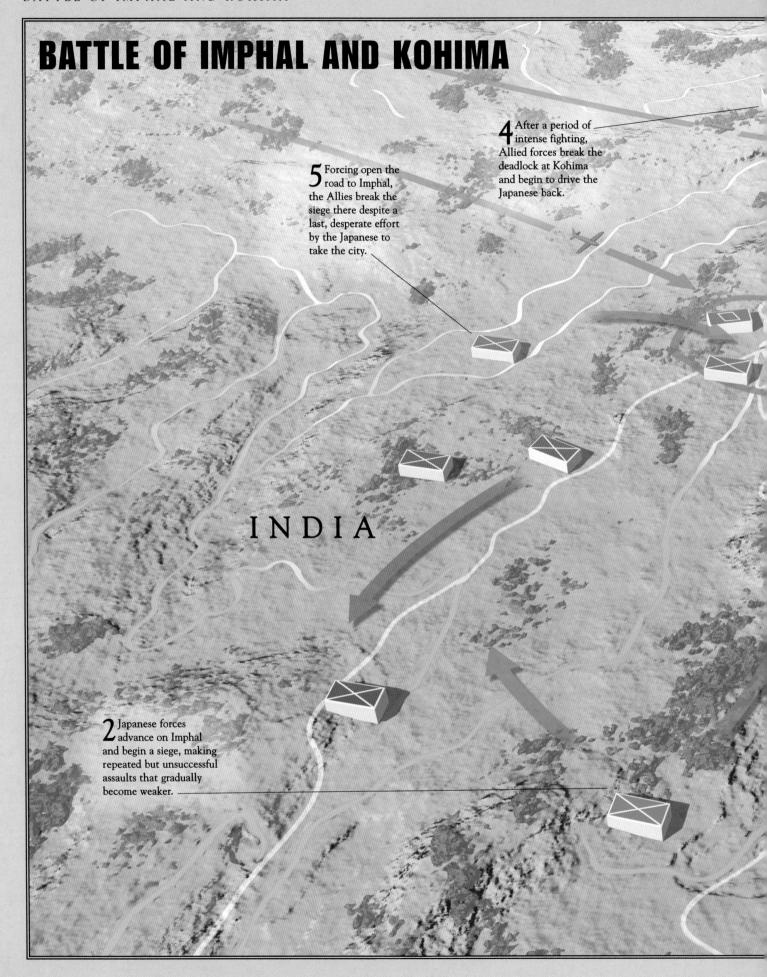

4 After a period of intense fighting, Allied forces break the deadlock at Kohima and begin to drive the Japanese back.

5 Forcing open the road to Imphal, the Allies break the siege there despite a last, desperate effort by the Japanese to take the city.

INDIA

2 Japanese forces advance on Imphal and begin a siege, making repeated but unsuccessful assaults that gradually become weaker.

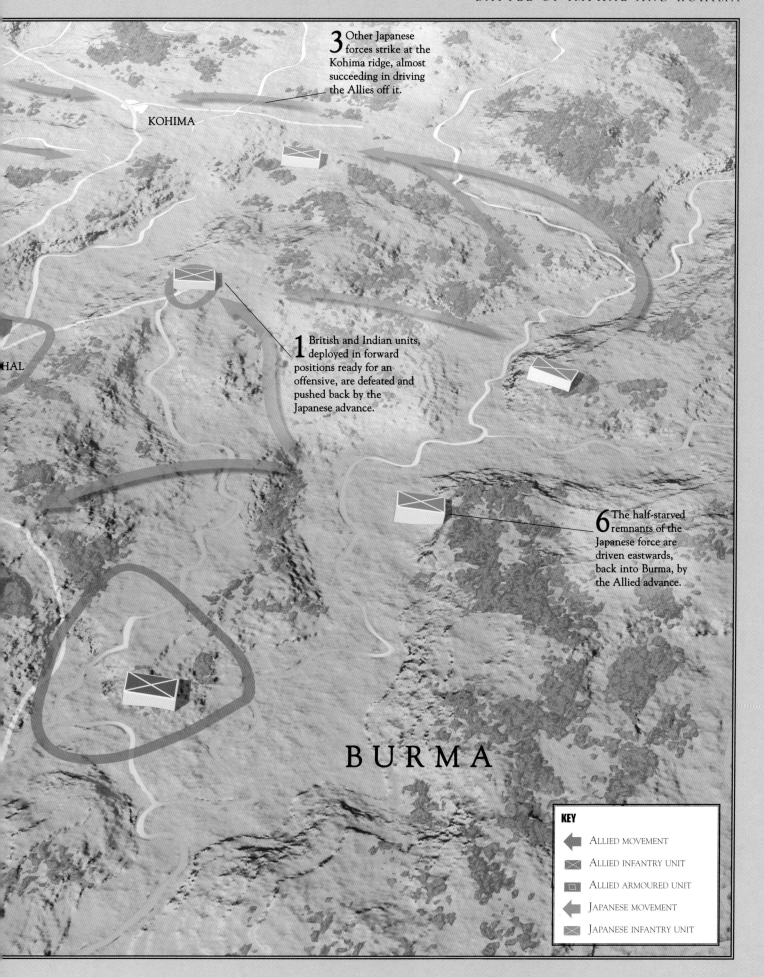

3 Other Japanese forces strike at the Kohima ridge, almost succeeding in driving the Allies off it.

KOHIMA

1 British and Indian units, deployed in forward positions ready for an offensive, are defeated and pushed back by the Japanese advance.

HAL

6 The half-starved remnants of the Japanese force are driven eastwards, back into Burma, by the Allied advance.

BURMA

KEY

←	ALLIED MOVEMENT
⊠	ALLIED INFANTRY UNIT
▱	ALLIED ARMOURED UNIT
←	JAPANESE MOVEMENT
⊠	JAPANESE INFANTRY UNIT

MONTE CASSINO 1944

The Battles of Monte Cassino between January and May 1944 represented something of an anomaly in the conduct of the war in Europe. In an unusually static period of warfare, the Allies took five months and four separate battles to break through the German Gustav Line, anchored around the position at Monte Cassino.

It cost the Allies – including the fighting at Anzio – 105,000 casualties and the Germans at least 80,000. Despite the breakthrough, the opportunity to destroy the Germans in Italy was missed and the slog up Italy would continue for another year.

Italy surrendered to the Allies on 8 September 1943. The British Eighth Army had already crossed the Straits of Messina five days before, and on 9 September the Fifth Army, a mixed US-British force, landed at Salerno. The near successes of the German counterattack against the Salerno beachhead

MONTE CASSINO FACTS

Who: II US Corps and II New Zealand Corps of General Mark Clark's (1896–1984) Fifth Army and subsequently General Oliver Leese's (1884–1978) British Eighth Army under overall command of General Harold Alexander (1891–1969) faced Lieutenant-General Fridolin von Senger und Etterlin's (1891–1963) XIV Panzer Corps.

What: A series of offensives against the Gustav Line, a German defensive line anchored around the imposing position of Monte Cassino.

Where: The area surrounding Monte Cassino and the nearby town, just over 100km (62 miles) south of Rome.

When: 24 January–18 May 1944

Why: Cassino controlled the mouth of the Liri Valley and thus the most straightforward route to Rome.

Outcome: Despite the efforts of Allied forces, the Germans held their position through the first three costly attritional battles, before the Gustav Line was finally broken across the front in May 1944.

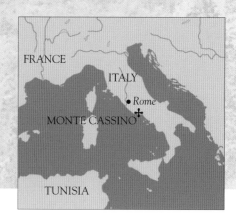

GERMAN PARATROOPERS OF *the 1ˢᵗ Paratroop Division man an MG 42 in the ruins of the monastery. The Allied bombing did little more than create even more defensible positions and legitimize the German occupation of the building.*

convinced Hitler to follow the advice of Field-Marshal Albert Kesselring (1885–1960) and resist the Allied advance as far south as possible. He also issued orders for the construction of the Gustav Line 160km (100 miles) south of Rome. This stretched from the Adriatic to the Tyrrhenian sea.

The key to the position was the entrance of the Liri valley, which offered the most obvious route to Rome. Monte Cassino dominated the approach, overlooking the rivers that crossed the mouth of the valley. The Germans built pillboxes and dugouts across the Liri, established positions in the surrounding mountains, fortified the town of Cassino and flooded the rivers. It was probably the most formidable defensive position in Europe.

ANZIO LANDINGS

Operation *Shingle*, a planned landing at Anzio behind the Gustav Line, forced the Fifth Army to push on to draw the German reserves from the Anzio area. General Mark Clark (1896–1984), the Fifth Army commander, launched the French Expeditionary Corps (FEC) against the German positions north of Cassino while the British X Corps

attempted to cross the river Garigliano to the west in mid-January. Neither operation was wholly successful, although they did draw the Germans south.

Then Clark committed US II Corps against the Cassino position. The 36th Division had two regiments destroyed trying to cross the Gari river between 20 and 22 January. The Anzio landings took place virtually unopposed on 22 January. Clark knew the Germans would throw everything available at the beachhead, so he committed his final division, the 34th Red Bull, north of Cassino to maintain the pressure. The 34th attacked on the night of 24 January. It took them three days to establish themselves in strength across the Rapido river.

On 29 January, the division pushed into the high ground behind the monastery and managed to secure a foothold in the outskirts of the town. It then inched its way across the Cassino massif before the attack petered out on 12 February. Despite the extraordinary efforts of the US infantry, the town and monastery remained in German hands. Aware

THE DOMINATING POSITION of the Monastery at Monte Cassino is clear in this photograph taken prior to the bombing of 15 February 1944. Castle Hill sits in front of the Monastery, while the town of Cassino nestles around its base.

that the Germans still intended to counterattack at Anzio, the Allies attacked again using II New Zealand Corps, made up of 2nd New Zealand and 4th Indian Divisions under Lieutenant-General Bernard Freyberg (1889–1963). The 4th Indian took over US 34th Division's positions, finding that the key piece of terrain, Point 593, had been retaken by the Germans. Much to the disgust of the divisional commander, Francis Tuker (1894–1967), Freyberg ordered a direct assault on the monastery.

Despite misgivings, the Allied commander in Italy, General Harold Alexander (1891–1969), authorized the bombing of the monastery. On the morning of 15 February, more than 250 bombers destroyed the abbey. However, due to an appalling lack of coordination, the lead formation of 4th Indian Division was unable to attack until the night of 16/17 February, 36 hours later, by which time German paratroopers had occupied the ruins. Despite strenuous efforts, 4th Indian Division failed to capture either Point 593 or the monastery over the next three days. On 17 February, the New Zealanders attacked the town from the east, managing to seize the railway station, but they were unable to advance further.

GERMAN COUNTERATTACK

Despite the efforts against Cassino, the Germans launched a massive attack on the Anzio beachhead. Still desperate to maintain pressure on the Gustav Line, Alexander ordered Freyberg to attack again. This time 4th Indian Division would attack the monastery on a slightly different axis,

ABOVE: THE ALMOST LUNAR appearance of the monastery after it had endured 309 tons of 227kg (500lb) bombs and incendiary bombs and 126 tons of 454kg (1000lb) bombs. It was the largest use of tactical airpower in the war to date.

RIGHT: A GERMAN 150MM (5.9IN) S-FH 18 artillery piece in action. Most German artillery at Cassino was located in the Liri Valley. As the Germans held most of the high ground, they could bring observed fire on the whole battlefield.

INDIAN SOLDIER

Soldiers of the British
Commonwealth rendered
outstanding service during
the Italian campaign.

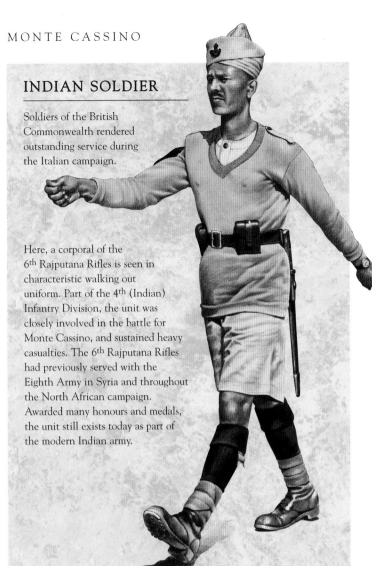

Here, a corporal of the
6th Rajputana Rifles is seen in
characteristic walking out
uniform. Part of the 4th (Indian)
Infantry Division, the unit was
closely involved in the battle for
Monte Cassino, and sustained heavy
casualties. The 6th Rajputana Rifles
had previously served with the
Eighth Army in Syria and throughout
the North African campaign.
Awarded many honours and medals,
the unit still exists today as part of
the modern Indian army.

above the town through Castle Hill, while the New
Zealanders attacked the town from the north. After air raids
and a massive bombardment, the two divisions attacked on
the morning of March 15 and managed to seize the railroad
station, but were unable to advance further.

Again the German paratroopers put up fierce resistance,
and even though the New Zealanders managed to clear most
of the town and 4th Indian Division took Castle and
Hangman's Hills, the Allies were not able to gain complete
control of Cassino or capture the monastery. Having
achieved very little, Freyberg called off the offensive.

EIGHTH ARMY TAKES OVER

As the weather improved, the Allies reorganized their
forces and Cassino became the responsibility of the Eighth
Army. Alexander's chief-of-staff, General John Harding
(1896–1989), was the driving force behind Operation
Diadem, the fourth battle of Cassino. He organized a
coordinated offensive across the front. In the west, US II
Corps would drive up the coastal plain toward Anzio, where
US VI Corps had been reinforced and was ready to break out
from the beachhead.

The FEC would attack through the Aurunci mountains
and break into the Liri valley behind the Gustav Line. The
British XIII Corps would attack up the mouth of the Liri with
Canadian I Corps ready to exploit up the valley. The Polish

*US ARTILLERY MEN demonstrating a massive 240mm (9.5in) M-1 Howitzer
to British troops. The largest piece of field artillery in the US armoury, the
M-1 was also used by the British Eighth Army at Cassino.*

RIGHT: A NORTH AFRICAN GOUMIER of the 2nd Moroccan Division of the French Expeditionary Corps. The achievements of these formidable troops in the Aurunci mountains were critical to Allied success in the fourth battle.

II Corps would attack Cassino, while British X Corps would conduct minor operations north of the town.

MONASTERY CAPTURED

Diadem opened at 11.00 p.m. on 11 May. The main thrust up the Liri by XIII Corps made slow progress, as did US II Corps on the coast. The French, however, achieved excellent results, threatening to turn the German flank.

The Poles took terrible losses up on the Cassino massif, but managed to seize Point 593 and the high ground around the monastery by 17 May. The Poles entered the abbey the following day to find it abandoned.

Threatened by Allied success in the valley, the Germans withdrew north. Alexander ordered VI Corps to break out of Anzio and cut off the German retreat. The German Tenth Army faced being trapped and destroyed. However, in an act of gross insubordination and military stupidity, Clark countermanded Alexander's order and turned US VI Corps towards Rome, which fell to him on 4 June. Much to his astonishment, Kesselring was able to extricate his forces and regroup on a defensive line north of Rome. The chance for a decisive victory had been lost.

The conduct of the Allied offensives round Cassino was uninspired and costly, but the vulnerability of the Anzio beachhead and the psychological importance of the monastery necessitated action. The chance to redeem the campaign was lost with Clark's vainglorious decision to capture Rome rather than defeat the enemy.

BELOW: ALLIED TRAFFIC MOVES through the town of Cassino in the aftermath of the fourth battle. The ravages of four months of bitter fighting are evident.

MONTE CASSINO

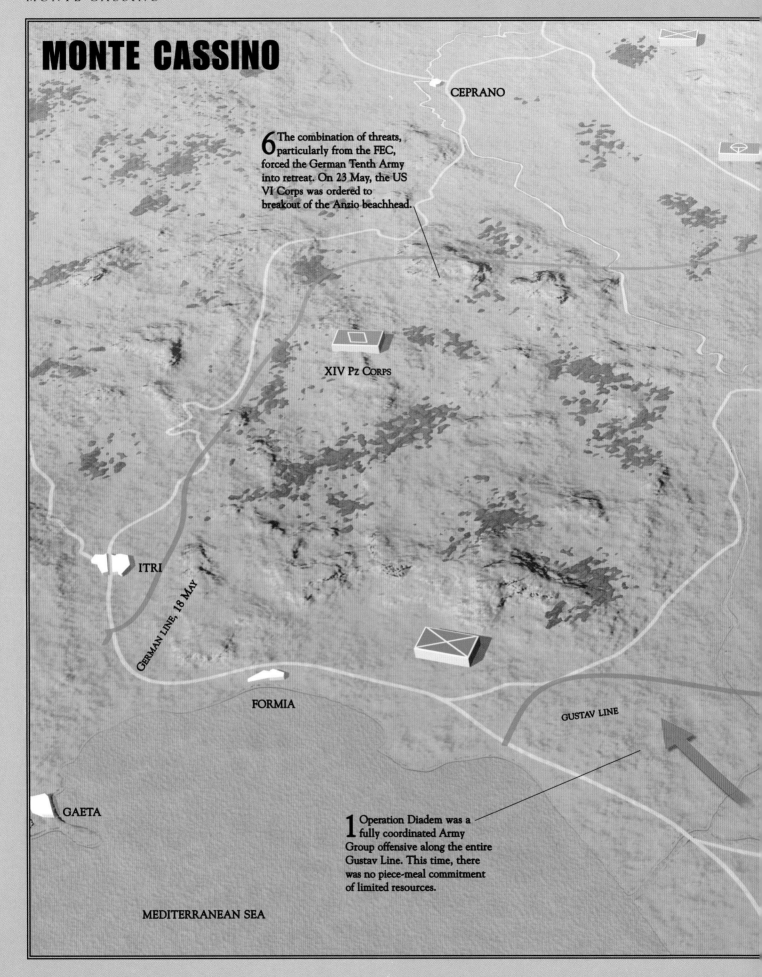

CEPRANO

6 The combination of threats, particularly from the FEC, forced the German Tenth Army into retreat. On 23 May, the US VI Corps was ordered to breakout of the Anzio beachhead.

XIV Pz Corps

ITRI

GERMAN LINE, 18 MAY

FORMIA

GUSTAV LINE

GAETA

1 Operation Diadem was a fully coordinated Army Group offensive along the entire Gustav Line. This time, there was no piece-meal commitment of limited resources.

MEDITERRANEAN SEA

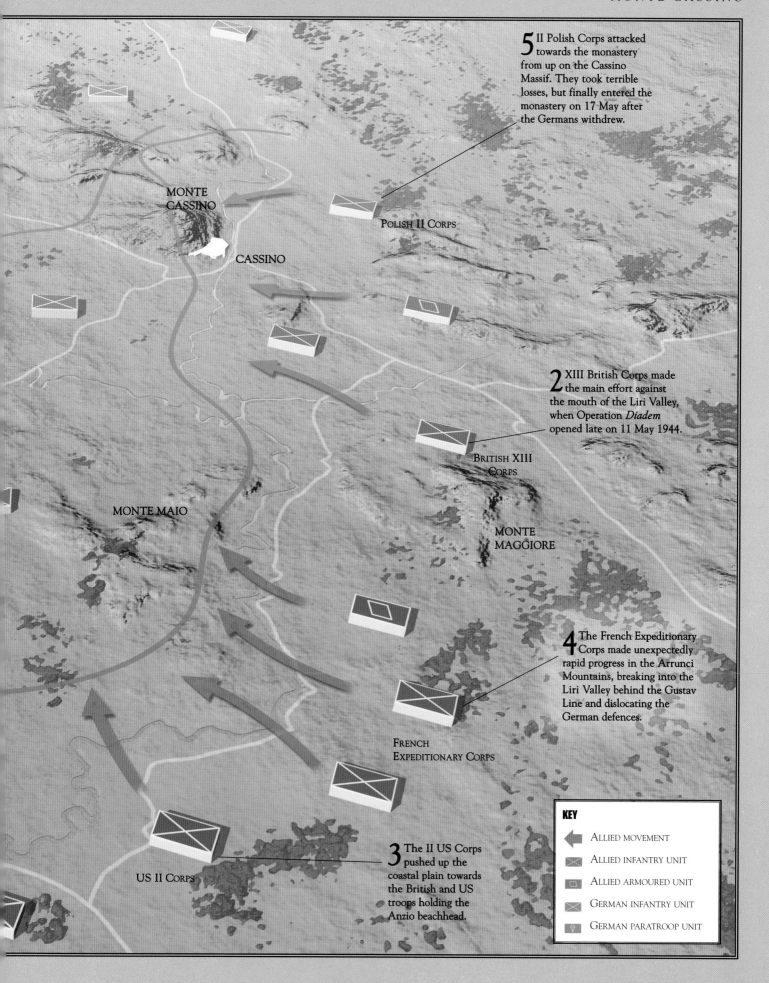

5 II Polish Corps attacked towards the monastery from up on the Cassino Massif. They took terrible losses, but finally entered the monastery on 17 May after the Germans withdrew.

POLISH II CORPS

MONTE CASSINO

CASSINO

2 XIII British Corps made the main effort against the mouth of the Liri Valley, when Operation *Diadem* opened late on 11 May 1944.

BRITISH XIII CORPS

MONTE MAIO

MONTE MAGGIORE

4 The French Expeditionary Corps made unexpectedly rapid progress in the Arrunci Mountains, breaking into the Liri Valley behind the Gustav Line and dislocating the German defences.

FRENCH EXPEDITIONARY CORPS

3 The II US Corps pushed up the coastal plain towards the British and US troops holding the Anzio beachhead.

US II CORPS

KEY

← ALLIED MOVEMENT

ALLIED INFANTRY UNIT

ALLIED ARMOURED UNIT

GERMAN INFANTRY UNIT

GERMAN PARATROOP UNIT

ALLIED VICTORY

Despite the tipping of the balance against the Axis countries, the nature of the regimes meant that they would fight to the bitter end. Thus the Allies had to fight their way across Europe and the Pacific towards the heartlands of Germany and Japan.

Although there were great and impressive military achievements from the Allies, such as the Normandy landings in June 1944 and the Soviet summer offensive the same year, the determination and remarkable resilience of the German and Japanese forces meant that the final campaigns would be extremely hard fought. Bitter defensive battles were fought at Monte Cassino and Iwo Jima, and the Allies suffered setbacks with the failed airborne operation at Arnhem in the autumn of 1944 and the surprise German offensive in the Ardennes in December of the same year. The final battles, for the island of Okinawa and the city of Berlin, proved costly outcomes to the most bloody war in world history.

THE END OF THE REICH: *as Soviet IS-2 tanks rumble along a Berlin street, refugees emerge from the cellars of gutted buildings, carrying their belongings with them. This photograph was taken in late April 1945, just days before the surrender of Germany.*

NORMANDY LANDINGS 1944

D-Day – the Allied landings on the Normandy coast of German-occupied France 6 June 1944 – was one of the most climactic days of World War II. Ever since 1943, the Western Allies had prepared for this operation, codenamed Neptune/Overlord. On D-Day, the Allies landed 160,000 US, British and Canadian forces (plus a small French contingent) to establish beachheads in Normandy.

With the 'Second Front' successfully established, the German Reich would subsequently find itself locked into a three-front war of attrition that would eventually overwhelm it. As Supreme Allied Commander, the US General Dwight 'Ike' Eisenhower (1890–1969) exercised overall control over the

NORMANDY LANDINGS FACTS

Who: Supreme Allied Commander General Dwight Eisenhower (1890–1969) commanded the US, British and Canadian forces of General Bernard Montgomery's (1887–1976) Twenty-First Army Group, which faced Field Marshal Erwin Rommel's (1891–1944) Army Group B.

What : The largest amphibious operation in history, marking the Western Allies return to North West Europe.

Where: The Baie de la Seine in Normandy, France.

When: 6 June 1944

Why: The British and Americans had long intended to return to Northern Europe, and

Normandy provided suitable beaches within range of land-based air cover.

Outcome: The Allies successfully established themselves ashore, thus opening the Second Front and marking a crucial turning point in the war.

BRITISH INFANTRY *gather on Sword Beach in preparation for the push inland. British troops were meant to push on to the strategically important town of Caen in the first day, and did make significant inroads.*

invasion while below him came the three British service chiefs: Admiral Bertram Ramsay (1883–1945), Air Chief Marshal Trafford Leigh-Mallory (1892–1944), and General Bernard Montgomery (1887–1976). Field-Marshal Erwin Rommel's (1891–1944) Army Group B controlled the German forces that opposed the D-Day landings.

NAVAL ARMADA

The D-Day plan began with the night-time passage across the Channel of a naval armada laden with Allied troops, to anchor opposite the five designated invasion beaches: in the east, the three Anglo-Canadian sectors – 'Sword', 'Juno' and 'Gold' and in the west the two US beaches, 'Omaha' and 'Utah'. Shortly before this, three Allied airborne divisions would land to secure the invasion's eastern and western flanks. Finally, after heavy aerial and naval bombardments, the assault forces would land on these five beaches. After these initial assaults had established small beachheads, follow-up forces would advance inland so that by the end of D-Day Allied forces would have captured Bayeux and consolidated the four eastern beachheads and the British airborne zone into a single salient.

BAD WEATHER

D-Day was slated to begin on 5 June, but bad weather forced Eisenhower to postpone the invasion. It nevertheless went ahead on the 6th despite the continuing rough seas. However, the launching of the invasion in bad weather enabled the Allies to surprise the Germans, whose slow

A PRIEST ADMINISTERS a blessing to US sailors and soldiers on 4 June 1944. Operation Overlord was scheduled to begin on 5 June, but was delayed by bad weather.

reactions let slip their best chance of defeating the invaders. On 5 June, 6939 vessels assembled off the coast of southern England and that evening headed south towards the Normandy coast. Next, from 11.30 p.m., 1100 Allied transport planes transported 17,000 airborne troops to Normandy. In the early hours of 6 June, British airborne forces landed northeast of Caen and seized key locations to protect the invasion's eastern flank. Simultaneously two US airborne divisions landed in the marshes behind 'Utah' to delay German ripostes against the invasion's western flank.

While local German forces concluded that these airborne landings were the start of the invasion, higher German authorities remained convinced that they were a diversion prior to the main Allied attack in the Pas de Calais. As these airborne operations unfolded, the naval armada weighed anchor off the Normandy coast. As dawn approached, the Allies commenced naval and aerial bombardments of the German coastal defences.

BEACH ASSAULTS

Next, between 6.30 a.m. and 7.45 a.m, the Allied amphibious assaults commenced on the five designated beaches. At the eastern beach, 'Sword', the British 3rd Division commenced its assault at 7.15 a.m.; here the assault force, as at the other beaches, comprised a combination of infantry, commando and specialized armoured units. Over

SHERMAN 'FLAIL' TANK

The Sherman Crab was one of a number of specialized armoured vehicles used during the D-Day landings. The Crab mounted a flail – a set of heavy chains suspended on a rotating drum in front of the tank – that was used to clear a path through a minefield. The method was first used, aboard a Matilda tank, at El Alamein. The Crab, mounted on the standard Allied medium tank the M4 Sherman, could clear a lane about 3.3m (11 ft) wide at the speed of 2km/h (1.2mph). The chains would need replacing after several detonations.

the next two hours, the British forces fought their way off the beach and captured the fiercely defended German strongpoint at La Brèche. Meanwhile, other Allied units fought their way east into the fringes of Ouistreham and advanced 3.2km (2 miles) inland to capture Hermanville. All morning, follow-up forces landed on 'Sword' beach, which became increasingly narrow as the tide rose. The resulting traffic jam prevented the supporting armour from moving inland, but eventually the British spearheads renewed their drive inland despite this lack of armour.

FOUR PATHFINDER OFFICERS of British 6th Airborne Division synchronize their watches in front of a Dakota C-47, before take-off at RAF Harwell.

169

LEFT: AMERICAN TROOPS *from the 1st Infantry Division, the 'Big Red One', board landing craft in preparation for Normandy landings.*

Meanwhile, at 7.45 a.m., 3rd Canadian Infantry Division commenced its assault on 'Juno'. In the face of fierce enemy resistance, it took over two hours to secure the first exits from the beach. Over the rest of the morning, British and Canadian units advanced through St-Aubin and Courseulles to create a defensive line 6.4km (4 miles) inland. Further west, the British 50th (Northumbrian) Infantry Division had commenced its assault on 'Gold' at 7.30 a.m. Here the preliminary bombardments suppressed German resistance and thus the spearheads established an initial beachhead despite their lack of armour, delayed by the heavy seas.

On the western flank, however, the German strongpoint of le Hamel had escaped much of the recent bombardment. British forces battled for many hours against intense enemy resistance to capture le Hamel. While this action raged, other British units both pushed inland and drove 6.4km (4 miles) west to seize Port-en-Bessin, narrowing the 14.5km (9-mile) gap that existed between 'Gold' and 'Omaha'.

BLOOD BATH AT OMAHA BEACH

The assault of 1st and 29th US Infantry Divisions on 'Omaha' commenced at 6.30 a.m. Even before this time, things had gone awry, with the fire support proving less effective than planned. The heavily loaded infantry that managed to struggle through the neck-high water to the shore then encountered murderous enemy fire that inflicted terrible casualties; Allied intelligence had failed to detect the recent

BELOW: THE SCALE OF OPERATION OVERLORD is clear here in this picture of beached landing craft and supply ships on Omaha Beach in the aftermath of the fighting.

ABOVE: WOUNDED MEN OF the US 3rd battalion, 16th Infantry Regiment pause to smoke and eat after capturing Omaha Beach on 6 June 1944.

reinforcement of the German defences here. Throughout the morning, US troops strove to fight their way off the beach and into the bluffs beyond, yet by midday the US foothold on enemy-occupied soil still remained precarious.

THE OTHER BEACHES

This stood in stark contrast to the less costly assault mounted at 'Utah', located along the southeast corner of the Cotentin Peninsula. Here, at 6.30 a.m., the 4th US Infantry Division commenced its assault after accurate naval gunfire had smashed the relatively weak German defences; the enemy believed that the marshes located behind 'Utah' would persuade the Allies not to land there. In the face of moderate resistance, the Americans soon advanced inland to close with the perimeter held by the US airborne forces.

Over the rest of D-Day, the Allies advanced further inland from these seven separate amphibious/airborne assaults, to create four larger beachheads. In the west, British units linked up with the airborne forces located east of the Orne. However, a German armoured counterattack north prevented the forces landed at 'Sword' from linking up with those landed on 'Juno'. Meanwhile, in the latter sector Canadian forces had linked up with British forces landed on 'Gold'. Further west at 'Omaha', US forces had secured a tenuous 1.6km (1-mile) deep foothold on French soil but at

the price of more than 2000 casualties, while at 'Utah' US forces had linked up with their airborne comrades.

By midnight on 6 June 1944, the 159,000 Allied troops ashore had established four sizable beachheads. While the Allied invasion front remained vulnerable to German counterattack, D-Day's success now made it virtually impossible for the enemy to throw the invaders back into the sea. The establishment of the 'Second Front' on 6 June 1944 represented a crucial step forward on the Allied march to victory over Nazi Germany, which was finally realized on 8 May 1945.

RIGHT: A PARATROOPER SERGEANT of US 101st Airborne Division. He carries .30 M1A1 Carbine with a folding stock, a weapon specifically designed for paratroopers.

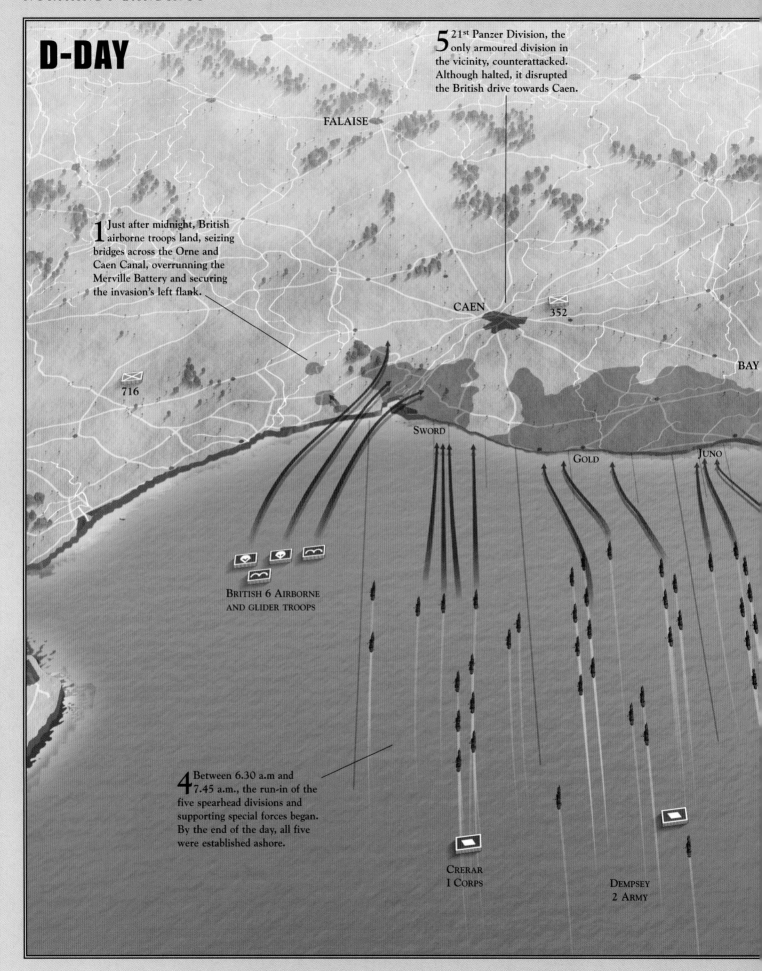

D-DAY

5 21st Panzer Division, the only armoured division in the vicinity, counterattacked. Although halted, it disrupted the British drive towards Caen.

FALAISE

1 Just after midnight, British airborne troops land, seizing bridges across the Orne and Caen Canal, overrunning the Merville Battery and securing the invasion's left flank.

CAEN

352

716

BAY

SWORD

GOLD

JUNO

BRITISH 6 AIRBORNE AND GLIDER TROOPS

4 Between 6.30 a.m and 7.45 a.m., the run-in of the five spearhead divisions and supporting special forces began. By the end of the day, all five were established ashore.

CRERAR
I CORPS

DEMPSEY
2 ARMY

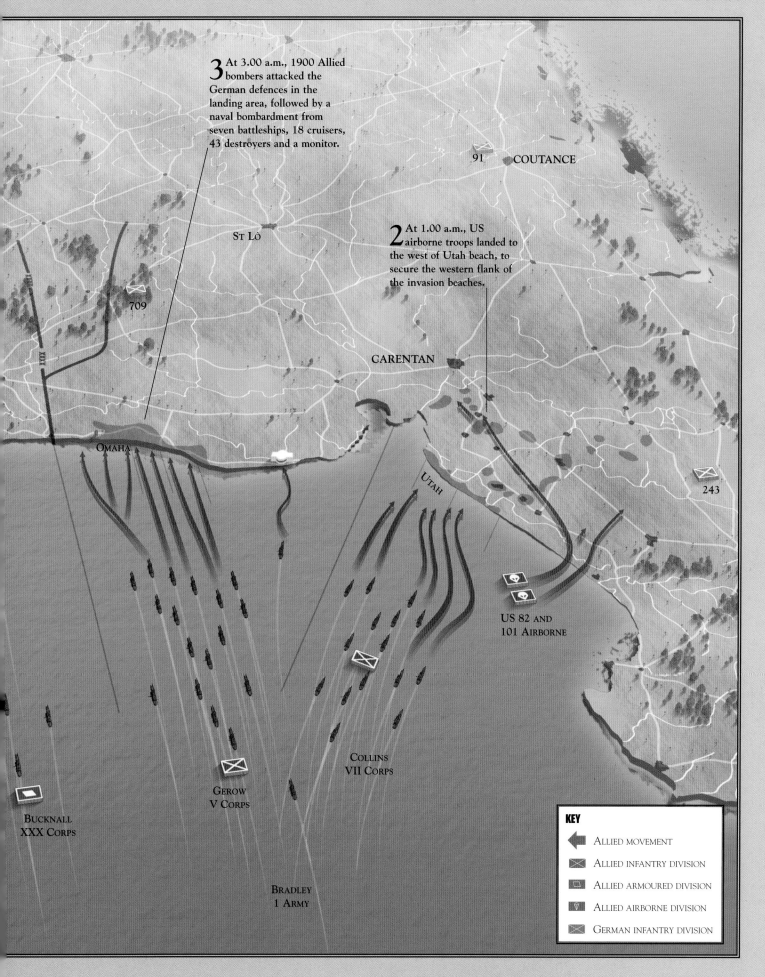

3 At 3.00 a.m., 1900 Allied bombers attacked the German defences in the landing area, followed by a naval bombardment from seven battleships, 18 cruisers, 43 destroyers and a monitor.

2 At 1.00 a.m., US airborne troops landed to the west of Utah beach, to secure the western flank of the invasion beaches.

91   COUTANCE

St Lô

709

CARENTAN

243

OMAHA

UTAH

US 82 AND
101 AIRBORNE

COLLINS
VII CORPS

GEROW
V CORPS

BUCKNALL
XXX CORPS

BRADLEY
1 ARMY

KEY

⬅ ALLIED MOVEMENT

⊠ ALLIED INFANTRY DIVISION

▭ ALLIED ARMOURED DIVISION

▯ ALLIED AIRBORNE DIVISION

⊠ GERMAN INFANTRY DIVISION

BREAKOUT FROM NORMANDY

1944

During late July and August 1944, the Western Allies successfully broke the stalemate that had emerged in the Battle for Normandy and subsequently translated this into a decisive strategic victory that saw the German forces expelled from the region.

The development of such a stalemate was far removed from Allied plans. Their expectations were that once the D-Day landings had established a beachhead subsequent operations would quickly force the Germans to withdraw behind the river Seine, where the decisive battle would ensue. Hitler, however, ordered his forces to prevent the Allies advancing inland, forcing the latter Allies to mount continual attacks against fierce resistance that turned the campaign into a bitter six-week attritional struggle.

BREAKOUT FROM NORMANDY FACTS

Who: Twenty-First Army Group and from 1 August 1944 US Twelfth Army Group commanded by Lieutenant-General Omar Bradley (1893–1981) under land commander General Bernard Montgomery faced Field Marshal Günther von Kluge (1882–1944) until 18 August, then field Marshal Walther Model's (1891–1945) Army Group B.

What: A series of Allied offensives that finally cracked the German line in Normandy and allowed the Allied forces to break out of the bridgehead.

Where: Normandy, France

When: 25 July–30 August 1944

Why: Rather than withdraw to behind the River Seine once the Allies established

their beachhead, German forces were ordered to hold their ground by Hitler, leading to a six-week attritional struggle.

Outcome: The German position in Normandy was broken and the Allies crossed the Seine, liberated Paris on 25 August and embarked on a rapid advance westwards across France towards Germany. It was a decisive strategic victory.

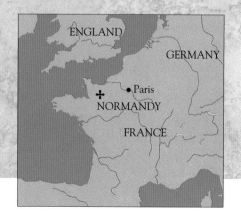

BRITISH MEDICS recover a wounded comrade and carry him to a Jeep, somewhere in Normandy, July 1944.

A BRITISH SECTION MOVES up a sunken lane in Normandy. The close nature of the Normandy bocage is well illustrated here.

These grinding battles began to bear fruit in mid-July as Allied numerical superiority wore down the Germans. In mid-July, General Bernard Montgomery (1887–1976) launched Operation *Goodwood*, an armoured assault to outflank Caen from the east. While the operation failed to achieve its objectives, it did facilitate the success of the subsequent US offensive – Operation *Cobra* – initiated on 25 July. To sustain their fierce defensive stands against *Goodwood*, the Germans had to divert most of their logistical supplies to the eastern sector of the front. Consequently, the German forces defending the Saint-Lô front were starved of vital logistical supplies just prior to *Cobra*, and their ensuing shortages of fuel and ammunition made it easier for the Americans to secure success.

WAR OF ATTRITION

On 25 July, General Omar Bradley's (1893–1981) First US Army initiated *Cobra*, a massed break-in operation preceded by massive aerial and artillery bombardments. Once these infantry forces had torn a hole in the German line, the Americans aimed to insert three mobile divisions that would advance through the enemy's rear areas to the coast near Coutances, thus cutting off sizable enemy forces. The heavy bombing strike so weakened the defending German forces that VII US Corps drove forwards 3.2km (2 miles) during that first day. Over the

next 48 hours, US audacity turned this break-in into a decisive breakout by securing a 27.4km (17-mile) advance. By 29 July, the Americans had ripped asunder the German front and so Bradley now widened the scope of *Cobra*. Between 29 and 31 July, US forces crossed the Sélune river at Pontaubault, thus rounding the base of the Cotentin peninsula and opening the gateway for further advances west into Brittany, south towards the Loire and east towards the Seine.

On 30 July, to widen this breach, Montgomery launched an improvised British offensive from Caumont towards Vire, codenamed *Bluecoat*. By 1 August, therefore, the grinding attritional battle of Normandy had been transformed by *Cobra* into a rapid campaign of mobile warfare. The growing US influence on the campaign was now underscored when Bradley's Twelfth US Army Group became operational and assumed command of the First Army and General George Patton's (1885–1945) Third Army.

GERMAN COUNTERATTACK

On 2 August, Hitler reacted to the US breakout by attempting to stuff the genie back into the bottle: he ordered Army Group B to mount a hasty counterattack against the

weak western flank of the breakout. By retaking Avranches, this would isolate the US forces located south of the penetration. During the night 6/7 August, a hastily assembled mobile force attacked down the narrow corridor between the Sée and Sélune rivers towards Mortain. Unsurprisingly, after some initial success this German riposte was halted. This failure now presented the Allies with a strategic opportunity to encircle and destroy the German forces in Normandy, either in the Argentan–Falaise area or via a larger envelopment along the Seine.

In early August, US forces were surging west against feeble enemy resistance, thus outflanking the still cohesive German line against the British around Caen. With this deep US advance into their rear areas, the only feasible German strategy was to withdraw behind the river Seine – but Hitler insisted that his forces stood and fought where they were.

ADVANCE TO FALAISE

By early August, given the scale of recent US success, it had become crucial for the British and Canadian forces bogged down near Caen to advance south towards Falaise. This

LEFT: A TIGER TANK *of the SS Schwere Panzerabteilung* 101 *moves through a Normandy town on 10 June 1944.*

BELOW: A US INFANTRY SECTION *lies prone on the edge of field. The time of year meant that the corn in Normandy was often chest high.*

ABOVE: A MIXTURE OF *jubilant American GIs and French civilians aboard what appears to be a tracked German AFV.*

advance would assist the British attacks being executed further west to widen the breach in the enemy lines created by *Cobra*. Thus between 7 and 8 August General Guy Simonds' (1903–1974) II Canadian Corps commenced Operation *Totalize*, its drive on Falaise. By using a novel night-infiltration attack, supported by strategic bombers, *Totalize* secured significant initial success. However, determined German resistance slowed Simonds' armour and so on 11 August he halted the attack.

Meanwhile, between 8 and 13 August US forces had raced northwest deep into the German rear to reach Alençon, just 32km (20 miles) away from Simonds' spearheads. If the two forces could link up in the Falaise–Argentan area, the German Seventh Army would be caught in a huge pocket. This led Simonds on 14 August to mount an improvised offensive towards Falaise, codenamed *Tractable*. On 15 August, however, bitter German resistance stymied Simonds' advance before it could secure the key high ground north of Falaise.

SEINE BRIDGEHEAD

But by then the Americans had halted their advance north from Alençon, partly due to supply shortages and fears about friendly fire from Simonds' forces. Instead, Bradley divided his forces and directed US V Corps to race eastwards to the Seine. Incredibly, by 19 August, this corps had secured a

bridgehead across the Seine at Mantes-Gassicourt. Despite the US halt at Alençon, the Falaise pocket was nevertheless well-formed by 16 August with the Germans holding just a precarious 16km (10-mile) wide neck around Trun.

FALAISE BREAKOUT

Between 16 and 19 August, Simonds' armour thrust southeast towards Trun and linked up with the Americans to close the pocket. This weak Allied blocking position could not withstand the ensuing German breakout, for as the battered remnants of Seventh Army desperately fought their way out of the pocket through these blocking positions, SS armour also attacked the latter from outside the pocket. These attacks enabled some 40,000 German troops to escape, albeit without their heavy equipment. With Seventh Army no longer cohesive and with the Americans racing into the interior of France, the Germans now had no choice but to withdraw back to the Seine.

Even before the Falaise pocket had been closed, Montgomery had initiated his own offensive towards the Seine, reflecting his desire to enact the 'long' rather than 'short' envelopment. By 21 August, four corps had struck northeast towards the Upper Seine north of Paris, seeking to

ABOVE: A FRENCH RESISTANCE *fighter armed with a sten submachine gun and an American officer crouch behind a car during a gun fight in a French city.*

catch up with the US advance. However, between 21 and 30 August, the battered remnants of Army Group B mounted a controlled withdrawal back to the northern bank of the Seine. At Vernon on 26 August, the first British bridgehead was established across the river. Just four days later, all German resistance south of the Upper Seine had ceased and with this the Normandy campaign ended. By this

ON 20 JUNE 1944, US troops pause for a break outside a small French café during their advance inland.

juncture, Paris had fallen and the Americans had raced north beyond the Seine and east into the interior of France. The Allies had won the Battle of Normandy and now their thoughts turned to advancing into the German Reich itself.

TIGERS IN NORMANDY

The PzKpfw VI Tiger Mark I heavy tank entered service in late 1942. The appearance of the Soviet T-34 spurred the production of the Tiger, mounting the formidable 88mm (3.46in) gun and extremely thick armour. It was automotively less impressive.

Nonetheless the Tiger – deployed in heavy tank battalions at the corps and army level – was the scourge of Allied tank crews in Normandy. It could deal with any of the British and US tanks deployed and was virtually invulnerable to the Sherman's 75mm (2.95in) gun from the front. It achieved massive tactical success on occasion, but there were never enough available to make a difference.

BREAKOUT FROM NORMANDY

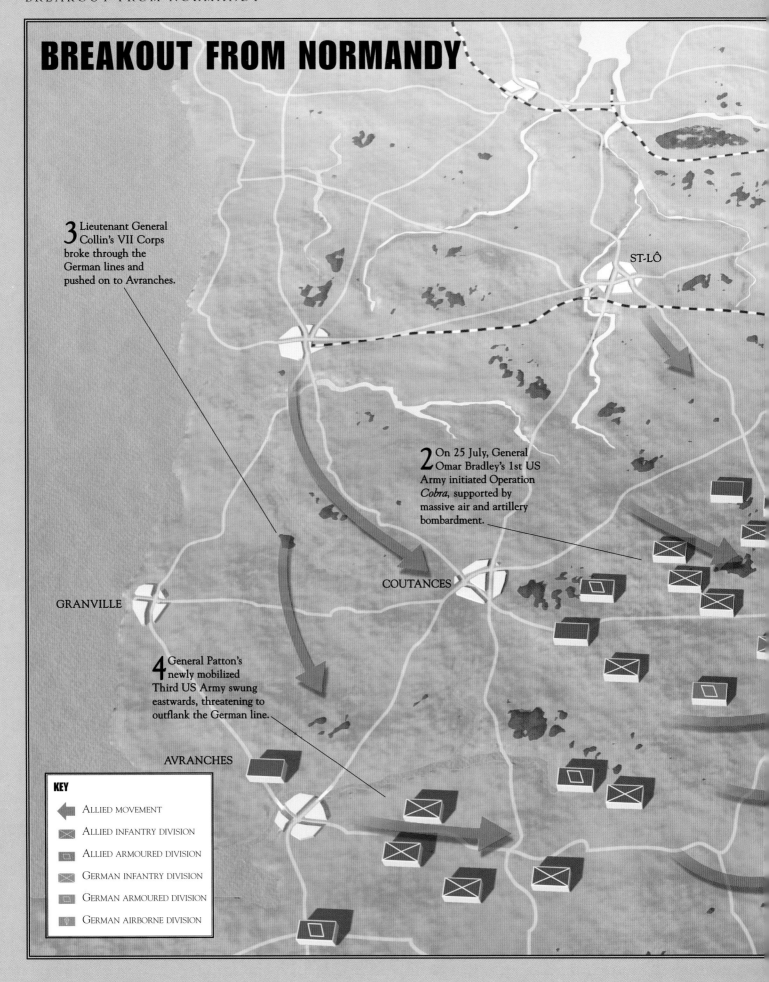

3 Lieutenant General Collin's VII Corps broke through the German lines and pushed on to Avranches.

ST-LÔ

2 On 25 July, General Omar Bradley's 1st US Army initiated Operation *Cobra*, supported by massive air and artillery bombardment.

COUTANCES

GRANVILLE

4 General Patton's newly mobilized Third US Army swung eastwards, threatening to outflank the German line.

AVRANCHES

KEY

ALLIED MOVEMENT

ALLIED INFANTRY DIVISION

ALLIED ARMOURED DIVISION

GERMAN INFANTRY DIVISION

GERMAN ARMOURED DIVISION

GERMAN AIRBORNE DIVISION

BAYEUX

CAEN

FALAISE

5 Hitler ordered a counterattack against Mortain, which opened on 7 August. It did little more than push the remaining German armour deeper into the pocket now forming.

6 The US forces made rapid progress to the south and finally linked up with British and Canadian forces on 19 August, sealing the Falaise pocket at last.

PHILIPPINE SEA 1944

Rising like the mythical phoenix from the devastation of Pearl Harbor, the United States Navy had become a veritable juggernaut by the spring of 1944. In support of amphibious operations which had wrested key bases and outposts from the Japanese in the Gilbert and Marshall Islands, the US Pacific Fleet was poised to accomplish another primary mission – the destruction of the Imperial Japanese Navy.

During 30 months of fighting, the grand strategy for victory in the Pacific – Island Hopping – had carried the US armed forces across vast expanses of ocean. On 15 June 1944, amphibious landings were conducted on the island of Saipan in the Marianas, an archipelago that lay in the path of the American advance toward the Philippines. The capture of Saipan, along with the islands of Guam and Tinian, would disrupt Japanese supply efforts to the far reaches of the Empire while providing bases from which long-range US bombers could regularly attack the Japanese home islands.

PHILIPPINE SEA: FACTS

Who: Admiral Soemu Toyoda (1885–1957), commander of the Japanese Combined Fleet, and Admiral Jisaburo Ozawa (1886–1966), commander of the First Mobile Fleet, versus Admiral Raymond Spruance (1886–1969), commander of the US Fifth Fleet and Admiral Marc Mitscher (1887–1947), commander of Task Force 58.

What: The Japanese committed the majority of their air power against the US fleet.

Where: The Philippine Sea in the Central Pacific.

When: 19–20 June 1944

Why: The Japanese hoped to stem the tide of the US advance across the Pacific.

Outcome: A decisive victory for the US Navy resulted in the virtual annihilation of Japanese carrier air power.

A DAMAGED US NAVY Curtiss SB2C Helldiver dive bomber is inspected by officers and crewmen on the flight deck of an aircraft carrier. The Helldiver replaced the ageing Douglas SBD Dauntless.

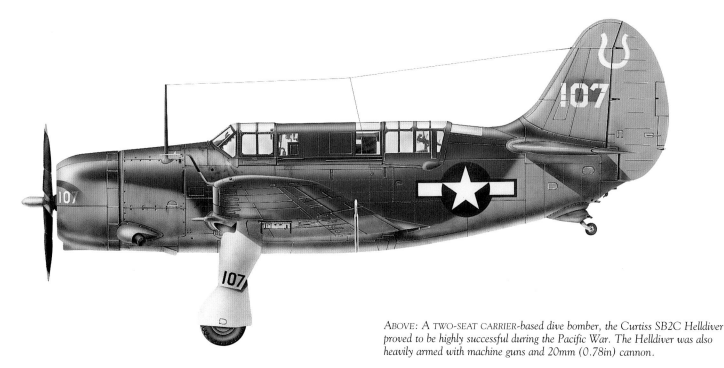

ABOVE: *A* TWO-SEAT CARRIER-*based dive bomber, the Curtiss SB2C Helldiver proved to be highly successful during the Pacific War. The Helldiver was also heavily armed with machine guns and 20mm (0.78in) cannon.*

ABOVE: ADMIRAL CHESTER W. NIMITZ *served as the US Navy Commander-in-Chief in the Pacific. Nimitz assumed command days after Pearl Harbor and led the revitalized fighting force to victory.*

Anticipating dire consequences if the Americans succeeded, Admiral Soemu Toyoda (1885–1957), Commander-in-Chief of the Japanese Combined Fleet, set in motion operation A-Go, a desperate gambit. Toyoda dispatched Admiral Jisaburo Ozawa (1886–1966) and the First Mobile Fleet to the waters of the Philippine Sea to confront the US naval armada, which was screening the Saipan invasion force and fully expecting such a response from the Japanese.

Ozawa hoped to utilize the one advantage his aircraft still possessed, that of greater range than the American planes, and to leverage land-based air power in the Philippines and surrounding islands to hit the Americans decisively before they could bring their overwhelming superiority to bear. Under his command was a still potentially lethal assemblage of five fleet and four light aircraft carriers, five battleships, 11 heavy cruisers, two light cruisers, 28 destroyers and more than 500 aircraft. The force included the super battleships *Yamato* and *Musashi*, each displacing 71,400 tonnes (78705 tons), the largest warships of their kind ever built.

Admiral Raymond Spruance (1886–1969), commander of the US Fifth Fleet, was in overall command of a striking force built around the core of Task Force 58, led by Admiral Marc Mitscher (1887–1947). Organized into four battle groups, Task Force 58 included a complement of seven large fleet carriers, eight light carriers, seven battleships, 21 cruisers, 69 destroyers and nearly 1000 aircraft.

Although the US naval contingent was quite capable of potent offensive action, Spruance realized that his mission was twofold. Not only was he to engage the Japanese when and where practical but he was also charged with protecting the Saipan invasion beaches and support shipping. Therefore he determined to conduct a defensive operation rather than concentrate wholly on annihilating Ozawa.

In retrospect, Ozawa's effort appears doomed from the start. Warned by Naval Intelligence and a cordon of picket submarines that the Japanese were on the move, Spruance was well prepared for the coming engagement. He did not have long to wait.

TURKEY SHOOT

On the morning of 19 June 1944, Ozawa launched 69 planes against the Americans, 45 of which were soon shot down. A follow-up strike of 127 planes met a similar fate, 98 of them splashing into the sea under the guns of US Grumman F6F Hellcat fighters. During four raids against Task Force 58, the Japanese managed to inflict only slight damage on one US carrier and two battleships. The slaughter of planes and pilots was so thoroughly one-sided that the action came to be known as the 'Great Marianas Turkey Shoot'. In effect, Spruance was allowing what remained of Japan's carrier air power to dash itself against the rocks of his formidable air defences.

Compounding Ozawa's troubles, the newest aircraft carrier in the Japanese fleet and the admiral's flagship, *Taiho*, was struck by a torpedo from the submarine USS *Albacore* on 19 June. The damage had not been fatal, but early in the afternoon a young officer ordered the ship's ventilation system to be turned on to clear fumes from ruptured fuel lines, and the *Taiho* quickly became a floating bomb. A spark ignited the fumes, causing a catastrophic explosion, and the carrier slid beneath the waves within an hour. Furthermore, just after noon the submarine USS *Cavalla* slammed three torpedoes into the aircraft carrier *Shokaku*. Hours later, the ship was shattered by a massive internal explosion and sank.

COME RETRIBUTION

US search planes hunted the Japanese warships throughout the next day, but it was late when Ozawa's force was finally discovered. Mitscher, aware that the enemy ships were steaming at the outermost range of his planes and his returning pilots would probably have to land on decks in gathering darkness, quickly turned his carriers into the wind and launched 240 aircraft.

The sun was low in the West when the US planes found their target. Sweeping in to attack, they seriously damaged the carrier *Zuikaku*, the lone surviving veteran of the Pearl Harbor attack 30 months before. The light carriers *Ryuho* and

A HEAVILY ARMED VERSION of the North American B-25 Mitchell medium bomber, with .50-cal. machine guns mounted in its nose, strafes a Japanese patrol craft off the Philippines in July 1944.

LEFT: STATIONED ABOARD A JAPANESE aircraft carrier, a naval officer keeps track of planes as they take off to attack US Navy ships during the Battle of the Philippine Sea.

Junyo were hit by bombs and the light carrier *Hiyo* was sunk. As combat operations ebbed, the most formidable foe faced by the Americans during the Battle of the Philippine Sea turned out to be darkness. Numerous accidents occurred as planes with nearly empty fuel tanks attempted to land on their carriers. Other pilots were forced to ditch in the open sea and await rescue. Courageously, Mitscher risked attack by enemy submarines in ordering his ships to turn on their lights and fire star shells to assist the returning pilots. Eighty-two planes were lost, but the majority of the downed airmen were plucked from the water the next day.

AIR POWER ON THE WANE

The Battle of the Philippine Sea resulted in the destruction of Japanese carrier air power. When the fighting was over, Ozawa had only 35 aircraft remaining. He had lost three

BELOW: BRACKETED BY BOMBS from US Navy aircraft, a Japanese warship takes evasive action during the Battle of the Philippine Sea. Japanese naval air power was virtually eliminated during the fighting.

AIRCRAFT BURN AS DAMAGE *control parties attempt to contain the flames aboard a US aircraft carrier that has been struck by a Japanese kamikaze. Another stricken carrier is visible in the distance.*

carriers and more than 400 planes over two disastrous days. More than 200 land-based planes had been shot down or destroyed on the ground as well. The victory had cost the Americans 130 aircraft and relatively few casualties. Some historians have criticized Spruance for failing to completely

destroy Ozawa's fleet and deliver the decisive blow against the Japanese navy. However, given his dual responsibilities, it must be concluded that Spruance accomplished both to the best of his ability.

In October, the Battle of Leyte Gulf, the last great naval engagement of the Pacific War, would settle the issue once and for all. After the Philippine Sea, however, the final defeat of Japan was a foregone conclusion.

PHILIPPINE SEA

2 Launched from the Philippines, Japanese land-based aircraft augment the carrier planes. Four major raids are attempted throughout the day on 19 June 1944.

1 Hoping to utilize the greater range of his carrier-based aircraft, Admiral Ozawa launches a series of airstrikes against the US fleet in the Philippine Sea.

OZAWA FLEET

4 *Taiho*, the newest aircraft carrier in the Japanese fleet and Ozawa's flagship, is torpedoed by the submarine USS *Albacore* and later explodes.

5 The Japanese are further shaken as three torpedoes from the submarine USS *Cavalla* sink the aircraft carrier *Shokaku* shortly after noon on 19 June.

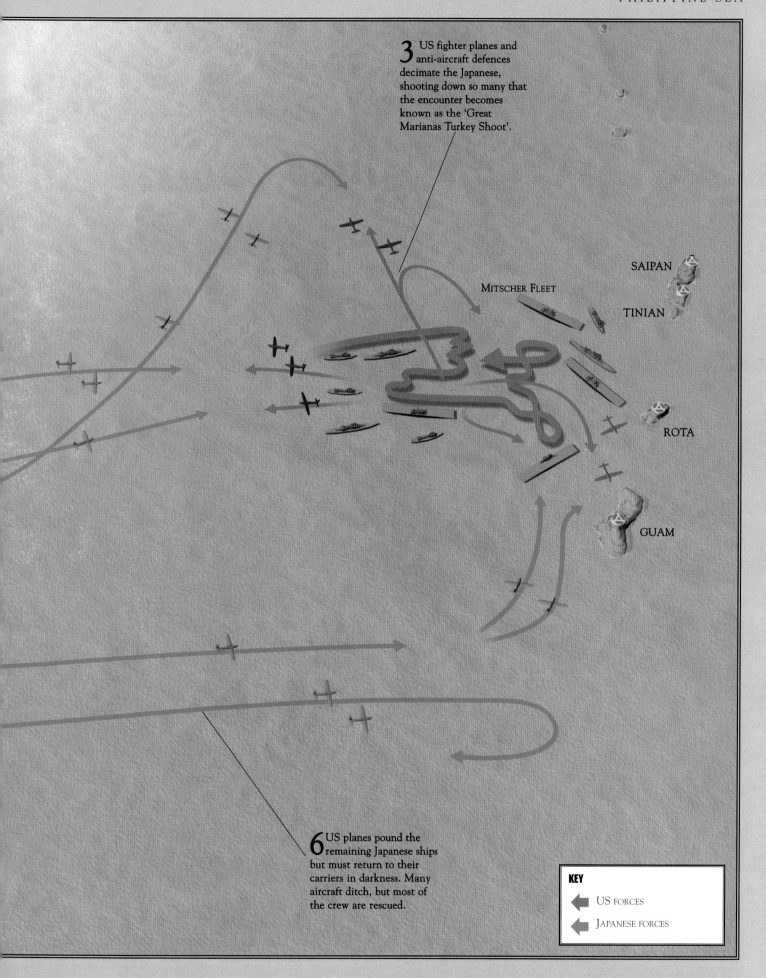

3 US fighter planes and anti-aircraft defences decimate the Japanese, shooting down so many that the encounter becomes known as the 'Great Marianas Turkey Shoot'.

MITSCHER FLEET

SAIPAN

TINIAN

ROTA

GUAM

6 US planes pound the remaining Japanese ships but must return to their carriers in darkness. Many aircraft ditch, but most of the crew are rescued.

KEY

US FORCES

JAPANESE FORCES

WARSAW RISING

1944

As the war moved towards its conclusion, the Allies agreed to divide Europe into spheres of influence. This was not acceptable to the Polish people, who wanted once again to be a free and sovereign nation. To demonstrate their independence, the Poles planned an uprising to liberate their capital before the advancing Red Army arrived.

Poland was one of the earliest victims of Nazi aggression, invaded in September 1939. The nation's army resisted as best it could, but defeat was inevitable even before the Soviet invasion from the other direction. However, this was not the end of Polish resistance. Free Polish forces were an important part of the war while resistance networks at home did all they could to further the Allied cause.

WARSAW RISING FACTS

Who: More than 40,000 Polish irregulars versus German occupying forces of roughly 25,000 troops.

What: The Uprising began on 1 August 1944 as part of a nationwide rebellion. It was intended to last for only a few days until the Soviet Army reached the city. However, it developed into a long urban guerrilla campaign against the occupiers.

Where: Warsaw, Poland.

When: August–October 1944.

Why: The Poles sought to re-establish their sovereignty after four years of Nazi-German occupation.

Outcome: The uprising was ultimately put down with great losses on both sides. It is estimated that more than 200,000 civilians died in the fighting, while 700,000 were expelled from the city.

IN AUGUST 1944, Polish volunteers equipped with whatever weapons they could obtain seized much of Warsaw from the German occupation forces, beginning a long and bitter struggle for the city.

191

MEN OF THE *Dirlewanger Brigade, a formation supposedly intended to rehabilitate criminals by military service. The brigade's career of atrocities reached its peak during the Warsaw Rising.*

Once the tide of the war had turned and German forces began the long retreat out of Russia, it became obvious that Poland was going to be 'liberated' by the Soviet Union, which meant inevitably falling into its sphere of influence. Indeed a pro-Soviet government was being readied for installation as soon as the Red Army pushed the Germans out. The Poles did not welcome this prospect. They wanted a free and independent state and that meant doing more than waiting for one foreign army to leave and another to arrive. The plan, named Operation *Tempest*, called for orchestrated risings in several cities and a campaign of attacks in various regions of the country.

This would hopefully drive the German occupiers out before the Red Army arrived and also assist the Allied cause by distracting German attention. Once the capital was liberated, members of the Polish government would come out of hiding and assume control.

No one had any illusions that there would not be bloodshed when the rising took place, but the Poles were willing to make the sacrifice. They had been fighting a hidden war for the entire occupation, hampering German efforts in Russia by disrupting the logistics chain running eastwards.

The largest resistance organization was named *Armia Krajowa* (Home Army). It had over 400,000 members, who were armed with weapons dropped by the Allies or obtained

from German sources – by theft, capture or sometimes black market purchase. In addition, there were stocks of weaponry concealed in the last days of freedom when it became apparent that the German advance could not be halted.

Thus there was no shortage of willing and experienced fighters available for the operation. The resistance forces had been fighting this kind of guerrilla war for years, albeit on a smaller scale. Now they saw their opportunity to win a decisive victory.

THE RISING

In July 1944, the Red Army was advancing on Warsaw and it seemed obvious that the battle for the city would soon begin if the German garrison did not retreat. This was unlikely as the city was a major logistics and transport centre and was also politically significant.

Plans were made to use Polish labour to construct fortifications around the city and a demand was made for men to come forward to do the work. Suspicious of the motives behind the order, the population largely refused to obey it. This increased tensions between the population and the occupiers even further and prompted the Home Army commanders to move up their timetable. The order was given to launch the rising on 1 August 1944.

The Home Army had about 45,000 members in Warsaw at the time of the rising, under General Antoni Chrusciel (1895–1960). About half of these personnel were equipped for combat, though it was necessary to get weapons to many of them just before the rising started.

ABOVE: FLAMETHROWERS PROVED VERY EFFECTIVE in the urban fighting for Warsaw. Their use was acceptable to a regime that did not care about damage to the city – indeed, much of it was deliberately destroyed.

Organizing such a large-scale operation was difficult, especially within an enemy-held city, and it was not possible to conceal from the occupiers that something was going on. The garrison and internal security forces, including SS troops and secret police, were alerted and able to prepare to an extent. The original plan had been for the first strikes to be made at night and by surprise. Instead, the Home Army had to attack alert troops in daylight. Success was mixed: in some areas, objectives were quickly overwhelmed where in others the attacks were met with intense machine-gun and small-arms fire and repelled.

There were about 11,000 German troops in the city under the overall command of Lieutenant-General Reiner Stahel. About half were regulars; the rest were mostly from the *Luftwaffe*. There were also more than 5000 SS personnel in the area under the command of Colonel Paul Giebel. Cooperation between these units was patchy at times and there was no coherent strategy for dealing with the uprising.

The result was a very confused situation with groups from both sides cut off from their allies by territory held by the enemy. Barricades were erected and control over captured areas consolidated, and gradually the insurgents took

RIGHT: HITLER TOOK A personal interest in the battle for Warsaw, allocating large resources and condoning the harsh measures used to suppress the insurgency.

ABOVE: A GERMAN OFFICER *directs his men during street fighting in Warsaw. In this sort of close-quarters battle, effective junior leadership was of paramount importance; in a fluid situation higher command could not react quickly enough.*

control of more and more of the city. By 4 August, most of Warsaw was under Polish control. All that was necessary was to hang on until the Red Army arrived.

GERMAN COUNTERMEASURES

Even as the Poles were reaching the high watermark of their uprising, an organized response began to unfold. German reinforcements came up, and all forces were placed under a single commander, General Erich von dem Bach (1899–1972), an SS officer who formulated plans to retake the city.

A spearhead of combat troops drove into the city, establishing a line behind which the streets were under firm German control. Here the SS and Gestapo were free to operate as they wished. There was no pretence of justice or justification – civilians were simply rounded up behind the German line and shot.

The massacre was intended to break the will of the population and bring the insurgency to an end without having to dig the Poles out house by house. In this, it failed. Resistance became ever more determined, partly from outrage and partly from the feeling that to surrender was a death sentence anyway.

Once it became apparent that reprisals were not the answer, a different approach was used. Instead of simply executing captured resistance fighters, some were accorded the status of prisoners of war and fairly treated in the hope that this would make it seem that it was worth surrendering. This also had little effect.

STREET FIGHTING

The uprising had been intended as a short campaign to end with the Red Army arriving at the city limits. Yet the Red Army remained strangely inactive, suddenly unable or perhaps unwilling to make much progress in its advance. Thus the Poles were forced to fight on.

The arrival of tanks on 7 August did not shift the balance much. The insurgents had prepared obstacles and barricades, and although some ground was lost the situation had stabilized by 9 August. The fighting reached a climax between 9 and 18 August, with large-scale urban combat raging across wide areas of the city.

By 2 September, the tide had turned. Under air attack and bombardment by distant artillery to which they had no reply, the Poles had to pull out of the old town, using the sewers to avoid detection. The fighting went on elsewhere, the German forces grinding their way through the city in a manner not dissimilar to the urban hell of Stalingrad.

THE SOVIETS APPROACH

By the middle of September, the advance units of the Red Army had almost reached the Vistula and were pushing the Germans back once again. Although Soviet forces seemed unwilling to help the insurgents, Free Polish units fighting with them moved into the city and joined their countrymen. They were not given support by their Soviet comrades in arms, however, and were badly defeated.

The Free Polish commander, General Zygmunt Berling (1896–1980), was relieved of command by his Soviet allies and the remainder of the Soviet army halted short of

LEFT: THE RED ARMY *had significant forces nearby and could perhaps have come to the aid of the insurgents, but did not. Instead, weapons like this Su-152 self-propelled gun stood idle while the battle raged.*

Warsaw and stayed there. There were solid tactical reasons – the Soviets were closely engaged with German armoured battle groups at the time – but there was more to it than this.

Although the Soviets had been calling for a Polish uprising for months, Stalin did not desire the Warsaw insurgency to succeed. He wanted Poland under Soviet control, not independent, and the insurgents had risen in the name of the pro-West government-in-exile based in London. By waiting until the rising was crushed and then moving in, he ensured that Poland would fall under the sway of Moscow.

Stalin also refused to allow the Western Allies to use Soviet airbases to fly supplies in to the insurgents. Some drops were

THESE WOUNDED POLISH insurgents were captured at the end of the uprising, and stood a good chance of being treated as prisoners of war. Earlier on, captured personnel were simply shot.

still made, but they had to fly out of distant bases and were not effective. Soviet troops at times fired on Allied aircraft making supply runs, though a re-supply mission was eventually permitted. By then, it was too late: the insurgents had been ground down to the point where they could no longer resist.

On 2 October 1944, General Tadeusz Bor-Komorowski (1895–1966), Chrusciel's superior in the Home Army, surrendered what was left of the forces in Warsaw after receiving a promise that the insurgents would be treated as regular combatants in accordance with the relevant conventions. The civilian population was also to be spared reprisals.

THE DESTRUCTION OF WARSAW

Some of the insurgents did not turn themselves in but tried to fade out of sight among the population. Of those who did surrender, some were treated as any other prisoners of war and sent west to camps in Germany. Of the remainder, some were sent to concentration camps, some to labour projects and most dispersed and released. None was allowed to remain in the city.

The city was then systematically destroyed by fire and explosives. Some houses escaped but all public and historic buildings were deliberately targeted. The Red Army finally entered Warsaw in mid-January 1945, by which time very little remained of the city.

A CITY DESTROYED

About a quarter of Warsaw was destroyed in the fighting that resulted from the uprising. After the Polish surrender, the population was driven out and an attempt was made to burn or demolish the remainder of the city. In fact, 85 per cent of Warsaw was destroyed in this manner, with special emphasis put on cultural buildings, from churches and schools to monuments and the university.

The city was rebuilt after the war, and considerable effort was put into recreating the historic city centre, which is now a World Heritage Site. In 2004, a ceremony was held to mark the 50th anniversary of the uprising, though it was suggested that the Russian delegation should observe from the far bank of the Vistula.

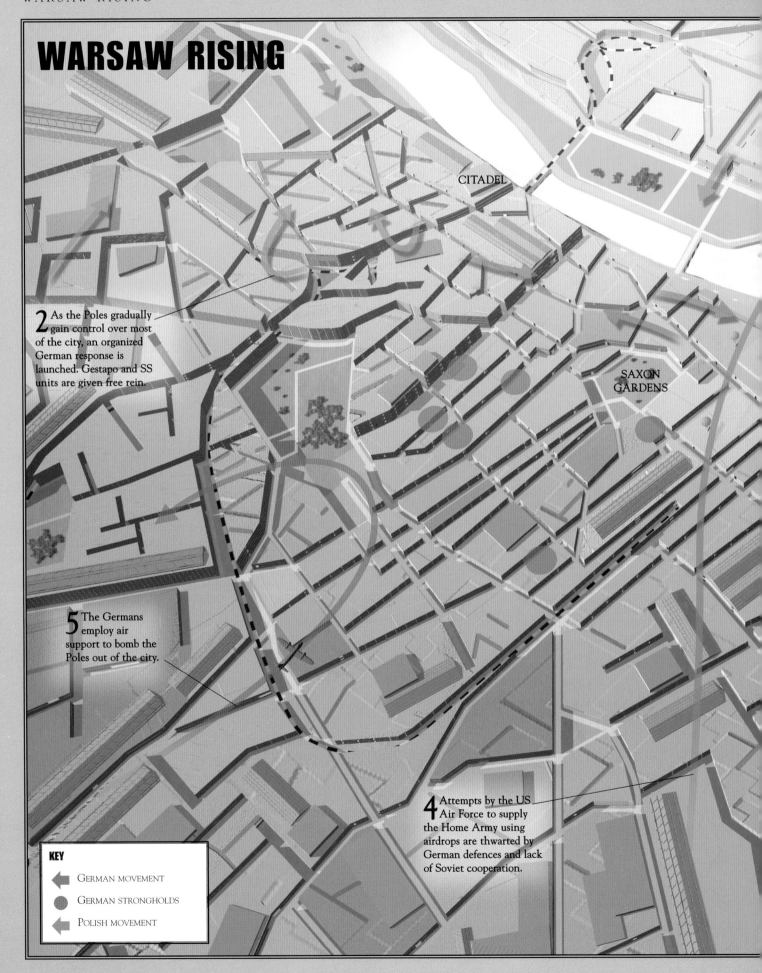

WARSAW RISING

CITADEL

2 As the Poles gradually gain control over most of the city, an organized German response is launched. Gestapo and SS units are given free rein.

SAXON GARDENS

5 The Germans employ air support to bomb the Poles out of the city.

4 Attempts by the US Air Force to supply the Home Army using airdrops are thwarted by German defences and lack of Soviet cooperation.

KEY

◄ GERMAN MOVEMENT

● GERMAN STRONGHOLDS

◄ POLISH MOVEMENT

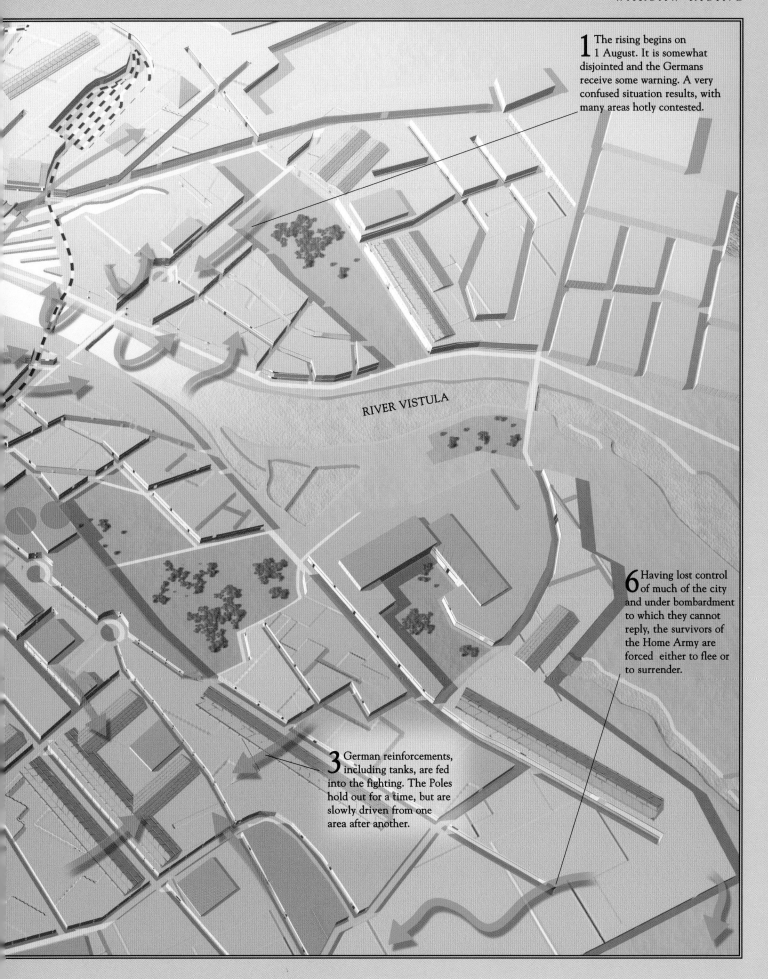

1 The rising begins on 1 August. It is somewhat disjointed and the Germans receive some warning. A very confused situation results, with many areas hotly contested.

RIVER VISTULA

6 Having lost control of much of the city and under bombardment to which they cannot reply, the survivors of the Home Army are forced either to flee or to surrender.

3 German reinforcements, including tanks, are fed into the fighting. The Poles hold out for a time, but are slowly driven from one area after another.

OPERATION 'MARKET GARDEN' 1944

Operations 'Market' and 'Garden' were complementary halves of a daring plan to seize strategic bridges with airborne troops, then rush ground forces up and across them. Had it succeeded, Market Garden might have shortened the war by a year.

The Siegfried Line, or Westwall, was a chain of fortifications facing France, constructed before the war. Rather than a solid line, it was a deeply defended zone covered by minefields, pillboxes, bunkers and antitank obstacles, all covered by artillery in protected emplacements. Entrenched in such positions, even third-line troops could inflict serious casualties.

In the summer of 1944, it was obvious that if the Allies were forced to assault the Siegfried Line they would suffer serious casualties. An alternative line of attack, into the heavily defended Ruhr, would be equally costly. So the Allies

OPERATION 'MARKET GARDEN' FACTS

Who: Allied airborne and ground forces, including the British 1st Airborne Division and Polish Brigade, opposed by German armoured and infantry units.

What: Although at first the advance was a success, German resistance was heavier than expected.

Where: The Netherlands, near the town of Arnhem, on the River Rhine.

When: 17–25 September 1944

Why: The Allies wanted to get across the Rhine quickly, bypassing major German defences and trapping large numbers of German forces in the Netherlands.

Outcome: The operation was a failure, prolonging the war in Northwest Europe by at least a few months.

PARATROOPS AND GLIDERBORNE *infantry land at Arnhem. Putting troops in a glider required less training than creating paratroops, though it was scarcely less dangerous. Glider troops were also less prone to being scattered.*

sought an alternative and found one that, with luck and daring, might be workable.

The plan was relatively simple. Attacking by surprise, the Allies would seize strategic bridges over the rivers Maas, Waal and Lower Rhine, enabling the establishment of a bridgehead behind the enemy's main defended zone and the most formidable natural obstacles. The only problem was that the first bridge might indeed be taken by *coup de main*, perhaps by light armoured forces racing up to grab it, but by the time the assault force got across and reached the next bridge, they might find it to be blown or strongly held.

The answer was for all the bridges to be captured at the same time, by paratroops and glider-borne infantry who would defend their objective until relieved by the rapidly advancing armoured spearhead. The airborne component was codenamed *Market* and the armoured advance *Garden*, but in reality neither had any point without the other. It was the whole, Operation *Market Garden*, that mattered. It was a bold plan – perhaps a little too bold. One Allied officer, feeling that the Allies were about to overextend themselves remarked, 'I think we're going a bridge too far'. But it was all

BRITISH PARATROOPERS EN ROUTE to Arnhem. Just getting onto the ground was a dangerous business; 'jump casualties' from enemy fire or a bad landing were inevitable on any operation.

or nothing – there was no point in grabbing just some of the bridges. *Market Garden* had to succeed completely or not at all.

The most serious threat to the operation was not the enemy but poor planning. Perhaps as a result of complacency following the success of the Normandy landings, much was taken for granted. As a result, re-supply operations came unstuck and cooperation between units failed. Sometimes this was due to problems with radios but just as often to a lack of good communications procedures.

OPENING MOVES

The operation began with paratroop landings by British, American and Free Polish units. RAF concerns about the air defences in the Arnhem region meant that the paras were dropped at a distance from their objectives, requiring a forced march and giving the enemy time to react to the threat.

This might not have been too serious but for two facts. Firstly, II SS Panzer Corps was in the region, rebuilding its strength after taking a battering in Normandy. This was an experienced and well-equipped unit that retained its offensive spirit. Secondly, Field-Marshal Walter Model (1891–1945) was in the immediate vicinity. Model had gained a well-deserved reputation as an excellent commander on the Eastern Front, where he staved off defeat again and again by scraping a battle group together from whatever was to hand and improvising a brilliant battle plan. Now, that experience came to the fore.

Model gave orders to prevent the paras from reaching their objectives, then went to his headquarters and began organizing a response to the overall situation. By this time, he knew that Allied armour was smashing its way towards him and that paratroops had landed along its projected route. It was not at all difficult to determine what the Allies were attempting.

Model's fast response meant that very few of the paras assigned to take the Arnhem bridges reached the town at all. Elements of 2nd battalion, the Parachute Regiment under Lieutenant-Colonel John Frost (1912–1993), along with an assortment of troops gathered along the way, were able to reach the north end of the bridge and hang on there, but this was the limit of the paras' success. Model assigned part of his force to contain the paras and began gathering everything else he could find to halt the armoured attack coming his way.

THE ALLIES ADVANCE

Although some of the airborne troops were still in England, unable to take off due to fog, the advance went ahead. There were several minor waterways to cross and plans had been laid to set up temporary bridges if necessary, but in the event the Allies were able to overrun what defenders there were and to gain control of the permanent bridges.

However, there were two waterways that could not be bridged: at Nijmegen and Arnhem the Allies had to cross

ABOVE: ALTHOUGH PARATROOPERS jumped in quick succession, a 'stick' could become widely separated if there was much wind. Paradrop operations always began confused, with lost personnel hoping to rejoin their units later.

BELOW: THE SDKFZ 251/22 mounted a heavy antitank gun on a proven half-track truck chassis. These vehicles were effectively used as mobile tank destroyers by SS troops fighting at Arnhem.

arms of the Rhine. There was no way for combat engineers to create a temporary crossing of such wide rivers. Here the bridges would have to be taken and that meant getting there while the paras still had control of the bridges.

Despite this, the ground assault had been delayed, waiting for confirmation that the airborne operation was a success. As a result, resistance along the roads towards the bridges firmed up and the advance fell behind schedule. Nightfall forced a stop and by the time the armoured spearhead reached Nijmegen an organized defence was in place. Attempts to break through were met by fire from 88mm (3.46in) antitank guns and repelled.

The original plan had called for all the bridges to be in Allied hands within 48 hours. However, by this time the ground forces were still trying to get on to the Nijmegen bridge while the airborne forces were fighting sporadic and scattered actions all over the countryside. Some were successful and more paras reached Arnhem, but overall the chances of success were diminishing fast.

Frost's paras were still clinging to the end of the Arnhem bridge, incidentally denying its use to the enemy, but they were under ferocious pressure from artillery and tanks. The Allies had to get across the Waal at Nijmegen and start making some headway before it was too late.

ABOVE: THE ROAD BRIDGE at Arnhem. Although the paratroopers were not able to capture the whole bridge, they held one end of it long enough to deny its use to a German counterattack.

BELOW: A KAMPFGRUPPE OF German infantry advances. In such a confused situation, an attack could come from anywhere and it was not always possible to tell whether a contact was a couple of lost paras or a major force.

The solution was daring and aggressive: US airborne troops would make an assault crossing in small boats and then storm the far end of the bridge. While their attack distracted the defenders' attention, the armoured forces would advance across at full speed.

The crossing was extremely difficult even without the intense enemy fire that came from the bank. Many paddles were missing from the boats so the troops used rifle butts and helmets to crawl slowly across the wide river. Even with assistance from tank guns and aircraft, many boats were riddled, yet somehow the paras got across and launched an attack up the bank.

As the assault boat crews took them back across to pick up more paras, those that had survived the crossing fell on the defenders and drove them from the banks. In a very confused action, where aggression counted for more than anything else, the armoured troops charged on to the bridges from one end while the paras attacked the other.

During the advance, the German commander on the spot tried to detonate previously laid demolition charges, which failed to work. The likely explanation is that a member of the Dutch Resistance cut the wires during the fighting. After the bridge was made safe, the armoured forces were able to advance across it.

The Allies were finally across the Waal and only 18km (11 miles) from where Frost and his paras were holding one end of the Arnhem bridge. A rapid advance might have been in order but the Allied force was tired and disorganized. It was not possible to put together a sufficient force to break through and achieve anything at Arnhem.

A BRIDGE TOO FAR

The situation was still very fluid, with German forces coming in from the flanks and at times cutting the Allied line of communications. Model's forces at Arnhem were gaining strength and Frost had finally been overrun.

It was clear that an assault was very unlikely to succeed. Worse, Model had managed to get some panzers across the river (using an alternate route since Frost's paras denied him the use of the bridge until it was too late) and was advancing down the road to Nijmegen.

An Allied armoured thrust up the Arnhem road was unable to break through and attacks along other axes ran into heavy resistance. The operation had obviously failed and it was time to salvage all they could. As many paras as possible were brought across the river in assault boats during the night of 25/26 September.

AFTERMATH

The goal of getting across the Rhine quickly and without fighting through heavy defences had not been achieved. A combination of mischance, poor planning and the determination of the enemy robbed the operation of success.

ABOVE: MAN-PORTABLE MORTARS *were the only artillery available to the lightly equipped paratroopers. They were effective in close-range urban fighting, but ammunition was limited by what could be carried.*

As a result, the allies were forced to fight their way in 'though the front door' and took heavy casualties as a result. The damage in still-occupied territory caused by the extra months of war was also considerable.

ABOVE: ALTHOUGH GOOD TACTICS *and use of cover could improve the odds, it was also possible to be in the wrong place at the wrong time. This German soldier may have made a mistake or simply been unlucky.*

OPERATION 'MARKET GARDEN'

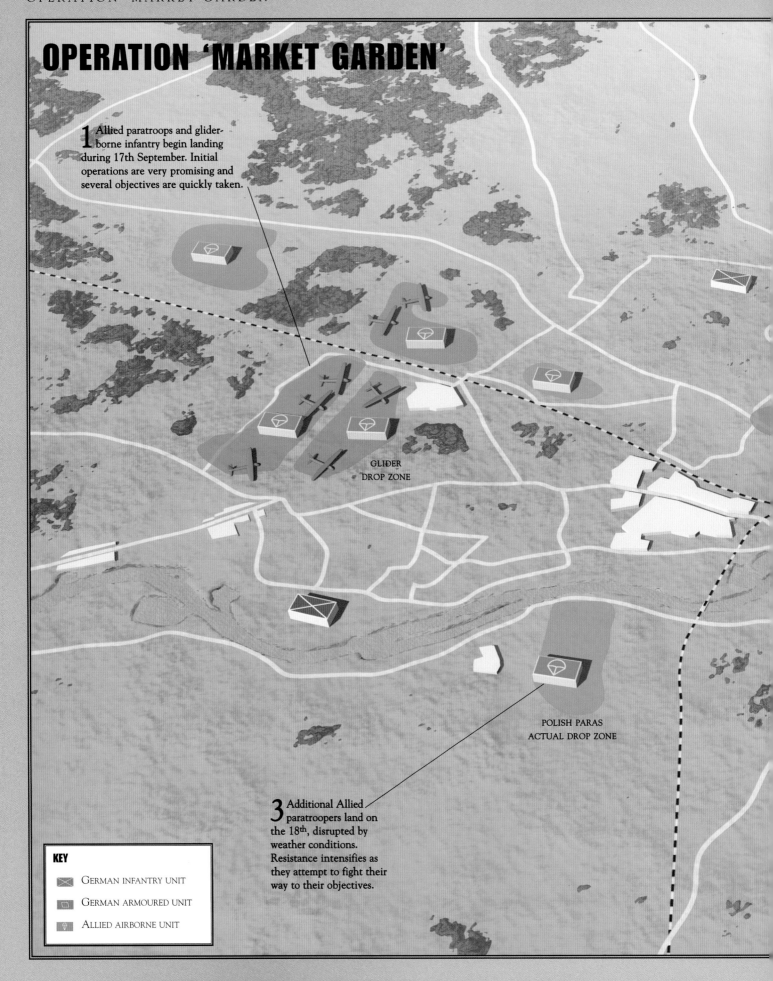

1 Allied paratroops and glider-borne infantry begin landing during 17th September. Initial operations are very promising and several objectives are quickly taken.

GLIDER
DROP ZONE

POLISH PARAS
ACTUAL DROP ZONE

3 Additional Allied paratroopers land on the 18th, disrupted by weather conditions. Resistance intensifies as they attempt to fight their way to their objectives.

KEY

⬌ GERMAN INFANTRY UNIT

▱ GERMAN ARMOURED UNIT

▽ ALLIED AIRBORNE UNIT

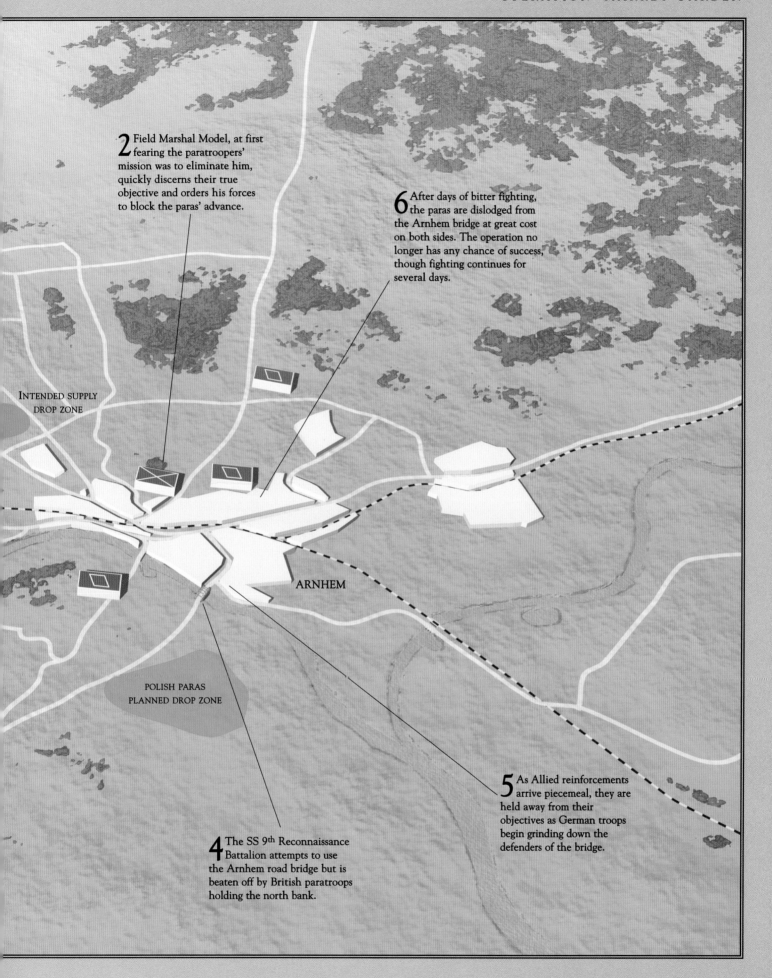

2 Field Marshal Model, at first fearing the paratroopers' mission was to eliminate him, quickly discerns their true objective and orders his forces to block the paras' advance.

6 After days of bitter fighting, the paras are dislodged from the Arnhem bridge at great cost on both sides. The operation no longer has any chance of success, though fighting continues for several days.

INTENDED SUPPLY DROP ZONE

ARNHEM

POLISH PARAS PLANNED DROP ZONE

5 As Allied reinforcements arrive piecemeal, they are held away from their objectives as German troops begin grinding down the defenders of the bridge.

4 The SS 9th Reconnaissance Battalion attempts to use the Arnhem road bridge but is beaten off by British paratroops holding the north bank.

BATTLE OF THE BULGE 1944–45

At 5.30 a.m. on the morning of 16 December 1944, the thunder of hundreds of German guns shattered the stillness of the Ardennes, a relatively quiet sector of the Allied lines on the German frontier. It was the beginning of Operation Wacht am Rhein *(Watch on the Rhine), a last gamble by Adolf Hitler in the West.*

The *Führer's* objective was to force a wedge between the Allied Twelfth and Twenty-First Army Groups with a fast-moving armoured thrust that would drive across the river Meuse and on to the vital Belgian port city of Antwerp. Hitler also hoped subsequently to shift forces to meet a coming offensive in the East, where the Soviet Red Army was poised to strike across the river Vistula into

BATTLE OF THE BULGE FACTS

Who: German forces under the command of *Führer* Adolf Hitler (1889–1945) and his generals versus Allied forces under General Dwight Eisenhower (1890–1969).

What: Hitler hoped to divide Allied army groups in the West, drive to the port of Antwerp and change the course of the war.

Where: The front lines in Belgium, France and Luxembourg.

When: 16 December 1944 to 15 January 1945

Why: Hitler sought to divide the Western Allies and gain time to confront the coming Soviet offensive along the river Vistula in the East.

Outcome: The battle resulted in a disastrous defeat for Nazi Germany. Less than four months later, World War II in Europe was over.

HALTED MOMENTARILY ALONG *an icy road in Belgium, German Panzer V 'Panther' tanks spearhead the German Ardennes offensive. With its large gun, the Panther was one of the best tanks of World War II.*

ABOVE: CAPTURED DURING THE opening phase of the Battle of the Bulge, American prisoners are marched by their German captors toward an uncertain fate. SS soldiers were guilty of atrocities during the fighting.

the heart of Germany. Bypassing Field-Marshal Gerd von Rundstedt (1875–1953), his commander in the West, Hitler instructed three armies – Sixth Panzer under SS General Josef 'Sepp' Dietrich (1892–1966) to the north, Fifth Panzer commanded by General Hasso von Manteuffel (1897–1978) in the centre, and Seventh Army under General Erich

Brandenberger (1892–1955) further south – to strike on a 97km (60-mile) front from Monschau, Germany, to the town of Echternach in Luxembourg.

THE STORM BREAKS

For months, Hitler had mulled over his plan. Finally, with 275,000 troops, hundreds of tanks and nearly 2000 artillery pieces, he launched his attack against a sector of the line that Allied commanders had considered virtually inactive. Warning signs of a pending offensive had been ignored and when the Germans jumped off, numerous American units were taken completely by surprise. However, pockets of stiff resistance formed along Elsenborn Ridge, particularly by troops of the 99th Division.

These determined efforts slowed Dietrich to a crawl until a shift of troops to the south outflanked some defensive positions along the Schnee Eifel, a cluster of hamlets and tree-covered hills in front of the high ground. Thousands of US soldiers were scooped up as prisoners. The untested troops of the 106th Infantry Division found themselves cut off in the Schnee Eifel, and on 19 December two entire regiments surrendered – but the Americans on Elsenborn Ridge stood their ground.

Dietrich's armoured spearhead, commanded by SS Colonel Joachim Peiper (1915–1976), pushed hard for several key bridges over the Meuse and other waterways, which would facilitate rapid crossings. In the process, however, the Germans were held up by groups of US combat engineers, one of which disabled Peiper's lead tank and blocked access to a bridge across the Amblève river at the town of Stavelot. Other bridges were blown up nearly in the Germans' faces by the engineers. Enraged by the delays, Peiper was also plagued by a shortage of fuel. His force, which originally numbered 4000, was eventually surrounded and only around 800 managed to escape. Peiper and his command gained lasting infamy in the fight, which would

BELOW: THE GERMAN TIGER II or King Tiger tank combined a high velocity 88mm (3.46in) cannon and sloped armour in a formidable fighting vehicle. The horizontal lines of anti-mine zimmerit coating are faintly visible.

RIGHT: SOLDIERS FROM KAMPFGRUPPE PEIPER on the road to Malmédy. In the background is a SdKfz 251 half-track armoured personnel carrier.

come to be known as the Battle of the Bulge. One of his units was guilty of murdering 85 captured Americans in a field near Malmedy in one of the most publicized atrocities of World War II.

As Allied troops held Elsenborn Ridge, the north shoulder of the great bulge began to form. Brandenberg's thrust ran into the veteran 9th Armoured and 4th Infantry Divisions of the US Army and made little or no progress along the southern edge of the offensive. In the centre, Manteuffel's tanks came closest to reaching the Meuse near Dinant, roughly 80km (50 miles) from their start line. A heroic stand by elements of the US 7th Armoured Division at the town of St Vith delayed the Germans for six days. The town did not fall until 23 December and British Field-Marshal Bernard Montgomery (1887–1976), placed in command of forces north of the bulge, used the time to consolidate his defences.

RIGHT: SOLDIERS FROM KAMPFGRUPPE PEIPER on the road to Malmédy. In the background is a SdKfz 251 half-track armoured personnel carrier.

BELOW: AS THE TIDE of the fighting in the Ardennes begins to turn in late December 1944, American infantrymen proceed through some abandoned, snow-covered buildings toward German positions.

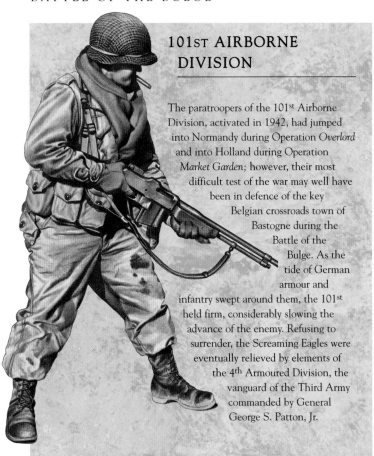

101st AIRBORNE DIVISION

The paratroopers of the 101st Airborne Division, activated in 1942, had jumped into Normandy during Operation *Overlord* and into Holland during Operation *Market Garden*; however, their most difficult test of the war may well have been in defence of the key Belgian crossroads town of Bastogne during the Battle of the Bulge. As the tide of German armour and infantry swept around them, the 101st held firm, considerably slowing the advance of the enemy. Refusing to surrender, the Screaming Eagles were eventually relieved by elements of the 4th Armoured Division, the vanguard of the Third Army commanded by General George S. Patton, Jr.

'NUTS!'

Southwest of St Vith, the Belgian crossroads town of Bastogne proved critical to the outcome of the Battle of the Bulge. Continued possession of Bastogne by the Americans would deny the Germans use of a key road network and slow their advance considerably. On 17 December, the vanguard of Manteuffel's forces reached the outskirts of the town. Unable to capture it by direct assault, the Germans bypassed Bastogne, which was defended by the lightly armed 101st Airborne Division and elements of other units.

The encircled paratroopers held on by their fingernails, but when heavy German forces drew the noose tighter on 22 December they were invited to surrender. The ranking US officer in the embattled town was Major-General Anthony McAuliffe (1897–1983), and his famous reply to the German ultimatum was simply, 'Nuts!'.

Although he was in dire straits, McAuliffe did have reason to hope. Foul weather, which had benefited the Germans, had begun to clear the previous day and allowed an airdrop of desperately needed supplies. Of even greater importance, relief for the beleaguered defenders of Bastogne was already on the way.

BARRICADES NOW OPEN, American troops move through a village in Belgium that shows signs of heavy fighting, late December 1944.

Americans in the Ardennes, and his gamble had reached the brink of success. In the end, a lack of fuel, unexpectedly stiff resistance and clearing weather had conspired to bring about a crushing defeat.

The offensive had cost the *Führer* dearly. More than 120,000 Germans had been killed, wounded or taken prisoner during a month of hard fighting. Scores of tanks and other armoured vehicles had been destroyed or abandoned. American casualties totalled nearly 80,000, with about 8500 dead, 46,000 wounded and more than 20,000 captured. Both sides had suffered terribly. For the Allies, the losses could be made good. For the Germans, they could not.

PATTON PIVOTS

On 20 December, under orders from the Supreme Allied Commander, General Dwight Eisenhower (1890–1969), elements of General George Patton's (1885–1945) Third Army disengaged from their own offensive in the Saar, wheeled 90° to the north and began slashing towards the surrounded town, which appeared on maps as an American island in a sea of German tanks and troops. Hardly stopping to rest or eat, the men of Third Army penetrated the German perimeter. Patton's spearhead, the 4th Armoured Division, made contact with the 101st Airborne on the day after Christmas.

The relief of Bastogne sealed the fate of the German offensive, while heroic defensive efforts at Elsenborn Ridge, St Vith and elsewhere had contained the German thrust within a week. Soon the great bulge began to resemble a gigantic Allied pincer movement rather than a tremendous German threat. As 1944 ebbed away, so too did Hitler's dream of ultimate victory in the West. By 15 January 1945, Allied forces had converged on the city of Houffalize, Belgium, effectively reducing the German salient.

IRREPLACEABLE LOSSES

With the failure of Operation *Watch* on the Rhine and the commencement of the Red Army winter offensive in the East on 12 January 1945, the endgame of World War II in Europe had begun. In two months, the Allies would be across the Rhine, the last imposing natural barrier to their advance. Soon the Soviets would be fighting in the suburbs of Berlin. Hitler had diverted precious troops and matériel from the Eastern Front for the all-out effort against the

RIGHT: GENERAL ANTHONY MCAULIFFE, acting commander of the 101st Airborne Division at Bastogne, issued the famous reply of 'NUTS!' to a German demand for surrender during the Battle of the Bulge.

BATTLE OF THE BULGE

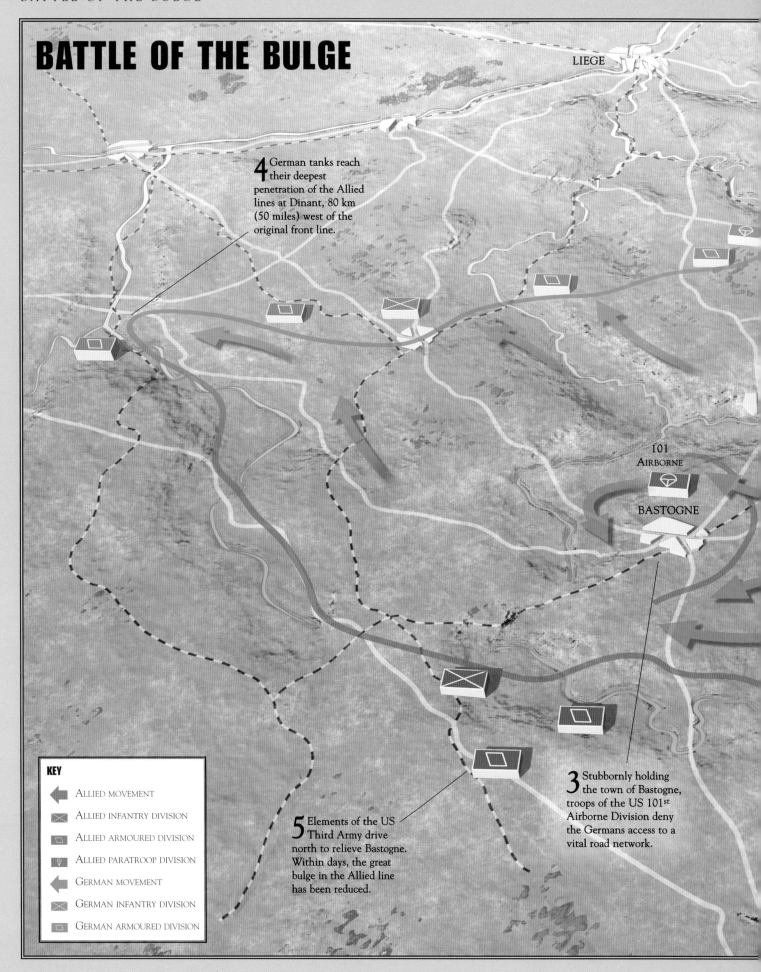

LIEGE

4 German tanks reach their deepest penetration of the Allied lines at Dinant, 80 km (50 miles) west of the original front line.

101 AIRBORNE

BASTOGNE

3 Stubbornly holding the town of Bastogne, troops of the US 101st Airborne Division deny the Germans access to a vital road network.

5 Elements of the US Third Army drive north to relieve Bastogne. Within days, the great bulge in the Allied line has been reduced.

KEY

◄	ALLIED MOVEMENT
⊠	ALLIED INFANTRY DIVISION
▱	ALLIED ARMOURED DIVISION
▽	ALLIED PARATROOP DIVISION
◄	GERMAN MOVEMENT
⊠	GERMAN INFANTRY DIVISION
▱	GERMAN ARMOURED DIVISION

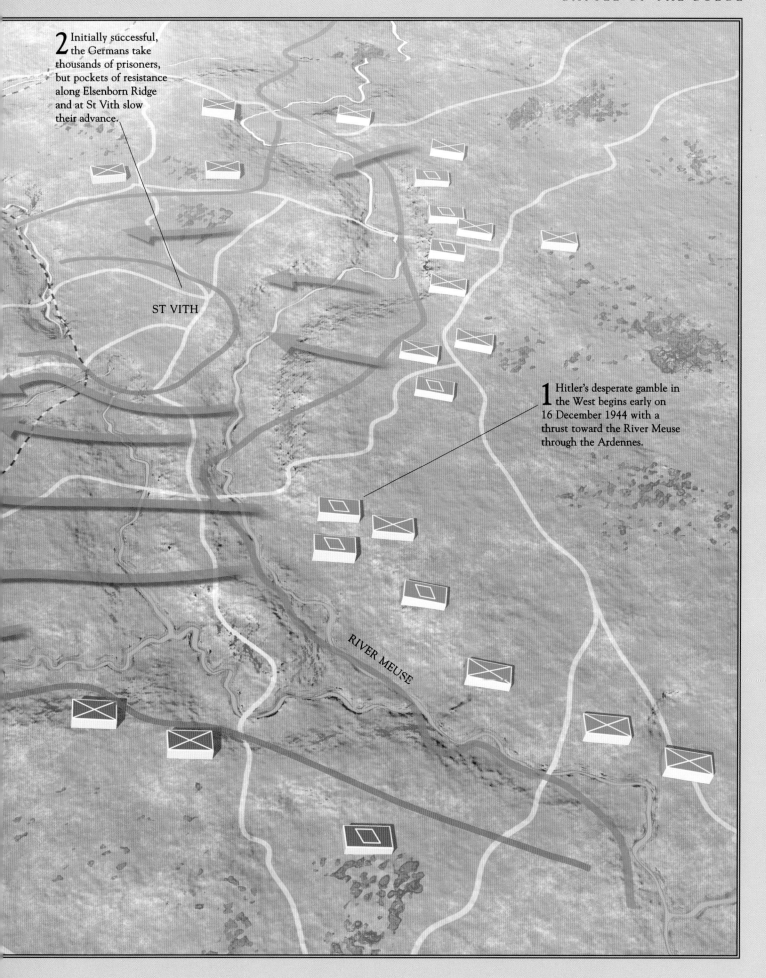

2 Initially successful, the Germans take thousands of prisoners, but pockets of resistance along Elsenborn Ridge and at St Vith slow their advance.

ST VITH

1 Hitler's desperate gamble in the West begins early on 16 December 1944 with a thrust toward the River Meuse through the Ardennes.

RIVER MEUSE

IWO JIMA

1945

The island road to Tokyo was long and bloody for the US military. Although the United States had seized the initiative in the Pacific, it was clear throughout the campaign that the Japanese were resourceful and tenacious foes – willing to fight to the death. As the war entered its fourth year, American planners had become resigned to the fact that final victory would necessitate an invasion of the Japanese home islands.

Such an undertaking would require extensive logistical preparation and suitable staging areas were needed. Already, long-range bombers were being deployed to rain death and destruction on Japanese cities. Crippled bombers returning to distant bases in the Marianas needed a safe haven to land. Aboard each bomber was a crew of 10–14 men.

The island of Iwo Jima in the Volcanoes Group seemed to fill both requirements. Situated only 1062km (660 miles) south of Tokyo, the Japanese had already constructed airfields there. Although taking the island promised to be a

IWO JIMA FACTS

Who: Japanese troops under Lieutenant-General Tadamichi Kuribayashi (1891–1945) versus US Marines under Lieutenant-General Holland M. Smith (1882–1967).

What: US Marines attempted to capture the island in the Volcanoes Group.

Where: The island of Iwo Jima in the Pacific Ocean, less than 1127km (700 miles) from the Japanese home islands.

When: 19 February to 26 March 1945

Why: Iwo Jima could provide a staging area for future operations and a safe haven for crippled bombers returning from raids on Japanese cities.

Outcome: US Marines captured Iwo Jima after more than a month of savage fighting. Over 20,000 Japanese soldiers were killed and just a few hundred captured. American forces suffered almost 7000 killed and 19,000 wounded.

CAPTURED BY PHOTOGRAPHER *Joe Rosenthal, this image of US Marines and a Navy corpsman raising the US flag on Mount Suribachi at Iwo Jima is perhaps the most enduring of World War II. In fact, the flag had been raised earlier that day but the action was restaged for the camera.*

IN THIS AERIAL VIEW of the American landings at Iwo Jima, assault craft approach the black, volcanic sand beaches. The Japanese waited for the landing areas to choke with men and equipment before opening fire.

LVT-4 'WATER BUFFALO'

At the landings on Iwo Jima, the LVT-4 (Landing Vehicle Tracked) was the latest in a series of amphibious assault vehicles deployed in the Pacific during operations against the Japanese. Thousands of LVT variants were produced during the war.

Based upon an initial design by Donald Roebling in 1935, the LVT demonstrated its worth during the landings at Tarawa in November 1943, and was improved with greater armour protection and both .50-cal. and .30-cal. Browning machine guns.

difficult affair, Admiral Chester Nimitz (1885–1966), Commander-in-Chief of the Pacific Fleet, authorized Operation *Detachment* to commence in February 1945, with US Marine Major-General Holland Smith (1882–1967) in command of the offensive against Iwo Jima.

SULPHUR ISLAND

Shaped like a pork chop, Iwo Jima is scarcely 8km (5 miles) long and 7.2km (4½ miles) across at its widest point. At the southern tip, the 170m (550ft) Mount Suribachi rises to dominate most of the island. Despite its relatively diminutive stature, Iwo Jima had been turned into a fortress by more than 25,000 Japanese troops and a large contingent of Korean labourers under the command of Lieutenant-General Tadamichi Kuribayashi (1891–1945).

Across the island the Japanese had constructed a labyrinth of pillboxes, bunkers, machine-gun nests, artillery emplacements and spider holes large enough only for a single soldier. Many of the Japanese guns were positioned with interlocking fields of fire, their positions reinforced with steel, concrete, coconut logs and heaps of sand to absorb the shock waves of American pre-invasion bombardment. The Japanese had also honeycombed Mount Suribachi itself with tunnels and artillery and machine-gun emplacements near the mouths of caves.

The US plan was straightforward: the 4th and 5th Marine Divisions with the 3rd Division in reserve, more than 40,000 strong, were to assault beaches on the southern end of Iwo Jima. From there, they would isolate and capture Mount Suribachi, fight their way across the island, take the airfields and subdue pockets of Japanese resistance.

TO THE SUMMIT OF SURIBACHI

On the morning of 19 February 1945, US Marines hit the beach on Iwo Jima. For 20 minutes, there was virtually no reaction from the Japanese defenders. Kuribayashi, who had instructed his soldiers to kill 10 Americans before sacrificing themselves for the emperor, had also told his men to hold their fire until the invasion beaches were choked with American troops and landing craft. With a thunderous crash, the eerie silence was broken. Japanese bullets and shells rained down on the Americans and inflicted heavy

ABOVE: SHAPED LIKE A pork chop, the island of Iwo Jima is dominated by the 170m (550ft) Mount Suribachi. Control of its airstrips saved the lives of thousands of American airmen.

BELOW: GRUMMAN F4F WILDCAT fighter planes prepare to take off on a support mission from the deck of the escort carrier USS Makin. US air superiority was complete by this stage in the war.

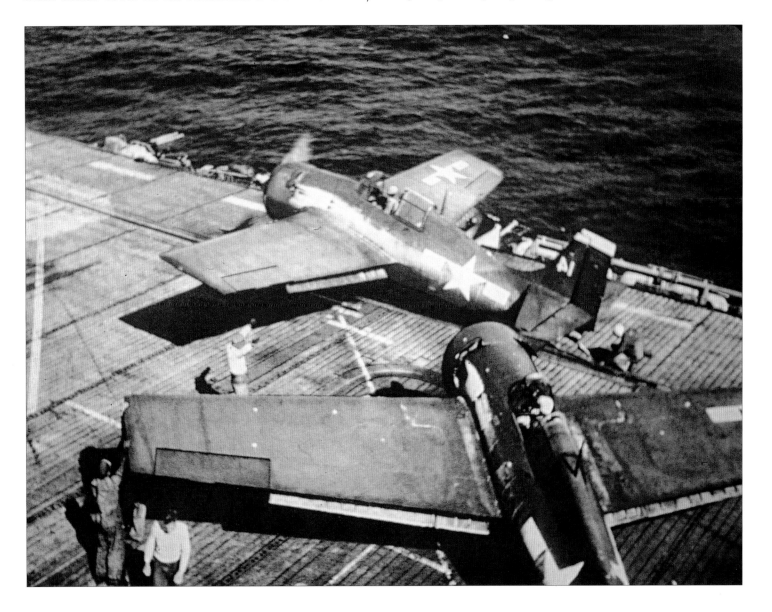

WARY OF JAPANESE SNIPERS and well camouflaged machine gun nests, a US Marine shouts to a comrade. After more than a month of bitter fighting, Iwo Jima was declared secure.

casualties. To make matters worse, the black volcanic sand of the island made footing difficult and impeded the progress of tracked vehicles.

Nevertheless, the Marines braved withering enemy fire and managed to cut off Mount Suribachi on the first day. Subsequently they fought their way to the base of the extinct volcano and began an arduous climb. Although the high ground was far from secure, on 23 February a patrol worked its way to the top of Mount Suribachi and triumphantly raised a small US flag amid exploding Japanese grenades and sniper fire.

Hours later a second, much larger flag was located and carried to the summit. It was the raising of this flag which Associated Press photographer Joe Rosenthal captured on film. At the sight of the banner, Americans fighting and even dying across Iwo Jima lifted a collective cheer. Naval vessels offshore sounded their horns and claxons. Rosenthal's frame became one of the enduring images of the twentieth century and made instant celebrities of the

group of six flag raisers, three of whom did not survive the battle for Iwo Jima to learn of their newfound fame. The image became the focus of a war bond tour across the United States and inspired the US Marine Corps Memorial in Washington DC.

YARD BY TERRIBLE YARD

In spite of this great boost to morale, more than a month of difficult fighting lay ahead for the Americans, whose numbers continued to grow on this small spit of land. Tanks were called upon regularly to fire point blank into Japanese fortifications. Individual acts of heroism occurred everywhere, and 26 Marines were awarded the Congressional Medal of Honor for their courage.

Progress was measured in yards, and otherwise nondescript locales earned lasting nicknames such as Bloody Gorge, the Amphitheater, Turkey Knob and the Meat Grinder. Marines crawled forward to fling grenades and satchel charges into the firing slits of Japanese bunkers or the mouths of caves. Flamethrowers burned defenders alive, routing them out of their defensive positions or immolating them where they stood. Some caves were sealed with explosives or bulldozers, burying their enemy occupants alive. Several times, the Japanese hurled themselves against well-entrenched Marines in suicidal banzai charges and died to the last man.

By 27 February, the two completed airstrips were in US hands and a third, which was under construction, had been taken as well. On 4 March, with the battle for the island still raging, the first four-engine Boeing B-29 Superfortress bomber made an emergency landing on Iwo Jima. During the remainder of the war, more than 2200 such landings were made and the estimated number of airmen saved topped 24,000. Fighters soon began flying escort missions with the big bombers as well.

IN THE MOUNTAIN'S SHADOW

Not until 26 March, after 36 days of combat, was Iwo Jima finally declared secure. The Japanese garrison on the island was virtually wiped out during the fighting. The Marines captured only 216 prisoners and some 3000 holdouts were still being eliminated months later. Although Kuribayashi's

body was never found, he was reported either to have committed suicide or to have been killed while leading a final desperate banzai charge. The Americans lost more than 6800 dead and 17,000 wounded at Iwo Jima, but the objectives of Operation *Detachment* had been achieved. Just days after the official end of the Iwo Jima battle, Marines and troops of the US Army landed on the island of Okinawa, moving another step closer to the home islands of Japan.

Iwo Jima stands as an epic of heroism and sacrifice by the men of the US Marine Corps. 'The raising of that flag on Suribachi means a Marine Corps for the next 500 years,' noted Secretary of the Navy James Forrestal (1892–1949). Admiral Nimitz captured the essence of the struggle, stating that at Iwo Jima 'uncommon valour was a common virtue'.

A US MARINE uses a flamethrower to silence a Japanese bunker on Iwo Jima. The island's fanatical defenders usually fought to the death, preferring even suicide to surrender.

IWO JIMA

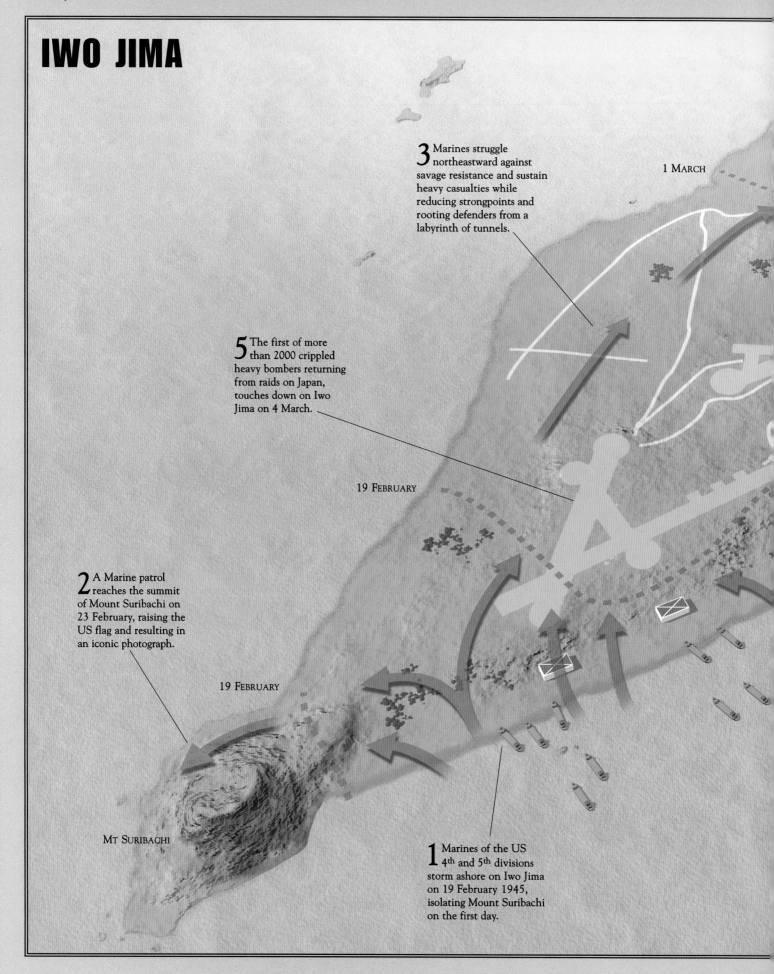

3 Marines struggle northeastward against savage resistance and sustain heavy casualties while reducing strongpoints and rooting defenders from a labyrinth of tunnels.

1 MARCH

5 The first of more than 2000 crippled heavy bombers returning from raids on Japan, touches down on Iwo Jima on 4 March.

19 FEBRUARY

2 A Marine patrol reaches the summit of Mount Suribachi on 23 February, raising the US flag and resulting in an iconic photograph.

19 FEBRUARY

MT SURIBACHI

1 Marines of the US 4th and 5th divisions storm ashore on Iwo Jima on 19 February 1945, isolating Mount Suribachi on the first day.

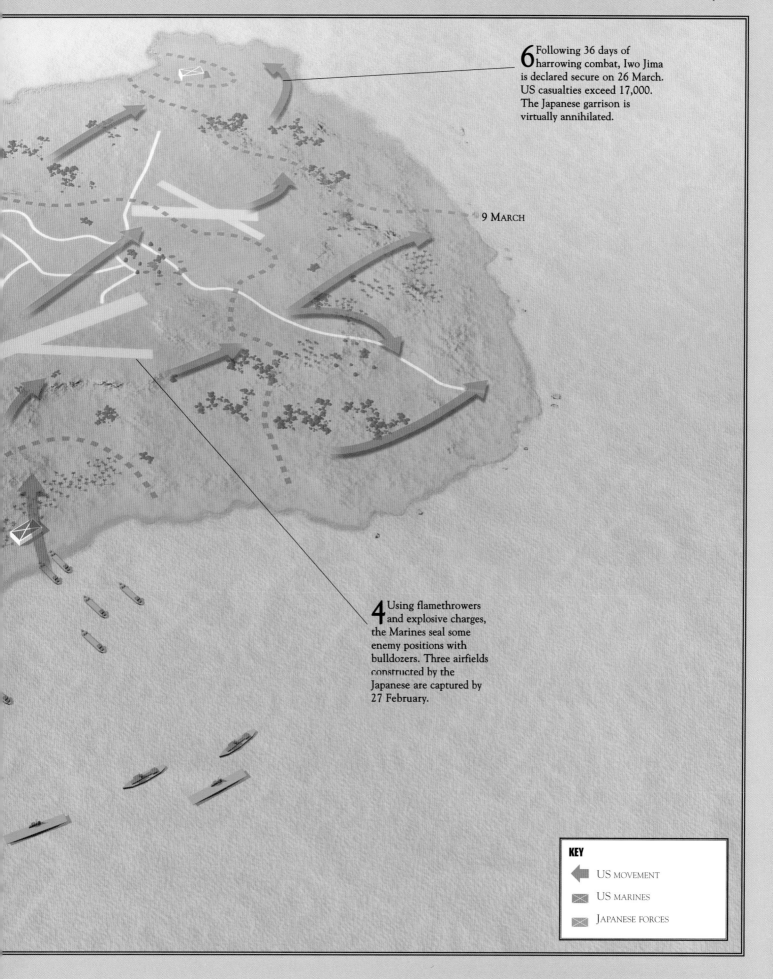

6 Following 36 days of harrowing combat, Iwo Jima is declared secure on 26 March. US casualties exceed 17,000. The Japanese garrison is virtually annihilated.

9 MARCH

4 Using flamethrowers and explosive charges, the Marines seal some enemy positions with bulldozers. Three airfields constructed by the Japanese are captured by 27 February.

KEY

⬅ US MOVEMENT

✉ US MARINES

✉ JAPANESE FORCES

BATTLE FOR BERLIN 1945

By the end of 1944, it was clear that Germany was losing the war. Two Red Army Fronts, commanded by Marshal Ivan Konev (1897–1973) and Marshal Georgy Zhukov (1896–1974), were advancing rapidly across western Poland. Further north, the 2nd Belorussian Front under Marshal Konstantin Rokossovsky (1896–1968) pushed into the Baltic states.

Here Colonel-General Gotthard Heinrici's (1886–1971) under-equipped Army Group Vistula was the sole barrier between Berlin and the Soviets. On the western front, German forces had smarted from the failed offensive in the Ardennes. By 3 April, Anglo-American forces had completed their encirclement of the Ruhr and prisoners were being taken at the rate of 15,000–20,000 a day.

BATTLE FOR BERLIN FACTS

Who: Red Army forces ordered by Stalin to capture Berlin, led by Marshal Ivan Konev (1897–1973) and Marshal Georgy Zhukov (1896–1974), versus Hitler's designated defender of Berlin, General Karl Weidling (1891–1955)

What: Victory was eventually assured for the Soviet Union as German forces, overwhelmed by sheer weight of men and armour, were encircled by eight Soviet armies smashing their way through Berlin.

Where: The Soviet Army's final offensive broke across the Oder and after vicious street-by-street fighting took the *Reich's* capital itself.

When: Between 16 April 1945 and 2 May 1945.

Why: The Allies believed that only with the successful assault on Berlin and defeat of the forces controlling it could the war be brought to a final, irreversible conclusion.

Outcome: Nazism was effectively defeated, leaving Berliners to count the cost. The daunting task of rebuilding a shattered Europe lay ahead.

LARGE ARTILLERY PIECES such as this tractor-borne 152mm (6.5in) gun formed a significant arm of Red Army forces shattering Berlin, along with assault guns, infantry and support troops.

assured that the Red Army would never reach Germany, soon realized that the enemy was edging into the city suburbs. Amid the rumble of Soviet guns, people of all ages were mustered to build fortifications. Houses and blocks of flats were transformed into concrete strong points. On Sunday 15 April, Adolf Hitler, confined to his bunker beneath the Chancellery garden, issued the last of his directives, which was given an optimistic gloss: 'The enemy will be greeted by massive artillery fire. Gaps in our infantry will have been made good by countless new units … The Bolshevik … must and shall bleed to death before the capital of the German *Reich* … ' The prospect of new units was the *Führer's* delusion. Manpower ranged from 15-year-old Hitler Youth personnel to men in their seventies. So-called 'infantry' consisted of 60,000 untrained, exhausted *Volkssturm* (Home Guardsmen) whose average ammunition supply was around five rounds per rifle and these, along with such machine guns as there were, had largely been salvaged from occupied countries.

At 3 a.m. Berlin time the next day, three red flares shot into the sky and the artillery opened fire. The sky was full of searchlight beams boring into dense smoke and boiling dust. Although many of the pontoon bridges had not been completed, Red Army infantry north and south of the bridgehead situated near the town of Kustrin, who had expected the arrival of assault boats, plunged into the river Oder, their log boats supporting guns and rafts heavy with supplies.

BRIDGEHEAD ATTACK

The troops of Zhukov's First Belorussian Front had been ordered by Stalin to make the attack on Berlin from the bridgehead. At the Seelow Heights, situated some 90km

By then, Berlin was an outnumbered fortress city: one million men were concentrated in the sector with 10,400 guns and mortars, 1500 tanks and assault guns and 3300 aircraft. The Soviets had 2,500,000 men, more than 42,000 guns and mortars, more than 6200 tanks and self-propelled guns and 8300 aircraft. Berliners, who had been

BELOW: *THE T34/85, part of the 4000-strong Soviet armada of tanks approaching Berlin, was a later variant on the USSR's highly effective leviathan, armed with enlarged turret and armament. By the war's end, the T-34 was accounting for around 70 per cent of Soviet tank production.*

30 APRIL 1945: Soviet infantrymen battle their way into the still defended Reichstag, fixing an improvised flag to one of its columns. The event was later restaged for cameras.

(60 miles) east of Berlin and overlooking the western flood plain of the Oder, reception was fierce and the Soviets were held off until late on 17 April. This was in contrast with Konev, who had crossed the Neisse to the south across open terrain more favourable to tanks and made rapid progress. Stalin ordered Konev to turn two of his tank armies northwards to aid Zhukov. The breakthrough to the Berlin suburbs was achieved on 19 April.

The next day was the *Führer's* birthday, marked by barrages of exploding artillery shells and the deafening howls of multi-barrelled rocket launchers. But still there were forces desperately fighting to hold their positions before the city. Ninth Army under General Theodor Busse had originally been given the task of blocking the Soviets' direct route to Berlin, while General Hasso von Manteuffel's 3rd Panzer Army had been positioned further north. Although von Manteuffel had some success and managed to hang on briefly, it was clear by 21 April that Busse's forces were on the point of total collapse. An appeal went out to Lieutenant General Hans Krebs of the High Command of the Army Chief of Staff, that Busse should

withdraw or face total destruction. The reply was predictable: Ninth Army was to stay where it was and hold on to its positions.

HOPES OF RESCUE

Hitler next seized on the presence of SS *Obergruppenführer* Felix Steiner's III SS *Germanische* Corps, situated in the area of Eberswalde to the north of Berlin. Steiner's Corps was directed to attack forthwith on von Manteuffel's flank, drive south to cut off the Soviet assault and re-establish contact between the Third and Ninth Armies. But there were no experienced troops available to Steiner. What Hitler called Army Group Steiner was mostly sweepings from the *Luftwaffe* personnel, local *Volkssturm* and assorted police. In no way could they challenge the strength of Rokossovsky's and Zhukov's fronts. Von Manteuffel was heard to comment, 'We have an army of ghosts.'

ABOVE: ON 20 APRIL, HIS 56TH BIRTHDAY, *Hitler in the Berlin Chancellery garden makes his last photographed appearance, awarding decorations to Hitler Youth, the youngest of whom was 12.*

BELOW: RED ARMY ARMOUR *passes through the suburbs of Berlin following the surrender of the city, May 1945.*

Frantically clutching at straws, Hitler next pinned his hopes on the Twelfth Army of General Walther Wenck, which was to be rushed from the Western Front. Wenck was ordered to disengage from the Americans to his west and attack to the east, linking up with Busse and together attacking the Soviets surrounding Berlin. Sole resources were raw recruits; there were no battle-worthy tanks. On 23 April, Hitler received a blunt report from General Karl Weidling, Battle Commandant of Berlin, that there was only sufficient ammunition for two days' fighting. Nevertheless, Weidling hung on with such forces as he possessed while the Soviet stranglehold grew tight around the city, now a few blocks from the bunker. There Hitler, rapidly declining in health and lost in his delusions, kept saying, "Where is Wenck? Where is Wenck?" But by now Wenck, a realist and severely disillusioned, was seeking to bring remnants of his own army and of Ninth Army, together with as many civilian refugees as possible, safely across the Elbe into US Army-occupied territory. By 30 April, Berlin was a raging inferno throughout. For the Soviets, there was a prime objective: the capture of the iconic *Reichstag*, still heavily defended by its garrison. Even so, by early afternoon the Soviet Red victory banner was flying from the dome.

UNCONDITIONAL SURRENDER

Later that same day Hans Krebs, a Russian speaker, was dispatched under a white flag to meet the Red Army's General Vasily Chuikov to discuss surrender terms and to

MARSHAL GEORGY ZHUKOV

A man of peasant background, Georgy Zhukov emerged as the most outstanding military figure in the Red Army during World War II. He was created First Deputy Supreme Commander-in-Chief Soviet Armed Forces in August 1942, serving in the post throughout the conflict. Responsible for the attack that relieved Stalingrad, he went on to coordinate the First and Second Belorussian Fronts in the 1944 summer offensive, and he commanded the First Belorussian Front in the final assault on Germany and capture of Berlin, becoming Commander-in-Chief of Soviet occupation forces. In 1955–57, he served as Soviet Minister of Defence, but had long incurred Stalin's jealousy, and was dismissed and disgraced for allegedly challenging the Communist Party leadership of the Armed Forces. Partly rehabilitated under Khrushchev, he died in June 1974, his ashes buried in the Kremlin wall with full military honours.

inform him that Hitler and his new spouse Eva Braun had committed suicide. Chuikov made it clear that the Soviets would not accept anything but unconditional surrender. Meanwhile, Soviet military action would be unremitting. Krebs also killed himself and his body was later found in the bunker. It was left to Weidling, the last commander of the Berlin defence zone, formally to surrender the city to the Soviets at 1.00 p.m. on 2 May. By 4.00 a.m., the fighting was over. Figures for the number of dead during the battle could never be calculated precisely, but it is generally thought that up to 100,000 German troops lost their lives and a likely equal number of civilians. Around the same number of Soviet soldiers died. Berlin, in effect, had to be recreated.

THE BERLIN POPULACE faces the reality of defeat, with hardly a building left intact. Here, women and children pass by the Brandenburg gate.

AFTERMATH

Defeat heralded a long period of decline for much of Germany. With the ending of the Nazi dictatorship, East Germany faced years of Communist oppression, economic misery and, for the ordinary citizen, many of the familiar trappings of dictatorship, notably the presence of the Stasi secret police, regarded by many as successors to the Gestapo. Not until 12 September 1990 was Germany formally reunified and many of the inequalities of the poor East and prosperous West consigned to history.

BATTLE FOR BERLIN

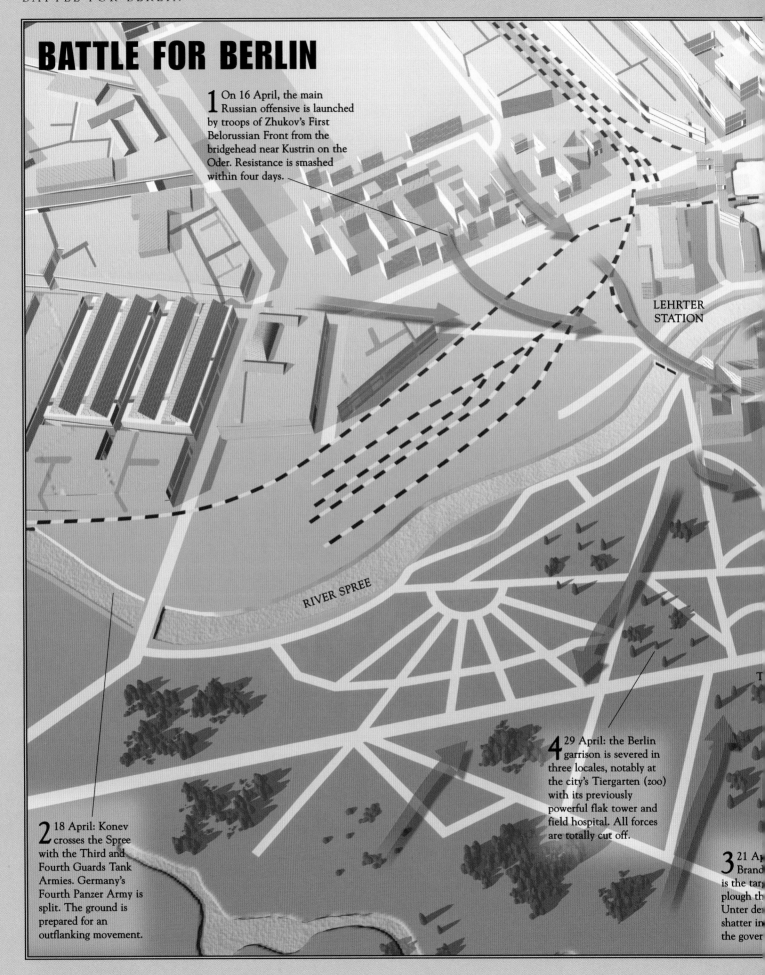

1 On 16 April, the main Russian offensive is launched by troops of Zhukov's First Belorussian Front from the bridgehead near Kustrin on the Oder. Resistance is smashed within four days.

LEHRTER STATION

RIVER SPREE

2 18 April: Konev crosses the Spree with the Third and Fourth Guards Tank Armies. Germany's Fourth Panzer Army is split. The ground is prepared for an outflanking movement.

4 29 April: the Berlin garrison is severed in three locales, notably at the city's Tiergarten (zoo) with its previously powerful flak tower and field hospital. All forces are totally cut off.

3 21 Ap Brand is the tar plough th Unter de shatter in the gover

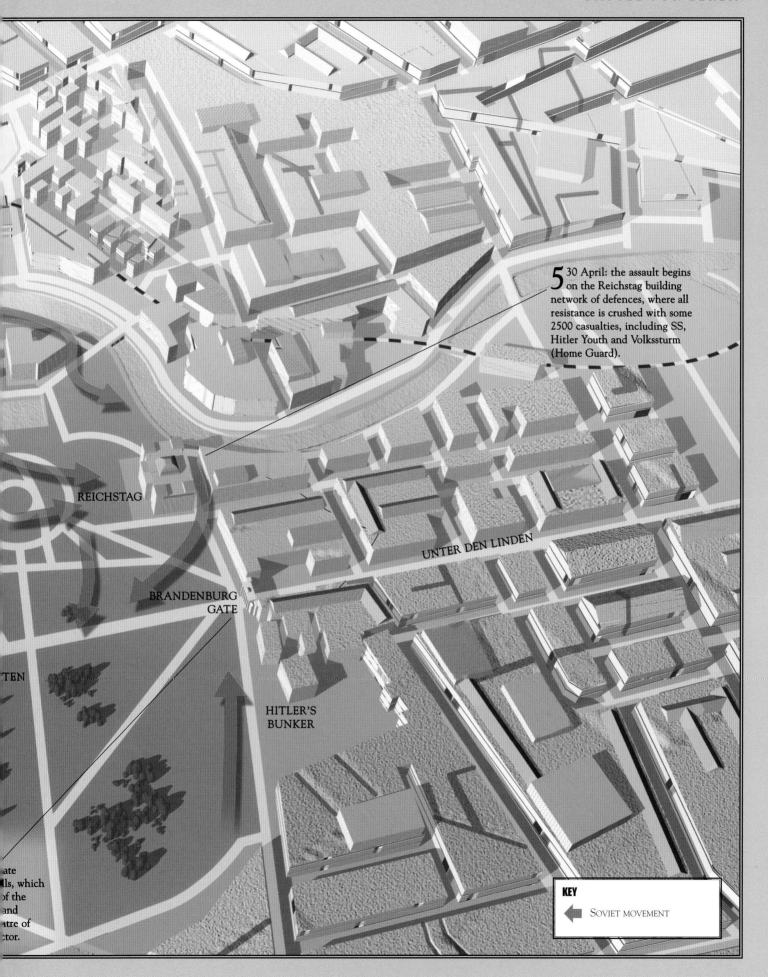

5 30 April: the assault begins on the Reichstag building network of defences, where all resistance is crushed with some 2500 casualties, including SS, Hitler Youth and Volkssturm (Home Guard).

REICHSTAG

UNTER DEN LINDEN

BRANDENBURG
GATE

TEN

HITLER'S
BUNKER

ate
ls, which
f the
and
tre of
ctor.

KEY

◄ SOVIET MOVEMENT

OKINAWA 1945

The Allies' amphibious invasion of Okinawa was a massive undertaking, against heavy and determined resistance. Japanese forces on the island were aware that they faced overwhelming opposition and were determined to exact as high a price as they could from the invaders.

The war in the Pacific was characterized by 'island-hopping' operations, which allowed the Allies to steadily encroach on the Japanese islands. Where possible, garrisons cut off by the Allied advance were bypassed and allowed to wither on the vine. Without amphibious transport, they were no threat and, lacking re-supply, would eventually become incapable of combat.

However, some objectives simply had to be taken. Okinawa was one – it was needed as a staging post for the final assault on Japan. This was obvious to the Japanese as well as the Allies and preparations were put in place well in advance. As the Japanese perimeter out in the Pacific gradually collapsed inwards, fortifications were dug and plans were laid to make the assault on Okinawa as expensive as possible.

OKINAWA FACTS

Who: Allied (mainly US) forces numbering 548,000 soldiers and 1300 ships, versus 100,000 Japanese ground, air and naval forces.

What: The Allies launched the largest amphibious operation of the Pacific campaign.

Where: Okinawa, in the Pacific Ocean

When: 1 April–21 June 1945

Why: The island was to be used as a staging point for the invasion of the Japanese homeland.

Outcome: The Allies captured Okinawa and 90 per cent of the buildings on the island were completely destroyed. Okinawa provided a fleet anchorage, troop staging areas and airfields in close proximity to Japan, allowing the Allies to prepare for the invasion of Japan.

US LANDING CRAFT bring stores ashore on 13 April 1945, during the battle for Okinawa. The packed horizon gives an indication of the size of the naval armada involved in the operation.

ABOVE: AIR SUPPORT FOR THE NAVAL *armada and the ground forces fighting on Okinawa was supplied by naval fighters and fighter-bombers, such as these F4U Corsairs, flying from more than 40 Allied aircraft carriers.*

With near-total command of the sea, the Allies could land more or less anywhere they pleased. It was not possible to prevent a landing and unlikely that a counterattack could contain one. The Japanese assumed that the Allies would get ashore, though they did what they could to make this costly. The defences of the island were centred on a medieval castle whose position guaranteed that the Allies would have no easy avenue of attack and would have to fight through the well-prepared fortifications.

While some of the islands the Allies assaulted were garrisoned by small forces, often with little artillery or air defence equipment, Okinawa was defended by several divisions with good support and, critically, plenty of artillery. These belonged to the Thirty-Second Army under the

command of Lieutenant-General Mitsuru Ushijima (1887–1945), who had his headquarters in the medieval fortress of Shuri Castle in the south of the island. Defence of the northern sector was the responsibility of Colonel Takehido Udo.

The Allied ground commander was Lieutenant-General Simon Buckner Jr (1886–1945), commanding the US Tenth Army. Buckner had a marine and an infantry corps under his command, each of two divisions, plus an additional marine and two more army divisions as a reserve.

THE ALLIES ARRIVE

The first phase of the battle was the Allied effort to establish air and naval supremacy in the vicinity of Okinawa. Forces from Britain, Australia and New Zealand contributed here, though the ground forces were exclusively American.

Marines were landed on nearby islands from 26 March onwards, clearing opposition to create a safe anchorage. Meanwhile carrier-borne aircraft attacked airfields while the Japanese struck back with air attacks including hundreds of kamikaze aircraft. These sank several vessels and damaged others; the US Navy suffered its heaviest battle casualties of the war off Okinawa.

The Allies also faced naval attacks. By this time, the Imperial Japanese Navy was a skeleton of its former power, short of fuel and with few ships remaining. However, the super-battleship *Yamato* was available along with the light cruiser *Yahagi* and eight destroyers. There was only enough fuel for a one-way mission, so the *Yamato* was to attack the Allied fleet while her fuel remained, then beach herself on Okinawa, where her 450mm (18in) guns would join the defence.

RIGHT: THE US INVASION *force moors off Okinawa, April 1945. The Americans committed more than half a million men and 1300 ships to capturing this small Japanese island.*

Yamato and her escorts sailed on 6 April under the command of Admiral Seiichi Ito (1890–1945), who had originally refused to carry out what he saw as a wasteful and hopeless gesture. Events proved him right.

Yamato was incredibly well protected, but the Allies had total air supremacy with large numbers of dive-bombers and torpedo aircraft available. The Yamato task force was sighted soon after leaving port. On 7 April, it came under intense air attack from more than 400 Allied planes. One by one, the escorts were sunk and the giant ship was hit by several bombs as well as ten torpedoes.

A battleship force was waiting in case Yamato somehow got through, but there was no need. After two hours of

THESE US MARINES' ARMAMENT includes rifles and carbines, which were handier for close-range combat in the jungles of the island. Semi-automatic operation allowed for a high rate of fire.

attack, the last Japanese battleship capsized and exploded, taking most of her crew with her. There was no further naval interference in the invasion.

THE ALLIES ADVANCE

US Marines began going ashore on Okinawa on 31 March 1945, when an advance force was put ashore. The main landings began the next day, assisted by diversionary operations to distract the enemy and slow their response.

USS INTREPID

Aircraft carriers were a vital weapon in attacking the islands of the Pacific, which were often out of range of land-based aircraft, and in defending the fleet against air attack. Although the Japanese naval air arm was irretrievably smashed by 1945, kamikaze aircraft and small-scale raids still posed a serious threat.

USS Intrepid, an Essex-class carrier, suffered a near miss and a hit from kamikaze aircraft while on station off Okinawa. Good damage control procedures kept her in action. She operated 90-100 fighters, dive bombers and torpedo bombers; her loss or withdrawal for repairs would have dented Allied air superiority, though not badly, as many other carriers were available.

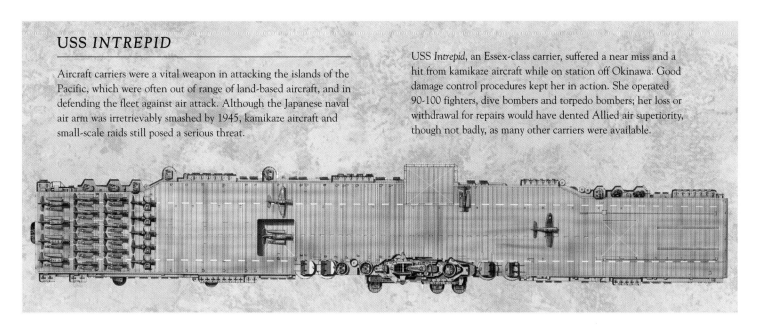

LEFT: THE LANDING VEHICLE (TRACKED) is an armoured fire support variant designated LVT(A)-4. Its 75mm (2.95in) howitzer had a short range but could provide vital fire support for troops assaulting a defended island.

The initial landings went well, largely because the defenders knew they could not be strong everywhere and had concentrated their forces where they would be most effective. Okinawa is a long, narrow island running broadly southwest–northeast with small peninsulas and a number of islands off the coast. The main Japanese force was concentrated in the southern end of the island and took some time to reduce. Defences were lighter to the north, and after clearing the immediate area the Allies were able to push northeast, driving the defenders steadily back.

The Allies made steady progress in the north, reaching the end of the island by 13 April, though the Motobu Peninsula and the island of Ie Shima were stubbornly held and not taken until 21 April. Pushing south was more of a problem: progress was slow and fiercely opposed by well dug-in Japanese troops. High ground, caves and artificial strongpoints had to be cleared by assault, resulting in hand-to-hand combat. Each was hotly contested and the Allies took heavy casualties as they pushed onwards.

After clearing what turned out to be a strong outpost line at Cactus Ridge, the advance became stalled for a time against the main Japanese line of resistance at Kakazu Ridge. Then from 12–14 April the Japanese counterattacked strongly.

Each assault was beaten off with heavy casualties on both sides and after this attempt the Japanese went back on the defensive.

On 19 April, the Allies made a renewed attempt to get the offensive moving. Under cover of diversionary operations and a huge artillery and naval bombardment, a powerful assault went in, supported by heavy air attack. However, the Japanese had ridden out the barrage in strong positions and were in good shape to resist the assault. Tanks – including flamethrowers – were of some assistance, but little headway was made.

Ushijima considered a counterattack but decided against it. His reserves were needed to counter a possible landing behind his lines by US 2nd Marine Division, which was making threatening movements by way of a diversion.

THE FIGHT FOR OKINAWA

The stalemate went on until the end of the month despite fresh US troops rotating into the line. On 4 May, the Japanese again counterattacked. The plan was ambitious and included an attempt to outflank US positions by amphibious operations. Despite determined efforts, the counterattack failed, and on 11 May Buckner went back over to the offensive. On 13 May US forces finally broke the Shuri defensive line. Infantry of the 96th Division and armoured supports ground their way into Japanese positions on Conical Hill as 6th Marine Division took Sugar Loaf Hill. With these key terrain features in US hands, the main Japanese line was compromised, but the monsoon weather made further advances difficult for a time.

The centre of the main line was Shuri Castle. With the flanks turned, the castle was exposed to attack and there was a chance to encircle the defenders. Major-General Pedro del Valle's (1893–1978) 1st Marine Division stormed the castle on 29 May. This not only broke the main defensive line but also greatly disheartened the Japanese forces on Okinawa, though they were able to fall back to a final position on the southern tip of the island.

The costly advance was then resumed, with the marines forced to dig fanatical defenders out of their positions. Many fought to the last or killed themselves to evade capture. Among them were Ushijima and his chief of staff, Lieutenant-General Isamu Cho. The remainder held their final line until 17 June, when the defence finally collapsed. This was a rare occasion on which significant numbers of Japanese troops surrendered. The

LEFT: A US MARINE FIRES his Thompson submachinegun during the fighting on Wana Ridge. Heavy shelling has reduced the vegetation to tree stumps and tangles of fallen branches.

RIGHT: A JAPANESE BOY CARRIES his baby sibling following the surrender of Okinawa. The civilian population suffered terribly, with an estimated 140,000 dying over the course of the three-month battle.

US Marines developed techniques to reduce casualties: for example, one method of clearing a cave involved the mouth being taken under heavy fire, after which a flamethrower tank approached and sprayed burning fuel into the interior, clearing any last defenders. However, despite such measures losses were very severe.

In the last days of the campaign, General Buckner was killed by enemy shellfire, making him the most senior US officer to be killed in action during the war. Heavy shellfire from both sides was a characteristic of the Okinawa campaign, which became known as the Typhoon of Steel.

The last organized resistance on Okinawa was the 24th Infantry Division, which was still fighting on 21 June. After this formation was broken, pockets of Japanese soldiers held out for another 10 days or so, but were mopped up one by one. The most senior Japanese officer captured alive was a major.

Many of those who survived tried to hide among the local population but were revealed by the Okinawans, who had no reason to shelter their enemies. Japanese soldiers had used Okinawan civilians as human shields or sent them to collect water under fire. In the closing stages of the battle, the Japanese encouraged locals to kill themselves rather than submit to the Allies.

AFTERMATH

Okinawa was firmly in Allied hands by the end of June. There was never any chance of the Japanese military holding the island. The defence was intended to delay the Allies as long as possible and to inflict as many casualties as possible. In this, the defence was a success. US forces suffered extremely heavy casualties, in part because of the refusal of Japanese troops to surrender even when surrounded and cut off. Once Okinawa was taken, it could be used as a base for the invasion of Japan itself. The nature of the resistance and the casualties incurred worried the Allies. An attack on the Japanese islands would be extremely costly. However, such a costly assault was made unnecessary by the use of atomic bombs in August 1945, which brought the war to an end.

BELOW: ALTHOUGH THE JAPANESE defence of Okinawa collapsed on 17 June, clearing out the last pockets of resistance took until the end of the month.

OKINAWA

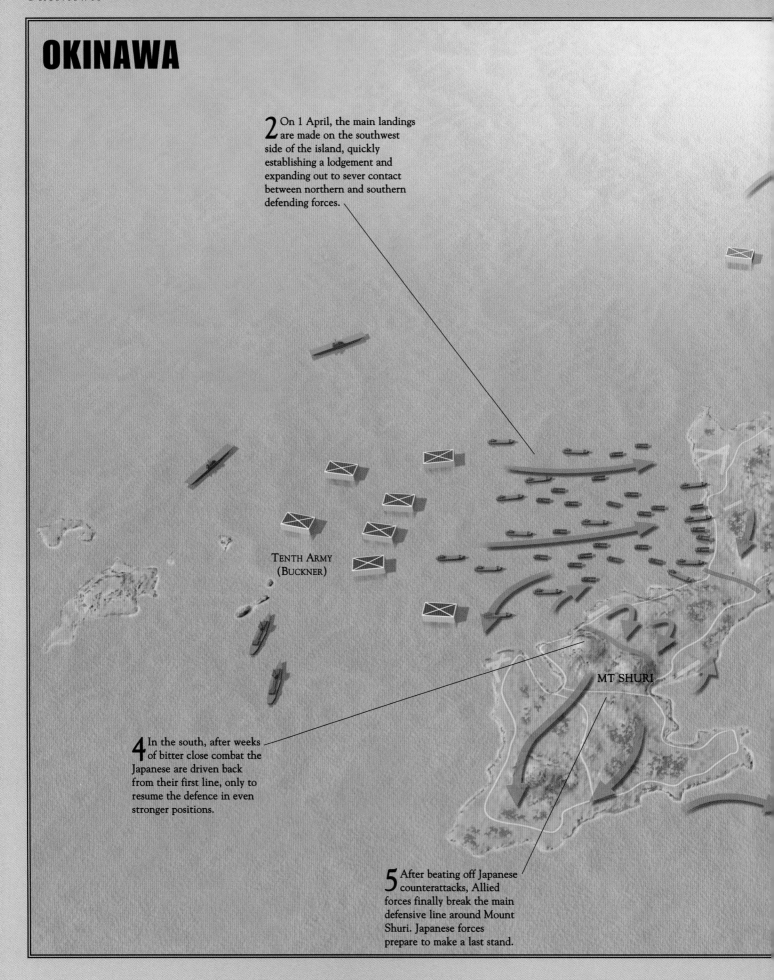

2 On 1 April, the main landings are made on the southwest side of the island, quickly establishing a lodgement and expanding out to sever contact between northern and southern defending forces.

TENTH ARMY
(BUCKNER)

MT SHURI

4 In the south, after weeks of bitter close combat the Japanese are driven back from their first line, only to resume the defence in even stronger positions.

5 After beating off Japanese counterattacks, Allied forces finally break the main defensive line around Mount Shuri. Japanese forces prepare to make a last stand.

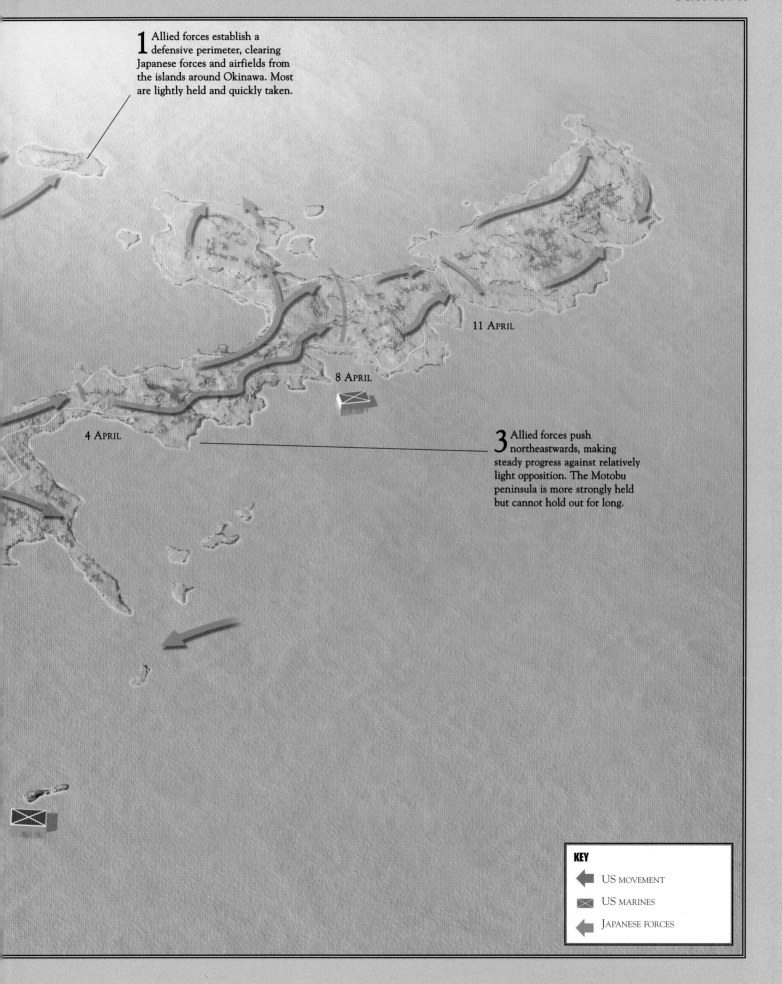

1 Allied forces establish a defensive perimeter, clearing Japanese forces and airfields from the islands around Okinawa. Most are lightly held and quickly taken.

11 APRIL

8 APRIL

4 APRIL

3 Allied forces push northeastwards, making steady progress against relatively light opposition. The Motobu peninsula is more strongly held but cannot hold out for long.

KEY

US MOVEMENT

US MARINES

JAPANESE FORCES

INDEX

1942

2 JANUARY British and Commonwealth forces in Malaya retreat in the face of Japanese forces.

8 FEBRUARY Red Army cuts off 90,000 German troops at Demyansk.

15 FEBRUARY Surrender of British and Commonwealth forces to the Japanese at Singapore.

24–29 OCTOBER British launch their big offensive at El Alamein, defeating Rommel's Africa Corps.

8 NOVEMBER Allied forces land unopposed in Vichy French North Africa.

24 DECEMBER German forces are encircled in Stalingrad.

---

1 FEBRUARY New Enigma cipher adopted by U-boat fleet, rendering communications traffic unreadable by British codebreakers.

7 FEBRUARY Supply convoys sail to Malta, carrying Spitfire fighters aboard aircraft carriers.

16 FEBRUARY U-boats launch a major anti-shipping offensive off the US eastern seaboard, sinking 71 ships during the remainder of the month. As a consequence, convoys are introduced.

7–8 MAY Battle of the Coral Sea.

4–5 JUNE Battle of Midway. All four Japanese aircraft carriers are sunk by the end of the 5 June.

12 NOVEMBER Battle for Guadalcanal begins.

---

19 FEBRUARY Japanese bomb Darwin, Australia.

5 APRIL Japanese bomb Colombo, Ceylon.

18 APRIL 'Doolittle raid' on Tokyo by US bombers.

30/31 MAY First 1000 bomber raid against Cologne, planned by new Air Chief Marshal Arthur 'Bomber' Harris.

25/26 JUNE Third and final 1000 bomber raid by RAF against Bremen.

10 AUGUST RAF's area bombing offensive threatened as Germans begin jamming the Gee navigation system.

---

12 JANUARY Japan declares war on Dutch East Indies.

25 JANUARY Siam declares war on Britain and US.

8 MARCH Japanese forces enters Siam, oil-rich Rangoon and land on Australian New Guinea.

9 MARCH Dutch East Indies surrender to Japan.

8 NOVEMBER Marshal Pétain secretly instructs the French High Commissioner in Algiers to open negotiations with the invading Allied forces of French North Africa.

11 NOVEMBER French forces in Morocco and Algeria sign armistice with the Allies; in retaliation, Germans occupy Vichy France.

1943

22 JANUARY German Sixth Army in Stalingrad cut in two: the final phase of the defeat of the Germans at Stalingrad begins.

1/2 FEBRUARY Japanese begin evacuation of Guadalcanal after Allied attack.

7 MAY Tunis falls to Allies.

5–12 JULY Germans launch Operation Citadel at Kursk in an attempt to gain the initiative on the Eastern Front. The operation is a failure.

3 SEPTEMBER Allied landings on mainland Italy begin.

6 NOVEMBER Soviets liberate Kiev.

27 DECEMBER In Italy, Eighth Army captures Ortona after fierce German resistance.

---

18 FEBRUARY US Navy bombards Japanese positions in the Aleutian Islands.

24 MAY Germany withdraws U-boats from North Atlantic after losing 33 U-boats in a month.

1 JULY Allies concentrate on attacking 'Milch Cow' refuelling U-Boats in Bay of Biscay.

10 JULY Allied landings in Sicily begin.

20 SEPTEMBER The Wolfpack U-boat campaign attacking Allied convoys reopens.

26 DECEMBER Scharnhorst sunk by British Home Fleet in last major gunnery duel in Royal Navy history.

---

18 FEBRUARY US Navy bombards Japanese positions in the Aleutian Islands.

17 MARCH The Axis powers now outnumbered in North Africa: while Britain and America have 3000 aircraft, the Axis powers have only 500.

13 MAY Sardinia bombarded by Allies from air for 14 days.

16/17 MAY RAF 617 Squadron carries out 'bouncing bomb' raids against German Ruhr dams.

17 AUGUST USAAF raid on Schweinfurt and Regensburg suffers heavy losses.

10 OCTOBER US Flying Fortresses begin attacks on Greece and Romanian oil fields.

---

9 MARCH Due to illness, Rommel is replaced as German commander-in-chief in North Africa.

18 APRIL Admiral Yamamoto, mastermind of the Pearl Harbor attack, is shot down and killed by American fighters.

25 JULY Mussolini arrested and deposed as Italian leader.

8 SEPTEMBER Italian surrender announced.

13 NOVEMBER Allies recognize Italy as a co-belligerent, formally accepting Italy's wish to change sides.

28 NOVEMBER–1 DECEMBER Tehran Summit between Churchill, Roosevelt and Stalin.